ISBN 978-1-5281-0860-7
PIBN 10912455

LAYER MARNEY: LAYER MARNEY HALL.
Gatehouse from the South-West; early 16th-century.

ROYAL COMMISSION ON HISTORICAL MONVMENTS

(ENGLAND.)

AN INVENTORY

OF THE HISTORICAL MONVMENTS

in

ESSEX

VOLUME III. (North-East)

ANNO DÑI·ᴁ·M·C·M·X·X·I·I

LONDON :
PRINTED & PUBLISHED BY HIS MAJESTY'S STATIONERY OFFICE

To be purchased through any Bookseller or directly from H.M. STATIONERY OFFICE
at the following addresses : Imperial House, Kingsway, London, W.C.2, and
28 Abingdon Street London, S.W.1 ; 37 Peter,Street, Manchester ;
1 St. Andrew s Crescent, Cardiff ; or 23 Forth Street,
Edinburgh.

Price £2 net.

TABLE OF CONTENTS

(6405) Wt.14535/520 1000 11/22 Harrow G. 51

LIST OF PLANS AND ILLUSTRATIONS.

WITH TITLES AND PRINCIPAL DATES.

___

PREFACE.

A FEW informal words will not, I trust, be out of place by way of introduction to this Inventory, and may help to explain both the arrangement of these pages and the manner in which the monuments have been recorded.

This volume contains (in addition to the terms of appointment and official report) a Sectional Preface which, under subject headings, calls attention to any particularly interesting examples mentioned in the Inventory; an illustrated Inventory, with a concise account of the monuments visited; a list of monuments that the Commissioners have selected as especially worthy of preservation; a glossary of architectural, heraldic and archæological terms; a map showing the topographical distribution of the scheduled monuments, and an index.

Under the heads of parishes, arranged alphabetically, will be found a list of their respective monuments, and an introductory paragraph which calls attention to the more noticeable monuments in the parish. The chronological sequence chosen is not perhaps scientifically perfect, but it has been found a workable basis for classification. The order adopted is as follows :—

    (1) Prehistoric monuments and earthworks.
    (2) Roman monuments and Roman earthworks.
    (3) English ecclesiastical monuments.
    (4) English secular monuments.
    (5) Unclassified monuments.

In addition to dwelling houses, the English secular class (4) includes all such earthworks as mount and bailey castles, homestead moats, etc. To the section of unclassified monuments (5) are assigned all undatable earthworks.

Each category of monuments has been under the care of separate Sub-Commissions, with the Earl of Crawford and Balcarres and myself as Chairmen.

The descriptions of the monuments are of necessity much compressed, but the underlying principle on which accounts of any importance are based is the same throughout.

In the first place, the Parish is located by letters in brackets which refer to the square where it is to be found in the map at the end of the volume; reference is also given where necessary to the Ordnance sheets (scale 6 inches to the mile) by small letters in front of the number of each monument. In the case of Churches, the description begins with a few words on the situation and material of the monument, together with a statement as to the development of its various parts. A second paragraph calls attention, when necessary, to its more remarkable features. This is followed by a concise description, mainly architectural, of its details. A fourth paragraph deals with the fittings in alphabetical order, while the concluding sentence gives a general statement as to structural condition. The accounts of less important buildings, whether secular or ecclesiastical, are still further compressed, and in the case of secular monuments consist of a single paragraph, or of a mere mention of their situation if they belong to a group with certain characteristics described in a covering paragraph.

The illustrations are derived from photographs taken expressly for the Commission, and reproduced by H.M.'s Stationery Office, whose work, I think, deserves special recognition. They have been chosen rather for their educational than their æsthetic value. Had appearance alone been made the test of selection, many more might easily have been included. The map at the end of the Inventory shows the distribution of the monuments, and incidentally throws some light on the concentration of population in the country at various times before the year 1714.

To ensure clearness of description, all ancient churches not illustrated by historically hatched plans have been provided with key plans to a uniform scale of 48 feet to the inch, with the monumental portions shown in solid black. The dimensions given in the Inventory are internal unless otherwise stated. Monuments with titles in italics are covered by an introductory sentence to which reference should be made. Further, the index has again been revised at the hands of the small Committee of the Commission, whose report and recommendations were adopted for the preparation of the index to Essex, Volume II.

It may also be well again to draw attention to the fact that our Record Cards may be consulted by any properly accredited persons, by giving notice of any such intention to our Secretary, at 66, Victoria Street, Westminster, S.W.1. The cards contain drawings of tracery and mouldings as well as plans and sketches of the monuments—forming in truth the complete National Inventory—and will ultimately be deposited for reference in the Public Records Office.

As in the past, no monument has been or will be included in our Inventories that has not been actually inspected and the account checked *in situ* by a member of our own investigating staff. In a work of such intricate detail there must be mistakes. But I hope these are neither numerous nor serious. A further guarantee of accuracy lies in the fact that my fellow Commissioners Mr. Page and Mr. Peers have revised the reports of the Inventories of secular and ecclesiastical monuments, while Mr. Montgomerie has visited and supervised the reports on earthworks. Further, the heraldry of the Inventory has been checked by the Reverend E. E. Dorling, F.S.A.; the descriptions of armour by Mr. J. Murray Kendall, F.S.A. (Assistant to the Secretary of the Imperial War Museum); the descriptions of glass by Dr. James; the description of brasses by Mr. Mill Stephenson, F.S.A.; the spelling of names and descriptions of costumes by Mr. O. Barron, F.S.A.; and the accounts of Roman monuments by our Assistant Commissioner, the late Mr. R. P. L. Booker, F.S.A., and Dr. R. E. Mortimer Wheeler, F.S.A. (Assistant Keeper of the Welsh National Museum). Nevertheless I shall welcome any corrections and criticisms that may be sent to me with a view to their possible inclusion in some future edition.

It is much to be regretted that, owing to the financial exigencies of the time, our staff has not only not been restored to its pre-war strength but has been further reduced during the present year, while the recent sudden death of Mr. R. P. L. Booker has added to our tale of loss, though I am glad to report that the account of Roman Colchester in the main body of the Inventory, as well as that part of the Sectional Preface which deals with the very important finds and Roman remains in the N.E. section of the County was written and revised by him before his death.

The success that has already attended the publication of the Commission's Inventories, and their value in securing the preservation of monuments of historical interest, that otherwise might have been destroyed, leads me to hope that the reduction of the work of investigation that must result will be only temporary.

PLYMOUTH.

26th July, 1922.

TERMS OF APPOINTMENT AND OFFICIAL REPORT.

WHITEHALL, 28TH OCTOBER, 1908.

The KING has been pleased to issue a Commission under His Majesty's Royal Sign Manual to the following effect :—

EDWARD, R. & I.

EDWARD THE SEVENTH, by the Grace of God, of the United Kingdom of Great Britain and Ireland and of the British Dominions beyond the Seas King, Defender of the Faith, to

Our right trusty and well-beloved Counsellor HERBERT COULSTOUN, BARON BURGHCLERE ;

Our right trusty and right well-beloved Cousin and Counsellor ROBERT GEORGE, EARL OF PLYMOUTH, Companion of Our Most Honourable Order of the Bath ;

Our right trusty and well-beloved Cousin HAROLD ARTHUR, VISCOUNT DILLON ; and

Our trusty and well-beloved :—

DAVID ALEXANDER EDWARD LINDSAY, Esquire, commonly called Lord Balcarres ;

SIR HENRY HOYLE HOWORTH, Knight Commander of Our Most Eminent Order of the Indian Empire, President of the Royal Archæological Institute of Great Britain and Ireland ;

SIR JOHN FRANCIS FORTESCUE HORNER, Knight Commander of Our Royal Victorian Order ;

JAMES FITZGERALD, Esquire, Companion of the Imperial Service Order, Assistant Secretary in the Office of the Commissioners of Our Works and Public Buildings ;

JOHN GEORGE NEILSON CLIFT, Esquire, Honorary Secretary of the British Archæological Association ;

FRANCIS JOHN HAVERFIELD, Esquire, Doctor of Laws, Camden Professor of Ancient History in the University of Oxford ;

EMSLIE JOHN HORNIMAN, Esquire ; and

LEONARD STOKES, Esquire, Vice-President of the Royal Institute of British Architects ;

GREETING !

Whereas We have deemed it expedient that a Commission should forthwith issue to make an inventory of the Ancient and Historical Monuments and Constructions connected with or illustrative of the contemporary culture, civilization and conditions of life of the people in England, excluding Monmouthshire, from the earliest times to the year 1700, and to specify those which seem most worthy of preservation :

Now know ye, that We, reposing great trust and confidence in your knowledge and ability, have authorized and appointed, and do by these Presents authorize and appoint you, the said Herbert Coulstoun, Baron Burghclere (Chairman) ; Robert George, Earl of Plymouth ; Harold Arthur, Viscount Dillon ; David Alexander Edward Lindsay (Lord Balcarres) ; Sir Henry Hoyle Howorth ; Sir John Francis Fortescue Horner ; James Fitzgerald ; John George Neilson Clift ; Francis John Haverfield ; Emslie John Horniman, and Leonard Stokes, to be Our Commissioners for the purposes of the said enquiry ;

And for the better enabling you to carry out the purposes of this Our Commission, We do by these Presents authorize you to call in the aid and co-operation of owners of ancient monuments, inviting them to assist you in furthering the objects of the Commission ; and to invite the possessors of such papers as you may deem it desirable to inspect to produce them before you.

And We do further give and grant unto you, or any three or more of you, full power to call before you such persons as you shall judge likely to afford you any information upon the subject of this Our Commission ; and also to call for, have access to and examine all such books, documents, registers and records as may afford you the fullest information on the subject, and to enquire of and concerning the premises by all other lawful ways and means whatsoever :

And We do by these Presents authorize and empower you, or any three or more of you, to visit and personally inspect such places as you may deem it expedient so to inspect for the more effectual carrying out of the purposes aforesaid :

And We do by these Presents will and ordain that this Our Commission shall continue in full force and virtue, and that you, Our said Commissioners, or any three or more of you, may from time to time proceed in the execution thereof, and of every matter and thing therein contained, although the same be not continued from time to time by adjournment :

And We do further ordain that you, or any three or more of you, have liberty to report your proceedings under this our Commission from time to time if you shall judge it expedient so to do :

And Our further will and pleasure is that you do, with as little delay as possible, report to Us, under your hands and seals, or under the hands and seals of any three or more of you, your opinion upon the matters herein submitted for your consideration.

And for the purpose of aiding you in your enquiries We hereby appoint Our trusty and well-beloved George Herbert Duckworth, Esquire, to be Secretary to this Our Commission.

> Given at Our Court at *St. James's*, the twenty-seventh day of *October*, one thousand nine hundred and eight, in the eighth year of Our Reign.
>
> By His Majesty's Command,
>
> H. J. GLADSTONE.

EDWARD, R. & I.

Edward the Seventh, by the Grace of God, of the United Kingdom of Great Britain and Ireland and of the British Dominions beyond the Seas King, Defender of the Faith, To Our trusty and well-beloved Sir Schomberg Kerr McDonnell (commonly called the Honourable Sir Schomberg Kerr McDonnell), Knight Commander of Our Most Honourable Order of the Bath, Commander of Our Royal Victorian Order, Secretary to Our Commissioners of Works and Public Buildings,

GREETING !

Whereas We did by Warrant under Our Royal Sign Manual bearing date the twenty-seventh day of October, one thousand nine hundred and eight, appoint Commissioners to make an inventory of the Ancient and Historical Monuments and Constructions connected with or illustrative of the contemporary culture, civilization and conditions of life of the people in England, excluding Monmouthshire, from the earliest times to the year 1700, and to specify those which seem most worthy of preservation :

And Whereas a vacancy has been caused in the body of Commissioners appointed as aforesaid, by the death of James Fitzgerald, Esquire :

Now know ye that We, reposing great confidence in you, do by these Presents appoint you the said Sir Schomberg Kerr McDonnell to be one of Our Commissioners for the purpose aforesaid, in the room of the said James Fitzgerald, deceased.

> Given at Our Court at *St. James's*, the tenth day of *April*, 1909, in the ninth year of Our reign.
>
> By His Majesty's Command,
>
> H. J. GLADSTONE.

WHITEHALL, 30TH MAY, 1910.

The KING has been pleased to issue a Warrant under His Majesty's Royal Sign Manual to the following effect :—

GEORGE, R. I.

GEORGE THE FIFTH, by the Grace of God, of the United Kingdom of Great Britain and Ireland and of the British Dominions beyond the Seas King, Defender of the Faith, to all to whom these Presents shall come,

GREETING !

Whereas it pleased His late Majesty from time to time to issue Royal Commissions of Enquiry for various purposes therein specified :—

And whereas, in the case of certain of these Commissions, namely, those known as—

The Ancient Monuments (England) Commission,

. . . .

the Commissioners appointed by His late Majesty, or such of them as were then acting as Commissioners, were at the late Demise of the Crown still engaged upon the business entrusted to them :

And whereas we deem it expedient that the said Commissioners should continue their labours in connection with the said Enquiries notwithstanding the late Demise of the Crown :

Now know ye that We, reposing great trust and confidence in the zeal, discretion and ability of the present Members of each of the said Commissions, do by these Presents authorize them to continue their labours, and do hereby in every essential particular ratify and confirm the terms of the said several Commissions.

And We do further ordain that the said Commissioners do report to Us under their hands and seals, or under the hands and seals of such of their number as may be specified in the said Commissions respectively, their opinion upon the matters presented for their consideration ; and that any proceedings which they or any of them may have taken under and in pursuance of the said Commissions since the late Demise of the Crown and before the issue of these Presents shall be deemed and adjudged to have been taken under and in virtue of this Our Commission.

Given at Our Court at *St. James's*, the twenty-sixth day of *May*, one thousand nine hundred and ten, in the first year of Our Reign.

By His Majesty's Command,

R. B. HALDANE.

GEORGE, R. I.

GEORGE THE FIFTH, by the Grace of God, of the United Kingdom of Great Britain and Ireland and of the British Dominions beyond the Seas King, Defender of the Faith, to

Our right trusty and well-beloved Counsellor HERBERT COULSTOUN, BARON BURGHCLERE ;

Our right trusty and right well-beloved Cousin DAVID ALEXANDER EDWARD, EARL OF CRAWFORD ;

Our right trusty and right well-beloved Cousin and Counsellor ROBERT GEORGE, EARL OF PLYMOUTH, Companion of our Most Honourable Order of the Bath ;

Our right trusty and well-beloved Cousin HAROLD ARTHUR, VISCOUNT DILLON ; and

Our trusty and well-beloved :—

SIR SCHOMBERG KERR MCDONNELL (commonly called the Honourable Sir Schomberg Kerr McDonnell), Knight Grand Cross of Our Royal Victorian Order, Knight Commander of Our Most Honourable Order of the Bath ;

SIR HENRY HOYLE HOWORTH, Knight Commander of Our Most Eminent Order of the Indian Empire, President of the Royal Archæological Institute of Great Britain and Ireland ;

SIR JOHN FRANCIS FORTESCUE HORNER, Knight Commander of Our Royal Victorian Order ;

JOHN GEORGE NEILSON CLIFT, Esquire, late Honorary Secretary of the British Archæological Association ;

FRANCIS JOHN HAVERFIELD, Esquire, Doctor of Laws, Camden Professor of Ancient History in the University of Oxford ;

EMSLIE JOHN HORNIMAN, Esquire ; and

LEONARD STOKES, Esquire, Past President of the Royal Institute of British Architects ;

GREETING !

Whereas We have deemed it expedient that the proceedings of the Royal Commission on the Ancient and Historical Monuments and Constructions of England shall cover the period up to the year 1714, instead of up to the year 1700, and that a new Commission should issue for this purpose :

Now know ye that We have revoked and determined, and do by these Presents revoke and determine, the Warrants whereby Commissioners were appointed on the twenty-seventh day of October, one thousand nine hundred and eight, and the tenth day of April, one thousand nine hundred and nine, and every matter and thing therein contained.

And we do by these Presents authorize and appoint you, the said Herbert Coulstoun, Baron Burghclere (Chairman) ; David Alexander Edward, Earl of Crawford ; Robert George, Earl of Plymouth ; Harold Arthur, Viscount Dillon ; Sir Schomberg Kerr McDonnell ; Sir Henry Hoyle Howorth ; Sir John Francis Fortescue Horner ; John George Neilson Clift ; Francis John Haverfield ; Emslie John Horniman, and Leonard Stokes, to be Our Commissioners to make an inventory of the Ancient and Historical Monuments and Constructions connected with or illustrative of the contemporary culture, civilization and conditions of life of the people in England, excluding Monmouthshire, from the earliest times to the year 1714, and to specify those which seem most worthy of preservation.

And for the better enabling you to carry out the purposes of this Our Commission We do by these Presents authorize you to call in the aid and co-operation of owners of ancient monuments, inviting them to assist you in furthering the objects of the Commission ; and to invite the possessors of such papers as you may deem it desirable to inspect to produce them before you :

And We do further give and grant unto you, or any three or more of you, full power to call before you such persons as you shall judge likely to afford you any information upon the subject of this Our Commission ; and also to call for, have access to and examine all such books, documents, registers and records as may afford you the fullest information on the subject, and to enquire of and concerning the premises by all other lawful ways and means whatsoever :

And We do by these Presents authorize and empower you, or any three or more of you, to visit and personally inspect such places as you may deem it expedient so to inspect for the more effectual carrying out of the purposes aforesaid :

And We do by these Presents will and ordain that this Our Commission shall continue in full force and virtue, and that you, Our said Commissioners, or any three or more of you, may from time to time proceed in the execution thereof, and of every matter and thing therein contained, although the same be not continued from time to time by adjournment :

And We do further ordain that you, or any three or more of you, have liberty to report your proceedings under this Our Commission from time to time if you shall judge it expedient so to do :

And Our further will and pleasure is that you do, with as little delay as possible report to Us, under your hands and seals, or under the hands and seals of any three or more of you, your opinion upon the matters herein submitted for your consideration.

And for the purpose of aiding you in your enquiries We hereby appoint Our trusty and well-beloved George Herbert Duckworth, Esquire, to be Secretary to this Our Commission.

> Given at Our Court at *Saint James's*, the twenty-ninth day of *November*, one thousand nine hundred and thirteen in the fourth year of Our Reign.

> By His Majesty's Command,

> R. McKENNA.

GEORGE, R.I.

WHITEHALL, 11TH AUGUST, 1921.

The KING has been pleased to issue a Warrant under His Majesty's Royal Sign Manual to the following effect :—

GEORGE THE FIFTH, by the Grace of God, of the United Kingdom of Great Britain and Ireland and of the British Dominions beyond the Seas King, Defender of the Faith, to

Our trusty and well-beloved :—

SIR ARTHUR JOHN EVANS, Knight, Doctor of Letters, Doctor of Laws, Fellow of the Royal Society ;

SIR CHARLES HERCULES READ, Knight, Doctor of Laws, President of the Society of Antiquaries of London ;

MONTAGUE RHODES JAMES, Esquire, Doctor of Letters, Doctor of Laws, Provost of Eton College ;

DUNCAN HECTOR MONTGOMERIE, Esquire ;

WILLIAM PAGE, Esquire ; and

CHARLES REED PEERS, Esquire.

GREETING !

Know ye that We reposing great trust and confidence in your knowledge and ability do by these Presents appoint you the said Sir Arthur John Evans, Sir Charles Hercules Read, Montague Rhodes James, Duncan Hector Montgomerie, William Page and Charles Reed Peers to be members of the Royal Commission on Historical Monuments (England).

Given at Our Court at *Saint James's*, the eighth day of *August*, one thousand nine hundred and twenty-one, in the twelfth year of Our Reign.

By His Majesty's Command,

EDWARD SHORTT.

ROYAL COMMISSION ON THE ANCIENT AND HISTORICAL
MONUMENTS AND CONSTRUCTIONS OF ENGLAND.

REPORT.

TO THE KING'S MOST EXCELLENT MAJESTY.

1. MAY IT PLEASE YOUR MAJESTY.

We, The undersigned Commissioners, appointed to make an Inventory of
the Ancient and Historical Monuments and Constructions connected with or illustrative of the contemporary culture, civilization and conditions of life of the people
in England, excluding Monmouthshire, from the earliest times to the year 1714, and
to specify those which seem most worthy of preservation, humbly submit to Your
Majesty the following Report on the Monuments in the N.E. Division of the County
of Essex, being the 6th Interim Report on the work of the Commission since its
appointment.

2. We have again to thank Your Majesty for the encouragement given to us
Your Commissioners and our executive staff, by the gracious words which accompanied
Your Majesty's acceptance of our Inventory of the Monuments in Central and
S.W. Essex.

3. We have pleasure in reporting the completion of our enquiries into
N.E. Essex, an area containing 1,311 monuments in 101 parishes, with an average
of 13 monuments per parish as compared with averages of 14·5 monuments in
Central and S.W. Essex, 24 per parish in N.W. Essex, 10 per parish in North Buckinghamshire, 15 per parish in South Buckinghamshire, and 8 per parish in Hertfordshire.

4. An illustrated volume containing the full inventory of these monuments is
issued under the advice of the Lords Commissioners of Your Majesty's Treasury as
a separate Stationery Office publication.

5. No alteration has been found to be necessary in the descriptions of the monuments, which follow exactly the order and method of the previous volume.

6. As in the previous volume, these descriptions have been referred for revision
to special representatives of the Essex Archaeological Society and to the Clergy
and principal owners in each parish. We are satisfied that no important example
dating from the earliest times up to the year 1714 has been omitted.

7. In order to comply with the recommendations of the Publications Committee
we have arranged with the Controller of Your Majesty's Stationery Office for the
accounts of the monuments in Colchester to be printed in such a way that it will
be easy to reprint them for sale as a separate publication should there be, as is
anticipated, a distinct local demand for their re-issue in this form.

8. We humbly recommend to Your Majesty's notice the following monuments, within the area investigated, which, in our opinion, are especially worthy of preservation. For the convenience of students we have subdivided the monuments selected for special mention as they fall under their respective subheads :—

(a) Earthworks and Roman.

(b) Ecclesiastical.

(c) Secular.

Earthworks and Roman.

14. COLCHESTER.

(1) ROMAN REMAINS ; including town walls, Balkerne Gate, and vaults under the Castle.
Condition—Good.

(265) THE LEXDEN EARTHWORKS ; an elaborate system of earthworks mainly between the Colne and Roman Rivers.
Condition—Well preserved only in parts.

96. WEST MERSEA.

(1) MERSEA MOUNT ; a large Romano-British tumulus.
Condition—Good.

(2) FOUNDATIONS of Roman circular building.
Condition—Have suffered from weather since being exposed.

Ecclesiastical :—

10. BRADWELL.

(1) PARISH CHURCH ; dating from the 12th century and later ; remarkable as being practically untouched, with interesting fittings.
Condition—Fairly good, some window tracery weathered.

11. BRIGHTLINGSEA.

(3) PARISH CHURCH ; mainly of the 15th and early 16th centuries, with fine tower.
Condition—Good.

14. COLCHESTER.

(3) HOLY TRINITY CHURCH ; with pre-Conquest W. tower, and rare mazer-bowl.
Condition—Good.

(5) ST. MARTIN'S CHURCH ; dating from the 12th century, with interesting woodwork in the chancel.
Condition—Fairly good.

(15) ST. JOHN'S GATE ; the 15th-century gatehouse of a Benedictine abbey.
Condition—Good.

(16) ST. BOTOLPH'S PRIORY ; ruins of 12th-century nave of a priory of Austin Canons.
Condition—Ruins well preserved : in care of H.M. Office of Works.

16. COPFORD.

(1) PARISH CHURCH ; a remarkable 12th-century building with restored paintings.
Condition—Good, much restored.

18. DEDHAM.

(1) PARISH CHURCH ; a large church of early 16th-century date.
Condition—Good.

24. ELMSTEAD.

(1) PARISH CHURCH ; dating from the 14th century and containing an oak effigy.
Condition—Good.

25. FEERING.

(1) PARISH CHURCH ; dating from the 14th century or earlier, with good early 16th-century brickwork in nave.
Condition—Good.

26. FINGRINGHOE.

(1) PARISH CHURCH ; dating from the 12th-century, with remains of paintings.
Condition—Of tower bad ; of masonry of chancel, etc., poor.

31. GREAT BENTLEY.

(1) PARISH CHURCH ; dating from the 12th century, with good doorways.
Condition—Good.

33. GREAT BROMLEY.

(1) PARISH CHURCH ; dating from the 14th century, with good early 16th-century roof and S. porch.
Condition—Generally good, but of nave roof, poor.

34. GREAT CLACTON.

(1) PARISH CHURCH ; a remarkable 12th-century building with good doorways.
Condition—Good, except roof of nave.

40. GREAT TEY.

(1) PARISH CHURCH ; with fine 12th-century tower and 14th-century chancel.
Condition—Fairly good.

45. INWORTH.

(1) PARISH CHURCH ; mainly of pre-Conquest date.
Condition—Good, much restored.

46. KELVEDON.

(2) PARISH CHURCH ; dating from the 12th century.
Condition—Good, except N. aisle, which is much decayed.

51. LAWFORD.

(1) PARISH CHURCH ; with very rich 14th-century chancel.
Condition—Good, except tower.

54. LAYER MARNEY.

(1) PARISH CHURCH ; of early 16th-century date, with fine monuments and a painting.
Condition—Fairly good, but unsatisfactory foundations tend to render the structure insecure.

59. LITTLE COGGESHALL.

(1 and 2) ABBEY and CHURCH ; remains of Cistercian abbey with 13th-century brickwork.
Condition—Good.

62. LITTLE HORKESLEY.

(1) PARISH CHURCH ; dating from the 12th century, with fine brasses and monuments.
Condition—Good, much restored.

64. LITTLE TEY.

(1) PARISH CHURCH ; with 12th-century apse.
Condition—Good.

79. ST. OSYTH.

(2) PARISH CHURCH ; dating from the 12th century, with brick 16th-century nave and good monuments.
Condition—Good.

81. STANWAY.

(3) CHURCH OF ALL SAINTS ; with 14th-century tower and 17th-century porch.
Condition—Ruinous.

82. STISTED.

(1) PARISH CHURCH ; dating from late in the 12th century.
Condition—Much restored.

86. TOLLESBURY.

(2) PARISH CHURCH ; dating from late in in the 11th century.
Condition—Good.

Secular :—

9. BRADFIELD.

(2) BRADFIELD HALL ; remains of an early 16th-century brick house.
Condition—Fairly good.

11. BRIGHTLINGSEA.

(4) JACOBES HALL ; an interesting early 16th-century brick house.
Condition — Good, timber ceilings recently uncovered.

14. COLCHESTER.

(18) THE CASTLE ; the largest (in area) Norman keep in this country.
Condition—Of ruins, good ; of earthworks, imperfect.

(30) RED LION HOTEL ; a rather elaborately ornamented timber house of late 15th-century date.
Condition—Good.

(39) GATE HOUSE ; a good example of a 17th-century timber building.
Condition—good.

(69) MARQUIS OF GRANBY INN ; an early 16th-century building of timber with an elaborately carved beam.

(231) THE SIEGE HOUSE ; a 15th-century timber-framed house with marks of bullets dating from the siege.
Condition—Good.

(263) BOURNE MILL ; a 16th-century brick building with interesting decorative features.
Condition—Good.

18. DEDHAM.

(2) SOUTHFIELDS ; a 15th-century court-yard building, formerly a 'bay and say' factory.
Condition—Good.

20. EARLS COLNE.

(2) EARLS COLNE PRIORY ; a modern house containing a series of mediaeval monuments to the Veres, Earls of Oxford.
Condition—Of monuments, good.

(23) COLNEFORD HOUSE ; a good example of 17th-century pargeting.
Condition—Good.

35. GREAT COGGESHALL.

(3) PAYCOCKS ; a richly ornamented timber house of early 16th-century date.
Condition—Good.

38. GREAT HORKESLEY.

(2) CHAPEL (now a cottage) ; an early 16th-century brick building.
Condition—Good.

54. LAYER MARNEY.

(2) LAYER MARNEY TOWERS or HALL ; a remarkable fragment of a great house with early Renaissance detail.
Condition—Good.

62. LITTLE HORKESLEY.

> (5) LOWER DAIRY FARM; c. 1600, with good carved bressumers, etc.
> Condition—Good.

79. ST. OSYTH.

> (4) PRIORY or ABBEY; a house incorporating interesting remains of an abbey of Austin Canons; fine 15th-century gatehouse.
> Condition—Good; ruins well preserved.

> (7) ST. CLAIR'S HALL; an interesting 14th-century and later house with an aisled hall.
> Condition—Good, except W. wing.

89. TOLLESHUNT MAJOR.

> (3) BECKINGHAM HALL; a 16th-century gatehouse and wall.
> Condition—Of house, good; of gatehouse and walls, poor.

98. WIVENHOE.

> (2) THE HALL; remains of an early 16th-century house of brick.
> Condition—Good, much altered.

> (6) HOUSE; with good ornamental pargeting of the 17th century.
> Condition—Bad.

9. The Index Committee, consisting of Mr. C. R. Peers, F.S.A., Mr. W. Page, F.S.A., and Mr. G. H. Duckworth, C.B., F.S.A., in a third interim report have suggested certain further emendations which we have adopted in this present volume. We attach their report.

10. We have also to thank the Publications Committee of the Commission, consisting of Lord Plymouth (Chairman), Mr. W. R. Codling, C.B.E., M.V.O., Mr. John Murray, C.V.O., Mr. C. T. Hagberg Wright, Mr. W. Page, F.S.A., and Mr. G. H. Duckworth, C.B., F.S.A., for a most valuable report on the steps that should be taken to curtail expenditure on publication and at the same time increase the sales of our Illustrated Inventories.

11. We offer our grateful thanks to Mr. J. Murray Kendall, F.S.A., for revision of the descriptions of Armour; to the Reverend E. E. Dorling, V.P.S.A., for revision of descriptions of Heraldry; to Mr. Oswald Barron, F.S.A., for revision of the descriptions of Costumes and spelling of names; to Mr. Mill Stephenson, F.S.A., for revision of descriptions of Brasses, and to Mr. R. P. L. Booker, F.S.A., and to Mr. R. E. M. Wheeler, M.C., Litt.D., F.S.A., for revision of descriptions of Roman Remains; to Mr. Albany Major, F.S.A., O.B.E., Secretary of the Committee on Ancient Earthworks and Fortified Enclosures, for revision of the accounts of Earthworks, and to Mr. F. E. Eden for his descriptions and illustrations of the Ancient Glass in the county.

12. We desire to call attention to the assistance given to our work by the members of the Essex Archaeological Society, and we have pleasure in acknowledging the courtesy and hospitality extended to ourselves by the Clergy and owners of houses in the county.

13. We have also to thank the Bishop of Chelmsford for his letter of introduction to the Clergy in his diocese; the Clergy who have freely opened their churches for investigation; the Reverend Canon Galpin and the Reverend T. W. Curling, respectively President and Secretary of the County Archaeological Society, and Mr. Wykeham Chancellor, F.R.I.B.A., Mr. Miller Christy, Dr. P. Laver, F.S.A., and Mr. A. G. Wright, Curator of the Colchester Museum, for assistance given to ourselves and to our investigators.

14. We desire to express our acknowledgment of the good work accomplished by our Executive Staff in the persons of Mr. A. W. Clapham, F.S.A., Mr. J. W. Bloe, F.S.A., Mr. W. H. Godfrey, F.S.A., Mr. W. Byde Liebert, Mr. G. E. Chambers, Mr. M. L. Logan, and Mr. P .K. Kipps ; Miss M. G. Saunders, on whom has devolved the work of checking the proofs of the Inventory and making the Index of this Volume, and Miss M. V. Taylor, M.A., who has investigated the Roman Remains of this portion of the County of Essex.

15. We desire to express our high appreciation of the admirable way in which our Secretary, Mr. G. H. Duckworth, adapts the work of the Commission to the economical pressure applied to all Government Departments. It is of the greatest importance that the work of the Commission should not come to a standstill, and it is only by our Secretary's extreme care in working out the details that we are able to maintain a regular publication of our volumes.

Signed :

PLYMOUTH.
DILLON.
CRAWFORD & BALCARRES.
HENRY H. HOWORTH.
J. F. F. HORNER.
J. G. N. CLIFT.
E. J. HORNIMAN.
LEONARD STOKES.
ARTHUR J. EVANS.
C. HERCULES READ.
M. R. JAMES.
D. H. MONTGOMERIE.
WILLIAM PAGE.
C. R. PEERS.

GEORGE H. DUCKWORTH
(*Secretary*).

22nd May, 1922.

NORTH-EAST ESSEX.

SECTIONAL PREFACE.

(i) EARTHWORKS, ETC., PREHISTORIC AND LATER.

The North-eastern quarter of Essex contains comparatively few earthworks of importance for the country is little suited to hill-forts and works of that description. Of the existing examples of earthworks the most interesting are the Red Hills, the Lexden Earthworks and the Romano-British barrow on Mersea Island.

Over two hundred Red Hills, so-called from the red earth of which they are composed, have been noted in Essex, chiefly near the estuaries of the Colne and the Blackwater. Similar works are found on the Lincolnshire coast, on the Upchurch marshes in Kent, and on the opposite shores of the Channel. They are usually situated by the sides of creeks and along what was the old high-water mark before the sea-walls were built. They are generally of low elevation and irregular in shape and frequently cover two or three acres. The red earth is extremely fertile, and is often removed and used for agricultural purposes. Careful investigation has been made of some of the hills, notably at Goldhanger and Canewdon, and here they consisted of powdery red earth containing pieces of roughly shaped and crudely baked clay, with grass as a binding material, in the form of fire-bars, fragments of small chambers (similar to ovens) and circular stems spreading out at the end. Late Celtic pottery, some pieces with rivet holes, and small pieces of Roman pottery (including a fragment or two of Arretine ware) have also been discovered. The mounds appear to be originally of pre-Claudian date, but their purpose is doubtful though many theories on the subject have been advanced. It is possible that the material was brought by water, perhaps as ballast, and dumped at the sides of the creeks to form 'hards' or landing places. The salt-marshes (known as Saltings) contain many mounds other than the Red Hills, and are crossed by ancient tracks, known as 'Peat ways.'

Of Hill Camps, the single example (see Plan, p. 128) is in Great Horkesley parish. Here the defensive works, except at the northern end, are gradually being destroyed by the plough.

The Lexden Earthworks (see Map, p. 72) are collectively the most interesting monument of their class in Essex. They are situated about two miles from the centre of Colchester and cover all the high ground W. of the town between the River Colne and Roman River and, to a certain extent, beyond both rivers. They consist of four main lines of entrenchments each with a rampart and a ditch on their western side, situated one behind the other and running roughly N. and S. On the line of Gryme's Dyke, the westernmost of the four, is a curious triangular work, perhaps covering a point where the three western lines of entrenchment converge, and further

N. is a large excavation, known as King Coel's Kitchen, perhaps a disused gravel-pit. There is also an original entrance through this dyke.   There are slight traces of minor banks near the main entrenchments.

Mersea Mount (see Section, p. 229), in West Mersea parish, contained a Romano-British burial (see Roman Remains below).

The mediaeval earthworks include the remains of three castles, the town ditch at Colchester and some sixty homestead moats.   The rampart and ditch of the Inner Bailey of Colchester Castle remain intact on the N. and E. sides, the northern rampart being thrown up over Roman walls and pavements.   Of the town ditch, fragments remain on the N. and E. arms.   At Mount Bures is a well-preserved moated mound with no traces of a bailey ;   it was possibly the seat of the Sackvilles. Of Birch Castle, mentioned by Morant as a moated mound, belonging to Sir William Gernon, only a semi-circular fragment of rampart and ditch remains.

The miscellaneous earthworks include a length of entrenchment in Layer Marney parish, two doubtful tumuli at Messing and Tolleshunt Major respectively, a fragment of a recently discovered work in Brinkley Grove, N. of Colchester, and a number of mill-dams.

The recorded occupation of Mersea Island by the Danes, in A.D. 895 (*Anglo-Sax. Chron.*), has left no recognizable trace ; the suggested identification of their camp with the moat in East Mersea (2) is almost certainly incorrect as the site is too high above the sea-level and too far from the coast.

(ii) ROMAN REMAINS.

The area included in the present volume is, in Britain, unrivalled for its wealth of historical associations with the latest pre-Roman and earliest Roman periods. These associations cluster round Colchester which had a flourishing population already in touch with Roman civilization before the Claudian invasion A.D. 43. Roman moneyers were employed by Cunobeline ; Roman amphorae have been found with late Celtic pottery at Colchester ; and Arretine ware has occurred in at least one of the mysterious 'Red Hills.' The adoption, therefore, of the elements of 'Romanization' was stimulated rather than initiated by the invasion.   South-eastern Britain was absorbed rather than conquered, and the (apparently) casual and unguarded occupation of Colchester itself by the first colonists indicates a comparatively settled and civilized countryside.   Under such conditions it is likely that country houses of Roman type began to spring up almost immediately after the invasion ; indeed a building at Pleshey, noted in Volume II of the Essex Inventory, was certainly occupied at this period, and excavation may be expected to yield similar evidence elsewhere.   Of military remains there is, on the other hand, no trace.   Such temporary fieldworks as must have been thrown up by the Claudian armies may be supposed to have vanished long since beneath the plough. Colchester has been claimed by some writers as in origin a legionary fortress, but the absence of supporting evidence is reflected in the diversity of opinion as to the precise legion stationed there, and the weight of Tacitus is, on the whole, opposed to any such view.

Towns and villages.—It is not improbable that some of the 'villas' noted in the district formed the nuclei of small settlements, and at Brightlingsea, near the mouth of the River Colne, there seems to have been a small village.   The only town definitely known to us, however, is Colchester, one of the four or five places in Britain which attained to colonial or to municipal rank.

Camulodūnum, the royal *oppidum* of Cunobeline, is an exceptionally large specimen of the promontory fortress. Here, two rivers, the Colne and the Roman River, approaching each other and then receding only to meet after a while, enclose a more or less pear-shaped plateau, of an elevation of about one hundred feet with tolerably steep sides, and measuring about three by four miles. The neck of the plateau is defended by a reinforced system of earthworks. There are four distinct lines of embankment across the space from the Colne to the Roman River, and, beyond the rivers to the north and south, other ramparts are found, which must have been designed as flanking works to the main defences. The outmost line, $3\frac{1}{2}$ miles in length, the straightest, and therefore perhaps the least ancient of the entrenched lines, is known as Gryme's Dyke. It shows a curious double bend at a place a little south of the centre, and not far to the north of the bend a gap, where presumably the ancient road passed. The dyke has been a boundary, time out of mind, and now marks the western confines of the borough of Colchester, and the *civitas* of the Domesday survey seems, in the opinion of many good judges, to correspond to the British *oppidum*.* The area included between rivers and dykes is as much as twelve square miles, and must have possessed great natural strength when forests enclosed it on the north and west, and the rivers, with the tides and marshes, offered a much broader expanse of water defences than now. Within the limits a considerable number of Celtic coins have been found, and a Celtic cemetery existed in Lexden Park, but no evidence of permanent dwellings of these people have come to light, such as abound at Alesia, Bibracte and other *oppida* of the latest pre-Roman period in Gaul.

To this place came Claudius, as conqueror, in A.D. 43, with his four victorious legions. Here in due course arose the Temple to Claudius, the Statue of Victory, the Curia and the Theatre which Tacitus mentions. The "Colonia Victricensis" seems to have been called into being by Ostorius Scapula sometime between the years 47 and 50. This general required all the regular troops he could muster for his expedition into Wales, but, as he could not afford to leave his rear completely unguarded, he established at Camulodunum a strong body of veterans "'as a defence against the rebels and as a means of imbuing the 'socii' with respect for our laws." (Tacitus Ann. XII. 32.) Thus, it would seem, in the north-east corner of the extensive area of Celtic Camulodunum, under Roman auspices, an intensive life was developing on the site of modern Colchester. The existing walls enclose 108 acres, which is exactly double the size of the legionary camp at York. But however tempting it may be to suppose that the walls of Colchester originated as a double legionary camp, there stands the definite statement of Tacitus that in A.D. 61 the colony was unprotected by defences such as a fortress would have required. Moreover, three instances of burial within the walls, and a case where the wall passes on the top of Roman pavements (see Inventory, No. 45), prove that the present walls are not coeval with the first Roman occupation of the site.

Anyhow, in A.D. 61, when the storm of Boudicca's (Boadicea) rebellion burst, there was only a small military force at hand to quell it. At that time the natives were chafing at the lawlessness of the veterans and the licence of the soldiers, and were further exasperated by eviction from their holdings, and by the spectacle of Roman luxury, while the veterans were scattered in the cultivation of their ill-gotten estates, and the legate Suetonius was far away in North Wales. There was no time to remove the women and infirm into safety ; no time to construct fosse or rampart, and though the young men and soldiers occupied the temple (all else was plundered or fired), it fell after a two days' siege. In London, Verulam, and Colchester, about 70,000 citizens and provincials were killed.

Roman Camulodunum had to make a fresh start, and the walls and other evidence indicate something of the general outline of the new work. It is quite certain that a road ran from the Balkerne Gate to the East Gate, almost certainly crossed by a road from Head Gate to the North Gate. The clue thus afforded may be reinforced by the known position of early churches within the walls, by sundry considerations concerning the Castle area, and by the excavation of an insula in 1920 in the Castle Park (No. 36, p. 26). The spade then revealed a block of about 440 ft. by 290 ft. built, as the pottery involved implies, in the latter half of the first century, over older buildings that had been destroyed by fire, and were differently orientated. · It established the facts that 330 ft. south of the N. wall of the city is a road running east and west parallel to the wall ; and that this road is cut by two others at right angles, respectively at 820 ft. and at 1,110 ft. from the E. town-wall. The last-mentioned of these roads is the main thoroughfare leading from the Roman Ryegate, and lies partially under the present Ryegate Road. As this line was seemingly the western boundary of the King's demesne in Domesday, extending from High Street northwards, and through the wall down to the River Colne, it is likely that the Roman way remained so far in evidence till the Norman Conquest. If continued southwards, it would meet the S. wall of the town at the point where the Mersea Road may be supposed to enter, at the lost Roman South Gate.

The width of the excavated insula suggests that it lies in the same longitudinal zone as the forum of the town, and it will be seen hereafter that this very likely is the case.

The bearing of the evidence of the churches on the town-plan is interesting. There were eight parish churches within the walls, and the date of their respective foundations is probably very remote. But it is noticeable that the parishes attached in all cases extend beyond the walls, while St. Botolph's is extra-mural as far as the building is concerned though its parish bounds penetrate within the *enceinte*. At Lincoln, on the contrary, in the upper city, town walls and parish boundaries are rigidly conterminous. It is likely that old churches would have been placed so as to be easily accessible from old streets, and at Colchester, St. Peter's, St. Runwald's (now destroyed), St. Nicholas', All Saints' and St. James' are approached by the High Street, while two others, St. Martin's and Holy Trinity, rest their west end on the same transverse line as St. Runwald's ; and St. Mary-at-the-Walls, though slightly away from a line of a probable Roman street, stands close to a Roman postern in the town-wall.

Of the buildings within the walls the schedule in the Inventory (subjoined) tells its own tale. Till recently no house had been properly planned, and no individual edifice possessed much distinctive interest. The points which proved a change of plan after the first occupation of the site had been noted, and the pavements irregularly recorded. But these were perhaps of no particular merit, they include no figure subjects, and the harvest of finds inside the town could not at all compare with the richness of the yield of the cemeteries outside. In particular, two monuments, both in Colchester Museum, deserve notice : (1) the tombstone of M. Favonius Facilis, a centurion of the twentieth legion, of 1st-century date, and (2) a sphinx, holding in its claws a human head of grotesque character. But the digging in the Castle Park has thrown new light on the plan of the Roman city, and the reinvestigation of the Castle has revealed the fact that it covers one of the most extensive surviving 'monuments' of Roman Britain.

The plan (p. 28) shows that the west end of the town, near the London road, was more thickly covered with buildings than the eastern quarter, though many may be waiting discovery in the still large gardens on this side. The Roman town never spread beyond its early walls and does not rank among the larger towns of Roman Britain. It was too near London and did not, like Verulam, stand on any important road. The small finds in the museum and elsewhere show that it was occupied to the end of the Roman period. No evidence exists as to its fate in the fifth century. The fire and first narrowing of the Balkerne Gate betoken an enemy in the Roman period, but the date is uncertain. The further reduction of the Gate and the destruction of the north-eastern postern were probably effected in the post-Roman period, but whether in struggles with Saxons or Danes is unknown. It is difficult to believe that in a place so exposed to sea-raiders, occupation was continuous from Roman to Saxon days, when other towns like Roman Canterbury, Verulam, and Silchester were either deserted for a time or abandoned altogether.

The Celtic name of the Claudian 'Colonia Victricensis' continued in use during the Roman period. The town is called both 'Colonia' and 'Camoloduno' in the Antonine Itinerary (474, 480), but 'Camuloduno' in the Peutinger Table. Camulodunum, spelt as on Cunobeline's coins, is mentioned in an inscription from Carnuntum at Vienna (*Corp. Inscr. Latin.* III. 11233) and possibly in another found 27th July, 1922, at Jedburgh Abbey. It is so used by Tacitus and is to be preferred to the spelling, Camalodunum, as in the elder Pliny (Nat. Hist. II. 187) and an unimportant inscription in the Vatican (*Corp. Inscr. Latin.* XIV. 3955). The name is connected apparently with a Celtic war god Camulus.

Farms and Country-houses.—These are fairly numerous, and the presence of bricks of Roman type in the walls of at least twenty-five churches (excluding Colchester) may be assumed to indicate the existence of a number of destroyed or undiscovered buildings within the area. Unfortunately, in no case have the known remains been completely or scientifically excavated, and it is not possible to reproduce an intelligible plan of a single example, with the small exception of the circular building on Mersea Island. There seems now to be little doubt that this building was not a ' pharos ' but was a peristyle monument of a plan which can be paralleled in existing monuments on the Appian Way (L. Canina, *Via Appia*) and elsewhere. On both sides of Colchester, at Stanway on the west and at Alresford on the east, extensive 'villas' have been partially excavated, but all detailed information regarding the former seems to have been lost, and the record of the latter is inadequate. At Rivenhall, trenches have revealed the existence of extensive remains which deserve further exploration ; and at Great Coggeshall, Dovercourt, St. Osyth, Tolleshunt Knights, and, less certainly, at Tollesbury and Kelvedon, evidence of settled Roman occupation has been found, but not properly investigated.

Burial-Mounds.—The mound on Mersea Island has been shown by excavation to have been built over a burial of late 1st-century date, and should therefore be classed with the Bartlow Hills (see Volume I of the Essex Inventory) as an example of a mode of sepulture which was common at this period both to south-eastern Britain and to Belgium. It is possible that the two mounds in Lexden Park, near Colchester, are of similar origin, but the partial excavation of one of them disclosed no burial, although Roman potsherds were found in its structure.

Roads.—Four roads in N.E. Essex are largely of Roman origin ; conjecture adds others, of which some are probable but all are unproved. The known roads all converge upon Colchester. The Stane Street, which emerges from Hertfordshire near Bishops Stortford and proceeds due eastwards (see Sectional Preface to Essex Inventory, Vol. I), was joined at Marks Tey by the Roman main road from London, and so carried both lines of traffic to the west or south-west gates of Colchester. It has been reasonably argued that this coincidence of the London Road with the natural course of Stane Street implies the pre-existence of the latter, but our know-ledge of the road-system in this district is very incomplete and alternative routes possibly existed.   Between Stanway and Colchester the problem is further compli-cated by the probability that the system was altered in Roman times.   Excavation has shown that the original road penetrated the Gryme's Dyke at an entrance half a mile south of the present Lexden Road, proceeded east-south-eastwards through the inner banks, and then, near Prettygate Farm, turned abruptly north-eastwards to the Balkerne Gate (H. Laver, *E.A.S.T.* (N.S.), III, 123; M. Christy, *ib.*, XV, 190, XVI, 127), passing close to the present Grammar School and the junction of Queen's Road with Victoria Road near West Lodge.   This is the quarter where the great 1st-century cemetery stood, and the road-metal is said to have been found 10 ft. north of the centurion tombstone, which was unearthed in the fifth garden on the east side of Beverley Road.

The route thus indicated between Colchester and Stanway was indirect, and was probably determined partly by the pre-existence of the Lexden earthworks. There is reason, however, to suppose that this road was superseded during the later Roman period by a more direct route which left Colchester at the site of the mediaeval Head Gate (beneath which the foundations of a Roman gate are said to have been noticed) and coincided approximately with the present Lexden Road.   It is on this line, and not on that of the earlier way, that the open-field system hinges, and it is possible, though not certain, that the modern cutting made for St. Clare Road, adjoining Lexden Park, has disclosed the ditch which formerly flanked the Roman Road.   Close to this route, south-west of Head Gate, have been found numerous 3rd and 4th-century inhumation·burials.

South of Colchester the Roman Road to Mersea can be traced intermittently. It is said to have been found by the eastern boundary-wall of St. John's Abbey, and to run near Plum Hall and Monk Wycke to the place called the Rampart on the E. side of Berechurch Park, where it remains to a height of two or three feet. Abberton. church stands on it, and it is supposed to pass by Peet Hall Causey to the Strood.   Traces of it, however, are scarce, and it has been thought that the old approach to Mersea Island was by a ferry some half mile or more east of the present causeway.

The Eastern Counties route in the Antonine Itinerary six miles beyond Camulo-dunum reaches '*Ad Ansam.*'   This halting-place must have been on the bank of the River Stour, near Stratford St. Mary.   The present road, from about two miles from Colchester, is a parish boundary almost all the way, but whether the Roman Road emerged from the Rye Gate or (like the modern road) from the East Gate is uncertain.

On leaving these four roads—Stane Street and the roads to London, Mersea and Stratford—evidence even of a general kind becomes precarious.   Near Dover-court, the "mutilated parts of a considerable large stone pavement" containing Roman coins is noted by Morant (*Hist. Essex*, I, 499), and may be part of a line of communication between Colchester and the destroyed fort at Walton by Felixstowe. North-west of Colchester a road from Cambridge should probably be looked for.   This route, which is clear over the Gogmagog Hills and may be followed dubiously as far as Ridgewell, must have descended the Colne Valley ; but in the area wherewith this volume is concerned no trace of it has been discovered.   (See Sectional Preface to Essex, Vol. I).   South-west of the town a road may have led in the direction of (though not necessarily to) Maldon ; but here again verification is not yet forthcoming.

LITTLE TEY : *c.* 1130 and later.

LAMARSH : 12th-century and later.

STISTED : late 12th-century and later.
East Windows, 13th-century.

BRADWELL-JUXTA-COGGESHALL.
Chancel, *c.* 1340 ; Nave, 12th-century and later.

BOXTED : 12th-century and later.

CRESSING : 12th-century and later.
Windows, 14th and 15th century.

PEBMARSH : 14th-century and later.

FINGRINGHOE : 12th century and later.

CHURCH PORCHES.

ARDLEIGH.
South Porch ; late 15th century.

LITTLE OAKLEY.
Porch and Window South of Chancel ;
mid 14th-century.

FINGRINGHOE.
South Porch ; late 14th and late 15th-century.

COLNE ENGAINE.
South Porch ; early 16th-century.

PEBMARSH.
South Porch ; early 16th-century.

LAYER MARNEY.
South Porch of Chancel ; early 16th-century.

(iii) ECCLESIASTICAL AND SECULAR ARCHITECTURE.

BUILDING MATERIALS : STONE, FLINT, BRICK, ETC.

There is little change in the general characteristics of both ecclesiastical and secular buildings in N.E. Essex from those described in the preceding volumes on the N.W., Central and S.W. parts of the county. The parts towards the E. coast show a greater use of septaria as building material, and the Colchester district displays, as might be expected, an extensive reuse of Roman material, both brick and stone. The N.E. is the only part of the county yet surveyed which provides examples of 13th-century or earlier brickwork. The bricks used at Coggeshall Abbey, of late 12th and early 13th-century date, are of a warm red tone and generally about 1¾ in. to 2 in. thick; the fact, that the majority of them are shaped to suit their present positions is an argument in favour of local manufacture. With the 14th century the use of brick became more general in this part of the county and examples are noted at Colchester, St. Martin and St. Leonard-at-the-Hythe; Stanway All Saints, and Fordham. The brick of this period is of a much lighter shade, varying from light red to a muddy yellow. The 15th and 16th-century brickwork reverts to the warm red colour of the earlier work; an instance of remarkably large bricks (11¼ in. by 5¼ in.) of this period occurs in the lower part of the tower of Weeley church.

Nearly all the purely secular buildings of earlier date than the 16th century are of timber; after that period a certain number of the larger houses were built of brick. Stone is confined to the domestic buildings of certain dissolved monastic houses, to the keep of Colchester Castle, and to the walls of a number of cellars in the town of Colchester.

ECCLESIASTICAL BUILDINGS.

The churches of N.E. Essex include a fairly high proportion of buildings of more than usual interest. The proximity to the Suffolk border is indicated by the presence of a number of large churches, such as Dedham (Plate, p. 80), Great Coggeshall and Great Bromley (Plate, p. 112), of the East Anglian type. Bradwell (juxta Coggeshall) church is worthy of special mention as it is untouched by modern restoration and presents a museum of church fittings of all periods down to the end of the 18th century. The two churches of Copford and Great Clacton are both buildings of a peculiar type of construction of which the only parallel in this country appears to be the nave at Chepstow Priory.

Chronologically, all the mediaeval periods are well represented except the 13th century, of which, as elsewhere in Essex, there are comparatively few examples. The tower of Holy Trinity, Colchester (Plate, p. 34), is a well-known example of pre-Conquest work and is built on to the W. gable of a still earlier church. Inworth retains both nave and chancel of pre-Conquest date, but the latter was subsequently extended. Of late 11th and 12th-century work there are many examples, Tollesbury, Heybridge (Plate, p. 131), and West Mersea tower being the earliest. The two 12th-century churches at Copford and Great Clacton (Plates, pp. 76, 114) have already been referred to; they were both roofed by a system of broad cross-arches with cross-vaults groined into the main span in each bay : both vaults were subsequently removed. The ruined priory church of St. Botolph, Colchester (Plates, pp. 46, 47), is in a class by itself as being the nave of a fairly large conventual church; it is largely built of Roman brick. Enriched work of this period occurs at Little Totham (Plate, p. 115), Great Bentley (Plate, p. 108), Great Tey (Plate, p. 130) and Middleton (Plate, p. 142). Great Tey has a massive 12th-century central tower and the W. towers of Heybridge and St. Martin, Colchester (Plate, p. 38), have features of interest. A series of plain early 12th-century vaults represents the E. range of the monastic buildings at St. Osyth. To the very end of the century belong the columns of the N. arcade at Stisted (Plates, pp. 212, 213). The best examples of the 13th century are to be found in the chancels of Stisted (Plate, p. xxviii) and Easthorpe (Plate, p. 92), the nave at Kelvedon (Plate, p. 141) and the monastic buildings of St. Osyth (Plate, p. 203) and Little Coggeshall (Plates, pp. 166–7). Fourteenth-century work is well represented in the district, the chancel of Lawford (Plates, pp. 150, 151) being an example of particular richness. Other good work of the period occurs at Colchester St. Martin (Plate, p. 39) and St. Nicholas; Langham (Plate, p. 148); Great Bromley (Plate, p. 113), Elmstead (Plate, p. 93) and Pebmarsh; the W. tower at All Saints, Stanway (Plate, p. 6), has a curious vault in the form of a saucer dome with applied ribs. The finest 15th-century building is probably the handsome W. tower at Brightlingsea (Plate, p. 11), and other good examples of the 15th and 16th centuries are to be found at Dedham, Great Bromley, Great Coggeshall, Feering (Plate, p. 96), St. Osyth (Plate, p. 198), Layer Marney (Plate, p. 155) and Colchester St. Leonard-at-the-Hythe (Plate, p. 35). The nave at St. Osyth, the S. side at Feering, and the whole church of Layer Marney are executed in brick. The only examples of post-Reformation work of any interest are the church at Manningtree, much altered, and the porch and other works at All Saints, Stanway, all of the 17th century.

Apsidal E. ends, all of the 12th century, occur at Copford, Little Tey (Plate, p. xxviii) and Little Braxted, the two latter being without chancel-arches. Remains of a former apse exist at Easthorpe and probable indications of another at Great Braxted. The church at Lamarsh has a round tower (Plate, p. xxviii), much repaired, and central towers exist at Great Tey and Mount Bures, but the last-named has been rebuilt; there is evidence also of a former central tower at Wakes Colne, of a central crossing at St. Nicholas, Colchester, and documentary evidence of a central tower at St. Peter's in the same town. The priory church of St. Botolph, Colchester, had two western towers, of which one still stands in part.

Western towers of brick are to be found at Layer Marney, Weeley, Thorpe-le-Soken, Great Holland, Tolleshunt Major (Plate, p. 220) and Colchester (Berechurch and Greenstead). The upper stages of Colne Engaine; St. Mary, Birch (Plate, p. 6); and Little Bromley, are also of this material.

There are handsome stone porches at Ardleigh (Plate, p. xxix), Great Bromley and Brightlingsea, and good brick examples at Feering (Plate, p. 96) and Pebmarsh (Plate, p. xxix). Of timber porches, those at Aldham (Plate, p. xxxvi) and Tendring (Plate, p. xxxvi) date from the 14th century, and later instances at Frating, Bradwell (Plate, p. 7) and Great Horkesley have features of interest.

Nine churches have low-side windows.

There is a fine hammer-beam roof at Great Bromley (Plate, p. 113) and others at Peldon, St. Osyth, and Colchester St. Leonard-at-the-Hythe (Plate, p. 35); a 17th-century example occurs at Manningtree (Plate, p. xxxvi). Good roofs of other types exist at St. Osyth, Dedham and Colchester St. James and St. Martin.

Stone or brick vaulting is used at Dedham (Plate, p. 213) and Stanway All Saints (W. tower) and Great Coggeshall and Feering (Plate, p. 133) (S. porches).

One desecrated chapel at Great Horkesley (Plate, p. 127) is scheduled in the inventory. It is a late 15th-century brick building and is now used as a cottage.

HOUSES WITH EXPOSED TIMBER-FRAMING.

From the South.

North Side of Main Block.

LITTLE HORKESLEY: Josselyns; late 15th or early 16th-century.

GREAT HORKESLEY.

(13) Baytree Farm; 15th-century.

DEDHAM.

(2) Southfields; late 15th or early 16th-century.   Courtyard, looking North-East.

From the South-West.

COLCHESTER.

(194) No. 17, East Hill; 16th-century.

Gable, South End of West Front.

LITTLE HORKESLEY: Lower Dairy Farm; c. 1601.

TOLLESBURY.
(20) House, S. Side of Main Street; late 15th
or early 16th-century.

KELVEDON.
(23) House, High Street; 15th-century and later.

ST. OSYTH.
(8) Priory Cottage; 15th-century and later.

ST. OSYTH.
(7) St. Clair's Hall; 14th-century and later.

STANWAY.
(14) Abbots Farm; 15th or early 16th-century.

RIVENHALL.
(13) Rivenhall Hall; early 16th century.

GREAT HORKESLEY.
(11) Whitehouse Farm; early 16th-century.

LANGHAM.
(5) Broomhouse; early 16th-century.

MONASTIC AND COLLEGIATE BUILDINGS.

The mitred Benedictine abbey of St. John at Colchester is now represented only by the gatehouse (Plate, p. 43) and some of the precinct wall. There are no remains above ground of the Priory of Earls Colne. The small Cluniac house of Little Horkesley apparently adjoined the church there, but the existing edifice was probably always parochial. Of the Cistercian order the only example was the Abbey of Coggeshall, of which there are interesting remains of the domestic buildings (Plates, pp. 166, 167), with the 'capella extra portas' now in the chapel of Little Coggeshall (Plate, p. 127). The Austin Canons are represented by the extensive and important remains of the Abbey of St. Osyth (Plates, pp. 198, 202), the ruined nave of the priory of St. Botolph at Colchester (Plates, pp. 46, 47), the earliest house of the order in England, and a single wall at Tiptree Priory, Great Braxted. The Benedictine nunnery of Wix adjoined the church there and the existing N. arcade may have formed part of the nuns' quire. Of the two houses of friars (Grey and Crossed or Crutched) at Colchester, and of Cressing Temple there are no remains above ground.

Two almshouses at Colchester (Winnock's and Winsley's) have 17th and late 16th-century buildings of some interest.

SECULAR BUILDINGS.

The N.E. division contains the single example in Essex of a walled town—Colchester. Its relative importance during the mediaeval period may be gauged by the fact that it had eight parish churches within the walls and three more immediately outside. Unfortunately, no ancient buildings connected with its corporate life have survived though there is handsome corporation plate dating from the 17th and 18th centuries and mediaeval seals to bear witness to its continuous commercial importance. A very large collection of municipal records dating from about 1300 onwards is stored in a carefully isolated apartment in the Castle Keep.

About two hundred and thirty-five houses in the N.E. part of the county have been assigned to the period preceding the Reformation; they are scattered fairly evenly over the whole area, except the N.E. coastal district, and are nearly all of timber. The earliest domestic work is of the 14th century. St. Clair's Hall, St. Osyth (Plate, p. xxxi), has an aisled hall with oak columns of this date, and another contemporary hall of similar character existed at Bourchiers Hall, Tollesbury, but of this the roof is now the only recognizable portion. In West Stockwell Street, Colchester, are remains of a timber building, probably of late 14th-century date. A number of houses on both sides of the High Street, Colchester, are provided with mediaeval stone-built cellars, many of them with 14th-century details. Their chief interest lies in the fact that they seem to indicate that the main building line of that period was set considerably back from the street frontage and had in front a line of cellars presumably covered in and perhaps supporting booths or shops.

The best examples of domestic work of the 15th century are monuments Nos. 5, 70, 71 and 75 in Great Coggeshall; Nos. 30, 86, 190 and 231 in Colchester; Feeringbury in Feering; Southfields in Dedham (Plate, p. 84); and Tolleshunt D'Arcy Hall, in Tolleshunt D'Arcy. There are houses with good early 16th-century detail at Paycocks in Great Coggeshall (Plates, pp. 118, 119), a very rich example; the Sun Inn at Kelvedon; the Marquis of Granby at Colchester (Plate, p. xxxvii); Tollesbury (No. 18) (Plate, p. xxxvii), and Jacobes Hall at Brightlingsea (Plate, p. 176). While later timber building is exemplified at Lower Dairy Farm, Little Horkesley (Plate, p. xxx); Gate House, Colchester (No. 39) (Plate, p. 122); Great Coggeshall

(Nos. 31, 69), etc.   Seventeenth-century pargeting remains largely intact at Colneford House, Earls Colne (Plate, p. 235) and Wivenhoe (No. 6) (Plate, p. 235); more fragmentary examples of the same work occur at Colchester (Nos. 29, 31, 53, 192, 227 and 234) and Mount Bures (No. 5).   There are remains of good early 16th-century brick houses at Bradfield Hall in Bradfield (Plate, p. 10) and Wivenhoe Hall in Wivenhoe (Plate, p. 234), and Beckingham Hall in Tolleshunt Major has a curious mid 16th-century gatehouse (Plate, p. 230) with remains of stencilled decoration on plaster.   Layer Marney Towers or Hall (Plates, Frontispiece, etc.) consists of the early 16th-century gatehouse and one range of a large courtyard house, probably never completed ; it is remarkable not only for its proportions but as providing one of the few examples of Renaissance ornament in this country before the Reformation. The abbey buildings of St. Osyth (Plates, pp. 198, 199) and Coggeshall were converted into houses soon after the Dissolution, and the remains of the Darcy mansion at St. Osyth are important.   At Wix (No. 2) (Plate, p. 231) and Tiptree Priory, in Great Braxted (Plate, p. 234), are late 16th-century houses built on the sites of former monastic establishments, and the curious structure of Bourne Mill, Colchester (Plate, p. 68), is largely built of reused material, probably from St. John's Abbey.   The main block at Beaumont Hall, Beaumont cum Moze (Plate, p. 234); is another brick building of a rather later date.

At Coggeshall is a bridge of three spans, which though much altered is probably of 13th-century date.

FITTINGS.

Altars.—At Great Tey there is part of a small altar with consecration crosses, presumably intended for insertion in a larger slab.   At the end of the tomb of John, 2ud Lord Marney, at Layer Marney, is an altar of the same materials and workmanship as the tomb but with a modern slab.   Other altar-slabs remain at Colchester St. Martin, Little Horkesley, St. Osyth and Thorrington.

Bells.—Forty-eight bells in N.E. Essex are of pre-Reformation date.   Of these, two by a predecessor of William Dawe, one by William Burford, and probably the uninscribed clock-bell at Lexden are of the 14th century.   Of the remainder, six are by Robert Burford and four each by H. Jordan and J. Danyell.   A large proportion of the post-Reformation bells were supplied by the Colchester foundry of the Grayes.

Brasses.—The earliest brass is the magnificent cross-legged effigy of Sir William Fitzralph, *c.* 1323, at Pebmarsh (Plate, p. 171).   To the beginning of the 15th century belong the handsome canopied brasses of the Swynbornes, father and son, at Little Horkesley (Plate, p. 171), one with the SS collar ; the brass of Sir William Pyrton, 1490, at Little Bentley, also has the SS collar.   At Wivenhoe are the large early 16th-century brasses, both with canopies, of William, Viscount Beaumont. and Elizabeth, Countess of Oxford ; of similar date and character is the brass of Bridget, Lady Marney, and her two husbands, at Little Horkesley.   There is an interesting series of family brasses at Tolleshunt D'Arcy of the Darcies, at Great Coggeshall of the Paycockes, and at Brightlingsea of the Beryffs ; the Paycockes and the Beryffs being rich merchants.   Only two brasses with effigies of priests remain ; at Great Bromley, of 1432, with a mutilated canopy, and at Wivenhoe, of 1535. Aldermen in their robes are represented at Colchester St. Peter, and a civilian at Wormingford has a collar, formerly inlaid, round his neck.   A single shroud brass occurs at Little Horkesley, and at Elmstead are a pair of hands holding a heart. Palimpsest brasses have come to light at Colchester St. James, Tolleshunt D'Arcy (two), Fingringhoe and Wivenhoe ; two of these are of Flemish workmanship.

GREAT BROMLEY.
Chest; early 17th century.

CRESSING.
Communion Table; dated 1633.

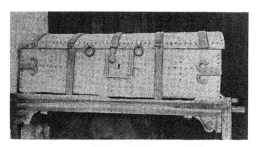

FINGRINGHOE.
Chest; Mediaeval, with later date 1684.   Bier; 17th-century.

LITTLE BENTLEY.
Chest; 14th or 15th-century.

MESSING.
Chest; 13th or 14th-century.

DOVERCOURT.
Poor-box; dated 1589.

TOLLESBURY.
Removed from (3) Bourchier's Hall, now at
Guisnes Court; early 17th-century.

GREAT COGGESHALL.
(36) House, Back Lane.   Overmantel; late 17th-century.

STANWAY.
(4) Stanway Hall; 17th-century.

LAYER MARNEY HALL.
In Passage, West Wing; early 17th-century.

LAYER MARNEY HALL.
In modern N.W. Wing; early 16th century.

There are early 14th-century indents with separate letters in the inscriptions at Great Horkesley (dated 1327), Tolleshunt D'Arcy and Wivenhoe.

Ceilings and Plaster Work.—In domestic buildings there are enriched plaster ceilings (Plate, p. 235) at Colchester (No. 114), Dedham (Nos. 9, 22 and 24), Manningtree (No. 13) and Harwich (No. 3, 20 and 31). The specimens of enriched pargeting have already been referred to (p. xxxii).

Chests.—Early dug-out and iron-bound chests remain at Messing (Plate, p. xxxii), Fingringhoe (Plate, p. xxxii), Langham and Stisted ; two of these, at Fingringhoe and Stisted, have dates in iron-work (1684 and 1676) added later. Other mediaeval or early 16th-century chests, heavily bound with iron, occur at Little Bentley (Plate, p. xxxii), Copford and Layer Marney. There are late 16th or 17th-century chests with carved fronts at Great Bromley (Plate, p. xxxii) and Great Henny. Two interesting foreign chests, one of iron painted and one with iron arabesque-ornament, remain at Great Tey and Wivenhoe. There is an interesting 16th-century alms-box at Dovercourt (Plate, p. xxxii).

Communion Table.—The only communion table of particular interest is the carved and dated example (1633) at Cressing (Plate, p. xxxii).

Doors.—The finest surviving door in the district is that at Colchester St. Peter (Plate, p. 42), with rich hammered and stamped iron-work of *c.* 1300, ascribed to Thomas of Leighton, the craftsman responsible for the grille on the tomb of Eleanor of Castille at Westminster. There is enrichment of similar date and character surrounding the handle-plate of a door at Aldham (Plate, p. 132). Fairly elaborate 12th-century iron-work remains on the S. door at Heybridge (Plate, p. 132). Of traceried doors of the late mediaeval period, the best examples are at Great Bromley (Plate, p. 132) (two), Dedham (with remains of carved figures, Plate, p. 42), Fingringhoe (Plate, p. 132) and Ardleigh (Plate, p. 132).

Fireplaces.—The most interesting fireplaces are those of late 11th-century date at Colchester Castle (Plate, p. 58), each with two flues ; they are amongst the earliest examples in the country. At Paycocks in Great Coggeshall are two fireplaces with early 16th-century carved oak lintels (Plate, p. 119) ; of rather later date and of early Renaissance design is the handsome carved stone fireplace at Stanway Hall in Stanway (Plate, p. xxxiii). Other examples of interest (Plate, p. xxxiii) are to be found at Marks Hall in Markshall, Colchester (Nos. 18 and 20) ; Great Coggeshall (No. 36) ; Langham (No. 11) ; Layer Marney Towers in Layer Marney, and Guisnes Court in Tollesbury.

Fonts (Plate, p. xxxiv).—There are comparatively few 12th and 13th-century fonts in the district and none of them are of particular interest. The 14th-century font at Dovercourt has a shafted stem and traceried bowl. Many good 15th and early 16th-century fonts survive, the more important being those at Colchester St. Martin, Great Tey, Little Totham, Stanway St. Albright, Thorrington, Great Clacton and East Mersea ; that at Great Clacton has carved figures and the font at East Mersea has a rich traceried bowl. The most interesting font, however, is one of carved oak at Marks Tey ; it has a traceried bowl and stem and remains of carved figures cut back. The font at Bradwell has a brick stem. A curious 18th-century font at Tollesbury is dated by the parish records a few years too late for inclusion in the Inventory. The fonts at Fingringhoe and Little Horkesley have buttressed and traceried covers of 15th and early 16th-century date respectively.

Glass (Plates, pp. 192, 193).—Very little pre-16th-century glass has survived in the churches of N.E. Essex, and what there is, is, for the most part, fragmentary. The largest quantity is at Lawford—excellent foliage, border and canopy work (14th-century). At Great Oakley, Little Oakley, Wormingford and East Mersea are small examples of the same kind and period. At Elmstead are the upper parts of two panels composed of foliage in grisaille set in a border of fleurs-de-lis and castles (*c.* 1300). Of the 14th century there is good tabernacle work at Feering. Of late 16th or early 17th-century date is one large and nearly complete window— the E. window at Messing with six of the corporal works of mercy in panels, the whole under a mutilated canopy. The four late 12th-century medallions in the E. window of the chancel of Rivenhall church call for special mention on account of their date and their excellent condition. They were brought from abroad and inserted in their present position in the 19th century. The 13th-century panel of the knight on horseback in the same window is also noteworthy. There are a few good examples of 14th-century heraldic glass—at Great Bromley is a coat of Martel and at Frinton are the shields of Warenne and Elderbeke. Most of the heraldry is of the 16th century; of that period we have the very interesting armorials of the Marney family in the North Chancel Chapel at Layer Marney, including three shields of Henry, Lord Marney, K.G. At Lawford Hall in Lawford there is a remarkable Swiss roundel with the arms of the Empire and Fribourg with its dependent towns. There, also, are some shields of the Bowyer family and a Tudor Royal Arms. At the Siege House, Colchester, are two roundels (removed from another Colchester dwelling) which are of rather special interest. The one, dated 1546, shows the quartered coat of Katherine Parr, surmounted by a Royal crown, and the other the full achievement of Thomas, 3rd Duke of Norfolk, K.G. It is noticeable that the Royal arms are placed in the first quarter, a fact which supplies contemporary evidence of the truth of one, at least, of the charges brought by Henry VIII against the Duke. At Dukes, in Layer Marney, and at Feeringbury, in Feering, among others, are roundels with Royal badges crowned and initials E.R. (probably for Queen Elizabeth). Of the last years of the 17th century, or the beginning of the 18th century, is a large oval panel with the arms of Henry Compton, Bishop of London, in the E. window of the N. aisle at the church of St. James, Colchester.

Hour-glass Stands.—Wrought-iron hour-glass stands remain at East Mersea, Thorrington and Little Bentley.

Monuments.—The N.E. quarter of Essex contains thirteen mediaeval effigies, of which four are at Earls Colne Priory (Plate, p. 91) and three each at Layer Marney (Plate, p. 158) and Little Horkesley (Plate, p. 170). All except one at Earls Colne and one at Little Horkesley (both ladies) are armed figures. The three at Little Horkesley are of the 13th century and of oak. The figure at Elmstead (Plate, p. 170) is also of oak and of *c.* 1310. The series at Earls Colne are to members of the family of Vere, Earl of Oxford; all the monuments are of alabaster, except the earliest, which is probably the figure of Robert, 5th Earl, 1296. The tombs have been moved more than once and have been wrongly ' re-assembled,' the great tomb of Richard, 11th Earl, and his wife, now forming two separate monuments. The tombs of the Marneys at Layer Marney consist of one 14th-century monument of alabaster and two early 16th-century tombs with effigies and slabs of touch and early Renaissance architectural work of terra-cotta, of which they form a remarkable example. The other two effigies are at Thorpe-le-Soken and Tolleshunt Knights. Other mediaeval monuments occur at Dedham with a panelled canopy, and at

BRADFIELD.
Late 12th or early 13th-century.

ALPHAMSTONE.
Late 12th-century.

GREAT CLACTON.
15th-century.

BRADWELL-JUXTA-COGGESHALL.
Bowl, 12th-century, re-cut ;
Stem, 16th-century.

DOVERCOURT.
Mid 14th-century.

EAST MERSEA.
15th century.

COLCHESTER : ST. MARTIN.
15th century.

LITTLE TOTHAM.
15th-century.

LITTLE BROMLEY.
Early 16th-century.

MARKS TEY.
Of Oak, 15th-century ;

COLCHESTER : ST. LEONARD, HYTHE.
Cup ; Elizabethan.   Mazer ; 1521.

COLCHESTER : HOLY TRINITY.
Mazer ; 15th-century.

EARLS COLNE.
Paten ; early 16th-century. Cup ; late 16th-century.

COLCHESTER : ST. MARY-AT-THE-WALLS.
Cup ; 1623.

LITTLE BENTLEY.
Communion Plate with Cases ; 1623.

Colchester St. Nicholas, a Gothic wall-tablet. There is an interesting incised slab of a priest at Middleton (Fig., p. 183), probably of Flemish workmanship, and a fragment of another at Bradwell. The best post-Reformation monuments are the two Darcy tombs at St. Osyth (Plate, p. 197) and other memorials at Rivenhall (Plate, p. 197), Colchester Berechurch (Plate, p. 97) and Little Totham (Plate, p. 97). There are wall-monuments or tablets of some interest at Bradwell (Plate, p. 97), Cressing (Plate, p. 97), Tollesbury and Colchester Holy Trinity.

Niches.—There is an interesting series of 15th or early 16th-century niches at Brightlingsea and other good examples are at Little Oakley, Ardleigh and Lawford.

Paintings.—The fine series of 12th-century paintings at Copford (Plate, p. 77), though considerably restored, are nevertheless still of extreme interest and give an excellent idea of the general appearance of such work when recently executed. Fingringhoe had also an extensive series of paintings, but most of these are in an advanced state of decay. At Bradwell, Easthorpe and Great Totham are painted figures more or less well preserved and at Layer Marney is an excellent representation of St. Christopher (Plate, p. 155) of early 16th-century date. Slight remains of painted decoration occur also at West Mersea.

There are no important remains of domestic decoration of this character, but a room in Colchester (No. 21) has early 18th-century painted panels, and remains of painted work occur at Josselyns in Little Horkesley and at Wivenhoe (No. 6). The Gatehouse of Beckingham Hall in Tolleshunt Major has remains of a painted stencil design on the external plastering.

Panelling.—The best linen-fold panelling occurs at Paycocks in Great Coggeshall (Plate, p. 119) and Tolleshunt D'Arcy Hall in Tolleshunt D'Arcy (Plate, p. 180), and there is good later 16th or 17th-century panelling at Messing church and Bradwell church.

Piscinae.—At Great Horkesley is a 12th-century pillar-piscina and the 13th-century examples at Bradfield and Little Coggeshall have features of interest. There is a long list of good 14th-century piscinae including those at Great Bromley, Lawford, Little Oakley, Pebmarsh, Great Tey, Alphamstone, Colne Engaine and Elmstead, of these the first four are the more noteworthy ; 15th or early 16th-century examples occur at Bradwell and Brightlingsea.

Plate (Plate, p. xxxv).—The earliest plate of the district are the two mazer-bowls mounted in silver at Holy Trinity and St. Leonard-at-the-Hythe, Colchester ; the former is of the 15th century and has a black-letter inscription referring to the three kings, and the latter apparently bears the date-mark for 1521. At Earls Colne is an early 16th-century paten with an incised figure of Christ in the middle. There are eighteen Elizabethan cups, of which an unusually large proportion have no date-mark ; one cup dates from 1561, four from 1562, one from 1563 and three from 1567. Of later plate the most interesting piece is the Irish Chalice (Plate, p. xxxv) from St. Mary-at-the-Walls, Colchester ; it is dated 1633 and formerly belonged to the Franciscan Friary of Rossereily, Galway. Other interesting pieces are the cup given by Laud, 1633, at Manningtree, and the two sets in their original cases at Little Bentley and Little Horkesley.

Pulpits.—The most interesting pulpits (Plate, p. 181) are those at White Colne and East Mersea, both of the 17th century ; the former has carved figures of saints and the latter retains its sounding-board.

Royal Arms.—There is a handsome carved panel of the Royal Arms, dated 1634, at Messing (Plate, p. 181).

Screens.—Screen-work is but poorly represented in the district, but at Bradwell (Plate, p. 34) is an interesting 15th-century example retaining its boarded tympanum. At Colchester St. Martin (Plate, p. 39) there was a 14th-century screen dividing the chancel into two portions and probably used for the Lenten Veil. Other screens with features of interest include those at Thorpe-le-Soken, Copford, and Ardleigh ; the first of these has a curious inscription. Secular screens occur at Marks Hall in Markshall (Plate, p. 180), Coggeshall Abbey in Little Coggeshall, St. Clair's Hall in St. Osyth and Kelvedon (No. 58).

Sedilia.—The finest sedilia are the finely carved 14th-century recesses at Lawford (Plate, p. 150) ; other notable examples of the same century occur at Elmstead and Alphamstone. To the 13th century belong those at Little Coggeshall and Easthorpe.

Stalls and *Seating.*—There is a very richly panelled back of a bench of *c.* 1500 at Inworth (Plate, p. 181), and at Langham are some carved bench-ends with popey-heads (Plate, p. 181). The early 17th-century stalls at Messing (Plate, p. 181) are good examples of their period.

Condition.

1. *Prehistoric and Roman.*—The earthworks at Lexden are fairly well preserved, as are the mounts at Lexden and Mersea ; Pitchbury Ramparts have nearly disappeared, except for the N. section. The Roman remains at Colchester are well looked after. The foundations at West Mersea have suffered from exposure.

2. *Mediaeval Churches, etc.*—Of the one hundred and nine churches of ancient foundation, eight have been almost entirely rebuilt and others retain only small portions of the old structure. The former churches of Moze, Layer Breton, Little Henny and Colchester Mile End are represented by foundations only, though the last place has a modern church some distance from the old site. Two churches at Walton-le-Soken have been destroyed by the sea. The churches of Little Birch, Stanway All Saints, Mistley, Virley and Colchester St. Botolph are roofless and ruined. Of the remaining ninety-four all but six are in fairly good condition ; the majority have been extensively restored.

About eight per cent. of the secular buildings are in a poor or bad condition, but most of these are of little importance except the pargeted house at Wivenhoe (6), which is a ' selected ' monument. The larger houses are nearly all in excellent condition and Layer Marney Towers has been recently restored. The earthworks of the castle of Mount Bures and Colchester are well preserved, at any rate in part, but those at Birch are much denuded.

MANNINGTREE CHURCH.
Detail of Nave Arcade and Roof; *c*. 1616.

PATTISWICK CHURCH.
Nave Roof; 14th or early 15th-century.

LITTLE BENTLEY CHURCH.
Nave Roof; early 16th-century.

TENDRING CHURCH.
Arch over North Door supporting
Roof-truss; 14th-century.

ALDHAM CHURCH.
South Porch; 14th-century.

TENDRING CHURCH.
North Porch; mid 14th-century.

COLCHESTER.
(47) The George Hotel.
King-post of Roof; 15th-century.

COLCHESTER.
(69) The Marquis of Granby Inn.
Ceiling in East Wing; early 16th-century.

GREAT COGGESHALL.
(5). The Woolpack Inn.
Roof-truss; 15th-century.

EARLS COLNE.
(9) House, High Street. Ceiling; early 16th-century.

TOLLESBURY.
(18) Black Cottage. Ceiling; c. 1520.

ALPHAMSTONE.
(4) Barn at Clees Hall; 15th-century.

ESSEX.

LISTS OF HUNDREDS, HALF-HUNDREDS AND PARISHES.

(The Parishes printed in italics are inclu^de^d in Volume III.)

CLAVERING.
Berden
Clavering
Farnham
Langley
Manuden
Ugley

UTTLESFORD.
Arkesden
Birchanger
Chrishall
Debden
Elmdon
Elsenham
Great Chesterford
Henham
Littlebury
Little Chesterford
Newport
Quendon
Rickling
Saffron Walden
Stanstead Mountfitchet
Strethall
Takeley
Wenden Lofts
Wendens Ambo
Wicken Bonhunt
Widdington
Wimbish

FRESHWELL.
Ashdon
Bardfield Saling
Bartlow End
Great Bardfield
Great Sampford
Hadstock
Helion Bumpstead
Hempstead
Little Bardfield
Little Sampford
Radwinter

DUNMOW.
Aythorpe Roding
Barnston
Berners Roding
Broxted
Chickney

DUNMOW—cont.
Good Easter
Great Canfield
Great Dunmow
Great Easton
High Easter
High Roding
Leaden Roding
Lindsell
Little Canfield
Little Dunmow
Little Easton
Margaret Roding
Mashbury
Pleshey
Shellow Bowells
Thaxted
Tilty
White Roding
Willingale Doe
Willingale Spain

HINCKFORD.
Alphamstone
Great Henny
Lamarsh
Little Henny
Middleton
Pebmarsh
Stisted
Twinstead
Ashen
Belchamp Otton
Belchamp St. Paul's
Belchamp Walter
Birdbrook
Bocking
Borley
Braintree
Bulmer
Castle Hedingham
Felstead
Finchingfield
Foxearth
Gestingthorpe
Gosfield
Great Maplestead
Great Saling
Great Yeldham
Halstead Rural
Halstead Urban
Liston
Little Maplestead

HINCKFORD—cont.
Little Yeldham
Northwood
Ovington
Panfield
Pentlow
Rayne
Ridgewell
Shalford
Sible Hedingham
Stambourne
Stebbing
Steeple Bumpstead
Sturmer
Tilbury-juxta-Clare
Toppesfield
Wethersfield
Wickham St. Paul's

HARLOW.
Great Hallingbury
Great Parndon
Harlow
Hatfield Broad Oak
Latton
Little Hallingbury
Little Parndon
Matching
Netteswell
Roydon
Sheering

LEXDEN.
Aldham
Birch
Boxted
Bures
Chapel
Colne Engaine
Copford
Dedham
Earls Colne
East Donyland
Easthorpe
Feering
Fordham
Great Coggeshall
Great Horkesley
Great Tey
Inworth
Langham
Little Horkesley

LEXDEN—cont.
Little Tey
Marks Tey
Markshall
Messing
Mount Bures
Pattiswick
Stanway
Wakes Colne
West Bergholt
White Colne
Wivenhoe
Wormingford

COLCHESTER.
Colchester

WITHAM.
Bradwell
Cressing
Great Braxted
Kelvedon
Little Braxted
Little Coggeshall
Rivenhall
Black Notley
Fairsted
Faulkbourne
Hatfield Peverel
Terling
Ulting
White Notley
Witham

CHELMSFORD.
Boreham
Blackmore
Broomfield
Buttsbury
Chelmsford
Chignall
Danbury
East Hanningfield
Great Baddow
Great Leighs
Great Waltham
Ingatestone & Fryerning
Little Baddow
Little Leighs
Little Waltham
Margaretting
Mountnessing

CHELMSFORD—*cont.*

Rettendon
Roxwell
Runwell
Sandon
South Hanningfield
Springfield
Stock
West Hanningfield
Widford
Woodham Ferrers
Writtle

TENDRING.

Alresford
Ardleigh
Beaumont-cum-Moze
Bradfield
Brightlingsea
Dovercourt
Elmstead
Frating
Frinton
Great Bentley
Great Bromley
Great Clacton
Great Holland
Great Oakley
Harwich
Kirby-le-Soken
Lawford
Little Bentley
Little Bromley
Little Clacton
Little Holland
Little Oakley
Manningtree
Mistley
Ramsey
St. Osyth
Tendring
Thorrington
Thorpe-le-Soken
Walton-le-Soken
Weeley
Wix
Wrabness

WINSTREE.

Abberton
East Mersea
Fingringhoe
Great Wigborough
Langenhoe
Layer Breton
Layer de la Haye
Layer Marney
Little Wigborough
Peldon
Salcott

WINSTREE—*cont.*

Virley
West Mersea

THURSTABLE.

Goldhanger
Great Totham
Heybridge
Little Totham
Tollesbury
Tolleshunt D'Arcy
Tolleshunt Knights
Tolleshunt Major
Langford
Wickham Bishops

DENGIE.

Althorne
Asheldham
Bradwell-juxta-Mare
Burnham
Cold Norton
Creeksea
Dengie
Hazeleigh
Latchingdon
Maldon All Saints
Maldon St. Mary
Maldon St. Peter
Mayland
Mundon
North Fambridge
Purleigh
St. Lawrence
Southminster
Steeple
Stow Maries
Tillingham
Woodham Mortimer
Woodham Walter

ROCHFORD

Ashingdon
Barling
Canewdon
Eastwood
Foulness
Great Stambridge
Great Wakering
Hadleigh
Havengore
Hawkwell
Hockley
Leigh
Little Stambridge
Little Wakering
North Shoebury
Paglesham
Prittlewell
Rayleigh

ROCHFORD—*cont.*

Rawreth
Rochford
Shopland
Southchurch
South Fambridge
South Shoebury
Sutton

BARSTABLE.

Basildon
Bowers Gifford
Brentwood
Bulphan
Canvey Island
Chadwell
Corringham
Doddinghurst
Downham
Dunton
East Horndon
East Tilbury
Fobbing
Great Burstead
Horndon-on-the-Hill
Hutton
Ingrave
Laindon
Laindon Hills
Lee Chapel
Little Burstead
Little Thurrock
Mucking
Nevendon
North Benfleet
Orsett
Pitsea
Ramsden Bellhouse
Ramsden Crays
Shenfield
South Benfleet
Stanford-le-Hope
Thundersley
Vange
West Horndon
West Tilbury
Wickford

ONGAR.

Abbess Roding
Beauchamp Roding
Bobbingworth
Buckhurst Hill
Chigwell
Chipping Ongar
Fyfield
Greensted
High Laver
High Ongar
Kelvedon Hatch

ONGAR—*cont.*

Lambourne
Little Laver
Loughton
Magdalen Laver
Moreton
Navestock
North Weald Bassett
Norton Mandeville
Shelley
Stanford Rivers
Stapleford Abbots
Stapleford Tawney
Stondon Massey
Theydon Bois
Theydon Garnon
Theydon Mount

CHAFFORD.

Aveley
Childerditch
Cranham
Grays Thurrock
Great Warley
Little Warley
North Ockendon
Rainham
South Ockendon
South Weald
Stifford
Upminster
Wennington
West Thurrock

HAVERING LIBERTY.

Havering-atte-Bower
Hornchurch
Noak Hill
Romford Rural
Romford Urban

WALTHAM.

Chingford
Epping
Epping Upland
Nazeing
Waltham Holy Cross

BECONTREE.

Barking
Dagenham
East Ham
Great Ilford
Little Ilford
Low Leyton
Walthamstow
Wanstead
West Ham
Woodford

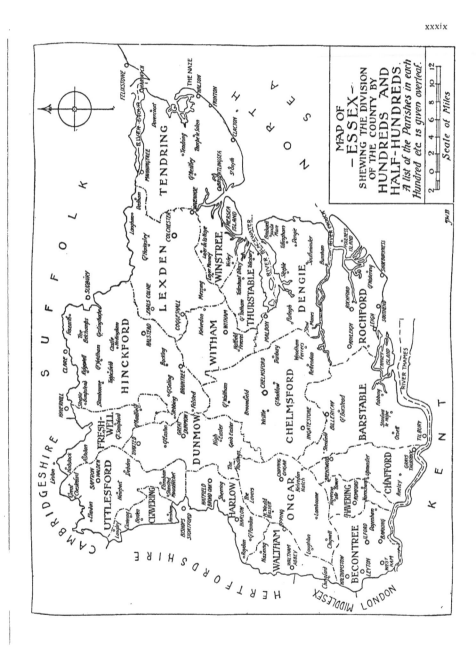

AN INVENTORY OF THE ANCIENT AND HISTORICAL MONUMENTS

IN NORTH-EAST ESSEX.

ACCREDITED TO A DATE ANTERIOR TO 1714,

arranged by Parishes.

(Unless otherwise stated, the dimensions given in the Inventory are internal. Monuments with titles printed in italics are covered by an introductory sentence, to which reference should be made. The key plans of those churches which are not illustrated by historically hatched plans are drawn to a uniform scale of 48 ft. to the inch, with the monumental portions shown in solid black.)

1. ABBERTON. (D.d.)

(O.S. 6 in. xxxvi. N.E.)

Abberton is a small parish 4 m. S. of Colchester.

Ecclesiastical :—

(1). PARISH CHURCH OF ST. ANDREW stands near the N. end of the parish. The walls are of mixed rubble with dressings of limestone ; the tower is of red brick. The roofs are tiled. The *Nave* and probably a chancel were built or rebuilt about the middle of the 14th century. Early in the 16th century the *West Tower* was added. The *South Porch* was added probably in the 18th century. The church was restored late in the 18th or early in the 19th century (when the chancel was rebuilt on the old foundations) and again subsequently.

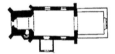

Architectural Description—The *Chancel* (19 ft. by 15½ ft.) is modern, but the lower courses of the walls are those of the mediaeval building. The plastered, two-centred chancel-arch is of uncertain date.

The *Nave* (29½ ft. by 18 ft.) has in the N. wall a mid or late 14th-century window of two plain pointed lights in a two-centred head ; further W. is the late 14th-century N. doorway, now blocked and with chamfered jambs, two-centred arch and moulded label. In the S. wall is a window similar to that in the N. wall ; further W. is the late 14th-century S. doorway, with moulded jambs, two-centred arch and label with defaced head-stops.

The *West Tower* (8½ ft. square) is of red brick, with some diapering in black brick, and is of early 16th-century date ; it is of three stages, with a

modern parapet. The two-centred tower-arch is of four chamfered orders ; the responds have plain splays. The W. window is of stone and of three cinquefoiled lights, with vertical tracery in a two-centred head with a moulded label ; the W. door-way, below it, is of brick with chamfered jambs and two-centred arch. The second stage has in the W. wall a single-light window, with a four-centred head. The bell-chamber has on each side a window formerly of three lights and with a four-centred head ; the mullions have been destroyed.

Fittings—*Bell :* one by Miles Graye, 1663. *Chest :* In S. porch, small, iron-bound, with two locks, probably 16th-century. *Communion Table :* with turned legs and moulded rail, early 17th-century. *Door :* In doorway to turret staircase, of overlapping battens, early 16th-century. *Font :* plain octagonal bowl, with moulded lower edge, stem and hollow-chamfered base, probably 15th-century. *Monuments :* In churchyard—(1) to George Kercley (?), 1701, head-stone with skull and cross-bones ; (2) to G.K., 1707, head-stone. *Plate :* includes an Elizabethan cup, with a band of incised ornament.

Condition—Fairly good, some ivy on tower.

Secular :—

(2). *Homestead Moat,* at Abberton Hall, N. of the church.

---

2. ALDHAM. (C.c.)

(O.S. 6 in. [a]xxvi. N.E. [b]xxvii. N.W [c]xxvii. S.W.)

Aldham is a parish with a small village at Fordstreet, 5½ m. W. of Colchester. The house (5) is the principal monument.

Ecclesiastical :—

[b](1). PARISH CHURCH OF SS. MARGARET AND CATHERINE stood ¾ m. W.S.W. of the modern church. The foundations indicate a building 72 ft. by 21 ft. The old church was pulled down and the

modern church erected on the present site in 1855. It contains much reused material in Barnack and limestone of the 13th, 14th and 15th centuries, distributed as follows :—

Architectural Description—The *Chancel* has a 15th-century E. window, with moulded and shafted splays with embattled capitals. In the N. wall are two 15th-century windows, each of two cinque-foiled lights in a square head and mostly old. Between them the arch over the doorway is hollow-chamfered and two-centred ; the jamb-shafts have moulded capitals and bases, all of the 14th century ; the doorway is mostly modern. In the S. wall are two windows similar to those in the N. wall, but mostly modern. The doorway between them is modern, except the moulded early 15th-century label.

The *North Vestry* has in the E. wall a much restored 14th-century window of two pointed lights in a two-centred head

The *Nave* has in the N. wall two windows, all modern except part of the splays.

The *South Aisle* has an E. window, modern except part of the splays ; further N. is a 14th-century doorway to a turret stairway, with moulded jambs and two-centred arch. The turret has two lights, one quatrefoiled and one traceried, both small and of the 14th century. In the S. wall are three lancet windows, mostly modern externally, but with 13th-century splays and rear-arches. Further W. is the 13th-century S. doorway, with roll-moulded jambs and two-centred arch, much restored. In the W. wall are two lancets and a round window, all of the 13th century internally.

The *West Tower* has in the S. wall a doorway with 13th-century chamfered jambs of Barnack stone. The W. window has some old jamb and splay-stones.

The *South Porch* (Plate, p. xxxvi) is of timber on modern walls, and of 14th-century date. The moulded two-centred outer archway has quatre-foiled and traceried spandrels ; above it is a moulded head-beam and foiled barge-boards ; flanking the arch are single lights with trefoiled ogee heads and tracery. The side walls are of two bays each of three similar lights and tracery. The roof is of two bays, with curved and hollow-chamfered braces to the tie-beams, ogee curved braces to the collars and double hollow-chamfered plates.

The *Roofs* of the chancel, nave, and S. aisle are each of trussed-rafter type, with moulded plates, and are probably of the 15th century. The E. bay of the chancel roof has more richly moulded and double embattled plates. The roofs of the vestry and tower have old rafters.

Fittings—*Bells* : Inaccessible, but said to be two ; 1st by Thomas Bullisdon, and inscribed "Sancta Margareta Ora Pro Nobis," early 16th-century ; 2nd by William Dawe, and inscribed

"Sum Rosa Pulsata Mundi Katerina Vocata," *c.* 1400. *Chest :* In vestry—plain with iron-bound angles, 17th-century. *Doors :* In chancel—in N. doorway, of nail-studded battens with hollow-chamfered fillets and frame, planted on, 14th-century. In S. doorway of chancel—of old battens with modern fillets, 15th-century. In S. doorway —of overlapping battens with strap-hinges and pierced traceried scutcheon - plate, 15th-century. In S. doorway of tower (Plate, p. 132)—of three wide battens with good domed scutcheon from which radiate four foliated iron branches, *c.* 1300. *Floor-slab :* On site of old church—to Sir George Sayer, 1650. *Piscinae :* In chancel—with modern jambs and 14th-century cinquefoiled head, quatre-foil drain. In S. aisle—in S. wall, with moulded jambs and two-centred head, square drain with stone rosette, 14th-century.

Condition—Good, rebuilt.

Secular :—

b(2). ALDHAM HALL, house and moat, 1,100 yards S. of the church. The *House* is of two storeys, timber-framed and plastered ; the roofs are tiled. It was built probably in the 16th century, and has 17th-century additions ; it is now of L-shaped plan, with the wings extending towards the N.E. and S.E. The N.E. wing has some exposed timber-framing. The porch on the N.W. side has 17th-century billeted barge-boards and a pendant ; the doorway has a fluted lintel. Two windows have moulded frames and mullions. One chimney-stack has two original octagonal shafts. Inside the building are exposed ceiling-beams and one room is lined with late 16th-century panelling and has an overmantel with two panels divided by fluted pilasters. Another room has an overmantel made up of 16th-century panelling. There are also two doorways, one with a four- and one with a three-centred head.

The *Moat* is fragmentary.

Condition—Of house, good.

a(3). CHECKLEY'S FARM, house and moat, about 1 m. W. of the church. The *House* is of two storeys, timber-framed and plastered ; the roofs are tiled. It was built late in the 16th or early in the 17th century, and has exposed ceiling-beams and joists.

The *Moat* is incomplete.

Condition—Of house, ruinous.

MONUMENTS (4–11).

The following monuments, unless otherwise described, are of two storeys, timber-framed and plastered ; the roofs are tiled or thatched. Some of the buildings have original chimney-stacks and exposed ceiling-beams.

Condition—Good, or fairly good.

b(4). *Bourchier's Hall*, 700 yards N.N.W. of the church, has been rebuilt except for the kitchen wing, which is of early 18th-century date and has a modillioned eaves-cornice.

FORDSTREET, *W. side* :—

b(5). *Boy Scouts' Hall*, house and tenement, ¾ m. N.N.E. of the church. The house was built early in the 16th century, with a two-storeyed Hall and cross-wings at the N. and S. ends ; the tenement is an early 17th-century addition. The upper storey projects, on curved brackets, at the E. ends of the cross-wings and also on the E. and W. sides of the addition. The gables of the original wings have moulded barge-boards. Inside the building the former Hall has original moulded ceiling-beams and joists, and the wide fireplace has a moulded lintel. The N. wing has an original window, with a four-centred head and a doorway with a two-centred head. The S. wing has two original windows with diamond-shaped mullions. The roof is original and of king-post type ; the tie-beams have curved braces.

b(6). *House*, now mission hall, 60 yards N. of (5), was built probably late in the 16th century, and has an original chimney-stack, with three octagonal shafts.

E. side :—

b(7). *House*, 50 yards S.E. of (6), was built probably early in the 18th century, and has a modillioned eaves-cornice on the W. front. The doorway has a pediment above it, carried on consoles. Inside the building is an original fireplace with a moulded architrave.

b(8). *House* and shop, 70 yards S. of (7), was built probably in the 16th century.

b(9). *House*, S. of (8), was built probably early in the 18th century and has a coved eaves-cornice of plaster on the W. front.

b(10). *House*, 60 yards S. of (9), was built probably in the 16th century, but was entirely remodelled early in the 18th century. It has a cross-wing at the N. end, and the main block has a coved cornice of plaster on the W. side. The porch has a pine-apple ornament in plaster and the date 1706. Inside the building one room has early 18th-century panelling, and the staircase has slight turned balusters of the same period.

b(11). *Cottage*, ½ m. S.W. of the church, was built in the 17th century and has exposed timber-framing.

3. ALPHAMSTONE. (B.b.)

(O.S. 6 in. (*a*)xii. S.E. (*b*)xvii. N.E.)

Alphamstone is a parish and small village 5½ m. N.E. of Halstead. The church is interesting.

Ecclesiastical :—

a(1). PARISH CHURCH (dedication unknown) stands towards the N. end of the parish. The walls are of flint rubble, except the S. wall of the chancel, which is partly of brick ; the dressings are of limestone and the roofs are covered with tiles and slates ; the bell-turret is weather-boarded. The *Nave* was built probably in the 12th century. A West tower was added at some uncertain date and subsequently demolished. Early in the 14th century the *Chancel* was rebuilt ; shortly afterwards the chancel-arch and S. arcade were built and the *South Aisle* added. In the 15th century the *North Porch* was added. In the 16th century the S. wall of the chancel was partly rebuilt and the *South Porch* added. The church was restored at the end of the 19th century, when the *Bell-turret* was repaired and the chancel largely refaced. There is a considerable collection of sarsen stones in and about the churchyard, which appear to have been brought together by human agency.

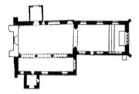

Architectural Description—The *Chancel* (34 ft. by 18½ ft.) is faced on the E. and N. with black flints ; it has a modern E. window, with some reset stones in the splays, rear-arch and the external sill. In the N. wall are three windows, the two eastern are modern except for the splays and rear-arches, which are of *c.* 1300 ; the westernmost window is of *c.* 1300, partly restored, and of two pointed lights with a quatrefoil in a two-centred head ; it is carried down below a transom to form a ' low side,' which is fitted with old iron grilles and modern shutters with old hinges. In the S. wall are two windows, the eastern is modern except for the 14th-century splays and rear-arch ; the western is uniform with the westernmost in the N. wall, but one of the shutters is ancient ; between the windows is a 14th-century doorway with chamfered jambs and segmental-pointed arch. The 14th-century chancel-arch is two-centred and of three chamfered orders ; the semi-octagonal responds have moulded capitals and bases.

The *Nave* (39 ft. by 20 ft.) has in the N. wall two windows, the eastern is of early 14th-century date and of two trefoiled ogee lights with tracery in a two-centred head with a moulded label ; the western window is of the 15th century and of three cinquefoiled ogee lights with tracery in a four-centred head with a moulded label; further W. is a 12th-century round-headed window, now blocked and only visible internally; W. of this window is the 13th-century N. doorway, probably reset, and with chamfered jambs and two-centred arch. The early 14th-century S. arcade is of three bays with two-centred arches of two chamfered orders; the octagonal columns and semi-octagonal responds have moulded capitals and bases. In the W. wall is a modern window and on either side of it and visible externally are the responds and springers of a 14th-century tower-arch.

The *South Aisle* (9½ ft. wide) has an early 14th-century E. window of three trefoiled ogee lights with net tracery in a two-centred head. In the S. wall are three windows, the two eastern are of the 14th century and of two trefoiled lights with tracery in a two-centred head; the westernmost has a 17th-century oak frame and a square head; between the two western windows is the early 14th-century S. doorway with chamfered jambs, two-centred arch and moulded label with head-stops.

The *North Porch* is timber-framed on modern dwarf brick walls. The timber-framing is partly of the 15th century and the outer archway has posts and a two-centred head of that period.

The *South Porch* is probably of the 16th or 17th century and has a four-centred outer archway and moulded barge-boards. In the E. wall is a plain loop.

The *Roof* of the chancel is probably of the 17th century and has plain and very light tie-beams and posts. The roof of the nave has tie-beams, collars and rafters probably of the 15th century. The 15th-century roof of the N. porch has a tie-beam with curved braces. The S. porch has old rafters and collar-beams.

Fittings—Bells: three, 1st and 3rd from the Bury foundry, c. 1500, and inscribed "Sancte Gorge Ora Pro Nobis" and "Sancta Maria Ora Pro Nobis"; 2nd by Austen Bracker, c. 1550, inscribed "In Honore Scaunte Marie." *Brass:* In chancel—to Margaret Sidey, widow, 1607, inscription only. *Chests:* In S. aisle—(1) panelled, each panel in front with a lozenge ornament, early 17th-century; (2) of hutch form with iron straps and lock, 16th or 17th-century. *Communion Table:* plain with square stop-chamfered legs, 16th or 17th-century. *Doors:* In N. doorway—of feathered and nail-studded battens, strap-hinges and pierced scutcheon-plate with drop-handle, 15th-century. In S. doorway—similar to that in N. doorway but without scutcheon-plate and handle, 15th-century. *Font* (Plate, p. xxxiv): square, Purbeck marble bowl, each side with five shallow, round-headed panels, late 12th-century, stem modern. *Font Cover:* of oak, domed and panelled, with turned ball-finial with

shaped supports, probably late 17th-century. *Glass:* In chancel—in N.E. window, blue and gold roundels; in N.W. window, grisaille quarries, 14th-century. In S.W. window, similar grisaille. In nave—in middle N. window, fragments of figures, suns and tabernacle work, etc., 15th-century. In S. aisle—in S.E. window, borders of yellow fleurs-de-lis and cups on a black ground, and fragments, 14th-century. *Locker:* In chancel —in N. wall, with moulded jambs and trefoiled ogee head with finial, early 14th-century, fitted with modern door. *Paving:* In chancel—slip-tiles with conventional patterns, 14th-century. *Piscinae:* In chancel—in range with sedilia with mutilated moulded and cinquefoiled head and moulded label, octofoiled drain, 14th-century, jamb-shaft modern; in N. wall, with chamfered jambs and two-centred head, damaged quatrefoiled drain, 13th-century, but probably not *in situ*. In S. aisle—in S. wall, with chamfered jambs and trefoiled ogee head, round drain, 14th-century. *Sedilia:* In chancel—in range with piscina, of three bays, with detached shafts with moulded bases and capitals, moulded and cinquefoiled arches with moulded labels, and horizontal string, early 14th-century. In nave—sill of N.E. window carried down low to form seat. In S. aisle—sill of S.E. window carried down to form seat.

Condition—Fairly good.

Secular :—

HOMESTEAD MOATS.

[a](2). At Moat Farm, 300 yards N.E. of the church.

[b](3). At Mosse's Farm, nearly 1 m. S.S.E. of the church.

[b](4). BARN and moat, at Clees Hall, ¼ m. N.W. of (3). The *Barn* (Plate, p. xxxvii) is timber-framed and weather-boarded. It was built in the 16th century, and is of ten bays and about 120 ft. long. The roof is of queen-post type.

The *Moat* is incomplete.

Condition—Of barn, fairly good.

[b](5). UPPER GOULDS FARM, house and moat, 600 yards W. of (4). The *House* is of two storeys, timber-framed and plastered; the roofs are tiled. It was built probably late in the 16th century with a cross-wing at the N. end. The upper storey projects at the W. end of the cross-wing. Inside the building the ceiling-beams and wall-posts are exposed.

The *Moat* is fragmentary.

Condition—of house, good.

[a](6). IVY COTTAGE, house and moat, about ¾ m. S.W. of the church. The *House* is of two storeys, refaced with modern brick; the roofs

are tiled. It was built early in the 17th century, and has an original chimney-stack with grouped diagonal shafts.

The *Moat* is fragmentary.

Condition—Of house, good, much altered.

ᵃ(7). COTTAGE, 700 yards S.S.W. of the church, is of two storeys, timber-framed and plastered ; the roofs are thatched. It was built in the 17th century and has exposed ceiling-beams.

Condition—Good.

ᵃ(8). COTTAGE, 60 yards N. of the church, is of two storeys, timber-framed and plastered ; the roofs are tiled. It was built in the 17th century and has exposed ceiling-beams.

Condition—Fairly good.

ᵃ(9). KING'S FARM, house, nearly 1¼ m. W.S.W. of the church, is of two storeys, timber-framed and plastered ; the roofs are tiled. It was built early in the 17th century, and has an original chimney-stack with grouped diagonal shafts. Inside the building are exposed ceiling-beams.

Condition—Good.

---

4. ALRESFORD. (E.d.)

(O.S. 6 in. xxxvii. N.E.)

Alresford is a parish on the left bank of the Colne estuary and 5 m. S.E. of Colchester.

Roman :—

(1) DWELLING HOUSE, of corridor type with detached building, possibly bath-block, on W., in a field now called "Eight acre or Near-ford field," and 300 yards S.E. of Alresford Lodge Farm. It was excavated in 1885 (*Essex Arch. Soc. Trans.*, N.S., III, pp. 136–9 ; *Essex Note Book*, Dec., 1884, 1.34, 38, 64, 88, 124 ; *Proc. Soc. Antiq.*, X, 178), (see also *Sectional Preface*, p. xxvii), but nothing is now visible on the site except loose fragments of brick and some tesserae. The corridor was 162½ ft. long by 10 ft. wide, turning S. at right angles at each end. The plan was indicated by the tessellated and other pavements only, all the walls having been removed. The associated finds included coins of Commodus and Faustina and some 'Samian' potsherds. Some fragments of painted plaster from the walls, one with a few letters in graffiti, and pottery are now preserved in the Colchester Museum.

Ecclesiastical :—

(2). PARISH CHURCH OF ST. PETER stands near the middle of the parish. The walls are probably of rubble, but are covered with cement ; the dressings are of limestone and the roofs are tiled. According to Morant, referring to an inscription to Anfrid de Staunton, the church was built or rebuilt

early in the 14th century, and this is probably the date of most of the structure, but the Roman brick quoins of the N.W. angle of the Nave are of the 12th-century, and the corresponding quoins of the S.W. angle have been recently exposed, showing that the 12th-century building was 21¾ ft. wide externally. The church was drastically restored in the 19th century, when the *Chancel* appears to have been partly rebuilt, the *South Vestry*, *South Aisle* and *North Porch* added, and the bell-turret rebuilt.

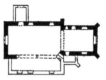

Architectural Description—The *Chancel* (22 ft. by 16 ft.) has no ancient features, except a tri-angular headed opening in the E. gable and part of the jambs and head of the window in the S. wall, which are of *c.* 1300.

The *Nave* (39 ft. by 21 ft.) has in the N. wall two modern windows and further W. a late 14th-century N. doorway with recut moulded jambs and two-centred arch. The S. arcade is modern, and in the W. wall is a modern window.

The *South Aisle* is modern, but reset in the S. wall are two early 14th-century windows of two plain lights, with a spandrel in a two-centred head ; the mullion of the western window is modern ; the modern S. doorway has reset splays and rear-arch of the 14th century.

The *Roof* of the nave has one old tie-beam and a moulded N. wall-plate, probably of the 14th century.

Fittings—*Indent :* In chancel—of marginal in-scription, slab mostly covered by choir-stalls *Monument :* In churchyard—S. side, to Sarah (Sparhawk), wife of Samuel Bridg, 1680, table-tomb of brick with stone slab.

Condition—Good, much altered.

Secular :—

(3). BROOK FARM, house, about ¾ m. E.N.E. of the church, is of two storeys, timber-framed and plastered ; the roofs are tiled. It was built late in the 15th or early in the 16th century, with a central hall and cross-wings at the N. and S. ends. There is a 17th-century addition on the N. side. Inside the building is some exposed timber-framing and an original doorway with a four-centred head. The roof has original cambered tie-beams.

Condition—Good, much altered.

5. ARDLEIGH. (D.c.)

(O.S. 6 in. [a]xix. S.W. [b]xix. S.E. [c]xxviii. N.W.)

Ardleigh is a parish and small village 4½ m. N.E. of Colchester. The church and house (6) are the principal monuments.

Ecclesiastical :—

[b](1). PARISH CHURCH OF ST. MARY stands in the village. The walls are of mixed rubble, with much pudding-stone ; the dressings are of limestone and brick, and the roofs are tiled. The W. bay of the *Nave* is of early to mid 14th-century date. The *West Tower* and the *South Porch* were added late in the 15th century. The rest of the church, including *Chancel, Chapels, Nave* and side *Aisles*, was entirely rebuilt in 1885.

The S. porch is a good example of the period, and among the fittings the S. door is noteworthy.

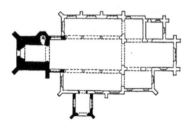

Architectural Description—The *Nave* (53 ft. by 21 ft.) is modern except for the W. bay, which has on each side a mid 14th-century window of three trefoiled ogee lights with tracery in an obtuse two-centred head with a moulded label and head-stops ; one stop on the N. is modern.

The *South Aisle* is modern, but reset in the S. wall is a late 15th-century doorway (Plate, p. 132) with moulded and shafted jambs and two-centred arch, enriched with carved heads and foliage ; the arch has a square head with a moulded label and spandrels carved with mutilated figures of Adam and Eve and a background of foliage.

The *West Tower* (15½ ft. by 12¼ ft.) is of late 15th-century date and of three stages (Plate, p. 221), with a moulded plinth of flint-inlaid work and a modern parapet. The two-centred tower-arch is of two moulded orders, the outer continuous and the inner resting on much restored semi-octagonal shafts, with moulded capitals and bases. The W. window is of three trefoiled ogee lights, with vertical tracery in a two-centred head with a moulded label ; the cusp points are foliated ; the partly restored W. doorway has a moulded two-centred head with moulded labels and defaced head-stops. The second stage has in each wall a

window of one cinquefoiled light ; the external reveals of those in the N., S. and W. walls are of brick. The bell-chamber has in each wall a much restored window of two trefoiled ogee lights with tracery in a two-centred head with a moulded label.

The *South Porch* (Plate, p. xxix) is of late 15th-century date and has a moulded plinth and embattled parapet, both with flint-inlaid panels ; the diagonal buttresses have stone panels with traceried heads to each stage, and are finished with octagonal shafts with embattled capitals, supporting seated figures of beasts. The S. front is of two stages and is entirely covered with flint-inlay in panels ; at the top of the lower stage runs the name Maria in black letter, and at the base of the upper stage is a row of chalices and hosts in stone ; below these is an ashlar band with the black-lettter inscription, " Orate p animabus Johīs Hūte at ȳ wode et Alicie uxoris ejus Johīs Hute Willī Hūte." The outer archway is two-centred and is of two moulded orders, the outer continuous and the inner resting on attached shafts with moulded capitals and bases ; the arch has a square head with double moulded labels, stopped with crowned lions on foliated brackets and spandrels carved with figures of St. George and the Dragon. Above the arch are three niches with buttressed jambs and elaborate traceried and crocketed canopies ; the pedestals have each a half-angel issuing from clouds. The side walls of the porch have each a window of three cinquefoiled lights, with embattled tracery in a segmental-pointed head with a moulded label.

The *Roof* of the porch is of late 15th-century date, partly restored, and has moulded and braced principals, forming four-centred arches, moulded ridge and wall-plates.

Fittings—*Bells :* eight ; 3rd by John Darbie, 1676 ; 4th by the same founder, 1675 ; 6th by Charles Newman, 1689 ; 8th probably by Robert Burford, early 15th-century, and inscribed " Sum Rosa Pulsata Mundi Maria Vocata." *Door* (Plate, p. 132) : In S. doorway—of two folds, each with three panels with elaborately traceried heads, moulded bars, late 15th-century, partly restored, old pierced scutcheon-plate. *Monument :* In S. porch—on S. wall, internally, to Barbara, wife of Henry Lufkin, 1706, and to Henry Lufkin, 1721, wooden ' marbled ' tablet with side pilasters and broken curved pediment. *Niches :* In S. chapel—in E. wall, but formerly in E. wall of old S. aisle, with moulded and buttressed jambs and defaced vaulted canopy with rosette bosses, remains of colour, late 15th-century. In S. porch—over S. doorway, with buttressed jambs and ogee cinquefoiled canopy with crocketed label, late 15th-century, much defaced. *Plate :* includes cup and cover-paten, the former dated 1584 and both with bands of engraved ornament. *Recess :* In tower—in S. wall, small niche with triangular head of brick, late 15th-century. *Screen*

STANWAY : CHURCH OF ALL SAINTS ; 14th-century and later.
From the North.

BIRCH : CHURCH OF ST. MARY (LITTLE BIRCH) ; 12th-century and later.
From the South-East.

LANGHAM: (3) VALLEY HOUSE.
Main Staircase; early 17th-century.

BRADWELL-JUXTA-COGGESHALL: PARISH CHURCH OF
THE HOLY TRINITY.
South Porch, c. 1340; Balusters, early 17th-century.

(Plate, p. 181) : Between chancel and nave—base of screen with moulded rail and two bays on each side doorway, flanked and divided by restored buttresses, each bay with two open panels with septfoiled ogee heads and tracery with spandrels richly carved with foliage, dragons, grotesque heads, etc., late 15th-century, partly restored. *Stoup :* In S. porch—with moulded jambs and cinquefoiled head, bowl cut away, late 15th-century.

Condition—Good, much restored and rebuilt.

Secular :—

[a](2). HOMESTEAD MOAT, at Ardleigh Wick, 1¼ m. W. of the church.

[a](3). ARDLEIGH HALL, 200 yards N.W. of the church, is of two storeys, timber-framed and plastered ; the roofs are tiled. It was built in the 15th century, but has a large modern block of brick added on the E. side. The upper storey projects and is gabled at the E. end of the N. side. Inside the building the N. wing has an original king-post truss and central purlin ; the S. wing has an original cambered tie-beam with shaped wall-posts. Some timber-framing and ceiling-beams are exposed.

MONUMENTS (4–13).

The following monuments, unless otherwise described, are of the 17th century and of two storeys, timber-framed and plastered ; the roofs are tiled. Many of the buildings have original chimney-stacks and exposed ceiling-beams.

Condition—Good, or fairly good.

[a](4). *Cottage,* two tenements, on W. side of road, 30 yards S.W. of the church.

[a](5). *House,* two tenements, S. of (4). The upper storey projects on the E. front.

[a](6). *House,* two tenements, on S. side of road 60 yards S.W. of (5), was built in the 15th century ; two wings were added at the back, one probably in the 16th century and one in the 17th century. The upper storey formerly projected on the N. front but has been underbuilt ; the original bressumer is moulded and. has defaced running foliage ornament. The upper storey has exposed timber-framing and three four-light windows with moulded sills and now blocked. In the E. wall is an original five-light window with moulded frame and mullions. Inside the building, two rooms on the ground floor have original moulded ceiling-beams and joists ; the beams are carved with running foliage. The roof at the E. and W. ends has original tie-beams, those at the W. end with curved braces and king-posts.

[b](7). *Abbott's Cottage,* about ½ m. E. of the church.

[c](8). *Bovill's Hall,* ½ m S. of the church, has been practically rebuilt except the N.W. wing.

[c](9). *Hull Farm,* house, 1 m. S.W. of (8), is of T-shaped plan with the cross-wing at the S. end.

[c](10). *Mose Hall,* ¼ m. W. of (9), was built in the 15th century with cross-wings at the N.E. and S.W. ends. On the S.E. side is a projecting chimney-stack with tabled offsets and there is a similar stack at the N.E. end. Inside the building the main block has an original roof of king-post type. There is also a door of 17th-century panelling.

[c](11). *Harvey's Farm,* house, about 1¾ m. W.S.W. of the church, was built probably in the 15th century, with a cross-wing at the N.W. end. The upper storey projects on curved brackets at the N.E. end of the cross-wing. Inside the building is a door with old strap-hinges. In the garden is some 15th-century moulded stonework probably of ecclesiastical origin.

[a](12). *Gatehouse Farm,* house, ¼ m. N.W. of (11), was built in the 15th century and has a cross-wing at the E. end. There are also modern additions on the E. The upper storey projects at the N. end of the cross-wing. The roof has an original king-post truss.

[a](13). *Clark's Farm,* house, 1 m. N.E. of (12), was built in the 16th century on an L-shaped plan with the wings extending towards the W. and N.

————

6. BEAUMONT CUM MOZE. (F.c.)

(O.S. 6 in. [a]xxix. S.E. [b]xxx. S.W.)

Beaumont cum Moze is a parish (formerly two parishes) 7 m. S.W. of Harwich.

Ecclesiastical :—

[a](1). PARISH CHURCH OF ST. LEONARD stands in the S.W. part of the parish. With the exception of the 14th or 15th-century E. buttresses and probably the chancel walls, the church was rebuilt in the 19th century. In the S. wall of the chancel is a doorway, probably of the 14th century, with chamfered jambs and two-centred arch.

Fittings—*Bells :* two ; said to be, 1st uninscribed ; 2nd by John Darbie, 16—. *Communion Table and Rails :* Table with turned and twisted legs and rails, early 18th-century. The Rails are of the same date and have twisted balusters. *Floor-slabs :* In chancel—(1) to Mrs. R. E. Rathborne, 1689 ; (2) to Rev. James Rathborne, early 18th-century. *Indent :* In S. porch—of figure and inscription, 15th-century. *Piscina :* In chancel—with moulded jambs, cinquefoiled head and sexfoiled drain, 15th-century. *Plate :* includes Elizabethan cup

and cover-paten and a paten of 1683. *Miscellanea :*
In nave—over chancel-arch, stone carved with
I H S.   The S. porch has some reused timbers
including a 15th-century moulded wall-plate
Condition—Rebuilt.

a(2). FOUNDATION MOUNDS on site of Moze
church, about 1½ m. N.E. of (1).

Secular :—

a(3). BEAUMONT HALL (Plate, p. 234), S.W. of
the church, is of two storeys with attics. The
walls are of brick and plastered timber-framing,
and the roofs are tiled. It was built probably
late in the 17th century with a semi-detached
wing on the N.E.   The main block has on each
side two curvilinear Dutch gables of brick with
oversailing copings. The wing has similar but
smaller gables. Inside the building, the early
18th-century staircase has moulded rails and
twisted balusters.
Condition—Good.

a(4). COTTAGE, at Moze Cross, 550 yards N.W.
of (2), is of two storeys, timber-framed and weather-
boarded ; the roofs are tiled. It was built late
in the 17th century, and has exposed framing and
ceiling-beams.
Condition—Good.

Unclassified :—

b(5). RED HILLS, several, within the sea-wall,
about 1½ m. E. of the church.

----

7. BIRCH. (C.d.)

(O.S. 6 in. *(a)*xxvii. S.W. *(b)*xxxvi. N.W. *(c)*xxxvi.
S.W.)

Birch is a parish 5 m. S.W. of Colchester. It
includes the former parishes of Great and Little
Birch. The church of the former, now the parish
church, has no ancient features. The ruined church
of Little Birch is interesting.

Ecclesiastical :—

b(1). CHURCH OF ST. MARY (Plate, p. 6), formerly
the parish church of Little Birch, stands ¾ m.
N.E. of the parish church of Great Birch. The
walls are of rubble with some brick ; the
rubble of the nave is coursed ; the dressings are
of limestone and brick. The *Nave* was built
early in the 12th century. About the middle
of the 14th century the *Chancel* was rebuilt and
the *West Tower* added. The Chancel-arch was
inserted *c.* 1400. In the 16th century the upper
part of the tower was rebuilt and the stair-turret
added. The church fell into disuse, probably
in the 17th century, and is now roofless and ruinous.

Architectural Description—The *Chancel* (26½ ft.
by 16½ ft.) has in the E. wall the jambs of a
14th-century window ; the head has gone and the
sill has been broken away. In the N. wall are
two mid 14th-century windows, with two-centred
heads and moulded labels ; the former mullion
and tracery of each has been destroyed. In the
S. wall are two similar windows but the outer
arch and label of the eastern window has been
destroyed ; between them is a mid 14th-century
doorway with moulded jambs, two-centred arch
and label. The chancel-arch was inserted *c.* 1400 ;
the arch has gone, but the late 14th-century
responds of cut brick have each an attached shaft,
with a moulded stone base.

The *Nave* (31½ ft. by 19 ft.) has in the N. wall
two windows, the eastern is of the 12th century,
now blocked, and has a Roman brick W. jamb and
splay with part of the round head of stone ; the
western window has moulded jambs perhaps of the
14th century and an early 16th-century brick head ;
it is set low in the wall and has a single pointed
light under a square moulded label ; E. of it is
the N. doorway of which only the splays and
segmental-pointed rear-arch, probably of the 14th
century, remain ; E. of the eastern window is a
small quatrefoiled opening of the 15th century
which formerly lighted the stairway to the rood-
loft ; the upper and lower doorways have been
removed and the openings blocked. At the E.
angles of the nave are pilaster buttresses of Roman
brick and the W. angles have quoins of the same
material. In the S. wall are two windows, the
eastern, formerly of two lights, is now only a
ragged opening with the sill and part of the E.
jamb remaining ; the western window is of the
12th century and is similar to that in the N. wall
but is complete and not blocked ; further W. is a
ragged opening representing the former S. doorway;
it has splays and rear-arch of Roman brick and
perhaps of the 12th century. In the S.W. angle
is the early 16th-century doorway to the stair-
turret of the tower ; it has chamfered jambs and a
four-centred head.

The *West Tower* (6½ ft. square) is of four
stages with a ruined parapet. The two lower
stages are of the 14th century but built on to the
12th-century W. wall of the nave ; the two upper
stages are of red brick and are of 16th-century
date. The 14th-century tower-arch is of brick
and has responds and two-centred arch of two
chamfered orders. The 14th-century W. window
is of two cinquefoiled lights with a quatrefoil
in a two-centred head with a moulded label and

carved stops, one with a head and one with a grotesque beast. The second stage has in the E. wall a square-headed opening ; above it are the marks of the former steep-pitched roof of the nave. In the W. wall is a 14th-century window of one cinquefoiled light with a moulded label. The bell-chamber has in the E., N. and W. walls an early 16th-century window of brick and of two four-centred lights in a square head ; the mullion of the W. window has been destroyed.

Fittings— *Coffin-lid :* Tapering slab used as threshold of S. doorway. *Piscina :* In chancel— with moulded jambs and trefoiled head, broken drain, 14th-century.

Condition—Ruinous and tower much overgrown with ivy.

Secular :—

b(2). BIRCH CASTLE, formerly belonging to the Gernon family (Morant, II, 182), stands a few yards S. of the parish church. A short length of rampart and ditch situated on a spur of high ground is all that remains of the earthworks of the Castle. Morant describes the work as a mount surrounded by a ditch.

In the valley to the N.E. of the castle is an old dam, now disused.

Condition—Fragmentary.

HOMESTEAD MOATS.

b(3). S.E. of Birch Holt and nearly 2 m. W.S.W. of the parish church.

b(4). At Birch Holt Farm, 150 yards N.W. of (3).

MONUMENTS (5–11).

The following monuments, unless otherwise described, are of the 17th century and of two storeys, timber-framed and plastered ; the roofs are tiled or thatched. Many of the buildings have original chimney-stacks and exposed ceiling-beams. Condition—Good, or fairly good.

b(5). *Winterflood's Farm,* house, nearly 2 m. W.N.W. of the parish church, is of L-shaped plan with the wings extending towards the S. and E.

b(6). *Cottage,* on S. side of road, 500 yards N.E. of (5).

b(7). *Claypit Farm,* house, nearly ¾ m. E.S.E. of (6), was built probably late in the 16th century, with a cross-wing at the N. and S. ends. The original central chimney-stack has grouped hexagonal shafts.

a(8). *Upper Hill Farm,* house, 1½ m. N. of the parish church, was built late in the 16th or early in the 17th century, and has a cross-wing at the W. end. The upper storey projects at the N. end of the cross-wing and on the E. side of the main block.

b(9). *Cottage,* about ¼ m. S.E. of St. Mary's church.

b(10). *Cottage,* on the E. side of the road at Birch Green, about ½ m. S. of the parish church, was built probably in the 16th century, and has a cross-wing at the N. end.

c(11). *Roundbush Farm,* house, about 1¼ m. S.W. of the parish church, has an original chimney-stack, with four octagonal shafts.

---

8. BOXTED. (D.b.)

(O S. 6 in. (*a*)xviii. N.E. (*b*)xviii. S.E. (*c*)xix. N.W. (*d*)xix. S.W.)

Boxted is a parish on the right bank of the Stour and 5 m. N. of Colchester. The church is interesting.

Ecclesiastical :—

a(1). PARISH CHURCH OF ST. PETER (Plate, p. xxviii) stands in the N. part of the parish. The walls are of mixed rubble, with some Roman brick and much iron pudding-stone in the tower ; the upper part of the tower is of brick ; the dressings are of limestone and the roofs are tiled. The *Chancel* and *Nave* are of mid 12th-century date and the *West Tower* was built perhaps rather later in the same century. In the 14th century the lateral walls of the nave were pierced with arches, but these were left in a rough state ; the *North* and *South* Aisles were added at the same time. About 1500, the chancel was largely rebuilt, and in the 16th century the upper part of the tower was rebuilt and a stage added ; the *South Porch* is perhaps of the same century. The church was much altered in the 17th and 18th centuries, and has been restored in modern times when the S. porch was practically rebuilt.

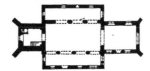

Architectural Description—The *Chancel* (24 ft. by 17½ ft.) has the stump of an early 16th-century gable-cross and a modern E. window. In the N. wall are two windows of *c.* 1500, partly restored, each of two cinquefoiled lights with vertical tracery in a four-centred head with a moulded label and head-stops. In the S. wall are two windows uniform with those in the N. wall, and between them is a doorway of the same date, with moulded jambs, two-centred arch and a label. The mid 12th-century chancel arch is semi-circular and of two orders, the outer roll-moulded and the inner plain ; the responds are plain with chamfered imposts ; the former side shafts or outer order have been removed and the N. respond has been partly cut away.

The *Nave* (41 ft. by 20 ft.) has in the E. wall above the chancel-arch two 14th or 15th-century windows, each of one trefoiled light ; below them is the line of the former steep-pitched roof of the nave. The N. and S. arcades are probably of the 14th century and each have rough pointed arches cut through the wall, three on the N. and four on the S. side ; on the N. side there are responds, but on the S. the arches die on to the end walls. The clearstorey has on the N. side two, and on the S. three, windows of uncertain date and with roughly cut rounded heads ; below the windows on the N. side are traces in the plaster of two semi-circular rear-arches, probably of 12th-century windows. Above the S. clearstorey is a gabled dormer of timber, probably of the 18th century, but much restored. On the N. side of the W. tower are the Roman brick quoins of the 12th-century nave.

The *North Aisle* (8½ ft. wide) is of the 14th century and has a partly restored E. window of three pointed lights with plain spandrels in a two-centred head. In the N. wall are two windows, each of a single pointed light ; further W. is the N. doorway, with moulded jambs and two-centred arch ; it is now partly blocked and converted into a window. W. of the doorway are traces, externally, of another window. In the W. wall is an 18th-century or modern window.

The *South Aisle* (8½ ft. wide) is of the 14th century, and has in the E. wall a window, perhaps originally of several lights but with all except one converted into a square-headed two-light window ; the remaining light is trefoiled and blocked internally ; the rear-arch is moulded and dies on to the arcade wall. In the S. wall are three windows, the eastern is of wood and set in a gabled head of timber ; the moulded lintel is dated 1604, but the window has been much restored ; the other two windows are each of one cinquefoiled light, badly formed, and are of the 14th century, but much altered ; the rear-arch of the eastern window is moulded ; between them is the S. doorway with jambs of two moulded orders and a modern head. In the W. wall is a window of one cinquefoiled light, partly restored.

The *West Tower* (13½ ft. by 12½ ft.) is of four stages internally, with an embattled brick parapet ; the top stage is also of brick and of the 16th century ; the lower part is of late 12th-century date. In the E. wall of the ground stage is a rough pointed doorway of brick and of 16th-century date. It is set in the blocking of the former two-centred tower-arch which appears in the second stage, and is of rough rubble retaining parts of the

boarding of the original centering ; it is probably of late 12th-century date. The W. window is of the 14th century, and of two trefoiled lights with a quatrefoil in a two-centred head. In the S. wall is a 12th-century single-light window of Roman brick with a round head, and now blocked. The second stage has in the N., S. and W. walls a single-light window, probably of late 12th-century date ; two of them are now blocked. The third stage (the early bell-chamber) has in the E., N. and W. walls a pair of late 12th-century pointed windows, all now blocked ; the S. wall was rebuilt in the 16th century. The bell-chamber has in each wall a reset 14th-century window, each formerly of two cinquefoiled lights in a two-centred head with a moulded label and head-stops.

The *Roof* of the nave is of late 14th-century date, and of four bays with king-post trusses, moulded wall-plates and tie-beams and king-posts with moulded capitals and bases. The roof of the S. porch incorporates some old timbers.

Fittings—Bells : two, 1st by Thomas Gardiner, 1714. *Chest :* In N. aisle—iron-bound, with two locks, 17th-century. *Door :* In tower stair-turret—of oak battens with strap-hinges, probably 17th-century. *Glass :* In chancel—in tracery of S. windows, fragments of ruby and blue glass, 14th-century. *Monuments* and *Floor-slabs.* Monuments: In chancel—on S. wall, (1) to Elizabeth (Maidstone), wife of Nathaniel Bacon, 1628, marble tablet with a double arch and figures of an angel, skeleton, and shield of arms ; " dedicated to ye memory of God's great favour in her dere love, N.B." In churchyard —(2) to Anne, wife of Thomas Goodall, 1714, head-stone with skull and cross-bones. Floor-slabs : In chancel—(1) to John Maidstone, 1672 ; (2) to Mrs. Mary Havers, 1679, Maidstone Havers, her son, 1687, and Anne, daughter of John Maidstone, 1698 ; (3) to John Maidstone, 1666, and Dorothy (Maidstone), widow of Timothy Felton, 1717 ; (4) to Anne, daughter of John Maidstone, 1692 ; (5) to Robert Maidstone, 1684. In nave—(6) to Alexander Carr, 1681, and John Marr, 1683, servants of Awbrey, Earl of Oxford, with shields of arms. In tower—(7) part of slab with moulded edge, mediaeval. *Niche :* In nave—in E. wall, S. of chancel-arch, tall plastered niche with round head, probably early 16th-century. *Piscina :* In chancel—with moulded jambs, cinquefoiled head and square drain, 15th-century. *Sedile :* In chancel—sill of S.E. window, carried down to form seat.

Condition—Good.

Secular :—

c(2). RIVERS HALL, house and moat, nearly ¾ m. E. of the church. The *House* is of two storeys, timber-framed and plastered ; the roofs are tiled.

BRADFIELD : (2) BRADFIELD HALL.
South Front ; c. 1520.

BRIGHTLINGSEA: PARISH CHURCH OF ALL SAINTS.
North Chapel and Aisle, 1520–40, and West Tower, *c.* 1500.

It was rebuilt probably in the 18th century and has some ornamental plaster-work at the back, dated 1713. One of the windows at the back has the scratched date 1713. Inside the building some rooms have original deal panelling. The *Moat* surrounds the house.
Condition—Of house, good.

MONUMENTS (3–10).

The following monuments, unless otherwise described, are of the 17th century and of two storeys, timber-framed and plastered ; the roofs are tiled or thatched. Many of the buildings have original chimney-stacks and exposed ceiling-beams.

Condition—Good, or fairly good.

a(3). *Cottage*, 50 yards N.E. of the church, has been almost entirely rebuilt.

a(4). *Almshouses*, 50 yards S.E. of the church, have exposed timber-framing at the N. end.

a(5). *Hill Farm*, house, about ½ m. S.E. of the church, was built probably late in the 16th century with cross-wings at the N. and S. ends.

a(6). *Cottage*, on W. side of road, ¼ m. S.S.W. of (5).

b(7). *Cottage*, 300 yards S. of (6).

b(8). *Cottage*, on S. side of road, nearly ½ m. S.W. of (7), has been refronted with brick.

b(9). *Barrett's Farm*, house, 600 yards W. of (8), was built probably in the 16th century.

d(10). *Cottage*, on S. side of road, 1¼ m. S.S.E. of the church.

Unclassified :—

c(11). MILL BASINS, between Cophedge and Ash Woods and ¾ m. E. of the church. Two basins, a dam between them and a strong outer dam at the N.E. end.
Condition—Fairly good.

_____

9. BRADFIELD. (E.b.)

(O.S. 6 in. xx. S.W.)

Bradfield is a parish and village 7½ m. W. of Harwich. The church and hall are the principal monuments.

Ecclesiastical :—

(1) PARISH CHURCH OF ST. LAWRENCE stands in the village. The walls are probably of rubble, but are entirely covered with cement ; the dressings are of limestone and the roofs are tiled. The *Chancel* and *Nave* were built about the middle of the 13th century. About the middle of the 14th century the *South Porch* was added and the *West Tower* was added early in the 16th century.

The church has been restored in modern times, the west tower partly rebuilt, and the *North* and *South Transepts, Vestry* and *Organ Chamber* added.

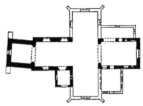

Architectural Description—The *Chancel* (26 ft. by 17½ ft.) has a modern E. window. In the N. wall is a 13th-century lancet window with a modern rear-arch, further W. is a modern doorway and arch. In the S. wall is a modern window and doorway ; further W. is a blocked window, probably of the 13th century. The two-centred chancel-arch is of doubtful date and of two chamfered orders ; the outer continuous and the inner resting on attached shafts with moulded capitals.

The *Nave* (45½ ft. by 18¼ ft.) has in the N. wall two late 13th-century windows each of two lancet lights and much restored. In the S. wall is a window uniform with those in the N. wall ; further E. is the 14th-century N. doorway with moulded jambs and two-centred arch, mostly covered with cement.

The *West Tower* (about 14 ft. square), is of three stages, the two lower of early 16th-century date, much repaired and the top stage modern. The two-centred tower-arch is of two chamfered orders, the outer continuous and the inner resting on attached shafts with moulded capitals and bases. The W. window is of two cinquefoiled lights in a three-centred head with a moulded label ; below it is the W. doorway with double chamfered jambs, two-centred arch and moulded label ; it is now blocked. The second stage has in the W. wall a window of one cinquefoiled light.

The *South Porch* has a modern outer archway. The side walls have each a mid 14th-century window, that on the W. of two trefoiled lights with a quatrefoil in a two-centred head ; that on the E. is blocked.

Fittings—*Bell* : one, said to be inscribed " I am koc of this floc wit gloria tibi Domine," late 14th-century. *Brasses* and *Indents.* Brasses : In chancel—on S. wall, (1) of Joane (Harbottell), wife of Thomas Rysbye, 1598, figure of woman in elaborately embroidered stomacher, etc., and shield of arms ; (2) to John Harbotle, 1577, inscription and shield of arms ; (3) to Jakys Reynford, *c.* 1520, inscription only ; (4) to Elizabeth, daughter of Edward Grimestone, 1604, inscription only.

Indents : In nave and by S. porch—two slabs, with traces of indents. *Chairs :* In chancel— two with carved or inlaid backs, turned and carved legs, etc., mid 17th-century. *Font* (Plate, p. xxxiv) : octagonal tapering bowl, each face with two shallow pointed panels, stem with plain round shafts at each angle, late 12th or early 13th-century. *Helm :* In chancel—on S. wall, combed funeral-helm, with vizor, 16th-century, carved crest, later. *Piscinae :* In chancel—with chamfered jambs and two-centred head, sexfoiled drain, probably 13th-century ; reset in N. ·wall, double, with moulded two-centred arches enriched with 'dog-tooth' ornament, moulded label with mask-stops, central shaft between bays with moulded capital and base, 13th-century. *Plate :* includes 17th-century cup, with restored stem. *Pulpit :* semi-hexagonal, with panelled sides, early 18th-century, with 16th and 17th-century carving and panels stuck on.
Condition—Fairly good.

Secular :—

(2). BRADFIELD HALL, house and moat, nearly 1¼ m. S.S.W. of the church. The *House* is of two storeys with attics ; the walls are of brick and the roofs are tiled. The remaining portion of the original house (Plate, p. 10) consists of a rectangular block of *c.* 1520, with a semi-octagonal stair-turret at the S.W. angle. The S. front has a crow-stepped gable, with cusped corbelling below the deeply moulded copings ; at the apex and on each side are crocketed pinnacles set diagonally ; the wall face is diapered and there are two original windows, both with four-centred heads and moulded labels ; the lower retains the intersecting tracery and heads of three lights ; but in the upper window the mullions and heads have been cut away. The stair-turret has small blocked windows with square moulded labels ; one of these windows is quatrefoiled. Inside the building are some 17th-century doors and panelling. The newel of the staircase is carried up to form a turned post ; the rails at the top have symmetrically turned balusters of *c.* 1600. In the E. wall at the attic level is the four-centred head of a large window, with a chamfered rear-arch springing from moulded corbels. There is also an original doorway with a four-centred head.
The *Moat* surrounds the house.
Condition—Of house, fairly good.

(3). HOUSE and shop, 70 yards N.W. of the church, is of two storeys, timber-framed and plastered ; the roofs are tiled. It was built late in the 17th century and has exposed ceiling-beams.
Condition—Good, much altered.

(4). COTTAGE (Plate, p. 189), three tenements, 150 yards S.S.W. of the church, is of two storeys, timber-framed and plastered ; the roofs are thatched. It was built early in the 17th century,

with a cross-wing at the S. end. The upper storey projects at the E. end of the cross-wing. Inside the building are exposed ceiling-beams.
Condition—Good.

———

BENTLEY, see GREAT BENTLEY · and LITTLE BENTLEY.

———

10. BRADWELL (-juxta-Coggeshall). (A.d.)

(O.S. 6 in. [d]xxv. S.E. [b]xxvi. S.W. [d]xxxiv. N.E.)

Bradwell is a small parish and village on the S. bank of the Blackwater, 4½ m. N. of Witham. The church and its fittings are noteworthy.

Ecclesiastical :—

[b](1). PARISH CHURCH OF THE HOLY TRINITY (Plate, p. xxviii) stands near the N.E. corner of the parish. The walls are probably of flint-rubble and are covered with plaster ; the dressings are of limestone and clunch ; the roofs are tiled. The *Nave* was built early in the 12th century. The *Chancel* was rebuilt and the *South Porch* added *c.* 1340. In the 16th or early in the 17th century the *Bell-turret* was built.
Amongst the fittings the 14th-century paintings and incised slab, the 15th-century screen, and the 17th-century monument are noteworthy.

Architectural Description—The *Chancel* (22¾ ft. by 21½ ft.) has an E. window of *c.* 1440, and of three cinquefoiled lights with vertical tracery in a two-centred head. In the N. wall are two windows, the eastern is of *c.* 1340 and of two trefoiled ogee lights with tracery in a segmental-pointed head ; the jambs and tracery are moulded internally ; the western window is of *c.* 1460, and of two cinquefoiled lights with vertical tracery in a two-centred head with a moulded label and head-stops. In the S. wall are two windows of *c.* 1340, both of two cinquefoiled ogee lights with tracery in a roughly semi-circular head with a moulded label ; the western window has carved flowers in two cusps of the tracery ; between the windows is a 14th-century doorway, with double chamfered jambs and a two-centred arch.
The *Nave* (33½ ft. by 21½ ft.) is undivided structurally from the chancel. In the N. wall are two windows ; the eastern is of *c.* 1340 and of two cinquefoiled ogee lights with tracery in a segmental head ; the western window is of early

12th-century date, and of one small round-headed light ; between the windows is the early 12th-century doorway, now blocked, with a modern window in the blocking ; it has plain jambs and a semi-circular arch. In the S. wall are two windows similar to those in the N. wall, but the western window is now blocked by a cupboard and is not visible externally ; between the windows is the round-headed S. doorway, similar to the N. doorway, but of brick and not blocked. In the W. wall is a window of c. 1460, of two cinquefoiled lights with tracery in a two-centred head with a moulded label ; above it in the gable is a small round-headed window, of uncertain date.

The *Bell-turret* is of timber and probably of late 16th or early 17th-century date ; it rests on large stop-chamfered posts and a cross-beam near the W. end of the nave, and is covered externally with modern weather-boarding and shingles.

The *South Porch* (Plate, p. 7) is of timber and of c. 1340. The S. gable has foiled barge-boards, and the E. and W. sides have each seven open lights with trefoiled ogee and traceried heads ; the mullions have been replaced by turned balusters of early 17th-century date on the E. side, and modern except for the half balusters on the W. side.

The *Roof* of the chancel is of the trussed-rafter type, plastered on the soffit, and with plain chamfered wall-plates. The 14th-century roof of the nave is of three bays with two king-post trusses ; the tie-beam of the western truss is moulded and of the 15th century ; the king-posts have moulded capitals and bases, and the eastern may be a later copy. The 14th-century roof of the S. porch has moulded wall-plates and two cambered tie-beams, one supported by curved braces.

Fittings—*Bells :* three ; all by Miles Graye ; 1st, 1621 ; 2nd, 1609 ; 3rd, 1632, cracked. *Brass Indents :* In chancel—(1) of figures and canopy, two shields, group of children (?) and inscription-plate, part hidden by foot-pace of altar ; (2) of inscription-plate. *Chests :* In nave—' dug-out ' with iron bands and two locks, possibly 17th-century, lid apparently modern ; in cupboard under bell-turret, ' dug-out ' with strap-hinges, 17th-century or earlier. *Communion Table :* with plain legs and moulded rails, 17th-century, top modern. *Door :* In S. doorway—of studded battens on square framing, stock-lock of oak and traceried scutcheon to modern handle, drop-handle to latch, strap-hinges, late 15th or early 16th-century. *Font* and *Cover* (Plate, p. xxxiv) : Bowl of limestone, originally square with small cheveron ornament round top, 12th-century, bowl cut octagonal, early in the 16th century ; stem of brick with moulded top and base, and sunk quatrefoil in each face, early 16th-century. Cover of oak, pyramidal, with panelled sides and ball top, 17th-century, bracket for pulley on framing of

bell-turret above. *Funeral Helm :* In chancel—on N. wall, with crest (dog's head razed), 17th-century. *Glass :* In chancel—in E. window, in tracery, fragments, 15th-century ; in N.E. window, fragments in tracery, with dog in roundel, 14th-century ; in N.W. window, fragments of figures and tabernacle work, etc., 15th-century ; in S.W. window, part of angel holding shield, *a bend with two scallops* (one lost) *thereon on a chief a leopard* (reversed), 15th-century ; fragments of tabernacle work, etc., 15th-century. In nave—in N.E. and S.E. windows, fragments, 14th-century, mostly *in situ. Monuments* and *Floor-slabs.* Monuments : In chancel—against E. wall, (1) of Anthony Maxey [1592], and Dorothy (Basset) [1602], his wife, wall-monument (Plate, p. 97) of marble and alabaster, erected by their son, Sir Henry Maxey, with two round-headed recesses flanked and divided by Corinthian columns, and containing kneeling figures of two men in plate-armour and wives at prayer-desks, entablature with quartered shield of Maxey and four smaller shields below ; on N. wall, (2) to Sir William Maxey, 1645, Helena (Grevill), his wife, 1653, and Grevill, 1648, and William, 1659, their sons, wall-monument of black and white marble with broken pediment and achievement of arms, above it a funeral helm and crest, partly of late 16th-century date. Floor-slabs : In chancel—(1) to Edward Beancock, M.D., 1665, with shield of arms ; (2) defaced and partly hidden by pew, probably 17th-century ; (3) lower part of priest, incised figure in mass vestments with incised marginal inscription in Lombardic capitals, with the date 1349. *Paintings :* In chancel—on E. wall, high up on N. side, remains of figure of angel with lozengy background, top border and foliated lower border ; on E. splay of N.E. window, a Trinity, the Dove obliterated ; on W. splay, full length Resurrection figure of Christ, with cross-staff ; on soffit of rear-arch, a Majesty in a vesica, flanked by angels, one holding cross and crown of thorns, 14th-century. In nave —on soffit of rear-arch of N.E. window, circular central panel with bird (? eagle) and scrolled foliage-ornament ; on N. wall, near W. end, small head, probably of Infant Christ, part of large figure subject ; on E. splay of S.E. window, the Incredulity of St. Thomas (hands only of St. Thomas) ; on W. splay, figure, probably of St. James the Great, with book, staff and scrip, diapered background ; on soffit of rear-arch, circular central panel with *Agnus Dei* and flowing foliage on each side, all paintings c. 1320. *Panelling :* In chancel—loose, broken panel, c. 1600. In nave— in pew on N.W., six moulded panels with lozenge patterns and foliated top-rail, late 16th-century ; W. of parclose screen, plain battened panelling with moulded top-rail, 15th-century ; beneath seats of two S. pews, some 17th-century panelling. *Piscina :* In chancel—with carved and chamfered jambs and cinquefoiled arch in a square head with foliated spandrels and moulded label having base of central pinnacle, moulded projecting basin resting on remains of carved head, quatrefoil drain with carved ornament in centre, 15th-century. *Royal Arms:* Over W. gallery, of Charles II, painted and subsequently repainted. *Screens:* Between chancel and nave (Plate, p. 34), of four bays with moulded posts, rail and head, head with mortices for former loft on the W. side, post between N. bay and doorway with mortice for former parclose, N. bay with traceried heads of seven lights, mullions removed, second bay forming doorway, with traces of former traceried head; third bay with traceried heads of five former lights, S. bay open probably as doorway to former pulpit, plain close lower panels, except two with traceried heads in third bay; above beam, boarded framing, forming E. side of former loft, and pierced with two trefoiled openings, on E. face painted diapered ornament, pink on green, 15th-century. In nave—N. side, W. end of former parclose, now forming division between pews, two close lower panels only, with traceried heads and chamfered posts, formerly having attached buttresses, boarding pierced with a quatrefoil, 15th-century. *Seating:* In nave—on S. side, five backs of seats with moulded rail and one bench-end, late 15th-century; in cupboard under bell-turret, two bench-ends (?) with shaped tops. *Tiles:* In chancel—on sill of S.W. window, a number, some with traces of pattern, 14th or 15th-century. *Miscellanea:* In chancel—on sill of S.W. window, fragments of two small and nude *alabaster figures,* probably 17th-century.

Condition—Fairly good, some window tracery weathered.

Secular :—

MONUMENTS (2–8).

The following monuments, unless otherwise described, are of the 17th century and of two storeys, timber-framed and plastered or weather-boarded; the roofs are tiled. Some of the buildings have exposed ceiling-beams and original chimney-stacks.

Condition—Good, or fairly good.

ª(2). *House,* at Perry Green, on the W. side of the road and about 1,100 yards W. of the church.

ª(3). *Cottage,* three tenements, 400 yards S. of (2). The upper storey projects on the E. side.

ᶜ(4). *Gosling's Farm,* house, about ½ m. S.S.W. of the church, is of L-shaped plan with the wings extending towards the S. and E.

ª(5). *Park Farm,* house and barns, 1,100 yards W.N.W. of the church.

ª(6). *Cottage* (Plate, p. 188), on the W. side of the road at Blackwater, about 1 m. N.W. of the church, was built probably early in the 16th century. The upper storey projects on the S.E. side and the gable at the N.E. end had original scalloped barge-boards.

ª(7). *Cottage,* adjoining (6) on the N., has an original central chimney-stack with grouped diagonal shafts.

ª(8). *Cottage,* two tenements, 70 yards E.N.E. of (7).

————

BRAXTED, see GREAT BRAXTED and LITTLE BRAXTED.

————

11. BRIGHTLINGSEA. (E.d.)

(O.S. 6 in. xxxvii. S.E.)

Brightlingsea is a parish and small town on the left bank of the Colne estuary, 7½ m. S.E. of Colchester. The church and Jacobes Hall are the principal monuments.

Roman :—

(1). In a garden on the N. side of a deserted cottage called "Noah's Ark," half a mile W. of Moveron's Farm, trenches made during the war revealed sections of walls, pavements, etc., of a fair-sized house, 2 or 3 ft. below the surface. The site is just above the saltings on the E. bank of the River Colne, close to the railway. Many portable objects, including "bricks with hieroglyphics on them," are said to have been dispersed by the Australian troops who occupied the trenches. A note of the place had previously been made.

(2). In Brightlingsea itself, on the top of the hill, near the waterworks, in laying pipes at the cross-roads, Church Road, Walnut Street, Park Chase and Spring Road, mosaic pavements were found in 1884. Roof and flue-tiles, with 'Samian' and other pottery, were turned up in 1888 in Well Street, and in 1900 similar finds were made in Spring Road, close to a spring. The site is now built over. (*Essex Arch. Soc. Trans.,* 1907, N.S., X, 88. E. P. Dickin, *Hist. of Brightlingsea,* 1913, p. 5.) (See also *Sectional Preface,* p. xxiv.)

Ecclesiastical :—

(3). PARISH CHURCH OF ALL SAINTS (Plate, p. 11) stands 1½ m. N.N.W. of the town. The walls are of flint-rubble, with knapped flint facing to the N. chapel (E. bay), S. vestry and W. tower. There is much brick in the rubble of the N. aisle. The dressings are of Reigate, Barnack and other free-stone. The roofs are slated, except the vestry and tower, which are leaded. The *Chancel* was built

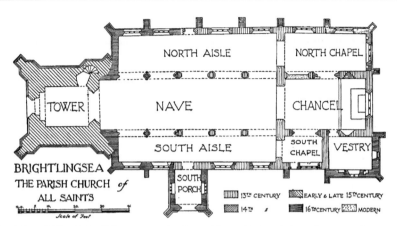

BRIGHTLINGSEA
THE PARISH CHURCH of
ALL SAINTS

Scale of Feet

⊞ 13ᵀᴴ CENTURY   ▨ EARLY & LATE 15ᵀᴴ CENTURY
▧ 14ᵀᴴ   ,   ▬ 16ᵀᴴ CENTURY ▦ MODERN

about the middle of the 13th century. At the end of the same century the *North Chapel* was added, and perhaps the *South Chapel* also, and the Nave and Aisles were rebuilt of three bays. In the 15th century the S. arcade was rebuilt with the old materials and the aisle remodelled; remains of 13th-century work are said to have been found between the two windows E. of the porch. Towards the end of the 15th century the *West Tower* was built well to the W. of the church. It was finished *c.* 1490–1500. The Nave was lengthened shortly afterwards by two bays to join it. The *South Vestry* was added *c.* 1518 and the *North Chapel* was lengthened towards the E. *c.* 1521; this was the Lady Chapel. About this time or shortly after the S. chapel arch and windows were built. About 1530–40 the *North Aisle* was reconstructed up to the W. bay (which is of *c.* 1500). The *South Porch* is also of early 16th-century date. The clearstorey and roofs fell in 1814, and the church has been restored in modern times.

The tower is a very lofty and handsome example of the period, the N. chapel and vestry are good examples of flint-inlay work, and the S. porch has good detail. The tower, S. vestry and N. chapel can be approximately dated from evidence furnished by wills. Among the fittings the many niches, all with remains of colour, and the image of a bishop are noteworthy.

Architectural Description—The *Chancel* (29 ft. by 18 ft.) has a 15th-century E. window of three cinquefoiled lights, with vertical tracery in a two-centred head with a moulded label, jambs and mullions. In the N. wall are two arches, the eastern is of early 16th-century date, four-centred and of two moulded orders, the outer continuous and the inner resting on round attached shafts

with moulded capitals and bases; the western arch is of *c.* 1300, two-centred and of two chamfered orders; the semi-octagonal responds have moulded capitals and bases; this arch is blocked on the S. face; E. of the eastern arch is a mid 13th-century lancet window, now blocked and only visible on the N. side. In the S. wall is an arch of *c.* 1530, four-centred and of two moulded orders, the outer continuous and the inner resting on round attached shafts with moulded capitals and bases; further E. is a doorway of *c.* 1520, with stop-moulded jambs and four-centred arch in a square head with traceried spandrels enclosing a rose and a fleur-de-lis; further E. is a mid 13th-century lancet window, blocked on the outside face. The chancel arch is modern.

The *North Chapel* (29½ ft. by 13½ ft.) has the eastern bay and buttresses, of *c.* 1520, faced with knapped flint; the moulded plinth embattled parapet and buttresses have flint-inlay work in traceried panels; the plinth has a series of shields, one with the sacred monogram, and nearly all the others with a merchant's mark (a variety of the Beriffe mark). In the E. wall is a window of three cinquefoiled lights, with vertical tracery in a two-centred head. In the N. wall are two windows of *c.* 1520 and each of three cinquefoiled ogee lights with transoms and vertical tracery in a segmental-pointed head with a moulded label; both are blocked below the tracery. In the W. wall is a plain plastered, four-centred arch of doubtful date.

The *South Vestry* is of *c.* 1520 and has walls faced with knapped flint, moulded plinth, embattled parapet and buttresses, both enriched with flint-inlay in traceried panels. In the E. wall is a window of one four-centred light in a square head with a moulded label and partly restored. In the

S. wall is a window of two trefoiled lights in a square head with a moulded label ; both windows are heavily barred with iron.

The *South Chapel* (15 ft. by 9¼ ft.) has in the E. wall, above the vestry roof, an early 16th-century window of three cinquefoiled ogee lights with cusped spandrels in a square head with a moulded label. In the S. wall is a window uniform with those in the N. wall of the N. chapel, but not blocked ; further W. is an early 16th-century doorway with moulded jambs and four-centred arch and a series of square carved flowers in the moulding. In the W. wall is a plain two-centred and plastered arch of doubtful date.

The *Nave* (64½ ft. by 18 ft.) has a N. arcade of five bays ; the three eastern bays are of *c.* 1300, with two-centred arches of two chamfered orders and finely jointed voussoirs ; the columns are octagonal and of small stones, with moulded capitals and bases (detail as N.W. arch of chancel) ; the corbel, from which the easternmost arch springs, is modern ; the two western bays are of early 16th-century date, with two-centred arches of two moulded orders, the outer continuous and the inner resting on round attached shafts, with moulded capitals and bases ; the third pier of the arcade consists of two half-columns of the different periods, set back to back as responds. The S. arcade is uniform with the N. arcade, except that the three eastern bays have apparently been rebuilt in the 15th century, reusing some of the old material, but with large stones in the arches ; the columns and respond of this part have double chamfered bases.

The *North Aisle* (13 ft. wide) has in the N. wall four windows, the three eastern are of *c.* 1510 and of three cinquefoiled lights, under a four-centred head with a moulded label ; the fourth window is of three ogee cinquefoiled lights, with vertical tracery in a segmental-pointed head ; between the two middle windows is the 14th-century N. doorway, reset ; it has hollow-chamfered jambs and two-centred arch. The parapet of the aisle has three carved gargoyles.

The *South Aisle* (9½ ft. wide) has in the S. wall four windows, the two eastern are uniform with that in the S. wall of the S. chapel ; the two western are uniform with the westernmost in the N. aisle ; between the second and third windows is the 13th-century S. doorway with jambs and two-centred arch of two chamfered orders and a moulded label with mask-stops. The parapet of the aisle has five carved gargoyles.

The *West Tower* (16¼ ft. by 14¼ ft.) is of *c.* 1500 and of four stages, faced with knapped flint and with a pierced and embattled parapet enriched with flint-inlay ; the moulded plinth has on the western face traceried panels with blank shields and the remainder ornamented with flint-inlay.

The buttresses have each a series of canopied niches, eight in the height, with moulded and foliated pedestals, and crocketed canopies, the lower six of which have ribbed vaults ; the buttresses are finished with restored pinnacles above the parapet. The stair-turret is lit by quatrefoiled openings and the parapet has two shields of St. George and a molet and rose. The two-centred tower-arch extends through two stages and is of three orders, the two outer continuous and the inner with attached shafts with moulded capitals and bases. The W. doorway has moulded and double-shafted jambs and a two-centred arch with a square head and a moulded and crocketed ogee label, carried through the square head and finished with a finial ; the spandrels are carved with oak foliage. The second stage is formed by an open gallery half the height of the tower-arch. In the W. wall is a window of four cinquefoiled lights with vertical tracery in a two-centred head with a moulded arch and crocketed ogee label with a traceried spandrel. The third stage has in the N., S. and W. walls a window of two ogee lights with plain vertical tracery in a four-centred head with a moulded label and a transom with four-centred heads beneath it. In the E. wall is a similar window without a transom ; below it is a blocked doorway with a four-centred head. The bell-chamber has in each wall a window of three cinquefoiled ogee lights with vertical tracery in a two-centred head with a moulded label ; the transom has four-centred heads beneath it.

The *South Porch* is of early 16th-century date and has a moulded plinth with flint-inlay orna-ment ; the carved and enriched parapet has two carved gargoyles, and is embattled at the sides and has a front gable with a series of blank shields divided by ' Tudor flowers.' The two-centred outer archway is of two moulded orders, the outer continuous and the inner resting on attached shafts with moulded capitals and bases ; the outer order of the arch has on the S. side carved square flowers alternating with diadems and two shields one with the arms of the Trinity and one defaced ; the outer order on the N. side has a series of blank shields, hanging from straps and some bearing scratches like masons' marks ; the archway has a double moulded label enclosing a square outer head and carved with square flowers ; the spandrels are foliated and have each a large shield, one with the crossed keys of St. Peter and one with the crossed swords of St. Paul and both with a small ship in base. Above the arch and in each side buttress is a niche with a moulded pedestal, trefoiled and sub-cusped head, with crockets, carved cresting and flanking buttresses. The side walls have each a window of three depressed trefoiled lights with embattled tracery in a segmental-pointed head with a moulded label ; they are mostly blocked.

The *Roofs* of the chancel and nave are modern but fixed to them are a number of square foliated bosses, which may be old; one has a molet and another a sheaf, both on shields. The S. vestry has plain 16th-century beams and joists. There is reused material in the roofs of both aisles. The floor of the third stage of the tower has moulded main beams and joists, with curved braces springing from moulded capitals. The early 16th-century roof of the porch is of two bays with moulded main timbers and curved braces to the principals. *Fittings—Bells:* one and sanctus; 1st by William Dawe, *c.* 1400 and inscribed " Dulcis Sisto Melis Vocor Campana Michaelis " ; sanctus uninscribed. *Brasses:* In N. chapel—(1) of William Beriffe of Jacobes, 1578, and John, his father, 1542, figure of civilian in gown and ruff and inscription-plate ; (2) of [John Beryf, 1496, and Margaret, Amy, and Margaret, his wives] figures of civilian in long gown with belt and pouch, woman in butterfly head-dress, five sons, four daughters, and merchant's mark, indents of figures of two wives, two groups of children and inscription-plate ; (3) of [Alice Beriffe, 1536, and her daughter Margaret] shaft and bracket of *c.* 1420 with indents of two figures on it, filled with figures of two women, one a widow and one with flowing hair, indents of shield and two inscription-plates ; (4) of [John Beriff, 1521, and Mary and Alice, his wives] figures of civilian in fur-lined gown and two women with pedimental head-dresses, four sons, one daughter and merchant's mark ; indents of group of children and inscription-plate. In nave—(5) of [William Beryff, 1525, and Joan, his wife] figures of civilian in fur-lined gown and woman in pedimental head-dress, two scrolls, indents of two groups of children, two scrolls and inscription-plate. In N. aisle—(6) of [Margaret Beriff, 1505] figure of woman in pedimental head-dress, indents of inscription-plates ; (7) to Mary Beryf, 1505, figure of woman in pedimental head-dress, four sons and one daughter, indent of inscription-plate. *Coffin-lid:* In N. chapel—with incised foliated cross, 13th-century ; four consecration crosses at angles, subsequently used as altar (?). *Doors:* In chancel—in doorway to vestry, of moulded battens with strap-hinges and stock-lock, early 16th-century. In tower—in W. doorway, with moulded fillets, planted on, and remains of former traceried heads, *c.* 1500 ; in doorway of staircase, of nail-studded battens, with strap-hinges, *c.* 1500. *Floor-slab:* In S. chapel—to Francis Wheeler, 1692, and Susan, his wife, 1679, and Francis, their son, 1694. *Font:* octagonal bowl, each face with a quatrefoil enclosing a rose, moulded underside with carved flowers, stem with sunk panels with cinquefoiled heads, traces of colour and gilding, late 15th-century. *Gallery:* Under tower—with moulded beams,

opening in middle with 18th-century balustrade, gallery front with moulded uprights and rail, *c.* 1500. *Glass:* In N. chapel—in N.W. window, two pieces of foliage and two small boar's heads in a border, early 16th-century. *Image:* In S. chapel—in niche in S. wall, of bishop blessing, in mass vestments, head gone, remains of colour and gilding, early 16th-century. *Lockers:* In tower, in third stage, four rebated for doors, two with inner recesses, *c.* 1500. *Niches:* In chancel —in S. wall, with double cinquefoiled canopy with crockets, finials, and cresting, remains of colour, 15th-century. In N. chapel, two flanking E. window, both cut back flush with wall and each with ribbed canopy remains of crocketed head and finial, remains of colour, early 16th-century, loose in N. niche, crested pedestal with remains of colour and powdered with I H C. In S. chapel—in E. wall, with cinquefoiled head and ribbed vault, carved crockets and cresting, small head at top of one jamb, moulded pedestal, remains of colour and below a black-letter inscription—" Ora Pro aibus Johīs Mors et Dionisii• ux ej(us) et p̄ aībus [oim] fideliū," in S. wall, in splay of S. window, with double cinquefoiled head and crocketed and crested canopy, remains of colour, early 16th-century. In nave—in second pier of N. arcade, with ogee head, 15th-century ; in second pier of S. arcade, two, one with ogee and one with trefoiled head, 15th-century. *Painting:* In tower—on W. wall, name Robert Cooe (?) in red colour, 16th-century ; *see also* niches, font, etc. *Piscinae:* In S. chapel—with hollow-chamfered jambs and cinquefoiled head, jambs with carved flowers, drain with carved boss, early 16th-century. In tower—in 1st stage, round drain, perhaps from chancel, date uncertain. *Plate:* includes two cups, large and small, both with band of incised ornament round bowl and both of 1620. *Recesses :* In vestry—in S. wall, square-headed recess with elbow-bend, possibly oven, early 16th-century. In S. aisle—W. of S. doorway, with plastered round head, jambs and sill, date and purpose uncertain. *Sedile:* In chancel—sill of S.E. window carried down to form seat, 13th-century. *Stoup:* In S. aisle—E. of S. doorway, with chamfered jambs and two-centred head and restored basin, 15th-century. *Table:* In tower—made up of early 17th-century material. Condition—Good.

Secular :—

(4). JACOBES HALL, house, two tenements and shop, on the S. side of High Street, 200 yards E.S.E. of the modern church, is of two storeys, timber-framed and plastered ; the roofs are tiled. It was built early in the 16th century, with a two-storeyed hall in the middle and cross-wings at the E. and W. ends. The W. cross-wing has been largely rebuilt and there is a modern shop between the wings.

The house has good carved detail of the period, and the brick stair-turret is noteworthy.

The upper storey projects at the S. end of the E. wing, but has been partly underbuilt. The brick stair-turret (Plate, p. 176) is semi-hexagonal and stands in the N. angle between the W. wing and the main block ; it has trefoiled corbelling between the stages, an embattled parapet, and a pyramidal capping with remains of crockets ; there is one blocked window of two pointed lights in a square head. Inside the building the ground floor of the main block has moulded main beams with twisted leaf ornament, foliated stops and moulded joists ; the wall-plates are moulded and embattled. In the W. wall are three doorways, two original and one of the 17th century ; the original doorways have four-centred heads and one has foliated spandrels and a door with pierced scutcheon-plate and strap-hinges. In the E. wall is a fireplace with an original moulded lintel with foliated spandrels and probably not *in situ*. In the passage at the E. end is an original doorway, with a four-centred head and another doorway now blocked. The beams and joists of the hall continue up to this partition. On the first floor of the main block is an original king-post with a moulded base ; the rest of the truss is concealed.

Condition—Good ; timbered ceilings recently uncovered.

MONUMENTS (5–13).

The following monuments, unless otherwise described, are of the 17th century and of two storeys, timber-framed and plastered ; the roofs are tiled. Some of the buildings have exposed ceiling-beams.

Condition—Good or fairly good, unless noted.

HIGH STREET, S. side :—

(5). *Inn*, opposite modern church and 200 yards W. of (4), was built probably early in the 18th century and has a modillioned eaves-cornice to the N. front.

(6). *House*, three tenements, 70 yards E. of (4), was built probably late in the 16th or early in the 17th century, with cross-wings at the E. and W. ends. The upper storey originally projected at the N. end of both wings, but has been underbuilt.

N. side :—

(7). *Swan Hotel*, 50 yards E. of the modern church, was built late in the 16th century, with cross-wings at the E. and W. ends. There is a 17th-century addition on the N. side and the house has been completely altered in recent years. Inside the building are some original moulded beams.

(8). *House*, three tenements, N.E. of (4), was built early in the 16th century, but was refronted in brick in the 18th century and the gables hipped back. Inside the building the middle block has original moulded joists.

HURST GREEN :—

(9). *House*, three tenements, on N.W. side and 50 yards from the junction with High Street, was refronted in brick early in the 18th century.

(10). *House*, range of three tenements, 50 yards N.E. of (9), has a cross-wing at the N.E. end.

(11). *Cottage*, on E. side of road, 100 yards N.E. of (10), was built in the 16th century with a cross-wing at the N. end. The upper storey projects at the W. end of the cross-wing on curved brackets.

Condition—Poor.

(12). *Malting Farm*, house, 1,200 yards S.E. of the old church, was built probably in the 16th century with cross-wings at the N.W. and S.E. ends. The house has been refronted and the roof raised.

(13). *Moverons*, house, 1,200 yards W. of the old church, has been rebuilt except for a wing on the W. side.

BROMLEY, see GREAT BROMLEY and
LITTLE BROMLEY.

12. BURES. (B.b.)

(O.S. 6 in. xvii. N.E.)

Bures is a parish on the Suffolk border and partly in that county, 8 m. N.W. of Colchester. The parish church is in the Suffolk portion of the parish.

Secular :—

MONUMENTS (1–11).

The following monuments, unless otherwise described, are of the 17th century and of two storeys, timber-framed and plastered or weather-boarded ; the roofs are tiled or thatched. Several of the buildings have original chimney-stacks and exposed ceiling-beams.

Condition—Good or fairly good, unless noted.

(1). *Old Toll House*, house and shop, 100 yards W. of Bures Bridge, was built early in the 16th century. The cross-wing at the W. end has an upper storey, projecting at the N. end. Inside the building is a considerable quantity of 17th-century panelling. The roof has remains of the original construction.

(2). *Eight Bells Inn*, 60 yards S.W. of (1), has extensive modern additions.

(3). *Cottage*, 180 yards S. of (2).
Condition—Poor.

(4). *Cottage*, W. of (3).

(5). *Cottage*, 300 yards W.N.W. of Bures Bridge.

(6). *Cottage*, W. of (5).
Condition—Poor.

(7). *Parsonage Farm*, house, 700 yards W.S.W. of Bures Bridge, was built probably in the 16th century and has a projecting upper storey on the E. side.

(8). *Cottage*, N. of Valley Green Farm and nearly 1¼ m. S.S.W. of Bures Bridge.

(9). *Upper Jennys*, house, nearly 1½ m. S.W. of Bures Bridge, was built in the 16th century. The plaster of the front is dated 1769.

(10). *Ravensfield Farm*, house, nearly 1¾ m. W.S.W. of Bures Bridge.

(11). *Hill Farm*, house 1,200 yards N.W. of Bures Bridge, has an original chimney-stack with two grouped hexagonal shafts.

---

13. CHAPEL. (B.c.)

(O.S. 6 in. (*d*)xvii. S.E. (*b*)xxvi. N.E.)

Chapel is a small parish and village on the River Colne, 5½ m. E.S.E. of Halstead.

Ecclesiastical :—

b(1). PARISH CHURCH (dedication unknown) stands at the N. end of the parish. The walls are of flint-rubble, covered with cement and the dressings are of clunch ; the roofs are tiled. The church was consecrated in 1352 as a chapel-of-ease to Great Tey and the *Chancel* and *Nave* are probably of this date. The *South Porch* was added probably in the 18th century. The building was restored in the 19th century when the *North Vestry* was added and the bell-turret added or rebuilt.

Architectural Description — The *Chancel* and *Nave* (53½ ft. by 18½ ft.) are structurally un-divided. The mid 14th-century E. window is of two pointed lights with a quatrefoil in a two-centred head ; on either side of it is a modern window. The N. wall has two modern windows and E. of them a modern doorway. In the S. wall are three windows, the easternmost is modern, the second is of the 15th century and of two cinque-foiled lights in a square head ; the westernmost window is of mid 14th-century date and of two-trefoiled lights with a quatrefoil in a two-centred

head ; the jambs and mullion are moulded ; further W. is the N. doorway with a wooden frame and square head, probably of the 17th century. In the W. wall is a late 15th-century window of three cinquefoiled lights in a three-centred head with a moulded label and three modern windows.

Fittings—*Door :* In S. doorway—of oak battens with strap-hinges, 17th-century. *Piscina :* In chancel—with two-centred head and octofoiled drain, 14th-century. *Plate :* includes pewter flagon and plate, early 18th-century. *Pulpit :* semi-octagonal with panelled sides, upper panels fluted, carved and shaped brackets to book-rest, mid 17th-century. *Reading-desk :* with two arcaded panels carved with foliage and carved and shaped brackets to book-rest, mid 17th-century. Condition—Good, but much ivy on S. wall.

Secular :—

MONUMENTS (2–6).

The following monuments, unless otherwise described, are of the 17th century and of two storeys, timber-framed and plastered ; the roofs are tiled. Some of the buildings have original chimney-stacks and exposed ceiling-beams. Condition—Good, or fairly good.

a(2). *Swan Inn*, 130 yards N.E. of the church, has later and modern extensions at the back.

b(3). *House*, 50 yards E. of the church.

b(4). *Hillhouse Farm*, house, ¼ m. S. of the church.

b(5). *Brook Hall*, 120 yards S. of (4), was built probably in the 16th century with cross-wings at the E. and W. ends. The front has been faced with modern brick.

b(6). *Pope's Farm*, house, ¼ m. S.E. of (5), was built probably in the 15th century with cross-wings at the N. and S. ends. There are two 17th-century additions on the W. side. Inside the building the main block and one cross-wing have original king-post trusses.

CLACTON, see GREAT CLACTON and LITTLE CLACTON.

COGGESHALL, see GREAT COGGESHALL and LITTLE COGGESHALL.

14. COLCHESTER (D.c.)

(O.S. 6 in. (a)xxvii. N E. (b)xxvii. S.E. (c)xxviii.
N.W. (d)xxviii. S.W. (e)xxxvi. N.E.)

Colchester is an ancient borough standing on the
crest of a high plateau above the right bank of the
Colne river.   The present civil parish, formed
in 1897, comprises the intra-mural parishes of
All Saints, Holy Trinity, St. James, St. Martin,
St. Mary at the Walls, St. Nicholas, St. Peter
and St. Runwald, the extra-mural parishes of
St. Botolph, St. Giles, St. Leonard at the Hythe
and St. Mary Magdalene, and the rural parishes
of Lexden, Berechurch, Greenstead, and Mile End,
In the following inventory the district is treated
as a single parish, and the monuments are grouped
under the usual sub-heads.

The parish contains important prehistoric earthworks including the various lines of intrenchments
covering the approaches from the west, Lexden
Mount, etc.   The Roman monuments include the
greater part of the town wall, the Balkerne Gate
and the substructure under the Castle.

Of mediaeval monuments the most important
are the ruins of St. Botolph's Priory Church,
St. John's Abbey Gate, the churches of Holy
Trinity, St. Martin, St. James and St. Leonard at
the Hythe, the Castle, the Red Lion Hotel (30),
and the Marquis of Granby Inn (69). Monuments
21, 39, 51, 60, 65, 86, 92, 105, 114, 128, 160, 189,
231, 262 and 263 also contain interesting features.
A remarkable survival is the number of 14th and
15th-century cellars remaining under many of the
houses in High Street and Head Street. Examples
of ornamental pargeting are to be found at Monuments 29, 31, 53, 192, 227 and 234.

There are certainly buildings, other than those
described, of a date anterior to 1714, but these
have been so much altered as to be practically
modern, and for this reason they have been
disregarded.

*LIST OF WORKS TO WHICH REFERENCE
IS MADE BY ABBREVIATIONS BELOW.*

A.J.—Journal of the Royal Archæological Institute.

Antiq.—The Antiquary.

*Arch.—Archæologia.   Published by the Society of
Antiquaries of London.*

*B.A.A.—The British Archæological Association
Journal.*

*Cutts, Colchester.—History of Colchester, by E. L.
Cutts (Historic Town Series, 1888).*

*E.A.S.T.—Essex Archæological Society Trans-
actions.*

Gent.'s Mag.—The Gentleman's Magazine.

*Gough's Camden—R. Gough's edition of Camden's
Britannia, 1789.*

*Morant—History of Essex, by P. Morant, 1768.
(Vol. i, Colchester section).*

(N.S.)—New Series.

(O.S.)—Old Series.

O.S.—Ordnance Survey.

*P. G. Laver—Information furnished by P. G. Laver,
Esq., F.S.A., of Colchester.*

P.S.A.—Proceedings of the Society of Antiquaries.

*Phil. Trans.—Philosophical Transactions (of the
Royal Society).*

*Vet. Mon.—Vetusta Monumenta, published by the
Society of Antiquaries.*

*Wire's MS.—The MS. Diary, plan, etc., of William
Wire. Mid 19th-century, now preserved in the
Colchester Museum.*

*Wright—History and Topography of Essex, by
T. Wright, 1836.*

(1) Roman Colchester :—

A.—WALLS AND GATES (*see* Map of Earthworks
and Plan of Roman Town, pp. 72 and 28).

On the N.E. side of the old British oppidum the
Romans enclosed an area of about 108 acres by a
wall 3,100 yards in length.   The Colne approaches
to within a few yards of the wall on the N. and the
lowest elevation recorded at that spot is 26 ft. The
ground rises steadily to a ridge half-way between
the N. and S. of the enclosure, and then falls away
again to a small depression outside the S. wall.
The ridge represents the axis of the Roman town,
and is closely followed by the High Street.   The
level falls from about 115 ft. above O.S. datum at
the W. end to about 65 ft. at the E. end of the
town.   The wall forms roughly a rectangle of
about 1,000 yards from E. to W. by 510 yards
from N. to S, with rounded angles (except perhaps
at the S.W. corner), and exhibits a long curving
sweep in the S.E. corner to suit the configuration
of the ground.   The course of the wall can be
traced throughout save for some distance in the
S.W. corner, which seems to have suffered special
damage in the siege of 1648.   Structurally, it
consists of layers of septaria, roughly faced, interlaced regularly with fourfold courses of brick, with
a core of rubble and cement, the lowest brick course
going right through the wall.   It has an average
thickness of about 8 ft.   Towards the E. end of
the N. wall and, less clearly, N. of the Balkerne Gate
are remains of an internal earthen rampart about
20 ft. in width.   At present the only indications
of a ditch outside the wall are at the N.E. and S.W.
angles.   At the N.E. angle the general appearance
of the broad, deep, V-shaped ditch suggests a
mediaeval origin.   At the S.W. angle in Crouch
Street the relationship of the ditch with the

foundations of Roman buildings, which either impinged upon it or were cut by it, is ambiguous. (*E.A.S.T.*, XII, 257; XIII, 107. *B.A.A.* (O.S.), IV, 83.)

The wall is strengthened by rectangular and semi-circular bastions; one of rectangular plan, the older form, 19½ ft. wide and 12 ft. high, projecting 13 ft. inwards, and bonded into the wall, stood at the foot of the Castle Park, in the N. wall. Another of similar plan was in the E. wall, N. of the E. gate. No others of this type are known. Of the semi-circular external bastions Morant shows six in the S.E. section of the wall. There are now but four (Plate, p. 23). They are apparently solid and are not bonded into the wall. The wall has been patched at various times, and much of the N. side is in ruinous condition and largely encumbered by buildings.

It may be presumed that the town had six gates, two each on the N. and S., one each on the E. and W., though the evidence is not in every case conclusive.

(1). The Head Gate, in the S. wall, near its western end, was the chief gate of mediaeval Colchester. It was taken down in Morant's day (Morant, I, 7). Traces of a Roman gate are said to have been found in draining operations here in 1913 (*E.A.S.T.*, XIII, 107), and both the fact that the survey of Domesday is based on the London road which issues from this gate and the numerous burials found close by, make out a fair case for the Roman origin of this gate (see *Sectional Preface*, p. xxvi).

(2). The Roman road from Mersea Island seems to have come up to a South Gate, which must have stood rather to the west of the mediaeval St. Botolph's Gate. This gate would have corresponded with the Roman Rye Gate in the N. wall, but no record of it is known.

(3). The East Gate, which fell in 1651, was apparently the original Roman building, and occupied the northern half of the present highway. It consisted, like Newport Gate at Lincoln, of a central and two small side arches. (Morant, I, 7. *E.A.S.T.* (O.S.), I, 33, *n.*)

(4). The Roman Rye Gate was still standing in the middle of last century. It was a few feet E. of the mediaeval Rye Gate and possibly gave access to the road from Stratford. (*E.A.S.T.* (O.S.), I, 53.)

(5). The North Gate has left no trace of itself, but North Hill seems to follow the line of a Roman street, though the frontage of Roman houses underlies the eastern margin of the present street and outside the walls Roman buildings are met with in the existing highway. Cremation burials were found during the building of the North Bridge. (Wire's MS. *Gent.'s Mag.*, 1843, II, 189, and c.f. Nos. (1) and (2), p. 29.)

(6). The Balkerne Gate (Plate, p. 22), on the W., is the most remarkable monument of its kind in Britain. It is now encumbered by the superimposed structure of a public house—the King's Head—which entirely masks the effect of the great works. These extend for 107 ft. and project outwards from the wall of the town a distance of 30 ft. Provision is made for four passageways, two of 17 ft. in width for vehicular traffic in the centre, and a 6-ft. side-walk for foot passengers at either end, flanked in its turn by a roughly quadrant-shaped bastion, which acted as a guard chamber, entered from the town by means of a passage 12 ft. in length and 6 ft. wide, partly vaulted. The sideways were vaulted in brick. The southern sideway, which is 32 ft. long, and the bastions are still standing, to a height of 15 ft., the southern 12 ft.

It would seem to be a specimen not so much of the fortified gateway as of the 'porte monumentale.' Such were often constructed to mark the completion of a road undertaking, and the gate of Augustus at Rimini and Trajan's gate at Benevento record their origin to have been of this kind. The triangle of roads between Colchester—London—Verulam was no doubt one of the earliest of Roman works of the kind in the province, and it is possible the Balkerne Gate put the seal on the achievement. This would suggest about A.D. 80 as the date of the gate, and the pottery associated with its first foundation, as discovered in the excavation of the site in 1917 (*E.A.S.T.*, XV, 182), points to the same conclusion. Moreover, though there is no exact parallel known among the gates of Gaul, the protuberant Balkerne Gate, with its four openings for traffic, seems to have the closest affinity with certain gates—among others, the Porte d'Auguste at Nîmes, and the two gates at Autun—which belong to the first century B.C. or A.D. Inasmuch as the city walls and the Balkerne Gate are homogeneous in structure, they are no doubt of one period, and the whole *enceinte* may fairly be set down as the work of the middle of the latter half of the first century. At a subsequent period the gate with its manifold openings and projecting defences seems to have proved a source of weakness to the town rather than of strength, and on two separate occasions blocking took place. While the Roman was still in the land the N. half of the gateway was destroyed, apparently by fire. On rebuilding, the foot-walk on this side disappeared, and the carriage-way was reduced. Yellow mortar, in place of red, proclaims the change of workmanship. In the post-Roman period a rough wall, without foundations, 8 ft. in breadth, was built across the whole of the northern half, foot and carriage-way as well. (*E.A.S.T.*, XV, 183.)

In addition to the main gateways two minor gateways or posterns are known. One in the

COLCHESTER   THE BALKERNE GATE

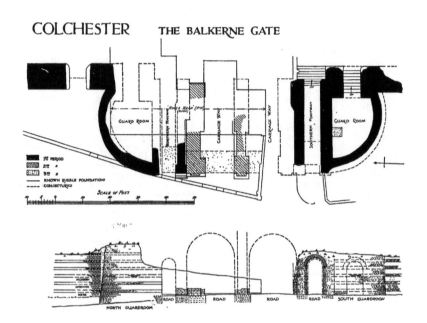

N. wall, to the E. of Rye Gate, was explored in 1849–1856 (*E.A.S.T.* (O.S.), I, 56, 217). The jambs stood 11 ft. apart and provided for a single passage-way. The other postern, in the W. wall near the S.W. corner of the town in St. Mary's churchyard, is in a fragmentary condition but retains on the N. side the springing of a brick arch.

At both these posterns, drains pass under the wall. In a building to the N.E. of the Castle area (see B (39), below) a spring or well has been found, and the surplus water from here flowed away in a culvert under the northern postern. The probable remains of a drain under the western postern were temporarily uncovered in 1920. Besides these, three other drains are known to have pierced the enclosing wall: one, between the Roman and the mediaeval Rye Gate (*E.A.S.T.* (O.S.), I, 53); another, in St. James's churchyard (*E.A.S.T.* (O.S.), I, 56), and, lastly, a curious tile-arched drain which went under the S. wall between the supposed Roman South Gate and the mediaeval Schere Gate (*E.A.S.T.* (O.S.), I, 57; XII, 257; Wire's MS., 31st March, 1846).

B.—Buildings within the Walls.

(See Plan, p. 28.)

The following is a list of the recorded finds of Roman structural remains within the walls. The numbers refer to the accompanying plan.

(1). Tessellated pavement, at S.W. end of North Hill, under 65 North Hill. (Wire.)

(2). Tessellated pavement and flues, behind 65 North Hill, doubtless part of the same house as (1). (P. G. Laver.)

(3). Foundations, floors, painted plaster, etc., have been found W. of North Hill in the garden of St. Peter's Vicarage at various times since 1844, at a depth of 3 to 4 ft. (Wire's MS. *E.A.S.T.* (O.S.), V, 155–6.)

(4). Tessellated pavement, W. of North Hill, under summer-house in garden formerly belonging to Mr. Halls. (P. G. Laver.)

(5). Part of house of at least six rooms, with mosaics, flues, etc., found in 1865 in a garden formerly belonging to Mr. Halls, 132 yards N. of Balkerne Gate and 32 ft. E. of W. wall of town.

Balkerne Gate and Town Wall.

Vault under the Castle.

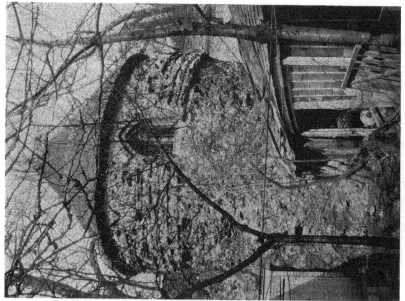

South Bastion.

South-East Bastion.

(*E.A.S.T.* (O.S.), IV, 53 (plan); V, 161. *B.A.A.* (O.S.), XXI, 169, note. O.S. 10 ft. and 25 in. xxvii. 12.)

(6). Single tesserae indicating a pavement were observed in 1843 N. or N.E. of (5), behind No. 47, North Hill (old number). (*E.A.S.T.* (O.S.), V, 155.)

(7.) Tessellated pavement, found in March, 1849, at back of " Mr. Stirling McLean's house " (now No. 45, North Hill). (*E.A.S.T.* (O.S.), V, 158.)

(8). Tessellated pavement W.S.W. of the former Bowler's Brewery Stores, W. of N. end of North Hill, perhaps the same as (10). (O.S. 10 ft. xxvii.)

(9). Tessellated pavement, found on 22nd May, 1845, in the field behind Bowler's Brewery Stores. (Wire's MS. *E.A.S.T.* (O.S.), V, 155.)

(10). Mosaic, recorded 27th September, 1844, found in making a saw-pit behind Bowler's Brewery Stores. (Wire's MS. *E.A.S.T.* (O.S.), V, 155. *B.A.A.* (O.S.), I, 54.)

(11). Tessellated pavement, perhaps the same as (8) and (10) was found on the 27th December, 1844, at Bowler's Brewery Stores. (Wire's MS.)

(12). Mosaics and tessellated pavements have been found at various dates E. of North Hill, in garden of No. 18 (formerly No. 16), Mr. Bryant's, S. of Nunn's Cut; also adjoining this on the S.W. under passageway between Nos. 17 and 18. (Wire's MS. and plan. *E.A.S.T.* (O.S.), V, 156. *E.A.S.T.*, X, 84 (fig.). *B.A.A.* (N.S.), XII, 289. *Antiquary*, II (N.S.), 447. *Essex County Standard*, 24th November, 1906 (photo). O.S. 10 ft. xxvii. P. G. Laver.)

(13). A trench cut in 1920, 100 yards S.E. of (12), in Mr. Frost's garden 100 yards E. of North Hill, revealed a hard gravelled surface (probably road or passage), and at a distance of 22 ft. further E. a tessellated pavement and foundations running N. and S. (P. G. Laver.)

(14). Tessellated pavement, found in 1855 in garden behind Chaise and Pair Inn. (*E.A.S.T.* (O.S.), V, 159.)

(15). Foundations, found on the 25th April, 1842, in North Hill, near E. side, opposite St. Peter's Church, running N. and S. in alignment with each other for a distance of 150 ft. or more. (Wire's MS. and sketch-plan.)

(16). Concrete floor, found December, 1842, in St. Peter's churchyard, a few feet S. of the S.W. angle of the S. aisle "in digging the grave adjoining Mr. J. Green's, senior, for his grand-daughter." (*E.A.S.T.* (O.S.), V, 155.)

(17). Tessellated pavement, found in December, 1849, N.E. of St. Peter's churchyard during the rebuilding of the People's or Public Hall adjoining the former Corn Exchange. The pavement lay "on the E. side of the building where the foundation is at the S.E. curve." (Wire's M.S. *E.A.S.T.* (O.S.), V, 158. O.S. 10 ft. xxvii.)

(18). Elaborate mosaic pavement, found in 1762-3, and near it, part of another pavement found during the demolition of a stable which was itself supposed to incorporate a Roman building, N. of High Street in rebuilding the Queen's Head or Falcon Inn, and in what was then "the garden of Bernard the Apothecary." Part of it was still *in situ* in 1836. (Gibson's *Camden*, 1772, I, 356. Gough's *Camden*, 1789, II, 58. Stukeley's *Letters and Diaries* (Surtees Soc.), II, 162-3. Morant, I, 184 (plate). Wright, I, 309, etc. *Phil. Trans.*, No. 255, August, 1699, p. 287.)

(19). Mosaic pavement and foundations, found about 1840 and 13th May, 1856, close to (18), on site of and near the Vegetable Market. (*E.A.S.T.* (O.S.), V, 155 and 160. *B.A.A.* (O.S.), II, 366. Wright, I, 295. Cutts, *Colchester*, plan, p. 34, I, 7. O.S. 10 ft. xxvii.)

(20). One or possibly two pavements, found before 1771, W. of West Stockwell Street (formerly Angel Lane), under the house (Dr. Richard Daniel's) next S. of (21). (*Arch.*, II, 290. Morant, I, 183.)

(21) and (22). Tessellated pavements and flue (?), found W. of West Stockwell Street, in kitchen garden of house opposite St. Martin's Church, 1768. In 1771 more was opened up at the S. end and under it was a stratum of burnt wheat. At the " further end" of same garden, another pavement "with something of an arch under it" was found in 1769. (*Arch.*, II, 287, 290.)

(23). Pavement, found before 1771, under or near house (then Mr. Wall's) next N. of (21). (*Arch.*, II, 290.)

(24). Tessellated pavement, partly destroyed and partly reburied, in yard of Inn (formerly the Bishop Blaise) at the N.E. corner of West Stockwell Street. (*E.A.S.T.*, X, 89.)

(25). Mosaic pavement with leaf border, about 22 ft. by 17 ft., found in 1793, W. of East Stockwell Street (formerly Bear Lane) "in the yard of one Bragg a baker" about 200 yards N.E. by N. of (23). It extended beneath a stone wall into the adjoining garden where it could not be excavated. In September, 1794, it was rapidly being destroyed. (*Vet. Mon.*, III, Plate xxxix. *Gent.'s Mag.*, 1794, II, 801. *Soc. Ant. MS. Minutes*, XII, 204, etc.)

(26). Mosaic pavement laid on a foundation of bricks set edgeways with a foot layer of broken granite chips on it (? an earlier road or passage). Found in November, 1855, N. of St. Helen's Lane and probably under it, in burial ground of the Independent Chapel (Herrick's), not far from (25) "but sadly mutilated." (*E.A.S.T.* (O.S.), V, 159, 160.)

(27). Tessellated pavement, found before 1846, in garden of house three doors N. of the Independent Chapel, St. Helen's Lane. (*E.A.S.T.* (O.S.), V, 156.)

COLCHESTER CASTLE.

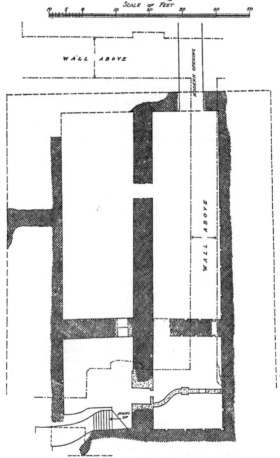

PLAN OF SUBSTRUCTURES

(28). Tessellated pavement and foundations found in 1920 in Truslove's Yard, in North Gate Street. (P. G. Laver.)

(29). The S. wall of the cellar of the house at N.E. corner of Maidenburgh Street, adjoining the site of N. wall of the town, incorporates a piece of Roman brick walling containing an arch, probably a drain, and now blocked. The wall and arch are now buried below the springing of the latter, but the wall is still visible to a height of 6 ft. and a similar breadth from E. to W. The work is good and probably not later than the second century A.D. (Wire's MS. *E.A.S.T.* (O.S.), I, 53.)

(30). Short length of walling of septaria surmounted by triple course of Roman brick, still visible and underlying N. wall of St. Helen's Chapel. Presumably Roman, but see monument (17), p. 50.

(31). Tessellated pavement, nearly 3 ft. by 6 ft., found in 1842 and 1845, 6 ft. deep and destroyed; at the S.E. corner of High Street and East Stockwell Street under the former Bear Inn. Near by were remains of a "circular building between 20 and 30 ft. in diameter." (Wire's MS., 13th December, 1845. *E.A.S.T.* (O.S.), V, 154–5.)

(32). Tessellated pavement on the N. side of High Street, found before 1907, in enlarging Mr. Wicks's wine cellar, next W. of the George Hotel; now destroyed. (*E.A.S.T.*, X, 89.)

(33). Fragment of wall, possibly Roman, running E. and W. found in 1917 under Museum Street. (P. G. Laver.)

(34). Vaulted structure under the Castle— Beneath the Castle is a vaulted building, 92¾ ft. long and 45½ ft. wide internally. It is divided longitudinally by a wall 5¾ ft. thick down the middle which is crossed by a wall of 5 ft. at about 30 ft. from the southern end.

The walls are of ragstone rubble and the vaults (Plate, p. 22) appear to have been built in layers about a foot deep, against boards; the marks of these boards are clearly visible on the E. wall at the S. end; the layers are divided by a joint of yellow sand or very sandy mortar. The walls below the springing of the vault have, where shown on the plan, rough chases, being the 'matrices' of former upright posts; these posts were in position when the vault was built and their heads were enveloped in the masonry, leaving a socket sometimes as much as 9 in. deep. These posts were probably constructional and a similar method of construction (at Rome) is illustrated in J. H. Middleton's *Remains of Ancient Rome* (1892), Vol. I, p. 48. The form of the vaults is a very irregular ellipse with flattened sides; the main W. vault has been cracked longitudinally, probably by the weight of the former Norman wall above. The foundations of the E. wall of the E. vault have been traced to a depth of 9½ ft. below the existing floor. There are no original openings in any of the walls.

In the N. wall is a cutting made at the end of the 17th century by Mr. John Wheely (Morant, I, 7, 10), who in 1693 bought the Castle for the sake of the building material it afforded, to facilitate the removal of the sand filling from the vaults. This cutting extends vertically to the underside of a course of Roman bricks and if this level is pursued a little to the W. of the cutting the Roman work can be traced some distance higher giving a section of the back wall with a facing of five courses of

septaria, six courses of brick, five of septaria and the two lowest of the next courses of brick; above this point the Roman face is not equally well defined, but it can nevertheless be traced about 4 ft. higher, the face of the uppermost foot being set back about 1 ft. from the main wall-face.

The thickness of the side walls has only been tested by excavation on the W. side, where a trench was cut in 1922. It proved that the walls extended as far as and were conterminous with the Norman foundations, there being remains of a cement-rendered face on the older work. Portions of four courses of bricks were found as facing to the Roman work and the brickwork extended into the foundations considerably further at one point than another.

An excavation made at the N. end of the W. vault proved that the Roman work there had been partially destroyed, probably at an early period, as the Norman foundation exhibited a further offset which could not have been built if the Roman wall had then been in existence.

The modern staircase which gives access to the vaults at the S. end cuts through the Roman vault and also the Roman S. wall. Above the core of the crown of the vault at this point can be seen a horizontal course of tiles of the same period. The tiles are irregularly jointed and seem to represent the levelling up for a pavement rather than the pavement itself. A small portion of the outer face of the S. wall has been recently uncovered immediately S. of this staircase; so far as it remained it was entirely of brick.

On the supposition that the foundations were of the same thickness on both long sides of the building, the total dimensions of the resulting platform (above the vaults) would be 105 ft. from N. to S. and 80 ft. from E. to W. See accompanying Plan, also Section on p. 53.

There is now no doubt that this building is Roman. Its structural independence of, and obvious priority to, the 11th-century castle above it are alone sufficient to suggest a Roman origin, and the evidence set forth in the *Journal of Roman Studies*, IX, 146; X, 87, has been confirmed and amplified by the results of the recent excavations recorded above. It has been noted that during the partial demolition of the Castle at the end of the 17th century a tunnel was cut through the northern Norman and Roman walls, and it may be of significance that "in breaking up the Foundation of one Part, an [ingenious gentleman] saw a Coin of Galba uncovered, which lay between the Bricks in that manner those pieces are found which have been industriously placed to discover the Age of a Building" (N. Salmon, *New Survey of England*, 1728, I, 137). This statement cannot rank as evidence, but Dr. T. Ashby states that vaulting of the present type was not uncommonly used at Rome in the 1st and 2nd centuries A.D.,

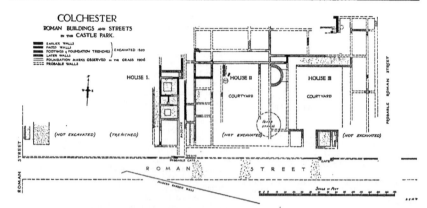

COLCHESTER
ROMAN BUILDINGS AND STREETS
IN THE CASTLE PARK.

and the complete absence of reused material in the structure may be regarded as strong evidence for an early date in a district such as Colchester, where good building material is far from abundant.

It is less certain whether, as has been tentatively suggested, this vaulted structure formed the podium of a temple (? the temple to Claudius). The transverse partition wall may have carried the front wall of the cella of a temple, and the excessive thickness of the W. wall and the relative thinness of the N. wall would seem to imply a range of columns on each flank, continued only as pilasters, at the back.

The measurements suggest an octostyle arrangement on the S. front and the resultant plan would thus bear a general resemblance to that of the temple of Mars Ultor at Rome.

(35). Walls and pavements under the ramparts of Castle Bailey found in 1842, 1892, etc. Under the earthwork round the northern end of the Castle area run two parallel walls about 2 ft. in thickness on a rectangular plan. The width of the enclosure thus formed is about 390 ft. Between the two walls is a distance of 25 ft., but on the N. side the outer wall at a distance of 45 ft. from the angle is set back 15 ft., and the space between the walls is there increased to that extent. This space was partially paved with blue lias slabs, and south of the main north-west corner were cement floors on which were found burials almost certainly of pagan Saxon date. These walls have been identified with much probability with the northern part of the forum of the Roman town. The excessive width of the excavated insula (36) to the N. of this site indicates that the forum lay in this longitudinal division of the town plan and the remains discovered are entirely consistent with this attribution. Definite proof, however, awaits a further excavation

of the site. (Journal of Roman Studies, IX, 145, plan.) There is a number of drains round about the Castle but their age is doubtful. (Jenkins' Colchester Castle (1853), 10, 18–20, 37, n.; App., pp. 21–2. E.A.S.T. (O.S.), I, 226–7; IX, 123–5. B.A.A. (O.S.), I, 53; (O.S.) II, 36–8.)

(36). Buildings and streets in Castle Park, found S. of town wall in 1906 and 1920. The remains represented the greater part of an insula measuring approximately 420 ft. from E. to W. and 300 ft. from N. to S. They indicate the general ground plan of three houses of fair size, the abodes apparently of good, easy citizens. The first belongs to the corridor type, the other two, which ultimately seem to have been united, are courtyard houses. They are dated with some precision by 'foundation offerings' as appertaining to the Flavian period. These offerings consisting of clay urns carefully buried close to the footing of a wall, and in one case still containing "some minute pieces of the unburnt bones of a small animal," constitute the chief interest of the site, but the buildings attest clearly the regular plotting ordained by the Roman surveyor at the re-edification of the colony after its destruction by Boudicca in A.D. 61 (E.A.S.T., X, 323; XVI, 7, and Sectional Preface, p. xxvi.)

(37). Burnt debris resting on "a long row of tesserae" so continuous that it was thought to be a path inside the wall, at N. end of Sheep's Head Field (now Castle Park) immediately S. of the town wall. (E.A.S.T. (O.S.), I, 54.)

(38). Tessellated pavement, found about 1848, N.E. of the N.E. angle of the Castle ramparts and immediately E. of the refreshment room in the Park. (Jenkins' Colchester Castle (1853), p. 37; note plan and App., p. 22. E.A.S.T. (O.S.), I, 226; V, 157. O.S. 10 ft. xxvii.)

(39). A building 30 ft. square with double walls, clay being rammed between them, and a concrete floor, furrowed by wide gutters and a spring still filling it, was partly excavated in 1853 by Duncan, N.E. of the Castle in the " Holly Trees " grounds. Three feet above the floor was an arched opening 2 ft. square, forming the mouth of a culvert which was traced for a distance of 200 ft. N. to a gateway in the town wall. The culvert after passing through the gateway branched into two and was traced for a distance of 56 ft. outside the walls. It was 1 ft. 9 in. wide and 4 ft. 4 in. high, built with tiles, and arched where it passed under the gateway. In the building from which it led was a large spiral spring for a trap which would close the culvert when the water in the well rose only 5 ft. high. (*E.A.S.T.* (O.S.), I, 210 (plan).)

(40). Tessellated pavement, 18 in. below the surface, found about 1852 under Castle Road, opposite Radnor Terrace, towards the W. end of former Botanical Gardens. A well-worn 'second brass' coin of Faustina the Elder was found underneath the concrete bed of the pavement which is probably the same as that described by another writer as black with a red border, 10 ft. by 30 ft. found 23 in. below the surface. (*E.A.S.T.* (O.S.), I, 215 ; V, 158–9.)

(41). Layers of wood ashes found 2½ ft. below surface, and a little further E. a flagstone floor 6 ft. square bearing traces of fire found about 1852 a little N. of (40). Still further E. a fragmentary floor of Roman tiles 3 ft. below surface, continued by a path of septaria and pebbles 3 ft. wide and of unknown length. (*E.A.S.T.* (O.S.), V, 159 ; cf. also (O.S.), I, 215.)

(42). Pavement, S. of High Street, 80 yards S. of East Hill House. (O.S. 10 ft. xxvii. 12, 4.)

(43). Mosaic pavement, red and white with 'star-like' pattern found, before 1768, in "Berry Field," now the grounds of East Hill House, probably within the N.E. corner of the meadow, 130 ft. W. of the E. wall as marked on the O.S. 10 ft. xxvii. 12, 9. (Morant, I, 183. *Arch.*, XVI, 147.)

(44). Large piece of tessellated pavement and 10 ft. from it a smaller piece in a geometrical pattern found February, 1907, S. of East Hill House, in levelling the bowling green. (*Daily Telegraph*, 4th February, 1907. *Essex Weekly News*, 1st February, 1907.)

(45). Pavements and foundations under S. wall of town. (*E.A.S.T.* (O.S.); I, 37, 57. *A.J.*, LXIV, 216.)

(46). Pavement found in 1920, E. of the former Theatre (now garage), near the S.E. corner of Queen Street, and about 20 ft. N. from the town wall. (P. G. Laver.)

(47). Pavement or paved way found in 1848 W. of Queen Street, opposite house No. 27. (*E.A.S.T.* (O.S.), V, 157. O.S. 10 ft. xxvii.)

(48). Roman brick floor found September, 1848, a little N. of (47), about half-way up Queen Street ; now destroyed. (*E.A.S.T.* (O.S.), V. 157.)

(49). Very hard foundation-wall crossing the street at right angles, in Culver Street, opposite garage on site of old Grammar School. (Wire's MS. (sketch-plan). *E.A.S.T.* (O.S.), V, 158. *B.A.A.* (O.S.), V, 86.)

(50). Very hard foundations of septaria and a floor of Roman tiles found October, 1848, under Culver Street, E. of Long Wyre Street, opposite the backway to the Cross Keys Inn. (*B.A.A.*, (O.S.), V, 86. *E.A.S.T.* (O.S.), V, 158. O.S. 10 ft. xxvii.)

(51). Two hypocaust flues, and near them three arched hypocaust fire-places or flues covered internally with soot, were found in August, 1848, at a depth of 6 ft. from the surface, under Long Wyre Street, about 150 ft. S. of Culver Street, opposite the entrance to Smith's Yard. More remains under the footpath were not opened. The remains were reburied except for one fire-place, which was damaged. (Wire's MS. (sketch-plan). *E.A.S.T.* (O.S.), V, 157. *B. A. A.* (O.S.), V, 87.)

(52). Mosaic pavement found before 1850, approximately E. of (51) under the soil-pit and garden of a house overlooking Long Wyre Street. (Wire's MS. (sketch-plan). *B.A.A.* (O.S.), V, 86.)

(53). Pavement under Long Wyre Street, at the entrance to Albion Court. (O.S. 10 ft. xxvii. 12, 9, perhaps a mistake for (54) below.)

(54). Pavement found September, 1848, opposite the third and fourth doors on the N. side of Albion Court, east of Long Wyre Street. (Wire's MS. (sketch-plan). *E.A.S.T.* (O.S.), V, 157. *B.A.A.* (O.S.), V, 87.)

(55). Foundation-wall, S. of (53), crossing Long Wyre Street "at an angle," found in 1848. (Wire's MS. (sketch-plan). *B.A.A.* (O.S.), V, 86.)

(56). At intervals, successively a tessellated pavement and a floor of Roman tiles, the latter close to the S. end of the street, found in 1848, S. of (55) under the same street. (Wire's MS. (sketch-plan).

(57). Mosaic with spiral border, found in 1892, E. of (55), in alterations at Mr. Lock's furniture shop, under an old chimney and extending under part of the house. (*Antiq.*, XXVII, 24. *E.A.S.T.* X, 89.)

(58) and (59). Two mosaic pavements in Victoria Place, at S.W. end of Long Wyre Street, each

130 ft. N. of Eld Lane and 140 ft. and 70 ft. W. of Long Wyre Street respectively. (*B. A. A.* (O.S.), V, 86. *E.A.S.T.* (O.S.), V, 157. O.S. 10 ft. xxvii.)

(60). Foundations found in 1848 under Culver Street, S. of St. Nicholas graveyard and immediately W. of Long Wyre Street. (Wire's MS. (sketch-plan). *B.A.A.* (O.S.), V, 86.)

(61). Foundations, etc., found 23rd December, 1842, in St. Nicholas churchyard. (Wire's MS.)

(62), (63) and (64). Foundations and tessellated pavement found in Culver Street, between Long Wyre Street and Trinity Street, and S. of Culver Street. (O.S. 10 ft. xxvii. Apparently no other authority.)

(65). Tessellated pavement found before 30th April, 1842, "on the premises of Mr. Salmon, linen-draper, No. 50 High Street," now No. 48. (Wire's MS. *E.A.S.T.* (O.S.), V, 154.)

(66). Fragments of Roman wall extending E. and W. and consisting of ten courses of brick on rubble footing, S. of High Street, 50 yards W. of Red Lion Inn, in E. wall of cellar of Messrs. Brand Bros., 34 High Street, 9½ ft. S. of the street wall. Still visible.

(67) and (68). Two, possibly three, pavements; one of black and white tesserae and another an elaborate mosaic, found before 1762, in June, 1849, and in 1857, under the yard of the Red Lion Inn. (Morant, I, 183. *B. A. A.* (O.S.), V, 87. *E.A.S.T.* (O.S.), V, 158 ; X, 87.)

(69). Pavement, found before 1849, in Lion Walk, at the N. end ; now destroyed. (Wire (sketch-plan). *B. A. A.* (O.S.), V, 86.)

(70). Mosaic pavement, found 1848 and 1849, in Lion Walk, near the S. end, about 20 ft. from Eld Lane, opposite a spirit warehouse. (Wire's MS. (sketch-plan). *E.A.S.T.* (O.S.), V, 157–8. *B.A.A.* (O.S.), V, 86.)

(71). Tessellated pavement, found 1843, in graveyard of Lion Walk Chapel, about 30 ft. E. of Lion Walk, where grave was being dug for T. B. Harvey. (Wire's MS. *E.A.S.T.* (O.S.), V, 155. *B.A.A.* (O.S.), V, 86.)

(72). Tessellated pavement, E. of (71), adjoining the wall dividing this graveyard from the next property on the E. (O.S. 10 ft. xxvii.)

(73). Tessellated pavement, nearly 3 ft. below the surface, found in 1748, etc., W. of Trinity Street, in garden of Trinity House (now Messrs. Cooper and Garrod's, formerly Sir Ralph Crefield's). (Morant, I, 183, hence Brayley and Britton, V, 293. Cutts, *Colchester* (plan I, 12). O.S. 10 ft. xxvii.)

(74). "Very hard foundations," at depth of 5 ft., found E. of Trinity Street, opposite the "house of Worts, Surgeon," Nos. 5 and 6 Trinity Street. (*E.A.S.T.* (O.S.), V, 158. O.S. 10 ft. xxvii.)

(75). Tessellated pavement, at a depth of 6 ft., found N. of (77), at the Culver Street back entrance of No. 1 Trinity Street. (*E.A.S.T.*, X, 88.)

(76). Foundations, found 1880, S.W. of (75), in garden of No. 1 Trinity Street. (P. G. Laver.)

(77). Tessellated pavement found W. of Trinity Street, in garden of " Mr. Francis, Solicitor" (*i.e.*, Tymperleys.) (Cutts, *Colchester* (plan I, 13). O.S. 10 ft. xxvii.)

(78). Pavement, in Sir Isaac's Walk under the Friends' Meeting House. (O.S. 10 ft. xxvii.)

(79). Tessellated pavement, under the house at the N. corner of Head Street and Sir Isaac's Walk. (Cutts, *Colchester* (plan I, 3). O.S. 10 ft. xxvii.)

(80). Mosaic pavement, with central vase, guilloche, ivy leaves, etc., and fragments of walls and coloured plaster, found May, 1881, at a depth of 5 ft., E. of Head Street, under part of Messrs. Mumford's Iron Foundry, formerly Mrs. Prosser's garden; reburied. (*E.A.S.T.* (N.S.), III, 140 (plate) ; X, 88. *P.S.A.* (2nd series), VIII, 543.)

(81). Mosaic and foundations, found 1886, partly under Culver Street and partly under adjacent buildings, at the gateway to Mumford's Iron Foundry, 60 yards E. of Head Street. Close by, down the former "Hitchcock's Backway," opposite Bank Passage, a tessellated pavement and roof tiles were found in 1856. (*Builder*, 5th November, 1886, 682. *Antiq.*, XV, 29. *E.A.S.T.* (N.S.) III, 207, and X, 88. *E.A.S.T.* (O.S.), V, 160.)

(82). Two walls of brick and septaria running E. and W., found January, 1920, in High Street, S. of tram-lines, about 300 ft. from W. end of Street. (P. G. Laver.)

(83). Foundations, etc., are known to exist beneath several of the buildings on S. side of High Street, at the W. end. (O.S. 10 ft. xxvii.)

(84). "A concrete road apparently Roman " seen W. of Head Street, at N. angle of Church Street and Head Street, and vaguely described. It can hardly be accepted as evidence, although a Roman street probably ran near this site. (Wire's MS.)

(85). Foundations and tessellated pavement found in 1893 W. of Head Street, at back of King's Head Inn, in making a strong-room for Mr. Howard's office. (P. G. Laver.)

(86). Tessellated pavement found N. of (85), in the garden of the house now known as St. Mary's, E. of St. Mary's Church. (P. G. Laver.)

(87). Foundations, etc., found 1892 in garden S. of (85). (P. G. Laver.)

(88). Tessellated pavement, found about 1871 a little S. of St. Mary's Church and Church Street South, in the garden of St. Mary's Cottage, formerly Mr. Unwin's ; taken up and relaid in the veranda of the house. (*E.A.S.T.* (O.S.), V, 160. Cutts, *Colchester* (plan I, 1). O.S. 10 ft. xxvii.)

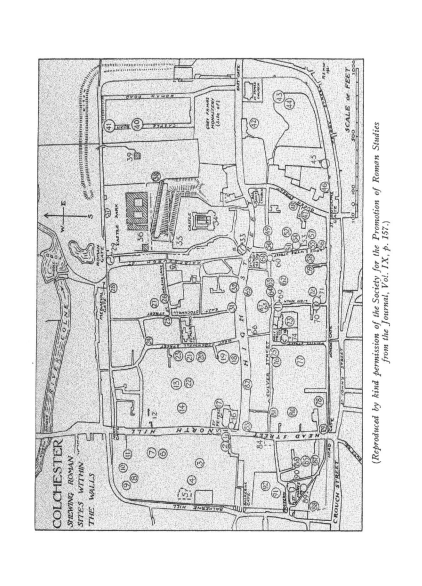

(Reproduced by kind permission of the Society for the Promotion of Roman Studies from the Journal, Vol. IX, p. 157.)

(89). Pieces of tessellated pavement found at considerable distances apart during the digging of graves in graveyard S. of St. Mary's Church. (Morant, I, 183.)

(90). Foundations and tessellated pavement found under E. end of St. Mary's Church, in 1871. (O.S. 10 ft. xxvii.)

(91). Tessellated pavement found in cherry garden, N. of the old Rectory which was immediately N. of St. Mary's Church tower. (Morant, I, 183.)

(92). Foundations and tessellated pavement found 1871 under E. wall of S.E. bay-window of the modern St. Mary's Rectory. (Cutts, *Colchester* (plans).)

C.—BUILDINGS OUTSIDE THE WALLS.

There was a number of buildings on the N.W., W. and S.W. of the town. Outside the Balkerne Gate there were houses on both sides of the road for some little distance, and under 23 St. Mary's Street is a tessellated pavement. Extensive foundations have also been met with in the grounds of the Union Workhouse. (P. G. Laver.) On other sides the marshes made the ground unfit for habitation. The foundations under Crouch Street suggest the former existence there of a house of some importance.

(1). Tessellated pavement found February, 1875, at a depth of 2½ ft. by the N. entry of the Victoria Inn and under the W. side of Station Road (as far as the middle of the road) in front of the Inn and opposite Albert Road. (*E.A.S.T.* (N.S.), II, 189; III, 129.)

(2). A strong "wall of Roman character" was found to support the northern abutment of North Bridge when it was rebuilt in 1843. (Wire's MS., 26th May, 1843. *Gent.'s Mag.* (1843), II, 189.)

(3). Tessellated pavement found August, 1876, between the Workhouse N. of Lexden Road and Blatch Square, close to the Hospital. (*A.J.*, XXXIII, 420. *E.A.S.T.*, X, 89.)

(4). Several fragments of red tessellated pavement found in excavations for the nurses' quarters at the Hospital, and therefore close to (3). (*E.A.S.T.*, X, 89. Some were left *in situ*.)

(5). Tessellated pavement laid on a foundation of septaria and brickbats, etc., found December, 1852, just outside the W. wall of the town, E. of Balkerne Lane. (*E.A.S.T.* (O.S.), V, 159; X, 89. O.S. 10 ft. xxvii.)

(6). A small piece of red tessellated pavement found 3 ft. below the surface in Lord's Land Nursery in March, 1895. (*Antiq.*, XXXIX, 130.)

(7). Tessellated pavement found behind St. Mary's Villa at the corner of Balkerne Lane and entrance of Lord's Land Nursery Gardens. (O.S. 10 ft. xxvii.)

(8). Red tessellated pavement, fragments of a wall, painted plaster, etc., found 30 in. below the surface in the middle of the Chantry Lands, 1st January, 1853. (Wire's MS. *E.A.S.T.* (O.S.), V, 159.)

(9). " Considerable masses of Roman masonry " and the footings of a large structure of septaria and white mortar found opposite No. 61 (Dr. Renny's) Crouch St., near the King's Arms Public House. (*E.A.S.T.*, XIII, 110.)

(10). A mass of Roman masonry with red mortar in it found at a depth of 8 ft. in Crouch Street, opposite to the entrance to the Bull Hotel, 150 ft. W. of Head Gate. Septaria in white mortar, sections of columns found a few feet further W. (*E.A.S.T.*, XIII, 110.)

(11). A pavement of large red tesserae found at a depth of 4 ft. in the middle of Osborne Street, near the Bath Hotel, which is 200 ft. W. of St. Botolph's Gate. (*E.A.S.T.*, X, 88.)

(12). A tessellated pavement found at a depth of 11 ft. near (11) in February, 1903. (*E.A.S.T.*, X., 88. *Antiq.*, XXXIX, 65. *Daily Graphic*, 7th February, 1903).

(13). A tessellated pavement found opposite St. Botolph's Terrace in Priory Street (Cutts, *Colchester*, Plan I, 4. O.S. 10 ft. xxvii.)

(14) Foundations partly under the S. wall of the town N. of (13). (*E.A.S.T.* (O.S.), I, 57. O.S. 10 ft. xxvii.)

(15). Recent discoveries observed by P. G. Laver include—(a) remains of pavement on N. side of Crouch Street opposite the Maldon Road. (b) Foundations, walling and tessellated pavement, found in the grounds of the Union Workhouse. (c) Foundations of buildings, tessellated pavements and roadway, found near the N.E. corner of the junction of Crowhurst and Papillon Roads. (d) Foundations and walling, near Burlington Road, at the S. end of Dr. Chichester's Garden. (e) Foundations and walling, S. of the main building of the Hospital and E. of the Kitchen wing.

D.—KILNS. (See Map, p. 72.)

(1). About half-way between Lexden Road and Sheepen Farm to the N., floors, rubbish pits and kilns of various forms have been found over an area of ¼ acre. One kiln is still preserved and roofed over. In the neighbourhood much Samian was found, including part of a Samian mould : early coins—Cunobeline, Claudius, etc., to M. Aurelius—and miscellaneous metal objects. (*E.A.S.T.* (N.S.), I, 192, plans. *B. A. A.* (O.S.), XXXIII, 230 and 267. *A. J.*, XXXIV, 302 ; XXXV, 70.)

(2). "On the S. side of Lexden Road," probably near St Mary's Lodge were found " vases standing on circular vents above the hollow chambers through which the heat was conveyed to them." (C. Roach Smith, *Coll. Ant.*, II, pl. xiii.)

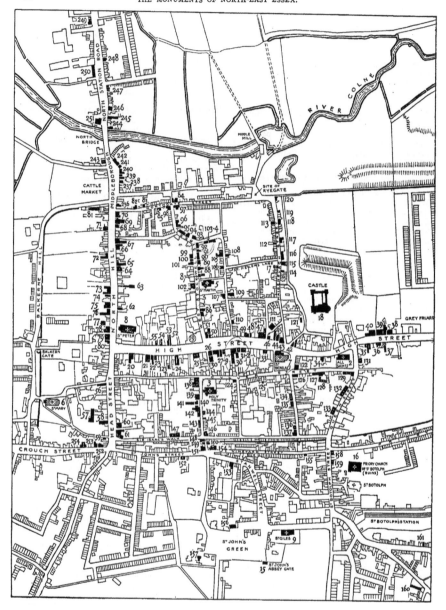

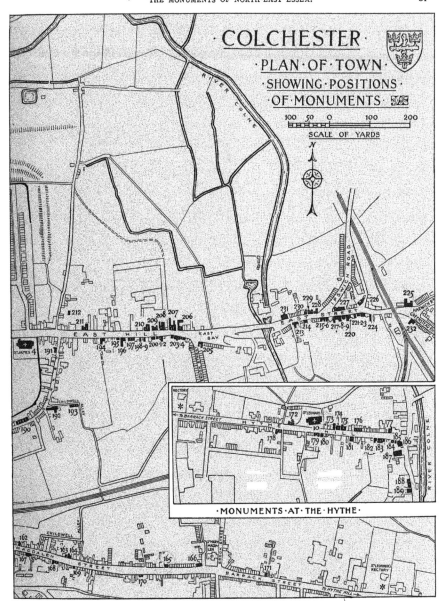

·COLCHESTER·
·PLAN·OF·TOWN·
·SHOWING·POSITIONS·
·OF·MONUMENTS·

100 50 0   100   200

SCALE OF YARDS

·MONUMENTS·AT·THE·HYTHE·

(3). On the N. side of the Colne, in a garden 500 yards N. of the town near the road from Middle Mill, was a 3-ft. layer of burnt earth mixed with brick, probably a brick clamp. Near the same place, adjoining the railways, E. of Mile End Road, a Roman pottery kiln was said to have been found, "some years before." (*E.A.S.T.*, X, 325. *Colch. Mus. Rep.*, 1908, p. 11. Wire's MS., 28th March, 1845.)

E.—CEMETERIES. (See Map, p. 72.)

Cemeteries existed all round the town where the soil was dry enough.

(1). North.—Between the town and the railway E. of the North Station, a tile tomb, cinerary urns and a skull with some bronze coins, including a fine one of Caligula, have been uncovered. (C. R. Smith, *Coll. Ant.*, II, 39. *B. A. A.* (O.S.), I, 238. *Arch.*, XXXI, 443. *Colch. Mus. Rep.*, 1908, 10–12. Wire's M.S. O.S. 6 in. xxvii. N.E.)

(2). South.—(*a*) In Mill Place, Butt Road, and about Denmark Street, cinerary urns and inhumations have been encountered with lead coffins and skeletons. This cemetery seems to be of late date. (Wire's M.S. C. R. Smith, *Coll. Ant.*, III, 52–4; II, 297. *Antiquary*, XXVIII, 45. *E.A.S.T.* (O.S.), IV, 265. *B. A.A.* (O.S.), II, 297. O.S. 25 in. xxvii.)

(*b*) Similar finds have been made in the vicinity of Chapel Street and in and near the N. end of the Artillery Barracks, and apparently in the grounds of Reed Hall. (*E.A.S.T.* (N.S.), III, 276. O.S. 25 in. xxvii.)

(3). The largest Cemetery by far is that near the Lexden Road, flanking the original Roman road to London, which led S.W. from the Balkerne Gate, and intersected the Lexden Road at the N.W. corner of the Hospital grounds. Its use was continuous throughout the Roman period ; both cremation and inhumation were practised here ; it extended full half a mile along the road and the earliest burials seem to be near the Hospital and West Lodge. (*E.A.S.T.* (O.S.), IV, 257 ; V, 162 ; (N.S.), III, 273 ; VI, 171. C. R. Smith, *Coll. Ant.*, II, 39. *Arch.*, XXXII, 404. *P. S. A.* (1st series), I, 159, 328 ; (2nd series), III, 381 ; IV, 271, 433 ; XII, 43. *B. A. A.* (O.S.), II, 42, 101 ; (O.S.) III, 57 ; (O.S.) IV, 401 ; etc.). The most noticeable finds have been :—

(*a*) The Sphinx, a freestone block 25 in. by 25 in. by 10 in. unearthed in March, 1821, in the garden of the Hospital. Early coins (Agrippa and Claudius) were associated with this find. (Drummond Hay, *Letter to the Committee* (Colchester, 1821). *Gent.'s Mag.* (1821), I, 367 ; (1822) I, 107. *E.A.S.T.* (O.S.), I, 64. C. R. Smith, *Coll. Ant.*, II, 37.)

(*b*). The 'Colchester Vase,' discovered 1853 in the grounds of West Lodge ; a very fine piece of slip-ware 9 in. high, decorated in barbotine with a gladiatorial scene and wild animals. (*E.A.S.T.* (O.S.), I, 128.) C. R. Smith, *Coll. Ant.*, IV, 82.)

(*c*). A tombstone commemorating a centurion of the XXth legion, found in 1868 in the garden of the fifth house on the E. side of Beverley Road, and a fragment found in the Hospital grounds in 1821 to another centurion of the same legion. (*E.A.S.T.* (O.S.), V, 87.)

(*d*). A 'Columbarium.' In a garden at the corner of Beverley and Queen's Roads, almost certainly modern.

(*e*). An embossed glass vase 3 in. high and 3¼ in. in diameter found near Wellesley, formerly Blatch Road, representing a scene in the circus with quadrigae and bearing the names of four popular charioteers. Vessels of this type were made probably in Belgium and were fashionable in the late 1st and early 2nd century. (Schuermans, *Annales de la Soc. Archéologique de Namur*, xx (1893). Kisa, *Das Glas im Altertume*, III, 730, 742, etc.) It probably commemorates the victory of Crescens, the champion of the blue faction, a Moor who had won over 1½ million sesterces when he was 22 years of age. (See Lanciani (1888), *Anc. Rome*, 214. *Corpus Inscriptionum Latinarum*, VII, 1273. *P.S.A.* (2nd series), III, 165.)

(*f*). A lead coffin was discovered in the Creffield Road with a lead pipe to the surface from over the mouth of the corpse. (*P.S.A.*, xii, 43. *E.A.S.T.* (N.S.), III, 273.)

(*g*). An altar dedicated to the Sulevian Mothers found in Balkerne Lane, in 1881, a short distance from the S.W. angle of the town wall. (*Proc. Soc. Ant. Lond.*, 2nd series, II, 266–283.)

(*h*). Funeral inscription in Purbeck marble found in digging foundations of Grammar School annexe in 1910. (*Essex Review*, xix (1910), 165. Haverfield, *Ephemeris Epigraphica Additamenta Quinta*, (1913), 522–23. *Corporation Colchester Museum Report*, 9 (plate I).)

Ecclesiastical :—

b(2). PARISH CHURCH OF ALL SAINTS stands on the S. side of High Street. The walls are of stone and flint-rubble mixed with brick ; the dressings are of limestone ; the roofs are covered with tiles and lead. The *Nave* was built probably in the 12th century or earlier, as Morant records that there was herring-bone work in the S. wall, which has now been refaced. Early in the 14th century the *Chancel* was largely rebuilt and late in the same century a W. tower was added. In the 15th century the *North Chapel* was added and the *North Aisle* rebuilt. Early in the 16th century the *West Tower* was rebuilt. The church was restored in the middle of the 19th century when the existing N. arcade of the nave replaced a previous one of iron.

Architectural Description—The *Chancel* (27½ ft. by 16 ft.) has a modern E. window. The 15th-century N. arcade is of two bays with two-centred arches of two moulded orders ; the column has four attached shafts with moulded capitals and bases ; the responds have attached half columns. In the S. wall are two modern windows of 14th-century character and between them are traces of a blocked doorway, covered externally by a modern buttress. The early 14th-century chancel-arch is two-centred and of two moulded orders ; the responds have each three attached shafts with moulded capitals and modern bases.

The *North Chapel* (27½ ft. by 15½ ft.) has an almost entirely modern E. window of three cinquefoiled lights with vertical tracery in a two-centred head. In the N. wall is a modern window much restored. In the W. wall is a 15th-century two-centred arch of two moulded orders, the outer continuous and the inner resting on attached shafts with moulded and embattled capitals and moulded bases.

The *Nave* (49½ ft. by 18 ft.) has a modern N. arcade. In the S. wall are two modern windows incorporating some old stones internally ; further W. is the modern S. doorway.

The *North Aisle* (12½ ft. wide) has an embattled parapet with cusped panels inlaid with flint. In the N. wall are three much restored 15th-century windows, similar to those in the N. chapel ; further W. is the late 15th-century N. doorway with moulded jambs and two-centred arch in a square head with a moulded label ; the spandrels carved with a lion and a unicorn ; this bay has the plinth enriched with quatrefoiled panels inlaid with flint. In the W. wall is a much restored window of two cinquefoiled lights with a quatrefoiled spandrel.

The *West Tower* (11 ft. by 10 ft.) is of three stages with a moulded plinth and embattled parapet ; the walls are faced with knapped flint. The late 14th-century, two-centred tower-arch is of two orders, the outer moulded and continuous and the inner chamfered and resting on semi-octagonal attached shafts with moulded capitals and bases. The early 16th-century W. window is much restored and of three cinquefoiled lights with an embattled transom and vertical tracery in a two-centred head.

(6405)

with a moulded label ; the reset late 14th-century W. doorway has moulded jambs and a two-centred arch with a moulded label. The second stage has in the N. and S. walls a much restored window of two cinquefoiled lights in a square head with a moulded label. The bell-chamber has in each wall a much restored window of three cinquefoiled and transomed lights with tracery in a square head with a moulded label.

The *Roof* of the chancel has modern boarding and 14th or early 15th-century moulded plates. The flat 15th-century roof of the N. chapel is of two subdivided bays with moulded main timbers and plates. The trussed-rafter roof of the nave is old but now covered with modern boarding. The roof of the N. aisle is similar to that of the N. chapel but of four bays.

Fittings—Bells : five ; first and second by Miles Graye, 1610 ; third by Richard Boler, 1587 ; fourth by Miles Graye, 1620 ; fifth by Miles Graye, 1682. Bell-frame old. *Communion Table :* with turned legs, shaped brackets and ball-feet, mid 17th-century. *Doors :* In N. aisle—in N. doorway, of two leaves, each with three panels, moulded fillets and frame planted on ; below springing level, band of Tudor flowers, *c.* 1500. In .tower—in doorway of turret staircase, of battens with strap-hinges, 15th-century ; in W. doorway, of battens with moulded fillets planted on, and strap-hinges, 15th‑century. *Floor-slabs :* In chancel—(1) to Elizabeth Rampley, 1688 ; (2) to Edmund Hickeringill, 1708, rector of the parish, Anne, his wife, 1708, and Edmund, their son, 1705, with shield of arms ; said to be under organ—(3) to John Phillips, town chamberlain, 1683. *Monument :* In churchyard, to George Davidson (?), 1701 (?), table-tomb. *Plate :* includes cup with baluster stem, early 17th-century ; large cup of 1714 and small paten of the same date.

Condition—Good.

ᵇ(3). PARISH CHURCH OF THE HOLY TRINITY stands on the S. side of Culver Street. The walls of the chancel, chapel and aisle are of flint-rubble and septaria with courses of Roman brick and dressings of Reigate stone ; the rubble of the tower is of the same materials but with much more Roman brick and with dressings of Roman brick ; the roofs are tiled. The W. wall of the *Nave* is part of a pre-Conquest church of uncertain date ; to this was added about the middle of the 11th century the *West Tower* and at the same time the tower-arch was inserted in the older wall. The *Chancel* was rebuilt about the middle of the 14th century and late in the same century the S. arcade of the nave was built and a S. aisle added. There are some indications (in the reuse of material) of the existence of a late 14th-century S. chapel. Late in the 15th century the *South Chapel* and its arcade were built or rebuilt ; the *South Aisle* refaced or

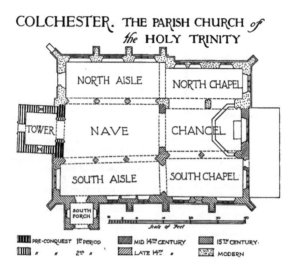

COLCHESTER. THE PARISH CHURCH of
the HOLY TRINITY

NORTH AISLE	NORTH CHAPEL	
TOWER	NAVE	CHANCEL
SOUTH AISLE	SOUTH CHAPEL	

SOUTH PORCH

Scale of Feet

▥ PRE-CONQUEST 1ST PERIOD ▨ MID 14TH CENTURY ◫ 15TH CENTURY.
▥ " " 2ND " ▧ LATE 14TH " ▦ MODERN

rebuilt together with the *South Porch*, both incorporating work of the 14th century. The church was restored in the second half of the 19th century when the *East Vestry, North Chapel* and *North Aisle* were added.

The W. wall of the nave and the W. tower are particularly interesting examples of two periods of pre-Conquest work and among the fittings the 15th-century mazer is noteworthy.

Architectural Description—The *Chancel* (27¾ ft. by 15 ft.) has an E. window all modern except the splays and rear-arch which are of probably the 14th century. In the N. wall is a modern arcade. In the S. wall is a late 15th-century arcade of two bays with moulded four-centred arches and moulded labels on both sides with carved stops, possibly earlier work reused ; the column has four attached shafts with moulded capitals and bases ; the responds have attached half columns, with earlier moulded bases, reused. The late 14th-century chancel-arch is two-centred and of two moulded orders, the outer continuous and the inner resting on attached and filleted shafts with moulded capitals and bases ; S. of it is a 15th or early 16th-century squint with a four-centred head.

The *South Chapel* (27¾ ft. by 13½ ft.) has a late 15th-century E. window of three cinquefoiled lights with vertical tracery, having embattled transoms and a segmental-pointed head ; further N. is a modern doorway. In the S. wall are two windows uniform with that in the E. wall ; between them is a late 15th-century doorway, now blocked,

with moulded jambs, four-centred head and label. In the W. wall is a late 15th-century, four-centred arch of two moulded orders, the outer continuous and the inner resting on attached shafts with moulded bases and embattled capitals ; the labels are moulded and that on the E. has earlier head-stops reused.

The *Nave* (34½ ft. by 18½ ft.) has a modern N. arcade. The late 14th-century S. arcade is of three bays with four-centred arches of two moulded orders with moulded labels ; the carved stops on the N. side are two dogs holding rabbits and a head and on the S. side three heads and a beast ; the piers have each four attached shafts with moulded capitals and bases and the responds have attached half piers. The W. wall is that of a pre-Conquest nave of earlier date than the tower with which it makes a straight joint ; the original wall is about 28 ft. high to the base of the gable, the line of which is indicated inside the tower by a raking break in the bonding ; below the gable in the present second stage of the tower are traces of a window or opening, now blocked. The tower-arch is a late pre-Conquest insertion and is built of Roman brick ; the plain responds have three plain offsets at the base and three oversailing courses for imposts ; the arch is semi-circular ; the opening is flanked on both faces by pilaster strips carried round the arch and interrupted by the imposts.

The *South Aisle* (11½ ft. wide) has in the S. wall two windows, both modern except for the splays and rear-arches which may be of the 14th century ;

BRADWELL-JUXTA-COGGESHALL:
PARISH CHURCH OF THE HOLY TRINITY.
Interior showing Nave Roof, 14th-century; Screen, 15th-century, etc.

COLCHESTER: (3) PARISH CHURCH OF THE HOLY TRINITY.
West Tower, from the North-West; Pre-Conquest.

COLCHESTER: (10) PARISH CHURCH OF ST. LEONARD, HYTHE.
Interior showing Nave Arcades, 14th and 15th-century, and Roof, early 16th-century.

between them is the restored 14th-century S. doorway, probably reset, and with moulded jambs, two-centred arch and label with defaced head-stops. In the W. wall is a 17th or 18th-century window of three pointed lights in a four-centred head ; the splays and rear-arch are of the 15th century.

The *West Tower* (11½ ft. square) is of late pre-Conquest date and is built on to the earlier wall on the E. side. It is of three stages (Plate, p. 34) with an offset plinth and courses between the stages all of Roman brick ; at the top are a few courses of 18th-century brick, a coved cornice and a pyramidal roof. The ground stage has in the N. and S. walls a double splayed window with a round head. The W. doorway (Plate, p. 142) is entirely of Roman brick and has a triangular head, three oversailing courses as imposts and pilaster strips at the sides continued over the head. The second stage has externally, in the N. and S. walls, a round-headed recess. In the W. wall are two double splayed windows with round heads, now blocked ; below them is a round-headed opening the imposts of which are formed by returning the string-course between the storeys. The bell-chamber has two ranges of windows ; the lower has one round-headed window in each wall ; the upper range is in each wall a window of two round-headed lights with a pier between them ; between the two ranges of windows are slight traces of a round-headed wall-arcade marked out by small fragments of brick, most of which have probably fallen out ; in the E. wall these arches are continued down as strips of upright bricks but the work is much weathered and is in no part very distinct.

The *South Porch* has an outer archway, probably of the 14th century reset ; it has moulded jambs, two-centred arch and label ; above the arch is a restored opening with a trefoiled head. The side walls have each a window all modern except for part of the splays and three-centred rear-arch which are probably of the 15th century.

Fittings—*Bell :* one by Miles Graye, 1633. *Chest :* In vestry—plain iron-bound, probably 16th-century. *Doors :* In S. doorway—of feathered battens, with three strap-hinges and pierced scutcheon-plate, 14th or early 15th-century. In W. doorway—of battens, with strap-hinges, probably 16th-century. *Font :* octagonal bowl, each face carved with foliage or blank shield, moulded lower edge with ribbon ornament, early 15th-century, stem and top of bowl, modern. *Glass :* In S. Chapel — in E. window, in tracery, coloured roundels set in tracery, partly restored, 15th-century. *Indent :* In S. aisle—of figure and inscription-plate. *Monuments* and *Floor-slabs :* Monuments : In N. chapel—on N. wall, (1) to William Gilberd, 1603, marble and alabaster tablet with side pilasters, cornice, achievement and thirteen shields of arms. In S. aisle—in S. wall, (2) recess, with moulded jambs and four-

centred head, altar-tomb, with panelled front and shields, much defaced, late 14th-century. Floor-slabs : In S. aisle—(1) to Thomas Talcott, 1686 ; (2) to Rev. Joseph Powell, 1698 ; (3) to Ann, widow of Gravely Hurst, 1688 ; (4) to Gravely Hurst, 1679 ; (5) to Sarah Cockerill, 1679. *Piscina :* In S. chapel—in S. wall, with trefoiled four-centred head and octofoiled drain, late 14th-century. *Plate :* includes alms-dish or mazer (Plate, p. xxxv) with maple wood bowl and moulded silver-gilt rim inscribed in black letter " Jaspar fert myrram tus Melchior Baltazar aurum," 15th-century, and a pewter flagon of c. 1700. *Seating :* In chancel—modern seat with 15th-century standard and popey-head. *Stoup :* In S. porch—E. of S. doorway, with trefoiled head, 15th-century, bowl missing.

Condition—Good.

b(4). PARISH CHURCH OF ST. JAMES stands on the S. side of East Hill. The walls are of flint and septaria-rubble, partly faced with knapped flints ; the tower has a large admixture of Roman brick ; the dressings are of limestone ; the roofs are covered with tiles and lead. The N.W. angle of a 12th-century *Nave* remains, but this is the only visible work of that period. The *West Tower* was perhaps added in the 13th century. The N. and S. arcades of the Nave suggest four different periods of the enlargement of the main body. The two E. bays of the S. arcade belong to late in the 13th century and there is some structural evidence that at this time the church had transepts. Early in the 14th century the two E. bays of the N. arcade were built or rebuilt. Early in the 15th century the chancel-arch was rebuilt, the western part of the S. arcade built or rebuilt, and the eastern part rebuilt with the 13th-century materials ; the western part of the *South Aisle* is of this date and was probably built to line with the S. face of the former transept, which was incorporated in it. Late in the 15th century the N. arcade was reconstructed on similar lines to the S. arcade and the *North Aisle* rebuilt, the former transept on this side being apparently reduced in length. About 1500 the *Chancel*, *North* and *South Chapels* and *North Vestry* were rebuilt. The W. tower appears to have been much rebuilt in the 15th century, but the exact extent of the work is uncertain. The church was restored in the 19th century when the tower-arch together with a *North Porch*, in place of an earlier one of unknown date, were rebuilt and the clearstorey added.

The building is of interest from its somewhat complicated history.

Architectural Description—The *Chancel* (43 ft. by 18½ ft.) is of early 16th-century date and is faced with knapped flints with a moulded and panelled plinth and buttresses ornamented with flint-inlay. The E. window is modern except for the moulded and shafted jambs and two-centred

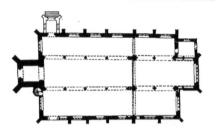

head. The N. and S. walls have each an arcade of two bays, with moulded two-centred arches, the outer members continued down the pier and responds and the inner springing from attached shafts with moulded capitals and bases ; further E. on each side is a wall-arch corresponding to the arcades and enclosing a window of three trefoiled ogee lights with flowered cusps and vertical tracery in a two-centred head ; the jambs and mullions are moulded. The side walls have a moulded external cornice or string with carved flowers and shields with the initials $\frac{S}{RC}$, T C and $\frac{SS}{T}$ all partly restored. The lofty chancel-arch is of early 15th-century date, four-centred and moulded ; the responds have each a large half-round attached shaft with small angle-rolls, moulded capitals and bases.

The *North Vestry* is of early 16th-century date and is faced externally with knapped flint ; the moulded parapet has a facing of quatrefoiled diapering with a carved flower in each quatrefoil ; at the N.E. angle is the base of a former pinnacle. In the E. wall is a modern doorway. In the N. wall is a window of three trefoiled lights in a square head. In the S. wall is a recess with a segmental-pointed head at the back of the recess (see Fittings) in the chancel ; further W. is a blocked doorway with a four-centred head. In the W. wall is a door-way with moulded jambs and four-centred arch in a square head with quatrefoiled spandrels, enclosing shields.

The *North Chapel* (29 ft. by 13 ft.) is of early 16th-century date and has a parapet ornamented like that of the vestry. The N.W. buttress is wider than the others and may represent the adapted end of the E. wall of the former transept. In the E. wall is a window similar to the side windows of the chancel. In the N. wall are two windows similar to that in the E. wall. In the W. wall is a two-centred arch of two moulded orders ; the responds have each an attached round shaft with moulded capital and base ; this arch is higher than the main level of the S. aisle roof which is canted up to cover it, a circumstance which indicates the former existence of a transept.

The *South Chapel* (29 ft. by 18 ft.) is of early 16th-century date and has an E. window of four lights and two windows of three lights in the S. wall, all similar in detail to those in the N. chapel. In the W. wall is a two-centred and moulded arch probably of 13th-century material, reset ; the responds have each an attached shaft with moulded capital and base.

The *Nave* (65 ft. by 18½ ft.) has a N. arcade of four bays, the two eastern bays are of early 14th-century date, reconstructed in the 15th century ; they have two-centred arches of two moulded orders ; the column is octagonal with moulded capital and base and the responds have attached half columns, the two western bays of the arcade are of late 15th-century date with two-centred arches of two moulded orders ; the outer continuous and the inner resting on attached shafts with moulded capitals and bases. The S. arcade is also of four bays of which the two eastern are of late 13th or early 14th-century date with the arches rebuilt in the 15th century ; the two-centred arches are of two moulded orders ; the column is octagonal with moulded capital and base and the responds have attached half columns ; the two western bays are of early 15th-century date and have two-centred arches of two moulded orders, the outer continuous and the inner resting on attached shafts with moulded capitals and bases. The clearstorey is modern.

The *North Aisle* (13 ft. wide) has in the N. wall three modern windows ; further W. is a much restored, late 14th-century doorway, probably reset with jambs and two-centred arch of two moulded orders. In the W. wall is a modern window and further S. is the Roman brick angle of the original nave.

The *South Aisle* (18 ft. wide) has in the S. wall four windows, all modern except the splays and rear-arches probably of early 15th-century date ; below the easternmost window is an early 14th-century string-course probably indicating part of the end wall of the former transept ; W. of the windows is the modern S. doorway. In the W. wall is a window, all modern except the 15th-century splays and rear-arch ; further N. is the partly restored 14th-century doorway to the tower stair-turret ; it has an ogee head.

The *West Tower* (11 ft. square) is of three stages but is divided externally into two only by a deep offset ; the parapet is embattled and above the buttresses the quoins are of Roman brick. The tower-arch, W. window and doorway are modern. The second stage has in the N., S. and W. walls a window of one pointed light ; the N. and W. windows are modern externally but the S. window and the splays and rear-arches of the others are perhaps of the 13th century and are of Roman brick. The bell-chamber has in each wall a window all modern except the splays and rear-arches which are of Roman and later bricks and perhaps of the 14th century.

The *Roof* of the N. chapel is flat and of early 16th-century date; it is of three bays with moulded main beams; the two middle principals have curved braces carved with the arms of the See of London and probably 17th-century repairs. The early 16th-century roof of the S. chapel is of similar character but has original curved braces, carved in the E. and middle trusses with large symbols of the four Evangelists. The roof of the N. aisle is modern but incorporates four pairs of brackets carved with foliage, flowers, etc. Incorporated in the supports of the modern spirelet are two 15th-century moulded beams.

Fittings—*Bells:* two, by Miles Graye, 1622. Bell-frame old. *Bracket:* In S. chapel—in E. wall, moulded bracket supported by angel with spread wings and holding a scroll, carved flowers in hollow of moulding, traces of colour, early 16th-century. *Brasses:* In S. chapel—on S. wall, (1) of John Maynarde, 1569, alderman, figure of man in fur-lined gown and inscription-plate; (2) of Ales, wife of John Maynard, 1584, figure of woman, upper part missing, and inscription-plate; palimpsest on figure part of large draped figure and an inscription part of a Flemish plate with a shield of arms, *a molet between three bugles and an engrailed border.* *Doors:* In N. chapel—in doorway to vestry, nail-studded, with moulded fillets and pierced scutcheon-plate, 15th-century. In tower—in doorway of staircase, of battens with strap-hinges, 15th-century. *Glass:* In N. chapel—in E. window, cartouche with the arms of the See of London impaling Compton, early 18th-century. *Monument* and *Floor-slab.* Monument: In ' tower— on W. wall, to Thomas Reynolds, 1665, mayor, and Margery (Decoster) his wife, 1649, oval tablet with enriched border and two shields of arms. Floor-slab: In tower—to Nathaniel Laurence, 171[4], and Martha [Greene], his wife, 1677. *Piscinae.* In chancel—square drain partly restored. In N. chapel—in E. respond, plain perforated shelf, early 16th-century. In S. aisle—in S. wall, with two-centred head and moulded drain, 14th-century. *Plate:* includes a salver of 1705. *Sedilia:* In chancel, S. chapel and S. aisle, sills of S.E. windows carried down to form seats.

Condition—Good.

b(5). PARISH CHURCH OF ST. MARTIN (Plate, p. 38) stands on the E. side of West Stockwell Street. The walls are of flint-rubble with much Roman and later brick; the dressings are of limestone and Roman brick and the roofs are tiled. The *Nave* was built early in the 12th century and had a narrow N. aisle. Late in the same century the *West Tower* was added. Early in the 14th century the *Chancel* was rebuilt and a N. chapel was

perhaps built at the same time; late in the 14th century the N. and S. arcades of the nave were built, the North aisle widened and the *South Aisle* and the *North* and *South Transepts* added. A S. porch was built probably at the same time. About the middle of the 15th century the chancel-arch was rebuilt. The upper part of the tower fell probably early in the 17th century and later in the century the *South Porch* was rebuilt. The church was restored in the latter half of 19th century and there is a temporary *Vestry* on part of the site of the former N. chapel.

The church contains interesting 12th and 14th-century work, the roof-truss forming an open screen in the chancel, being an unusual feature.

Architectural Description—The *Chancel* (32 ft. by 15 ft.) has an early 14th-century E. window of three trefoiled ogee lights with net tracery in a two-centred head; the splays and rear-arch are moulded; the external jambs are modern. In the N. wall is a window, all modern except for the 14th-century splays and rear-arch; further W. is a late 15th-century, four-centred and moulded arch, awkwardly cut into the chancel-arch on the W. side and now blocked; in the W. jamb is a squint from the N. aisle; further E. is a 14th-century doorway with moulded jambs and two-centred arch. The exterior of the wall shows traces of the junction of the former E. wall, of the N. chapel. In the S. wall are two windows, the eastern is uniform with the corresponding window in the N. wall, the western is modern except for the early 16th-century splays and four-centred rear-arch; between them is a doorway all modern except parts of the splays and rear-arch, which are probably of the 15th century. The mid 15th-century chancel-arch is two-centred and of two chamfered orders, the outer continuous and the inner resting on attached shafts with moulded capitals and bases.

The *Nave* (46 ft. by 16 ft.) has late 14th-century N. and S. arcades of three bays with two-centred arches of two hollow-chamfered orders and partly restored; on the nave side are labels with animal and head-stops; the octagonal columns have moulded capitals and bases and the responds have attached half columns; the N.E. respond is partly restored. E. of the S.E. respond is a 15th-century doorway, with a four-centred head to the roof-loft staircase, the upper doorway has also a four-centred head. The S.E. external angle of the nave has 12th-century quoins of Roman brick.

The *North Transept* (14¼ ft. by 16¼ ft.) is of late 14th-century date and has brick quoins. In the E. wall is a two-centred arch of one chamfered order. In the N. wall is a much restored window of three cinquefoiled lights with vertical tracery in a two-centred head; the jambs and head are moulded. On the W. side is a modern arch to the N. aisle.

COLCHESTER *The* PARISH CHURCH *of* S*t* MARTIN

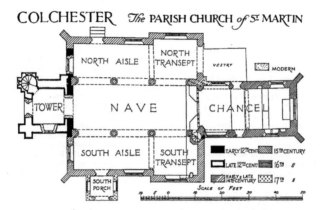

The *North Aisle* (12 ft. wide) has in the N. wall a window, nearly modern except the late 14th-century rear-arch, splays and internal jambs ; further W. is the late 14th-century N. doorway with moulded jambs, two-centred arch and segmental rear-arch. The W. wall is partly of the 12th century with Roman brick quoins to the original angle ; in it is a window, modern except for the splays and rear-arch which are probably of the 14th century.

The *South Transept* (14 ft. by 16 ft.) has in the S. wall a late 14th-century window, generally similar to the window in the N. transept, but with restored mullions. On the W. side is a 15th-century four-centred arch of two hollow-chamfered orders ; the inner order springing on the S. side from a moulded corbel.

The *South Aisle* (12 ft. wide) has in the S. wall a partly restored window of *c.* 1400 and of three cinquefoiled lights with vertical tracery in a two-centred head with a moulded label ; further W. is the late 14th-century S. doorway with jambs and two-centred arch of two wave-moulded orders with a moulded label. In the W. wall is a partly restored early 14th-century window, possibly reset, and of two trefoiled ogee lights with a quatrefoil in a two-centred head with a moulded label.

The *West Tower* (11½ ft. by 12½ ft.) is of late 12th-century date and is now of one stage with part of the ruined second stage ; the pilaster buttresses have quoins of Roman brick and in the N. and S. walls are rough construction arches, of Roman brick, possibly inserted to avoid interference with the foundations of the pre-existing nave. The stair-turret is lit by small quatrefoiled openings of the 14th or 15th century. The tower-arch is modern and above it is a blocked doorway

of uncertain date. In the W. wall is a doorway of *c.* 1400 with moulded jambs and two-centred arch in a square head with quatrefoiled spandrels and a moulded label, partly restored.

The *South Porch* has a reset late 14th-century outer archway with moulded jambs and two-centred arch. The side walls have each a square 17th-century window fitted with four turned oak balusters ; the balusters in the W. window are modern.

The *Roof* of the chancel is of early 14th-century date and of two bays with a central king-post truss ; the tie-beam is moulded and is supported below by moulded wall-posts extending to the floor, and curved and moulded braces forming a two-centred arch (Plate, p. 39) with traceried spandrels and a boss at the apex carved with a face and foliage ; the braces rest on 17th-century carved consoles ; at the springing level are the sawn-off ends of a moulded cross-beam ; the octagonal king-post has a moulded capital and base and four-way struts ; this arched truss probably served as a screen from which to hang the lenten-veil ; each bay of the roof has eight pairs of moulded and curved rafters, twelve of which have, at the apex, carved bosses of foliage, grotesque heads, etc. ; against the walls are double moulded wall-plates forming a frieze formerly panelled ; the traceried head of one panel remains on the N. side. The nave, transepts and aisles have plain braced collar-beam roofs probably of late 14th-century date ; that over the S. transept has been much rebuilt and that over the S. aisle has a moulded wall-plate on the S. side. Above the arch on the S. of the N. transept are remains of timbering, apparently to the former eaves before the erection of the transept.

COLCHESTER: (5) PARISH CHURCH OF ST. MARTIN; 12th-century and later.
West Tower, etc., from the South-West.

COLCHESTER : (5) PARISH CHURCH OF ST. MARTIN.
Interior showing Arched Truss in Chancel ; early 14th-century.

Fittings—*Altar :* In chancel—slab with chamfered under-edge, five consecration crosses, two possibly modern. *Chair:* In chancel—with panelled back, fluted top rail, shaped arms and turned front legs, 17th-century. *Chests:* In N. aisle—(1) panelled, with fluted top rail, one lock, early 17th-century ; (2) plain panelled, possibly late 17th-century. *Coffin-lid :* In chancel—with foliated cross, 13th-century. *Doors :* In chancel—in N. doorway, made up of late 17th-century and modern work, with swags and bolection mouldings. In N. aisle—in N. doorway, of feathered battens with straphinges, probably late 14th-century. In S. aisle—in S. doorway, modern, with reused strap-hinges, 15th-century. *Font* (Plate, p. xxxiv): octagonal bowl with traceried panels and crocketed ogee heads, pinnacles at angles, stem with attached shafts having moulded capitals and bases, 15th-century. *Niche :* On S.W. buttress of porch, with canopied and crocketed head and side buttresses, late 14th-century, partly restored. *Piscinae :* In chancel—with square jambs and moulded ogee head and label, with crockets and remains of finial, side pinnacles with traceried panels and carved finials, octofoiled drain, 14th-century. In S. transept—in S. wall, with trefoiled head and sexfoiled drain, late 14th-century, modern sill ribbed mould, late 14th-century, under modern sill 14th-century head-corbel. *Poorbox :* In nave—incorporating mouldings and panels carved with arabesque ornament and a figure-subject, mid to late 17th-century. *Pulpit :* incorporating four carved panels with conventional foliage and other designs, 16th and 17th-century. *Recess :* In chancel—in N. wall, with trefoiled and sub-cusped ogee head and moulded label, 14th-century, possibly Easter Sepulchre. *Screen :* Under chancel-arch, incorporating, below the rail, six trefoiled, sub-cusped and richly traceried heads, cusp points with carved heads, foliated spandrels to tracery, early 15th-century. *Sedilia :* In chancel—sill of window carried down to form seat, 14th-century, restored. In S. transept—similar sedile. *Miscellanea :* In chancel—incorporated in seat, two traceried heads, 15th-century.

Condition—Fairly good, but some ivy on ruined tower.

b(6). PARISH CHURCH OF ST. MARY-AT-THE-WALLS stands in the S.W. angle of the walled town. The walls of the tower are of stone, with limestone dressings ; the upper stage is of brick. The *West Tower* is of mid to late 15th or early 16th-century date as to its two lower stages. The church was ruined during the siege and rebuilt 1713–14, but this building was pulled down in the second half of the 19th century and the present church erected 1872. The top stage of the tower was added in 1729.

Among the fittings the 17th-century chalice is particularly noteworthy.

Architectural Description — The *West Tower* (15 ft. by 13¾ ft.) is of three stages the two lower of rubble and the top stage of brick with an embattled parapet. The moulded plinth, partly restored, has stone panels alternately with pointed heads and circles cusped and enclosing blank shields. There are diagonal buttresses at three angles and a stair-turret at S.E. angle. The unusually lofty tower-arch is two-centred and of two moulded orders the outer continuous and the inner resting on semi-circular shafts with moulded capitals and bases. In the S. wall is a modern doorway to the stair-turret. The W. window is of three cinquefoiled lights with vertical tracery in a two-centred head, with an embattled transom, all restored except the splays and rear-arch. The W. doorway has stop-moulded and shafted jambs and moulded two-centred arch, with a crocketed label, finial, square head and traceried spandrels, modern or restored. The second stage has in the N., S. and W. walls a window with a three-centred head, all of brick. The bell-chamber has in each wall a brick window with plain jambs and three-centred head, all of early 18th-century date.

Fittings—*Bell :* one by John Darbie, 1679. *Monuments :* In tower—on N. wall, (1) of John Rebow, 1699, erected by Sir Isaac Rebow, and to others of later date, black and white marble monument, with seated figure of man, before an arched panel with Corinthian side-columns and achievement of arms. In churchyard—S. side, (2) to Richard Rootrey, 1707 ; headstone ; (2) to seven children, 1689, headstone, names buried. *Plate :* includes a richly decorated chalice (Plate, p. xxxv) inscribed " Maria monty Jonasn me fieri fecit pro conventu fratrum minorum de Rosriala Pro cujus anima oretur Ano: 1633 " ; on the bowl is I.H.S. and on the knop " Ave Maria " ; the cup has scale ornament and the knop is pierced and engraved with the instruments of the passion ; on the foot is an engraved crucifixion ; (Rosriala is probably Rossereily, county Galway) there is also a cup and cover-paten of 1714. *Pulpit :* In vestry —cupboard made up of carved work and inlaid panels of former pulpit ; panels have monograms of the Rebow family and H.C. with a mitre, for Henry Compton, Bishop of London, early 18th-century.

Condition—Good, mostly rebuilt.

b(7). PARISH CHURCH OF ST. NICHOLAS stands on the S. side of High Street. The walls are of mixed rubble with dressings of limestone ; the roofs are covered with tiles and lead. The church was entirely rebuilt early in the 14th century when it consisted of *Chancel,* N. Vestry, *Crossing,* probably N. and S. Transepts, and *Nave* with *North* and S. Aisles ; there was also a S. chapel of uncertain date. According to Morant a tower fell late in the 17th century and as this ruined the chancel it probably stood over the crossing. The building was restored in the 18th century and the *North Tower* built or rebuilt in its present position N. of the crossing. In 1875 the church was generally restored, the chancel largely rebuilt, the S. aisle and Transept Chapel destroyed and a new church of much larger size added to the S. of the old building; the north tower was refaced and partly rebuilt and a spire added.

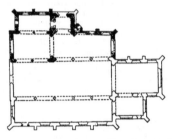

Architectural Description—The *Chancel* of the old church (25 ft. by 15½ ft.) has a modern E. window. In the N. wall are two modern windows copying old features and below the western is a 14th-century doorway modern internally but with an old rear-arch on the outer face of the wall, indicating the former existence of a vestry. The S. arcade is modern.

The *Crossing* of the old church (14 ft. by 15½ ft.) had originally on each side an early 14th-century arch, two-centred and of two moulded orders; the responds had each three attached shafts with moulded capitals and bases; of these arches the eastern only retains its much restored N. respond; the N. arch has been thickened by the addition of two modern orders with their responds and with the old outer order on the N. reset in a new position; the S. arch has been replaced by the modern W. arch of the arcade mentioned above, but the W. respond incorporates some of the old stones; the W. arch is intact.

The *Nave* of the old church (27 ft. by 17¾ ft.) has an early 14th-century N. arcade of two bays with a moulded column of quatrefoiled plan and with other details similar to the W. arch of the crossing; in the spandrel over the column is a round quatrefoiled opening of the 14th century. The S. arcade is uniform with the N. arcade, but the eastern and part of the western arch are modern and there is no opening in the spandrel. In the W. wall is a large window all modern except the 15th-century moulded and shafted splays and the two-centred rear-arch.

The *North Aisle* of the old church (11½ ft. wide) now a vestry, has in the E. wall a modern doorway set in the blocking of a plain segmental-pointed

half-arch. In the N. wall are two 14th-century windows, much restored and each of two trefoiled lights with tracery in a two-centred head. Set high in the W. wall is a single light window, entirely restored; below it there is said to have been a doorway, removed at the restoration.

The *North Tower* has been entirely restored but the core of the lower walls may be old and the S.E. turret staircase is old internally.

Reset in the S. wall of the modern S. aisle is an early 15th-century doorway with moulded and shafted jambs and moulded two-centred arch; it is flanked by buttresses from which springs an ogee crocketed label, either much restored or modern. In the W. wall of the same aisle is a window incorporating a moulded and shafted 15th-century S. splay and part of a moulded rear-arch of the same date.

Fittings—*Bells*: six with a clock-bell and one additional bell; 3rd by Richard Hille, 15th-century, inscribed "Sancte Jacobe Ora Pro Nobis"; 5th by Henry Pleasant, 1701; 6th by Joanna Hille, 15th-century, inscribed "In Multis Annis Resonet Campana Johannis"; additional bell, from St. Runwald's church, by Miles Graye, 1621. *Bracket*: In old nave—in N.E. angle, moulded corbel with stiff-leaf foliage and trumpet stem curved back into wall, early to mid 13th-century. *Chests*: In old nave—with carved and panelled front, three panels with lozenges of carving, conventional fleur-de-lis ornament to top rail, 17th-century. In modern S. aisle—carved front with two arcaded panels and frieze, early 17th-century. In N. tower —plain with cambered lid and tapering sides, 17th or 18th-century. *Communion Table*: In modern vestry—with turned legs, shaped brackets and carved top rail, c. 1660. *Monuments*: In old chancel—on N. wall, (1) stone tablet with recessed panel having cinquefoiled ogee head with crockets and finial and cinquefoiled super-head with spandrels carved with thistles; in main panel slab with indents of kneeling figure of a civilian, scroll, Trinity, roundel and inscription-plate; above it a square boss carved with a doubtful figure, said to be a mermaid; in top panel two shields with merchant's mark and the initials W.I. and O.I., c. 1500, brought from St. Runwald's church. In old nave—(2) to Samuel Great, 1706, and Susan, his wife, 1722, shaped marble tablet with cherubheads and cartouche. *Niches*: In old N. aisle— on E. wall, with ogee head, formerly cinquefoiled, ribbed vault and rosettes, very small, 15th-century; in W. wall, externally, with trefoiled ogee head and tracery above it, 14th-century. *Painting*: In new nave—at W. end, altar-piece painted on canvas, the dead Christ and women, early 18th-century, brought from St. Runwald's church. *Piscinae*: In old chancel—in E. wall, with moulded jambs and trefoiled head, late 14th-century, probably not *in situ*, sill modern. In old N. aisle—loose, scalloped capital of pillar-piscina with nail-head ornament and square drain, 12th-century. *Plate :* includes cup with incised ornament and cover-paten, dated 1569 ; Elizabethan cup with band of incised ornament ; large cup and cover-paten probably of 1667, the former with baluster stem, and stand-paten of 1708 ; all except the first cup and paten belonged to St. Runwald's parish. *Recess :* In old chancel—in N. wall, large with segmental-pointed head, date and use uncertain. *Stoup :* In old N. aisle—in W. wall externally, recess with two-centred head, probably stoup to former doorway, date uncertain. *Miscellanea :* In churchyard— N. and S. of church, worked and moulded stones including tracery and one head-corbel or stop. 14th and 15th-century.

Condition—Good, much restored.

b(8). PARISH CHURCH OF ST. PETER stands on the E. side of North Hill. The walls, where ancient, are of mixed rubble with septaria, brick and ragstone ; the dressings are of Reigate and other limestone. The roofs are covered with lead and tiles. The

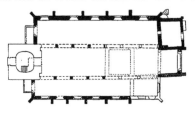

earliest part of the structure are the four western bays of the S. arcade of the *Nave* with the *South Aisle*, which are of early 15th-century date ; later in the same century the corresponding bays of the N. arcade with the *North Aisle* were built. At this time the church included a central tower occupying the space between the third and part of the second arcades of the existing arcades. Early in the 16th century the *North Vestry* with the *Bone-hole* beneath it were added. There is no evidence of the date of the *Chancel*. The church was injured by an earthquake in 1692 and probably soon after the windows of the aisles were remodelled. In 1758 the central tower was removed, the N. and S. arcades extended, partly with old materials over its site, and the West Tower added ; shortly after the chancel was reduced to half its length by extending the nave arcades eastwards and at the same time the S. aisle was extended to the same point. The church was restored in the 19th century when the clearstorey was added and the chancel-arch built.

The vaulted bone-hole is interesting and among the fittings the early 14th-century ironwork of the S. doorway is noteworthy.

Architectural Description—The *Chancel* (12 ft. by 17 ft.) has no ancient features.

The *North Vestry* is of early 16th-century date and has at the eastern angles square projecting buttresses each with remains of flint-inlay panelling partly restored and having the base of a pinnacle at the top. The parapet of the N. wall has richly cusped panelling or diapering with carved rosettes ; on the E. wall the parapet has been rebuilt in brick but it incorporates some portions of the old work on which are two shields, one *a cheveron with a molet in the sinister quarter* and the other *a cross.* In the E. wall is a modern doorway with the square head and moulded label with head-stops of a former window. In the W. wall is a doorway with chamfered jambs and segmental-pointed arch, with a moulded label.

The *Bone-hole,* beneath the vestry, is of early 16th-century date and is of two bays with a quadripartite vault of plastered brick having chamfered main, diagonal and wall-ribs. In the E. wall are two windows each formerly of three quartrefoiled openings ; of these the middle quartrefoil in each window remains with traces of another in the northern window. In the N. wall was a similar window but only the rear-arches remain ; further N. is a doorway with a four-centred stone head ; it is approached by a flight of steps.

The *Nave* (87 ft. by 20½ ft.) has N. and S. arches of seven bays, of these the second and third bays probably occupy the site of the former central tower. The piers and arches of the first three bays on the N. side are largely composed of reused material and 18th-century imitations of 15th-century work ; the rest of the N. arcade is of 15th-century date, perhaps partly reset and with two-centred arches of two orders, the outer sunk-chamfered and continuous and the inner moulded and resting on shafts with moulded capitals and bases ; there is a moulded label on each face ; the responds have attached half-columns, that on the E. having been altered into a column in the 18th century. The S. arcade has the three eastern bays of the 18th century but with a reset 15th-century E. respond similar to those of the N. arcade, a reset third arch and reused materials in the columns ; the remaining four bays of the S. arcade are of early 15th-century date and have two-centred arches of two moulded orders with a moulded label on the N. side and remains of a similar label on the S. side ; the columns have attached shafts with moulded capitals and bases and the W. respond has an attached half-column. The clearstorey is modern and the W. gallery is of the 18th century.

The *North Aisle* (17 ft. wide) has a large 18th-century gallery. In the E. wall, above the vestry is a 15th-century window of two cinquefoiled lights with vertical tracery in a two-centred head with a moulded label. In the N. wall are five 18th-century windows with round heads, key-stones and imposts ; each is set in a partly blocked 15th-century window opening of which portions of the much weathered jambs, sill and head are visible ; in the fourth bay are traces of a 15th-century doorway with a two-centred head. In the W. wall is an 18th-century window set in an earlier opening, similar to those in the N. wall.

The *South Aisle* (12 ft. wide) has an 18th-century gallery. The easternmost bay is entirely of mid 18th-century date. The remaining bays of the S. wall, except the fifth, have each an 18th-century window set in an earlier opening, similar to those in the N. aisle ; in the fifth bay is a 15th-century S. doorway with moulded and shafted jambs and two-centred arch. In the W. wall is a window similar to those in the S. wall and below it is an 18th-century doorway.

Fittings—*Brasses* and *Indents*. Brasses : In N. aisle—on N. wall, (1) of Richard Sayer, 1610, and Alse (Spooner) and Ellen (Lawrence), his wives, rectangular plate with kneeling figures of man, wives, one son and one daughter with an achievement of arms and inscription ; (2) of Agnes (Woodthorpe), wife successively of Aleyn Dister and Robert Leache, 1553, rectangular plate with kneeling figures of two men (Robert Leache) in red aldermanic gown in enamel, wife with widow's veil, four sons and five daughters, architectural background, ornamental border and inscription ; (3) of William Brown, 1572, and Margaret, his wife, 1573, kneeling figures of man and wife at prayer-desks, five sons, two daughters, achievement of arms and foot-inscription. In S. aisle—on E. wall, (4) of John Sayer, 1563, rectangular plate with kneeling figures of man at prayer-desk, architectural background, achievement of arms and inscription ; on S. wall, (5) of John Sayre, alderman, 1509, and Elizabeth, his wife, 1530, rectangular plate with kneeling figure of man in red aldermanic gown in enamel, wife with widow's veil, four sons and one daughter in butterfly head-dress, architectural background and inscription. Indents : In N. aisle—(1) of inscription-plate. In tower—(2) and (3) defaced. *Chair :* In chancel—with carved and upholstered back, turned or twisted legs and rails, shaped arms, late 17th-century. *Communion Table :* small with twisted legs, carved and shaped top rails, probably late 17th-century. *Communion Rails :* In tower—twisted and turned balusters, rail carved with acanthus ornament, reused in gallery staircase, *c.* 1710. *Doors :* In N. aisle—in doorway to vestry, of feathered battens and a frame of fillets planted on, two strap-hinges and domed scutcheon-plate with ornamental edge and drop handle, probably 14th-century, latch and key-plate, probably 16th or 17th-century. In S. aisle—in S. doorway, in two folds with moulded feathered battens and two

enriched strap-hinges (Plate, p. 42) with scrolled foliage terminating in leaves or rosettes of stamped iron, *c.* 1300, ascribed to Thomas of Leighton (Buzzard) ; intermediate strap-hinge, without scroll-work is interrupted by round scutcheon-plate, probably a later 14th-century addition, with pierced traceried panels and a raised rim of fret pattern ; lower hinge much damaged. *Monuments* and *Floor-slabs*. Monuments : In chancel—on N. wall, (1) of Martin Basill, 1623, and Elizabeth, his wife, 1625, marble wall-monument with two niches containing kneeling figures of man and wife, flanked by Corinthian columns supporting an entablature with achievement of arms, below, figures in relief of six sons and seven daughters ; on S. wall, (2) to Mary (Thurston) wife of William Eldred, 1671, marble oval tablet with wreath and cartouche of arms ; (3) of George Sayer, 1577, and Agnes (Wesden), 1556, and Frances (Sammon), small wall-monument with kneeling figures of man, two wives, four sons and three daughters, three Corinthian columns supporting entablature and achievement of arms. Floor-slabs : In chancel—(1) to [John Cole ?] alderman 16—, and Anne ? (Thurston ?), his wife, 1668. (2) to Danyell Cole, 1642, last Bailiff and first Mayor of Colchester. In nave—(3) to [Aquila], wife of Edmund Thurston, 16[81], with lozenge of arms. In N. aisle—(4) to Sir William Campion, killed 1648, with defaced shield of arms ; (5) to Elizabeth R[ayner, daughter of William Swallow], 1693, also to Mary, wife of William Rayner, and others ; against N. wall, (6) to John Stilleman, 1699 ; against W. wall, (7) to Mary, daughter, 1710, four other daughters and four sons of John Potter, 1699, and others later ; (8) to John Freeman, 1714, with achievement of arms. In S. aisle—(9) to Mrs. Jasper Waters, 1683, six sons and five daughters unnamed, and to Jasper Waters, 1706, and Sarah his wife, 1724 ; (10) to James Lemyng, 1671, and Mary (Batten), his wife, 1671 ; *Piscina :* In S. aisle—in S. wall, with septfoiled ogee head, early 15th-century. *Plate :* includes stand-paten of 1698. *Pulpit :* hexagonal, each face with raised inlaid panels, foliage fruit and flowers, cherub-heads, two cherubs supporting a shield of St. Peter under book-board, early 18th-century, stem mostly modern. *Royal Arms :* In nave—on N. wall, of William III carved and painted woodwork. *Table :* In vestry—large, with turned legs and shaped top rail, early to mid 17th-century. *Miscellanea :* In churchyard—various fragments of worked stones, 15th and 16th-century.

Condition—Good, but external stonework badly perished.

b(9). PARISH CHURCH OF ST. GILES stands a short distance to the E. of St. John's Green. The walls are of mixed rubble with some septaria and brick ; the porch is mainly of brick and the tower

COLCHESTER.: (8) PARISH CHURCH OF ST. PETER.
South Door, showing Ironwork of c. 1300, ascribed to Thomas of Leighton (Buzzard).

DEDHAM: PARISH CHURCH OF ST. MARY.
North Doorway and Doors; c. 1500.

COLCHESTER: (15) ABBEY OF ST. JOHN THE BAPTIST.
Gatehouse ; late 15th-century.

is timber-framed and weather-boarded ; the dress-ings are of limestone and brick and the roofs are covered with tiles, slates and lead. The S. wall of the *Nave* was built probably in the 12th century. The *Chancel* has one 13th-century window and may be of that date. A North Aisle, now included in the nave, was built or rebuilt probably late in the 14th century. Early in the 16th century the *North Chapel* and the *South Porch* were added. The *West Tower* is probably of late 17th or early 18th-century date. Early in the 19th century the nave and aisle were thrown into one and the existing colonnades and galleries erected. Early in the 20th century the church was restored and the *South Chapel* added.

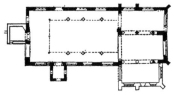

Architectural Description—The *Chancel* (30 ft. by 17½ ft.) has an E. window all modern except the splays and a few reset, external stones. In the N. wall is a brick arcade of two bays all modern except a few bricks of the eastern arch and the column which has four attached shafts with partly restored moulded capitals of early 16th-century date ; further E. is an early 16th-century doorway of brick with chamfered jambs, partly restored and a moulded four-centred arch ; it is now blocked. In the S. wall is a modern arcade of two bays and E. of it is a mid 13th-century lancet window entirely covered with cement. The chancel-arch is modern except for the moulded capital and some reset stones of the S. respond which are of the 15th century.

The *North Chapel* (31 ft. by 14 ft.) has an E. window all modern except parts of the splays, rear-arch and some external stones, which are of early 16th-century date ; further S. is a modern doorway. In the N. wall are two early 16th-century windows both much restored and each of three cinquefoiled lights with vertical tracery in a segmental-pointed head with a moulded label. In the W. wall is a modern archway.

The *South Chapel* is modern but in the S. wall is a doorway with an old rear-arch, reset. Above the doorway is a wooden tablet bearing the names of churchwardens and the date 1665.

The *Nave* (64½ ft. by 35¾ ft.) has modern colonnades. In the N. wall are three windows probably of the 17th century and each of three plain segmental-pointed lights with uncusped tracery in a segmental-pointed head with a moulded

label ; between the two western windows is the late 14th-century N. doorway with moulded and double-shafted jambs and two-centred arch with a moulded label ; on either side of it are traces of the existence of a former porch. In the S. wall are four windows, the easternmost is of early 16th-century date and of three trefoiled ogee lights with rosettes to the cusps and vertical tracery in a two-centred head ; the jambs and mullions are moulded and the splays have shafts with moulded capitals and bases ; the second window is of the 18th century and is set in the lower part of a blocked, early 14th-century window formerly of two trefoiled ogee lights with a cusped spandrel in a two-centred head ; the two western windows are apparently entirely modern ; W. of the porch is a wide single-light window with a roughly pointed head, all of Roman brick and perhaps of the 12th century ; it is now blocked ; E. of it is the modern S. doorway with traces of the brick jamb of a 16th-century doorway W. of it ; the S.W. angle of the nave has quoins of Roman brick. In the W. wall is a modern doorway set in the blocking of a rough tower-arch of doubtful date ; N. of it is a modern doorway and S. of it externally are traces of the former square-headed W. window of the nave ; above this is a quatre-foiled opening probably modern.

The *West Tower* is partly timber-framed and weather-boarded and has no ancient features visible.

The *South Porch* is mainly of red brick with a little rubble ; it is of early 16th-century date and has an outer archway with jambs and four-centred arch of two moulded orders. The side walls have each a window of two four-centred lights in a square head ; the mullions are modern.

The *Roof* of the N. chapel is of early 16th-century date and of four and a half bays with moulded main timbers, moulded and hollow-chamfered principals, moulded collars with curved braces and moulded side purlins with curved wind-braces. The early 16th-century roof of the S. porch is of two bays with braced collar-beams and curved wind-braces, the main timbers are moulded and the E. plate is carved with twisted foliage ; the W. plate is missing.

Fittings—Bell : one, said to be by Miles Graye, 1657. *Bracket* : In N. chapel—in E. wall, prob-ably with angel, but defaced, early 16th-century. *Coffin-plates* : In N. chapel—on S. wall, (1) to John, Lord Lucas, 1671 ; (2) to " the Lady Anne Lucas," 1660. *Door* : In N. doorway—of two leaves with elaborately traceried head, late 14th-century. *Monuments* and *Floor-slab*. Monuments : In N. chapel—on N. wall, (1) probably to Sir Thomas Lucas, 1611, and Mary, his wife, 1613, modern recess, marble shelf set above the recess, and carved rosettes and strap-ornament on soffit of arch. In nave—in S. wall, (2) to William Cock,

1619, pastor of the church, and Anna, his wife, 1625, plain inscribed stone. *Floor-slab* : In N. chapel—on N. wall, to Sir Charles Lucas and Sir George Lisle, shot in 1648. *Pall :* Funeral pall of the Lucas family, oval shape and of purple velvet, with fringe, embroidered initials and date E. L., 1628, G. S., I H S, and true lovers' knot. *Panelling :* In S. chapel—partition made up of late 16th-century panelling. *Piscina :* In chapel—with modern jambs and two-centred head, recut, old drain. *Stoup :* W. of N. doorway externally, blocked recess, possible stoup. *Miscellanea :* In nave, memorial tablet recording benefactions of Jeremiah Daniell, 1695.

The *Churchyard* has incorporated in the N. and E. walls many worked stones from the abbey including several portions of an interesting wall-arcade of the 12th century. Extending W. from the tower is a length of 16th-century brick walling. Condition—Good, except S. wall of nave, rest much altered and restored.

ᵈ(10). PARISH CHURCH OF ST. LEONARD-AT-THE-HYTHE stands on the N. side of Hythe Hill. The walls are of mixed rubble, septaria, flint, pebbles, brick and freestone ; the dressings are of limestone and the roofs are covered with lead and tiles. The *Chancel* and the N. arcade of the *Nave* and the *North Aisle* were built *c.* 1330–40 and at the same time or soon afterwards the *North Vestry* was added ; the *West Tower* was built late in the 14th century. In the 15th century the S. arcade was built, the *South Aisle* and *South Porch* added and the chancel-arch rebuilt. About 1500 the *North* and *South Chapels* were added or rebuilt and the clearstorey added ; *c.* 1530 the rood-stair was rebuilt. The church has needed continuous restoration owing to subsidence or to the insufficient strength of the old work. The top stage of the tower is modern and the S. porch has been largely rebuilt.

The nave has a good hammer-beam roof and among the fittings the mazer-bowl of 1521 is note-worthy.

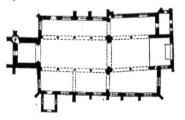

Architectural Description—The *Chancel* (42½ ft. by 20 ft.) has an E. window, all modern except parts of the jambs and shafted splays which are of the 15th century. In the N. wall is a two-light window of 14th-century character but all modern except parts of the jambs, splays and rear-arch ; further W. is an arcade of *c.* 1500 and of two bays with four-centred arches of two moulded orders, the outer continued down the responds and the inner resting on attached shafts with moulded capitals and bases. In the S. wall is a window and arcade, uniform with those in the N. wall ; between them is an early 16th-century squint with a rounded head. The late 15th-century chancel-arch is four-centred and of two moulded orders, the outer continuous and the inner resting on shafts with moulded capitals and bases ; the arch is much distorted.

The *North Vestry* has in the E. wall a loop-light and N. of it a modern doorway. In the N. wall is an early 16th-century window, heavily grated and formerly of two lights ; it now has a flat four-centred head and a plastered label. In the S. wall is the recess of the former 14th-century doorway from the chancel ; it is now reset in the W. wall ; it has double sunk-chamfered jambs and a moulded two-centred arch.

The *North Chapel* (32¾ ft. by 12½ ft.) has in the E. wall a window of *c.* 1500 and of three cinque-foiled lights in a segmental-pointed head, with moulded splays, jambs and label. In the N. wall are two windows similar to that in the E. wall. In the N.W. angle are the two early 16th-century doorways of the rood-loft staircase ; the lower one has rebated jambs and four-centred head, the upper has chamfered jambs and a square head. In the S.W. angle and set in a corbelled projection is a doorway at the level of the loft and with chamfered E. jamb and square head ; in the thickness of the wall are stairs leading up to the higher level of the main loft across the chancel-arch. In the W. wall is an early 16th-century arch, two-centred and of two moulded orders, the outer continuous and the inner resting on attached shafts with moulded capitals and bases.

The *South Chapel* (34 ft. by 15½ ft.) has a modern E. window. Close to the junction with the chancel is a straight joint indicating the position of a former buttress. In the S. wall are three modern windows and below the middle one is a doorway originally of early 16th-century date but reconstructed in the 18th century and covered with Roman cement. In the W. wall is an arch uniform with the W. arch of the N. chapel but much distorted.

The *Nave* (49 ft. by 20 ft.) has an early 14th-century N. arcade of four bays with two-centred arch of two moulded orders ; the columns are of quatrefoil plan with moulded capitals and bases and the responds have attached half-columns ; the third column and the fourth arch have been rebuilt in the 15th century to match the earlier work. The 15th-century S. arcade is of four bays with four-centred arches of two moulded orders, the outer confined down the responds and the inner resting on attached shafts with moulded capitals and bases ; the columns have each four similar shafts but of these the shaft of the first has been rebuilt and the whole of the second is modern. E. of the arcades on each side is a carved head-corbel, one defaced, to support the former rood-beam. The clearstorey has on each side six windows each of two lights and originally of early 16th-century date but now almost completely restored.

The *North Aisle* (11 ft. wide) has in the N. wall three windows of *c.* 1500 and uniform with those in the N. chapel ; further W. is the 14th-century N. doorway with restored jambs and two-centred arch of two orders the inner rounded and the outer chamfered ; the label is moulded. In the W. wall is a 14th-century window almost completely restored and of three lights, two plain and one cinquefoiled, with tracery in a two-centred head.

The *South Aisle* (14 ft. wide) has in the S. wall three modern windows ; further W. is the 15th-century S. doorway with moulded jambs and two-centred arch in a square head with traceried spandrels, a moulded label and stops carved with half-angels ; the head is partly restored ; further W. and set high in the wall is a square-headed doorway to the room over the porch. In the W. wall is a modern window and further N. the wall incorporates a buttress of the tower, formerly external.

The *West Tower* (13 ft. square) is of three stages, the two lower of late 14th-century date and the top stage modern. The moulded plinth has flint chequer-work and above it as far as a modern string-course the wall is faced with alternate bands of brick and knapped flint. The tower-arch is two-centred and of two moulded orders, the outer continuous and the inner resting on semi-octagonal shafts with moulded capitals and widely spreading bases. The W. window is modern except for the splays and rear-arch ; below it is a plain pointed doorway of the 14th century ; it is now blocked. In the N.W. angle is the doorway to the turret staircase with moulded jambs and ogee head. The second stage has in the N., S. and W. walls a quatrefoiled opening with a modern label.

The *Roof* of the N. chapel is of early 16th-century date and of flat pent form ; it has moulded main timbers and curved brackets under the principals, resting on angel-corbels of stone. The roof of the S. chapel is uniform with that of the N. chapel but the main timbers at the E. end are not moulded and there are no brackets on the S. wall. The early 16th-century roof of the nave (Plate, p. 35) is of hammer-beam type and of six bays with seven trusses ; the purlins, principals and posts are moulded and the hammer-beams and collars are moulded and embattled and have curved braces beneath them ; the spandrels above the collars

and hammer-beams are traceried and the moulded wall-plates have carved rosettes ; four figures of angels fixed on the hammer-beams are now preserved in the vestry. The roof of the N. aisle is uniform with that of the N. chapel but has two bosses carved as roses at the intersection of the intermediate principals and remains of painted decoration in bands at the E. end. The S. porch has a boarded ceiling with moulded cornice and ribs having flowered bosses at the intersections ; much of this appears to be modern but part of it is of late 15th-century date.

Fittings — *Bells :* five ; 2nd by H. Jordan, 15th-century, and inscribed " Benedictum Sit Nomen Domini" ; 3rd by Kebyll, 15th-century, and inscribed " In Multis Annis Resonet Campana Johannis." *Chairs :* In chancel—three with carved backs and lower rail, turned and shaped legs, early 18th-century ; one with carved back and arms, turned and shaped legs and rails, early 18th-century. In S. chapel—one with turned legs and back carved with lozenge ornament, early 17th-century ; another with plain back and turned legs, late 17th-century. *Chest :* In N. chapel—of oak with panelled and arcaded front, 17th-century. *Clock :* On tower—on S. wall externally, clock-face of stone, circular dial with radiating figures and carved spandrels, *c.* 1500. *Doors :* In N. chapel, in doorway to vestry—of battens with moulded fillets, strap-hinges and drop handle, 16th-century. In S. doorway—of battens with ornamental strap-hinges and pierced scutcheon-plate, 15th-century ; woodwork pierced with several holes, said to be loopholes made during the siege of 1648. In upper doorway, by S. doorway—of plain battens, with strap-hinges, 15th-century. *Floor-slabs :* In N. chapel—(1) name covered by organ, 1708. In S. chapel—(2) to Alice, wife of Robert Bell, 1646 ; (3) to Isaac Sherley, 16(92). *Font :* octagonal bowl with panelled sides alternately blank shields in quatre-foils and chalice and host, Agnus Dei and flowers, stem with trefoil-headed panels, 15th-century. *Indent :* In N. chapel—of priest and inscription-plate. *Niche :* In chancel—in N. wall, with cinquefoiled head, 15th-century. On tower—on S. wall externally, with moulded jambs and cinque-foiled head, 15th-century. *Piscinae :* In chancel —in S. wall, with moulded jambs and cinquefoiled head, sexfoiled drain, 15th-century, restored. In S. chapel—in S. wall, similar to that in chancel, 15th-century. *Plate* (Plate, .p. xxxv) : includes mazer-bowl with silver-gilt rim of 1521, and mid 18th-century inscription, raised silver-gilt moulded boss at bottom with the initials I H C in black letter ; large Elizabethan cup with two bands of incised ornament ; large cup probably of 1624 and a paten of 1713. *Screen :* In chancel—under S.W. arch, lower part of parclose with moulded rail and close traceried panels, early 16th-century.

Miscellanea: In chancel—low down in N. wall, square quatrefoiled sinking or panel, 15th-century.

Condition—Arcades and walls out of perpendicular and various arches much distorted, building still subject to settlement and needs constant attention.

ᵉ(11). PARISH CHURCH OF ST. MICHAEL, BERE-CHURCH stands about 2 m. S. of Colchester. The walls are of brick with stone dressings ; the roofs are tiled. The church has reused detail of the 14th century but the whole building consisting of *Chancel, Nave* and *West Tower* was rebuilt *c.* 1500. At a slightly later date the *North Chapel* was added and the chancel widened towards the N. The church was restored in the 19th century when the N. walls of the chapel and nave were rebuilt.

The early 16th-century roof of the N. chapel is noteworthy.

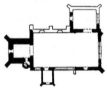

Architectural Description—The *Chancel* (17 ft. by 24¼ ft.) is structurally undivided from the nave. On the E. wall towards the N. is a diagonal buttress not at the true angle and indicating the widening of the chancel. The E. window is of three cinquefoiled lights with tracery in an acute two-centred head of plastered brick and is probably of early 17th-century date. In the N. wall is a four-centred arch probably of the 16th century but entirely covered with cement. In the S. wall is a much restored doorway with moulded jambs and two-centred arch of the 14th century reset.

The *North Chapel* (17½ ft. by 14½ ft.) has in the E. wall an early 16th-century brick window of three four-centred lights with intersecting tracery in a four-centred head with a moulded label and round stops. The N. wall is modern. In the W. wall is a doorway with moulded jambs and four-centred arch in a square head with a moulded label all of brick.

The *Nave* (31¼ ft. by 24¼ ft.) has a modern N. wall. In the S. wall are two modern windows and between them is a reset 14th-century doorway with moulded jambs and two-centred arch.

The *West Tower* (9¾ ft. square) is of three stages with an embattled parapet. The four-centred tower-arch is plastered and of three square orders ; the responds have oversailing capitals and moulded bases. The reset late 14th-century W. window is of three cinquefoiled and sub-cusped lights with vertical tracery in a two-centred head with a moulded label and head-stops ; the reset 14th-century W. doorway has moulded and shafted jambs and two-centred arch with a moulded label. The second stage has in the W. wall a reset late 14th-century window of one trefoiled light with moulded label. The bell-chamber has in the E. and N. walls a brick window of *c.* 1500 and of two four-centred lights under a square head ; in the S. and W. walls are reset late 14th-century windows of stone and each of two cinquefoiled and sub-cusped lights, under a square head.

The *Roof* of the N. chapel is of early 16th-century date and of the hammer-beam type, with moulded rafters ; the embattled wall-plates, the hammer-beams, braces and wind-braces are moulded and richly carved with faces, foliage and flowers of varying designs ; below the middle of the collar-beams are carved pendants and at the ends of the hammer-beams and at the feet of the wall-posts are carved and painted cartouches of the arms of Audley of Walden, added early in the 17th century.

Fittings—*Brass :* In N. chapel—on E. wall, to Thomas Awdeley, 1584, and John Awdeley, 1588, inscription only. *Doors :* In S. doorway—made up of linen-fold and traceried panelling, with strap-hinges and ring handle, early 16th-century. In doorway to turret staircase, of oak battens with moulded fillets, 16th-century. *Font :* octagonal bowl, each face quatrefoiled and enclosing a flower, plain stem and moulded base, 15th or early 16th-century. *Monuments* and *Floor-slabs.* Monuments : In N. chapel—against N. wall, (1) of Sir Henry Audley and Anne (Packington), his wife, erected 1648, in his lifetime, black and white marble monument (Plate, p. 97) with reclining figure of man in armour, in front of base kneeling figures of two sons and three daughters, at back inscribed tablet with side pilasters pediment and cartouche of arms ; on S. wall, (2) to Robert Awdeley, 1624, erected by Katherine (Windsor), his wife ; black and white marble tablet with ornamental border and three shields of arms. Floor-slabs : In chancel—(1) to Anne, daughter of Robert Barker, 1647. In N. chapel (2) to Catherine, wife of Robert Audley, 1641 ; with shield of arms. (3) To Robert Awdeley, with three shields of arms. *Niches :* In N. chapel—in E. wall, two with four-centred heads, early 16th-century, covered with cement. *Paving :* In N. chapel—of black and white marble squares, 17th-century. *Piscina :* In chancel—sill with heptagonal drain, date uncertain. *Recess :* In N. chapel—in S. wall, with four-centred head, early 16th-century, covered with cement. *Screen :* In archway to N. chapel—of wrought-iron with plain strikes, arched bar over entrance, with partly twisted standards and a finial all terminating in large ornamental fleurs-de-lis, 16th or 17th-century.

Condition—Good, but much ivy on walls.

ᵈ(12). PARISH CHURCH OF ST. ANDREW, GREEN-STEAD, stands on a hill to the E. of the Colne. The

COLCHESTER : PRIORY CHURCH OF ST. BOTOLPH ; 12th-century and later.

West Front.

COLCHESTER: PRIORY CHURCH OF ST. BOTOLPH ; 12th-century and later.

walls are of mixed rubble and the W. Tower is of red brick; the roofs are covered with tiles and slates. The W. part of the N. wall of the *Nave* is perhaps of the 12th century. Late in the 16th century the *West Tower* was added. The *Chancel* and the E. part of the nave were refaced but perhaps not entirely rebuilt late in the 18th century and are covered with rough-cast. The *South Chapel* and *Aisle* and the *North Porch* are modern.

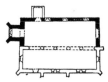

Architectural Description — The *Chancel* and *Nave* (53 ft. by 18 ft.) are structurally undivided. The E. wall is probably old up to the springing of the window-head, where there is a set-off; the E. window is of the 18th century. In the N. wall are three modern windows and further W. is the plastered N. doorway with plain jambs and a round head; the N.W. angle has quoins partly of Roman brick and perhaps of the 12th century. The S. arcade is modern.

The *West Tower* (6 ft. square) is of late 16th-century date and of red brick; it is of three stages with some diapering in black brick and a modern parapet. The plastered tower-arch is two-centred and of two chamfered orders, the outer continuous and the inner resting on modern corbels. The 18th-century W. window is set in an opening with moulded stone jambs of reused material. The second stage has in the N., S. and W. walls a window with a plain segmental head and a modern inserted mullion. The bell-chamber has in each wall a similar but larger window with two inserted mullions.

The *Roof* of the nave is of trussed-rafter type and ceiled, but the old timbers are exposed under the eaves of the N. wall.

Fittings—*Floor-slab:* In chancel—to Thomas Shaw, M.A., 1692, rector of the parish. *Piscina:* In chancel—reset in E. wall, with hollow-chamfered jambs and trefoiled head, cinquefoiled drain, late 13th or early 14th-century. *Plate:* includes an early 17th-century cup. *Recesses:* In chancel— in E. wall, with chamfered jambs and two-centred head, plastered and perhaps modern; in N. wall, with chamfered jambs and segmental-pointed arch, all plastered, probably a 14th-century tomb-recess. In W. tower—in N., S. and W. walls, three, of brick with segmental or three-centred heads, late 16th-century.

Condition—Good, much restored.

b(13). PARISH CHURCH OF ST. LEONARD, LEXDEN, on the S. of the main road, was entirely rebuilt in the 18th and 19th centuries and occupies a site several yards S. of the original church. It contains from the old church the following :—

Fittings—*Bells:* twelve and clock bell; clock-bell uninscribed but probably mediaeval. *Chairs:* In chancel—two, one with enriched and inlaid arcaded back, shaped arms and turned legs, early 17th-century, the other with panelled back, fluted top-rail with brackets, shaped arms and turned legs, early 17th-century. *Monuments:* In church-yard—slabs to (1) Jonathan Woodthorpe, 1683; (2) to Nathaniel Cuffley, 1676 (?); (3) to Penelope (Lucas), wife of Isaac Selfe, 1700, with achievement of arms; headstone (4) to Anne Wilshere, 1707. *Plate:* includes cup of *c.* 1670 with shield of the Lucas arms.

a(14). PARISH CHURCH OF ST. MICHAEL, MILE END, stood on the E. side of the road. The old church fell down in the 19th century and a new church was built in the village in 1854-5. On the site are remains of the rubble foundations of the nave about 18 ft. wide and of indeterminate length; the chancel has entirely disappeared. Near the entrance to the churchyard are two pieces of 14th or 15th-century moulded stonework.

b(15). ABBEY OF ST. JOHN THE BAPTIST, gate-house and precinct wall lies to the S. of St. John's Green. The Abbey was founded late in the 11th century for Benedictine monks by Eudo Dapifer. The buildings have completely disappeared except for the great gatehouse and portions of the precinct wall.

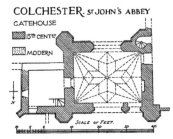

COLCHESTER. ST JOHN'S ABBEY

GATEHOUSE

15ᵀᴴ CENTᵞ

MODERN

SCALE OF FEET.

The *Gatehouse* is of two storeys, the walls are partly of rubble and partly of brick with limestone dressings; the roofs are covered with lead and tiles. It was built probably in the 15th century and has been considerably restored.

Elevations—The *N. Front* (Plate, p. 43) has a moulded plinth, modern parapet and walls faced with knapped flint set in stone panels with cusped heads; this work is mainly original to the ground storey and mainly restored to the upper storey;

the restored work includes a series of lily-pots in stone. Flanking the gate are two octagonal *turrets* of two stages with ornamental cresting, partly restored between the stages and crocketed pinnacles restored at the top. The main outer archway has stop-moulded jambs and four-centred arch of two orders with a moulded label and a square-headed outer label with defaced carved spandrels; the small archway further W. is similar but without labels or spandrels; flanking the main arch are two large niches with trefoiled and crocketed canopies, semi-octagonal on plan and each having a ribbed lierne vault with a central rosette and small supporting shafts in the angles; the brackets are moulded and supported by large half-angels holding shields, that on the E. with the *Agnus Dei* and that on the W. defaced; flanking the niches are shallow buttresses. The upper storey has two windows all modern except the lower part of the jambs of the eastern window; between the windows is a large niche almost entirely restored. The front of the *porter's lodge* adjoining the gatehouse on the E. has a moulded plinth and remains of the junction of a thin wall extending towards the N. Further E. are remains of an original window with a square head, subsequently used as a doorway and now blocked with bricks. The *S. front* has an inner archway with stopped jambs and four-centred arch of two hollow-chamfered orders with a moulded label and head-stops and partly restored. Above it is a window almost entirely modern and the parapet is also modern. The octagonal turrets are finished with crocketed pinnacles.

The *Gate Hall* has a ribbed lierne vault of stone with moulded ribs and ashlar web; at the middle intersection is a defaced carved boss; the ribs spring from moulded corbels carved with two human heads and two lions, one of them winged; in the N.E. angle are marks of the impact of a cannon-ball, probably dating from the period of the siege in 1648. In the E. wall is a doorway with stop-moulded jambs and four-centred head. In the W. wall is a recess with moulded jambs and four-centred head and further S. is a doorway with similar mouldings and head. The porter's lodge, now of two storeys with attics, has no ancient features internally. The rough S. wall seems to indicate that it formerly extended further in that direction. Adjoining the W. side of the gatehouse was a building now destroyed; from it the staircase in the S.W. turret was entered and has two doorways one above the other, each with a four-centred head.

The *Precinct Wall* remains standing for a considerable length on the N.E. and S. sides; it is of rubble and 16th-century brick. There are numerous worked and moulded stones built into a wall on the W. side of the site and also into a pier near the middle of the site. Near the E. wall is a

round construction entirely composed of vaulting ribs and other fragments. Some 12th-century fragments are incorporated in the internal walls of the gatehouse. Other fragments are incorporated in the churchyard wall of St. Giles's Church and the wall N. of the St. John's Green School.

Condition—Of gatehouse, good.

b(16). PRIORY CHURCH OF ST. BOTOLPH, ruins (Plates, pp. 46, 47), stand to the E. of St. Botolph Street. The walls are of flint-rubble and the dressings of Roman brick with a few dressings of Barnack and limestone. The Priory was founded at the close of the 11th century, being the first house of Austin Canons in the country. After the suppression of the priory in 1536 most of the buildings were destroyed, but the nave, or such part of it as was parochial, was retained. The building was entirely ruined in the siege and has ever since remained in that condition. The whole of the existing remains, with the exception of minor alterations, belong to the middle of the 12th century.

The ruins are those of the nave of a conventual church planned on an imposing scale. The use of Roman brick so extensively in a building is unusual and the whole of the wall surfaces were no doubt originally plastered. The detail of the W. front in general and of the W. doorway in particular is noteworthy.

Architectural Description—There are no remains of the eastern arm or crossing of the church.

The *Nave* (27 ft. wide) has remains of the seven western bays; it was originally at least of eight bays and probably of more. The N. arcade has cylindrical piers with bands of Roman brick and capitals of two projecting courses of the same material; the semi-circular arches, of two plain Roman brick orders, remain only in the third, sixth and seventh bays from the W. The triforium has similar arches of two plain orders and all of these remain except that in the W. bay; between the bays are plain pilasters. The clearstorey has been entirely destroyed. The S. arcade has been uniform with that on the N. but only the three W. bays remain and the triforium arch of the third bay has fallen.

The *North Aisle* (9¾ ft. wide) has plain pilaster buttresses to the N. wall and similar responds on the inside from which sprang the former quadri-partite vault; the transverse arch between the seventh and eight bays from the W. remains. The N. wall extends one bay E. of the arcade and has in this bay an original window with a round head; in the next bay is a window of c. 1280 and formerly of two lights in a two-centred head; the mullion has gone; the sixth bay from the W. has a mid 14th-century window of two cinquefoiled lights in a two-centred head; the second, third and fifth bays from the W. have each remains of a similar window; in the fourth bay is an original doorway with a round arch and jambs formerly of

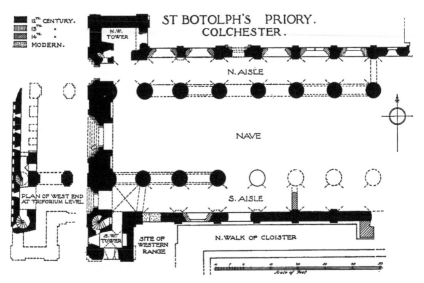

two orders, each with a round shaft; the chamfered bases and part of the inner pair of shafts remain; above the doorway is a round-headed window of the same date.

The *South Aisle* (10 ft. wide) is generally similar to the N. aisle but has remains of a 14th-century window only in the third bay from the W., there are traces of a former doorway in the next bay to the W. and between that and the W. bay the transverse arch of the former vault remains. Across the aisle opposite the fifth column are remains of an inserted wall, indicating the former existence of a chapel.

The *West Front* (Plate, p. 46) extends as one composition the full width of the nave and aisles and was flanked by the two western towers; of these the northern is ruined to near the ground, while of the southern the lowest stage is standing; of the front itself a fragment at the end of the S. arcade rises almost to the full height but the rest is more or less ruined. In the middle of the front is the W. doorway (Plate, p. 50) with round arch of five orders richly ornamented, the outer with a roll-moulding and the rest with various forms of cheveron ornament; the jambs have each six shafts of which two were coupled and attached to the reveal of the doorway; of the others the outer has a cushion capital and the rest richly carved capitals of the same form; three of these remain on the S. and two on the N. side; above the doorway are remains of raking lines of a low

gable of Roman brick; flanking the doorway both inside and out are recesses with round heads and beyond them the two doorways at the ends of the aisles; each of these was of four round orders but of the northern only the base of the jambs remain with four shafts; two of them coupled as in the main W. doorway; of the southern doorway the opening is complete but the stone enrichments and shafts have been removed. Above these doorways and extending across the front are two tiers of wall-arcade with interlacing round arches of Roman brick; at the back of the upper arcade is the triforium passage with small round-headed windows pierced through the back of the arcade. Above this the middle bay has about half of a large round window flanked on the S. by a large round-headed window; in the S. bay at this level are four round-headed recesses in two tiers and above them a round recess. Of the topmost stage of the front only a fragment remains with traces of a wall-arcade.

The *North West Tower* (12½ ft. by 8 ft.) is ruined to the base of the walls.

The *South West Tower* (8½ ft. by 8 ft.) is of the same plan as the N.W. tower and has a barrel-vault, groined back on the N. and S. In the N. wall is a round arch to the aisle and in the W. wall is a round-headed window; there was a similar window in the S. wall, but the wall here is much broken away.

The *Domestic Buildings* lay to the S. of the church, but of these nothing remains except the base of the N. arcade wall of the cloister. A thick rubble wall incorporated in the house, now shop, No. 37 Botolph Street, is probably part of the entrance or gateway to the Priory.

Fittings—*Glass :* In case in S.W. tower—fragments found in the excavations. *Niches :* In nave —in first column from E. of N. arcade, with round head and stone jambs, 12th-century. In cloister— in W. bay of N. wall, with cinquefoiled ogee head and crocketed pinnacles at sides, 14th-century. *Painting :* In N. aisle—on plaster on N. wall, masoned lines, etc., probably 14th-century. *Paving :* In nave and aisles—remains of paving *in situ*, slip-tiles with geometric patterns and shields of arms, (*a*) Clare, (*b*) *a lion passant*, also plain red tiles.

Condition—Now a National Monument, in care of H.M. Office of Works.

b(17). St. HELEN'S CHAPEL, now a parish hall, stands on the W. side of Maidenburgh Street. The walls are of rubble with bonding courses of brick ; the dressings are of limestone and the roofs are tiled. The chapel appears to have been entirely rebuilt late in the 13th century, but under the later walling on the N. side are a few courses of septaria and Roman brick, not quite in the same alignment and either of 12th-century or Roman origin. The building has been restored and partly rebuilt in modern times.

Architectural Description—The *Chapel* (33¼ ft. by 14½ ft.) has an E. window all modern except the late 13th-century chamfered rear-arch and part of the jambs. In the N. wall are two late 13th-century windows each of one pointed light ; the western window has been partly restored. In the S. wall is a similar window, now blocked. In the W. wall are a modern doorway and window ; above the doorway is a pointed relieving arch of Roman brick.

Condition—Good, much restored.

Secular —:

b(18). The CASTLE (Plates, pp. 51, 55, 58, etc.) stands on the N. side of High Street, between it and the N. wall of the town. It consisted of an inner bailey, with the keep or great tower in the middle and an outer bailey covering the ground between the inner bailey and the N. wall of the town. The High Street appears to have been diverted so as to skirt the outer edge of the moat of the inner bailey.

The Keep or Great Tower was built and the earthworks raised late in the 11th century on the site of what has been provisionally identified as the Forum of the Roman town, the keep standing on substructures of Roman date. The walls of the keep show evidence of two ' builds,' following

probably on one another, with only a short interval during which the unfinished walls were provided with a temporary crenelation. No alteration appears to have been made during the rest of the mediaeval period, but there is documentary evidence that the building became ruinous early in the 17th century. The precise date of the destruction of the bailey walls, outer gates, and the filling up of most of the moat is uncertain. In 1693 and the succeeding years the destruction of the keep was begun, but it only extended to the upper storeys. About the middle of the 18th century the existing structures on the tops of the N.E. and S.W. turrets were added. There are modern prison and museum buildings in the S. part of the Keep.

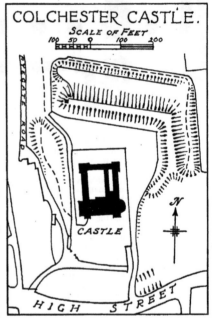

COLCHESTER CASTLE.

The castle is amongst the most important remains of mediaeval military architecture. In area it is the largest Norman keep now remaining in the country.

The *Earthworks* now consist of an inner bailey with a strong rampart and ditch on the N. and E. sides, and traces of a rampart and ditch on the W. Morant states that the bailey was formerly surrounded on the S. and W. sides by a strong wall, in which were two gates. The W. wall reached

THE CASTLE.
South Doorway ; late 11th-century.

PRIORY CHURCH OF ST. BOTOLPH.
West Doorway ; 12th-century.

COLCHESTER.

COLCHESTER CASTLE; late 11th-century and later.
South Front.

nearly as far as the E. side of St. Helen's Lane (now Maidenburgh Street) and the S. wall almost as far as the High Street. The northern rampart is 32 ft. high above the bottom of the ditch and is thrown up upon a Roman wall. The defences on the S. have been destroyed, but recent excavations on the N. side of the High Street indicate that the ditch ran roughly parallel with the street on this side.

The KEEP, or Great Tower (110 ft. by 151½ ft. externally), is now of two storeys with substructures; it was formerly of three storeys or more. The walls are of coursed rubble, consisting of septaria, Roman brick and ragstone, with dressings of Roman brick, Barnack, Caen, and other freestones. The building is of two bays on the N. side and of three on the E. and W., divided by flat pilaster buttresses and having square projecting turrets at three angles and an apse projecting E. from the S.E. angle. The walls have a plain chamfered plinth course of Barnack stone, below which they batter outwards. The lower storey generally has quoins of ashlar while those of the upper storey are chiefly of Roman brick ; near the base of the upper storey on the E. and N. faces is a course of Roman bricks set on edge.

Above this course on the E. and W. faces and on the S.W. turret and lining with the termination of the stone quoins is a series of upright joints, probably representing a temporary crenellation erected during a pause in the building operations. The lower or ground storey is entered by an original doorway (Plate, p. 50) at the W. end of the S. front (Plate, p. 51) ; the round arch is of three moulded orders with a moulded label enriched with a double billet ornament ; the jambs are of two orders ; the side shafts have been removed but the capitals remain, the inner pair being of ornamental cushion form while the outer have crude volutes and a row of conventional leaves ; the capitals also have moulded abaci continued as imposts ; portions of one moulded base remain on the W. side. The reveals of the arch are grooved and slotted for a portcullis. This entrance gives access to a lobby with a modern wall on the E. side ; from the lobby a round-headed arch opens into the main staircase in the S.W. turret. In the space to the E. of the lobby is a large stone and brick steened well. The main building is divided unequally from N. to S. by a cross-wall (Plate, p. 58) and the larger hall was further subdivided by a longitudinal wall or arcade, now destroyed, except at the S. end. This main hall (Plate, p. 58) had in the N. wall two windows with round heads and deep embrasures of two round-headed orders, the outer of Roman brick and the inner of ashlar ; the western of these embrasures has been cut through to form a modern doorway. In the W. wall are three similar windows and embrasures. In the E. wall is a doorway with a round-headed

arch of brick and jambs ; it opens into the smaller hall (Plate, p. 62) which has in the N. wall one and in the E. wall three embrasures and windows similar to those in the large hall except that the southern has been cut through for a modern doorway ; a third window further S. has also been cut through for a doorway, now blocked. S. of the main hall is a room with a plain barrel-vault of rubble and a modernized window in the S. wall. At the S. end of this room is a rectangular sinking (9 ft. by 8 ft.) in the floor, enclosed with stone walls and of doubtful purpose but possibly a cistern. The apse (Plate, p. 54) is divided into five bays externally by pilaster buttresses and contains a barrel-vaulted room with an apsidal end, half-domed ; across the W. end is a cross-vault groined into the main vault ; there are modernized windows in the E. end and at the S. end of the cross-vault. The two northern turrets are solid at this level.

The second storey has an original entrance (Plate, p. 59) in the N. wall of the main hall, now blocked ; it has a plain round arch and was approached by an external flight of steps, now destroyed, but of which the marks are visible on the external wall ; this entrance is commanded by a narrow loop in the N.W. turret, which also contains a circular staircase to the floor above and two garde-robes, one now blocked. In the N. wall of the main hall are four windows and embrasures similar to those in the ground floor but with larger windows. In the W. wall are three pairs of similar windows and embrasures, but the windows of the northernmost pair have been partly restored ; between these pairs of windows are two large fireplaces with rounded backs of herring-bone brickwork and round arches of brick set in a slight projection ; they have double flues. The E. wall at this level is entirely of herring-bone brickwork and has a round-headed doorway with reveals also of herring-bone work. In the N. wall of the smaller hall is a window similar to those in the main hall. The N.E. turret has a barrel-vaulted room and entrance and a modernized window in the E. wall and a narrow original window in the N. wall. The main E. wall has four windows similar to those in the main hall ; the southernmost is now blocked. S. of the third window is a garde-robe in the thickness of the wall with a small barrel-vaulted lobby adjoining it ; there are also two fireplaces similar to those in the main hall. The sub-chapel in the S.E. angle of the building now forms part of the museum, it has a barrel-vault with a half dome over the main apse and groined cross-vaults over the side apses also with half domes. An entrance has at some period been cut at the back of the middle apse on the N. side but the original entrance appears to have been in the western apse on the same side. Here is now a ragged gap, but the original

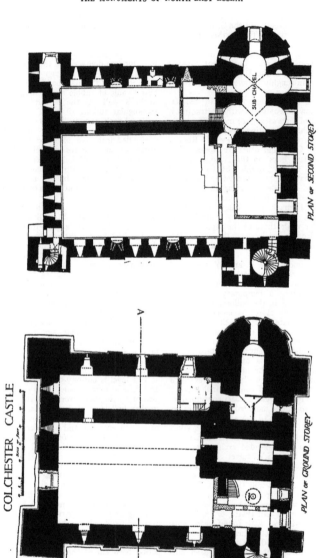

PLAN OF SECOND STOREY

SUB-CHAPEL

PLAN OF GROUND STOREY

COLCHESTER CASTLE

A

B

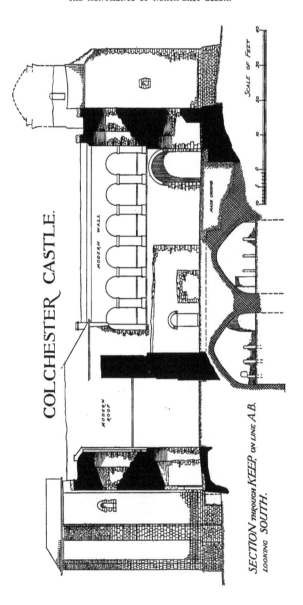

COLCHESTER CASTLE.

SECTION THROUGH KEEP, ON LINE A.B. LOOKING SOUTH.

SCALE OF FEET

drawbar hole remains on the E. side. There is also a ragged gap in the W. wall broken through the back of an apsidal bay in the adjoining part of the building. The windows have been modernized except the two side windows of the main apse which are original. W. of the sub-chapel is a large room with modern N. wall and ceiling and modernized windows. In the S. wall is a reset stone fireplace of late 15th or early 16th-century date, with a moulded segmental-pointed arch with traceried spandrels enclosing shields, one blank and one with a merchant's mark. Flanking the fireplace are early 17th-century carved terminal figures of oak supporting a carved shelf and an overmantel of two bays each with a pair of arcaded panels, which are divided and flanked by carved and coupled Ionic columns standing on open pavilions and supporting a richly carved entablature; the woodwork is not *in situ* and the design is, in places, incomplete. The main staircase in the S.W. turret has a ramped barrel-vault below the stairs (Plate, p. 59).

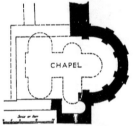

PLAN OF THIRD STOREY.

The third storey has been destroyed except for the base of the walls. The walls of the chapel in the S.E. angle are standing about 4 ft. high and have plain internal responds round the apse. The comparative thinness of the outer wall compared to the thickness of the walls of the sub-chapel below seems to indicate the former existence of an arcade and ambulatory similar to those of the White Tower, London. The projecting turret on the S. of the apse contains at this level a small side chapel with an eastern apse. Remains of stone paving are visible against the S. wall, further W.

There are several carvings and graffiti in various parts of the building. These include in the main entrance (1) inscription in Lombardic capitals " AL YAT FOR ROGER CHANNBYRLEYN & FOR HYS WYF GOD (Y?)EF HEM AL? GODE (L)YF," mid 14th-century, for Robert Chamberlayn, gaoler, and Elena his wife; (2) four sunk panels each with a trefoiled-head and one with a figure in relief of St. Christopher, another man with a staff, and the other two with mitres and crosiers, 14th-

century; on opposite reveal, (3) a trefoil-headed panel with a damaged Crucifixion, 14th or 15th-century. In doorway in cross-wall between main and lesser halls, (4) several roughly cut figures with a spear, bow, etc., a double fleur-de-lis ornament, probably mediaeval and the name JOHN, probably 17th-century. Adjoining doorway on W. face, (5) carved Crucifixion with two attendant figures, 15th-century. In an embrasure in W. wall, (6) design with crossed keys.

The substructures are described under Roman, B (34).

Condition—Of ruins, good; of earthworks, imperfect.

b(19). TOWN HALL on N. side of High Street is modern but the tower contains a bell (from former Town Hall) inscribed " Thomas Marie Sonat In Ethere Clare" and probably of *c.* 1400.

HIGH STREET, S. side :—

b(20). HOUSE (6 and 7 High Street), now the Colchester Club and formerly the White Hart Inn, about 40 yards E. of Head Street. The house was built probably in the 16th century but has been complete altered externally. Inside the building is a fine late 17th-century staircase with close strings, turned and twisted balusters, moulded rails and square newels. There is also an original fireplace of stone with moulded jambs, four-centred arch and spandrels carved with blank shields and foliage. On the ground floor is a late 17th-century panelled door.

Condition—Good, much altered.

b(21). HOUSE and shop (11 High Street), 30 yards E. of (20), is partly of two and partly of three storeys; the walls are timber-framed but the house has a late 18th-century front of brick. The house was built in the 17th century and at the back is a wing of *c.* 1700 forming practically a separate building. The back gable of the main block has original moulded barge-boards. The detached wing has on the S. side a modillioned eaves-cornice and inside is a complete panelled room of *c.* 1700 with bolection-moulding and a dentilled cornice; all the panels have rough paintings of architecture or landscape. The fireplace in the W. wall has a panelled overmantel flanked by pilasters carved with conventional foliage.

Condition—Good.

b(22). HOUSE and shop (12 High Street), E. of (21), is of three storeys; partly of brick and partly of plastered timber-framing. The cellar is probably mediaeval but the house was rebuilt *c.* 1700. The front is of brick with a band between the upper storeys and a modillioned eaves-cornice. Inside the building the cellar has the front and part of one side wall of rubble; the floor above is supported on heavy chamfered beams. On the upper floors

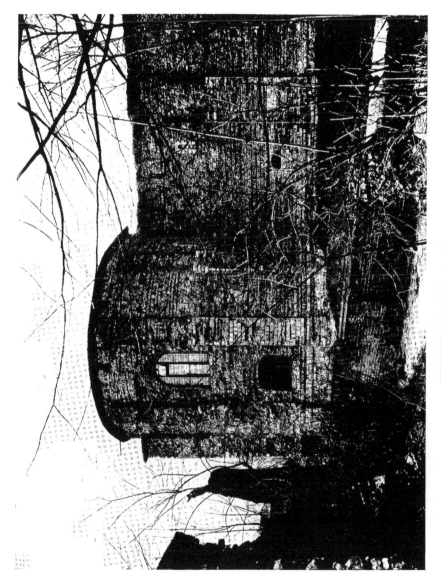

COLCHESTER CASTLE; late 11th-century.
Apse at South End of East Front.

From the North-East.

From the North-West.

COLCHESTER CASTLE ; late 11th-century.

is some early 17th-century panelling and the top part of the staircase is of *c.* 1700 with heavy twisted balusters and moulded string and rail. The E. boundary wall at the rear of the house is of brick and probably of late 16th-century date. Condition—Good.

b(23). HOUSE (13 High Street), E. of (22), was rebuilt late in the 18th century but the cellars are partly of 16th or 17th-century brickwork. Condition—Rebuilt.

b(24). HOUSE, now two houses and offices (23 and 24 High Street), 40 yards E. of (23), is of two storeys, timber-framed and plastered; the roofs are tiled. The house was built probably in the 16th century but there is little to indicate the date. At the back of No. 23 is a detached brick building of *c.* 1660 with moulded band-course between the storeys and between it and the main building is a gallery formerly open and divided into two bays by an oak post in the form of a column with a moulded capital and egg ornament. One window at the back of No. 24 has a 17th-century moulded bracket beneath the sill. Inside the building both parts have some late 16th or early 17th-century panelling. The back staircase of No. 24 is of *c.* 1600 and has a moulded rail, symmetrically turned balusters and ·similar but larger newels with ball caps; a doorway at the foot of the stairs has a rounded head of the same date. The detached building has on the S. wall a reset overmantel, made up of early 17th-century material; it has arcaded panels and moulded pilasters carved with two full length and one terminal figure. Condition—Fairly good.

b(25). HOUSE, now shops (28–30 High Street), 35 yards E. of (24), is of three storeys with attics, partly timber-framed and·plastered and partly of brick; the roofs are tiled. It was built early in the 18th century and has a modillioned eaves-cornice to part of the front. Inside the building is part of an early 18th-century staircase with close string and twisted balusters. Condition—Good.

b(26). HOUSE, now shop (34 High Street), 20 yards E. of (25), is of two storeys with attics, partly timber-framed and plastered and partly of brick; the roofs are tiled. The cellar is probably mediaeval but the house was rebuilt early in the 18th century and has modillioned eaves-cornices both in front and behind. Inside the building the cellar has rubble walls and a lamp-niche in the S. wall; incorporated in the E. wall is a section of Roman building. In the shop is some reused late 16th-century panelling. Condition—Good.

b(27). HOUSE and shops (35–37 High Street), E. of (26), has been completely rebuilt except the cellar which is of the 14th century. In a rubble

wall about 12 ft. S. of the street frontage is an original doorway, with chamfered jambs, two-centred arch and moulded label; E. of the doorway is a square-moulded bracket and W. of it is a fireplace, probably of the 16th century, with chamfered jambs and a back built of alternate courses of brick and tiles; above the modern lintel is a square vent-hole. Condition—Good.

b(28). HOUSE and shop (38 High Street), E. of (27), has a late 14th-century cellar. The house above is perhaps of the 17th century but has been entirely altered. The cellar has rubble walls and a cross-wall running E. and W.; the ceiling has heavy beams resting on posts with massive curved brackets. In the cross-wall is an original doorway with moulded jambs and two-centred arch; the crown is broken away and the doorway has been reset *c.* 1500; an original splay probably of this doorway remains further W. The cross-wall has also two niches with pointed heads and a moulded and embattled bracket of *c.* 1500. The front cellar has two recesses with curved backs and a lamp-niche with a triangular head. Condition—Good.

b(29). HOUSE and shop (39 High Street), E. of (28), is of two storeys with attics partly timber-framed; the roofs are tiled. It was built early in the 16th century but has an 18th-century block on the street front. At the back is a projecting wing with remains of elaborate pargeting of *c.* 1650 on the E. face, consisting of floral scrolls and the initials R. C. D. Inside the building the cellars have mediaeval rubble walls and a pointed niche on the E. side; the floor above has heavy beams and posts with curved brackets. On the first floor one room has original and elaborately moulded ceiling-beams and joists. In the wing is a 16th-century window with moulded jambs and mullion and diamond-shaped intermediate mullions. The staircase landing has a painted dado of late 17th-century date, representing balusters and handrail. Condition—Good.

b(30). RED LION HOTEL (Plate, p. 63), 10 yards E. of (29), is of three storeys, with cellars; the walls are timber-framed and plastered and the roofs are tiled. The cellars have rubble walls and two doorways of *c.* 1400. Of the house, the earliest part is the present kitchen and the bedroom above it which formed part of a two-storeyed hall of *c.* 1470 with the 'screens' at the W. end; there are slight indications of a former cross-wing at the E. end, but if any cross-wing existed at the W. end it must have stood on the adjoining property. About 1500 the house appears to have been turned into an inn; the main block on the street front was built, with two lighting areas, at the back of it and a cart entrance in the middle; to allow of this entrance communicating with the inn-yard at the back, the eastern part of the older hall was pulled down and a new two-storeyed hall built on the W. side of the courtyard. Probably late in the 16th century the E. lighting area was incorporated in the building and late in the 17th century a staircase was inserted between the old and the later halls. Probably in the 18th century the building was extended S. on both sides of the courtyard and still further extensions were made in the 19th century. Early in the 20th century the building was carefully restored.

The house is an important and richly ornamental example of late 15th-century work.

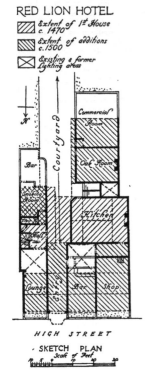

RED LION HOTEL

HIGH STREET

- SKETCH PLAN
Scale of Feet

Elevations — The *North Front* has exposed timber-framing and the two upper storeys and the eaves project ; the roof is finished towards the street with four hipped gables, probably of the 18th century. The projection of the first floor has been underbuilt, except the entrance archway, which is of *c.* 1500, with moulded posts and a four-centred

arch in a square head ; the spandrels are carved with figures of St. George and the dragon ; E. of the archway is a large curved bracket, to the overhang, with carved spandrels and terminating in a carved face ; the moulded bressumer has other carved faces indicating where the former brackets occurred. The second storey is divided into bays by eight shafts with little tabernacles at the top and moulded bases ; from these shafts spring carved brackets terminating in faces and supporting the moulded bressumer above ; the windows on this storey are all modern but the blocked openings of two original windows remain ; the wall-face between the studding is ornamented with two ranges of traceried panels, of which twenty-nine remain in the lower range and six in the upper range. The third storey is divided into bays by shafts of simpler form than those of the storey below ; the moulded bressumer of the eaves is supported on curved brackets, four of them carved. The wall-space has two ranges of traceried panels of which sixteen remain in the lower range and three in the upper ; of the latter, two have a painted decoration of zig-zag bands in white, slate-colour and brown.

The *W. Lighting Area* is built over on the ground floor, but above this level the E. and W. sides are treated in a similar manner to the N. Front. Six traceried panels are preserved on each side. The N. side of the area is covered by modern work.

The *Wing* on the W. side of the courtyard is of two storeys and the upper storey projects on the E. side ; it rests on curved brackets springing from buttressed shafts, with moulded capitals, all of *c.* 1500.

Interior—The *Cellars* have rubble outer walls and a series of brick piers and arches inserted to carry the cartway above. In the N. wall are two doorways of *c.* 1400, with double chamfered jambs ; the former arches have been mostly destroyed, but the jambs retain their old door-hooks.

All the original rooms of the *ground and first floors* of the front block except the shop but including the cartway have moulded ceiling-beams and joists of *c.* 1500 and there are similar joists in the smoking room on the E. side of the courtyard. The former E. lighting area forms the back part of the lounge on the ground floor and has a modern timbered ceiling ; above, it is occupied by a modern staircase and has in the W. wall a window of *c.* 1500 and formerly of eight lights, with moulded mullions and two-centred heads ; half of this window has been removed and the remainder now forms an unplastered partition. On the *second floor* above this window is another with bar-mullions set diagonally ; this window has been partly cut away for a late 16th-century doorway with a four-centred head. In the E. wall of the front block, at this level is a blocked window of three lights with moulded mullions and two-centred heads ; it is set in the wall with the mouldings reversed as though intended to light the adjoining building, but this is probably only a carpenter's error.

The original *Hall block* of *c.* 1470 reduced in length at the E. end now forms the Kitchen and a bedroom above it. The Kitchen has moulded wall-plates, longitudinal beams and tie-beams ; the tie-beam has curved brackets with spandrels richly carved with conventional pomegranate ornament, and springing from much damaged shafts with moulded capitals. The plates and longitudinal beam run into the E. wall and this with the spacing of the bays shows that the Hall formerly extended about 8 ft. further E. Near the W. end of the room is a plain tie-beam with mortices for a partition on the soffit ; it probably formed part of the 'screen.' The bedroom above the Kitchen is similar in arrangement and ornament to the room below, but the details are better preserved. The window in the N. wall has below it an original moulded sill, and in the S. wall an original window of one light with a four-centred head. A room on the first floor of the former E. cross-wing has a moulded ceiling-beam of *c.* 1470, its position indicating that the cross-wing was three bays long. The roof of the original Hall has a plain king-post truss ; the rafters on the N. side retain some of the lathing for the former tiles before the addition of the roof of the front block *c.* 1500.

The *Block* on the W. side of the courtyard is separated from the old Hall by a staircase of *c.* 1700 with turned balusters, close string and moulded handrail ; the ceiling at the foot of the staircase has reused moulded joists of *c.* 1500. The upper storey of this block was originally open to the roof and has a central truss dividing it into two bays ; the truss has a king-post of *c.* 1500 with moulded capital and base.

Condition—Good.

b(31). House, two tenements and shops (45–47 High Street), E. of (30), is of three storeys, timber-framed and plastered ; the roofs are tiled. The cellars below the house are of the 14th century but the house itself was rebuilt probably in the 16th century and much altered early in the 18th century. The wing at the back is possibly of the 17th century. The front has an 18th-century eaves-cornice. At the back the upper storey projects and has a moulded bressumer and carved brackets. The E. face of the back wing has remains of good 17th-century pargeting with strapwork and foliage in panels. Inside the building the cellar has rubble walls and a cross-wall about 12 ft. back from the street frontage. In the cross-wall is a mid 14th-century doorway with widely chamfered jambs and segmental-pointed

arch with a moulded label and one head-stop with a liripipe hood ; further E. is a window of the same date and of a single pointed light ; W. of the doorway is a pointed niche. The shop on the W. has some 16th-century moulded ceiling-beams.

Condition—Good.

b(32). House and shops (48 and 49 High Street), E. of (31), are entirely modern except the cellars which are mediaeval and have rubble walls. The cellar under No. 49 has traces of former ceiling-beams dividing it into four bays and in the N. wall is a rough stone corbel.

Condition—Good.

b(33). Houses and shops (56 and 57 High Street), 45 yards E. of (32), have been practically rebuilt about the middle of the 18th century but stand upon mediaeval cellars with rubble walls. That under No. 57 has heavy ceiling-beams with one curved brace and was formerly of three bays.

Condition—Good.

b(34). House (65 High Street), 35 yards E. of All Saints Church, is of two storeys with attics ; the walls are partly timber-framed and plastered and partly of red brick ; the roofs are tiled. The back wing was built probably in the 17th century but the front block was rebuilt early in the 18th century. The N. front is of brick and has an early 18th-century modillioned eaves-cornice. The upper storey projects on the W. side of the back wing. Inside the building the early 18th-century staircase has a close string, turned balusters and square newels ; in the back wing is a door of moulded battens.

Condition—Good.

b(35). House, three tenements and shops (69–72 High Street), about 50 yards N.E. of All Saints Church, is of three storeys, partly timber-framed and partly of brick ; the roofs are tiled. The back wing of the front block was built early in the 17th century and further S. is a block of the same date and formerly detached ; the block between these two is probably of late 17th-century date and early in the 18th century the block fronting the street was rebuilt. There are extensive modern additions. The N. front is of brick and has an early 18th-century moulded band between the two lower storeys. Inside the building are some 17th-century ceiling-beams and two doorways of the same date with heavy frames.

Condition—Good.

b(36). House and shop, 20 yards E. of (35), is of three storeys, timber-framed and plastered ; the roofs are tiled. It was built probably early in the 17th century but was refronted in brick late in the 18th century. At the back is an early 18th-century addition with a staircase having twisted balusters and square newels. The cellars have heavy ceiling-beams and some of the ceiling-beams are exposed in the main block.

Condition—Good.

b(37). House, called the Minories, E. of (36), is of two storeys with attics, timber-framed and plastered ; the roofs are tiled. The back wing is of early 16th-century date as are the cellars under the main block, which was itself rebuilt and fronted with brick late in the 18th century. Inside the building the cellars of the front block have rubble walls, a number of arched recesses and heavy ceiling-beams. The cellars below the back wing have brick walls with arched recesses and a pavement of bricks set herring-bone wise. In the ground storey of this wing is an original moulded ceiling-beam and on the first floor is an original doorway of moulded and V-shaped battens with moulded frame and muntins. The staircase is of *c.* 1600 and has symmetrically turned balusters and square newels with incised ornament ; there is also some late 16th-century panelling.

Condition—Good.

N. side :—

b(38). Winsleys, house 130 yards W.N.W. of St. James' Church, is of two storeys, timber-framed and plastered ; the roofs are tiled. It was built probably early in the 18th century and has on the S. front an original eaves-cornice, with carved modillions.

Condition—Good.

b(39). Gate House and house adjoining (Plate, p. 122) (83 and 84 High Street), W. of (38), is of two storeys with attics, timber-framed and plastered ; the roofs are tiled. The main block was built late in the 16th or early in the 17th century, but in the second half of the latter century the S. front was rebuilt and an L-shaped addition made on the N. side. The upper storey projects on the whole of the S. front and has a moulded bressumer and large shaped and moulded brackets ; a wall-post at the E. end has a panel with the initials and date $_W{}^B{}_S$ 1680 (probably for William Boys and Sarah his wife). The four gables also project and have a moulded bressumer and barge-boards with carved pendants. The wall faces below the gables are treated with rusticated plasterwork. There are four projecting bay-windows on the first floor, and in the middle is an oval window with a moulded frame. There are also three projecting bays on the ground floor, the space under the fourth above being occupied by a cartway. Inside the building there is some late 17th-century panelling and a door of the same date.

Condition—Good.

b(40). House, now two houses (85 and 86 High Street), W. of (39), is of two storeys with attics, timber-framed and plastered ; the roofs are tiled. It was built late in the 16th century and extended

W. in the 17th century. There is a late 18th-century wing at the back. The upper storey formerly projected both at the front and the back of the main block but has been underbuilt. Inside the building are some exposed ceiling-beams and there is an original doorway with hollow-chamfered frame and four-centred head.

Condition—Good, much altered.

b(41). House and shop (105 High Street), 170 yards W. of (40), is of two storeys with attics, timber-framed and plastered ; the roofs are tiled. It was built in the 17th century but has been much altered. Inside the building are exposed ceiling-beams.

Condition—Good.

b(42). House and shop (106 High Street), at corner of Museum Street and W. of (41), is of two storeys with attics, timber-framed and plastered ; the roofs are tiled. It was built in the 16th century. The upper storey projects on the S. and W. sides and has a curved diagonal bracket at the angle. In the cellar of the building is a fragment of brick and rubble walling.

Condition—Good, much altered.

b(43). House and shop (108 High Street), at W. corner of Maidenburgh Street, is of three storeys, timber-framed and plastered ; the roofs are tiled. It was built probably early in the 16th century, but was entirely remodelled *c.* 1700. The second storey projected on the E. and S. sides, but has been underbuilt on the S. ; at the angle is an original heavy curved bracket. Inside the building the S. room on the first floor has an elaborate early 18th-century plaster ceiling with moulded panels and in the middle an oval wreath of foliage with acanthus · ornament and enclosing sprigs of oak and a sunflower. The space from which the main staircase has been removed has an enriched cornice and a panelled plaster ceiling with a wreath of foliage ; on the E. side is a narrow gallery formerly with a balustrade towards the staircase ; the gallery has a panelled soffit.

Condition—Fairly good, much altered.

b(44). Swán Hotel, 10 yards W. of (43), is of three storeys, timber-framed and plastered ; the roofs are tiled. It was built probably in the 17th century and has a cellar with brick walls and heavy ceiling-beams.

Condition—Good, much altered.

b(45). House and shop (111 High Street), W. of (44), is partly of three and partly of two storeys, timber-framed and plastered ; the roofs are tiled. The back wing is of 15th or early 16th-century date, but the front block was rebuilt early in the 18th century. The S. front has an early 18th-century modillioned eaves-cornice. The upper storey of the back wing projects on the W. side and has an original roof with king-post trusses.

Condition—Good.

Courtyards from top of wall, South-West angle.

West Courtyard from the South-East.
COLCHESTER CASTLE ; late 11th-century.

Staircase in South-west Turret.

Part of North Wall showing original Entrance, now blocked.

b(46). HOUSE and shop (113 High Street), 10 yards W. of (45), is of three storeys, timber-framed and plastered; the roofs are tiled. It was built in the 17th century, but has been almost entirely altered.
Condition—Good, much altered.

b(47). GEORGE HOTEL, 10 yards W. of (46), is of three storeys, timber-framed and plastered; the roofs are tiled. There are remains in the middle of the house of a 15th-century building with a main block and cross-wings; the cellars also are mediaeval but probably of rather later date. The building was probably brought into its present form in the 17th century when the earlier house was entirely enveloped and wings were added at the back. Inside the building the cellars consist of two parallel rooms running E. and W. and each of six bays with heavy ceiling-beams and rubble walls; in the dividing wall is an early 16th-century doorway with chamfered jambs and two-centred head of brick; in the same wall are two fireplaces with four-centred heads and each with a vent-hole above the arch; there are also two early 16th-century niches in the cellar, one with a two and one with a four-centred head. On the ground floor the kitchen has a ceiling-beam with a curved brace resting on a corbel carved with a bearded head. On the second floor at the head of the stairs is an original king-post (Plate, p. xxxvii) with a moulded base and embattled capital; it apparently formed part of the middle truss in the hall of the 15th-century house. In the roof are the original moulded wall-plates of the former E. cross-wing; an early 16th-century beam carved with foliage and nude figure is incorporated in the later roof.
Condition—Good.

b(48). HOUSE and shop (118 High Street), 20 yards W. of (47), is of three storeys, timber-framed and plastered, with modern brick front; the roofs are tiled. It was built in the 15th or early in the 16th century but has no ancient features except the roof which is of two bays with a plain king-post truss, central purlin and curved wind-braces.
Condition—Good, much altered.

b(49). HOUSE, two tenements and shops (119 and 120 High Street), W. of (48), is of three storeys, timber-framed and plastered, with a modern brick front; the roofs are tiled. The cellar is probably mediaeval, with rubble walls and heavy beams dividing it into four bays. The superstructure is perhaps of the 17th century and contains some late 16th-century panelling.
Condition—Good, much altered.

b(50). HOUSE and shops, 80 yards W. of (49), is of two storeys with attics, timber-framed and plastered; the roofs are tiled. It was built in the 17th century or perhaps earlier. The upper storey projects on the S. front.
Condition—Good, much altered.

b(51). ANGEL HOTEL, W. of (50), is modern except for the cellar and a two-storeyed block at the back which is of early 17th-century date. The upper storey of this block projects on the W. side on two brackets richly carved with foliage and a bearded head. Inside the building is some original panelling and the cellar has mediaeval walls of rubble; in one corner is a round stone well-shaft and there is a stone doorway with chamfered jambs and four-centred head; there are three later openings of brick and the cellar has heavy ceiling-beams and joists.
Condition—Good.

b(52). HOUSE and shop (145 High Street), 90 yards W. of (51), is of three storeys, timber-framed and plastered; the roofs are tiled. It was built in the 17th century but has been refronted and a one-storeyed extension built at the back. The two upper storeys project at the back and both of these have original shaped and moulded brackets; the higher projection has a moulded bressumer.
Condition—Good, much altered.

b(53). HOUSE and offices, W. of (52), is of three storeys, timber-framed and plastered, with a modern front; the roofs are tiled. It was built in the 17th century and has a projecting wing at the back. The W. side of this wing has remains of good pargeting enriched with foliage and scrollwork in panels. Inside the building is some original panelling.
Condition—Good, much altered.

b(54). HOUSE and offices (149 High Street), 15 yards W. of (53), is of two storeys, timber-framed and plastered; the roofs are tiled. It was built late in the 15th or early in the 16th century and has an open cartway at the W. end. The upper storey formerly projected in front and on one side of the cartway is an original post with an attached embattled capital with a curved bracket above it. The adjoining house on the E. may have been part of the same building.
Condition—Poor, much altered.

b(55). HOUSE and shop (151 High Street), 10 yards W. of (54), is of three storeys, timber-framed and plastered; the roofs are tiled. It was built probably in the 16th century but the timber-framing in front has been renewed except one curved bracket. The upper storeys both project in front.
Condition—Good, much altered.

HEAD STREET, W. side :—

b(56). HOUSE and shop, No. 21, at S. corner of Church Street North, is of two storeys, timber-framed and plastered; the roofs are tiled. It was built early in the 16th century. The upper storey projects on the E. and N. sides with a heavy curved bracket at the angle. The projection on the N. has an original moulded bressumer and curved brackets springing from attached shafts with moulded capitals.

Condition—Good, much altered.

b(57). HOUSE, now offices and formerly the King's Head Inn, stands back from the road about 60 yards S.W. of (56). It is of two storeys, timber-framed and plastered; the roofs are tiled. The main block was built probably late in the 16th or early in the 17th century but it was remodelled in the 18th century. The base of the chimney-stack at the N. end is original. Inside the building are some original ceiling-beams and panelling. The building N. of the front courtyard and also part of the King's Head Inn is timber-framed and plastered, and probably of the same date.

Condition—Good, much altered.

b(58). HOUSE on street front S.E. of (57), also part of the King's Head Inn, is of two storeys, timber-framed and plastered and with a modern front; the roofs are tiled. It was built in the 16th or 17th century but little of the original work is visible.

Condition—Good, much altered.

b(59). HOUSE, at S. corner of Church Street South, is modern but has an early 17th-century wing at the back, of two storeys, timber-framed and plastered. The upper storey projects on the N. side and under the eaves are original shaped and moulded brackets. The projecting gable at the W. end has a moulded bressumer.

Condition—Good.

E. side :—

b(60). HOUSE (54 Head Street), nearly opposite (58), is of two storeys with attics, timber-framed and plastered. The front is modern. The roofs are tiled. It was built early in the 17th century. The upper storey projects at the back on shaped and moulded brackets, below which are Ionic pilasters carved with terminal figures.

Condition—Good, much altered.

b(61). HOUSE (60 Head Street), S. of (60), is of two storeys with attics, timber-framed and plastered and with an 18th-century front; the roofs are tiled. The cellar is probably mediaeval but the upper part of the house appears to date from the end of the 17th century. It is of half H-shaped plan with the wings extending towards the E. The back has a coved eaves-cornice of plaster, returned round the wings. Inside the building the cellar has rubble walls and heavy hollow-chamfered ceiling-beams with curved braces; the main room (now cut up) is of five bays and there is a small projecting room on the W. The staircase to the cellar has some reused 17th-century panelling. The upper part of the house contains

much bolection-moulded panelling of *c.* 1690 and one room on the ground floor has a fireplace with a marble architrave of the same date.

Condition—Good.

MONUMENTS (62–264).

The following monuments, unless otherwise described, are of the 17th century and of two storeys, timber-framed and plastered; the roofs are tiled. Many of the buildings have exposed ceiling-beams.

Condition—Good, or fairly good, unless stated.

NORTH HILL, E. side :—

b(62). *House* and shop (2 North Hill), 35 yards N. of St. Peter's Church.

b(63). *House* (8 North Hill), 50 yards N. of (62), has a modern front block. At the back there are additions, extending eastwards; the middle one is of the 16th century and has a projecting upper storey on the N. side; the other two are of the 17th century the easternmost being of brick. There is a blocked five-light window in the S. wall of the middle building.

b(64). *House* and shop (12 North Hill), 45 yards N. of (63), is probably of the 16th century and has, at the S. end, a cartway into Crispin Alley.

b(65). *House* and shops (13–15 North Hill), N. of (64), was built in the 15th century on an L-shaped plan with the wings extending towards the E. and S. In the 17th century the W. part of the S. wing was rebuilt and the N. wing of the street front added. The upper storey projects on the S. side of the E. wing; in the ground storey is an original window of two cinquefoiled ogee lights with a square head; further W. is a blocked doorway with a four-centred head. In the N. wall of the same wing are two late 16th-century windows one of five and one of three lights and with moulded mullions. Inside the building on the first floor part of the original block has a moulded and embattled wall-plate. One room has remains of painted decoration, foliage and geometric patterns, in green, yellow and red and of late 16th-century date. The roof of the E. wing has original king-post trusses.

b(66). *Durlston House* (18 North Hill), 25 yards N. of (65), is perhaps of the 16th century but has been much altered; there is a 17th-century kitchen wing at the back.

b(67). *House* and shop (19 and 20 North Hill), N. of (66), has a front block of the 16th century, refaced with brick in the 18th century; at the back is a long early 17th-century wing and a later wing in the angle between it and the front block.

b(68). *House* (24 North Hill), 25 yards N. of (67), was built probably in the 16th century but has an 18th-century brick front.

Condition—Poor.

b(69). *Marquis of Granby Inn*, N. of (68), was built early in the 16th century on an L-shaped plan with the wings extending towards the E. and S. ; there is a modern addition in the angle. The E. wing has particularly good carved detail. The upper storey projects on the W. front and also on the N. side of the E. wing ; below it are two original windows each of six lights, with moulded mullions. At the S. end of the S. wing is a passage with original moulded ceiling-beams and two doorways (Plate, p. 100) with four-centred heads and spandrels carved with foliage and grotesque heads. Inside the building the main room of the E. wing has original moulded ceiling-beams and joists, it is divided into two bays by a heavy transverse beam (Plate, p. xxxvii) richly carved with acanthus foliage, birds, beasts, boys, griffons, eagles and grotesques ; in the middle is a shield with the initials H. M. or W., intertwined with a knot ; the beam rests on wall-posts with capitals carved with figures in early 16th-century costume ; the wall-plates have acanthus enrichment. The modern fireplace has an original lintel, moulded and carved with seven medallions of male and female heads. A cupboard in the room has linen-fold panelling. The other rooms on the ground floor have original moulded ceiling-beams and joists and one beam has in the middle a cartouche carved with a crowned grotesque head and foliage. On the first floor the main room in the E. wing has an original moulded ceiling-beam.

b(70). *House*, four tenements and shops (26–29 North Hill), N. of (69), was built late in the 15th or early in the 16th century, but has been much altered. The upper storey projects on most of the W. front. Inside the building is an original doorway with a four-centred head.

W. side :—

b(71). *House and shop*, nearly opposite (68), was built early in the 16th century but this part of the building is now largely pulled down, only the W. and S. walls remaining ; the rest of the house was rebuilt probably in the 17th century. The ruined building has an original moulded door-frame in the E. wall and two original doorways in the S. wall, both blocked ; the passage between it and the 17th-century part has original moulded ceiling-beams.
Condition—Partly ruinous.

b(72). *House* (45 and 46 North Hill), 50 yards S. of (71), is partly of three storeys ; it was built in the second half of the 16th century. The front block was remodelled early in the 18th century and has a coved eaves-cornice of plaster. The upper storeys project on the N. side of the back wing and have original shaped brackets.

b(73). *Cock and Pye Inn* and house (55 and 56 North Hill), 75 yards S. of (72), is of half H-shaped plan with the wings extending towards the W. The N.W. wing is probably of 15th or early 16th-century date with a 17th-century extension on the W. The S.W. wing, extending to the street, was built late in the 16th century. The rest of the building was rebuilt and the whole refronted in the 18th century. The upper storey projects on the N. side of the original N.W. wing and on part of the N. side of the S.W. wing ; on the first floor of the latter is the moulded sill of a projecting 16th-century window with two shaped brackets.

b(74). *House* (57 North Hill), S. of (73), has a projecting upper storey on the E. front. The door to the cellar is original and of moulded battens. Inside the building is a moulded ceiling-beam, probably reused.

b(75). *St. Peter's Vicarage*, 15 yards S. of (74), has walls of red brick. It was largely rebuilt late in the 18th century except for a portion of an early 18th-century house at the S.W. angle. The staircase is original but not *in situ ;* it has twisted balusters, square newels and moulded close string.

b(76). *House* (60 North Hill), S. of (75), has an early 17th-century back wing. The front block was rebuilt about the middle of the 18th century but incorporates an earlier staircase. Inside the building the early 18th-century staircase is of the dog-legged type with square panelled newels, turned balusters and moulded strings. There is also some moulded panelling probably of the same date. The back wing has original ceiling-beams resting on an octagonal post with a moulded capping. There are several old battened doors.

b(77). *House* (63, North Hill), 25 yards S.W. of (76), has been much altered. Inside the building is a carved bracket of early 16th-century type, reused.

b(78). *House* (64 and 65 North Hill), S.E. of (77), is of three storeys and has been almost completely altered.

b(79). *Waggon and Horses Inn*, S. of (78), is of three storeys, has been very much altered and restored ; the upper storeys project on the E. front.

b(80). *House* and shop (67 North Hill), S. of (79), is of three storeys. The second wing projects on the E. front.

———

b(81). *Range of tenements* on N. side of Cistern Yard and 45 yards W. of (70). The western part was built probably in the 17th century but the eastern is of early 18th-century date. The whole range stands partly on the N. wall of the town. A doorway at the E. end of the S. side has an oval plaster panel, above it, with the date 1702. On the N. side the upper storey of the W. block projects. Inside one tenement are two 15th-century moulded beams, reused.

NORTHGATE STREET, N. side :—

b(82). *House,* two tenements (4 and 6 Northgate Street), 45 yards E. of North Hill.

b(83). *House* (10 Northgate Street), 15 yards E. of (82).

b(84). *House,* now tenements (34 Northgate Street), 70 yards E. of (83). The walls are of red brick. It was built *c.* 1620 on an L-shaped plan with the wings extending towards the W. and N. The storeys are divided by a moulded brick string and the eaves-cornice has shaped modillions also of brick. There are many original windows which formerly had moulded mullions and square moulded labels ; some are now blocked but one, on the E. side, is of four lights.
Condition—Bad.

S. side :—

b(85). *House,* two tenements (13 and 15 Northgate Street), 35 yards W.S.W. of (84), has a projecting upper storey on the N. front, supported by three heavy shaped brackets.

WEST STOCKWELL STREET, E. side :—

b(86). *House* (Plate, p. 63), (3–6 W. Stockwell Street), 55 yards N. of High Street, was built late in the 15th century. The front part of No. 6 appears to be of rather earlier date and to have been the original Hall with a two-storeyed wing at the back. The double-gabled building (No. 3) incorporates the ' screens ' passage at the N. end and has a projecting upper storey with a moulded bressumer and curved brackets springing from shafts with capitals carved as angels ; the timber-framing of this part is exposed and has been partly restored but the framing for the windows is mostly original. The northernmost light on the ground floor, and the N. half of the window above it have original traceried heads. The two doorways have four-centred heads ; that on the N. opens into the former ' screens,' a passage with three original doorways across it and two on the S. side all with four-centred heads. Inside the building the front block of No. 6 has an original moulded wall-plate and remains of the former king-post roof-truss ; the back wing has an original king-post truss. The roof of the N. part of No. 3 is similar. Braced beams in the S. wall of the front rooms show that the building formerly extended further to the S. It was said to have formed part of the Angel Inn.

b(87). *House* (10 W. Stockwell Street), 15 yards N.W. of St. Martin's Church, has a 16th-century wing at the back forming two tenements ; the front block was rebuilt early in the 18th century. The back wing has an original window of three lights with moulded mullions.
Condition—Poor.

b(88). *House* (13 W. Stockwell Street), 10 yards N. of (87), has a projecting upper storey on the W. front.

b(89). *House* (14 W. Stockwell Street), N. of (88), was built probably in the 16th century and has a cross-wing at the N. end. The upper storey projects on the N. and W. sides of the cross-wing with a 17th-century shaped bracket. The gable has moulded barge-boards.

b(90). *House,* three tenements (14A–16 W. Stockwell Street), N. of (89), has a projecting upper storey on the W. front.

b(91). *House* (17 W. Stockwell Street), N. of (90). The former projecting upper storey on the W. front has been underbuilt.

b(92). *Stockwell Arms Inn,* N. of (91), was built probably late in the 15th or early in the 16th century but the S. part of the house has been either rebuilt or completely altered. There is a cross-wing at the N. end with a projecting upper storey on the N. and W. sides, with a moulded and embattled bressumer ; at the angle is a heavy diagonal bracket springing from a moulded capital carved with a defaced angel ; the subsidiary brackets are curved and spring from small shafts with moulded capitals ; the shafts are mostly cut away or buried. Inside the building are some original moulded ceiling-beams.

b(93). *House,* three tenements (20–22 W. Stockwell Street), 10 yards N. of (92). The upper storey projects and is gabled in the middle and W. bays of the S. front.

b(94). *House,* two tenements (23 and 24 Stockwell Street), 10 yards N.W. of (93), was built in the 15th century and has a cross-wing at the E. end. The upper storey projects on the S. front on curved brackets. The E. side has exposed timber-framing and an original doorway with a four-centred head.
Condition—Bad.

b(95). *House,* three tenements (25–27 W. Stockwell Street), N.W. of (94). The upper storey projects on the S.W. front of the two eastern tenements.

b(96). *House* (Plate, p. 65), three tenements (29–32 W. Stockwell Street), 15 yards N.W. of (95), is of three storeys and was built *c.* 1600. The upper storeys project on the W. front and there are three gables ; the projections have elaborately shaped brackets and the upper one a moulded bressumer.

b(97). *House,* two tenements (35 W. Stockwell Street and 21 Northgate Street), at corner, 25 yards N. of (96), has an early 18th-century wing on the S. side. On the S. side is an original shaped bracket to the eaves.
Condition—Poor.

W. side :—

b(98). *House,* two tenements (36 and 37 W. Stockwell Street), opposite (97), was built early in the 16th century and has a cross-wing at the

COLCHESTER CASTLE ; late 11th-century.
East Courtyard from the South.

(30) Red Lion Hotel, High Street. North Front; *c.* 1500.

(86) House, No. 3 West Stockwell Street; late 15th-century.
COLCHESTER.

N. end.   Inside the building are some original moulded joists and some 17th-century doors of moulded battens.

Condition—Partly ruinous.

ᵇ(99). *House* (Plate, p. 123), two tenements and shop (53 and 54 W. Stockwell Street), opposite (90), was built in the 15th century with cross-wings at the N. and S. ends. The N. cross-wing was rebuilt in the 17th century. The upper storey projects at the E. ends of the cross-wings on curved brackets. Inside the building are original cambered tie-beams and wall-posts.

ᵇ(100). *House* (Plate, p. 123) (55 W. Stockwell Street), S. of (99), has a projecting upper storey on the E. front.

ᵇ(101). *House* (Plate, p. 123) (56 W. Stockwell Street), S. of (100), was built in the 16th century and has an extension of *c.* 1700 at the back. The upper storey projects at the E. end with curved brackets.

ᵇ(102). *House* (62 W. Stockwell Street), 45 yards S. of (101), was built *c.* 1600 but the S. part of the house is a late 17th-century addition. The front is modern. Inside the building is some early 17th-century panelling and an overmantel of four arched bays resting on pilasters and having a strapwork frieze. There is one original window, with moulded mullions and now blocked.

Stockwell S. side :—

ᵇ(103). *House*, two tenements and formerly Workhouse, 15 yards E. of (92).

ᵇ(104). *House*, two tenements, E. of (103).

East Stockwell Street, W. side :—

ᵇ(105). *House*, now three tenements Nos. 30–32 and 30 yards S. of Stockwell. The S. tenement is probably part of a late 14th-century house and includes the 'screens' of a former Hall extending towards the N. In the 15th century a wing was added W. of the original block and about the middle of the 16th century a three-storeyed building replaced the former Hall. The N. tenement is of *c.* 1500 and may have been a separate building. At the back is a small almost detached wing, partly of the 17th century. The upper storey projects at different levels on the whole of the E. front ; the gable of the middle block also projects and has a 16th-century moulded bressumer. The former 'screens' has at the E. end an original doorway, but with the head removed. Further S. are remains of the head of a 15th-century doorway or window. On the N. side of the W. wing is a 15th-century window with diamond-shaped mullions ; further W. are two late 17th-century windows with solid frames. Inside the building the former 'screens' has in the S. wall two original doorways with moulded jambs and two-centred heads ; in the N. wall are two square-headed doorways ; one of the 15th or 16th

century and one later ; at the W. end of the passage is a doorway with an ogee head, probably original. The middle block has 16th-century moulded ceiling-beams. The W. wing has a 16th-century fireplace with a moulded lintel and on the first floor are remains of a 15th-century king-post roof.

ᵇ(106). *House*, two tenements, Nos. 38 and 39, 25 yards S. of (105), was built in the 16th century with a cross-wing at the S. end. The upper storey projects at the E. end of the cross-wing ; a door on this side is of moulded battens.

ᵇ(107). *Stockwell House*, 60 yards S. of (106), has an early 18th-century front of brick with a moulded band-course between the storeys. Inside the building are some early 17th-century moulded ceiling-beams and moulded wall-posts. The staircase of *c.* 1700 has twisted balusters and a moulded rail. There is also an early 17th-century door of moulded battens.

E. side :—

ᵇ(108). *House*, No. 14, 25 yards N. of St. Helen's Lane, has a projecting upper storey on the W. front.

Condition—Poor.

ᵇ(109). *The Gables*, house opposite (107), has a projecting upper storey at the W. end. Inside the building the wall running N. and S. on the W. of the staircase is of rubble.

ᵇ(110). *House*, 60 yards S. of (109), has been much altered.

ᵇ(111). *House*, No. 1, and shop on E. side of George Street, 20 yards N. of (46), has a projecting upper storey on the S.E. side. In the cellar is a rubble wall running E. and W.

Maidenburgh Street, W. side :—

ᵇ(112). *House*, No. 61, 55 yards N. of St. Helen's Chapel, is part of a larger 15th-century house. The roof has an original king-post truss.

Condition—Poor.

ᵇ(113). *House*, two tenements, Nos. 51 and 52, 45 yards N. of (112), has a projecting upper storey on the E. and S. sides, with three heavy shaped brackets in front.

E. side :—

ᵇ(114). *Cottage* and shop, No. 10, 15 yards S.E. of St. Helen's Chapel, was built late in the 16th or early in the 17th century and no doubt formed part of a larger building. The front is of modern brick. Inside the building the shop and the room behind it, formerly one room, have a rich plaster ceiling of *c.* 1600 and divided into panels by intersecting ribs with foliated bosses and terminals ; two panels have rose sprigs. The ceiling has been partly cut away for the staircase. Above the fireplace in the S. wall is a plaster panel representing a pot from which a conventional orange tree is growing.

b(115). *House*, two tenements and shop, Nos. 14 and 15, 15 yards N. of (114), has a projecting upper storey on the W. side.

b(116). *House*, three tenements, Nos. 18–20, 10 yards N. of (115), has an early 18th-century front of brick.

b(117). *House*, No. 23, 25 yards N. of (116), has a S. part of rather later date than the rest. The upper storey projects on the W. side and has one original shaped bracket. Inside the building are two original battened doors.

b(118). *House*, three tenements, Nos. 27–29, 30 yards N. of (117).
Condition—Poor.

b(119). *House*, No. 33, 15 yards N. of (118).

b(120). *House*, two tenements, Nos. 39 and 40, 30 yards N. of (119), has walls of red brick and was built early in the 18th century. There is a band-course dividing the storeys.

----

b(121). *House*, on W. side of Ryegate Road, and 30 yards S.W. of the castle, is modern but incorporates a 16th-century lintel or the base beam of a gable ; it is carved with foliage and has a diamond-shaped boss in the middle.

CULVER STREET, N. side :—

b(122). *House*, at corner of St. Nicholas Street, is of three storeys with two gables on the W. front. The second storey projects on the W. and S. sides and the two gables also project on large shaped brackets.

b(123). *House*, No. 12, standing back from the road 100 yards W. of Pelham's Lane, was built early in the 18th century and has a brick front with a band-course between the storeys and a modillioned eaves-cornice.

(123A). *House*, on S. side of road, 90 yards W. of Trinity Street, was built probably in the 17th century, but was largely rebuilt and refitted early in the 18th century.

S. side :—

b(124). *House*, now office, at W. corner of Lion Walk, has a projecting gable on the E. side. Inside the building on the W. of the main block is a short length of mediaeval rubble wall with a reset doorway of stone with a segmental head.

b(125). *Finch Almshouses*, 70 yards E. of (124), have been entirely rebuilt but reset at the end of the courtyard is a 17th-century stone tablet recording the foundation by Ralph Finch in 1552.

b(126). *Cross Keys Inn*, at the E. corner of Long Wyre Street, has at the back a small early 16th-century block with a projecting upper storey on the E. side. Inside this wing are some original moulded ceiling-beams and joists. The cart entrance has old timber-work with curved brackets.

b(127). *House*, formerly Grammar School, now garage, 40 yards E. of (126), was built early in the 16th century and the ground floor has original moulded ceiling-beams and joists.

b(128). *All Saints Court*, tenements E. of (127). A T-shaped block on the W. side of the court was built late in the 16th century the cross-wing being at the N. end ; to the N. of this is a cellar of about the same date. The N. range of the courtyard is of the 16th or 17th century and the rest of the buildings of the 18th century. There are some 16th-century windows with moulded mullions. Inside the building the cellar has rubble walls, a doorway with a two-centred head and a number of recesses ; on the S. side are three narrow bays with quadripartite vaulting and divided up by modern partitions. The cross-wing of the original building appears to have been originally of one storey and three bays long ; it has richly moulded wall-plates, hollow-chamfered tie-beams and collars with curved braces forming two-centred arches ; the trusses have been partly cut away. The staircase is of late 17th-century date with turned balusters and moulded hand-rail. The wing extending S. has original moulded wall-plates and beams ; in the W. wall is a moulded corbel formerly supporting a curved brace.

b(129). *Range of two houses*, Nos. 69 and 71, at the W. corner of Queen Street, are of red brick with a moulded band between the storeys. They were built probably early in the 18th century and have sash windows with flush frames. The western house has an oval window in addition and an eaves-cornice. The eastern house has a later parapet and inside it one room is lined with original panelling and has a fireplace with egg and tongue ornament and swags.

----

b(130). *House*, now workshop, on E. side of Pelham's Lane and S. of (26), has a projecting upper storey on the W. side.

QUEEN STREET :—

b(131). *House*, two tenements, Nos. 7 and 9, on E. side of road opposite All Saints' churchyard, has a cross-wing at the N. end with a projecting upper storey.

b(132). *Range of four houses*, Nos. 6–12, on W. side of road 30 yards S.W. of (129), is of red brick, with a band-course between the storeys. It was built *c*. 1698 the date on a small panel near the middle of the front. The S. part of the building retains its original modillioned eaves-cornice but the rest has a later parapet. One doorway has an original architrave with egg and tongue ornament. Inside the building is some 17th-century panelling and an original fireplace with a moulded architrave.

Schere Gate : (148–151) Houses ; 16th and 17th-century.

East Street : North side, showing (231) Siege House ; late 15th-century, etc.

COLCHESTER.

(96) Nos. 29–32 West Stockwell Street; *c.* 1600.

(194, etc.) East Hill, South Side ; 16th century and later.

(217) Nos. 29–33 ; late 16th-century ; Front dated 1692.

(214–216) Nos. 24–26 ; 15th to 17th-century.

EAST STREET, SOUTH SIDE.

(191) Nos. 5–7 Priory Street; 17th-century.

(228–230) Nos. 60–65; 15th to 17th-century.

EAST STREET, NORTH SIDE.

b(133). *House,* Nos. 20–24, now shop, 30 yards S. of (132), has a projecting upper storey on the E. front; the interior has been completely gutted.

Long Wyre Street, W. side :—

b(134). *House* and shop, 45 yards S. of Culver Street has a projecting and gabled upper storey on the E. front.

b(135). *Range of houses* and shops, Nos. 17–23, S. of (134), has a projecting upper storey on the E. front.

b(136). *House,* two tenements and shops, Nos. 33 and 35, 55 yards S. of (135), has a projecting upper storey in front.

b(137). *House,* No. 37, and shop at corner of Eld Lane and S. of (136), was built early in the 16th century. The upper storey projects on the E. and S. sides with a heavy diagonal bracket at the angle and has four curved brackets on each face.

Trinity Street, W. side :—

b(138). *The Bays* and two adjoining houses, at W. corner of Culver Street, have walls of brick, now covered with rough-cast. A timber-framed wing at the back may be of early 17th-century date but the whole of the front block appears to have been rebuilt about the middle of the same century. There is a plain band-course between the storeys and above this the E. and W. walls are divided into bays by shallow pilasters; those on the W. side have Ionic capitals but on the E. these have been removed. The N. end has a series of sunk panels and pilaster strips. Inside the building the middle tenement has some late 16th-century panelling, reused.

b(139). *House,* 15 yards S. of (138), has walls partly of brick and partly timber-framed. It was built early in the 18th century and has a red brick front with a band-course between the storeys and a modillioned eaves-cornice. Inside the building there is some original panelling and a staircase with turned balusters and a close string.

b(140). *House,* S. of (139), was built in the 16th century, but has no old features externally. Inside the building, both the ground and first floors have original moulded ceiling-beams.

b(141). *Tymperleys,* house W. of (140), was built late in the 15th or early in the 16th century and has a lower wing, little later in date, at the E. end. The upper storey projects on the S. front and has curved and hollow-chamfered brackets. On the first floor, at the E. end, is an original doorway with a four-centred head; it is now blocked but may have opened on to an external staircase; that the house extended further in this direction is negatived by the existence of the almost contemporary E. wing. Inside the building the ground floor has some original moulded ceiling-beams and the roof

has an original octagonal king-post with moulded capital and base and four-way struts. The staircase projects at the back, and has late 17th-century twisted balusters, close string and square newels with turned pendants. The E. wing has original moulded ceiling-beams.

b(142). *House,* S. of (140), was built probably in the 15th century and is of L-shaped plan with the wings extending towards the S. and W. The W. wing has exposed timber-framing, formerly internal, on the N. side and two original blocked doorways with pointed heads. The S. wing has been much restored; the upper storey projects on most of the E. side and there is a short length of original embattled bressumer. Near the S. end is an archway with some reset 17th-century panelling. Inside the building the W. wing has an original roof-truss with an octagonal king-post with a moulded capital. A room on the first floor has the initials and date in plaster—E. R. A. R. M. R. 1670. Another room is lined with panelling of *c.* 1700 and a short length of staircase has turned balusters and moulded rail of the same date.

b(143). *House,* three tenements, Nos. 12–14, 10 yards S. of (142), was built probably in the 16th century but has been much altered. It is of half H-shaped plan with the wings extending W. The upper storey projects on part of the E. side and at the ends of the wings.
Condition—Poor.

E. side :—

b(144). *House,* two tenements, Nos. 25 and 26, opposite (142), has a cross-wing at the N. end. The upper storey projects at the W. end of the cross-wing.

b(145). *House* and shop, No. 22, 10 yards S. of (144), has a projecting upper storey on curved brackets at the W. end.
Condition—Poor.

b(146). *Clarence Inn,* 30 yards S. of (145), was built probably in the 16th century, but has been much restored. The upper storey projects on the W. and S. sides.

———

b(147). *House,* three tenements, Nos. 12–14, on N. side of Sir Isaac's Walk, 50 yards W. of Trinity Street, was built probably early in the 18th century. The S. front has a coved eaves-cornice of plaster with the date, probably 1711, but a modern painted 16 replaces the 17. In the roof are a series of hipped dormers.

b(148). *Schere Gate* (Plate, p. 64), house, gateway and shop, opposite (146), has a projecting upper storey on the whole of the N. front, with curved brackets. The house is built partly on the town wall and the gateway of old timber-framing, but without character, replaces a former postern.

b(149). *House* and shop (Plate, p. 64), S. of (148) and on W. of Schere Gate, has a projecting upper storey on the E. side with one original shaped bracket.

b(150). *House* and shop (Plate, p. 64), opposite (149), has on the W. front a coved eaves-cornice of plaster and an oval panel with the date 1692.

b(151). *House* and shop (Plate, p. 64), 10 yards S. of (149) and at corner of St. John's Street, was built probably in the 16th century. The upper storey projects on the S. and E. sides with an original heavy diagonal bracket at the angle, carved on both faces with conventional foliage and springing from a moulded capital. Inside the building is an original beam carved with foliage, but not *in situ.*

b(152). *House*, on S. side of St. John's Street, 50 yards W.S.W. of (151), has a projecting upper storey on the N. side with original shaped brackets.

b(153). *House*, No. 23, on S. side of Stanwell Street, 55 yards E. of Abbeygate Street. The front has a moulded eaves-cornice of *c.* 1700 ; the back wing is probably of rather earlier date.

b(154). *House*, two tenements, Claudius House and the next house, on N. side of Vineyard Street, 10 yards E. of Schere Gate. The E. part of the house has a moulded eaves-cornice with carved modillions and below it a plaster frieze with vine enrichment. The W. part has a coved cornice of plaster. Inside the building is a late 17th-century staircase with close string, twisted balusters and newels with turned pendants.

b(155). *House*, on S. side of Vineyard Street, 50 yards W. of St. Botolph's Street, is an 18th-century building but incorporates a late 16th-century doorway with stop-moulded frame and square head.

b(156). *House*, four tenements, Nos. 11–14, on N. side of St. John's Green, 120 yards W. of St. Giles' Church, was built probably in the 16th century. The upper storey projects on the S. front on curved brackets.

b(157). *House*, at S.W. corner of St. John's Green, 100 yards S.W. of (156).
Condition—Poor.

St. Botolph's Street, E. side :—

b(158). *House* and shop, at S. corner of Priory Street, has a projecting upper storey on the W. side.

b(159). *House*, two tenements and shops, Nos. 40 and 41, 15 yards S. of (158). The projecting eaves on the W. side have two original brackets carved with acanthus ornament and a small head.

b(160). *Winnock's Almshouses*, on S. side of Military Road, 320 yards E.S.E. of St. Giles'

Church, is a long block of tenements of red brick. It was built *c.* 1678 and is a good example of the brickwork of the period. The N. front is divided into two bays by pilasters and into storeys by a continuous entablature ; the middle bay has a plain pediment and the two middle doorways (Plate, p. 176) are combined to form an architectural composition with pilasters surmounted by half-balls and a broken voluted pediment ; under the pediment are two sunk panels with the initials and date I^WM 1678. The doors of the six tenements are original and have each two large panels, bolection-moulded. The back is plain but the doors to the ground floor mostly have old frames.

Magdalen Street, N. side :—

b(161). *House*, No. 187, 320 yards E. of St. Giles' Church. The upper storey projects on the E. side on heavy hook-shaped brackets. There is a late 17th-century addition on the street front. Inside the building the former projection of the upper storey on the S. of the original block is visible.

b(162). *House*, No. 181, 35 yards E. of (161).

b(163). *House*, No. 166, 110 yards E. of (162), has a projecting upper storey on the street front.
Condition—Bad.

b(164). *House*, two tenements, Nos. 164–5, E. of (163), has a cross-wing at the W. end. The upper storey projects at the end of the cross-wing.
Condition—Bad.

b(165). *Baker's Arms Inn*, 240 yards E. of (164), has a projecting upper storey on the S. side but has been almost completely altered.

b(166). *House* and shop, No. 111, W. of St. Mary Magdalene churchyard. The upper storey formerly projected but has been underbuilt.

S. side :—

b(167). *House*, No. 35, now institute, 25 yards S.E. of (162). The upper storey projects on the N. side.

b(168). *House*, three tenements, Nos. 43–5, 60 yards E. of (167), has a gabled cross-wing at the E. and W. ends.
Condition—Poor.

b(169). *House*, No. 53, including entry to Brown's Yard, 40 yards E. of (168).

b(170). *House*, two tenements and shop, Nos. 81 and 82, 170 yards E. of (169).

b(171). *Inn*, No. 29, on N. side of Barrack Street, 120 yards E. of St. Mary Magdalene Church, has a modern block on the street front.

Hythe Hill, N. side :—

d(172). *House*, No. 133 (Plate, p. 123), now tenements, W. of Hythe churchyard, was built probably in the 15th century. The upper storey projects on the whole of the S. front, on curved brackets. Inside the building the main block has an original king-post roof-truss.

Condition—Poor.

d(173). *Dolphin Inn* and house, No. 127, 30 yards E. of Hythe Church, has cross-wings at the E. and S. ends. The upper storey of the main block and E. wing project on the S. front. Inside the building the W. wing has an early 18th-century staircase with close string and twisted balusters.

d(174). *House*, two tenements, Nos. 124–5, E. of (173).

Condition—Poor.

d(175). *House*, two tenements and post-office, Nos. 122–3, E. of (174), was remodelled or rebuilt early in the 18th century. The front has a modillioned eaves-cornice and original first floor windows ; at this level is a panel surrounded by a much damaged plaster wreath ; the plaster face of the wall has large square panels.

d(176). *House*, three tenements, 20 yards E. of (175).

d(177). *House*, No. 103, 70 yards E. of (176), has a projecting upper storey on the S. side.

S. side :—

d(178). *House* (Plate, p. 123), three tenements, Nos. 50–2, 30 yards S.W. of (172), has a cross-wing at the E. end. The upper storey projects on the N. front and there is a small original window on this side with moulded frame and mullion.

d(179). *House*, three tenements, Nos. 68–70, 80 yards E. of (178), has a projecting upper storey on the N. side with original shaped brackets.

Condition—Poor.

d(180). *House*, two tenements, Nos. 71–2, E. of (179), is probably of the 16th century but has been much altered. There is an original moulded ceiling-beam in the E. tenement.

d(181). *Queen's Head Inn*, 70 yards E. of (180), was built early in the 16th century but has recently been much altered and restored. The upper storey projects on the N. front and rests on two original curved brackets springing from attached shafts with moulded capitals. Inside the building is a heavy original ceiling-beam with curious mouldings.

d(182). *House*, two tenements, Nos. 89 and 90, 55 yards E. of (181), was built probably in the 16th century and has a cross-wing at the E. end. A cartway in the middle of the house has original moulded beams and plates.

d(183). *House*, three tenements and shops, Nos. 91–3, E. of (182), was built early in the 16th century with cross-wings at the E. and W. ends. The upper storey projects at the N. end of the E. wing. Inside the building in the main block is an original moulded ceiling-beam carved with twisted-leaf foliage and a shield bearing the initials I. G. (or C.) and crescent, triangle and square.

Condition—Poor.

d(184). *House* and shop, No. 97, 20 yards E. of (183), has weather-boarded walls and two gables on the N. front. It was built early in the 16th century and has original moulded ceiling-beams and joists in the shop.

d(185). *House*, two tenements and shop, Nos. 98-9, E. of (184), was built probably in the 16th century and has a weather-boarded cross-wing at the W. end. The upper storey projects on the N. side of the main block.

HYTHE QUAY :—

d(186). *House*, two tenements, Nos. 4 and 5, S. of (185), was built probably in the 15th century. The upper storey projects on the E. side. Inside the building the N. tenement has an original moulded oak corbel, bracket and wall-plate on the S. wall.

d(187). *House*, S. of (186), was built *c.* 1720 but contains some early 17th-century panelling and in the cellar is an early 16th-century beam, carved with twisted leaf ornament.

d(188). *Warehouse*, 60 yards S. of (187), was built probably in the 16th century and there is one original window.

d(189). *Neptune Inn*, S. of (188), was built in the 15th century with a central Hall. The exterior is quite modern and the original part has been much altered. The Hall formerly extended on to the site of the adjoining warehouse and in the partition is part of an original roof-truss. A curved and moulded brace springs from a moulded wall-post and supports the tie-beam ; the spandrel is filled with traceried panels divided by moulded uprights ; the spandrels of the tracery have carved foliage.

PRIORY STREET :—

b(190). *Range of seven tenements*, Nos. 76–82, on N. side, 270 yards E. of St. Botolph's Street. The tenements differ slightly in period but are all of late 17th or early 18th-century date.

b(191). *House* (Plate, p. 65), three tenements, Nos. 55–7, on W. side of road 30 yards S. of East Hill. The upper storey projects on the E. front.

b(192). *House*, now The Convent School, on E. side of road at S. corner of Childwell Alley, is of L-shaped plan with the wings extending towards the W. and S. The W. wing was extended late in the 17th century. Both sides of the S. wing (Plate, p. 101) and the S. side of the W. wing have projecting gables with original shaped brackets and moulded bressumers ; below the southern gable on the E. front are remains of a former bay-window and the wall-face has pargeted panels of flowers or foliage, but now much damaged. The later extension has mullioned and transomed windows. Inside the building is an early 16th-century fascia, reused and carved with running foliage.

b(193). *House*, five tenements, Nos.1–5, Childwell Alley, 35 yards E. of (192). The two E. tenements are a late 17th-century addition. In the middle of the N. front is a projecting gable with original shaped brackets. The upper storey formerly projected at the W. end but has been underbuilt. Condition—Poor.

EAST HILL, *S. side* (Plate, p. 65) :—

b(194). *House*, two tenements, Nos. 16 and 17, 100 yards E. of Priory Street, was built early in the 16th century and has an early 17th-century wing at the back. The upper storey projects in front and has one original curved bracket and a late 16th-century shaped bracket. There is one late 16th-century window, on the ground floor, with moulded frame and mullion and five similar windows under the eaves, all now blocked. At the E. end is a late 16th-century door (Plate, p. xxx) of square moulded panels with a lozenge-shaped enrichment in each panel. The timber-framing is exposed in front.

b(195). *Whalebone Inn*, 30 yards E. of (194).

b(196). *House*, two tenements, Nos. 23–4, E. of (195), has a projecting upper storey in front.

b(197). *House*, three tenements, Nos. 25–7, 10 yards E. of (196), has three gables at the back. Inside the building is an original moulded ceiling-beam.

b(198–199). *Houses*, Nos. 29 and 32, 15 yards E. of (197), are possibly the cross-wings of one house of which the main block, between them, has been rebuilt. Both are probably of the 17th century but the back part of the W. house is of early 16th-century date. The upper storey projects on the front of both buildings and the W. one has shaped brackets with moulded pendants. Inside the W. house the back part has an original moulded ceiling-beam. Condition of both—Poor.

b(200). *House*, No. 35, 15 yards E. of (199), was built probably late in the 16th century with a wing at the back. The upper storey projects on the N. front and has original hook-shaped brackets.

b(201). *House*, two tenements, Nos. 36–7, E. of (200), has a projecting upper storey on the N. front with hook-shaped brackets.

b(202). *House*, two tenements, Nos. 38–9, E. of (201), was built probably in the 15th century. At the back is a 16th or 17th-century extension. The upper storey projects on the N. front on

curved brackets and also on the E. side of the extension. Inside the building at the back of the front block was an original doorway with a four-centred head ; the head is now lying loose in the garden.

b(203). *House*, No. 47, 20 yards E. of (202), was perhaps originally of one storey. It has been refaced with brick and has a modern upper storey and back addition.

b(204). *House*, now four tenements, Nos. 48–51, E. of (203), was built early in the 16th century and has a 17th-century addition at the back. The upper storey in front has exposed timber-framing and formerly projected, but has been underbuilt. There are two original windows under the eaves with moulded frames and mullions. Inside the building one of the middle tenements has richly moulded original ceiling-beams and joists both on the ground and first floors. The E. tenement has also an original moulded ceiling-beam.

b(205). *House*, two tenements Nos. 1 and 2, East Bay, 35 yards E. of (204). The E. half of the front block is a wing of a 15th-century house, including the 'screens.' The rest of the block was rebuilt in the 17th century and there are 17th and 18th-century wings at the back. The upper storey projects in front and below it is an original doorway with a four-centred head. Inside the building the 'screens' are now represented only by the heavy beams of the former partitions. There are remains of the original king-post roof.

N. side :—

b(206). *House*, two tenements, 60 and 61, opposite (204), was built probably in the 15th century with a cross-wing at the W. end. In the 16th century a wing was added at the back and in the 17th century a long wing adjoining this addition on the N. was built ; about the same time two gables were added to the main block and a room built over the cartway further W. The added gables project in front of the main block on two 17th-century shaped brackets and have moulded barge-boards, and there is another bracket of the same date in the cartway. Inside the building the main block has original moulded ceiling-beams and remains of a king-post roof-truss.

b(207). *House*, Nos. 63–4, 10 yards W. of (206), has a 15th-century wing at the back. The front block which is of L-shaped plan was built early in the 16th century and there is a 17th-century addition in the angle between the wings. The front is modern. Inside the building the original wing has an oak post in the middle and above it a king-post roof-truss. The 16th-century building has an original moulded ceiling-beam and there are two original windows of three lights, now blocked.

b(208). *House*, No. 67, 15 yards W. of (207), has in the middle a mid 17th-century building of

COLCHESTER : (263) BOURNE MILL ; *c.* 1591, with earlier material.

COPFORD : PARISH CHURCH OF ST. MICHAEL AND ALL ANGELS ; c. 1100 and later.

From the South.

brick ; the front block is of late 17th-century date and there is an 18th-century addition on the E. Condition—Poor.

b(209). *House*, two tenements and shops, Nos. 68–9, W. of (208), has an 18th-century extension on the E. and a modern brick front.

b(210). *Goat and Boot Inn*, No. 70, 10 yards W. of (209), has been much altered. The upper storey projects on part of the E. side.

b(211). *House*, three tenements, Nos. 79–81, 140 yards W. of (210).

b(212). *House*, two tenements on E. side of Land Lane and 50 yards N.W. of (211), has been partly refaced with brick.

EAST STREET, S. side :—

d(213). *House*, five tenements, Nos. 11–13, 60 yards E. of the bridge, was built probably early in the 16th century. The W. part was altered and the S. wing added in the 17th century. The upper storey projects on the N. front. Inside the building the E. part of the front block has original moulded ceiling-beams and joists.

d(214). *House* (Plate, p. 65), two tenements, Nos. 17 and 18, 15 yards E. of (213), has a projecting upper storey in front.

d(215). *House* (Plate, p. 65), two tenements and shops, Nos. 24–5, 30 yards E. of (214), was built probably in the 15th century with cross-wings at the E. and W. ends ; the main block and the front part of the E. wing were rebuilt late in the 17th century and the W. wing extended S. The upper storey projects at the front end of the W. wing. On the W. side of the E. wing is the head of an original window. Inside the building are remains of the original roof construction.

d(216). *House*, No. 26 (Plate, p. 65), E. of (215), was built probably in the middle of the 16th century. The upper storey projects in front and has an early 18th-century modillioned eaves-cornice.

d(217). *Range of three houses* and shops, Nos. 30–33 (Plate, p. 65), 15 yards E. of (216). The E. part of the front block is of early 16th-century date ; the rest of the front is of rather later date. There are late 17th or early 18th-century additions at the back. The upper storey projects on the whole of the N. front ; at the E. end is an original curved bracket with carved foliage. The upper storey is plastered in panels and near the middle is an oval wreath enclosing the initials and date $_{RA}^{W}$ 1692. The eaves have a modillioned cornice of that period. Inside the building the E. part of the front block has original moulded ceiling-beams and some panelling of *c.* 1600.

d(218). *House*, two tenements, Nos. 34–5, E. of (217), has an 18th-century block on the N. front. The rear block is of late 17th-century brickwork.

d(219). *House*, and shop, No. 36, E. of (218), was built probably late in the 16th century.

d(220). *House*, No. 37, E. of (219), was built probably late in the 15th or early in the 16th century. The upper storey projects in front on curved brackets.

d(221). *House*, No. 38, 10 yards E. of (220), was built probably late in the 16th century and has a later addition at the back. The upper storey projects in front. Inside the building is an original moulded ceiling-beam.

d(222). *House*, two tenements, Nos. 39 and 40, E. of (221), was built probably in the 15th century with a cross-wing at the W. end. The upper storey projects in front.

d(223). *House*, No. 41, E. of (222), has a projecting upper storey in front and a later addition at the back.

d(224). *House* and shop, 15 yards E. of (223), has been much altered.

N. side :—

d(225). *Clarendon Inn*, and house, 100 yards E.N.E. of (224), was built probably late in the 16th century and has 17th-century additions at the back. In the roof are two reused beams with early 16th-century carving.

d(226). *House*, three tenements, at W. corner of the old Ipswich road, was built in the 15th century with cross-wings at the E. and W. ends and a wing projecting towards the N. In the 17th century this wing was extended and an addition made at the back. The upper storey projects at the S. end of both cross-wings and on the side of the N. wing. Inside the building the N. wing has an original king-post roof-truss.

d(227). *House*, three tenements, Nos. 58–9, 40 yards W. of (226), was built about the middle of the 16th century ; the W. end is a late 17th-century addition. The upper storey projects on the S. front of the original block and has an original moulded fascia and curved brackets. At the back the upper storey has remains of 17th-century pargeting with conventional foliage in panels.

Condition—Of E. part, poor.

d(228). *House* (Plate, p. 65), two tenements, Nos. 60 and 61, 40 yards W. of (227), has a projecting upper storey on the S. front with heavy shaped brackets.

d(229). *House* (Plate, p. 65), two tenements and shop, Nos. 62-3, W. of (228), was built in the 16th century with a cross-wing at the W. end. The upper storey formerly projected in front, but has been underbuilt.

d(230). *Houses* (Plate, p. 65), two tenements and shops, Nos. 64–5, W. of (229), were built in the 15th century and now consist of two blocks both gabled towards the S. and both having original roof construction, of king-post type.

d(231). *Siege House* and adjoining house, No. 74, (Plate, p. 64), 45 yards W. of (230), was built late in the 15th or early in the 16th century, and is of L-shaped plan with the wings extending towards the E. and N. The upper storey projects on the S. and W. sides with a heavy diagonal bracket at the angle springing from a moulded capping. The exterior is very much restored, but the E. part of the moulded bressumer is original and near the middle of the upper storey is an original window with diamond-shaped mullions. On the W. side is an original shaft with a moulded capital, supporting a curved brace ; part of the moulded frame of the adjoining window is also original. The timber-framing is much pitted with bullet holes, dating from the period of the siege. Inside the building several rooms have original moulded ceiling-beams. The N. room on the first floor has a modern fireplace with a mid 16th-century overmantel, of two panels with carved male and female heads ; on the E. wall-plate is carved one of the beatitudes and in the S. wall is an original doorway with a four-centred head and now blocked. In the window are two medallions of arms in glass reported to have been removed from a house in another part of Colchester : (1) the quartered coat of Katherine Parr, with an ornamental border including the initials and date W. S. 1546, and a merchant's mark ; (2) the quartered coat of Howard, Duke of Norfolk (with Brotherton in the first quarter) with an ornamental border, 16th-century. The roofs have remains of the original construction of king-post type.

GREENSTEAD ROAD, S. side :—

d(232). *House*, No. 1, two tenements and shops, 35 yards S. of (225), was built early in the 16th century and has a 17th-century wing at the back. The front has been faced with modern brick. Inside the building the ground floor has original moulded ceiling-beams, one in the E. tenement being unusually elaborate with a band of running foliage ; below its junction with the wall-plate is a carved shield with foliage. In the front wall is a window of c. 1600 with moulded frame and mullions.

d(233). *House*, No. 137, 350 yards E.S.E. of (232), was built early in the 16th century. The upper storey is gabled and projects on the N. front with a moulded bressumer and curved brackets, carved with foliage. Inside the building is an original moulded ceiling-beam.

d(234). *House*, three tenements, Nos. 283–7, 620 yards S.E. of (233), was built probably late in the

16th century. On the N.E. front are remains of 17th-century pargeting with large panels of scroll-work and vine ornament.
Condition—Poor.

d(235). *House*, No. 309, 130 yards S.E. of (234), has an 18th-century extension on the S.E.
Condition—Poor.

MIDDLEBOROUGH, E. side :—

b(236). *House*, No. 1, 10 yards N. of Northgate Street, adjoins the town wall on the N. The upper storey projects at the back.
Condition—Bad.

a(237). *House*, No. 10, 50 yards N. of (236), has been much altered.

a(233). *House*, two tenements, No. 11, N. of (237). The upper storey formerly projected at the W. end but has been underbuilt.

a(239). *House*, two tenements, Nos. 12 and 13, N. of (238), has a later addition at the back. The upper storey formerly projected on the W. front, but has been underbuilt.
Condition—Poor.

a(240). *House*, two tenements, N. of (239).

a(241). *House* and shop, No. 16, N. of (240), has been refaced with modern brick.

a(242). *House*, three tenements and shop, Nos. 17–19, N. of (241), was built in the 15th century with cross-wings at the N. and S. ends. The main block has been rebuilt and the whole is faced with modern brick. The roofs of the two cross-wings are original, the king-post remaining in the N. wing. There are some 17th-century battened doors.

W. side :—

a(243). *House*, two tenements, opposite (242), has walls of brick with a moulded string-course between the storeys on the E. front ; below it are the segmental heads of three original windows.

NORTH STATION ROAD, E. side :—

a(244). *House*, No. 1, four tenements, N. of North Bridge. The back part is of early 17th-century date and the front part an addition of later in the same century. The W. front is faced with modern brickwork.

a(245). *House* and shop, No. 3, 20 yards N. of (244), has been faced with modern brick. There is a later addition at the back.
Condition—Poor.

a(246). *House*, two tenements, Nos. 7 and 9, 20 yards N. of (245), has on the W. front a panel with the initials and date $\begin{smallmatrix} & M & \\ I & & H \end{smallmatrix}$ 1621.

a(247). *House*, three tenements and shops, Nos. 25 and 27, at S. corner of Albert Road. It has three gables on the W. front but the two side bays are probably 18th-century additions.

a(248). *House,* two tenements and shops, Nos. 45 and 47, 60 yards N. of (247), was built early in the 16th century. Inside the building the ground floor has original moulded ceiling-beams and joists.

W. side :—

a(249). *Range of four tenements,* Nos. 52–58, 90 yards N.N.W. of (248). The S. half is of early 17th-century date and the N. half was added later in the same century.

a(250). *Range of seven tenements,* Nos. 12–24, 100 yards S. of (249), was built probably early in the 18th century.

a(251). *Castle Inn,* N. of North Bridge, has been much altered. Inside the building is an original door of twelve moulded panels. At the back is an original window of two lights, now blocked.

CROUCH STREET, N. side :—

b(252). *House* and shop, No. 5A, 10 yards W. of Head Street, has a projecting upper storey on the S. front.

b(253). *House,* two tenements and shops, W. of (252), has a projecting upper storey on the S. front.

b(254). *House,* two tenements and shops, No. 17, 20 yards W. of (253), has a projecting upper storey on the S. front.

LEXDEN. Main Road, N. side :—

b(255). *House,* 160 yards N.E. of Lexden Church. The gable at the E. end has original moulded barge-boards with a pendant at the apex.

b(256). *House,* 200 yards W. of (255), was built in the 16th century with cross-wings at the E. and W. ends. The upper storey projects at the front end of the cross-wings. Inside the building the 17th-century staircase has turned balusters, square newels with terminals, and moulded strings. In the upper storey is an original window of three lights, with moulded frame and mullions and now blocked.

S. side :—

b(257). *House,* 350 yards W. of Lexden Church, was built in the 16th century or earlier and has a cross-wing at the E. and W. ends. The upper storey projects at the front end of both cross-wings. The roof of the E. wing has been altered.

b(258). *House,* now tenements, 30 yards W. of (257), was built probably in the 15th century with cross-wings at the E. and W. ends. The upper storey projects at the front end of the cross-wings. In the roof is an original king-post with two-way struts.

a(259). *Church Farm,* house, 100 yards N.N.E. of the modern church at Mile End, was built probably in the 16th century. The upper storey projects on the S. front.

a(260). *Pest House,* cottage between Mill Road and Clay Lane and ½ m. E.N.E. of Mile End new Church, has been much altered in the 18th century. Condition—Poor.

a(261). *House,* 270 yards S. of (260), was built in the 16th century. The upper storey projects at the E. end.

d(262). *Winsley's Almshouses* and farmhouse, about ½ m. S.S.W. of the Hythe Church. The middle block of the almshouses and the W. wing of the farmhouse, S. of it, belong to a fairly large late 16th-century house of brick and of courtyard or half H-shaped plan. The E. block of the farmhouse was added probably early in the 17th century. The almshouses were founded *c.* 1726 and incorporated the main block of the house which was much altered and flanking wings were added on the E. and W. sides forming an open courtyard ; these wings have been subsequently extended. The farmhouse was separated from the almshouses by breaking down a section of the building immediately S. of the latter. The main block of the almshouse has been much altered and has a projecting porch in the middle with original octagonal turrets at the angles, but entirely covered with cement and with applied features of 1726 ; the outer archway has double-chamfered jambs and three-centred arch in a square head ; the inner archway has a four-centred arch and set in it is an original stop-moulded oak frame and a door of moulded battens. The W. wall of the farmhouse has an original doorway with double-chamfered jambs and four-centred arch in a square head. The 17th-century addition has a window of three lights, with plastered mullions. Inside the building two tenements on the E. side of the entrance have each a 17th-century fireplace with a carved oak lintel, one has masoned decoration, carved stops and the date and initials H B 1649 (Henry Barrington, Mayor, 1648) ; the other has egg and dart ornament and other decoration of Jacobean character. There are also two doorways in these tenements with original stop-moulded frames and square heads. In the entry behind the porch is a similar door-frame and a 17th-century door elaborately panelled and with a small cut opening at the bottom. On the first floor the middle of the main block and the space over the porch is fitted up as a chapel but has no features earlier than 1726. The original part of the farmhouse has a moulded ceiling-beam.

b(263). *Bourne Mill* (Plate, p. 68), ¾ m. S.E. of St. Giles' Church, was built *c.* 1591. The walls are freestone rubble with some brick ; the stone is mostly spoil from some 12th and 13th-century building, probably St. John's Abbey. The front has four original windows with stone mullions and moulded labels ; the doorway (Plate, p. 100) has double-chamfered jambs and three-centred arch in

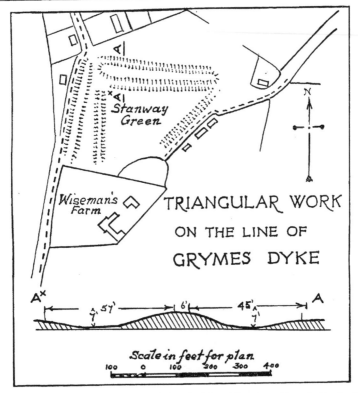

Stanway Green

Wiseman's Farm

TRIANGULAR WORK

ON THE LINE OF

GRYMES DYKE

A⁀   57′   6′   45′   A

Scale in feet for plan.
100   0   100   200   300   400

a square head with a moulded label; above it in a raised and moulded panel is an achievement of the Lucas arms. There is also a doorway to the upper storey, with a moulded label. The gables of the two ends are elaborately treated in the Dutch manner with curved and voluted offsets from which spring pinnacles of varying form; in the S. gable is a stone panel inscribed "Thomas Lucas, miles, me fecit Ano domini 1591 "; at the apex of each is an octagonal chimney-shaft. The back elevation has three windows, similar to those in front, and a doorway with a keyed three-centred head with carved spandrels and flanked by fluted pilasters. The reused material in the walls includes numerous moulded stones and the base of a 12th-century shaft.

ᵇ(264). *Monkwick*, house 1,100 yards N.E. of Berechurch Church, was built probably in the 16th century. The upper storey projects on the

S. side and has two gables. Inside the building one room has early 17th-century panelling and an overmantel of three enriched arcaded bays divided by fluted pilasters supporting a fluted frieze.

Unclassified :—

(265). THE LEXDEN EARTHWORKS.—These earthworks may be described as four main dykes, shown on the plan as A, B, C and D, each consisting of a rampart with a ditch on the west side.

The first four are situated at some distance apart, one behind the other, and running roughly north and south. The entrenchments protect the area elsewhere enclosed by the Colne and Roman Rivers and have flanking works extending beyond both rivers. There are slight traces of minor banks in the vicinity of the main entrenchments.

The date of the work is doubtful, but the evidence, which is negative in character, suggests a pre-Claudian origin.

A.—Gryme's Dyke, or the outward trench of Wyldenhey, situated partly in Stanway parish, is the westernmost of the four dykes, and extends for a distance of about 3 m.

It is first apparent, though almost obliterated by the plough, on the west side of the Bergholt road, near New Bridge, south of the Colne, and continues to near the Halstead road, where it is obliterated by gardens. Near the gravel-pits, east of the Union it is well defined and from this point the ditch is occupied by the road which runs past New Farm. About 300 yards S. of the farm is an original entrance which cuts obliquely through the bank. The dyke continues southwards in strong outline to a spot east of Stanway Green, where it turns sharply towards the west and again, after about 300 yards, to the south. The defences at this angle are double and further strengthened by a ditch across the base of the triangle, forming a small defensive work (see plan 73). Following the footpath which runs along the ditch, the dyke carries on across the Maldon road, along the western boundary of Butcher's Wood down to Baymill Cottages, near a ford of Roman River. (See *Sectional Preface*, p. xxiii.)

The rampart at a point south of Stanway Green is 10 ft. above the ditch, which is 50 ft. wide from crest to crest.

Condition—Fairly good.

B.—Partly in Layer de la Haye parish is shown on an 18th-century plan to commence S. of the London road. The position of the northern extremity of this line is doubtful. It is now visible in a field S.W. of Heath Cottage, where there would seem to have been a junction of the several lines of entrenchment, and is indicated by a scarp running past Well House and across the Maldon road to the N.E. corner of Oliver Thick's Wood. This section of the work is very indefinite. From Oliver Thick's Wood the course of the dyke can be followed running S.E. and S., past " Olivers" and across a ford of Roman River. Through Chest Wood and the garden of the Vicarage at Layer de la Haye, a stream runs along the ditch.

Total length, about 2 m.

Condition—Poor.

C.—This length of entrenchment is first visible in a plantation on the E. side of Lexden Straight Road, about 400 yards S. of London Road. For a distance of 350 yards it consists of a treble rampart and ditch, the ramparts being 5 ft. above the ditches, which are 50 ft. wide from crest to crest. On leaving the plantation it is much denuded and consists only of a single rampart and ditch, but is still easily traceable through the fields towards a small wood near Heath Cottage, which is said to be the site of a small earthwork. The total length is slightly over ½ m.

Condition—Good in parts.

D.—" The Sunken Way," or " Hollow Way," is the easternmost line of entrenchment and is said to be visible under certain conditions from the turning near Great Horkesley Church, across St. Botolph's Brook and the golf links to the Bergholt road near " Achnacone." From this point the outline of the work is well defined, running west of south across the railway cutting, where a good section of the work can be seen, and on past Lexden Lodge to the River Colne. Immediately east of the dyke at Lexden Lodge is a wide rectangular moat wrongly shown on the O.S. maps as " site of Roman fort."

The work is next evident in considerable strength in Lexden Park, and continues through the Park and across the road in a S.E. direction with a road on the crest of the rampart, to a point N.E. of Prettygate Farm. The supposed site of the old Roman road to London crosses the dyke close to this spot. A slight bank running, with intervals, S.W. past Prettygate Farm and Heath Farm, to a point E. of Stanway Green, may be a continuation of this work.

A section taken near Lexden Lodge shows the rampart to be 10 ft. above the ditch, which is 50 ft. wide from crest to crest.

Total length from Great Horkesley, about 3½ m.

Condition—Good.

Earthwork in Brinkley Grove, about 2 m. N. of the town, consists of the S.W. angle of an apparently rectangular site defended by a ditch 60 ft. wide and 9 ft. deep, with both an internal and external rampart. This work is not shown on the O.S. maps.

Condition—Imperfect.

Tumulus, in Lexden Park, about 7 ft. high. Opened 1860 and some pottery found.

Condition—Fairly good.

Lexden Mount, about ¼ m. S.W. of the church, is about 12 ft. high and 110 ft. in diameter at the base. The excavations of 1910 were largely negative in their results but some fragments of Roman Pottery were found. (See *Sectional Preface*, p. xxiii.)

Condition—Good.

King Coel's Kitchen, on the W. side of Gryme's Dyke, N. of the London Road. A large excavation, possibly a disused gravel-pit. (See *Sectional Preface*, p. xxiv.)

_____

15. COLNE ENGAINE. (B.c.)

(O.S. 6 in. [d]xvii. N.E. [b]xvii. S.W.)

Colne Engaine is a parish and small village 2 m. E. of Halstead. The church is the principal monument.

Ecclesiastical :—

[b](1). PARISH CHURCH OF ST. ANDREW stands near the middle of the parish. The walls are of

flint and stone-rubble mixed with Roman bricks and tiles ; the porch and the upper stages of the tower are of brick ; the dressings are of Barnack and limestone ; and the roofs are tiled. The *Nave* was built early in the 12th century. The *Chancel* was probably rebuilt in the 13th century. The *West Tower* was added possibly in the 14th century. Early in the 16th century the top stages of the tower were rebuilt and the *South Porch* added. The church was restored in the 19th century when the chancel-arch was rebuilt, the E. wall raised and the *North Vestry* added.

The top stage of the tower and the S. porch are interesting examples of brickwork ; the porch is in part a replica of that at Pebmarsh.

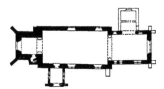

Architectural Description—The *Chancel* (26 ft. by 18½ ft.) has a modern E. window with some reused stones in the splays. In the N. wall are traces of a tile relieving-arch over the head of a blocked lancet window, only visible internally ; further W. is a single light 'low-side' window of the 14th century with a trefoiled ogee head and tracery ; between the windows is a modern opening to the organ chamber. In the S. wall are two windows, the eastern is of early 14th-century date and of two septfoiled lights with tracery in a two-centred head with richly moulded jambs and label with head-stops ; the western window is of the same date and is a 'low-side' window similar to that in the N. wall ; between the windows is a 13th-century doorway with chamfered jambs, two-centred arch and moulded label with head-stops, one modern ; it is now blocked ; above the doorway are traces of a relieving-arch similar to that in the N. wall. The chancel-arch is modern.

The *Nave* (48 ft. by 24 ft.) has W. quoins of Roman brick and in the S. wall are well-defined courses of similar bricks. In the N. wall are two modern windows. In the S. wall are two windows all modern except the rear-arch and splays of the eastern, which are of the 14th century ; W. of this window is a 12th-century window, now blocked ; further W. is the S. doorway with double chamfered jambs and moulded two-centred arch of the 14th century.

The *West Tower* (11 ft. square) is of three stages, the lowest probably of the 14th century and the two upper of early 16th-century date ; the embattled brick parapet has crocketed angle

pinnacles and projects on a trefoiled corbel-table above which is a band of cusped ornament ; on the E. side this band has a shield and the Vere molet ; the buttresses have each a trefoil-headed panel at the level of the second stage. The tower-arch and W. window are modern. The second stage has a loop in the N. and S. walls. The bell chamber has in each wall an early 16th-century window of two four-centred lights with a pierced spandrel in a four-centred head and a moulded label.

The *South Porch* (Plate, p. xxix) is of brick and of early 16th-century date. The outer archway has moulded jambs, two-centred arch and label all set in a projection with a crow-stepped head surmounted by a niche. The side walls have each a window of two four-centred lights with a pierced spandrel.

The *Roof* of the nave is of the 15th century and of four bays with moulded wall-plates and tie-beams with curved braces and square king-posts with moulded capitals and bases ; two braces rest on grotesque stone corbels. The 15th-century roof of the porch evidently belonged to an earlier structure and has moulded wall-plates and tie-beam with king-post, two-way struts and central purlin ; the cusped and sub-cusped barge-boards are much decayed.

Fittings—Bells : six ; 3rd by Miles Graye, 1624. *Brass :* On S. respond of chancel-arch—to Agnes Hunte, widow, and Agnes, Alys and Elyzabeth, her daughters, early 16th-century, inscription only. *Chest :* In vestry—plain, with ring-handles and strap-hinges, probably 17th-century. *Niche :* On porch—with moulded base and four-centred head, early 16th-century. *Piscina :* In chancel—with moulded jambs and trefoiled ogee head with carved spandrels, crocketed label and finial, octofoiled drain, 14th-century. *Sedile :* In chancel —sill of S.E. window carried down to form seat, splays stopped with trefoiled ogee heads, 14th-century.

Condition—Good, but some ivy on N. wall.

Secular :—

MONUMENTS (2–8).

The following monuments, unless otherwise described, are of the 17th century and of two storeys, timber-framed and plastered or weather-boarded ; the roofs are tiled or thatched. Some of the buildings have original chimney-stacks and exposed ceiling-beams.

Condition—Good, or fairly good, unless noted.

b(2). *Row of Cottages*, 300 yards W. of the church, has an original chimney-stack with grouped diagonal shafts.

b(3). *Goldington's Farm*, house and barn, nearly 1 m. W. of the church.

b(4). *Cottage*, 300 yards S. of (3), has the modern date 1620 on the W. gable. The central chimney-stack has four octagonal shafts and an original bay-window at the W. end of the house is of six transomed lights with moulded mullions.

b(5). *The Grove*, house on Boose's Green, nearly ½ m. N.N.W. of the church, has large modern additions and the modern date 1684 on the S.W. end. Inside the building is some original panelling and a moulded ceiling-beam.

b(6). *Cottage*, 180 yards E.N.E. of (5), has a wing on the E. with a projecting upper storey on its N. side.

b(7). *Brickhouse Farm*, house, ¼ m. E.N.E. of (6), is built of brick and has at the back an original window with a moulded frame.

a(8). *Hungry Hall*, house and barn, 1½ m. N.E. of the church. The *House* has been refaced with modern brick, but the chimney-stack has two original octagonal shafts.

The *Barn*, W. of the house, is probably of the 17th century and is of seven bays.

---

16. COPFORD.   (C.c.)

(O.S. 6 in. *(a)*xxvii. N.W. *(b)*xxvii. S.W.)

Copford is a parish 4½ m. W.S.W. of Colchester. The church is interesting.

Ecclesiastical :—

b(1). PARISH CHURCH OF ST. MICHAEL AND ALL ANGELS (Plate, p. 69) stands at the S.E. corner of the parish. The walls are of coursed rubble, septaria and Roman brick, except the S. aisle, which is of uncoursed rubble ; the dressings are of limestone and the roofs are tiled. The *Apse, Chancel* and *Nave* were built *c.* 1100 with a barrel-vault and a chamber above it. Late in the 12th century the easternmost arch of the S. arcade was inserted and a S. transept or chapel added. Probably at the end of the 13th century this chapel was extended W. to form a *South Aisle*. The barrel-vault of the main building was removed probably late in the 14th century. The church was restored in the 19th century, when the *South Vestry* and *South Porch* were added.

The church is an extremely interesting example of its period and the remains of the vaulted roof indicate a most unusual form, comparable with that at Great Clacton. The series of paintings, though much restored, are the finest and most complete in the county.

Architectural Description—The *Apse* (12 ft. by 20 ft.) of *c.* 1100 (Plate, p. 140) has flat pilaster buttresses and a plain half-domed vault groined back above the windows. There are three windows, each with a round head of two orders of Roman brick ; the external jambs and the splays have each a free shaft, but externally these are modern except for the bases and part of the shafts of the E. window ; internally the shafts have carved or scalloped capitals and moulded bases. The apse-arch is semi-circular and stilted and of two plain orders with chamfered imposts.

The *Chancel* and *Nave* (66 ft. by 21 ft.) are structurally undivided and consist of four bays with wide pilaster buttresses formerly supporting a barrel-vault of which the abutments remain on each side with the springing of the transverse arches and chamfered imposts at the springing line ; round lines on each side-bay of the walls indicate the line of the keying of the former cross-vaults and afford evidence of a roof consisting of a main barrel-vault with a series of four very stilted cross-vaults groined into it ; the former room above the vault was approached by a doorway cut through the upper part of the second buttress of the N. wall and now blocked. In the N. wall are three windows ; the two eastern are modern, but the westernmost is similar to those in the apse and has scalloped capitals to the side shafts ; it is much restored ; in the easternmost bay is a small doorway of *c.* 1100, with plain jambs, round arch, and lintel with the tympanum filled with Roman bricks ; the doorway is now blocked ; in the westernmost bay is the 12th-century N. doorway of three round orders, the two outer moulded and the inner plain and of Roman brick ; the two outer orders of the jambs have each a shaft with voluted or cushion capital, moulded abacus and base ; the inner order, lintel and tympanum are modern. In the S. wall (Plate, p. 76) are four arches, the easternmost is modern ; the second is of late 12th-century date, two-centred and of one chamfered order ; the responds have moulded angles and imposts ; the third arch is of late 13th-century date, two-centred and of three chamfered orders, the outer of Roman bricks and the others of contemporary bricks ; the responds continue the form of the arch, but the two inner orders have a moulded impost ; the westernmost arch is of uncertain date ; it is two-centred and of one chamfered and plastered order with plain imposts of stone ; above the easternmost arch is a round-headed recess indicating the head of an original window ; above the second arch is a more complete window-head, also blocked but retaining part of the side-shafts with cushion capitals with voluted ornament and no abaci. In the W. wall are two windows, one above the other ; the lower window is of mid 14th-century date and of two pointed lights in a two-centred head ; it is set in an original opening with internal shafts on the splays having scalloped capitals ; the original Roman brick jambs are invisible externally ; the upper window is original and has Roman brick jambs and a round head ; flanking it are two small round openings now blocked on the inside.

COPFORD : PARISH CHURCH OF ST. MICHAEL AND ALL ANGELS.

Interior, showing inserted Arches, 12th and 13th-century, and Nave Roof, late 14th or early 15th-century.

COPFORD: PARISH CHURCH OF ST. MICHAEL AND ALL ANGELS.
Wall Paintings in the Apse; mid 12th-century, restored.

COPFORD. THE PARISH CHURCH.

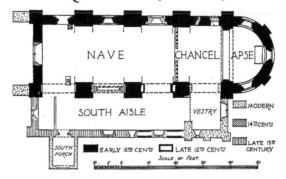

The *South Aisle* (11½ ft. wide) has in the E. wall a modern archway. In the S. wall are three windows, the two eastern are modern, but the westernmost is of the 14th century and of two trefoiled ogee lights with a quatrefoil in a two-centred head and partly restored; further W. is the modern S. doorway incorporating some old stones. In the W. wall is a modern window.

The *Roof* of the body of the church is of trussed-rafter type with moulded wall-plates and two trusses with octagonal king-posts having moulded capitals and bases probably all of late 14th or early 15th-century date. The bell-turret at the W. end of the nave stands on two heavy posts with a tie-beam and curved braces probably of the 15th century.

Fittings—Bells : three said to be ; 1st by Henry Jordan, mid 15th-century; 2nd by John Bird inscribed " Sum Rosa Pulsata Mundi Katerina Vocata," 15th-century ; 3rd by Thomas Draper and William Land, 1574. *Chest :* In nave— rectangular, iron-bound with two locks and four hasps, possibly 14th-century. *Door :* In N. doorway—of battens with marks of former ornamental iron-work, 12th-century. *Floor-slab :* In nave— to John Poole, 1677. *Font :* square bowl of Purbeck marble, each face with four round-headed panels but on one side the panels are unfinished, late 12th-century, stem modern. *Glass :* In nave— in W. window, shield of the arms of Tey—*argent a fesse between three martlets azure in chief and a cheveron azure in base, a crescent for difference,* ornamental border, irradiated rose above it and at sides part of black-letter inscription, late 15th-century. *Paintings :* There are remains of mid 12th-century paintings on the whole of the original building ; they were discovered in 1865 but have been, with some exceptions, considerably restored.

The apse (Plate, p. 77) has elaborate diapering, borders and banding around the three windows and on the splays of the side windows ; the splays of the middle window have figures of St. Michael and St. Gabriel ; between the windows and to the W. of them are standing figures of ten apostles including SS. Peter and Paul flanking the E. window ; each figure stands under a round-headed canopy surmounted by elaborate architecture ; the vault has in the middle a Majesty encircled by a rainbow supported by four angels ; in the background are the buildings of New Jerusalem, and in the main spandrels are large throned figures of angels one with an open and one with a closed book ; the groined vaults over the side windows have each an angel holding a palm and a cross respectively. The arch of the apse is richly diapered and has on the soffit twelve panels formed by interlacing foliage and containing the signs of the Zodiac. In the spandrels of the W. face are flying angels with trumpets and scrolls, and above them is a band of wavy ornament continued along the side walls ; this work must be later than the destruction of the former vault. The N. wall of the body of the church has in the first bay much restored diaper and conventional ornament ; the second bay has an unrestored painting said (improbably) to be of Christ and the Centurion, with a woman at the back ; the respond between the second and third bays has diaper work and a medallion with a nimbed head, and, on the springing of the arch, the lower part of a figure subject possibly Samson and the lion. The third bay has two figures of armed men, one unrestored and one modern ; the old figure has a gambeson, long mail hawberk and a coif. The respond between the third and fourth bay has diapering and a medallion enclosing a head and on the springing are remains of a figure subject. The S. wall has in the first bay remains of unrestored paintings, including a crowned figure holding an orb and two angels said to be holding bread and a paten, but now much faded. In the second bay is diapering and part of an unrestored armed figure with conical helmet, and mail; he holds a sword and spear. The respond between the second and third bays is similar to that on the N. and on the springer are remains of a figure subject, possibly the Flight into Egypt. The next respond is similar to that on the N.; the painting on the springer has been entirely restored. On the W. wall are traces of two large figure subjects, that to the N. almost obliterated and that on the S. with a central figure and three armed figures. *Scratching:* On E. respond of second bay of S. arcade—shield with symbol of the Trinity, 15th-century. *Screen:* Between chancel and nave—with moulded posts, central doorway with cinquefoiled and sub-cusped head with carved points and spandrels and traceried main spandrels; side bays each with five open panels with trefoiled, sub-cusped and ogee heads and tracery, early 15th-century, cornice and buttresses modern.

Condition—Good, much restored.

Secular :—

MONUMENTS (2–7).

The following monuments, unless otherwise described, are of the 17th century and of two storeys, timber-framed and plastered or 'weather-boarded; the roofs are tiled or thatched. Several of the buildings have original chimney-stacks and exposed ceiling-beams.

Condition—Good or fairly good, unless noted.

[b](2). *Vineyard Cottages,* range of tenements, ¼ m. W.S.W. of the church. On the N. side is an oval plaster medallion with date and initials, 1702 $\frac{L}{R A}$. One chimney-stack has three diagonal shafts.

Condition—Poor.

[b](3). *Cottage,* 350 yards W. of (2).

[b](4). *Cottage,* 130 yards N.W. of (3), has the timber-framing exposed.

Condition—Poor.

[b](5). *Mascott's Farm,* house, nearly 1 m. N.W. of the church, was built probably at the end of the 16th century but has been much altered.

[b](6). *Cottage,* 1 m. N. of the church, was built in the 16th century and has some exposed timber-framing.

Condition—Poor.

[a](7). *Mantill's Farm,* house and barn, 2¼ m. N. by W. of the church. The *House* has a cross-

wing at the S. end. One original chimney-stack has grouped diagonal shafts.

The *Barn,* N. of the house, is of five bays with a S. porch.

———

[b](8). MOUND, probably mill-mound, on N. side of road, 1,500 yards N. of the church.

———

17. CRESSING. (A.d.)

(O.S. 6 in. [a]xxv. S.E. [b]xxxiv. N.E [c]xxxiv. S.E.)

Cressing is a parish and village 3 m. S.E. of Braintree. The principal monuments are the church and Cressing Temple.

Ecclesiastical :—

[b](1). PARISH CHURCH OF ALL SAINTS (Plate, p. xxviii) stands at the S. end of the village. The walls are of flint-rubble with some brick; the dressings are of limestone and clunch, and the roofs are tiled. The *Nave* is probably of the 12th century, but there is no detail *in situ* of that date. The *Chancel* was rebuilt *c.* 1230. In the first half of the 15th century the walls of the nave were raised and early in the 16th century the S. wall of the chancel was rebuilt, the chancel possibly shortened and the *Bell-turret* added. The church was restored early in the 19th century, when the E. wall was rebuilt and the *North Vestry* added; the *South Porch* is also modern.

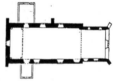

Architectural Description—The *Chancel* (17 ft. by 20 ft.) has a modern E. window. In the N. wall are two windows of the first half of the 13th century, each of one lancet light; the western has been completely restored externally. In the S. wall is an early 16th-century window of two cinquefoiled lights with a quatrefoil in a four-centred head, the external jambs and head are moulded, and the mullion and sill are modern; further W. is a doorway, all modern, except the internal splays and rear-arch, which are of early 16th-century date.

The *Nave* (50¾ ft. by 21¾ ft.) is structurally undivided from the chancel, but the internal angles of the set back in the N. and S. walls are splayed. In the N. wall are two windows of *c.* 1440, and each of two cinquefoiled lights with tracery in a two-centred head and a moulded label; further W. is the 14th-century N. doorway with chamfered jambs and two-centred arch;

the moulded label has mutilated head-stops ; above the rear-arch is set a voussoir carved with cheveron ornament, of *c*. 1130. In the S. wall are two windows ; the eastern is of *c*. 1340 and of two trefoiled ogee lights with tracery in a two-centred head ; the external label and rear-arch are moulded ; the western window is similar in date and detail to those in the N. wall ; at the E. end of the wall is a recess of uncertain use and date, with splayed jambs and a segmental arch ; W. of the windows is the late 14th-century S. doorway, with moulded jambs, two-centred arch and label. In the W. wall is a window, all modern, except the splays and rear-arch, which are of *c*. 1440.

The *Bell-turret*, probably of early 16th-century date and placed over the W. end of the nave, is square, covered with modern boarding, and has a short shingled spire. It rests on four hollow-chamfered posts set against the walls of the nave, with chamfered cross-beams and curved braces supporting a timber-frame with diagonal bracing ; between the posts on the N. and S. sides are horizontal struts with arched braces.

The *Roof* of the chancel is of early 16th-century date and of the trussed-rafter type, with moulded and embattled wall-plates. The 15th-century roof of the nave is steep pitched and of four bays ; the trusses have chamfered tie-beams with curved braces, and two collar-beams, the lower with curved braces and pierced traceried filling between it and the tie-beam ; the upper collar supports a king-post with four-way struts.

Fittings—*Brass :* In chancel—of Dorcas (Bigg), wife of Thomas Musgrave, of Norton, Yorks, 1610, seated figure of lady, left hand pointing to figure of infant, two inscription-plates. *Communion Table* (Plate, p. xxxii) : In vestry—of oak, with square and turned legs, top-rail with raised panels, lower rails carved with incised inscription : " Dorcas Smith wife of William Smyth Esquier gave this to the churche, A. dom, 1633." *Glass :* In nave—in tracery of two windows in N. wall, fragments of figures, foliage, etc., 15th-century. *Helms :* In chancel—at W. end, two, one with crest of Smith, early 17th-century. *Monument* and *Floor-slab.* Monument (Plate, p. 97) : In chancel—on S. wall, of Anne (Grene), wife of (*a*) Thomas Newman, (*b*) Henry Smith, of Cressing Temple, 1607, alabaster and marble tablet, with kneeling figures of man in plate-armour, and lady, with four shields of arms ; panelled base with small figures of a daughter and a swaddled infant. Floor-slab : In chancel—to Willyam Smith and Dorcas, his wife, mid 17th-century. *Piscinae :* In chancel —with chamfered jambs and four-centred head, early 16th-century ; octofoil drain, probably 14th-century. In nave—in sill of S.E. window, rough sinking to drain, date uncertain. *Royal Arms :* In nave—on S. wall, of Queen Anne before the Union, on canvas in carved frame. *Sedilia :* Sills

of S.E. window of chancel and N.E. and S.E. windows of nave carried down to form seats. *Miscellanea :* In nave—on sill of W. window, two carved *heads*, 14th-century

Condition—Good.

Secular —:

b(2). HOMESTEAD MOAT at Wright's Farm, about ¾ m. W.N.W. of the church.

b(3). CRESSING TEMPLE, house, outbuilding, barns and moat, about 1¼ m. S.S.E. of the church. The *House* is of two storeys, timber-framed and plastered ; the roofs are tiled. It was built *c*. 1600 on a T-shaped plan, with the cross-wing at the S.W. end. There are modern additions on the N.W. side. Inside the building, one room is fitted with original panelling, having a carved frieze ; the panelled overmantel has reeded pilasters and carved conventional foliage and dragons.

The *Garden*, E. of the house, is surrounded by late 16th-century walls of red brick. In the walls are two doorways with moulded jambs and four-centred arches with square labels ; a third doorway is similar, but with chamfered jambs, and is flanked by pilasters on the inside face.

The *Outbuilding*, E. of the house, is of two storeys, partly of brick and partly of plastered timber-framing ; it was built probably early in the 17th century. S. of the house is another outbuilding, now stables, also of two storeys and timber-framed. It was built *c*. 1623. the date on a carved panel on the N.W. side ; the gable above this has barge-boards carved with conventional foliage.

The *Barn*, N.E. of the house, is timber-framed, with brick nogging. It was built probably late in the 16th century, and is of five bays with two half-bays and a porch. The second barn, N. of the house, is timber-framed and weather-boarded. It was built early in the 16th century and is of similar plan to the larger barn ; the roof has king-post trusses.

There are traces of foundation mounds in the area enclosed by the above buildings.

The *Moat* is fragmentary.

Condition—Of all buildings, good.

b(4). HAWBUSH FARM, house, barn and moat, ½ m. W. of the church. The *House* is of two storeys, timber-framed and plastered ; the roofs are tiled. It was built probably early in the 16th century but has 17th-century and modern additions on the W. side. On the W. side is an old door of overlapping battens. A 17th-century chimney-stack on the W. side has two diagonal shafts. Inside the building are exposed ceiling-beams including one original moulded beam. There is also some late 16th-century panelling. The roof has remains of the original king-post construction but has been much altered,

The *Barn* N.E. of the house is timber-framed and probably of the 16th century.

The *Moat* is incomplete.

Condition—Of house, fairly good.

a(5). LANGHAM FARM, house and moat, about ¾ m. N. of the church. The *House* is of two storeys, partly timber-framed and plastered and partly of brick ; the roofs are covered with slate. It was built in the 16th century but was altered in the 17th century and the roof rebuilt in the 19th century. The W. end of the main block is of original brickwork. In the N. wall are several original doorways with four-centred heads ; there are also indications of a former N. wing. Inside the building one room is lined with early 17th-century panelling with a fluted frieze and fluted pilasters flanking the windows.

The *Moat* surrounds the house.

Condition—Of house, fairly good.

MONUMENTS (6–15).

The following monuments, unless otherwise described, are of the 17th century and of two storeys, timber-framed and plastered or weather-boarded ; the roofs are tiled. Several of the buildings have original chimney-stacks and exposed ceiling-beams.

Condition—Good or fairly good, unless noted.

a(6). *Field's Farm*, house, ¼ m. N.N.E. of (5).

b(7). *Rook Farm*, house and barns, 300 yards N.W. of the church. The *House* was built *c.* 1600 and has an original central chimney-stack with four detached shafts having ornamental caps. Inside the building are some original doors of moulded battens.

The *Barns* S.E. of the house are probably of the 17th century.

b(8). *House*, three tenements, 80 yards N.W. of the church.

b(9). *Cottage*, three tenements, 700 yards W. of the church.

b(10). *Newhouse Farm*, house, nearly ¾ m. S.S.E. of the church, has an original central chimney-stack with four detached octagonal shafts on a rectangular base with a moulded capping. The N. stack is of later date than that in the centre but was built to correspond with it.

c(11). *Hungry Hall*, about 1½ m. S.S.E. of the church, has an original central chimney-stack with the lower parts of several octagonal shafts.

b(12). *Cottage*, two tenements, 750 yards S.S.W. of the church.

b(13). *Cottage*, with outbuildings, 1,600 yards W. of the church, has been reduced to one storey in height. The E. gable has original barge-boards.

Condition—Poor.

b(14). *Jeffrey's Farm*, house, N. of (13), has inside the building two original moulded wall-plates.

b(15). *Cottage*, nearly 1 m. W.N.W. of the church, was built late in the 16th or early in the 17th century. The upper storey projects at the S. end.

---

18. DEDHAM. (D.b.)

(O.S. 6 in. *(a)*xix. N.W. *(b)*xix. N.E. *(c)*xix. S.W. *(d)*xix. S.E.)

Dedham is a parish and small town (Plate, p. 122) 6½ m. N.E. of Colchester. The church, Southfields, the Sun Hotel and Boxhouse Farm are the principal monuments.

Ecclesiastical :—

b(1). PARISH CHURCH OF ST. MARY (Plate, p. 81) stands in the village. The walls are of flint-rubble and brick ; the tower is faced with knapped flints ; the dressings are of limestone ; the roofs are lead covered. The church was practically rebuilt at the end of the 15th and the beginning of the 16th century, but incorporates a few fragments of earlier walling at the W. end. The rebuilding began on the S. side and comprised *Nave* with *North* and *South Aisles, Chancel, South Porch, West Tower* (finished in 1519) and *North Porch*. The church was restored in the 18th century and in modern times.

The church is a handsome example of the East Anglian type ; the vaulted passage under the tower is a curious feature and amongst the fittings the panelled door and early 16th-century monument are noteworthy.

Architectural Description—All the details not otherwise described are of *c.* 1500. The *Chancel* (45 ft. by 20 ft.), has in the E. wall a modern window. In the N. wall are three windows each of three trefoiled ogee lights with tracery in a two-centred head with a moulded label and moulded jambs ; all have been much restored. In the S. wall are three windows, similar to those in the N. wall but less restored ; below the middle window is a modern doorway. The four-centred chancel-arch is of two moulded orders, the outer dying on to the walls and the inner resting on moulded corbels with carved grotesque heads.

The *Nave* (95½ ft. by 20 ft.) has N. and S. arcades each of six bays with moulded four-centred arches of two moulded orders, the inner resting on attached shafts with moulded capitals and bases ; the outer order is continuous in alternate piers, the outer member in the other piers springing from a moulded capital and shaft ; from the piers and from the apex of each arch spring wall-shafts terminating in moulded capitals under the wall-posts of the roof. The clearstorey has on each side twelve windows each of three trefoiled ogee lights with tracery in a four-centred head with a moulded label, and partly restored.

DEDHAM : PARISH CHURCH OF ST. MARY.
West Tower, from the South-East ; *c.* 1519.

DEDHAM : PARISH CHURCH OF ST. MARY ; *c.* 1500.
Interior, looking East.

DEDHAM.

𝒯𝒽𝑒 PARISH CHURCH 𝑜𝑓 S^T MARY.

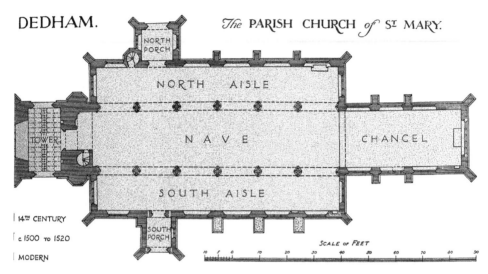

14TH CENTURY

c 1500 TO 1520

MODERN

SCALE OF FEET

The *North Aisle* (13 ft. wide) has in the E. wall a partly restored window of three trefoiled ogee lights with tracery in a four-centred head with moulded jambs and label. In the N. wall are five windows of similar design to that in the E. wall, and all partly restored; between the two western-most is the N. doorway (Plate, p. 42), with moulded and shafted jambs and moulded two-centred arch and label. In the W. wall is a window similar to that in the E. wall.

The *South Aisle* (13¾ ft. wide) has windows similar in number and character to those in the N. aisle and all partly restored. Between the two westernmost windows in the S. wall is the reset S. doorway of *c.* 1350, with double chamfered jambs and two-centred arch with a moulded label; above this doorway is a doorway of uncertain date to a former gallery. Between the two eastern windows in the S. wall are the upper and lower doorways of the rood-loft staircase, both with four-centred heads.

The *West Tower* (about 16 ft. square) is of early 16th-century date and of four stages (Plate, p. 80), with an embattled parapet of flint-inlay work, crocketed pinnacles rising from octagonal turrets or buttresses, and a moulded plinth with cusped panels of flint-inlay (Plate, p. 133) enclosing blank shields and crowned monograms of the Virgin. The ground stage forms a passage from N. to S. and is roofed with a segmental-pointed vault of stone; the soffit (Plate, p. 213) is enriched with a double range of cinquefoiled panels with tracery on

each side, enclosing carved flowers, portcullises and two heads, a crown, a mitre, and a hand holding a sword; there is also a series of small shields bearing (*a*) *party palewise;* (*b*) *a cheveron between three lozenges and three martlets on the cheveron* for Welbeck; (*c*) *a cross charged with a rose;* (*d*) *a cross,* (*e*) merchants' marks and the initials I.H., I.W. and T.W. In the E. wall is a lofty arch, the full height of the nave, with moulded responds and four-centred arch; it has a brick filling, in the lower part of which is the early 16th-century W. doorway with elaborately moulded jambs and four-centred arch in a square head with a moulded label and quatrefoiled spandrels enclosing shields; the rear-arch has traceried panelling on the face and a panelled and traceried soffit; further N. on the E. face is a blocked doorway with moulded jambs and four-centred arch; S. of the doorways on the E. side is an inserted stair-turret leading to a stone gallery with a parapet, all modern except a frieze with three lozenge-shaped panels with rosettes and a shield with a merchant's mark and a trefoil-headed panel at the N. end. The upper part of the filling of the main arch is pierced with a modern opening with a plain rounded head. The passage in the ground stage of the tower has at the N. and S. ends an archway with a moulded two-centred arch of two orders, the outer continuous and the inner resting on attached shafts with moulded capitals and bases; the arch has a square moulded label with traceried and carved spandrels. The second stage has the springers of a ribbed stone vault, never completed ; they rest on moulded corbels ; in the W. wall is a window partly restored and of four cinquefoiled lights with tracery in a two-centred head with moulded jambs and label. The third stage has in each wall a window of two cinquefoiled lights in a four-centred head with a moulded label. The bell-chamber has in each wall a window of three cinquefoiled lights with vertical tracery in a four-centred head with a moulded label.

The *North Porch* is of early 16th-century date and of two storeys, with an embattled parapet, moulded plinth and diagonal buttresses, all enriched with flint-inlay in panels with cusped heads ; the two-centred outer archway is of two moulded orders, the outer continuous and the inner resting on attached shafts with moulded capitals and bases ; the arch has a double label enclosing a square head and having crowned lions as stops ; the traceried spandrels have each a shield—(*a*) the Trinity (defaced) ; (*b*) *quarterly a bend with three crosses crosslet thereon* for Fastolf. The side walls have each a much restored window of three trefoiled lights with vertical tracery in a four-centred head with a moulded label. The upper storey has in the N. wall a much restored window of two cinquefoiled lights in a two-centred head with a moulded label ; flanking it, externally, are niches, each with moulded and buttressed jambs, moulded pedestal and trefoiled traceried and crocketed canopy.

The *South Porch* has an early 16th-century moulded plinth with panels of flint-inlay and a 14th-century two-centred outer archway of two chamfered orders reset ; above it is a window of one cinquefoiled ogee light in a square head with a moulded label.

The *Roof* of the chancel is flat-pitched and of four main bays with moulded main timbers and embattled wall-plates ; the principals have curved braces, springing from wall-posts and forming four-centred arches. The roof of the nave is flat-pitched and of thirteen bays with moulded main timbers and carved and embattled wall-plates ; the curved braces beneath the principals spring from wall-posts having attached shafts with moulded capitals and bases and standing on embattled corbels. The roofs of the N. and S. aisles are of flat pent form with moulded main timbers with curved braces and wall-posts.

Fittings—*Bells :* eight ; 6th by W. Burford, *c.* 1400 and inscribed "In Multis Annis Resonet, Campana Johannis " ; 7th by John Darbie, 1675. *Door :* In N. doorway (Plate, p. 42)—of two leaves with moulded and carved fillets planted on ; defaced angel at apex ; each vertical panel with traceried ornament to lower part and above it six shallow niches each formerly having a figure and canopy, all now cut away ; in head, four double panels or niches each with remains of carved figures including probably St. Catherine

and St. Margaret, and two female and four male figures all unidentifiable, early 16th-century. *Font :* octagonal bowl with panelled faces, carved with symbols of the evangelists and angels ; moulded lower edge with carved angels' heads, almost entirely defaced, moulded base, 15th-century. *Glass :* In N. aisle—in N.E. window, 16th-century quarry with knot and initials E.S. ; in N.W. window, fragments of tabernacle work, *c.* 1500. At vicarage—a few fragments. *Indents :* In churchyard—S. of chancel, (1) of cross and four round plates at angles ; W. of N. aisle, (2) of two figures, scrolls, inscription-plate, groups of children, Trinity and round plates at angles, 15th-century. *Monuments* and *Floorslab.* Monuments : In chancel—on N. wall, (1) to Edmund Chapman, 1602, lecturer to the church, alabaster and black marble tablet with broken pediment and achievement of arms (see also (5)) ; (2) of John Roger, 1636, minister of the church, tablet with niche containing bust in skull-cap and gown, represented in pulpit (see also (6)) ; on S. wall, (3) to William Burkitt, 1703, minister of the church, draped white marble tablet with cornice, lamps and achievement of arms. In N. aisle—against N. wall, (4) to [Thomas Webbe, early 16th-century, erected by his son John], altar-tomb with plinth partly enriched with quatrefoils, side of tomb with square quatrefoiled panels enclosing shields and rosettes ; the shields have the initials I.W., and T.W. and merchants' marks ; grey marble slab with moulded edge ; at back four-centred arched recess flanked by octagonal panelled piers carried up as embattled pinnacles, cusped and sub-cusped arch with foliated cornice and traceried spandrels ; at back of recess, range of quatrefoiled panels with three shields having the initials T.W. and merchant's mark, and one with initials I.W., cresting of Tudor flowers ; soffit of recess panelled with quatrefoils ; above cornice, a high attic with panelled and embattled parapet and cornice enriched with an angel holding a shield with a cross and small shields repeating the initials and mark in the recess ; on front of attic, indents of two kneeling figures, scrolls, groups of children and a square plate ; on edge of altar-tomb socket for marginal inscription. In churchyard—(5) to Edmund Chapman, 1602 ; slab ; (6) to John Roger, 1636, table-tomb ; (7) to Robert Alefounder, 1630, table-tomb ; (8) slab of 1638, defaced. Floor-slab : In chancel—to Martha (Wilkinson), wife of William Burkitt, 1698, with achievement of arms. *Niches :* See under N. porch. *Piscinae :* In chancel—with cinquefoiled and sub-cusped head and traceried spandrels enclosing shields with a sprig and the arms of the Trinity respectively, square drain, *c.* 1500, much recut. In S. aisle—in S. wall, with moulded jambs and trefoiled head, quatrefoiled drain, probably 14th-century reset. *Recess :* In

chancel—in S. wall, with segmental brick head and flue, date and purpose uncertain. In room over N. porch—in W. wall, small with square head, early 16th-century. *Scratchings :* on piers of arcades, doorways and window jambs, many masons' marks, *c.* 1500. *Miscellanea :* Near tower—carved figure (Plate, p. 133) of kneeling angel holding scroll, formerly on parapet of tower, early 16th-century.
Condition—Good.

Secular —:

b(2). SOUTHFIELDS (Plate, p. 84), house, said to have been formerly a "bay and say" factory, about 300 yards S.S.E. of the church. It is of two storeys with attics, timber-framed and plastered ; the roofs are covered with tiles and slates. It was built late in the 15th or early in the 16th century on a courtyard plan, with an entrance gateway on the N. There are small modern additions to the N. and S. ranges and the building has been altered to form ten tenements.

The building is of great interest as an example of a large timber-framed structure of its period.

Elevations—Much of the original timber-framing is exposed both in the courtyard (Plate, p. xxx) and in the external walls. The *N. Front* has in the middle the entrance archway with exposed ceiling-beams and a projecting and gabled upper storey ; hung from the middle posts of the entry is an original door of two folds and nail-studded with strap-hinges. The E. end of the N. front has a projecting upper storey. The upper storey of the *E. Front* also projected but has been underbuilt with modern brick. The *S. Front* has a projecting wing at the W. end, with an overhanging upper storey, original moulded bressumers and massive corner-posts with moulded capitals and curved diagonal and rectangular braces ; the diagonal braces are moulded ; the weather-boarded gable also projects. The *W. Front* has at the S. end an original projecting bay-window (Plate, p. 100) of five transomed lights with one light on the return ; the frame and mullions are moulded ; adjoining this window on the S. is another window of two lights, with similar mouldings. The large chimney-stack has tabled offsets and two octagonal shafts, modern at the top. On the rest of this front the upper storey formerly projected but has been underbuilt. The *Courtyard* (60 ft. by 40 ft.) has on the E. side an original doorway with a four-centred head and now blocked, and a four-light window with bar mullions, also blocked. The W. side (Plate, p. 85) has a small original porch ; the outer archway has a flat triangular head. S. of the porch the upper storey projects and there are two original windows of four lights with moulded frames and sills and both now blocked. The upper storey has a blocked doorway, formerly approached by an external staircase.

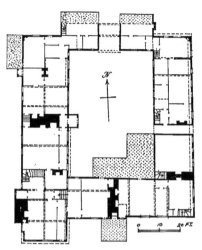

Interior—The most important part of the house is the projecting S.W. wing, called the "Master Weaver's House." Both storeys have original moulded ceiling-beams and joists and in the S. wall is a blocked window of six lights, with moulded mullions. There is an original doorway with a four-centred head and some 16th and 17th-century doors. The staircase of *c.* 1700 has turned balusters. The rest of the building has exposed timber-framing and chamfered ceiling-beams and some tie-beams with curved braces. The upper storey of the E. range appears to have formed one long room, all the existing partitions being modern.
Condition—Good.

MONUMENTS (3–34).

The following monuments, unless otherwise described, are of the 17th century, and of two storeys, timber-framed and plastered or weather-boarded ; the roofs are tiled or thatched. Many of the buildings have original chimney-stacks and exposed ceiling-beams.
Condition—Good, or fairly good, unless noted.

b(3). *Dedham Hall*, 300 yards N.E. of the church, was built early in the 17th century on a T-shaped plan with the cross-wing at the E. end ; late in the same century a wing was added on the N. of the main block.

b(4). *"Dael Holme,"* formerly Mill House, 200 yards W. of (3), was built *c.* 1600, and has later modern additions at the W. end. The N. front has an original timber porch with moulded framing and a dentilled lintel ; at the sides are symmetrically turned balusters. On the S. side are two projecting gables on original shaped brackets. The gables of the N. and W. additions also project on shaped brackets.

HIGH STREET, N. side :—

[b](5). *Cottage,* three tenements, at W. end of Brook Street and 160 yards E.N.E. of the church.

[b](6). *House* and barn, 30 yards W. of (5). The *House* was built late in the 15th or early in the 16th century on an L-shaped plan with the wings extending towards the E. and N. Inside the building several rooms have original moulded ceiling-beams and joists, and there is an early 17th-century door.

The *Barn,* N. of the house, is of three bays with a porch. In the garden are some jamb-stones of a 14th-century window.

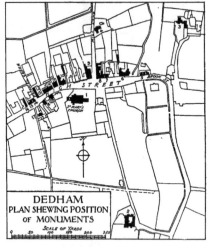

DEDHAM
PLAN SHEWING POSITION
OF MONUMENTS
SCALE OF YARDS

[b](7). *House* and shop, 30 yards W. of (6), is of three storeys, fronted with 18th-century brick.

[b](8). *Marlborough Head Inn,* adjoining (7) on W. side, was built *c.* 1500 on an L-shaped plan, with the wings extending towards the E. and N. There are 17th-century additions at the end of the N. wing. Inside the building the S.W. room has original moulded ceiling-beams carved on the soffit with foliage or cusped tracery ; the lintel of a recess in the S.E. corner has curved braces with foliated spandrels. A room on the first floor has an original moulded ceiling-beam and joists. The roof of the E. wing is original and of king-post type.

[b](9). *House* and shops, at W. junction of Mill Lane and High Street, was built early in the

16th century or possibly earlier. The upper storey projects on the E. side. Inside the building are some original moulded ceiling-beams. A room on the first floor has a late 17th-century plaster ceiling of two bays divided by a beam with vine and oak leaf ornament ; one bay has four panels with bosses of conventional foliage ; the other bay has similar bosses, irregularly placed.

[b](10). *Sun Hotel,* 60 yards W. of (9), was built early in the 16th century on a half H-shaped plan with the wings extending towards the N. The N.W. wing was twice extended in the 17th century. Under the E. end of the main block is a cartway, the lintel of which has curved braces. On the E. side of the early 17th-century extension is an external covered staircase (Plate, p. 100) with exposed timber-framing ; the landing at the top has a gable with a moulded bressumer and shaped brackets. Inside the building is an original moulded ceiling-beam and wall-posts with moulded heads. On the E. side of the yard is a block of stables, of early 16th-century date ; the main partition in the middle of the building consists of vertical panels formed by original moulded studs. The roof is of four bays with braced tie-beams and wind-braced purlins.

[b](11). *House* and shop, W. of (10), has on the E. wall some original pargeting with a design of polygonal panels and cross-shaped panels ; the gable above has moulded barge-boards with conventional foliage. The main chimney-stack has four grouped octagonal shafts, on a square base with a moulded coping.

[b](12). *House* and shop, W.S.W. of (11), was built possibly in the 15th century, but has been completely altered. The shop windows have trefoiled cusping at the angles, said to have come from Boxted church. Inside the building are some 17th-century doors. The staircase has an octagonal newel with a shaped top ; the roof has original cambered tie-beams.

[b](13). *House,* 15 yards W.S.W. of (12), was built probably late in the 16th century, and has a 17th-century addition at the back. In front there is an elaborate early 18th-century frame, of wrought iron, for an inn sign. The original chimney-stack has tabled offsets.

[b](14). *House* and shop, at W. corner of Princel Green and High Street, was built probably early in the 18th century.

[b](15). *House* and shop (Plate, p. 123), W.S.W. of (14), was built *c.* 1600, and has a late 17th-century wing at the back. The upper storey projects in front and on the same side are two projecting gables with original shaped brackets. Inside the building are original moulded ceiling-beams and joists, one with shafted dentils.

[b](16). *House* and shop, W.S.W. of (15).

DEDHAM : (2) SOUTHFIELDS : late 15th or early 16th-century.
From the South-West.

torey
g are
m on
eiling
d oak
with
y has

built
plan
The
tury.
tway,
1 the
is an
with
e top
uaped
ulded
eads.
es, of
on in
anels
l is of
raced

he E.
poly-
gable
tional
uped
ulded

built
com-
foiled
from
17th-
gonal
ignal

built
17th-
ere is
ought
-stack

rincel
rly in

DEDHAM: (2) SOUTHFIELDS; late 15th or early 16th-century.
Courtyard, showing West Range.

S. side :—

b(17). *House*, standing back from the road and 80 yards W.S.W. of the church.

b(18). *House* and shop, 20 yards N.N.E. of (17).

b(19). *House* and shop, 15 yards N.E. of (18). The upper storey formerly projected on the N. and E. sides.

———

a(20). *Rookery Farm*, house, 1,100 yards W.S.W. of the church, has inside the building some original doors and a window with moulded mullions, now blocked.

a(21). *Cottage*, by the river, about 1 m. W.N.W. of the church, was built *c*. 1500. The upper storey projects on the W. side and S. end and has an original moulded and embattled bressumer, exposed joists and curved brackets. Inside the building are original moulded ceiling-beams and joists.

a(22). *Boxhouse Farm*, house, ½ m. W. of (20), has a W. wing of 15th-century date ; the main block was rebuilt early in the 17th century. The upper storey of the W. porch projects in front ; above the entrance is a defaced date 16—, in plaster ; the window on the first floor is largely modern. In the S. wall is an opening with original turned balusters and above it is a band of running foliage in plaster. To the S. of the porch, above the lower window, is a band of scallops and conventional honeysuckle in plaster. N. of the porch is an early 17th-century window. Inside the building the S. room has a late 17th-century plaster ceiling (Plate, p. 235), divided into four bays by moulded trabeations with rich conventional foliage on the soffits ; the cornice is also enriched and the bays have central foliated bosses and sprays of fruit, etc., at the angles. The room above has a similar ceiling. There is one 17th-century door and the E. wing has remains of the original roof.

a(23) *Blackbrook Farm*, house, 650 yards S.W. of (22).

c(24). *Mount Pleasant*, house, about 1¼ m. S.W. of the church, was built probably in the first half of the 16th century, with a cross-wing at the S.W. end. The upper storey projects at the S.W. end and did formerly also on the S.E. front. Inside the building both wings have original moulded ceiling-beams. In the S.W. wing is a mid 17th-century plaster ceiling divided into square bays, with enriched borders and centre-pieces and fleurs-de-lis at the angles.

c(25). *Lamb Inn*, 50 yards N.E. of (24).

c(26). *House* (Plate, p. 189), 170 yards N.E. of (25), was built probably in the 16th century. Inside the building are some original moulded joists.

c(27). *Rye Farm*, house, 200 yards S.E. of (26), was built probably late in the 16th century, with a cross-wing at the W. end.

b(28). *Cottage*, two tenements, in Cooper's Lane, ½ m. S. of the church, was built in the 16th century and has a projecting upper storey on the W. side. Condition—Poor.

b(29). *Cottage*, S. of (28), has exposed timber-framing. Condition—Bad.

b(30). *House*, formerly Prince of Wales Inn, 120 yards E. of (29), was built in the 15th century, with a central hall and cross-wing at the W. end. The upper storey projects at the W. end of the cross-wing, but is covered by a modern annexe. Inside the building are original moulded ceiling-beams and king-post roof-trusses.

a(31). *Castle House*, 70 yards S.E. of (30), has been almost completely altered.

b(32). *House*, 160 yards E.N.E. of (31), has an original chimney-stack, with four octagonal shafts on a square base. The timber-framing is partly exposed at the back. Condition—Poor.

d(33). *Lufkin's Farm*, house, 1¼ m. S.S.E. of the church, has an original chimney-stack with diagonal pilaster-strips.

d(34). *Hill Farm*, house, 550 yards E.N.E. of (33), was built possibly in the 16th century. The gable projects at the N.W. end.

———

19. DOVERCOURT. (G.b.)

(O.S. 6 in. *(a)*xxi. S.W. *(b)*xxi. S.E.)

Dovercourt is a parish and town adjoining Harwich on the S.W. The church is the principal monument.

Roman :—

b(1). A tessellated pavement and a wall built entirely of Roman bricks is recorded by Morant on a small farm belonging to Dovercourt Vicarage, apparently in Beacon Hill field near a 'tumulus' on which stood a windmill about half a mile S. of Harwich. He also mentions various earthworks, which have now disappeared, and the "mutilated parts of a considerable large stone pavement," running hence to Harwich. This was the high road, and was called 'the Street,' and Roman coins were found in it. His information points to the site of a house, and possibly to traces of a Roman road from Colchester to Harwich, and across the harbour to the former fort at Walton. (Morant, *Hist. Essex*, 1768, I, 499 ; hence *Gough's Camden*, 1789, II, 60 ; Brayley and Britton, *Beauties of England*, V, 330 ; S. Dale, *Antiquities of Harwich*, 1732, p. 19.) (See also *Sectional Preface*, p. xxvii.)

Ecclesiastical :—

ᵃ(2). PARISH CHURCH OF ALL SAINTS stands on
the W. side of the parish. The walls are of septaria-
rubble with dressings of limestone ; the roofs
are tiled. The *Nave* was built in the 12th century.
Early in the 14th century the *Chancel* was rebuilt
and a porch was probably added during the same
period. About 1400 the *West Tower* was added.
The chancel-arch was replaced in timber *c.* 1615.
The church has been restored in modern times,
the chancel partly rebuilt. the top stage of the
tower rebuilt, the *North Vestry* added and the
South Porch rebuilt.

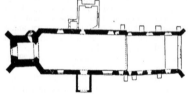

Architectural Description—The *Chancel* (35¾ ft.
by 23½ ft.) has a modern E. wall and window.
In the N. wall are three windows, the two eastern
of early 14th-century date but completely restored
externally ; they are each of two pointed lights
in a two-centred head ; the westernmost window
is a 'low-side' of a single lancet light of the same
period but modern externally. In the S. wall are
three windows similar to the corresponding windows
in the N. wall ; between the two eastern windows
is a modern doorway. Between the chancel and
the nave is a moulded and richly carved beam
with acanthus and conventional foliage ornament
and consoles at each end ; it rests on moulded
posts and has on the W. face three shields, two
with the date and initials 1615, G.W. ; on the soffit
of the beam are the initials R.H.

The *Nave* (61½ ft. by 23½ ft.), has in the N. wall
two windows, both of early 14th-century date
and similar to the eastern windows in the chancel ;
both are partly restored ; between them is the
14th-century N. doorway with hollow-chamfered
jambs and two-centred head ; further W. is a
12th-century window of one round-headed light,
now blocked ; E. of the eastern window is the
15th-century rood-loft staircase ; the lower doorway has restored jambs and rebated four-centred
head ; the upper doorway incorporates the jamb-
stones of a 12th-century opening. In the S. wall
are three windows, the easternmost is modern
except part of the jambs and rear-arch which
are of the 16th century ; the middle window is
of *c.* 1340 and of two trefoiled ogee lights with
flowing tracery in a two-centred head ; the
westernmost window is modern except for part
of the rear-arch ; between the two western

windows is the mid 14th-century S. doorway with
moulded jambs, two-centred arch and label ;
near the W. end of the wall is a blocked 12th-
century window, similar to that in the N. wall.

The *West Tower* (11½ ft. square) is of three
stages of which the two lower are of the 15th
century and the top stage modern. The two-
centred tower-arch is of three orders, the two
outer chamfered and moulded and continuous
and the inner hollow-chamfered and resting on
attached shafts with moulded capitals and bases.
There are indications of a former ringing-gallery
on the N. and S. walls. The W. window is of *c.* 1400,
partly restored, and of two cinquefoiled lights
with tracery in a two-centred head with a moulded
label ; the W. doorway is of the same date and
has double-chamfered jambs, two-centred arch
and label. The second stage has in the S. and
W. walls a blocked window of one trefoiled light.

The *South Porch* is modern except for the re-set
14th-century outer archway which has a moulded
two-centred arch ; the responds have attached
shafts with recut capitals and defaced bases.

Fittings—Bells : two ; 1st by Robert Mot,
1572 ; 2nd by William Burford, late 14th-century
and inscribed " In Multis annis resonet campana
Johannis." *Brass :* In chancel—on N. wall, of
civilian in fur-trimmed gown and belt, inscribed
scroll, mid 15th-century. *Coffin-lid :* In nave—
with foliated cross in relief, 13th-century. *Door :*
In S. doorway—of four upright panels, with
moulded fillets, plain strap-hinges and stock lock,
17th-century. *Font* (Plate, p. xxxiv) : octagonal
bowl with moulded edges and traceried panels
of various designs, square stem with attached shaft
at each angle, moulded base, mid 14th-century.
Panelling : In vestry—incorporated in modern
cupboard, three traceried heads, mid 15th-century.
Piscina : In nave—in S. wall, with chamfered
jambs and two-centred head, 14th-century. *Poor-
box* (Plate, p. xxxii) : iron-bound oak box with two
strap-hinges to lid, painted date on side 1589.
Condition—Good.

Secular :—

MONUMENTS (3–6).

The following monuments are of the 17th
century and of two storeys, timber-framed and
plastered or weather-boarded ; the roofs are tiled.
All the buildings have exposed ceiling-beams.
Condition—Good.

ᵃ(3). *Cottage*, about 700 yards E. of the church.

ᵃ(4). *Manor House*, 70 yards E. of (3), has a
modern addition on the N.

ᵃ(5). *Dovercourt Hall*, 600 yards S. of (4), is of
L-shaped plan with the wings extending towards
the S. and E.

ᵃ(6). *House*, nearly 1 m. W.S.W. of the church,
has an original chimney-stack with grouped diagonal
shafts.

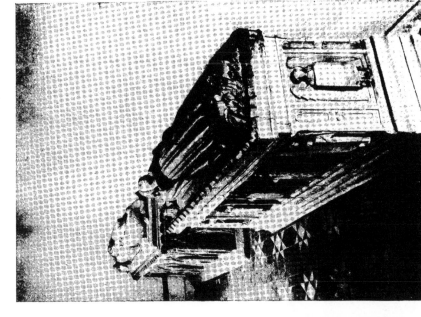

Tomb of Alice, wife of Richard, 11th Earl of Oxford; c. 1417.

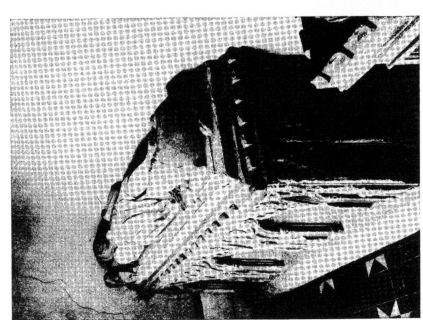

Tomb of Robert de Vere, 5th Earl of Oxford; c. 1340.

EARLS COLNE PRIORY.

with
abel;
12th-
all.
three
15th
two
two
uous
g on
pases,
allery
1400,
lights
ulded
; and
arch
. and
light.
re-set
ulded
ached

Mot,
ntury
pana-
ll, of
ribed
ave—
Door:
with
lock,
gonal
panels
shaft
ntury.
odern
ntury.
ltered
Poor-
h two
589.

17th
1 and
tiled.

hurch
has a

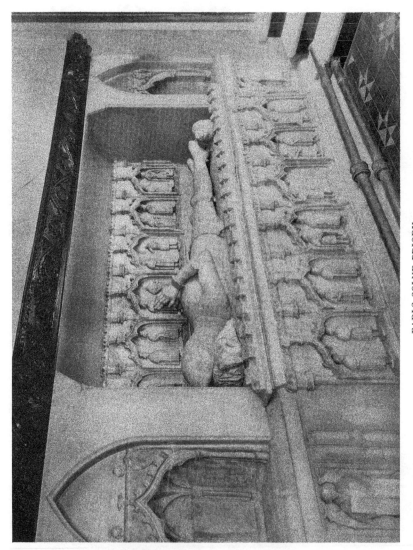

EARLS COLNE PRIORY.
Tomb of Thomas de Vere, 8th Earl of Oxford ; 1371.

20. EARLS COLNE. (B.c.)

(O.S. 6 in. (a)xvii. S.W. (b)xvii. S.E. (c)xxvi. N.W. (d)xxvi. N.E.)

Earls Colne is a parish and village (Plate, p. 123) 4 m. N. of Great Coggeshall. The church, Priory and Colneford House are the principal monuments.

Ecclesiastical —:

a(1). PARISH CHURCH OF ST. ANDREW stands at the E. end of the village. The walls are of flint-rubble, with limestone dressings ; the roofs are tiled. The history of the building is much obscured by restoration, but the earliest detail is the S. arcade of the *Nave* and a reset window in the N. chapel which are of *c.* 1340 ; the *Chancel* and *South Aisle* are probably also of this date. The *West Tower* was added *c.* 1460, but it was restored and partly rebuilt by John Earl of Oxford in 1534. A South porch was added in the 15th century. In the 19th century the church was restored, the *South Porch* rebuilt and the *North* and *South Chapels* and *North Aisle* added.

The W. tower is a handsome example of its period. Among the fittings the pre-Reformation paten is noteworthy.

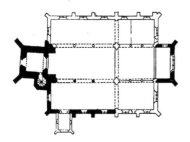

Architectural Description—The *Chancel* (38¾ ft. by 23 ft.) has no ancient features.

The *North Chapel* is modern but reset in the N. wall is a window of *c.* 1340, partly restored and of two trefoiled ogee lights with tracery in a two-centred head.

The *South Chapel* is modern, but the W. arch incorporates some 14th-century moulded voussoirs.

The *Nave* (50½ ft. by 22¾ ft.) has a modern N. arcade of three bays. The 14th-century S. arcade is of three bays with two-centred arches of two moulded orders ; the octagonal columns and semi-octagonal W. respond have moulded capitals and modern bases ; the E. respond is modern, the E. arch has been rebuilt and most of the other work has been scraped.

The *South Aisle* (19½ ft. wide) has in the S. wall two 14th-century windows almost entirely restored

and each of two cinquefoiled lights with a quatre-foil in a two-centred head, with a moulded label ; further W. is the S. doorway, all modern except the 14th-century moulded rear-arch and part of the splays. In the W. wall is a modern window, incorporating some old stones.

The *West Tower* (13 ft. by 14 ft.) is of three stages (Plate, p. 221) with a crow-stepped and embattled parapet enriched with panels of flint-inlay having cinquefoiled or trefoiled heads ; the larger panels have each the Vere molet in the middle ; in the middle of the E. and W. sides is a carved achievement of arms, with supporters and the Garter, on the E. side the shield bears Vere impaling Trussell for John 15th Earl of Oxford and his wife, and has below it the date 1534 and regnal year H.8. 25 ; the shield on the W. side bears Vere quartering Collroke, Clare, Sergeaux, Badlesmere, Samford, and Fitz Hamon ; the parapet of the stair-turret also has flint-inlay and the Vere molets. The 15th-century tower-arch is moulded and two-centred and springs from moulded and shafted responds with moulded capitals to the shafts. The W. window is of *c.* 1460 and of three cinquefoiled lights with tracery in a four-centred head with a moulded label and stops carved with busts of women holding hearts ; the W. doorway is modern, but the 15th-century string-course on either side of it has carved flowers and heads. The second stage has in the E. and W. walls a single 15th-century light with a trefoiled head ; a similar window in the N. wall has been removed ; in the E. wall is also an early 16th-century doorway of brick, with a four-centred head. The bell-chamber has in the E., S. and W. walls a 15th-century window of three cinquefoiled lights with tracery in a square head. In the N. wall is a much restored early 16th-century window of three cinquefoiled lights in a square head.

The *Roof* of the nave is of early 16th-century date and of five bays with moulded principals, collars and purlins, and a carved boss in the middle of each collar. The roof of the S. aisle is similar in date and detail to that of the nave, but is of six bays and has moulded wall-plates ; one of the bosses is carved with the Vere molet. The 15th-century roof of the S. porch has moulded and embattled wall-plates and tie-beam ; the other tie-beam is plain, but both support king-posts.

Fittings—*Chairs :* In N. chapel—with carved and inlaid back, turned legs and shaped arms, inlaid front-rail, early 17th-century. In chancel—two with richly carved backs and front rails, turned legs and shaped arms, probably late 17th-century and foreign work. *Monuments :* In S. chapel—(1) of Richard Harlakenden, 1602, and Elizabeth (Hardres), Elizabeth (Blatchenden), Jane (Josceline) and Anne (Dewhurst), his wives, small painted wall-monument of alabaster with kneeling figures of man and wives flanked by pilasters supporting an entablature, achievement and four shields of arms, restored early in the 18th century ; (2) to Jane and Mabell Harlakenden, 1614, plain rectangular tablet ; (3) to Mehetabell, daughter of Edward Eileston, 1657, oval tablet with white marble frame ; on S. wall—(4) to John Eldred, 1646, rectangular tablet with marble frame and cornice and resting on two carved stone heads. In churchyard—S. of church (5) to Francies (Fletcher), wife of John Hutchinson, 1712, head and foot-stones. *Plate* (Plate, p. xxxv) : includes early 16th-century paten with sexfoiled sinking and incised figure of Christ in a circle in the middle, cross formy in a circle on the rim ; large late 16th-century cup with bands of incised ornament. *Table :* In N. chapel—with turned legs and shaped brackets to top rail, 17th-century. *Weather-vane :* with copper corona and cock, late 17th or early 18th-century.

Condition—Good, much restored.

b(2). EARLS COLNE PRIORY, monuments, walls and fragments at house, ¼ m. E. of the church. The Priory was founded in the first year of the 12th century for Benedictine monks and as a cell to Abingdon Abbey. The lines of some of the original buildings are reported to have been visible in the turf on the N. side of the present house during the dry summer of 1921. The existing house has no ancient features, but in a covered passage at the back of the house are preserved four altar-tombs, formerly in the priory church—(1) probably of Robert de Vere, 5th Earl of Oxford, 1296, altar-tomb (Plate, p. 86) of *c.* 1340, with moulded and embattled slab of Purbeck marble richly arcaded sides and end, side with three main niches with cinquefoiled ogee and crocketed heads and shafted jambs ; three smaller niches with trefoiled heads and crocketed gables ; between the niches are small buttresses with pinnacles and in the spandrels above the larger niches are blank shields suspended by their straps ; in the smaller niches are much mutilated figures ; the freestone effigy of *c.* 1296 is in mail with kneecops, a long surcoat and prick spurs ; the head rests on a cushion supported by angels, and the feet on a boar ; there are traces of colour and gesso on the effigy and of colour on the tomb. Four niches with figures from the destroyed sides of this tomb are now built into the gate-piers of the stable yard and three others are fixed in the wall near tombs (3) and (4). (2) and (3) were formerly one large tomb (Plates, pp. 86, 90) of alabaster and probably of Richard de Vere, K.G., 11th Earl of Oxford, 1417, and Alice (Sergeaux), his wife ; the two long sides form the fronts of the two altar-tombs as at present arranged ; at the head of (2) is a square cusped panel probably part of

the monument of Robert, 9th Earl of Oxford and Duke of Ireland, 1392. The long sides of the two tombs have each five panels with angels holding rectangular shields and divided by traceried panels ; the moulded cornice is embattled ; the shields bear (*a*) Vere, (*b*) Vere impaling Badlesmere, (*c*) Vere, (*d*) Vere impaling Fitzwalter, (*e*) Vere. On tomb (3) (*a*) Vere, (*b*) Vere impaling *a saltire between* 12 *cherries* for Sergeaux, (*c*) Vere, (*d*) Vere quartering *checky* for Coucy, (*e*) Vere. The earlier panel at head of tomb (2) has a shield with the arms of Bohun. At the foot of tomb (2) and fixed into the wall elsewhere are four other fragments of the tomb of the 11th Earl with angels bearing shields (*a*) Vere with scutcheon of pretence, (*b*) defaced, (*c*) St. George and (*d*) France ancient quartering England. The effigy of the woman (Plate, p. 91) on tomb (2) has an elaborate horned head-dress, collar, low-necked gown with tight sleeves, loose cloak with cord fastenings, head on cushions with two supporting angels and at feet two small dogs. The man's effigy (Plate, p. 91) is in plate-armour with a wreathed bascinet inscribed across the front in black letter "Ihs : nazarenus," plate gorget and besagues, collar of S.S., breastplate with the arms of Vere, skirt of taces with mail beneath, remains of sword and dagger, garter on left leg, head on helm with boar crest, feet on lion. (4) Probably of Thomas de Vere, 8th Earl of Oxford, 1371, alabaster altar-tomb (Plate, p. 87) with moulded and embattled cornice, front with six niches divided by shafts and having trefoiled ogee and crocketed heads ; each niche has two weepers, all men in civilian dress ; the corresponding work of the other side of the tomb has been reset in the wall at the back of the modern recess ; it has similar weepers including one bishop. The effigy (Plate, p. 91) is in mixed mail and plate with bascinet, camail, jupon with the arms of Vere and with enriched edge, ornamental hip-belt, etc. Across the head of the modern recesses of tombs (3) and (4) is an early 16th-century carved oak beam, removed from the old Priory House which was pulled down in 1825, with running foliage, the Vere molet, and six grotesque heads.

The boundary wall of the grounds on the S.E. and S.W. sides is largely of late 16th-century date and of red brick. It contains the initials R.H., W. and X.W. in black bricks. On the S.W. side is a modern doorway with a door made up of 15th and 16th and 17th-century panelling ; above the doorway is a reset 15th-century niche with a cinquefoiled head and containing two figures. The lower part of the wall contains some reused worked stones. In the garden is a 15th-century panelled stone stem of octagonal form and possibly part of a font.

In the summer-house near the Priory pond is the bressumer of a fireplace, carved with the

Vere molet and boar, with other beasts and birds and with conventional leaf-ornament of the 16th century.

Condition—Of monuments, good.

Secular :—

ᶜ(3). LODGE FARM, house and moat, nearly 1¾ m. S.W. of the church. The *House*, now two tenements, is of two storeys, timber-framed and plastered ; the roofs are tiled. It was built probably early in the 16th century and altered late in the 17th century. Inside the building are exposed ceiling-beams and joists and one wall-plate has the mortices for the diamond-shaped mullions of a former window.

The *Moat* is incomplete.

Condition—Of house, good.

MONUMENTS (4–34).

The following monuments, unless otherwise described, are of the 17th century and of two storeys, timber-framed and plastered or weather-boarded ; the roofs are tiled or thatched. Several of the buildings have original chimney-stacks and exposed ceiling-beams.

Condition—Good or fairly good, unless noted.

HIGH STREET, N. side :—

ᵃ(4). *House*, two tenements and shop, 120 yards W.N.W. of the church, has a late 15th or early 16th-century outbuilding at the back, but the building itself is of the 17th century. The out-building has an original king-post roof of three bays.

ᵃ(5). *House* and shop, W. of (4), was built in the 16th century and has a 17th-century addition on the N. Inside the building are original moulded ceiling-beams and a doorway with a four-centred head. There is a little 17th-century panelling.

ᵃ(6). *Castle Inn*, W. of (5), is of half H-shaped plan with the wings extending towards the N. It has two original chimney-stacks, one of five shafts set diagonally on a rectangular base and one of three octagonal shafts. Inside the building the middle room has an original moulded ceiling-beam resting at one end on a wall-post with enriched mouldings. The E. room has above the fireplace a 17th-century painted panel with the verse " The houer Runneth | and T(ime flieth) | As Flower Fadeth | So Man Dieth | Sic transit Gloria | Mundi " ; on each side of it is an hour-glass, cherub's head, flower and skull and beyond a pair of crouching lions with swags above.

ᵃ(7). *House*, now club, shop and tenement, W. of (6), has a cross-wing, with a projecting upper storey, at the E. end.

ᵃ(8). *Cottage*, 150 yards W. of (7) and on the E. side of Queen's Road.

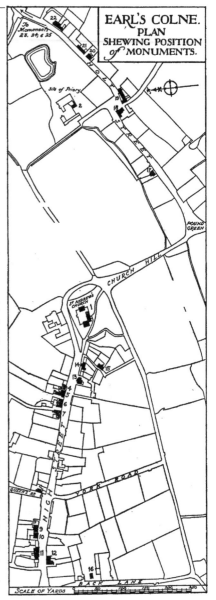

a(9). *House*, now Bank, 80 yards W. of (8), was built early in the 16th century and has a long wing at the back ; the front has been faced with modern brick.   Inside the building the W. room has original moulded ceiling-beams and moulded joists ; the beams and plate are carved with running foliage (Plate, p. xxxvii) and a shield with the molet of the Veres.   The back wing has an original king-post roof.

a(10). *House* and shop, W. of (9), was built probably early in the 16th century and has an original king-post roof.

a(11). *Lion Inn* and house, 20 yards W. of (10). The W. end of the house is of late 16th-century date and has original moulded ceiling-beams.   The E. front has been rebuilt.

S. side :—

a(12). *House*, four tenements, 20 yards S.W. of (11), was built probably in the 15th century, with cross-wings at the E. and W. ends.   The W. gable in front has plain old barge-boards with curved brackets.

a(13). *House* (Plate, p. 188), two tenements and shop nearly opposite (4), was built *c.* 1500.   The upper storey projects in front and has a moulded bressumer, carved with twisted leaf ornament and, at intervals, with the molet of the Veres. Inside the building are original moulded ceiling-beams and joists.   The roof has original king-post trusses.

a(14). *House*, two tenements, 30 yards E. of (13), has two projecting gables in front with carved fascias, one with the date and initials 1674 E.P.

a(15). *Cottage*, two tenements, S. of (14).

---

a(16). *Cottage* (Plate, p. 177), 80 yards S.S.W. of (12), has an original chimney-stack with four octagonal shafts.

POUND GREEN :—

b(17). *Cottage*, on N. side of road, 300 yards S.E. of the church, was built early in the 18th century.

b(18). *George Hotel*, on S. side of road, 130 yards N.E. of (17), was built probably in the 16th century and has a cross-wing at the W. end.

b(19). *House*, E. of (18), has a cross-wing at the E. end.

b(20). *Cottage*, two tenements, 90 yards N.E. of (19), has a cross-wing at the W. end.

b(21). *Range of three tenements*, N.E. of (20).

b(22). *House*, 45 yards N.E. of (21), was built probably late in the 16th century, but has been much altered.

---

b(23). *Colneford House*, 240 yards N.E. of (22). The S.E. wing is of late 16th-century date, but

the front is probably entirely of *c.* 1685.   The front has an upper storey richly ornamented between the windows with pargeting (Plate, p. 235) ; the panels have elaborate designs of conventional foliage and foliated borders ; one panel has the initials and date $\frac{T}{GE}$ 1685, probably for George and Elizabeth Toller.   Inside the building are some fireplaces with moulded architraves of late 17th-century date and some bolection-moulded panelling of the same period.   The staircase of dog-legged type has turned balusters and moulded rails.   The S.E. wing has original moulded ceiling-beams and joists.

b(24). *Range of six cottages*, 70 yards N.E. of (23).   The upper storey projects in three gabled bays on the N.W. front.

b(25). *Cottage* (Plate, p. 189), on N.E. side of the road, 700 yards E.S.E. of the church, has on the W. side an original dormer window with a moulded head to the window carved with the date and initials 1640 E.S.

d(26). *Mill's Farm*, house, ¾ m. S.S.E. of (25).

d(27). *Burnt House Farm*, house, ½ m. S.S.E. of (26).

d(28). *Becklandwood Farm*, house, 1,200 yards W. of (27).

e(29). *Whitegate*, house, about 1,000 yards S.W. of (28).

e(30). *Cottage*, on W. side of road, about ½ m. N. of (29).
Condition—Ruinous.

e(31). *Cottage*, 100 yards N. of (30).

e(32). *Range of three tenements*, on N. side of Curd's Road, 650 yards N. of (31).

e(33). *Cottage*, 180 yards N.W. of (32).

e(34). *Cottage*, 150 yards N.N.E. of (33).

---

21. EAST DONYLAND.   (D.d.)

(O.S. 6 in. xxxvii. N.W.)

East Donyland is a parish with a village at Rowhedge on the right bank of the Colne, 3 m. S.E. of Colchester.

Ecclesiastical :—

(1). PARISH CHURCH OF ST. LAURENCE stood 700 yards S.W. of the modern church.   It was entirely destroyed about 1837.   The modern church contains from the old building the following :—
Fittings — *Brasses :* On wall—(1) of Nicholas Marshall, 1621, figure of man in ruff, puffed breeches and cloak, erected by Alice (Brooke), his second wife ; (2) of Mary, wife of Nicholas Marshall, and after of William Graye, 1627, figure of woman

EARLS COLNE PRIORY.

Tomb of Richard de Vere, K.G., 11th Earl of Oxford ; 1417.

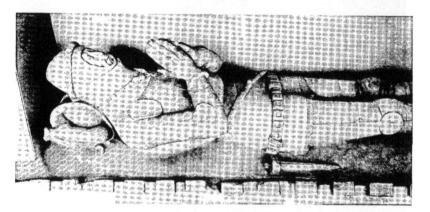

Thomas de Vere, 8th Earl of Oxford ; 1371.

Richard de Vere, K.G., 11th Earl of Oxford ; 1417.

Alice (Sergeaux), wife of Richard, 11th Earl of Oxford.

EARLS COLNE PRIORY : EFFIGIES.

in ruff, full gown, etc. *Monuments :* On W. wall—(1) of Elizabeth Marshall, 1613, marble monument with seated figure of woman in niche flanked by obelisks, entablature, figures of three children, two dead, two shields and achievement of arms In churchyard of old church—(2) to Susanna, wife of Ralph Turpin, 1706, headstone.
Condition—Rebuilt.

Secular :—

(2). EAST DONYLAND HALL, house and moat, 750 yards S.S.W. of the modern church. The *House* is of two storeys, with attics ; the walls are of brick and plastered timber-framing ; the roofs are tiled. It was built early in the 17th century, but reconstructed *c.* 1700 and refronted *c.* 1800. Inside the building the main staircase has turned and twisted balusters and moulded rails of *c.* 1700. The *Moat* surrounds the house.
Condition—Of house, good, much altered.

Unclassified :—

(3). MOUND, 270 yards N.N.W. of (2), is about 65 ft. in diameter and 8 ft. high.
Condition—Fairly good.

---

22. EASTHORPE. (C.d.)

(O.S. 6 in. (a)xxxv. N.E. (b)xxxvi. N.W.)

Easthorpe is a small parish 6 m. W.S.W. of Colchester. The church is the principal monument.

Ecclesiastical :—

b(1). PARISH CHURCH OF ST. MARY (Plate, p. 92) stands at the E. end of the parish. The walls are of mixed rubble and septaria partly coursed, the dressings are of Roman brick and clunch ; the roofs are tiled. The *Nave* with an apsidal chancel was built early in the 12th century. About the middle of the 13th century the apse was destroyed and the *Chancel* extended towards the E. A south porch was added in the 15th century. The church was restored in 1910 when the *South Porch* was rebuilt. The bell-turret is apparently modern.
The church has interesting remains of 12th and 13th-century work.
Architectural Description—The *Chancel* (30¾ ft. by 20 ft.) is structurally undivided from the nave. In the E. wall is a graduated triplet of mid 13th-century lancet windows ; the splays are enriched with dog-tooth ornament and have detached shafts with moulded capitals and bases ; the capitals of the two middle shafts are foliated ; the rear-arches and labels are much restored or modern but two of the head-stops are original. In the N. wall are two windows ; the eastern is a

13th-century lancet ; the western is of mid 14th-century date, much restored and of two cinque-foiled lights in a two-centred head with a moulded label and head-stops ; between the windows are slight traces, externally, of the jambs of a former doorway. In the S. wall are four windows, the two easternmost are uniform with the N.E. window, but much restored ; the third window is the upper part of a round-headed 12th-century light of Roman brick ; the lower part of the windows was blocked when the westernmost window was inserted in the 14th century ; this window has a modern mullion and tracery and a two-centred head ; E. of it is a 13th-century door-way with chamfered jambs and two-centred arch with a moulded label ; E. of the doorway, externally, the wall has been cut back to show the spring of the former apse.
The *Nave* (34 ft. by 20 ft.) has in the N. wall three windows ; the easternmost is of early 14th-century date and of two trefoiled ogee lights with a quatrefoil in a two-centred head ; the middle window is a 13th-century round-headed light of Roman brick ; the westernmost window is of the 16th or 17th century and is a single round-headed light of brick ; above the easternmost window is the head of a blocked 12th-century window similar to the middle window ; between the two western windows is the early 12th-century N. doorway with plain jambs and round arch of Roman brick ; at the E. end of the wall are two 15th-century doorways to the former rood-loft staircase ; the lower doorway has moulded jambs and two-centred arch ; the upper with rebated jambs and two-centred arch is probably of 13th-century material reused ; after the staircase has been removed, and reset in the outer wall is part of a former window with a cinquefoiled head. In the S. wall are three windows of which the easternmost and westernmost are of the 12th century and similar to that in the N. wall ; the middle window is of late 14th-century date and of two cinque-foiled lights with tracery in a two-centred head. W. of the windows is the S. doorway similar but larger than the N. doorway and fitted with a wooden frame ; beneath the easternmost window is a recess (see Fittings) and in the back of it is a single quatrefoiled window of the 14th century. In the W. wall is a mid 14th-century window of two cinquefoiled lights with a quatrefoil in a two-centred head with a moulded label ; above it is a window of one round-headed light and apparently all modern.
The *South Porch* has been rebuilt but incorporates the two-centred outer archway of oak, the tie-beam above it and a king-post truss, all of the 15th century.
Fittings—*Communion Table :* In chancel—with turned legs, shaped brackets and carved front rail, 17th-century. *Floor-slabs :* In chancel—

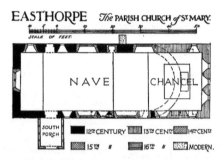

EASTHORPE *The* PARISH CHURCH *of* S.ᵗ MARY.

SCALE OF FEET

NAVE   CHANCEL

SOUTH PORCH

■ 12ᵗʰ CENTURY   ▥ 13ᵗʰ CENᵗ   ▨ 14ᵗʰ CENᵗ   ▨ 15ᵗʰ "   ■ 16ᵗʰ "   ▨ MODERN.

(1) to Thomas Greene, 1698, and his wife, 1719, with achievement of arms ; (2) to Anne (Blagrave), widow of George Kingesmyll, 1680, with shield of arms ; (3) to Margaret, daughter of George Kingesmyll, 1652. *Glass :* In chancel—in S.W. window, figure subject of Christ preaching, foreign, 16th-century, property of rector. *Niche :* In nave—above lower doorway to rood-loft, with rebated jambs and round head, date uncertain. *Paintings :* In nave—on splays and head of S.E. window, remains of figures in black and red including resurrection figure and angels holding instruments of the passion (?), also a band of indented ornament, 13th-century. *Piscina :* In chancel—with moulded jambs and segmental-pointed head, two round drains, 13th-century, much restored. *Plate :* includes late 16th-century cup and cover-paten, both remodelled. *Recesses :* In chancel—in N. wall, plain plastered recess, date uncertain. In nave—in S. wall at E. end, with shafted jambs, capitals formerly carved, moulded ogee arch, early 14th-century, probably tomb-recess. *Seating :* two benches with shaped ends and one with remains of popeys, 15th-century. *Sedilia :* In chancel—of two bays with moulded and trefoiled arches and labels enriched with dog-tooth ornament and having one old head-stop, shafted jambs and free shaft of grey marble in middle, with moulded capital and base, mid 13th-century, probably restored. *Stoup :* In nave—in S. wall, with moulded jambs and cinquefoiled head, probably 15th-century, bowl destroyed. *Miscellanea :* At vicarage—clunch stone, formerly built into wall above S. doorway, with erotic carving of woman and inscription E L U I . . ., 12th-century or earlier.
Condition—Good.

Secular :—

ᵃ(2). BADCOCK'S FARM, house and moat, about ¾ m. W.S.W. of the church. The *House* is of two storeys, timber-framed and plastered ; the roofs are tiled. It was built in the 16th century with cross-wings at the E. and W. ends. The upper storey of

the main block projects on the N. front and has a moulded bressumer carved with twisted leaf ornament and the date 1585. Inside the building the main block has exposed ceiling-beams and joists. The *Moat* formerly surrounded the house.
Condition—Of house, good.

ᵃ(3). EASTHORPE HALL, 70 yards W. of the church, is of two storeys, timber-framed and plastered ; the roofs are tiled. It was built in the 15th century with a central Hall and cross-wings at the E. and W. ends. In the 16th century the wings were extended towards the S. and in the 17th century a wing was added on the N. of the Hall-block. The main chimney-stack has three square detached shafts of the 17th century. Two other chimney-stacks have diagonal shafts also of the 17th century. Inside the building are exposed ceiling-beams and joists ; the original roof of the E. wing has a king-post truss. Two fireplaces have four-centred arches of brick and there are some late 17th-century panelled doors.
Condition—Good, much altered.

ᵇ(4). RECTORY, ¼ m. E. of the church, is of two storeys with attics ; the walls are partly of plastered timber-framing and partly of brick ; the roofs are tiled. The long cross-wing at the W. end of the house is of the 15th century, but the main block was rebuilt in the 17th century and extended eastwards in the 18th century ; there are various modern additions. Inside the building the original wing has cambered tie-beams. There are also some 17th-century panelled doors.
Condition—Good, much altered.

ᵇ(5). HOUSE (Plate, p. 188) opposite the church, is of two storeys, timber-framed and plastered ; the roofs are tiled. It was built probably late in the 15th century and is of L-shaped plan with the wings extending towards the S. and W. The upper storey projects on the E. and N. sides of the S. wing ; the angle-post has a much weathered capital and the timber-framing is exposed. Inside the building the W. wing has an original roof of rough king-post type.
Condition—Good.

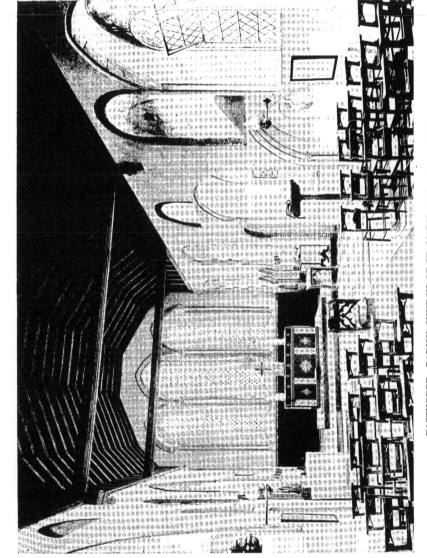

EASTHORPE: PARISH CHURCH OF ST. MARY; 12th-century and later.
Interior, looking East.

as a
orna-
ding
usts.

the
and
the
rings
the
17th
Hall-
quare
other
the
posed
the
laces
are

two
tered
roofs
of
main
nded
rious
iginal
also

urch,
; the
te in
with
The
es of
hered
inside
of

ELMSTEAD: PARISH CHURCH OF ST. LAURENCE.

23. EAST MERSEA. (D.d.)

(O.S. 6 in. xlvii. N.W.)

East' Mersea is a parish comprising the E. half of Mersea Island, 7½ m. S.S.E. of Colchester. The church is interesting.

Ecclesiastical —:

(1). PARISH CHURCH OF ST. EDMUND stands on the S. side of the parish. The walls are of septaria and flint-rubble with dressings of limestone; the roofs are covered with tiles and slates. The S. wall of the *Chancel* is thicker than the N. wall and may be of the 12th or 13th century. The S. wall of the *Nave* is probably of the same date and the upper part is of less thickness than the lower. In the 14th century the chancel was widened towards the N. and probably extended one bay to the E. Late in the 15th or early in the 16th century the *North Chapel, North Aisle* and *West Tower* were added. The *South Porch* was added probably late in the 18th century, when various other alterations were made.

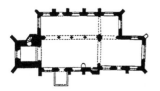

Architectural Description—The *Chancel* (30½ ft. by 19 ft.) has in the E. wall a 15th-century window of four cinquefoiled lights with vertical tracery in a two-centred head; in the gable is an opening with a trefoiled head and a moulded label. In the N. wall is an early 14th-century window of two trefoiled ogee lights with tracery in a two-centred head; further W. is a late 15th-century arch, two-centred and of two hollow-chamfered orders; the responds have each three attached shafts with moulded capitals and bases. In the S. wall are two 15th-century windows, both partly restored, and each of three cinquefoiled lights with vertical tracery in a four-centred head with a moulded label; between them is a late 15th-century doorway, with moulded jambs and two-centred arch and label. The late 15th-century chancel-arch is two-centred, but is otherwise similar in detail to the arch in the N. wall.

The *North Chapel* (14 ft. by 14 ft.) has in the E. wall a late 15th-century window of three cinquefoiled lights in a three-centred head; the middle light has an embattled transom. In the N. wall is a similar window. The late 15th-century W. archway is segmental-pointed and of two chamfered orders; the responds have each a semi-

octagonal attached shaft with concave faces and moulded capitals and bases; adjoining the S. respond is a squint with a rounded head.

The *Nave* (42½ ft. by 20 ft.) has a late 15th-century N. arcade of four bays with two-centred arches of two hollow-chamfered orders; the piers have each four attached shafts with moulded capitals and bases; the responds have attached half columns. In the S. wall are two windows originally of the 15th century, but with 18th-century wooden frames and mullions; between them is the 15th-century S. doorway, with moulded jambs and two-centred arch; at the E. end of the wall is a projection enclosing the rood-loft staircase; it has late 15th-century upper and lower doorways with four-centred heads.

The *North Aisle* (14 ft. wide) has in the N. wall three windows, the easternmost and westernmost are of late 14th or early 15th-century date and are each of two cinquefoiled ogee lights with tracery in a three-centred head with a moulded label, probably reset; the middle window is similar to those in the S. wall of the nave; between the two western windows is the 15th-century N. doorway with moulded jambs and two-centred arch. In the W. wall is a 15th-century window similar to the windows in the N. chapel.

The *West Tower* (12 ft. by 11 ft.) is of late 15th-century date and of three stages with a modern parapet and old carved gargoyles at the angles; on each face of the middle stage is a rough cross in knapped flints. The two-centred tower-arch is of two hollow-chamfered orders on the E. and of three on the W. side; the responds have each two attached shafts with moulded capital and base. In the N. wall is the doorway to the stair-turret, with moulded jambs and two-centred arch. The W. window is of three cinquefoiled lights with tracery in a segmental-pointed head with a moulded label; the mullions are modern. The second stage has in the N., S. and W. walls a square-headed loop; below the loop in the S. wall is a small blocked window with a decayed head. The bell-chamber has in each wall a window of two cinque-foiled lights in a square head with a moulded label; the S. window has been repaired with modern brick.

The *Roof* of the chancel has old wall-plates. The roof of the nave is ceiled and has on the N. side a moulded and embattled wall-plate of the 15th century with traces of colour.

Fittings—Bell: one; by Richard Hille, and inscribed: "Sum Rosa Pulsata Mundi Maria Vocata," early 15th-century. *Brass:* In chancel—to Maudlin Owtred, 1572, inscription only. *Doors:* In N. doorway, with moulded and studded fillets and strap-hinges, trellis framing, 16th-century. In S. doorway—modern, but with band of quatrefoiled panelling at bottom, 15th-century. In doorway to turret staircase of tower, plated with iron and nail-studded, 16th-century. *Font* (Plate, p. xxxiv) : octagonal bowl, each face with a trefoiled and crocketed head with tracery above and vaulting' or tracery below, shallow pedestals at base of panels, top edge carved with square flowers, lower edge with half-angels, stem with cinquefoiled and crocketed panels, moulded base, 15th-century. *Glass :* In chancel—in N. window, fragments, blue roundel, etc., 14th-century. *Hour-glass Stand :* on pulpit, of wrought iron, 17th-century. *Monument* and *Floor-slab.* Monument : In nave— on S. wall, to Lieut.-Col. Edward Bellame, 1656, framed wooden panel with painted achievement of arms. Floor-slab : In N. aisle—to James Fox, 1710. *Niches :* In N. chapel—flanking E. window, two wide recesses with mutilated cusped heads, 15th-century. *Painting :* In N. chapel—at back of niches, remains of painted decoration. *Piscina :* In chancel—with hollow-chamfered jambs and cinquefoiled head, second opening into splay of S.E. window, rectangular drain, 15th-century. *Plate :* includes Elizabethan cup with two bands of incised ornament. *Pulpit* (Plate, p. 181) : octagonal, panelled sides with lozenge-ornament, carved cornice, high plastered base, sounding-board with carved standard and frieze with turned pendants at the angles, early 17th-century, now painted. *Sedile :* In chancel—sill of S.E. window carried down to form seat, 15th-century. *Stoups :* In chancel—E. of doorway, recess with two-centred head, no bowl, possibly stoup, 15th-century. In nave—E. of S. doorway, with two-centred head, no bowl. *Tiles :* In chancel—in sills of S. windows and stoup, plain glazed tiles, probably 15th-century. *Miscellanea :* In N. chapel—worked stones, 14th and 15th-century.

Condition—Poor, external stonework much weathered.

Secular :—

(2). HOMESTEAD MOAT, around church and Hall, is fragmentary.

(3). DOG AND PHEASANT INN, 700 yards N.E. of the church, is of two storeys, partly timber-framed and partly of brick ; the roofs are thatched. It was built probably late in the 17th century and has exposed ceiling-beams.

Condition—Fairly good.

(4). WEIR FARM, house, about ¾ m. W. of the church, is of two storeys, timber-framed and weather-boarded ; the roofs are tiled. It was built probably in the 16th century and has cross-wings at the E. and W. ends. The walls have been partly faced with brick. The upper storey projects at the S. end of the W. cross-wing. Inside the building are exposed ceiling-beams.

Condition—Good.

Unclassified :—

(5). RED HILLS, two near Reeve's Hall, about 1 m. N.W. of the church. Now levelled.

---

24. ELMSTEAD. (D.c.)

(O.S. 6 in. [(a)]xxviii. N.W. [(b)]xxviii. N.E. [(c)]xxviii. S.W. [(d)]xxviii. S.E.)

Elmstead is a parish and village 4 m. E. of Colchester. The church, Hall and Allen's Farm are the principal monuments.

Ecclesiastical :—

[b](1). PARISH CHURCH OF ST. ANNE AND ST. LAURENCE stands in the N.E. corner of the parish. The walls are of mixed rubble with some puddingstone ; the dressings are of limestone and the roofs are covered with tiles and lead. The *Chancel, Nave* and *South Tower* were built probably c. 1310 but the nave may possibly be earlier ; about twenty years later the *South Chapel* was added and the chancel-arch rebuilt. The tower was probably never completed. The church has been restored in modern times.

The church with its South Tower is of some architectural interest and has been little touched by modern restoration. Among the fittings the wooden effigy is noteworthy.

Architectural Description—The *Chancel* (34 ft. by 19½ ft.) is of early 14th-century date and has a modern E. window set in the old opening with a two-centred head and moulded labels with external stops carved as kneeling angels. In the N. wall are two windows each of two pointed lights with a spandrel in a two-centred head with a moulded label and head-stops. In the S. wall are two windows, similar to those in the N. wall, but the label of the eastern has a carved head at the apex ; between the windows is a doorway with hollow-chamfered jambs, two-centred arch and moulded label with defaced head-stops. The mid 14th-century chancel-arch is two-centred and of two moulded orders ; the chamfered responds have each an attached and filleted shaft with a moulded capital cut back on the face ; S. of the arch is a squint with a round sexfoiled opening.

The *Nave* (42½ ft. by 21½ ft.) has in the N. wall three windows, the easternmost is of the 14th century and of two trefoiled ogee lights with tracery in a segmental-pointed head, with a moulded label ; the middle window is of c. 1400 and of three cinquefoiled lights with vertical tracery in a two-centred head with a moulded label ; the westernmost window is of early 16th-century date and of three cinquefoiled lights in a four-centred head with a moulded label ; between the two western windows is the N. doorway with a round

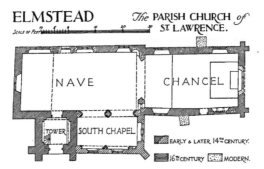

ELMSTEAD *The* PARISH CHURCH *of* St LAWRENCE.

NAVE   CHANCEL

TOWER SOUTH CHAPEL

EARLY & LATER 14TH CENTURY.

16TH CENTURY MODERN.

plastered head of uncertain date; it is now blocked. At the E. end the wall has been cut back to provide access to the former rood-loft and the N. rebated jamb of the former lower doorway remains. The mid 14th-century S. arcade (Plate, p. 93) is of two bays with two-centred arches of two moulded orders; the column is of quatrefoiled plan with moulded capital and base and the responds have attached half columns; further W. is the 14th-century S. doorway with double chamfered jambs and two-centred arch; above and to the W. is a second doorway, at the gallery level, with moulded jambs and two-centred arch. In the W. wall is a window similar to those on the N. side of the chancel.

The *South Chapel* (22¼ ft. by 10¼ ft.) is of *c.* 1340 and has an E. window of three lights with moulded jambs and shafted splays; the head has been replaced by a flat lintel and the lights are mostly blocked. In the S. wall is a wall-arcade of two bays with two-centred arches and labels with head-stops; the pier and responds are of semi-quatrefoiled plan and have moulded capitals and bases; each bay has a window similar to the N.E. window in the nave but with head-stops to the label. Below each is a small trefoiled ogee light set low in the wall and now blocked.

The *South Tower* (8½ ft. square) is of the 14th century and of one and half stages high and finished with a pyramidal roof. The ground stage forms the S. porch and has on the N.E. and N. sides a wall-arch with chamfered jambs and two-centred head; in the S. wall is a doorway with a two-centred arch of two moulded orders; the jambs have each an attached shaft with a moulded capital. The upper part of the tower has in the S. and W. walls a plain loop.

The *Roof* of the S. chapel incorporates some moulded tie-beams, rafters and a wall-plate of *c.* 1500 but has been much restored.

Fittings — *Brass* and *Indents.* Brass: In chancel—two hands issuing from clouds and holding

a heart inscribed "credo," above a scroll, indent of inscription-plate. Indents: In chancel—(1) of figure; in S. chapel (2) of armed figure, inscription-plate and four shields, 15th-century. *Communion Table:* with heavy turned legs, moulded end rails, early 17th-century, top and sides modern. *Door:* In S. doorway—of battens with broken strap-hinges, date uncertain. *Glass:* In vicarage —grisaille foliage, with border of castles and fleurs-de-lis, from heads of pointed lights, *c.* 1300. *Monuments* and *Floor-slab.* Monuments: In chancel—on E. wall, (1) to Thomas Martin, 1672, vicar of the parish, and to William, his son, 1664, two small rectangular wooden panels with moulded frames. In S. chapel—(2) on sill of E. window, carved oak effigy (Plate, p. 170) of man in mail with pointed bascinet, short surcoat, knee and elbow cops, heater-shaped shield, legs crossed, head on lion, feet against female figure, *c.* 1310. Floor-slab: In nave—to William Bendische, 1627. *Panelling:* In chapel—incorporated in 18th-century pews, early 17th-century. *Piscinae:* In chancel—in range with sedilia and forming together four bays each with moulded jambs and cinquefoiled head with a moulded label and head-stops including a king and bishop; the jambs of the third bay have carved stops of a stag and a male head; trefoiled drain to piscina, late 14th-century. In S. chapel—in S. wall, with shafted jambs and moulded trefoiled head with moulded label, sexfoiled drain, moulded sill and plain shelf, 14th-century. On wall in S.E. angle, moulded shelf. *Plate:* includes Elizabethan cup with engraved bands, and cover-paten with Tudor rose on foot. *Sedilia:* See Piscina.

Condition—Good.

Secular :—

[d](2). HOMESTEAD MOAT at Parsonage Farm, 600 yards S.S.W. of the church.

[b](3). ELMSTEAD HALL, W. of the church, is of two storeys with attics, timber-framed and

plastered ; the roofs are tiled. It was built *c.* 1500 with a central Hall and cross-wings at the E. and W. ends. The back part of the E. wing was rebuilt and heightened probably late in the 16th century. The gables at the S. end of the E. wing, at the back of the main block and the three gables of the W. wing have moulded barge-boards. Inside the building is a considerable amount of 17th and 18th-century panelling ; the room above the Hall has fluted pilasters and a moulded cornice. There are some original doorways with four-centred heads and on the first floor is a doorway with original jambs and square head. The room above the kitchen has a 16th-century door with moulded vertical fillets. The W. staircase leading to the attics has solid winding treads. In the attic of the W. wing is a 16th-century window of six lights with moulded mullions. There are several 16th and 17th-century doors.

Condition—Good.

MONUMENTS (4–9).

The following monuments, unless otherwise described, are of the 17th century and of two storeys, timber-framed and plastered or weather-boarded ; the roofs are tiled or thatched. Some of the buildings have original chimney-stacks and exposed ceiling-beams.

Condition—Good, or fairly good.

a(4). *Allen's Farm,* house, about ¾ m. W. of the church, was built *c.* 1584. The upper storey projects on the N. front and the ground storey is divided into bays by five posts carved with two-stage panelled buttresses on which stand crested shafts supporting curved brackets with foliated spandrels, two of these have shields each charged with a mill-rind cross. Beside the front door is a carved panel with two similar shields and the date 1584. Inside the building, above the fireplace of a room on the first floor is a 17th-century panel with a reversed fleur-de-lis between two wreaths.

ELMSTEAD MARKET :—

d(5). *Cottage,* three tenements at S.E. corner of cross-roads, about 1 m. S. of the church.

d(6). *King's Arms Inn,* E. of (5), has been completely altered.

d(7). *House* and shop, 30 yards E. of (6).

d(8). *Cottage,* three tenements 200 yards N.E. of (7), is of L-shaped plan with the wings extending towards the N. and W.

e(9). FEN FARM, house, 1¼ m. S.S.W. of the church, was built in the 15th century with a central Hall and cross-wings at the N. and S. ends. In the 16th century the N. wing was extended towards the E., the S. wing probably rebuilt and the Hall divided up and a gable added. The

upper storey projects at the W. end of the N. wing and the W. gables of the main block and the W. wing also project. Inside the building the S. room has an original moulded ceiling-beam. The top staircase has late 17th-century turned balusters. The roof of the N. wing is original and of two bays with a cambered tie-beam, stop-chamfered king-post and four-way struts. The roof of the main block has been much altered but has an original king-post with a moulded capital and stop-chamfered central purlin and base ; the timbers are smoke blackened ; the roof extended down over an annexe or aisle on the W., but whether this was the original arrangement is doubtful. There are some 17th-century doors.

25. FEERING. (B.d.)

(O.S. 6 in. *(a)*xxvi. N.W. *(b)*xxvi. S.W. *(c)*xxvi. S.E. *(d)*xxxv. N.E.)

Feering is a parish and small village 2 m. S.E. of Great Coggeshall. The church, Feeringbury, Sun Inn and Houchin's Farm are the principal monuments.

Ecclesiastical :—

d(1). PARISH CHURCH OF ALL SAINTS (Plate, p. 96) stands at the S. end of the parish. The walls are of flint and septaria rubble except the S. wall of the nave and the porch which are of red brick ; the dressings are of brick, clunch and limestone ; the roofs are covered with tiles and lead. The *Nave* is the earliest part of the structure and may be of the 12th or 13th century, but of this there is no definite evidence The *Chancel* was rebuilt early in the 14th century except possibly part of the N. wall ; *c.* 1330 the *North Aisle* and arcade were built. Early in the 15th century the *West Tower* was added. At the beginning of the 16th century the S. wall of the nave was rebuilt and the *South Porch* added. The church was restored in the 19th century and the *North Vestry* added.

The N. arcade and aisle are of good 14th-century work and the S. porch and S. wall of the nave are excellent examples of elaborate brickwork.

Architectural Description—The *Chancel* (38 ft. by 21¼ ft.) has an early 14th-century E. window of three pointed lights with plain intersecting tracery in a two-centred head. The N. wall, W. of the vestry, is of roughly coursed rubble and may be earlier than the rest of the chancel. In the N. wall are two windows similar to the E. window but of two lights and completely restored externally; between the windows is a modern doorway. In the S. wall are two windows similar to those in the N. wall ; further W. is an early 14th-century doorway, partly restored and now blocked ; it has

FEERING: PARISH CHURCH OF ALL SAINTS; from the South.

West Tower, early 15th-century; Brickwork of Porch, etc., early 16th-century.

CRESSING CHURCH.
To Henry and Anne Smith; 1607.

COLCHESTER: BERECHURCH CHURCH.
To Sir Henry Audley and Anne his Wife; erected 1648.

TOLLESHUNT D'ARCY CHURCH.
To Thomas Darcy, 1593, and Camylla his Wife.

LITTLE TOTHAM CHURCH.
To Sir John Samms and Isabell his Wife;
mid 17th-century.

BRADWELL-JUXTA-COGGESHALL CHURCH.
To Anthony Maxey (1592) and Dorothy his Wife (1602); erected by
Sir Henry Maxey, their Son.

FEERING *The* PARISH CHURCH *of* ALL SAINTS.

NORTH AISLE

VESTRY

TOWER

NAVE

CHANCEL

SOUTH PORCH

LATE 12TH or EARLY 13TH CENT.

14TH CENTURY

15TH   "

16TH   "   MODERN.

SCALE OF FEET

chamfered jambs and a two-centred arch ; above it is a blocked early 16th-century window of brick and of three four-centred lights in a four-centred head. The chancel-arch is modern but is said to be a copy of the former arch of *c.* 1200.

The *Nave* (52½ ft. by 24 ft.) has a N. arcade of *c.* 1330 and of four bays with two-centred arches of two moulded orders ; the columns have each four attached shafts with moulded capitals and bases ; the responds have attached half-columns. The S. wall is built of or faced with early 16th-century brick and has a moulded plinth with panels of flint-inlay and an embattled parapet resting on a trefoiled corbel-table. In the S. wall are three windows all of brick and of early 16th-century date ; the easternmost is of four four-centred lights with plain tracery in a four-centred head with a moulded label ; the second window is similar but of two lights with a spandrel in the head ; the westernmost window is similar but of five lights without tracery ; between the two western windows is the S. doorway, all modern externally but with an early 16th-century four-centred rear-arch.

The *North Aisle* (8½ ft. wide) has in the N. wall three 14th-century windows, the easternmost is of three pointed lights in a segmental-pointed head with a moulded label ; the two western windows (Plate, p. 143) are each of two trefoiled ogee lights with tracery in a two-centred head and a moulded label ; between them is the 14th-century N. doorway with jambs and two-centred arch of two moulded orders ; above it is a modern gabled weathering, probably indicating the former existence of a porch. In the W. wall is a window similar to the western window in the N. wall.

The *West Tower* (12 ft. square) is of three stages with an embattled parapet and is of early 15th-century date. The two-centred tower-arch is of three hollow-chamfered or moulded orders of which the inner two die on to the square responds ; the outer order is continuous ; N. of it is the staircase doorway with moulded jambs and two-centred arch. The W. window is of two cinquefoiled lights with tracery in a two-centred head ; below it is a doorway with moulded jambs, two-centred arch and label. The second stage has in the N., S. and W. walls a window of one trefoiled light in a square head with a moulded label. The bell-chamber has in each wall a window of two cinquefoiled lights under a square head with a moulded label.

The *South Porch* is entirely of red brick with black brick diapering and is of early 16th-century date ; it has a trefoiled corbel-table and an embattled parapet, crow-stepped at the S. end and finished with crocketed pinnacles at the angles and a truncated pinnacle at the apex. The moulded plinth has trefoil-headed panels of flint-inlay. The outer archway has moulded jambs and four-centred arch with a double label, four-centred and square ; above it is a projection on moulded corbelling and enclosing a niche with a four-centred head surmounted by three trefoil-headed panels with a stepped and moulded label. The side walls have each a window of three transomed and four-centred lights in a four-centred head with a moulded label. The roof has a brick vault (Plate, p. 133) with diagonal, cross and intermediate ribs springing from moulded corbels and having in the middle a shield with a merchant's mark. Above the S. doorway of the nave and below the vaulting is a four-centred and moulded wall-arch resting on

G

splayed angles with four-centred niches and on a squinch sprung across the N.W. angle of the porch. The bench on each side of the porch is supported on two three-centred arches of brick.

The *Roof* of the nave is of early 17th-century date, much restored; it is of four bays with moulded wall-plates with arabesque and other ornament; the middle tie-beam has small pendants at the base of the principals; the other tie-beams and the intermediate principals have small brackets.

Fittings—*Bells*: eight; 6th, 7th and 8th by Miles Graye, 1624. *Brass*: In chancel—on N. wall, to Judith (Gaell), wife of Robert Aylett, LL.D., 1623, inscription only. *Chair*: In chancel—with carved back and rail, late 17th-century. *Chests*: In vestry—(1) dug-out with cambered lid, three locks, one hasp missing, mediaeval; (2) panelled and carved front, with remains of inlay, c. 1600, partly restored. *Coffin-lid*: Under N. arcade—tapering slab, with double hollow-chamfered edge and cross in relief with trefoiled ends, late 13th-century. *Doors*: In S. doorway, of overlapping battens with strap-hinges and stock-lock, early 16th-century. On modern door to turret staircase, strap-hinges and key-plate with protective device, 16th-century. *Glass*: In nave—in S.E. window, crowned rose with initials E.R. and fragments of border, 16th-century. In N. aisle—in middle window in N. wall, heads of tabernacle work; in tracery foliated designs, 14th-century, *in situ*. *Monuments*: In N. aisle—in N. wall, (1) tomb-recess with shafted jambs, moulded ogee arch, label and foliated finial, late 14th-century, restored in cement. In churchyard—(2) to John Butcher, 1707, vicar of the parish, head-stone; (3) to John Andrews, 1687, head-stone; (4) to John Angier, 1695, head-stone with skull and cross-bones; (5) to John Joscelyn, 1704, head-stone. *Niche*: See Architectural Description, S. porch. *Piscinae*: In chancel—with trefoiled head and moulded label, early 14th-century, much restored. In S. aisle—in S. wall, with moulded jambs and defaced cusped head, broken octofoiled drain, c. 1330. *Sedile*: In chancel—sill of N.E. and S.E. windows carried down to form seat. *Stoup*: In nave—E. of S. doorway, with plain pointed head, date uncertain, basin destroyed. *Table*: In vestry—small, with turned legs and fluted front to drawer, 17th-century. *Tiles*: In vestry—loose incised and slip-tiles, one with the arms of Vere, the other with those of (?) Shirley, 14th-century.

Condition—Good.

Secular:—

*(2). HOUCHIN'S FARM, (Plate, p. 188) house, barn, and moat, nearly 2 m. N. of the church. The *House* is of three storeys with attics, timber-framed and partly plastered and partly weather-boarded; the roofs are tiled. It was built c. 1600 and is of L-shaped plan with the wings extending towards the E. and N. The second and third storeys of the main block project on the S. side and at the W. end with moulded bressumers and carved male and female grotesque figures set diagonally at the angles to serve as brackets. At the W. end are two original windows with moulded mullions and now blocked. Inside the building several rooms have original chamfered ceiling-beams and there is some original panelling in the hall. The E. room has an original oak overmantel divided into three bays by pilasters; each bay has a richly carved arched panel with pilasters at the sides and a pendant key-block; the carved frieze is divided into bays by modillions.

The *Barn*, S.E. of the house, is of c. 1600 and of eleven aisled bays with two porches. It is timber-framed and weather-boarded.

The *Moat* surrounds the house.

Condition—Of house, good.

*(3). PRESTED HALL, house and moat, about ¾ m. S.E. of the church. The *House* is of two storeys with attics, timber-framed and plastered; the roofs are tiled. Parts of the structure may be of c. 1527, the modern date on the W. porch, but there is little evidence of this as the house has been almost completely altered. Inside the building are some exposed ceiling-beams and a little panelling of c. 1600.

The *Moat* is fragmentary.

Condition—Of house, good, much altered.

*(4). FEERINGBURY, house and outbuilding, nearly 1 m. N.W. of the church. The *House* is of two storeys, timber-framed and plastered; the roofs are tiled. It was built in the 15th century with a central Hall and cross-wings at the N. and S. ends. The Hall was divided into two storeys in the 17th century and there are large modern additions on the W. side. The early 17th-century chimney-stack (Plate, p. 177) of the main block has a moulded capping and three octagonal shafts; there is a similar stack on the S. of the S. wing. Inside the building are some exposed ceiling-beams and two overmantels made up of early 17th-century carved panelling. The bay-window of the N. room has two pieces of late 16th-century glass, (a) an achievement of the arms of Heygate with the initials R.H,. (b) a crowned rose with the initials E.R. There are remains of the original roof of the Hall of three bays and the roof of the N. wing has an original king-post truss.

The *Outbuilding*, S.E. of the house, said to have been a chapel, is timber-framed and weather-boarded. It was built in the 15th century but the original S. wall has been removed. The roof is of two bays with moulded plates and tie-beams; the central truss has curved braces and a king-post with two-way struts.

In the garden is a 14th or 15th-century stone boss from a vault, carved with a head and having the springings of moulded ribs.

Condition—Of house and outbuilding, good.

MONUMENTS (5–30).

The following monuments, unless otherwise described, are of the 17th century and of two storeys, timber-framed and plastered or weather-boarded ; the roofs are tiled or thatched. Many of the buildings have original chimney-stacks, exposed ceiling-beams and wide fireplaces.

Condition—Good or fairly good, unless noted.

[c](5). *Cottage,* ½ m. N.E. of (4), has an original chimney-stack with rebated angles.

[c](6). *Surrex Farm,* house, ½ m. N. of (5), was built of brick in 1714, the date with the initials M.W. on a small stone above the original entrance. There is a projecting band-course between the storeys. One of the back doors has a flat head with shaped brackets.

[c](7) *Lees Farm,* house, 600 yards W. of (6), was built probably in the 16th century.

[c](8). *Maltbeggar's Hall,* 1,100 yards N.N.W. of (2), has a cross-wing at the W. end.

[b](9). *Palmer's Farm,* house, nearly ½ m. N.N.W. of (8).

[a](10). *Hopgreen Farm,* house, ¾ m. N.W. of (9), has various repairs dated 1788 and 1807.

[c](11). *House* at Langley Farm, now three tenements, 1 m. N.N.E. of the church has a N.E. wing probably of early 16th-century date. The rest of the house was rebuilt late in the 17th century except the early 17th-century chimney-stack of three grouped diagonal shafts. The upper storey projects at the E. end of the original block. Inside the same wing is an original king-post truss.

Condition—Bad (now demolished).

[d](12). *Diddles,* cottage, 600 yards E.S.E. of (11), was built probably in the 15th century and may once have had cross-wings at the ends. The roof construction is original, the middle truss being supported on two posts of which one has been cut away. This arrangement brings the building into the class of aisled halls but the construction is of the simplest character.

Condition—Poor (now demolished).

[c](13). *Hornigals,* house, nearly ½ m. N.E. of (12), was built probably early in the 16th century with a cross-wing at the N. end. The upper storey projects at the W. end of the cross-wing.

[d](14). *Poplar Hall,* formerly Oldhouse Farm, 500 yards S.W. of (12), has a cross-wing at the S. end. The upper storey projects at the W. end of the cross-wing.

[d](15). *Old Will's Farm,* house, about ¼ m. S.S.W. of (14), was built early in the 16th century and has a late 17th-century addition on the S.E.

The upper storey projects and is gabled in front at the E. end of the original block.

[d](16). *Cottage,* ¼ m. N.N.W. of (15), has an original chimney-stack with rebated angles.

[d](17). *Hill House,* house and barns, 600 yards E. of (15). The *House* has been much altered, but has a chimney-stack with diagonal shafts.

The *Barns* stand E. and W. of the house.

[d](18). *The Vicarage,* 50 yards N. of the church, has been almost completely rebuilt.

[d](19). *House,* 50 yards S.S.E. of the church, was built possibly in the 15th century and has an original roof with two king-post trusses.

[d](20). *Bell Inn,* 40 yards W.S.W. of (19), is of L-shaped plan with the wings extending towards the W. and S. The upper storey projects at the end of the S. wing and there is an original chimney-stack with plain pilasters. Inside the building is a little original panelling, reset.

[d](21). *Range of two tenements,* 30 yards W.S.W. of (20), was built early in the 18th century.

[d](22). *Cottage,* adjoining (21) on W.

[d](23). *Cottages,* on S. side of road 100 yards S. of the church, have been almost completely altered and partly faced with modern brick.

[d](24). *Chambers Farm,* house, 70 yards E. of (23), has been almost completely altered.

GORE PIT :—

[d](25). *House,* on S.E. side of road, nearly ½ m. S. of the church, was built probably *c.* 1600.

[d](26). *Cottage,* three tenements, 70 yards S. of (25), was built probably early in the 18th century.

Condition—Poor.

[d](27). *House,* 50 yards W. of (26), has cross-wings at each end. The central chimney-stack has two grouped diagonal shafts. Inside the building is a little original panelling, reset.

[d](28). *Cottage,* 100 yards W.S.W. of (27).

Condition—Poor.

[d](29). ST. ANDREWS, formerly Feering House, ¼ m. W.S.W. of (28), is modern but incorporates some old material including some bricks inscribed M D X in flowing capitals.

[d](30). SUN INN (Plate, p. 123) and tenements, 130 yards W.S.W. of (29), was built *c.* 1525. The upper storey projects on the S.E. front. The bressumer of the main block is carved with twisted foliage as are the barge-boards of the three gables above. These gables project and have moulded pendants from which spring curved straining pieces with foliated spandrels. Further E. is a small porch with original carved barge-boards. Inside the porch is an original doorway with a four-centred head. One room at the W. end has 17th-century panelling.

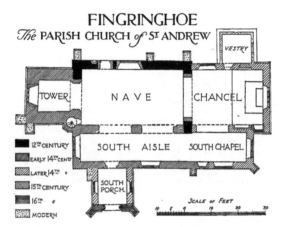

FINGRINGHOE
The PARISH CHURCH *of* St ANDREW

VESTRY

TOWER   N A V E   CHANCEL

SOUTH AISLE   SOUTH CHAPEL

SOUTH PORCH.

■ 12TH CENTURY
▨ EARLY 14TH CENT^Y
▨ LATER 14TH "
▨ 15TH CENTURY
■ 16TH "
▨ MODERN

SCALE OF FEET

26. FINGRINGHOE. (D.d.)

(O.S. 6 in. xxxvii. N.W.)

Fingringhoe is a parish on the right bank of the Colne estuary, 4 m. S.E. of Colchester. The church is the principal monument.

Ecclesiastical :—

(1). PARISH CHURCH OF ST. ANDREW (Plate, p. xxviii) stands in the village. The walls are of flint and limestone-rubble with septaria and some Roman brick ; the dressings are of limestone and Roman brick and the roofs are tiled. The *Nave* was built in the 12th century. Early in the 14th century the chancel-arch was rebuilt, the S. arcade built and the *South Aisle* and *West Tower* added. Later in the 14th century the *Chancel* was rebuilt and the *South Chapel* and *South Porch* were added. In the 15th or early in the 16th century the S. end of the porch was rebuilt. Various buttresses have been added in modern times, but the church generally has been little restored. The *North Vestry* is modern but stands on old foundations. The S. porch has interesting detail and among the fittings the remains of paintings are noteworthy.

Architectural Description—The *Chancel* (26¼ ft. by 19¾ ft.) has an E. window, all modern except perhaps the mid 15th-century splays and rear-arch and part of the external label. In the N. wall is a late 15th-century window of three cinquefoiled lights in a segmental head ; further E. is a doorway possibly of the same date but with a modern lintel. E. of the doorway is a window probably of the 14th century but now blocked and only visible internally ; it has a segmental rear-arch. In the S. wall is a 16th-century window of two plain square-headed lights ; further W. is a late 14th-century arch with moulded responds and two-centred head. The 14th-century chancel-arch is two-centred and of one continuous moulded order ; the responds have been for the most part restored.

The *South Chapel* (18¼ ft. by 10½ ft.) has an E. window all modern except the splays and rear-arch which are perhaps of late 14th-century date. In the S. wall is a window probably of the 14th century but with a 15th-century window of three cinquefoiled lights in a four-centred head with a moulded label and head-stops inserted in the older openings ; further W. is a 14th-century doorway with moulded jambs and two-centred head ; it is now blocked.

The *Nave* (38 ft. by 20 ft.) has N.E. and N.W. angles of the 12th century and of Roman brick ; the building was heightened probably in the 15th century. In the E. wall above the chancel-arch is the mark of the former steep-pitched gable of the nave and a 15th-century window of two cinquefoiled lights, now covered by the chancel roof. In the N. wall is a window with a two-centred head and a moulded label with head-stops ; it is probably of the 14th century, but without mullions or tracery ; further W. are remains of a 12th-century window with Roman brick jambs ; it is now blocked ; W. of this window is the 14th-century N. doorway with chamfered jambs and two-centred arch. In the S. wall is an early 14th-century arcade of two bays with responds and two-centred arches of one moulded order ; the E. respond has a square rebate cut in the N. angle with the moulding mitred back on to it ; E. of this arch is a blocked doorway to the former rood-loft.

GREAT COGGESHALL.
(69) House, East Street.   Bressumer; dated 1585.

GREAT COGGESHALL.
(8) House, Church Street   Doorhead ; Brackets ;
early 17th century.

COLCHESTER.
(263) Bourne Mill.   Doorway and
Achievement with Arms of Lucas ;
1591.

COLCHESTER.
(69) Marquis of Granby Inn.
Doorway; early 16th-century.

TOLLESHUNT D'ARCY HALL.
Doorway, N.E. wing ; c. 1500.

ST. OSYTH.
(14) Park Farm. Doorway with painting, in Screen; 15th-century.

Main Staircase; early 17th-century.

Detail of South Porch; early 17th-century.

LANGHAM: (3) Valley House.

LANGHAM.
(3) Valley House; early 16th and early 17th-century.

COLCHESTER: (192) House, now Convent School; early 17th-century.

The *South Aisle* (10 ft. wide) has in the S. wall a 15th-century window of three cinquefoiled lights in a four-centred head and mostly modern externally; further W. is the late 14th-century S. doorway (Plate, p. 132) with moulded jambs, two-centred arch and label. In the W. wall is a partly restored 15th-century window of three cinquefoiled lights with vertical tracery in a four-centred head with a moulded label.

The *West Tower* (11½ ft. square) is of three stages and is built in bands of flint-rubble and limestone. The moulded plinth has flint chequer-work. The tower-arch has chamfered responds and two-centred arch of uncertain date. The 16th-century W. window is of three plain ogee lights with uncusped tracery in a four-centred head with a moulded label. The roof has a quadripartite vault all plastered and with chamfered ribs. The second stage has in the E. wall a wide round-headed opening of Roman brick. The N., S. and W. walls have each a 14th-century window of one pointed light with jambs and heads of brick. The bell-chamber has in each wall a 14th-century window of two cinquefoiled lights with a quatrefoil in a two-centred head with a moulded label; they are in a bad condition and parts are missing or blocked.

The *South Porch* (Plate, p. xxix) is of flint with an embattled parapet of chequer-work and a moulded plinth with trefoil-headed panels of flint-inlay; the diagonal buttresses have similar panels, and above them, on each buttress is a mutilated niche with a three-centred head. The two-centred outer archway (Plate p. 142) is of two moulded orders, the outer continuous and the inner resting on round attached shafts with moulded capitals and bases; the double moulded label has defaced angel stops and a square head enclosing carved spandrels with St. Michael and the dragon; above the arch is a much mutilated niche with a carved woman's head corbel. The side walls have each a late 14th-century window of three cinquefoiled lights with vertical tracery in a two-centred head with a moulded label; the window in the E. wall is much broken and both are blocked; below the W. window is part of the 14th-century plinth.

The *Roof* of the chancel is of collar-beam type and of early 16th-century date; it is of two bays with moulded main timbers, embattled plates and curved braces forming four-centred arches and springing from engaged shafts with moulded capitals and bases. The early 16th-century roof of the nave is of collar-beam type and is generally similar to that of the chancel but beneath the middle of the curved braces, on each side, are bosses carved with heads, some of them grotesques. The flat pent-roof of the S. chapel and aisle is of the 15th century with moulded main timbers, and curved braces to the principals, partly missing.

Fittings—*Bells:* three; 1st by Miles Graye, 1625; 2nd from the Bury foundry, early 16th-century and inscribed, "Sancta Maria Ora Pro Nobis"; 3rd, uninscribed; bell-frame probably 17th-century. *Bier:* In S. aisle—with moulded rails and carved brackets, 17th-century. *Brasses:* In S. chapel—on N. wall, (1) of John Alleyn and Ailse, his daughter, late 16th-century, with figures of man and daughter in costume of period; palimpsest on inscription-plate, inscription with Latin texts; on floor, (2) to Richard Bryan, 1592, inscription only; (3) to Mary, wife of Richard Bryan, 1587, inscription only; (4) to Marcie, wife of Richard Wade, 1601, inscription only. *Chest* (Plate, p. xxxii): In S. aisle—dug-out with five ring handles, two ring handles and studded with nails in patterns and the date 1684, the chest is, however, probably mediaeval. *Consecration Cross:* In nave—on S.W. respond, incised cross formy in circle, probably 13th-century. *Door:* In S. doorway (Plate, p. 132), of four panels with moulded fillets and frame, traceried heads to panels, much damaged, moulded middle rail and cusped heads to lower panels, iron drop-handle and scutcheon-plate, late 14th-century. *Font:* octagonal bowl with moulded under-edge, plain stem and moulded base, late 14th-century. *Font-cover* (Plate, p. 181): of oak, octagonal and of three stages, panelled lower stage with pierced and traceried buttresses and cresting; much restored second stage; third stage with open ogee-shaped ribs with crockets and moulded terminal, 15th-century. *Monuments:* In chancel—on N. wall, (1) of George Frere, 1655, alabaster and marble tablet with bust in round recess with laurel wreath border, segmental pediment and three shields of arms, restored in 1779. In churchyard—S.E. of porch, (2) to Henry Simon, 1681, and Grace (Lock?), his wife, 1712, table-tomb with defaced achievement of arms. *Paintings:* In chancel—on E. wall, foliated diaper pattern in red, probably early 16th-century. In nave—on E. wall, round head of arch, late 16th-century foliated cresting with traces of earlier ornament in dark red, limited by line of early gable; on N. wall, high up, remains of early 16th-century diapered pattern of white flowers and feathery foliage on red ground; above N. doorway, remains of large figure of St. Christopher bearing the Holy Child, figures much defaced, background of meadow and foliated border on E. side, 15th-century or earlier; on S. wall, red wash on E. respond with traces of earlier ornament beneath; traces of foliage ornament above rood-loft doorway; on pier between arches, seated figure of the Virgin with Child, much defaced and traces of a figure probably of donor with black lettered scroll; above main figure a large scroll, formerly inscribed; background powdered with capital Ms; higher up figure of a crowned woman and remains of a censing angel, all probably 14th-century with traces of 16th-century ornament superimposed; on E. respond of second arch, remains of figure subject with cross at back, much defaced background of brocade design with painted rings and nails at top to imitate a hanging cloth ; on S. side of same pier St. Michael with a seated figure of a woman with long hair and an ermine tippet and smaller figures below ; on W. respond of second arch, said to be a risen Christ with hands in foreground holding instruments of the Passion (?), but almost obliterated ; above a half-angel with a scroll inscribed " In omni opere memento finis " ; below it an earlier sexfoiled circle. In S. aisle—on N. wall between it and chapel, embattled cresting in red with 16th-century ornamental cresting superimposed, slight traces of late 16th-century ornament in S. chapel and nave and of plain colouring elsewhere. *Piscina :* In chancel—with plain pointed head and round drain, probably 14th-century. *Sedile :* In chancel—with hollow-chamfered jambs and four-centred head, all plastered, possibly 15th-century. *Royal Arms :* In nave—on N. wall, Stuart arms in carved and painted wood, given in 1763.

Condition—Of tower, bad ; masonry of chancel, etc., poor.

Secular :—

(2). FINGRINGHOE HALL, 100 yards S.E. of the church, is of two storeys with attics and cellars ; the walls are of brick and plastered timber-framing ; the roofs are tiled. It was built early in the 17th century but was almost entirely reconstructed in the first half of the 18th century. Inside the building, are some original panelled doors.

Condition—Good, much altered.

(3). COTTAGE, at Hyde Park Corner, about ½ m. E.N.E. of the church, is of two storeys, timber-framed and plastered and partly faced with modern brick ; the roofs are tiled. It was built in the 16th century with a cross-wing at the W. end. Late in the 17th century the main block was rebuilt. The upper storey formerly projected at the N. end of the cross-wing but has been underbuilt.

Condition—Good, much altered.

(4). HAM'S FARM, house, three tenements, 1¼ m. S.W. of the church, is of two storeys, timber-framed and plastered ; the roofs are tiled. It was built probably in the 15th century with a cross-wing at the S. end. Early in the 16th century the main block was extended towards the N., probably on the site of a former cross-wing. The upper storey projects at the N. end of this extension and has a moulded bressumer. The W. gable of the cross-wing has an original moulded bracket. Inside the building the original part has exposed ceiling-beams and a cambered tie-beam. The extension has early 16th-century moulded ceiling-beams on the ground floor and hollow-chamfered ceiling-beams on the first floor.

Condition—Good.

27. FORDHAM. (C.c.)

(O.S. 6 in. [a]xviii. S.W. [b]xxvii. N.W.)

Fordham is a parish 5 m. N.W. of Colchester. The church is the principal monument.

Ecclesiastical :—

[b](1). PARISH CHURCH OF ALL SAINTS stands in the S. part of the parish. The walls are mainly of flint and pebble-rubble with some Roman and later brick, the dressings are of Barnack and soft lime-stone ; the roofs are tiled or covered with lead. The whole church was rebuilt in the 14th century, beginning with the *Chancel c.* 1330 and followed by the *Nave* and *North* and *South Aisles, South Porch,* and the lower part of the *West Tower, c.* 1340. The upper part of the tower was finished late in the same century. In the 16th century the S. aisle and porch and part of the N. aisle were refaced or rebuilt. In the 18th century the W. side of the tower was much damaged, perhaps by the fall of a spire, and early in the 19th century the greater part of the bell-chamber was rebuilt.

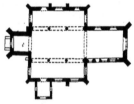

Architectural Description—The *Chancel* (27½ ft. by 20 ft.) has a mid 14th-century E. window with a two-centred head and a moulded label ; the tracery is modern. In the N. wall are two mid 14th-century windows, partly restored, and each of two cinquefoiled lights with a quatrefoil in a two-centred head. In the S. wall are three windows of which the two eastern are uniform with those in the N. wall ; the westernmost window is a single trefoiled light, probably of the same date ; E. of it is a mid 14th-century doorway with chamfered jambs, two-centred arch and label. The mid 14th-century chancel-arch is two-centred and of two chamfered orders ; the responds are semi-octagonal and have moulded capitals and bases, partly cut away.

The *Nave* (39 ft. by 20 ft.) has N. and S. arcades of three bays and of similar date and character to the chancel-arch ; the columns are octagonal and the arches bear some evidence of having been rebuilt. The clearstorey has on each side three trefoiled windows of mid 14th-century date.

The *North Aisle* (11½ ft. wide) has an E. window, all modern externally but with splays and four-centred rear-arch of the 15th century. In the

N. wall are two windows, the eastern of mid 14th-century date and of two trefoiled ogee lights with a quatrefoil in a two-centred head; the western window is uniform with that in the E. wall; further W. is the N. doorway probably of the 13th century reset; it has moulded jambs and two-centred arch. In the W. wall is a window all modern externally but with splays and rear-arch probably of the 14th century.

The *South Aisle* (11½ ft. wide) has an E. window all modern except parts of the jambs, the splays and rear-arch which are probably of the 15th century; the recess is carried down below the sill. In the S. wall are two windows uniform with the 15th-century windows in the N. aisle but with some old stones in the jambs; further W. is the 15th-century S. doorway with stop-moulded jambs and two-centred arch. In the W. wall is a window uniform with the corresponding window in the N. aisle.

The *West Tower* (10 ft. square) is of three stages, undivided externally and with a modern parapet. The 14th-century tower-arch is two-centred and of two moulded orders, the outer continuous and the inner resting on attached semi-octagonal shafts with moulded capitals and bases. The W. window is modern except perhaps the splays and rear-arch. In the second stage in the S. wall is a single trefoiled light probably of the 14th century. The bell-chamber has in the N. wall a window formerly of two cinquefoiled lights in a two-centred head, but now without its mullion; it is probably of the 14th century. In the S. and W. walls are modern windows.

The *South Porch* has a 15th-century outer arch-way with a moulded, two-centred arch and label; the moulded jambs have attached shafts with moulded capitals and bases. The side walls have each a 14th-century window of two trefoiled ogee lights with a cusped spandrel in a two-centred head with a moulded label and head-stops.

The *Roof* of the chancel is ceiled but has 14th or early 15th-century moulded plates and pole-plates. The roof of the S. porch incorporates two late 14th-century tie-beams and moulded wall-plates.

Fittings—*Bell:* one, said to be by Miles Graye, 1637. *Inscriptions* and *Scratchings:* On chancel —arch and arcades, rough mason's marks. On jambs of S. doorway, 15th-century *graffiti*. *Monuments:* In churchyard—S. of chancel, (1) to Elizabeth (Abbott), wife of James Stubbin, early 18th-century head-stone; (2) to Ann, wife of John Stubbin, 1711, head-stone. *Niches:* In S. aisle— flanking E. window, two, (1) square-headed recess, early 16th-century; (2) smaller recess, with four-centred head, probably early 16th-century; in jambs of N E. window, two with round heads, 15th-century. *Panelling:* Incorporated in modern pulpit, early 17th-century carved panels. *Piscinae:* In chancel—with cinquefoiled head and moulded

label, shelf and sexfoiled drain, 14th-century. In N. aisle—in E. wall, with two-centred head moulded label and octofoiled drain, 14th-century. In S. aisle—in S. wall, with trefoiled segmental-pointed head and octofoiled drain, 15th-century.
Condition—Fairly good.

Secular :—

HOMESTEAD MOATS.

a(2). At Moat Hall, ½ m. N.N.E. of the church.

a(3). At Houd's Farm, about 1 m. N. of the church.

b(4). FORDHAM HALL, house and barn, S.W. of the church. The *House* is of two storeys, timber-framed and plastered; the roofs are tiled. It was built probably late in the 15th century with cross-wings at the N. and S. ends, but the whole building was much altered in the 17th century and there are modern additions at the back. The upper storey projects at the E. ends of the cross-wings; on the N. wing there are 17th-century moulded brackets. Inside the building the main block has remains of the original roof and a plaster fragment is preserved, painted with foliage and the date 1586.

The *Barn*, E. of the house, is of the 17th century, timber-framed and weather-boarded and of seven bays.
Condition—Of house, good, much altered.

MONUMENTS (5–11)..

The following monuments, unless otherwise described, are of the 17th century and of two storeys, timber-framed and plastered; the roofs are tiled or thatched. Several of the buildings have original chimney-stacks and exposed ceiling-beams.
Condition—Good or fairly good, unless noted.

b(5). Range of two cottages, E. of the church. Inside one cottage is a moulded ceiling-beam.
Condition—Poor.

b(6). *Cobb's Farm*, house, 180 yards E. of (5).

b(7). *Barnard's Farm*, house, ¾ m. S.W. of the church, was built probably in the 15th century and has a cross-wing at the N. end. The upper storey projects at the E. end of the cross-wing, which has remains of the original roof-construction.

b(8). *Shoulder of Mutton Inn*, 200 yards S.S.E. of (7), is of two storeys with attics. It was built in the 16th century with cross-wings at the N. and S. ends. The roof of the main block was raised in the 18th century and there are modern additions on the E. side. The main block has a modilloned eaves-cornice.

a(9). *Cottage*, on the S. side of the road, ½ m. N. of the church.

a(10). *Archendine's Farm*, house, ¼ m. W.N.W. of (9).

a(11). *Cottage*, on W. side of road, ¼ m. N. of (2).

28. FRATING. (E.c.)

(O.S. 6 in. [a]xxviii. S.E. [b]xxxvii. N.E.)

Frating is a small parish 6 m. E.S.E. of Colchester.

Ecclesiastical :—

[b](1). PARISH CHURCH (dedication unknown), stands on the S.W. side of the parish. The walls are mostly of iron pudding-stone with some pebbles; the dressings are of limestone and the S.W. angle of nave has Roman brick quoins. The roofs are tiled. The S. wall of the *Nave* is of early 12th-century date. The *Chancel* was rebuilt *c.* 1300. The *N. Chapel* is possibly of the 14th century but there is little evidence of this; the *West Tower* was added about the middle of the 14th century and the *South Porch* is perhaps of the same date. The church was drastically restored in the 19th century when the N. chapel was extended W. to form a *North Aisle*, the tower and chancel-arches rebuilt and the S. wall largely refaced.

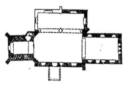

Architectural Description—The *Chancel* (23½ ft. by 15½ ft.) has a modern E. window. In the N. wall are three early 14th-century windows each of one trefoiled ogee light. In the S. wall are three windows, the easternmost is of two trefoiled ogee lights with a trefoil in a gabled head with a moulded label and head-stops; it is of *c.* 1300 with the head restored; the second window is uniform with those in the N. wall; the third window is similar but partly restored and carried down below a transom to form a 'low-side' with a modern shutter; between the second and third windows is a doorway of *c.* 1300 with chamfered jambs and two-centred arch. The chancel-arch is modern.

The *Nave* (35 ft. by 20½ ft.) has a modern N. arcade. In the S. wall are three windows, the easternmost and westernmost are modern; the middle one is an early 12th-century light with Roman brick jambs and round head; between the two western windows is a modern S. doorway with a round cemented rear-arch, possibly of the 12th-century.

The *North Aisle* (13½ ft. wide) has old walls to the E. bay which formed a N. chapel. The E. window is modern except the 14th-century splays and moulded segmental rear-arch. The eastern window in the N. wall is modern except the splays and hollow-chamfered rear-arch which are possibly of the 14th-century.

The *West Tower* (about 9 ft. square) is of mid 14th-century date and of three stages with a modern parapet. The tower-arch is modern and is set within a cemented two-centred arch dying into the side walls and perhaps of the 14th century. The W. window is modern; the W. doorway has stop-moulded jambs and two-centred arch. The second stage has in the W. wall a single light window with brick jambs and trefoiled ogee head of stone. The bell-chamber has in each wall a window of two cinquefoiled lights in a two-centred head with a moulded label, all much restored.

The *South Porch* is timber-framed and probably of the 14th century. It has a plain two-centred outer archway and the sides are each divided into five lights by diamond-shaped mullions.

The *Roof* of the N. chapel (E. bay of N. aisle) is flat with a moulded ridge-beam and joists; the beam has an oval panel in the middle with ' umbrella ' flutings and is probably of the 17th century. The 14th-century roof of the S. porch has ogee curved braces under the trussed collar-beams.

Fittings—*Bells :* three; said to be, 1st possibly by William Dawe, *c.* 1400 and inscribed, " Johannes Est Nomen Ejus "; 3rd by Kebyll, 15th-century and inscribed, " Sit Nomen Domini Benedictum." *Glass :* In chancel—in the N.W. window, border of foliage and ruby glass, 14th-century. *Monument :* In N. aisle—against E. wall, to Thomas Bendish, 1603, and Elinor (Ford), his wife, altar-tomb of alabaster and black marble, inscription with ornamental cresting, two shields of arms. *Piscina :* In chancel—with chamfered two-centred head and round drain, 14th-century. *Plate :* includes cup of 1584. *Recess :* In chancel—in N. wall, with moulded jambs and four-centred arch, enriched with small flowers, square head with foliated spandrels, early 16th-century, probably Easter Sepulchre. *Sedile :* In chancel—sill of S.W. window carried down to form seat.

Condition—Good, much restored.

Secular :—

[b](2). FRATING HALL, 200 yards N. of the church, is of two storeys; the walls are of modern brick and the roofs are tiled. It was built early in the 16th century and has four original tie-beams with curved braces in the roof and a central purlin. E. of the house is a 16th-century gateway of brick. The outer archway has two modern inserted piers; the inner archway has a four-centred arch and a square label, above which is a moulded cornice and capping. The garden wall is of similar date and of red brick with a modern coping; the wall contains several round-headed niches. In the garden are several moulded stones of the 13th or 14th century and probably brought from the church.

Condition—Of house, good.

[a](3). COTTAGE, at Frating Green, about ¾ m. N.E. of the church, is of two storeys, timber-framed and weather-boarded. It was built probably late in the 17th century and has an original chamfered ceiling-beam.

Condition—Good.

[a](4). FISH PONDS or duck-decoy, 200 yards N. of (2), consists of two rectangular islands, surrounded by wide ditches.

---

29. FRINTON. (G.d.)

(O.S. 6 in. xlviii. N.W.)

Frinton is a small parish and town by the sea, 5 m. N.E. of Clacton.

Ecclesiastical :—

PARISH CHURCH OF ST. MARY stands about 160 yards from the cliffs. The walls are of septaria and flint-rubble with dressings of limestone ; the roofs are tiled. The *Nave* was built probably in tle 14th century. The *South Porch* was added in the 16th century. The church fell into ruin in the 17th or 18th century. The *Chancel* was added in 1879 and the church restored ; there is a modern extension to the nave.

Architectural Description—The *Nave* (25 ft. by 18½ ft.) has been partly refaced. In the N. wall are two modern windows and between them is the 14th-century N. doorway with chamfered jambs and a modern head. In the S. wall are two modern windows and between them the 14th-century S. doorway with chamfered jambs and two-centred arch with a moulded label.

The *South Porch* is of *c.* 1600 and of brick. The outer archway has a four-centred head. The side walls have each a window of two restored four-centred lights in a four-centred head.

Fittings—*Glass* (Plate, p. 192) : In chancel—in N. window, two 14th-century shields, partly restored—(*a*) *checky or and azure* for Warenne ; (*b*) *gules three cheverons ermine* for Elderbeke. *Stoup :* In nave—in S. wall, with cinquefoiled head, 15th-century, no basin.

Condition—Good, much restored.

---

30. GOLDHANGER. (C.e.)

(O.S. 6 in. [a]xlv. S.E. [b]liv. N.E.)

Goldhanger is a village and parish on the N. side of the Blackwater estuary and 3½ m. E.N.E. of Maldon. The church is interesting.

Roman :—

[b](1). During the excavation of a Red Hill in 1908 and 1909 near the outlet of the creek, in the northern part of Fish Pit Marsh, evidence of the intrusion of a Romano-British settler was disclosed. Below the extreme eastern edge of the red earth on the old salting surface was found a kitchen midden of considerable size, containing masses of oyster and mussel shells, animal bones, many of which had been cut and split, and Roman pottery, including "large jars with a heavy roll rim." Over this had been spread red earth from the mound on the west side, and over this again was a layer of brown mould. In the red earth and mould of the mound had been built some seven flues, and three or four fire-floors filled with Roman pottery. The flues were chiefly in parallel pairs, and were from 18 to 30 in. wide, 2 ft. deep and from 5 to 8 ft. long. They were carefully made and lined with puddled clay about an inch thick and were filled with black ash and burnt clay. Some of the flues were laid on the floors, some below them. The floors consisted of hard material burnt yellow, and from 1 to 3½ ft. in thickness, and measured from 9 ft. by 13 ft. to 12 ft. by 18 ft. 'Samian' and other ware, bones of domestic animals and shells were abundant in and about the flues, but details of the smaller finds are lacking, and the date of the occupation cannot be fixed. It was the opinion of the excavators that while the Red Hill itself had been built on the open marsh, the mould could only have formed after the sea-wall had been constructed. Hence they would assign a pre-Roman date to the Hill itself, and conjecture the sea-wall to have been built possibly in Roman times. The Roman occupation of a Red Hill, of which this is the only recorded instance, may possibly have been due to a recrudescence of the industry—whatever it may have been—with which the original formation of the Red Hill was connected. (*Proc. Soc. Ant.*, XXIII, 69–76.) (See *Sectional Preface*, p. xxiii.)

Ecclesiastical :—

[b](2). PARISH CHURCH OF ST. PETER stands in, the village. The walls are of coursed flint-rubble with dressings of Roman brick and limestone ; the roofs are tiled. The *Chancel* and *Nave* were built in the 12th century and there are some indications that a S. aisle existed at the same time. The *South Aisle* was probably rebuilt late in the 14th century. In the second half of the 15th century the *West Tower* was added and the W. end of the church rebuilt. The *South Chapel* was added shortly afterwards. The church was restored in the 19th and 20th centuries when the chancel-arch and S. arcade were rebuilt and the *South Porch* added.

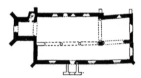

Architectural Description—The *Chancel* (21 ft. by 16½ ft.) has E. quoins of Roman brick. The E. window is modern. In the N. wall is a 12th-century window with jambs and round head of Roman brick. In the S. wall is a late 15th-century four-centred arch of two moulded orders ; the responds have semi-octagonal shafts with moulded capitals and bases. The chancel-arch is modern.

The *South Chapel* (20 ft. by 11¾ ft.) has in the E. and S. walls a window all modern or completely restored.

The *Nave* (45¾ ft. by 18½ ft.) has in the N. wall three windows, the easternmost and westernmost are modern ; the middle window is of the 12th century and is similar to that in the N. wall of the chancel ; between the two western windows is the N. doorway, possibly of the 12th century but much altered and with a two-centred arch of the 15th century. The E. quoins of the wall are of Roman brick. The S. arcade is modern.

The *South Aisle* (10¼ ft. wide) has in the S. wall two modern windows ; between them is the late 14th-century S. doorway, partly restored, and with stop-moulded jambs and two-centred arch with a moulded label.

The *West Tower* (10 ft. square) is of the 15th century and of three stages, with an embattled parapet. The two centred tower-arch is of two hollow-chamfered orders ; the responds have each a half-round shaft with moulded capital and base. In the N. wall is the doorway to the turret stair-case, with a two-centred head. The W. window is of two cinquefoiled lights with vertical tracery in a two-centred head with a moulded label ; below it is the W. doorway with moulded jambs, two-centred arch and label. The second stage has in the N., S. and W. walls a window of one trefoiled light. The bell-chamber has in each wall a window of two cinquefoiled lights in a square head with a moulded label and partly restored.

The *Roof* of the nave is of the 15th century and of three bays with moulded wall-plates, and tie-beams with curved braces and king-posts with four-way struts. The ground stage of the tower has 15th-century moulded ceiling-beams.

Fittings—*Bells :* six ; 4th by Miles Graye, 1652. *Brass :* See Monument. *Door :* In second stage of tower—of battens with strap-hinges, probably 15th-century. *Monument :* In S. chapel—in N.E. angle to [Thomas Heigham, 1531, and Alys, Awdrie, and Frances, his wives] altar-tomb of Purbeck marble, sides, of disarranged stones, panelled with cinquefoiled and traceried heads and traces of former buttresses, each bay on S. side with shields having defaced charges (*a*) *a pall with a cross erect ;* (*b*) *a fesse between three* (*roses ?*) ; (*c*) *a cheveron between three* . . . . . . ; on N. side one plain shield and one with the letters IHC ; slab with moulded edge and brass figure of woman in pedimental head-dress, indents of man in armour and two other wives and four shields of arms ; inserted later at top, brass inscription to Anthony Heyham, 1540, and Anne, his wife, with two shields of arms inserted in earlier indents—(*a*) *a cheveron, over all a bend* (*b*) (*a*) *impaling a lion within a border engrailed ;* tomb either rebuilt or made up of pieces from another monument. *Painting :* slight traces on roof timbers of nave. *Piscinae :* In chancel—with chamfered jambs and two-centred head, foliated drain, probably 13th-century. In S. chapel—in S. wall, with moulded jambs and ogee head, octofoiled drain, 15th-century. *Miscellanea :* In chancel—W. of S. arch, piece of *carving* with figures of angel bearing away soul of a bearded man, ivy foliage and dragon, possibly 14th-century, but of doubtful antiquity.

Condition—Good.

Secular :—

b(3). COBB'S FARM, house, ¾ m. W.S.W. of the church, was built in the 17th century but has been almost entirely rebuilt except for the central chimney-stack.

Condition—Good.

a(4). FALCON'S HALL FARM, house, about ½ m. N.N.W. of the church, is of two storeys with attics ; the walls are timber-framed and plastered, and the roofs are tiled. It was built early in the 16th century with cross-wings at the E. and W. ends. The upper storey projects at the N. end of the cross-wings ; the gable of the W. wing also projects and has a moulded and carved bressumer ; in the wall of the ground floor is an original window with moulded mullions and now blocked. Two chimney-stacks are of the 17th century and have diagonal shafts. Inside the building are exposed ceiling-beams and some 16th-century doors with strap-hinges. The roof of the W. wing has curved braces to the tie-beams and curved wind-braces.

Condition—Good.

a(5). FOLLY FAUNTS FARM, house, 200 yards E. of (3), is of two storeys with attics. The walls are timber-framed and the roofs are tiled. It was built late in the 16th or early in the 17th century and has a modern block on the S. front. The wing at the back was added *c.* 1700. Inside the building, is some exposed timber-framing and some of the ceiling-beams are also exposed.

Condition—Good, much altered.

Unclassified :—

[b](6). RED HILL, in Fish Pit Marsh, west of Gold-hanger Creek. There are many others along the line of the sea-wall.

---

31. GREAT BENTLEY. (E.d.)

(O.S. 6 in. [a]xxix. S.W. [b]xxxviii. N.W.)

Great Bentley is a parish and village 3½ m. N.N.E. of Brightlingsea. The church is interesting.

Ecclesiastical :—

[b](1). PARISH CHURCH OF ST. MARY (Plate, p. 108) stands in the village. The walls are of very regularly coursed iron pudding-stone, largely laid herring-bone-wise and of small stones ; there are some courses of septaria ; the quoins and dressings of the doorways are of Barnack stone but the original windows have pudding-stone jambs and heads. The extension of the chancel contains a larger proportion of septaria. The tower is of the same materials with much brick and a certain amount of water-worn granite, trap and other igneous stones. The roofs are tiled. The *Chancel* and *Nave* are of c. 1130–40. The chancel was extended towards the E. probably in the 14th century. Late in the same century the *West Tower* was added. The *North Porch* was built in the 14th or 15th century. The church was restored in the 19th and 20th centuries ; the chancel-arch is modern and the N. porch mostly rebuilt.

The church is a very complete example of careful 12th-century building.

Architectural Description—The *Chancel* (36 ft. by 20¾ ft.) has an E. window, modern except the splays which are possibly of the 14th century. The quoins of the E. angles are reused 12th-century material. In the N. wall are two windows, the eastern is a mid 13th-century lancet with wide splays ; the western is an early 12th-century window of pudding-stone, but with ashlar splays and rear-arch. In the S. wall are three windows, the easternmost is a very small 15th-century cinquefoiled light, above the piscina ; the two western windows are 13th-century single lights, with modern trefoiled heads and all modern externally ; above the westernmost window are traces of the head of a former 12th-century window ; between the two western windows is a doorway, all modern except one stone of the label. The chancel-arch is modern.

The *Nave* (54 ft. by 24½ ft.) has in the N. wall three windows, the eastern is of the 15th century and of three cinquefoiled lights with vertical tracery in a two-centred head, with a moulded label and head-stops ; in the E. splay is a doorway with a four-centred head, to the rood-loft stair-case ; the two lowest steps are cut in the sill of the window ; the stair is set in a thickening of the

wall, with a tabled top ; the two western windows are of the 12th century and similar to that in the chancel ; the westernmost is very much restored ; between them is the 12th-century N. doorway, with plain jambs and round arch, each voussoir of which has axe-worked diapering ; the impost stones have a boldly projecting volute worked on the inner face of each. In the S. wall are three windows, the easternmost is of the 15th century and of three cinquefoiled lights with vertical tracery in a four-centred head ; the two western windows are uniform with the corresponding windows in the N. wall ; between them is the 12th-century S. doorway, with a round arch carved with cheveron ornament and a label with cable ornament, and terminating on the E. in an upright grotesque head ; the inner order has a segmental arch supporting a tympanum and with each voussoir carved with two sunflowers ; the jambs have each a free shaft with cushion capitals carved with leaf ornament, moulded bases and chamfered abaci continued round the plain inner order.

The *West Tower* (12 ft. by 10¾ ft.) is of late 14th-century date and of three stages, with an embattled parapet. The two-centred tower-arch is cemented and of uncertain date. The W. window is modern except for the head, label and head-stops ; the W. doorway has double hollow-chamfered jambs and two-centred arch with a moulded label ; the hollow-chamfers of the head have a series of carved square flowers. The second stage has in the N., S. and W. walls a pointed window of brick. In the E. wall is a four-centred doorway of brick now appearing in the nave above the collar-beams. The bell-chamber has in each wall a window of two cinquefoiled lights with a quatrefoil in a two-centred head with a moulded label and head-stops ; the N. and W. windows are mostly modern and the other windows partly restored ; above the E. and N. windows is a cross in brickwork, and W. of the S. window is set a round stone bored through.

The *North Porch* is of timber on modern dwarf walls ; the old timbers are of the 14th or 15th century and include the inner pair of posts, curved outwards at the top and the hollow-chamfered plates with the mortices for diamond-shaped mullions now replaced by modern work.

The *Roof* of the Chancel has moulded 15th-century plates (now [1921] being opened out). The early 15th-century roof of the nave is of trussed-rafter type and of four bays with curved and chamfered principals, with moulded and formerly embattled wall-plates and moulded wall-posts.

Fittings—*Bells :* eight ; 6th by Miles Graye, 1683 ; 7th by Henry Pleasant, 1703. *Chest :* In tower—with cambered lid and iron straps, chest covered with skin, late 17th-century. *Coffin-lid :* In nave—upper half of tapering slab with hollow-chamfered edge and remains of formy cross, 13th-

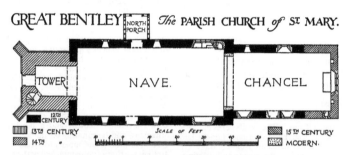

GREAT BENTLEY. *The* PARISH CHURCH *of* S⧠ MARY.

century. *Font:* octagonal bowl with double-trefoiled panels and shields alternately, three shields with traces of crosses, moulded under-edge with carved flowers, stem with plain pointed panels, 15th-century. *Niches:* In chancel—flanking E. window, two with hollow-chamfered jambs carved with flowers, ogee crocketed heads and finials, carved spandrels, side pinnacles and embattled head, late 14th-century, head of N. niche, modern. *Paving:* In chancel floor, nine slip-tiles with various patterns, including a greyhound, and a stag, late 13th or early 14th-century. *Piscinae:* In chancel—with chamfered jambs and two-centred head, quatrefoiled drain, 14th-century. In nave—in S. wall, with chamfered jambs and trefoiled head, remains of colour, 15th-century. *Plate:* includes cover-paten without date mark and a pewter flagon perhaps of early 18th-century date. *Scratchings:* On font and W. doorway, date and other marks, 17th-century ; on E. jamb of S. doorway, two sundials. *Stoup:* In nave—W. of S. doorway, recess for former stoup.
Condition—Good.

Secular :—

ᵃ(2). PARSONAGE FARM, house, barn and moat, ¾ m. N.N.E. of the church. The *House* is of two storeys, timber-framed and plastered ; the roofs are tiled. It was built probably in the 17th century and has cross-wings at the N. and S. ends. Inside the building the main block has exposed ceiling-beams and joists.
The *Barn*, E. of the house, is timber-framed and weather-boarded. It was built in the 16th century and is of four bays with a porch on the N. side.
The *Moat* is fragmentary.
Condition—Of house, good.

MONUMENTS (3–10).

The following monuments, unless otherwise described, are of the 17th century and of two storeys, timber-framed and plastered or weather-boarded ; the roofs are tiled or thatched. Many of the buildings have original chimney-stacks and exposed ceiling-beams.
Condition—Good, or fairly good.

ᵃ(3). *Crabtree Farm*, house, nearly 1¼ m. N. of the church, with large modern additions.

ᵇ(4). *House*, two tenements, at Green Corner, 500 yards N.N.E. of the church. The front half is probably part of a 16th-century house ; the back half is modern.

ᵇ(5). *House*, two tenements, standing back from the road, 250 yards S.S.W. of (4), built probably late in the 16th century.

ᵇ(6). *House*, 100 yards E. of the church, with walls of red brick.

ᵇ(7). *House*, adjoining (6) on the W., built probably in the 16th century. Inside the building some of the timber-framing is exposed.

ᵇ(8). *House*, called the Poplars, 300 yards N.E. of the church, has been refronted with modern brickwork.

ᵇ(9). *Eden's Farm,* house, nearly 1 m. E. of the church, was built probably late in the 16th century with a cross-wing at the E. end. There is a modern addition on the N. side. The gable of the cross-wing has the date 1717 probably indicating some alteration.

ᵇ(10). *Tye Homestead*, house, two tenements, nearly 1½ m. E.S.E. of the church.

ᵇ(11). *Moat* and *Fish Pond* in Hall Field, S. of the church.

---

32. GREAT BRAXTED. (B.d.)

(O.S. 6 in. ⁽ᵃ⁾xxxv. S.W. ⁽ᵇ⁾xlv. N.W. ⁽ᶜ⁾xlv. N.E.)

Great Braxted is a parish and hamlet 2½ m. E. of Witham. The church and Tiptree Priory are the principal monuments.

GREAT BENTLEY: PARISH CHURCH OF ST. MARY; *c.* 1130 and later.
South Wall, showing original masonry.

lany
acks

V. of

ner,
half
the

back
built

with

built
lding

N.E.
odern

E. of
16th
e is a
of the
ating

nents,

S. of

2½ m.

GREAT BRAXTED: PARISH CHURCH OF ALL SAINTS; from the South-east.
Chancel, 12th and 13th-century; Nave, 12th-century, with later Windows.

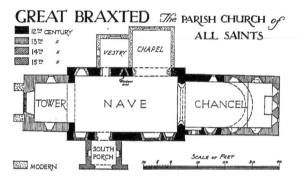

GREAT BRAXTED *The* PARISH CHURCH *of*
ALL SAINTS

■ 12ᵀᴴ CENTURY
▥ 13ᵀᴴ "
▨ 14ᵀᴴ "
▧ 15ᵀᴴ "

VESTRY CHAPEL

TOWER N A V E CHANCEL

Window arch

SOUTH PORCH

SCALE of FEET

▨ MODERN

Ecclesiastical :—

b(1). PARISH CHURCH OF ALL SAINTS (Plate, p. 109) stands in Braxted Park. The walls are of septaria mixed with flint, freestone and Roman bricks ; the dressings are of clunch and Roman bricks, and the roofs are tiled. The *Nave* and the W. half of the *Chancel* were built early in the 12th century when the church probably terminated eastwards in an apse. Early in the 13th century this apse was removed and the chancel extended to its present length ; shortly afterwards the *West Tower* was added but it is doubtful whether it was ever completed. The *South Porch* was added in the 15th century. The church was restored in the 19th century when the *North Chapel* and *Vestry* were added, the chancel-arch rebuilt and the timber belfry and spire probably renewed.

The coursed rubble walling of the chancel is interesting.

Architectural Description—The *Chancel* (32 ft. by 16½ ft.) has in the E. wall three 13th-century lancet windows, almost entirely modern externally. There is a break in the N. and S. walls of the chancel showing the junction of the 12th and 13th-century work ; the 12th-century work shows traces of an inward curvature at this point suggesting the spring of a former apse ; this is most apparent in the N. wall ; the 12th-century walls are of coursed rubble and on the N. side have regular courses of tufa and Roman tiles, two courses being set herring-bone-wise. In the N. wall are three windows, the two eastern are 13th-century lancets both partly restored ; the westernmost window is of early 12th-century date and with a round head of tufa. In the S. wall are four windows of which the three eastern are 13th-century lancets completely restored externally ; the westernmost window is in two divisions, the upper a lancet light and the lower a square-headed 'low-side' window, much restored externally,

both are probably of the 13th century ; W. of the second window are the external jambs of a 13th-century doorway, now blocked. E. of the easternmost window on each side are the socket holes for a beam formerly across the chancel. The chancel-arch is modern.

The *Nave* (38 ft. by 20 ft.) has S. quoins of Roman brick and a plastered N. wall. In the N. wall is a modern arch and two windows, the eastern window is of the 12th century but widened and altered in the 17th or 18th century ; the western window is modern as is the doorway E. of it ; high in the wall a round patch probably indicates a former round window like those in the S. wall. In the S. wall are three completely restored windows in the lower range, except the 14th-century splays and rear-arch of the middle window ; in the upper range are two round and sexfoiled windows probably of the 14th century but with modern jambs ; around the eastern the jambs and round head of a 12th-century window are indicated internally ; above the second window of the lower range is the Roman brick head of another 12th-century window. The 14th-century S. door-way has jambs and two-centred arch of two orders, the inner modern and the outer chamfered.

The *West Tower* (12 ft. by 14 ft.) rises as high as the nave and is surmounted by a timber bell-turret and spire. Between the two modern W. buttresses is sprung a segmental-pointed arch of which the chamfered outer order appears to be of the 13th century. The 13th-century tower-arch is two-centred and of one chamfered order. In both the N. and S. walls is a 13th-century lancet window. The W. window is modern.

The *South Porch* has a 15th-century outer archway, two-centred and of two moulded orders, the outer continuous and the inner resting on attached shafts with moulded capitals and bases ; the label is moulded. The side walls have each a

15th-century window of two cinquefoiled lights in a square head with a chamfered label.

The *Roof* of the chancel is probably of the 17th century towards the E. and of the 15th century towards the W.; both parts are of the trussed collar-beam type and ceiled; the W. part has moulded wall-plates. The late 15th or early 16th-century roof of the nave is much restored and has three king-post trusses with moulded and embattled tie-beams with curved braces, traceried spandrels and half-angels at the point of junction; the curved principals and the central purlin are moulded. The 15th-century roof of the S. porch has moulded and embattled tie-beams with curved braces forming four-centred arches, king-posts, wall-posts, moulded brackets and carved stone corbels, two with angels and two with faces; the wall-plates are moulded and embattled.

Fittings — *Monument* and *Floor-slabs*. Monument: In tower — to Robert Aylett, LL.D., 1654, tablet with emblems of mortality and two shields of arms. Floor-slabs: In chancel—(1) to Richard Milward, D.D., 1680, canon of Windsor and rector of the parish, with shield of arms; (2) to Anthony Carew, 1705, now covered by pulpit. *Locker:* In chancel—in N. wall, large with rebated jambs and two-centred head, slots for wooden shelf, 13th-century. *Panelling:* In chancel—dado of moulded panelling, with fluted frieze, early 17th-century, brought from elsewhere. *Piscina:* In chancel—with corbelled head and shelf in E. jamb, round drain, 13th-century, enlarged in the 16th century. *Plate:* includes a cup of 1562, an Elizabethan cover-paten, cover-paten of 1711, a flagon of 1660 and an alms-dish of 1646. *Sedile:* In chancel—plain recess with two-centred arch, possibly 13th-century. *Sundial:* On jamb of S.W. window of chancel, incised and much worn. *Miscellanea:* Incorporated in modern chancel furniture, part of 17th-century *table* with moulded top.

Condition—Good.

Secular :—

c(2). TIPTREE PRIORY (Plate, p. 234), house, about 1½ m. E.S.E. of the church, is of three storeys; the walls are of brick and the roofs are tiled. It stands on the site of a small priory of Austin Canons, founded in the 12th century, and dedicated to St. Mary and St. Nicholas. The only remaining portion of this structure is a rubble wall extending to the E. of the existing house, but the lay-out of the house may have followed the lines of the N., E. and W. sides of the canons' cloister. The house was built *c.* 1570 and then consisted of a main block, lying E. and W., and of which the western half is still standing, and probably two

wings projecting towards the S. from either end of the main building; these wings have both been destroyed. At the N.W. angle is a projecting turret added *c.* 1600, and there are later and modern additions at the back.

The *S. Front* has two ranges of four-light transomed windows with moulded labels and dressings of plaster, five windows in each range; of these the four easternmost of each range are original and the other two are old windows reset, as this end of the wall was covered by the former W. wing. The fourth window from the E. on the ground floor has been partly blocked and a doorway with chamfered jambs and three-centred head inserted in the opening. Below the westernmost window are traces of a former doorway and the lines of the former gabled roof of the W. wing remain on the wall at the first floor level. Adjoining the S.E. angle of the house and in continuation of the front is a doorway with moulded jambs and four-centred arch, surmounted by a moulded pediment springing from small brackets; this feature was no doubt the main entrance to the house before the destruction of the E. part of the main block and seems to indicate that the Great Hall occupied the portion now destroyed.

The *W. End* is of three storeys and there are lines indicating the original gable which has been heightened. The main block has three windows of similar character to those on the S. front but of varying sizes. A joint indicates the addition of the later turret on the N. side; this turret is semi-octagonal on plan and has three two-light windows on the W. side, the two lower being each surmounted by a cornice.

The *E. end* was formerly an internal wall and has reset in it three windows of similar character to those on the S. front. The space to the E. of the existing house was probably occupied by the Great Hall and is bounded on the N. by a rubble wall probably of mediaeval date; in it is a large 16th-century fireplace, with moulded jambs and four-centred arch.

Inside the building the existing divisions are probably mostly modern but the middle room on the ground floor has a wide fireplace, partly filled in, and to the E. of it is a long closet. The upper windows have each an iron casement with an ornamental latch.

The garden S. of the house is enclosed on the E. and W. sides by brick walls, that on the W. is bonded into the house and adjoining it a length of 40 ft. of rebuilt wall may indicate the dimensions of the destroyed W. wing.

Condition—Fairly good.

b(3). COTTAGE, two tenements, on the N. side of the village, and 1 m. S.E. of the church, is of two storeys, timber-framed and plastered; the roofs are tiled. It was built early in the 17th century, and has an original central chimney-stack with grouped diagonal shafts. Inside the building the ceiling-beams are exposed.

Condition—Fairly good.

[b](4). COTTAGE, about 1½ m. S.S.E. of the church, is of two storeys, timber-framed and plastered; the roofs are tiled. It was built early in the 17th century and has exposed ceiling-beams.

Condition—Good.

[b](5). NOAKS CROSS FARM, house, 1,050 yards S.E. of the church, is of two storeys, partly timber-framed and plastered and partly of brick; the roofs are tiled. It was built late in the 16th century on an L-shaped plan with the wings extending towards the S. and W. In the N. wall is an original window of brick with moulded jambs and mullions and now blocked. A window on the first floor has part of the corbels of a former bay-window, carved with foliage. Inside the building is a late 17th-century panelled door and some exposed ceiling-beams.

Condition—Good.

[a](6). GREENLEAF COTTAGE, three tenements, about 1¼ m. N.N.E. of the church, is of two storeys, timber-framed and plastered; the roofs are tiled. It was built probably early in the 17th century and has exposed ceiling-beams of that date.

Condition—Good.

33. GREAT BROMLEY. (E.c.)

(O.S. 6 in. [(a)]xxviii. N.E. [(b)]xxviii. S.E.)

Great Bromley is a parish 5½ m. E.N.E. of Colchester. The church is the principal monument.

Ecclesiastical:—

[a](1). PARISH CHURCH OF ST. GEORGE (Plates, pp. 112, 113) stands near the middle of the parish. The walls are of mixed rubble and some brick, with dressings of limestone; the roofs are covered with tiles and lead. The *Chancel, Nave* and *South Aisle* were built early in the 14th century. The *North Aisle* and the N. arcade were built about the middle of the 15th century, and the S. aisle was largely rebuilt; the *South Chapel* was added about the same time. About 1500 the clearstorey of the nave was built and the *West Tower* and *South Porch* were added. The church was generally restored in the 19th century, the chancel-arch being rebuilt.

The church is of considerable architectural interest, the late 15th-century hammer-beam roof of the nave being particularly rich.

Architectural Description—The *Chancel* (24½ ft. by 18¼ ft.) has an E. window, modern except for the 15th-century shafted splays. In the N. wall are two modern windows. In the S. wall is a mid 15th-century archway, two-centred and of two hollow chamfered orders, the outer continuous and the inner resting on attached shafts with moulded capitals and bases, all partly restored. The chancel-arch is modern.

The *South Chapel* (22 ft. by 14½ ft.) has a moulded plinth with trefoiled headed panels of flint-inlay. The E. window is modern. In the S. wall is a 15th-century window of three cinque-foiled lights with vertical tracery in a segmental-pointed head with moulded jambs and label; further W. is a 15th-century doorway with moulded jambs, three-centred arch and label.

The *Nave* (41¼ ft. by 22 ft.) has a 15th-century N. arcade of three bays, with two-centred arches of two chamfered orders; the columns are octagonal with moulded capitals and bases; the responds have attached half columns; the thickening of the wall behind the W. respond may indicate a portion of the earlier nave; E. of the E. respond is a round-headed recess, probably a former squint. The S. arcade is of early 14th-century date and of three bays, with two-centred arches of two chamfered orders; the octagonal columns have moulded and carved capitals with restored bases; the E. respond has an attached shaft but the W. respond is plain; the capitals of the E. respond and of the first column are carved with oak foliage; the capital (Plate, p. 213) of the second column is carved with grotesque beasts, including one swallowing a man, another with a woman's head preyed upon by reptiles and an angel supporting a woman. The clearstorey (Plate, p. 143) has walls faced with knapped flints in traceried panels of freestone, and an embattled parapet of similar character ornamented with shields bearing the cross of St. George. On each side are seven late 15th-century windows each of two trefoiled ogee lights with vertical tracery in four-centred heads with moulded jambs and labels.

The *North Aisle* (11½ ft. wide) has a late 15th-century E. window of three cinquefoiled and transomed lights with vertical tracery in a two-centred head with a moulded label and head-stops. In the N. wall are two windows similar to that in the E. wall but much restored; further W. is the late 15th-century N. doorway with moulded jambs and two-centred head and label, with head-stops; the moulding and label are carved with flowers. In the W. wall is a window similar to that in the E. wall.

The *South Aisle* (average 12¼ ft. wide) has at the E. end of the N. wall the blocked lower doorway of the rood-loft staircase. In the S. wall is a window similar to the S. window of the S. chapel and partly restored; further W. is the S. doorway of *c.* 1400, with moulded jambs, two-centred arch and label all carved with running foliage; above the doorway are the reset spandrels of a late 15th or early 16th-century doorway carved

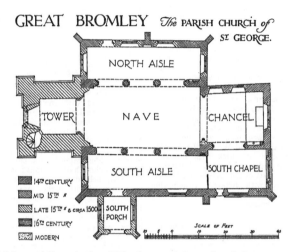

GREAT BROMLEY *The* PARISH CHURCH *of* S.^T GEORGE.

NORTH AISLE

TOWER   NAVE   CHANCEL

SOUTH AISLE   SOUTH CHAPEL

14TH CENTURY
MID 15TH ″
LATE 15TH ″ & CIRCA 1500   SOUTH PORCH
16TH CENTURY
MODERN

SCALE OF FEET

with figures of Adam and Eve ; in the middle of the head is a defaced moulded corbel. In the W. wall is a window of *c.* 1500 of three cinquefoiled ogee lights with vertical tracery in a segmental-pointed head with moulded jambs and label.

The *West Tower* (14½ ft. by 12½ ft.) is of late 15th-century date and of three stages with a moulded plinth enriched with quatrefoiled panels and a crow-stepped parapet with pinnacles at the angles ; the buttresses are square on plan at the base developing above into octagonal turrets and triple buttresses ; on the S.W. buttress is a shield of St. George. The tower-arch is two-centred and of three hollow-chamfered orders, the two outer continuous and the inner resting on attached shafts with moulded capitals and bases. The W. window is modern except for the moulded jambs, two-centred head and label with head-stops ; the W. doorway (Plate, p. 132) has moulded jambs and two-centred arch enriched with square flowers and set in a square head with a moulded label and stops carved with an angel with a shield and a griffon holding a scroll ; the spandrels have foliage and quatrefoiled circles, one enclosing the letters I H C. The second stage has in the E. wall a blocked doorway to the roof. The N., S. and W. walls have each a window of one trefoiled light in a square head with a moulded label. The bell-chamber has in each wall a transomed window of three cinquefoiled lights in a four-centred head with a moulded label.

The *South Porch* has a moulded plinth and parapet and the whole of the wall-face of the S. end is finished with knapped flints with elaborately

traceried panels of freestone ; the buttresses have on the outer face moulded panels with crocketed heads and are finished with embattled pinnacles set diagonally ; a similar but square pinnacle rises above the apex of the gable, the outer archway is two-centred and of two moulded orders, the outer continuous and the inner resting on attached shafts with moulded capitals and bases, the double label forms a square head, the spandrels of which are carved with figures of St. George and the dragon ; below the stops are carved figures standing on small attached shafts, one of the figures is missing. ·Above the doorway is a large niche with triple buttressed jambs terminating in pinnacles and a rich canopy with three-sided cinquefoiled head, crockets and cresting, terminating in a crocketed and finialed spire. The side walls have each a window of three trefoiled ogee lights with tracery in a two-centred head with moulded jambs and label.

The *Roof* of the nave is of *c.* 1500 and of seven bays ; the trusses are of the double hammer-beam type, with moulded main timbers and curved braces beneath the collars and hammer-beams, these last are foliated and either embattled or crested ; the spandrels of the braces have boldly carved conventional foliage and the braces and wall-posts terminate in crocketed and canopied niches in which are defaced figures of saints ; the stone corbels below them have carved cresting and alternate corbels are carved with half-angels ; the richly moulded and embattled wall-plates have a deep band of traceried panelling enclosing shields, three of which bear the cross of St. George, a lower

GREAT BROMLEY : PARISH CHURCH OF ST. GEORGE ; from the South.
Porch, Clearstorey, and Tower ; *c.* 1500.

GREAT BROMLEY : PARISH CHURCH OF ST. GEORGE.
Interior, showing South Arcade, early 14th-century, and Clearstorey and Nave Roof, *c.* 1500.

band of carving includes wings, crowns and flowers the two E. bays of the roof are painted. The 15th-century roof of the N. aisle is of pent type and of six bays with moulded main timbers. The roof of the S. chapel and S. aisle is continuous and incorporates some moulded 15th-century timbers. *Fittings — Brass and Indents. Brass :* In S. chapel—of [William Bischopton, 1432], figure of priest in mass vestments with scroll and mutilated inscription, cinquefoiled canopy with crocketed gable and buttressed standards, pinnacles missing. Indents : In S. chapel—(1) of man in armour and wife, with inscription-plate and two shields, late 15th-century ; (2) of man in armour, and wife, inscription-plate, shield, and two groups of children, 15th-century ; (3) of civilian and wife, three shields, inscription-plate and one child, late 16th-century. In nave—(4) defaced ; (5) of inscription-plate ; (6) defaced ; (7) of civilian, two wives, and inscription-plate, early 16th-century. In N. aisle—(8) white marble slab, with indent of head and hands of man, remains of figure in incised lines, with pedestal, canopy and side shafts, all much defaced. On same slab is another figure almost hidden by pews, late 15th-century. *Chest* (Plate, p. xxxii) : In S. chapel—of hutch type, with carved and arcaded front of three bays, early 17th-century. *Communion Table :* In S. chapel—with turned legs, carved top rail and carved brackets, c. 1650. *Doors :* In N. doorway—with moulded vertical ribs, 16th or 17th-century. In S. doorway—of two folds, each divided into three vertical panels with trefoiled and sub-cusped heads and elaborate tracery in three tiers above them, pierced scutcheon-plate, late 15th-century, part of tracery lost. In W. doorway (Plate, p. 132)—of two folds generally similar to above, but with tracery of different design, partly restored, same date. In doorway to turret staircase, with moulded frame and vertical rib planted on, 16th-century. *Glass :* In S. chapel — in S. window, shield of arms — *gules three hammers or, handles argent*, for Martel, wings at sides, 15th-century, below it quatrefoils with two roses, same date. *Floor-slab :* In the S. chapel—to Elizabeth Giels, 1699 (?). *Niches :* In S. chapel—in E. wall, two shallow recesses without ornament, 16th-century. In N. aisle—shallow recess with rough four-centred head, 15th-century. In S. aisle—in S. wall, round-headed recess, 15th-century. See also Architectural Description, S. porch. *Painting :* In nave—traces of red and black paint ; on first pier in S. arcade, lower part of figure in red lines, probably of 15th-century. *Piscinae :* In chancel—with chamfered jambs and quatrefoiled drain, date uncertain, head modern. In S. chapel—in S. wall, with trefoiled head surmounted by crocketed and finialed gable, quatrefoiled frieze and embattled cornice, side buttresses with embattled capitals and finials, octofoiled drain, 14th-century. In N. aisle—in

;S. wall, with moulded jambs and cinquefoiled head, plain drain, 15th-century. *Seat :* In chancel —incorporating 15th-century carved fragments, *Sedilia :* In chancel—two bays with cinquefoiled head and moulded jambs, 15th-century, middle shaft modern. *Miscellanea :* In chancel—in N. wall, moulded cornice with carved flowers, possibly head of blocked recess, 15th-century. In church-yard, S. side—worked stones from tower pinnacles and parts of window jambs and mullions, 15th-century.

Condition—Generally good, nave roof recently repaired.

Secular :—

MONUMENTS (2–7).

The following monuments, unless otherwise described, are of the 17th century, and of two storeys, timber-framed and plastered or weather-boarded ; the roofs are tiled or thatched. Several of the buildings have original chimney-stacks and exposed ceiling-beams.

Condition—Good, or fairly good, unless noted.

ᵃ(2). *Farm House*, about ½ m. S.E. of the church, is of L-shaped plan, with the wings extending to the N. and W. ; the N. wing was extended late in the 17th century.

ᵃ(3). *Hillyards*, house, about 1 m. E.N.E. of the church.

ᵇ(4). *House*, three tenements, on N. side of Hare Green, about 1 m. S.E. of the church, has a cross-wing at the W. end.

ᵇ(5). *Cottage*, three tenements, about 230 yards S.S.W. of (4).

Condition—Bad.

ᵇ(6). *Cottage*, two tenements, at N. end of Balls Green, 600 yards S.S.W. of (5).

ᵇ(7). *Cottage*, on W. side of the road, ¼ m. S.S.W. of (6).

---

34. GREAT CLACTON. (F.d.)

(O.S. 6 in. ⁽ᵃ⁾xxxviii. S.E. ⁽ᵇ⁾xlviii. N.E.)

Great Clacton is a parish, village and seaside town 12½ m. S.E. of Colchester. The church is the principal monument.

Ecclesiastical :—

ᵇ (1). PARISH CHURCH OF ST. JOHN THE BAPTIST (Plate, p. 114) stands in the village of Great Clacton. The walls are of septaria and mixed rubble ; the dressings are of limestone and Roman brick ; the roofs are tiled. The *Chancel* and *Nave* were built about the middle of the 12th century when the nave had a stone vault, removed at some uncertain period. The chancel was altered and partly refaced in the 14th century. The *West Tower* was added in the 15th century ; it was

GREAT CLACTON. *The* PARISH CHURCH *of* St JOHN *the* BAPTIST.

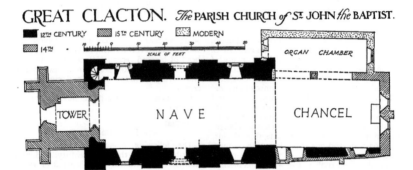

either never completed or the top stage was subsequently removed and is now replaced by a timber bell-chamber. The church was restored in the 19th century when the N. *Organ Chamber* with its arcade were built.

The church is extremely interesting from the remains of its unusual system of vaulting, very similar to that at Copford. The N. and S. doorways have good 12th-century detail.

Architectural Description—The *Chancel* (38¾ ft. by 24 ft.) has in the E. wall two modern windows and a modern round window above thèm. The N. wall has a modern arcade. The S. wall is of a curious tapering plan, the inside being 12th-century work and the outside face probably a 14th-century repair; in the wall are three windows, the two eastern have 12th-century shafts with scalloped capitals to the splays, probably reused material or a 12th-century alteration to the original design which is represented by the lower part of the western splay-shafts of two former windows set higher in the wall and with a recessed order of Roman brick; the eastern of the later windows has two 14th-century trefoiled lights with a quatrefoil in a two-centred head; the western window has a modern filling; further W. is a third window of the 15th century and of a single cinquefoiled light set low in the wall. E. of the modern window is a square label of the 15th century, but with no traces of a doorway below it. The chancel-arch is modern but springs from the original wide 12th-century responds with Roman brick quoins and chamfered imposts.

The *Nave* (56 ft. by 24½ ft.) is entirely of mid 12th-century date and is of three bays divided by wide pilaster buttresses with Roman brick quoins and partly restored. Corresponding with these buttresses, internally, are wide pilaster responds from which sprang the wide transverse ribs of the

main vault; the grooved and chamfered imposts and springers remain on the eastern responds on both sides. Each bay had apparently round cross-vaults groined into the main structure and the marks of these are visible in the E. bay of the S. wall. In the N. wall are three round-headed windows, all entirely restored externally and with plastered internal splays and rear-arches; below the middle one is the 12th-century N. doorway (Plate, p. 115) with a round arch of three orders; the two outer are roll-moulded and the inner encloses a brick tympanum with a plain lintel below it; the jambs have each two detached shafts, the outer plain, with a cushion capital and the inner diapered on one jamb and cable moulded on the other; the inner capitals are scalloped; the doorway has a few modern stones and the outer shaft and capital on the E. are modern; the doorway is set in a recess of which the head is carved with partly restored diaper ornament. In the W. bay of the N. waîl is a 12th-century doorway to a turret staircase, with a stone lintel enriched with diaper ornament and a round arch of Roman brick enclosing a plain tympanum; the staircase probably led formerly to the space above the vault, but now communicates with the tower. In the S. wall are two windows similar to those on the N.; the S. doorway between them is similar to the N. doorway but the shafts are all plain and the work has been more restored; the head of the recess is similar to that on the N. side. At the W. end of the nave is the framework of a former bell-turret, consisting of two tie-beams supporting uprights; it is of 16th or 17th-century date.

The *West Tower* (13 ft. by 12 ft.) is of three stages, including the modern timber bell-chamber; the two lower stages are of the 15th century. The two-centred tower-arch is of two orders, the outer moulded and continuous and the inner chamfered

GREAT CLACTON : PARISH CHURCH OF ST. JOHN THE BAPTIST.

From the South-East, showing 12th and 14th-century Work.

and resting on attached shafts with moulded capitals and bases. The W. window is of three cinquefoiled lights with vertical tracery in a two-centred head with a moulded label; the W. doorway has moulded jambs, two-centred arch and label. The second stage has in the N., S. and W. walls an opening of one trefoiled light; the heads of the N. and W. lights are modern.

Fittings—*Bells:* five; 4th and 5th by Miles Graye, 1649. *Floor-slabs:* In chancel—(1) to Larry Roris, 1648; (2) to Phillip Gardiner, 1704; (3) to Joseph Long, minister of the parish, and Ann, his wife, 1660. *Font* (Plate, p. xxxiv): octagonal bowl with panelled sides carved with three seated figures and two angels holding shields bearing the arms of the Trinity and a cross, 15th-century. *Piscina:* In chancel—in E. splay of S.E. window, with two pointed heads, octofoiled drain, 14th-century. *Royal Arms:* In nave—on W. wall, of Queen Anne after the Union, on canvas. *Sedile:* In chancel—sill of S.E. window carried down low to form seat.

Condition—Good, except roof of nave.

Secular :—

b(2). SHIP INN, 120 yards S.S.W. of the parish church, is of two storeys, timber-framed and plastered; the roofs are tiled; it was built early in the 16th century and has a cross-wing in the middle; the E. part of the house is probably an addition. The upper storey projects on the original part of the N. front and has a moulded bressumer to the cross-wing. Inside the building are original moulded ceiling-beams.

Condition—Good.

b(3). COTTAGE, 400 yards S.E. of the parish church, is of one storey with attics, timber-framed and weather-boarded; the roofs are thatched. It was built in the 17th century and has rough ceiling-beams.

Condition—Fairly good.

a(4). CANN HALL, house, nearly ¾ m. W.N.W. of the parish church, is of two storeys, timber-framed and plastered; the roofs are tiled. It was built probably late in the 16th century. The upper storey projects on the S. front. Inside the building are some exposed ceiling-beams.

Condition—Poor.

b(5). FOUNDATIONS, in garden of Church Hall, N. of the church. Rubble foundations of uncertain character were dug up during the autumn of 1921.

35. GREAT COGGESHALL. (B.c.)

(O.S. 6 in. xxvi. S.W.)

Great Coggeshall is a parish and small town 9 m. W. of Colchester. The church and Paycock's House are the principal monuments. In the town there are a number of interesting mediaeval buildings, especially Nos. 5, 70, 71 and 75.

Roman :—

(1). A considerable quantity of bricks, coins dating from Nero to Theodosius, and a large number of urns with much black ash were found in the middle of the 19th century in digging gravel; the urns being 2 ft. below the surface and extending over an area of 3 acres, in two fields called Crow Barn and Garden Fields near Highfields, about ½ m. W. of the town and to the N. of Stane Street, and the River Blackwater. (E. L. Cutts in *Essex Arch. Soc. Trans.,* I (1858), 103 ff., and *Arch. Jour.,* XVIII, 95.) They probably indicate the existence of a building in the neighbourhood, as well as a cemetery. To the latter may belong a curious burial recorded in the 17th century, found "adjoining to the rode called Coccill-way, which to this towne leadeth" (*i.e.,* Stane Street). It consisted of "an arched Vault of bricke, and therein a burning lampe of glasse" covered with a tile 14 in. square, a 'thumbed' urn containing ashes and bits of bone, and two Samian saucers, one stamped COCCILLI.M (seemingly a Banassic potter of S.W. Gaul, cf. Déchelette, *Les vases ornès de la Gaule romaine,* I, 118, n.). (Weever, *Funeral Monuments* (1631), p. 618, and Méric Casaubon, *Meditations of Marcus Aurelius* (1635); *Notes,* p. 34 and fig., hence Burton, *Commentary on the Itinerary of Antoninus* (1658), p. 231, and *Archaeologia,* V, 141.) In a piece of ground, recently added to the S.W. of the churchyard, tesserae and ridge-tiles have been found indicating the approximate position of a building. (See also *Sectional Preface,* p. xxvii, and Little Coggeshall (1A)).

Ecclesiastical :—

(2). PARISH CHURCH OF ST. PETER AD VINCULA stands N.E. of the town. The walls are of flint-rubble with fragments of Roman bricks, partly faced with ashlar and with limestone dressings; the roofs are covered with lead. The whole church consisting of *Chancel, North* and *South Chapels, Nave, North* and *South Aisles, West Tower* and *South Porch* was rebuilt in the first half of the 15th-century beginning with the tower.

The building is a good example of a large parish church of the 15th century.

Architectural Description—All the ancient details are of the 15th century. The *Chancel* (50 ft. by 26 ft.) has walls faced with ashlar and a plinth enriched with quatrefoiled panels and shields, mostly restored and bearing *two keys saltirewise;* the buttresses have plain and trefoil-headed panelling. The much restored E. window is of seven cinquefoiled ogee lights with vertical tracery in a two-centred head; the internal and external reveals are moulded. In the N. wall is an arcade of three bays with two-centred arches of two moulded orders; the moulded columns have each

GREAT COGGESHALL. The PARISH CHURCH of S.ᵗ PETER ᴬᴰ VINCULA.

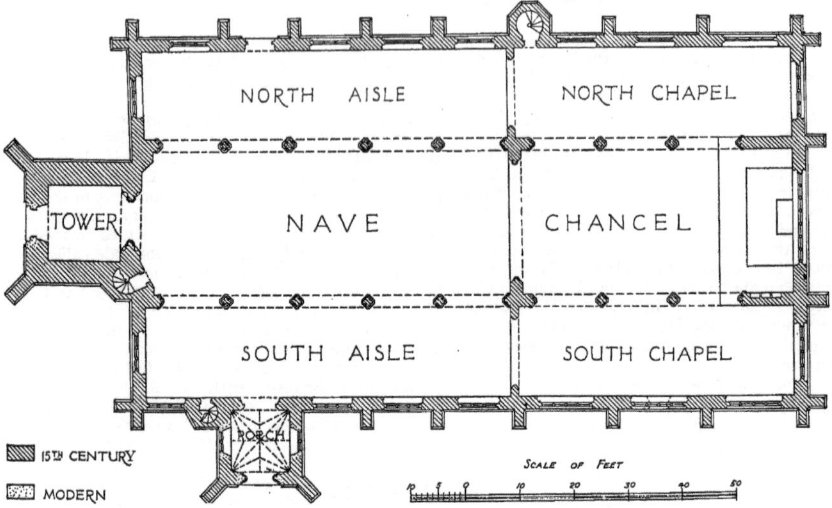

15ᵀᴴ CENTURY

MODERN

SCALE OF FEET

four attached shafts with moulded capitals and bases ; the responds have attached half columns. In the S. wall is an arcade uniform with that in the N. wall. The two-centred chancel-arch is of two moulded orders, the outer continuous and the inner resting on attached shafts with moulded capitals and bases. The clearstorey has on each side three much restored windows each of three cinquefoiled ogee lights with tracery in a four-centred head.

The *North Chapel* (51 ft. by 16 ft.) has walls and plinth similar to those of the chancel. In the E. wall is a much restored window of four cinquefoiled ogee lights with tracery in a four-centred head. In the N. wall are three much restored windows, the easternmost is uniform with the window in the E. wall ; the other two windows are each of three cinquefoiled lights with tracery in a segmental-pointed head. At the W. end of the wall is a doorway with moulded jambs and four-centred head opening into the semi-octagonal rood-stair turret. The W. archway is two-centred and of two continuous chamfered orders.

The *South Chapel* (51 ft. by 16 ft.) is generally similar to the N. chapel and has an E. window uniform with the E. window of the N. chapel. In the S. wall are three similar windows and under the middle window is a doorway with moulded jambs and four-centred arch in a square head with a moulded label, the spandrels are carved

with lions. The W. arch is uniform with that in the N. chapel.

The *Nave* (65½ ft. by 26 ft.) has N. and S. arcades each of five bays and with two-centred and moulded arches with moulded labels ; the columns and responds are similar to those of the arcades of the chancel. The clearstorey has a moulded internal string-course and has on each side five much restored windows, each of three cinquefoiled lights with tracery in a segmental-pointed head.

The *North Aisle* (16 ft. wide), has in the N. wall four windows, all much restored and each of three cinquefoiled lights with tracery in a segmental-pointed head ; between the two western windows is the N. doorway with moulded jambs and restored two-centred head with a moulded label. In the W. wall is a window uniform with those in the N. wall.

The *South Aisle* (16 ft. wide) is uniform in detail with the N. aisle except that the partly restored S. doorway has moulded jambs, four-centred arch in a square head with cusped spandrels enclosing shields and a moulded label ; W. of it is a small doorway with moulded jambs and three-centred arch in a square head.

The *West Tower* is of three stages with a restored embattled parapet. The two-centred tower-arch is of two moulded orders, the outer continuous and the inner resting on attached shafts with moulded capitals and bases. The W. window and doorway have been completely restored except for the splays and rear-arches. The second stage has in the E. wall a pointed light opening into the nave ; the N., S. and W. walls have each a single light window with a trefoiled head and completely restored externally. The bell-chamber has in each wall a much restored window of three trefoiled lights with tracery in a square head.

The *South Porch* is of two storeys and appears to have been largely rebuilt and has a modern outer entrance and side windows. The ribbed stone vault with its shafts is also modern except for some stones, and has a central boss carved with a pelican in her piety and three smaller bosses carved with leopard's faces and one with a woman's head. The upper stage has three windows all completely restored.

The *Roofs* are modern but incorporate some old material ; that of the chancel has old corbels carved with angels holding shields bearing a chain between two keys, a cross, saltire, a crown of thorns, etc. Some corbels in the aisle are old and carved with grotesques ; in the S. aisle also are two carved bosses, one of an angel and the other of a civilian, and on the wall is fixed a shield from the former roof, dated 1587.

Fittings—*Bells :* eight ; 4th by Miles Graye, 1681. *Brasses* and *Indents.* Brasses : In N. chapel—(1) of [John Paycocke, 1533, and his wife], figures of man and woman in civilian costume of the period, indents of foot and marginal inscriptions, five scrolls, figure of Virgin and child, two groups of children and four shields ; (2) of Thomas Peaycocke, 1580, figure of man in gown, foot and part of marginal inscription, indents of five plates and a scroll ; (3) to George Laurence, 1594, inscription and merchant's mark. In N. aisle— on N. wall, (4) to Thomas Aylet, 1638, plate with achievement of arms and inscription ; (5) figures of two women with butterfly head-dress, c. 1480 ; (6) said to be of William Goldwyre, 1514, figures of man in fur-lined gown and woman in pedimental head-dress ; (7) to John Oldam, 1599, inscription only. Indents : In S. porch—a number of slabs with defaced indents. In churchyard—S. of tower, of man and wife, two groups of children and foot inscription, 15th-century. *Door :* In doorway to turret staircase of porch—of plain studded battens, 15th-century. *Font :* round bowl with shallow arcade of trefoiled arches resting on pilasters with imposts and stepped bases, round stem with four detached shafts, partly restored and having moulded capitals and bases, early 13th-century. *Monuments* and *Floor-slabs.* Monuments : In S. chapel—against N. wall, (1) to Thomas Guyon, 1664, black, grey and white marble altar-tomb with moulded slab and plain pilasters at the angles. In churchyard—(2) to John Mullings, 1713, head-stone ; (3) to John, 1678, and Thomas Wilsher, 1703, head-stone ; (4) to John Richardson, 1693,

and Anne Richardson, 1712, table-tomb ; (5) to Thomas Co . . . ., 1675. Floor-slabs : In churchyard—(1) to Thomas Aylett, 17th-century ; (2) to Anne, wife of John Wilsher, 1675 ; (3) to Elizabeth French, 1686 ; (4) to Hannah Townsend, 1691 ; (5) slab carved with part of female figure in relief, late 17th-century. *Piscinae :* In N. chapel—recess with segmental-pointed head, date uncertain. In S. chapel—with moulded jambs and four-centred arch with foliated spandrels, octagonal drain, 15th-century. *Recess :* In E. wall, externally, with hollow-chamfered jambs and defaced cinquefoiled and sub-cusped head, with carved spandrels, moulded label and defaced stops, at back of recess, remains of defaced crucifix and figures of the Virgin and St. John, 15th-century. *Scratchings :* On all arcades—mason's marks, 15th-century. *Sedilia :* In chancel—three bays with cinquefoiled four-centred heads and moulded labels, moulded and shafted jambs with capitals and bases, 15th-century, now painted. *Sounding Board :* In S. chapel—circular with inlaid star pattern, made up into table, early 18th-century. *Stoup :* On S. chapel—E. of doorway, round bowl, broken, base of pedestal below, 15th-century.

In the churchyard is the octagonal base of a 15th-century churchyard cross with traces of mouldings.

Condition—Good, much restored.

Secular :—

(3). PAYCOCK'S HOUSE (Plates, pp. 118, 119), on the S. side of West Street and ¼ m. W.S.W. of the church, is of two storeys, timber-framed and partly plastered ; the roofs are tiled. It was built c. 1500 and has two wings at the back, of which the S.E. wing is either original or of slightly later date and the S.W. wing is a late 16th-century addition with a 17th-century extension towards the S.

The building is a remarkably complete example of a richly ornamented merchant's house of c. 1500.

Elevations—The *N. Front* has exposed timber-framing with modern brick filling. The upper storey projects and has a moulded and carved fascia with running foliage ornament, various small heads and figures and a shield with a merchant's mark or badge resembling an ermine tail and the initials T.P. for Thomas Paycock. Both storeys are divided into five bays by restored buttresses supporting curved brackets. At the top of the ground storey, under the overhang, is a plate with a band of sunk tracery. At the E. end is a large archway with a four-centred head and spandrels carved with foliage ; the lower parts of the side posts are also foliated and the upper parts have moulded pedestals and canopies with two carved figures of men, one holding a shield ; the double doors have moulded frames, rails and muntins and linen-fold panels. Adjoining the archway on the W. is a small blocked doorway, all restored except the moulded E. jamb. The two square bay-windows are entirely modern except the moulded jambs; in the W. bay of the wall there was a similar window of which only the E. jamb remains; in the same bay is a modern doorway fitted with an original door with moulded frame, rail and muntins and linen-fold panels. The upper storey has a plate below the eaves, carved with twisted leaf ornament; the bay-windows, generally similar to those of the lower storey, are entirely modern except the moulded jambs. The *S.E. Wing* has a projecting upper storey and gable at the S. end both with moulded bressumers. The wing has a number of windows with moulded mullions and an original doorway, now blocked, with chamfered jambs and moulded head. The *S.W. Wing* has exposed timber-framing.

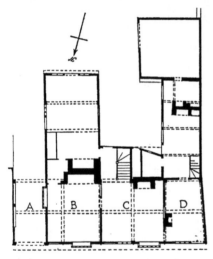

Interior—The main room (C) of the front block has original and elaborately moulded plates, ceiling-beams and joists, all with flowing blind tracery cut on the soffits; on the joists occur the initials T.P. and M.P. and the merchant's mark. The room (D) W. of this has moulded ceiling-beams and joists. In the S. and E. walls are reset original doorways with moulded jambs and four-centred heads with foliated spandrels. The room (B) has ceiling-beams and joists similar to those in (D). A transverse beam towards the E. side marks the extent of the original apartment, the space beyond being formerly open to the cartway (A) and having

chamfered beams and joists. On the S. side of the room the ceiling is framed round the opening of a former staircase, the original entrance to which remains in the partition between B and C. In the S. wall is a fireplace with a reused lintel, carved with animals, a shield bearing the merchant's mark. and scrolls with the name of Thomas Paycock; The walls are covered with original linen-fold panelling and incorporating three elaborately traceried panels. The S.E. wing has exposed ceiling-beams and above the fireplace is a fragment of plaster with remains of painted decoration. The S.W. wing has exposed ceiling-beams and a short length of moulded wall-plate. On the first floor the rooms over (B and C) have original moulded ceiling-beams and joists. The room over (B) has in the S. wall a fireplace with an original lintel carved with grotesque beasts and the merchant's mark of Paycock; further E. is a doorway with an original four-centred head and carved spandrels. There are several other original doorways and the other rooms have exposed ceiling-beams. The roofs have mostly been reconstructed, but that over the S.W. wing has remains of 16th-century queen-post trusses.

Condition—Good.

MONUMENTS (4–99).

The following monuments, unless otherwise described, are of the 17th century, and of two storeys, timber-framed and plastered or weather-boarded; the roofs are tiled or thatched. Many of the buildings have original chimney-stacks, wide fireplaces and exposed ceiling-beams.

Condition—Good or fairly good, unless noted.

CHURCH STREET, N.W. side :—

(4). *Cottage*, two tenements, 120 yards E. of the church.

(5). *Woolpack Inn*, 80 yards S.S.W. of the church, was built in the latter part of the 15th century with a central Hall of two storeys and cross-wings at the N. and S. ends. The N. cross-wing does not line with the rest of the building and may perhaps be earlier. Early in the 16th century additions were made on the W. side of the N. and S. cross-wings.

The building is an interesting example of a mediaeval house.

The upper storey projects at the E. end of the S. cross-wing and has a moulded and embattled bressumer; there is a similar bressumer at the base of the gable; on the ground floor of this wing is the original entrance to the 'screens,' with moulded jambs and four-centred head. The E. front of the Hall has the moulded and doubly embattled head of a large bay-window; above it is the moulded and embattled sill of a small bay-window, enriched with foliage and cresting.

GREAT COGGESHALL: (3) PAYCOCK'S HOUSE.
North Front ; c. 1500.

Ceiling of Main Room, Ground Floor.

Detail of Ceiling, Main Room,
Ground Floor.

Ceiling of Main Room, First Floor.

Fireplace to Room, First Floor, above B.

Fireplace and Panelling to Room B (see Plan).

Gateway in North Front.

The upper storey projects at the N. end of the N. W. addition and there are two late 17th-century sash windows in the W wall of the same part.

Interior—The lower Hall has moulded ceiling-beams and joists. The upper Hall has original moulded wall-plates and a central king-post truss (Plate, p. xxxvii), with moulded tie-beam and octagonal king-post with moulded base and embattled capital. There is also some 16th and 17th-century panelling on the walls. The ' screens ' are included in the S. cross-wing and there are on the ground floor in the S. wall two original doorways with moulded jambs and four-centred heads ; between them is an attached shaft with moulded base and capital from which springs a curved brace ; the screen itself has gone but the hollow-chamfered head remains. On the first floor part of the arched head of a fireplace remains. The N. cross-wing has an original king-post roof-truss with curved struts to the king-post. The N.W. addition has an early 16th-century door with strap-hinges. The roof has a king-post truss with curved braces. The S.W. addition is of four bays with king-post roof-trusses.

(6). *House*, two tenements, 40 yards S.W. of (5). Timber-framing recently exposed.

(7). *Range of three tenements*, 60 yards S.W. of (6). The upper storey of the S.W. tenement projects in front.

(8). *House*, four tenements, 40 yards S.W. of (7), was built early in the 18th century. Over a doorway at the side are two early 17th-century brackets (Plate, p. 100) carved with crouching satyrs.

(9). *House*, S.W. of (8), was built in the 16th century, much altered *c.* 1800 and again in 1922. The upper storey projects in front. The timber-framing has recently been exposed.

(10). *House*, two tenements, S.W. of (9), has a projecting upper storey in front.

(11). *House* and shop, S.W. of (10), was built probably late in the 16th century but has been much altered.

(12). *House*, S.W. of (11), was built probably late in the 16th century and has original moulded ceiling-beams. The roof has three cambeerd tie-beams.

(13). *House*, and shop and office, S.W. of (12), has a rebuilt cross-wing at the S.W. end.

(14). *House*, two tenements, S.W. of (13), has a projecting upper storey on the S. front.

(15). *House* and shop, S.W. of (13), was built *c.* 1700. The S.E. front is of brick and has a modillioned eaves-cornice. At the back the staircase had until recently an original window with solid mullion and transom. Inside the building the original well-staircase has turned and twisted balusters, square newels and close moulded strings.

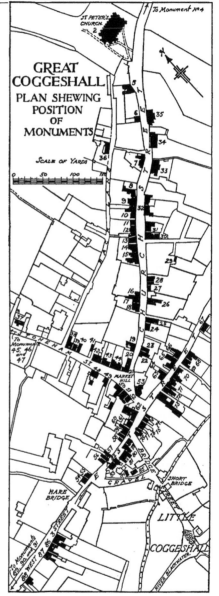

GREAT COGGESHALL

PLAN SHEWING POSITION OF MONUMENTS

SCALE OF YARDS

The large room on the first floor has original bolection-moulded deal panelling; the fireplaces have
moulded architraves and there is a moulded cornice
and dado rail.

(16). *House*, 50 yards S.W. of (15), was built
early in the 16th century and much altered early
in the 18th century. It has a projecting wing at
the back. The upper storey projects on the S.E.
front. At the W. corner of the front is a slender
shaft with a capital supporting a bracket. The
back wing has a late 17th-century window with
moulded mullions. Inside the building a room on
the first floor has original moulded ceiling-beams.
The back wing contains some original linen-fold
panelling and a panel with a carved and painted
shield bearing a merchant's mark and the initials I.S.
The roof of the back wing has original chamfered
tie-beams.

(17). *House* and shop, S.W. of (16), was built
about the middle of the 16th century. The upper
storey projects in front and inside the building are
two original moulded ceiling-beams.

(18). *House* and shop, S.W. of (17), was built
c. 1700 and has a moulded eaves-cornice.

(19). *House* (Plate, p. 188), two tenements and
shops, 60 yards S.W. of (18), was built about the
middle of the 16th century and has a cross-wing
at the N.E. end. The upper storey projects on the
S.E. front, with curved brackets to the cross-wing.
The timber-framing is exposed on the N.E. side
of the same wing.

(20). *House* and shop, 15 yards S.W. of (19),
was built probably in the 15th century but has
been almost completely altered. The roof has an
original king-post truss of plain character.

(21). *House* and shop, S.W. of (20), and at the
corner of Stoneham Street, has been much altered.
The upper storey formerly projected on both
fronts.

S.E. side :—

(22). *House* and shop, opposite (19), has been
much altered.

(23). *House*, N.E. of (22), was built early in the
18th century and has a brick front with a coved
eaves-cornice, a moulded band between the storeys
and a moulded cornice above the doorway.

(24). *House* and shop, 30 yards N.E. of (23).

(25). *House* and shop, N.E. of (24), has inside
the building two wall-posts with moulded ornamental heads.

(26). *Greyhound Inn*, 25 yards N.E. of (25),
was built *c.* 1600 but has been much altered.

(27). *Range of three tenements*, 15 yards N.E.
of (26).

(28). *Constitutional Club*, house, N.E. of (27), is
of three storeys and has been much altered in the
19th century. The upper storeys both project
on the N.W. front and have original moulded and
dentilled bressumers; the upper overhang has
four brackets, carved as consoles.

(29). *Cottage*, 50 yards E. of (28), standing
back from the road.
Condition—Poor.

(30). *House*, three tenements, 60 yards N.E. of
(28), was built probably early in the 16th century
but has been much altered. The front block has
on the N.W. and S.W. sides an original moulded
bressumer with twisted leaf ornament, at the first
floor level. Inside the building are original moulded
ceiling-beams.

(31). *House*, two tenements, N.E. of (30), was
built *c.* 1565. The front has been refaced with
modern brick but retains the moulded bressumer
to the former overhang; it is carved with conventional designs including birds, heads, etc., and
the date and initials, 1565, T.C. (? for Thomas
Clark).

(32). *Range of two, formerly of three, tenements*,
15 yards N.E. of (31), was built originally in the
16th century but has been almost completely
rebuilt in the 18th century. At the end of the
passage in the middle of the range is a doorway
with an original four-centred head.

(33). *House*, 40 yards N.E. of (32), was built
in the 16th century but has a plastered 18th-
century front of brick. Inside the building are some
original cambered tie-beams.

(34). *House*, 25 yards N.E. of (33), is almost
entirely of *c.* 1800 but incorporates part of an
early 17th-century building at the back, with
original moulded ceiling-beams.

(35). *House*, 15 yards N.E. of (34), is modern
but incorporates part of a 16th-century building.

(36). *House*, now three tenements, on N. side
of Back Lane, 180 yards S.W. of the church.
Inside the building are two late 17th-century
fireplaces with moulded architraves; the N.E. one
has an overmantel (Plate, p. xxxiii) with a cornice,
and central panel flanked by two oval wreaths
and by two amorini holding swags; the panel has
painted verses on the vanity of life. The other
fireplace has a moulded architrave and a panelled
overmantel with pilasters carved with flowers;
the mantelshelf has a carved cartouche.

STONEHAM STREET (Plate, p. 122), *E. side :—*

(37). *House*, 190 yards N.W. of Church Street,
has an original chimney-stack with plain pilasters
at the angles. On the W. front is a porch with a
projecting upper storey and remains of ornamental
plaster work on the N. side. Inside the building
there are some original moulded ceiling-beams and

a staircase with square newels having turned tops and pendants.

(38). *House*, now tenements, 80 yards S.E. of (37).

(39). *House* (Plate, p. 123), two tenements, S.E. of (38), has a projecting upper storey on the S.W. front. Inside the building are three original battened doors.

(40). *House*, two tenements, S.E. of (39). The upper storey projects and is gabled in front.

(41). *Cottage*, standing back from the road, 30 yards S.E. of (40).

(42). *House* and shop (Plate, p. 123), 10 yards S. of (41), has a projecting upper storey in front. Inside the building is some original panelling.

(43). *House*, two tenements and shop, S.E. of (42), was built probably in the 15th century with a central Hall and cross-wings at the N. and S. ends. The Hall was divided into two storeys in the 16th or 17th century and the front of the main block made flush with that of the cross-wings. Inside the building are original cambered tie-beams.

(44). *House*, two tenements and shop, S.E. of (43), has a wing at the back with a projecting upper storey on the S. side.

W. side :—

(45). *House*, two tenements, at the end of Robins Road, has a cross-wing at the W. end.

(46). *Range of four tenements*, S.E. of (45), appears to have been rebuilt in the 18th century except one chimney-stack with two diagonal shafts (*since demolished*).

(47). *House*, five tenements, 40 yards S.E. of (46), has a back wing of early 16th-century date. The main block was built late in the 16th or early in the 17th century. The upper storey projects in front and on the S. side of the back wing. The eaves of the front have a moulded cornice. Inside the back wing an original brick fireplace with chamfered jambs and four-centred arch.
Condition—Good (*wing since destroyed.*)

(48). *House* and shop, 170 yards S.E. of (47), was built c. 1500 and has, in the shop, original carved and moulded ceiling-beams and moulded joists. An outbuilding at the back may be of the 17th century.

(49). *House* and shop, 15 yards S.E. of (48).

(50). *Chapel Hotel*, 20 yards S. of (49), was built probably in the 16th century, but has been much altered. At the back is a block, formerly detached with a projecting upper storey on the N. side.

(51). *House*, two tenements and shop, S. of (50), has an 18th-century front.

(52). *House* and shop, S. of (51).

(53). *House* and shop on E. side of Market Hill, opposite (52), was built late in the 16th century. At the back is an original window with moulded frame and mullion. Inside the building are three original doors of moulded battens and an original brick fireplace with a segmental head.

EAST STREET, N. side :—

(54). *House*, 25 yards E. of Hare bridge. The upper storey formerly projected in front but has been underbuilt.

(55). *House*, now two tenements, E. of (54), was built about the middle of the 16th century. The upper storey formerly projected in front but has been underbuilt. The eaves have an early 18th-century cornice. The 17th-century chimney-stack has attached pilasters. Inside the building is an original carved and moulded ceiling-beam and moulded joists.

(56). *Cottage*, 30 yards E. of (55).

(57). *Block of two tenements* and shop, E. of (56). The E. part has been refronted and the whole much altered.

(58). *Cottage*, two tenements, 30 yards E. of (57), was built early in the 16th century. The front has been partly faced with modern brick. Inside the building are original moulded ceiling-beams, plates and joists, and an external cornice, moulded and embattled.

(59). *Cottage*, E. of (58), was built probably in the 16th century.

(60). *House* and shop, E. of (59), has a back wing of early 16th-century date ; the front has been entirely altered or rebuilt.

(61). *House*, two tenements and shop, E. of (60), was built c. 1500, but has been refronted with modern brick. Inside the building are remains of the original roof of king-post type.

(62). *House* and shop, E. of (61). The back wing, formerly a separate house, may be of the 16th century ; the front part was built in the 17th century. A modern building has been added on the E. side. The front has an early 18th-century modillioned eaves-cornice.

(63). *House*, two tenements and shops, 70 yards E. of (62), was built late in the 16th or early in the 17th century and has an added top storey. The second storey projects in front. Inside the building are two 17th-century doors.

(64). *House* and shop, E. of (63), has a projecting upper storey in front.

(65). *House*, two shops and offices, 15 yards E. of (64), was built probably early in the 16th century and has a 17th-century added wing on the N.E. The front has a moulded eaves-cornice.

Inside the building are original moulded and carved ceiling-beams and moulded joists. At the W. end are remains of an original roof of king-post type.

(66). *House*, now two tenements, E. of (65).

S. side :—

(67). *House*, 50 yards E. of (66), has a projecting upper storey on the N. front.

(68). *House*, two tenements, 40 yards W. of (67), was built in the 16th century. The upper storey formerly projected in front and has an original moulded bressumer. In the garden is a scalloped 12th-century capital, probably from Little Coggeshall Abbey.

(69). *House*, four tenements, W. of (68), was built *c.* 1585. The upper storey formerly projected in front and has a moulded bressumer (Plate, p. 100) carved with the date, conventional scrolls and a cartouche with defaced initials and grotesque unicorn supporters. At the W. end is an original door of moulded battens with an ornamental scutcheon-plate.

(70). *House*, now three tenements and shop, 10 yards W. of (69), was built *c.* 1500 with a central Hall, probably of two storeys, and cross-wings at the E. and W. ends. A little later the W. wing was extended at the back. Inside the building the ground floor of the main block has original moulded ceiling-beams and joists and a moulded and carved beam on the N. side, probably indicating the former extent of the building in that direction. In the W. wall are two original doorways, now blocked, and with moulded jambs and lintels and plain three-centred heads. The roof of the main block has remains of the original construction. The W. cross-wing has on the ground floor an original moulded ceiling-beam and wall-posts with attached shafts, having moulded capitals and bases. The first floor has moulded wall-plates and a central tie-beam with curved braces forming a four-centred arch. In the S. wall is a blocked doorway with a four-centred head. The E. cross-wing has an original cambered tie-beam and the later extension has a king-post roof-truss.

(71). *House*, two tenements and shops, W. of (70), was built in the 15th century with a central Hall and cross-wings at the E. and W. ends. The W. wing was extended at the back early in the 16th century and the Hall divided into two storeys in the 17th century. The upper storey projects at the front end of the E. wing. Inside the building the early 16th-century extension has moulded ceiling-beams and there are original tie-beams in the main block and cross-wings.

(72). *House* and shop, W. of (71), was built probably early in the 16th century. There is a 17th-century wing at the back. The upper storey projects on the W. side of the back wing and there

are the mortices of the bar-mullions of a former window. Inside the building are remains of original moulded ceiling-joists.

(73). *House* and outbuildings, W. of (72). The *House* was built in the 16th century and has a wing at the back with a projecting upper storey (Plate, p. 100) on the E. side. Inside the building is a staircase with solid oak treads and some early 17th-century panelling. An *Outhouse* has a roof of rough king-post type and of 16th-century date. The *Barn* incorporates an early 16th-century carved and moulded beam.

(74). *House* and shop, 35 yards W. of (73), was built in the 16th century and is of three storeys. The front has an early 18th-century moulded eaves-cornice. At the back the projection of the second floor has a plain curved bracket.

(75). *House* and shop, W. of (74), was built in the 15th century as a small one-storeyed Hall. Late in the 16th century it was divided into three storeys and a gable with a moulded bressumer added in front. Inside the building the former Hall was of one bay with no free roof-truss ; the end walls are framed with cambered tie-beams with curved braces and supporting queen-posts with semi-octagonal shafts having moulded capitals and bases and curved braces below the purlins ; the collar-beams have curved braces also.

(76). *White Hart Hotel*, W. of (75), is of three storeys and was built probably in the 16th century, but was much altered in the 18th century.

(77). *House*, W. of (76). The upper storey projects in front but has been partly underbuilt.

(78). *House* and shop, W. of (77).

(79). *House* and shop, 15 yards W. of (78), was built possibly in the 15th century but has been almost completely altered. Inside the building are indications of a former projecting upper storey on the N. and E. sides.

(80). *House* (Plate, p. 231), W. of (79), has a front block of red brick built *c.* 1700. There is a moulded band-course between the storeys, a modillioned eaves-cornice and a hipped roof. Some of the windows have original solid frames. Inside the building is some deal panelling of *c.* 1700 and moulded architraves to the fireplaces.
Condition—Bad (*since demolished*).

(81). *House*, four tenements, S.W. of (80), has inside the building one room lined with early 18th-century deal panelling.

(82). *Cricketers Inn*, W. of (81), was built probably in the 16th century but has been much altered and refronted.

(83). *House*, W. of (82), was built probably in the 16th century.

GREAT COGGESHALL.
Stoneham Street, looking North from Market Hill.

KELVEDON.
High Street, looking North-East from Church Street, showing Monuments (15), (16), (38), etc.

DEDHAM.
High Street, looking West, showing Monuments (10) to (15).

COLCHESTER.
High Street, North Side, showing (39) Gate House, etc.

COLCHESTER: HYTHE HILL.
Showing Monuments (172) and (178).

EARLS COLNE: HIGH STREET, LOOKING EAST.
Showing the Church and Monuments (5) to (7), etc.

COLCHESTER: WEST STOCKWELL STREET.
Showing Monuments (99) to (101).

FEERING.
(30) The Sun Inn; c. 1525.

DEDHAM: HIGH STREET.
(15) House and Shop; c. 1600.

KELVEDON: CHURCH STREET.
(6) Cottages; 17th-century.

Showing Monuments (38) to (40); 17th-century.

Showing Monuments (42) to (44); 17th-century.

GREAT COGGESHALL: STONEHAM STREET.

Gravel, N. side :—

(84). *Cottage*, 20 yards S.E. of (83).
Condition—Bad (*since demolished*).

(85). *House*, E. of (84).

West Street, S. side :—

(86). *Fleece Inn*, W. of (3), has a S.W. wing, probably of early 16th-century date. The main block was built early in the 17th century. The upper storey projects in front and has part of the early 17th-century moulded bressumer.

(87). *House*, six tenements, W. of (86), was built in the 15th century. Early in the 16th century an addition was made at the back and subsequently twice extended. In a passage next to the E. tenement, representing the former ' screens,' are two original doorways with chamfered jambs and ogee heads. The 16th-century addition W. of the passage has moulded ceiling-beams and joists.

(87A) *House*, three tenements, W. of (87), was built *c.* 1500. Part of the original timber-framing is exposed in front including two panels each of three trefoiled ogee lights with traceried heads. Inside the building are plain joists and a moulded beam.

(88). *House*, two tenements, 40 yards W. of (87).

(89). *House*, two tenements, 400 yards W. of (88).

N. side :—

(90). *House*, three tenements, 40 yards W.N.W. of (89), was built *c.* 1600. Inside the building is an original door with arcaded panels and a fluted frieze. There is also some original panelling, refixed in the archway in the middle of the building.

(91). *House*, two tenements, W. of (90), has a cross-wing at the W. end.

---

(92). *Highfields*, house, 200 yards N. of (90), is of three storeys. It was built *c.* 1600 but has been much altered and added to in the 19th century. Inside the building the middle room on the ground floor has original panelling and a panelled overmantel with coupled columns and dentilled cornice.

(93). *Cottage*, now two tenements, ¾ m. W. of (92).

(94). *Stockstreet Farm* (Plate, p. 177), house, 200 yards W.N.W. of (93), was built in the second half of the 16th century, but has been refronted. The central chimney-stack has an original base with a moulded capping. The original stack on the N. side has tabled offsets at the ends, and an embattled offset on the N. face. Inside the building is an original moulded wall-plate.

(95). *Cottage*, now two tenements, 50 yards S. of (94), was built probably late in the 16th century. The upper storey projects on part of the N. side and has an original moulded bressumer.

(96). *Gate House*, nearly 1 m. N.W. of the church, was built late in the 16th century with a cross-wing at the W. end. The upper storey projects at the N. end of the cross-wing and has an original moulded bressumer.

(97). *Pest House*, cottage, ½ m. N.W. of the church, has been refaced with 18th-century brick.

(98). *Bouchier's Grange*, house, ¾ m. N. of the church, was built probably early in the 16th century but has an 18th-century or modern block on the S. side. The upper storey projects on the W. side of the N. wing. Inside the building is an original king-post roof-truss.

(99). *Cottage*, two tenements, on S. side of Stane Street, 420 yards S. by E. of the church.

36. GREAT HENNY. (B.b.)

(O.S. 6 in. (a)xii. N.E. (b)xii. S.E.)

Great Henny is a small parish on the Suffolk border 6 m. N.E. of Halstead. The church is interesting.

Ecclesiastical :—

b(1). PARISH CHURCH OF ST. MARY stands near the middle of the parish. The walls are of flint-rubble with limestone dressings. The roofs are of tiles ; the spire is covered with shingles. The two lower stages of the *West Tower* are perhaps of late 11th or early 12th-century date. The rest of the church consisting of *Chancel*, *Nave* and the upper part of the W. tower were apparently rebuilt about the middle of the 14th century. Early in the 16th century the *South Porch* was added. The church was restored in the 19th century when the E. wall was rebuilt and the *North Vestry* and *Transept* added.

Architectural Description—The *Chancel* (34¼ ft. by 19½ ft.) has no ancient features, except the 14th-century splays and moulded rear-arch of the S.W. window and a ' low-side ' loop further W. and probably of the same date.

The *Nave* (50 ft. by 20½ ft.) has in the N. wall two 14th-century windows, much restored and each of two pointed lights with a two-centred head with a moulded label ; further W. is a 14th-century doorway with jambs and two-centred arch of two chamfered orders and now blocked. In the S. wall are three windows, the eastern and westernmost are uniform with those

in the N. wall ; the middle window is of early
16th-century brick, partly restored, and of two
four-centred lights with vertical tracery in a two-
centred head. E. of the windows are the late
15th-century upper and lower doorways of the
former rood-loft staircase ; the lower is of brick
with a four-centred head ; the upper is similar but
plastered and is now blocked. W. of the windows
is the S. doorway uniform with the N. doorway but
not blocked.

The *West Tower* (9½ ft. square) is of three stages,
undivided externally, and with a wooden cornice
at the base of the spire. The tower-arch is modern.
In the W. wall is a modern window. The second
stage has in each of the N., S. and W. walls two
internal recesses, with rough round heads and without dressings ; they are of late 11th or early 12th-
century date. The bell-chamber has in each wall
a 14th-century window of one trefoiled light with a
moulded label ; below the window in the E. wall
are the weatherings of a former gabled roof of the
nave.

The *South Porch* is of early 16th-century date
and is of brick ; it has a plain outer archway
with a four-centred head. The side walls have
each a single-light window with a four-centred head.

The *Roof* of the nave is of the 15th century and of
four bays with moulded main timbers and curved
braces springing from corbels carved with figures
holding musical instruments ; two of the trusses
have queen-posts and curved braces to the collars.
The early 16th-century roof of the S. porch has
moulded and embattled wall-plates, a moulded
and cambered tie-beam and a moulded ridge.

Fittings—*Bells :* three ; 1st by Robert Burford,
inscribed " Sancta Katrina Ora Por Nobis," early
15th-century ; 2nd and 3rd by Miles Graye, 1655
and 1652 respectively. *Brasses* and *Indent.*
Brasses : In chancel—on S. wall, (1) of William
Fyscher and Anne, his wife, *c.* 1530, with figures
of man and wife in civil dress, six sons and nine
daughters. In nave—on S. wall, (2) to George
Golding, 1617, inscription only. Indent : In tower
—of brass (1). *Chair :* In vestry—with carved
back, with enriched arched panel, turned legs,
and shaped arms, early 17th-century. *Chest :*
In tower—front with fluted pilasters and enriched
arcaded panels enclosing inlaid ornament, moulded
base and drop handles, 16th-century, partly
restored, probably Italian. *Door :* In N. doorway
—of battens with moulded fillets, probably 15th-
century. *Floor-slab :* In nave—to Thomas Sewell,
1707, with shield of arms. *Niche :* In gable of
porch—of brick with segmental-pointed head, early
16th-century. *Piscinae :* In chancel—double with
shafted jambs and column having moulded capitals
and bases, trefoiled heads, one sexfoiled and one
octofoiled drain, early 14th-century, column
modern. In nave—in S. wall, with moulded
jambs and trefoiled head, sexfoiled drain, 14th-

century. *Recess :* In S. porch—in S. wall, square-
headed recess, date uncertain. *Sedilia :* In chancel
—in recess with segmental-pointed arch, three
stepped seats, probably 14th-century. *Table :*
In vestry—with turned legs, late 17th-century.
Scratchings : On jamb of S. doorway, crosses, etc.
Condition—Good, much restored.

Secular :—

MONUMENTS (2–8).

The following monuments, unless otherwise
described, are of the 17th century and of two
storeys, timber-framed and plastered ; the roofs
are tiled or thatched. Some of the buildings have
original chimney-stacks and exposed ceiling-beams.
Condition—Good or fairly good, unless noted.

b(2). *Cottage,* 1,000 yards W. of the church.
Condition—Poor.

a(3). *Sheepcote Farm,* house, ¾ m. N.N.E. of the
church.

a(4). *Cottage* (Plate, p. 189), at N. end of Henny
Street, and nearly 1 m. N.E. of the church.

a(5). *Street Farm,* house, 350 yards S. of (4), has
cross-wings at the N. and S. ends, with projecting
upper storeys in front.

b(6). *Cottage,* 1 m. E. of the church, has two
gabled dormers in the roof, one with the date 1677.

b(7). *Snell's Farm,* house, 120 yards S. of (6),
was built probably in the 16th-century and has
cross-wings at the N. and S. ends.

b(8). *Cottage,* opposite (7).

---

37. GREAT HOLLAND (F.d.)

(O.S. 6 in. xxxix. S.W.)

Great Holland is a parish and small village
4 m. N.E. of Clacton. The church is the only
monument.

Ecclesiastical :—

PARISH CHURCH OF ALL SAINTS stands towards
the E. side of the parish. It was entirely rebuilt
in 1866 except the early 16th-century *West Tower*
which is of red brick with black brick diapering.

Architectural Description — The *West Tower*
(13 ft. by 9 ft.), is of three stages with a
moulded plinth, embattled parapet, S.E. stair-
turret and semi-octagonal turrets or buttresses
at the other angles. The tower-arch is two-
centred and of four chamfered orders dying on to
the side walls and entirely covered with cement.
The W. window is of four pointed lights with
vertical tracery in a two-centred head with a
moulded label and probably all of brick, but
mostly covered with cement ; the brick W. doorway has jambs and two-centred head of three

orders, moulded in the arch and chamfered in the jambs, with a moulded label. The second stage has in the N. and S. walls a small opening with a four-centred head. The bell-chamber has in each wall a modern window set in an old brick opening with a two-centred head and moulded label of brick.

Fittings—*Bells :* two ; 1st *c.* 1400 and inscribed " Omnes sancti orate pro nobis " in Lombardic capitals ; 2nd by John Danyell, mid 15th-century and inscribed " Vox Augustini Sonet In Aure Dei."

Condition—Good, mostly rebuilt.

---

38. GREAT HORKESLEY. (C.b.)

(O.S. 6 in. (a)xviii. N.E. (b)xviii. S.E.)

Great Horkesley is a parish 4 m. N.N.W. of Colchester. The church and the desecrated chapel (now a cottage) are the principal monuments.

Ecclesiastical :—

b(1). PARISH CHURCH OF ALL SAINTS stands in the N. part of the parish. The walls are of limestone and flint-rubble with some pudding-stone and septaria ; the dressings are of limestone and brick and the roofs are tiled. The *Nave* was built in the 12th century. In the 14th century the *Chancel* was rebuilt, the *North Vestry* and *Chapel* added and the *West Tower* built. Early in the 15th century the *North Aisle* and arcade were built and later in the same century the *South Porch* was added. The church was restored in the 19th century when the chancel-arch was rebuilt. The detail of the N. arcade is interesting.

Architectural Description—The *Chancel* (24½ ft. by 15¾ ft.) has a 15th-century E. window of three cinquefoiled lights with vertical and embattled tracery in a two-centred head with a moulded label and head-stops. In the N. wall is a 14th-century archway, partly restored ; it is two-centred and of two chamfered orders ; further E. is a 14th-century doorway with chamfered jambs, two-centred arch and moulded label. In the S. wall are two 15th-century windows, the eastern is of two cinquefoiled lights in a square head with a moulded label ; the western is similar but is continued down below an embattled transom with cinquefoiled heads beneath it ; between the windows is a 15th-century doorway with moulded jambs and two-centred arch in a square head with a moulded label and quatrefoiled spandrels. The chancel-arch is modern.

The *North Vestry* has in the E. wall a window all modern except the moulded internal lintel which is perhaps of the 16th century. The late 15th-century N.E. diagonal buttress has a moulded plinth with quatrefoiled panels enclosing a shield and two roses.

The *North Chapel* (14¼ ft. by 15¼ ft.) has in the N. wall two 14th-century windows each of two cinquefoiled lights with a quatrefoil in a two-centred head with a moulded label ; between them is a buttress similar to that of the vestry and with two shields of the Trinity and St. George and a rosette. In the W. wall is a 15th-century archway, four-centred and of two moulded orders, the outer continuous and the inner springing from attached shafts with moulded capitals and bases ; S. of it is a squint.

The *Nave* (40½ ft. by 19 ft.), has an early 15th-century N. arcade (Plate, p. 126) of three bays with two-centred arches of two moulded orders and a label on the S. side with head-stops ; the inner order of the arches is carved with square flowers and bosses of foliage, shields with (*a*) five bells and (*b*) five chalices and hosts, crowns, an angel, man's head and a woman's head with head-dress of the period ; the moulded columns have each four moulded and attached shafts with moulded capitals alternately plain and embattled, and moulded bases ; the responds have each one attached shaft ; piers and responds have been partly restored ; E. of the arcade is a modern opening. In the S. wall are two much restored 15th-century windows each of three cinquefoiled lights with vertical tracery in a segmental-pointed head with a moulded label ; further W. is the 15th-century S. doorway with moulded and shafted jambs and two-centred arch with a moulded label and angel stops ; the doorway has small square flowers carved in the hollow mouldings. The buttresses are similar to that of the N. vestry and carved with rosettes on the plinth ; the S.W. angle of the nave has 12th-century quoins.

The *North Aisle* (17½ ft. wide), is of the 15th century and has in the N. wall two windows similar to those in the nave and partly restored ; further W. is the N. doorway with hollow-chamfered jambs and two-centred arch with a moulded label. In the W. wall is a window uniform with those in the N. wall.

The *West Tower* (10½ ft. square) is of four stages the three lower of the 14th century and the uppermost of late 15th-century date with an embattled parapet. The tower-arch is two-centred and of one plain order and above it is the 12th-century window of the former nave and of one pointed light. The W. window is partly restored and of two pointed lights in a two-centred head. The second stage has in the N. and S. walls a single-light window with a two-centred head. The third stage has in each wall a single-light window with a two-centred head, all blocked and only the E. window showing externally. The bell-chamber has in each wall a late 15th-century window originally of two cinquefoiled lights in a four-centred head with a moulded label, but with mullion, etc., mostly broken away.

The *South Porch* is of late 15th-century date, much restored and of timber on modern dwarf walls. The outer archway is modern but above

GREAT HORKESLEY *The* PARISH CHURCH *of* ALL SAINTS.

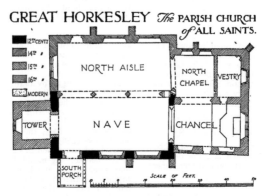

12TH CENT.
14TH ,
15TH ,
16TH ,
MODERN

NORTH AISLE

NORTH CHAPEL

VESTRY

TOWER

NAVE

CHANCEL

SOUTH PORCH

SCALE OF FEET.

it is a moulded and embattled lintel. The side walls have each seven open lights with moulded mullions and cinquefoiled and traceried heads.

The *Roof* of the chancel is of mid 15th-century date and of two bays ; it is of braced collar-beam type with moulded main timbers, curved braces forming two-centred arches with moulded pendants and springing from moulded and embattled corbels. The flat 15th-century roof of the N. chapel has curved braces to the principals and wall-posts resting on embattled stone corbels carved with heads ; the moulded and embattled wall-plates have carved flowers. The early 15th-century roof of the nave is of braced collar-beam type and of three bays with moulded main timbers ; the braces form two-centred arches and spring from wall-posts standing on stone corbels carved with heads, etc. ; one wall-post has a figure holding a shield. The 15th-century roof of the N. aisle is of three bays and similar to that of the N. chapel but with intermediate tie-beams and moulded main timbers.

Fittings—Bells : six ; 3rd by Miles Graye, 1679 ; 4th and 9th from the Bury Foundry, late 15th or early 16th-century, and inscribed respectively "Sancta Maria Ora Pro Nobis" and "Virgo Nos Ad Regna Coronata Duc Beata." *Chair :* In chancel —with richly carved and inlaid back, carved arms and turned legs, early 17th-century. *Coffin-lid :* In tower—tapering slab with double hollow-chamfered edge, 13th - century. *Communion Table :* In vestry—with turned legs, late 17th-century. *Doors :* In chancel—in doorway to vestry, of overlapping battens with moulded frame planted on, strap-hinges, probably 14th-century. In nave—in S. doorway, of overlapping battens with strap-hinges, 15th-century. *Floor-slab :* In chancel—to Samuel Gibbs, 1692, with shield of

arms. *Font-cover :* modern, but incorporating pierced and traceried panels, crocketed canopy, heads, etc., 15th-century. *Glass :* In N. aisle, in N.W. window, coloured fragments. *Indents :* In chancel—(1) of foliated cross springing from beast, marginal inscription in single Lombardic capitals " Dominus (?) Richardus Oliver quondam huius ecclesie rector qui obiit 11 die Junii Anno Domin MCCCX(X ?) VI (I ?)." In nave—(2) of inscription-plate. *Piscinae :* In chancel—with chamfered jambs and two-centred head, quatre-foiled drain, 14th-century. In N. chapel—in E. wall, with two-centred head and multifoiled drain, 14th-century. In N. aisle—in front of squint, pillar-piscina with scalloped capital and chamfered shaft, square drain, 12th-century. *Pulpit :* octagonal with band of carved vine ornament at top, moulded panels in lower stage, carved arcaded panels above, early 17th-century. *Sundial :* On Nave buttress — scratched circle with Roman numerals.

Condition—Fairly good.

Secular :—

[b](2). CHAPEL OF ST. MARY THE VIRGIN (Plate, p. 127), now a cottage, 1 m. S.S.E. of the church. The walls are of red brick and the roofs are tiled. It was built probably late in the 15th century, the eastern part forming the chapel and the western part a priest's house of two storeys. The walls have a moulded plinth and crow-stepped gables at the E. and W. ends. In the E. wall is a large blocked window with a two-centred head ; above it, in the gable, is a small niche with a cinquefoiled head. In the N. wall is an original doorway of stone with moulded jambs and four-centred arch in a square head with a square moulded label and spandrels carved with foliage,

GREAT HORKESLEY: PARISH CHURCH OF ALL SAINTS.
North Arcade of Nave ; early 15th-century.

GREAT HORKESLEY: (2) Cottage formerly Chapel of St. Mary ; late 15th-century.

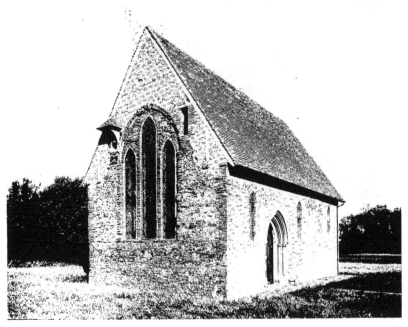

LITTLE COGGESHALL : CHAPEL OF ST. NICHOLAS ; *c.* 1220.
From the South-West.

a shield and a rose ; further W. is a window with a cinquefoiled head and now blocked. In the S. wall are two modern windows with traces of old openings above them ; between them are remains of the moulded label of the S. doorway. At the W. end is a chimney-stack with two shafts, set diagonally ; further S. is a blocked window with a two-centred head.

Inside the building the division between the chapel and house has been removed on the ground floor, but the moulded head of the former partition remains ; the upper storey of the house projected into the chapel and the moulded joists of this projection remain. In the S. wall is an original piscina with a four-centred head, and a cinquefoiled drain with a carved boss in the middle. The roof of the chapel has collar-beams and chamfered wind-braces ; in the S.E. angle is a carved corbel. Condition—Good.

MONUMENTS (3–19).

The following monuments, unless otherwise described, are of the 17th century and of two storeys, timber-framed and plastered or weatherboarded ; the roofs are tiled or thatched. Many of the buildings have original chimney-stacks and exposed ceiling-beams.

Condition—Good or fairly good, unless noted.

b(3). *The Causeway*, house, two tenements, 320 yards S. of (2).

b(4). *Barrack Yard* (Plate, p. 189), house, four tenements, 220 yards S. of (3), was built in the 15th century and is of L-shaped plan with the wings extending towards the E. and S. Inside the building is an original king-post roof-truss.

b(5). *Woodlands*, house, 120 yards N.E. of (4), was built in the 15th century with cross-wings at the N. and S. ends. It has been much altered but the roof has remains of the original king-post trusses.

b(6). *New Barn*, house, 300 yards W. of (3).

b(7). *Knight's Farm*, house, about 1,000 yards W.S.W. of (6).

b(8). *Cottage*, near Mount Hall, and 750 yards S.W. of the church.

b(9). *The Grove*, house, 1,000 yards S.S.E. of the church, has been almost completely altered and refaced. There is an original chimney-stack with three grouped diagonal shafts.

b(10). *Grove Cottage*, two tenements, 100 yards N.E. of (9), was built in the 16th century on a half H-shaped plan with the wings extending towards the E. In the 17th century the space between the wings was filled in. Inside the building is a blocked doorway with a four-centred head.

b(11). *Whitehouse Farm* (Plate, p. xxxi), house, 100 yards E.S.E. of (10), was built early in the 16th century with cross-wings at the N. and W.

ends. The upper storey projects at the W. end of the cross-wings. Inside the building one room has original moulded ceiling-beams and hollow-chamfered joists.

b(12). *Hospytt*, house, 300 yards S. of (11), was built in the 16th century or earlier with a cross-wing at the E. end.

b(13). *Baytree Farm* (Plate, p. xxx), house, ¼ m. N.E. of (11), was built in the 15th century with cross-wings at the E. and W. ends. The upper storey projects at the S. end of the cross-wings and the whole of the timber-framing is exposed on the S. front.

b(14). *House*, opposite (13), was built in the 15th century with a cross-wing at the S.W. end. There it a 17th-century addition, possibly on the site of the other cross-wing. The upper storey projects at the S.E. end of the cross-wing. Inside the building is an original doorway with a four-centred head. The cross-wing has an original roof with a king-post truss. Condition—Bad.

b(15). *Rookery Farm*, house, ¼ m. E. of (14).

a(16). *Potter's Farm*, house, 600 yards N.N.E. of (15), was built possibly in the 15th century but has been much altered. The 17th-century chimney-stack has two grouped diagonal shafts.

a(17). *Ridgenall*, house, 300 yards W. of (16). has a mid 16th-century N. wing and an L-shaped 17th-century addition to the S. of it. The rest of the building is modern. Inside the building are two original moulded ceiling-beams and some 17th-century panelling.

a(18). *Whitepark Farm*, house, nearly ¾ m. N.E. of the church, was built in the 16th century on a half H-shaped plan with the wings extending towards the S. The central chimney-stack has four grouped diagonal shafts.

a(19). *Bridge House*, 1 m. N. by E. of the church, was built probably early in the 16th century. The upper storey formerly projected in front, but has been underbuilt. Inside the building the W. room has original moulded ceiling-beams and joists.

Unclassified :—

b(20). PITCHBURY RAMPARTS, in Pitchbury Wood, about 2 m. S. of the church, are the N. end of a large camp, roughly oval in shape, and defended by a double rampart and ditch. The defences are well preserved in the wood, the inner rampart being 10 ft. above the ditch, which is 60 ft. wide from crest to crest, but the greater part of the work has been almost obliterated by the plough, and is now only faintly discernible in a large field S. of the wood. The camp appears to have been 800 ft. long and 600 ft. wide. (Plan over page.) Condition—Imperfect.

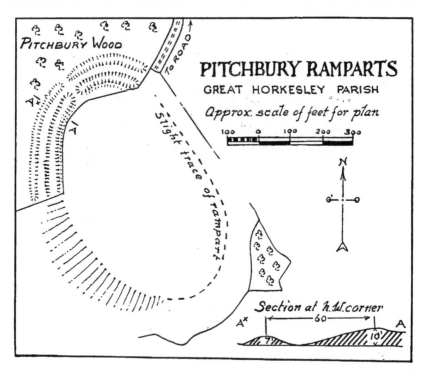

PITCHBURY RAMPARTS

GREAT HORKESLEY PARISH

Approx. scale of feet for plan

Section at N.W. corner

39. GREAT OAKLEY. (F.c.)

(O.S. 6 in. xxix. N.E.)

Great Oakley is a parish and village 5½ m. S.W. of Harwich.

Ecclesiastical :—

(1). PARISH CHURCH OF ALL SAINTS stands W. of the village. The walls are of flint and septaria-rubble, with dressings of limestone ; the roofs are tiled. The *Nave* is of the 12th century but has been lengthened at some uncertain period. Early in the 14th century the *Chancel* was rebuilt and probably late in the 15th century a W. tower was added. The *West Tower* was rebuilt in the 18th century and the church has been restored in modern times when the walls generally were refaced ; the *South Porch* is an 18th-century addition.

Architectural Description—The *Chancel* (37½ ft. by 18 ft.) has an E. window of *c.* 1420 and of four cinquefoiled ogee lights with vertical tracery

in a four-centred head with a moulded label and head-stops ; high in the wall is a small opening with a pointed head. In the N. wall are two windows, the eastern is of the 14th century, much restored, and of one trefoiled light ; the western window is of late 14th-century date and of two trefoiled ogee lights under a segmental-pointed

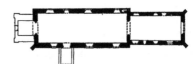

head with a moulded label and defaced head-stops ; E. of the windows is a doorway of *c.* 1500 (Plate, p. 142), now blocked but formerly opening into a vestry ; it has hollow-moulded jambs and four-centred arch, all enriched with carvings, heads in foliage, crowns and half-angels holding crowns or shields, the latter (a) *a border,*

(b) a cross engrailed in a border engrailed. In the S. wall are three windows, the easternmost is modern, except for the splays and rear-arch, which are probably of early 14th-century date; the middle window is of late 14th-century date and of one trefoiled light; the westernmost window is similar in form and date to the western window in the N. wall; between the two western windows is a late 14th-century doorway with chamfered jambs and two-centred arch. The late 14th-century chancel-arch is two-centred and of two chamfered orders, the outer continuous and the inner resting on attached shafts with moulded capitals.

The *Nave* (67 ft. by 21 ft.) has in the N. wall three windows, the easternmost is similar to the N.W. window of the chancel and is partly restored; the middle window is modern except for the 14th-century splays and rear-arch; the westernmost window is of mid 16th-century date and of three four-centred lights in a four-centred head with a moulded label; between the two western windows is a blocked 12th-century window of one round-headed light; the E. jamb of a similar window remains further E.; below the blocked window is the N. doorway of c. 1300 with double-chamfered jambs and two-centred arch, it is now blocked; at the E. end of the wall is the 15th-century rood-loft staircase; the lower doorway has hollow-chamfered jambs and two-centred head carved with square flowers. In the S. wall are three windows, the two eastern are modern except for the early 14th-century splays and rear-arches; the westernmost window is of late 14th-century date, much restored and of two trefoiled lights with tracery in a segmental-pointed head, with a moulded label; E. of it is the late 14th-century S. doorway with double-chamfered jambs, two-centred arch and moulded label, with head-stops.

The *West Tower* is of the 18th century except the late 15th-century tower-arch with responds and two-centred arch of two chamfered orders on the E. side; the responds have moulded bases.

Fittings—*Communion Table :* with turned legs, panelled rail with jewel ornament and curved brackets, early 17th-century. *Font :* square bowl, each face with five round-headed panels, moulded lower edge, moulded base of Purbeck marble, late 12th-century, stem modern. *Floor-slabs :* In chancel—(1) to Elizabeth (Cole), wife of Rev. Richard Drake, 1706. In nave—(2) to Sara, daughter of Thomas Savell, 1619, white marble slab. *Glass :* In chancel—in S.W. window, fragments of tabernacle work, etc., late 14th-century. *Indents :* In chancel—(1) of figure, probably of woman under canopy, three shields and marginal inscription, 15th-century; (2) of figure; (3) defaced; (4) of foliated cross, enclosing shield, and marginal inscription, late 14th-century. *Piscinae :* In chancel—double, with moulded jambs and

pointed heads under an ogee arch, octofoiled drains, 14th-century. In nave—in S. wall, with moulded jambs and two-centred head, octofoiled drain, mid 14th-century. *Recess :* In chancel—in N. wall, with plain square head, date uncertain. *Sedile :* In chancel—sill of S.E. window carried down to form seat. *Stoup :* In S. porch—with reused trefoiled head,· 14th-century. *Tiles :* In chancel—stamped with rose designs, mediaeval. *Miscellanea :* In walls of chancel—fragments of cheveron ornament, 12th-century; on sill of S.E. window, stone quatrefoiled panels, 15th-century.

Condition—Good.

MONUMENTS (2–6).

The following monuments, unless otherwise described, are of the 17th century and of two storeys, timber-framed and plastered or weather-boarded; the roofs are tiled or thatched. Some of the buildings have original chimney-stacks and exposed ceiling-beams.

Condition—Good or fairly good, unless noted.

THE VILLAGE :—

(2). *Cottage,* on N. side of road, 700 yards E.N.E. of the church, was built in the 15th century. The upper storey projects on the S.E. side In the N.W. wall is an original two-light window. The king-post roof is original and of two bays.

Condition—Ruinous (*now demolished.*)

(3). *House,* 50 yards E. of (2), was built probably early in the 16th century.

(4). *House,* 120 yards N.E. of (2).

Condition—Good, except roof.

---

(5). *Wash Farm,* now Brook Farm, house, 300 yards S.W. of the church, is of T-shaped plan with the cross-wing at the E. end.

(6). *Cottage,* three tenements, at Stones Green, about 1¼ m. W.S.W. of the church.

Condition—Poor.

---

40. GREAT TEY. (B.c.)

(O.S. 6 in. [a]xxvi. N.E. [b]xxvi. S.E.)

Great Tey is a parish and village 3½ m. N.W. of Great Coggeshall. The church and Abraham's Farm are the principal monuments.

Ecclesiastical :—

[a](1). PARISH CHURCH OF ST. BARNABAS (Plate, p. 130) stands in the village. The walls are of flint-rubble mixed with Roman bricks and some freestone; the dressings are of limestone and the roofs are covered with tiles and lead. The *Central Tower* with the remains of the S. arcade of the *Nave* were built early in the 12th century. Early in the 14th century the *Chancel* was rebuilt and

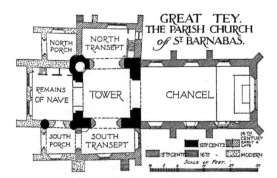

GREAT TEY.
THE PARISH CHURCH
of S^T BARNABAS.

later in the same century the *North* and *South Transepts* were built. In the 15th century the S. arch of the tower was inserted. The greater part of the nave and both the side aisles were pulled down in 1829 and the W. wall built; the *North* and *South Porches* on the site of part of the former aisles are modern and the church was restored in the 20th century.

. The central tower is a remarkable example of its period.

Architectural Description—The *Chancel* (40 ft. by 19½ ft.) has an E. gable with kneelers carved with grotesque heads and ball-flowers; in the apex is a 14th-century cusped panel with a modern inscription; the early 14th-century E. window is of five lights, one cinquefoiled and the rest trefoiled and with tracery in a two-centred head; the rear-arch and both labels are moulded and have grotesque and head-stops. In the N. wall are three early 14th-century windows each of two trefoiled lights with tracery in a two-centred head with a moulded label and head-stops. In the S. wall are three windows similar to those in the N. wall; one stop has a bishop's head; below the middle window is an early 14th-century doorway (Plate, p. 142) with moulded jambs, two-centred arch and label carved with square and ball-flowers.

The *Central Tower* (18 ft. by 17½ ft.) is of four stages divided externally by projecting courses of Roman brick and is entirely of *c.* 1100 except the N. and S. arches and the embattled parapet. The circular N.W. stair-turret rises above the parapet, but the lower part is now blocked. The E. and W. arches are of *c.* 1100 and are each semi-circular and of two plain orders on the W. face with chamfered imposts. The late 14th-century N. arch is two-centred and of two moulded orders, the outer continuous and the inner resting on semi-octagonal shafts with moulded and carved capitals. The late 14th-century S. arch is of distorted, two-centred form and of three chamfered orders, the two outer

continuous and the inner resting on semi-octagonal shafts with moulded capitals. Above the adjoining roofs in both the N. and S. walls are two small blocked openings with round heads; between them in the S. wall is a modern opening. The second stage has in the E. wall externally two round-headed recesses or panels of Roman brick. The N. and S. walls have each two groups each of three similar recesses and forming a wall-arcade. The third stage has in each wall two round-headed windows of two plain orders and built partly of stone and partly of Roman brick. The bell-chamber has in each wall three windows; the middle one is of two round-headed lights with a central column, having a voluted or cushion capital with a Roman brick abacus; the whole is enclosed in a round-headed outer order forming a tympanum; the other two windows are plain round-headed openings of two square orders.

The *North Transept* (19½ ft. by 10½ ft.) has in the E. wall a modern doorway. In the N. wall is a late 14th-century window of three trefoiled lights with tracery in a segmental-pointed head and partly restored.

The *South Transept* (19½ ft. by 9 ft.) has a 15th-century E. window of three cinquefoiled lights with vertical tracery in a segmental-pointed head; the splays are shafted and the rear-arch moulded. In the S. wall is a mid 14th-century window of two trefoiled lights with tracery in a two-centred head. In the W. wall is a reset arch perhaps of the 16th century; it is three-centred and of three chamfered orders the inner resting on attached shafts with crudely moulded capitals.

The *Nave* has no ancient features except the early 12th-century capitals of the E. respond and first column of the S. arcade, buried in the S. wall; the capitals have voluted angles, remains of carving and square chamfered abaci; the columns were apparently cylindrical; between them is set a two-centred 15th-century arch, visible

GREAT TEY : PARISH CHURCH OF ST. BARNABAS ; from the North-East.
Tower, early 12th-century ; Chancel and Transept, 14th-century.

HEYBRIDGE: PARISH CHURCH OF ST. ANDREW.
West Tower, from the North-West; 12th-century.

on the S. side and of two moulded orders, the inner resting on attached shafts with moulded capitals ; the arch is now blocked and contains a modern doorway.

The *Roof* of the chancel has 14th-century moulded wall-plates. Part of the 15th-century roof of the N. transept is visible in the modern staircase to the tower. The floor of the bell-chamber is supported on 15th-century curved transverse braces, with a carved boss at the intersection ; this may at one time have been open to the church.

Fittings—Altar : In chancel—in recess of piscina, Purbeck marble slab with three incised consecration crosses, slab originally about 2 ft. long and possibly for insertion in larger slab. *Bells :* eight, 1st and 2nd by John Darbie, 1682 ; 3rd by the same founder, 1671 ; 7th and 8th by Miles Graye, 1626 and 1629. *Chairs :* In chancel—two with cane backs, one with turned and twisted legs and posts, the other with curved arms and carved legs, late 17th-century. *Chests :* In nave—of iron and iron-bound, painted with foliage and figures of a man and woman, mid 17th-century and probably foreign. In N. porch—iron-bound and with convex lid, probably 16th-century. *Coffin-lids :* Outside S. porch and nave—three, one plain, one with traces of cross, and one coped and with a cross in relief, 13th-century. *Communion Table :* with plain turned legs, early 17th-century. *Font :* octagonal bowl, with quatre-foiled and octofoiled panels, flowers and defaced heads carved on underside, traceried panels on stem, early 15th-century. *Piscinae :* In chancel—with moulded jambs and trefoiled ogee head with traceried spandrels, early 14th-century. In S. transept—with trefoiled head, shelf and octofoiled drain, 14th-century. *Plate :* includes cup and cover-paten of 1561 with bands of incised ornament. *Royal Arms :* In S. porch—of Charles II, painted on canvas. *Seating :* Incorporated in reading-desk, four bench-ends with traceried panels and popeys carved with a crowned head and a man playing the bagpipes, 15th-century. *Sedilia :* In chancel—three bays with cinquefoiled heads, shafted jambs and two free columns, early 14th-century, almost completely restored. *Miscellanea :* Built into the walls of an outhouse at the Vicarage, several 12th-century carved capitals from the nave of the church ; another similar capital is in the garden of the Vicarage.

Condition—Fairly good.

Secular :—

HOMESTEAD MOATS.

*(2). At the Vicarage, 100 yards S.E. of the church.

*(3). At Florie's Farm, 1¼ m. W.N.W. of the church.

b(4). At Eastgore, nearly 1½ m. S.S.W. of the church.

b(5). TRUMPINGTONS, house, barn and moat, nearly 1¼ m. S.W. of the church. The *House* is of two storeys, timber-framed and plastered ; the roofs are tiled. It was built in the 17th century on an L-shaped plan. Inside the building are exposed ceiling-beams.

The *Barn*, N. of the house, is of the 17th century, timber-framed and weather-boarded. It is of eight bays with an aisle and two porches.

The *Moat* is fragmentary.

Condition—Of house, good.

MONUMENTS (6–31).

The following monuments, unless otherwise described, are of the 17th century and of two storeys, timber-framed and plastered or weather-boarded ; the roofs are tiled or thatched. Several of the buildings have original chimney-stacks and exposed ceiling-beams.

Condition—Good or fairly good, unless noted.

a(6). *House,* formerly Inn, 40 yards N.W. of the church, has been much altered.

a(7). *Cottage,* 110 yards W. of (6), was built in the 16th century. Inside the building is some late 16th-century panelling.

a(8). *House* and smithy, 100 yards N.W. of the church, was built probably in the 15th century. Inside the building are two of the original doorways in the former 'screens' and an original king-post roof-truss.

a(9). *House,* two tenements, on W. side of churchyard.

a(10). *Cottage,* 50 yards S. of the church, had a cross-wing at the S. end. A gabled dormer had the date 1642 in plaster. This cottage was demolished in 1922.

a(11). *House,* two tenements, S.E. of (10) The upper storey projects at the N. end.

b(12). *Teybrook Farm,* house and barn, about ½ m. S. of the church. The *House* has an addition of c. 1700 at the W. end. The upper storey projects on the S. side. Attached to the chimney-stack on the N. side is a small round stair-turret of brick, from which the stairs have been removed. The front door is original and has moulded rails forming a diamond pattern ; the back doorway has a four-centred head and a door of overlapping battens. Inside the building are some original doors and panelling.

The *Barn*, S. of the house, is of eight bays.

b(13). *Salmon's Farm,* house, 1½ m. S.S.W. of the church.

b(14). *Barn,* at Elm Farm, 650 yards S.E. of (13), is of four bays with an aisle.

b(15). *Cottage,* on N. side of road at Broad Green, ½ m. W. of (14).
Condition—Poor.

b(16). *Cottage,* two tenements, 100 yards W. of (15).

b(17). *Broadgreen Farm,* house, now two tenements, 50 yards S. of (16).

b(18). *Cottage,* two tenements, 70 yards W. of (17).

b(19). *Cottage,* at Cramer's Green, about 1½ m. S.W. of the church.

b(20). *Gull's Farm,* house, 900 yards N. of (19), has an original chimney-stack of one diagonal shaft.

a(21). *Cottage,* 750 yards E.N.E. of (20).

a(22). *Baldwins Farm,* house, nearly 1½ m. W. of the church.

a(23). *Abraham's Farm,* house and barn, ½ m. E. of (22). The *House* was built in the 15th century with cross-wings at the E. and W. ends. The Hall block was divided into two storeys probably early in the 17th century. Inside the building are two original doorways each with double chamfered jambs and a four-centred arch in a square head. There is also a panelled door of *c.* 1600.

The *Barn,* E. of the house, is of five bays with a porch.

a(24). *Windells,* house, nearly 1 m. N.W. of the church, has an original central chimney-stack, cross-shaped on plan.

a(25). *Cottage,* two tenements, ½ m. N. by W. of (24).

a(26). *Lambert's Farm,* house and outbuilding, 250 yards S. of (25). The *House* is of late 16th or early 17th-century date. The *Outbuilding,* W. of the house, has lower walls of brick and of the same date ; the upper part has been rebuilt.
Condition—Bad.

a(27). *Cottage,* two tenements, 500 yards S.E. of (26), has on the S. side a plaster wreath with the date and initials $\frac{L}{RA}$ 1700.

a(28). *House,* 320 yards S.E. of (27), has an original moulded ceiling-beam.

a(29). *House,* 200 yards S.E. of (28), was built probably late in the 16th century. The N.W. gable has original barge-boards with much weathered carving. The original chimney-stack on the N. side has tabled offsets. Inside the building are original moulded ceiling-beams.

a(30). *Cottage* (Plate, p. 177), 600 yards E. of (29), was built late in the 16th century and has an original chimney-stack with tabled offsets and a diagonal shaft.

a(31). *Collopsbarn,* barn, 550 yards W.N.W. of the church, is of five bays with a porch.

41. GREAT TOTHAM. (B.e.)

(O.S. 6 in. *(a)*xlv. N.E. *(b)*xlv. S.W. *(c)*xlv. S.E.)

Great Totham is a parish 3 m. N. of Maldon.

Ecclesiastical :—

b(1). PARISH CHURCH OF ST. PETER stands near the middle of the parish. The walls are mainly of boulder-clay and the dressings are of oolite and hard limestone ; the roofs are tiled. The *Chancel* may be of the 13th century but the earliest detail there or in the *Nave* is of the 14th century. The church was restored in the 19th century. The *North Aisle, Organ Chamber, South Vestry* and *Porch* were added and the bell-turret rebuilt.

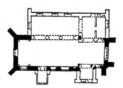

Architectural Description—The *Chancel* (19½ ft. by 15½ ft.) has S.E. quoins possibly of the 13th century. All the windows and archways are modern but a lancet window in each side wall may represent an ancient feature. There is no chancel-arch.

The *Nave* (35 ft. by 19 ft.) has a modern N. arcade. In the S. wall are three windows, the easternmost is probably of early 16th-century date, partly restored ; it is of three cinquefoiled lights with vertical tracery and embattled transoms under a three-centred head with a moulded label ; the middle window is of early 14th-century date and is said to have been brought from the chancel ; it is of two trefoiled ogee lights with a quatrefoil in a two-centred head ; the westernmost window is modern as is the S. doorway E. of it. In the W. wall is a 14th-century window of two cinquefoiled ogee lights with tracery in a square head.

The *Roof* of the chancel is of braced collar-beam type and boarded ; it has 15th-century moulded wall-plates and a moulded tie-beam at the W. end. The roof of the nave is of similar form and has similar moulded wall-plates ; the moulded tie-beams have curved braces. The bell-turret at the W. end of the nave rests on four posts, all modern except that on the N.E.

Fittings—*Brasses :* In chancel—of Elizabeth (Pilborough), wife of Richard Coke, 1606, and Elizabeth, their daughter, wife of Thomas Wilde, figures of two women in ruff and farthingale and three shields of arms. *Glass :* In nave—in S.E. and middle S. windows, quarries with roses, conventional flowers, foliage, etc., early 16th-century.

CHURCH DOORS AND IRONWORK.

ALDHAM.
South Door of Tower; c. 1300.

LITTLE TOTHAM.
North Door; late 12th century.

HEYBRIDGE.
South Door; 12th-century.

FINGRINGHOE.
South Door; late 14th-century.

ARDLEIGH.
South Door; late 15th-century.

GREAT BROMLEY.
West Door; 15th-century.

VARIOUS ECCLESIASTICAL DETAILS AND FITTINGS.

RIVENHALL CHURCH.
Helmet and Crest from the Wyseman Monument; c. 1608.

LITTLE TOTHAM CHURCH.
Bell, by John Sturdy;
15th-century.

LAWFORD CHURCH.
Woodwork in South Porch; mid 14th-century.

FEERING CHURCH.
Brick Vaulting, South Porch;
early 16th-century.

DEDHAM CHURCH.
Plinth of Tower, and Figure from Parapet;
early 16th century.

MISTLEY CHURCH.
Detail of Plinth to South Porch; c. 1500.

Paintings : In nave—in N.E. corner, above wall-plate, remains of three winged figures in black and green on a yellow ground, probably 15th-century ; on E. splay of S.E. window, figure of a crowned saint under a canopy, much defaced, early 16th-century. *Plate :* includes cup and paten of 1630. *Piscinae :* In chancel—with two-centred head and octofoiled drain, probably 14th-century, jambs modern. In nave—in S. wall, with two-centred head and square drain, 14th-century. *Miscellanea :* In nave—built into S. wall 6 ft. in advance of E. wall, fragment of moulded beam to rood-loft with one buttressed standard and part of moulded rail with painted trefoils and quatrefoils, 15th-century.

Condition—Good, much restored.

Secular :—

b(2). GREAT TOTHAM HALL and moat, 160 yards N. of the church. The *House* is of two storeys, partly timber-framed and plastered and partly of brick ; the roofs are tiled. It was built probably early in the 17th century and has modern additions. The original central chimney-stack has attached shafts on a rectangular base.

The *Moat* formerly surrounded the house.

Condition—Of house, good.

MONUMENTS (3–7).

The following monuments, unless otherwise described, are of the 17th century and of two storeys, timber-framed and plastered ; the roofs are tiled. Several of the buildings have original chimney-stacks and exposed ceiling-beams.

Condition—Good, or fairly good.

b(3). *Shoulder of Mutton Inn*, about ¾ m. W. of the church, was built in the 15th century with a cross-wing at the N. end, and has early 17th-century additions on the S. and E. There are also some modern additions. The upper storey projects at the W. end of the cross-wing and in this wall is an original window with diamond-shaped mullions and now blocked.

b(4). *Bull Inn*, 1,100 yards N.N.W. of the church, has been refaced with modern brick.

a(5). *Cottage*, on the W. side of road at Totham Hill, and 1 m. N.N.E. of the church, was built in the 16th-century. The upper storey projects on the E. front.

e(6). *Jepcracks Farm*, house, about ¼ m. E. of the church, was built early in the 16th century, but has been considerably altered. The upper storey projects and is gabled at the N. end of the W. front.

b(7). *Sain's Farm*, house, nearly ¾ m. S.S.E. of the church, was built late in the 16th century. Early in the 17th century a second block was built to the S.W. of the original building and connected

with it by a corridor and staircase wing. The original central chimney-stack has four octagonal bases on which has been planted a single short rectangular shaft. Inside the building is an early 17th-century ceiling-beam carved with conventional foliage. There are some panelled doors of the same date ; the staircase has turned newels and symmetrically turned balusters.

---

42. GREAT WIGBOROUGH. (C.d.)

(O.S. 6 in. *(a)*xxxvi. S.E. *(b)*xlvi. N.E.)

Great Wigborough is a parish 7 m. S. of Colchester.

Ecclesiastical :—

b(1). PARISH CHURCH OF ST. STEPHEN stands towards the N. end of the parish. The walls are of mixed rubble and septaria with dressings of limestone ; the roofs are tiled. The *Nave* and chancel were built late in the 14th century. Late in the 15th century a W. tower and a S. porch were added. The church was seriously damaged by the earthquake of 1884, and was subsequently restored ; the *Chancel* and *West Tower* being rebuilt and the *South Vestry* added. The *South Porch* was rebuilt in 1903.

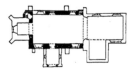

Architectural Description — The *Chancel* is modern except for some reused material of the 14th century in the N.E. and S.E. windows.

The *Nave* (37½ ft. by 21 ft.) has in the N. wall two windows ; the eastern is modern except for the reset 14th-century splays and rear-arch ; the western window is modern ; between them is the late 14th-century N. doorway, with moulded two-centred arch and label and defaced head-stops ; it has been partly reset and is now blocked ; at the E. end of the wall is the late 14th-century rood-loft staircase ; the lower doorway has hollow-chamfered jambs and two-centred head ; the upper doorway has a round head and has been reset and partly restored. In the S. wall are two windows, both modern except for the W. splay of the eastern window ; between them is the mid 15th-century S. doorway with a moulded two-centred arch and label with defaced head-stops ; the moulded jambs have each an attached shaft, with moulded capital and base ; above the doorway externally is a rough arch of doubtful purpose.

The *West Tower* has been almost entirely rebuilt but incorporates much of the late 15th-century material. The two-centred tower-arch is of two hollow-chamfered orders, the outer continuous and the inner dying on to the side walls. The W. window incorporates some old work in the jambs and splays.

The *South Porch* was rebuilt in 1903 but incorporates late 15th-century material. The two-centred outer archway is of two moulded orders, the outer continuous and the inner resting on attached shafts with moulded capitals and bases. The side walls have each a window, mostly modern but incorporating in one the head of two trefoiled lights with a moulded label and in the other some stones in the jambs.

The *Roof* of the nave is modern but incorporates some 15th or early 16th-century timbers, including a moulded principal and moulded and carved wall-plates.

Fittings—*Bells :* two ; 1st by John Danyell, inscribed "Nomen Magdalene Campana Geret Melodie," late 15th-century ; 2nd by Miles Graye, 1622. *Brass :* In nave—on N. wall, to Henry Bullocke, 1609, inscription only ; indent of this brass now forms threshold of S. doorway. *Door :* In tower—in doorway to turret, of overlapping battens with strap-hinges, 15th-century. *Font :* octagonal bowl with moulded upper and lower edges, panelled sides, four with quatrefoils enclosing blank shields, two with roses, the others with a pair of feathers and a heart respectively, each with a scroll, buttressed stem, 15th-century, lower part of stem and the base modern. *Floor-slabs :* In chancel—(1) to Henry Bullocke, 1628. In nave—(2) to Ann, widow of Edward Marke, 1621 ; (3) to Richard Wiseman, 1616. *Niche :* In nave—in N. wall, W. of N.E. window, with shafted jambs and ribbed vault, moulded pedestal, late 15th-century, much defaced. *Plate :* includes cup probably of late 16th-century date and remodelled, with knop and cone-shaped stem ; late 16th-century cover-paten with incised ornament. *Stoups :* In nave—adjoining N. doorway, with chamfered jambs and two-centred head, probably 15th-century and reset ; adjoining S. doorway, similar to above but *in situ*. *Miscellanea :* In splay of S. doorway—stone with 12th-century ornament. In churchyard—S. of tower, various worked stones, 14th or 15th-century.

Condition—Poor, serious cracks in walls.

Secular :—

b(2). HYDE FARM, house, 220 yards W. of the church, is of two storeys, partly timber-framed and partly of brick ; the roofs are tiled. It was built in the 15th century with a central hall and cross-wings at the E. and W. ends. Built into the E. chimney-stack is a gargoyle from Little Wigborough church. Inside the building the hall has been divided into two storeys in the 16th century, but retains an original king-post roof-truss. The

fireplace in the main chimney-stack has a four-centred head of the 16th century and in the E. wall of the hall is a doorway with chamfered jambs and four-centred head. There are remains of the original roof construction in the E. wing.

Condition—Good, much altered.

b(3). ABBOT'S HALL, ⅜ m. S.S.W. of the church, has been practically rebuilt, but the kitchen has 17th-century ceiling-beams and joists, apparently part of the original building.

Condition—Good, rebuilt.

a(4). MOULSHAM'S FARM, house, 300 yards N.E. of the church, is of two storeys, timber-framed and plastered ; the roofs are tiled. It was built early in the 17th century and has a late 17th-century addition on the W. side and modern additions both on the E. and W. Inside the building one room is lined with original panelling and there are some exposed ceiling-beams.

Condition—Good.

Unclassified :—

b(5). RED HILLS, several near Abbot's Hall saltings, about 1 m. S. of the church.

---

43. HARWICH. (G.b.)

(O.S. 6 in. xxi. N.E.)

Harwich is a town and port, forming with Dovercourt a municipal borough. It stands on the extreme N.E. point of the Essex coast and is about 18 m. E.N.E. of Colchester. The principal monuments are (3), (20) and (25).

Ecclesiastical :—

(1). PARISH CHURCH OF ST. NICHOLAS was entirely rebuilt in 1821 but contains from the earlier building the following :—

Fittings—*Brass :* In chancel—on N. wall, to John Rychemond [1530] and Joanne and Christiane his wives. *Font :* octagonal bowl, each face with two panels with pointed heads, late 12th-century, stem and base modern. *Monuments :* In chancel—on S. wall : (1) of William Clarke, 1666, marble tablet with Corinthian side columns and entablature with bust and blank shield of arms. In churchyard—to Frances, daughter of Richard Gray, 1701, to Richard Gray, 1711, and to John and George Rolfe, 1709, table-tomb. *Plate :* includes paten of 1683.

Secular :—

(2). THE OLD NAVAL YARD, in the N. angle of the town, contains a few old fittings, including a bell inscribed Abbot 1666, C.R., and a crane and tread-wheel of oak, perhaps as early as 1700 but partly renewed.

MONUMENTS (3–32).

The following monuments, unless otherwise described, are of the 17th century and of two storeys, timber-framed or weather-boarded ; the roofs are covered with tiles or slates. Several of the buildings have original chimney-stacks and exposed ceiling-beams.

Condition—Good or fairly good, unless noted.

CHURCH STREET, N.E. side :—

(3). *Three Cups Hotel*, N.W. of the church, was built early in the 16th century on an L-shaped plan with the wings extending towards the S.E. and N.E. There is a 17th-century addition between the wings. Inside the building two rooms have original moulded ceiling-beams or joists. The staircase of *c.* 1700 has turned and twisted balusters, close string and moulded handrail. A room on the first floor has a late 16th-century plaster ceiling (Plate, p. 235) with oval wreaths, Tudor roses, fleurs-de-lis and conventional foliage.

(4). *House* and shop, 40 yards N.W. of (3), was built in the 15th century but has been much altered. The upper storey projects on the N.W. side with a moulded bressumer ; here the timber-framing has recently been exposed by demolitions. Inside the building the roof has an original king-post truss.

(5). *House* and shop, 60 yards N.W. of (4). The upper storey projects in front.

S.W. side :—

(6). *House*, two tenements, 80 yards N.W. of (5), was built late in the 16th century but has been refronted with brick. The back has three projecting gables. Inside the building are two original moulded ceiling-beams.

(7). *House*, two tenements, S.E. of (6), was built early in the 16th century but has an 18th-century brick front. Inside the building is an original moulded ceiling-beam.

(8). *House*, two tenements and shops, 100 yards S.E. of (7), was built probably in the 15th century ; the S.E. tenement was added or rebuilt in the 16th century. The front is entirely modern. Inside the building are some late 16th-century ceiling-beams and remains of the original roof construction.

(9). *Duke's Head Inn*, S.E. of (8), has an 18th-century front of brick. Inside the building is some original panelling. The cellars have rubble walls.

(10). *House* and shops, 20 yards S.E. of (9), was built *c.* 1698, the date on a wreathed plaster panel on the front. The double-gabled attics project in front.

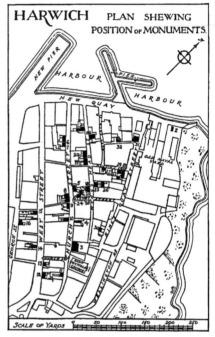

HARWICH   PLAN SHEWING POSITION of MONUMENTS.

SCALE OF YARDS

(11). *Forester's Arms Inn*, 110 yards S.E. of (10), was built probably in the 15th century. The upper storey projects in front. Inside the building are remains of the original roof construction.

WEST STREET, N.E. side :—

(12). *House* and shop, 40 yards S.W. of (11).

(13). *House*, two tenements, 15 yards N.W. of (12), is of two storeys with attics ; the upper storey and the attics project in front and the lower overhang has an original dentilled fascia board. Inside the building is an original moulded ceiling-beam.

S.W. side :—

(14). *House*, two tenements, 40 yards W.N.W. of (13) has been rebuilt, except the back wing which has a projecting upper storey on the N.W. side. Inside the building are two original panelled doors.

(15). *House*, 70 yards N.W. of (14), was built probably in the 16th century and has a 17th-century wing at the back.

(16). *House*, on the N.E. side of George Street, 30 yards S. of (15).

King's Head Street, S.W. side :—

(17). *House* and shop, 150 yards N.W. of the church, was built possibly in the 16th century, but has been much altered.

(18). *House* and shop, N.W. of (17), is of three storeys and was built probably late in the 16th century. The front is of 18th-century brick. The upper storeys project at the end of the back wing.

(19). *House*, two tenements, 45 yards N.W. of (18), has a projecting upper storey in front and an added storey on part of the front, which also projects.

(20). *House* and shop, N.W. of (19), has inside the building some original moulded ceiling-beams and panelling. A room on the first floor has an original plaster ceiling decorated with roses and fleurs-de-lis and divided into six panels by moulded trabeations.

(21). *House*, three tenements, 40 yards N.W. of (20), has a projecting upper storey with two gables in front.

N.E. side :—

(22). *House*, 20 yards E. of (21), was built in the 15th century and has a 17th-century wing at the back. The upper storey formerly projected in front, but has been underbuilt. The front block has remains of the original roof construction.

(23). *House*, two tenements, 90 yards S.E. of (22). The upper storey projects in front and has three gables.
Condition—Bad.

———

(24). *Royal Oak Inn*, on N.W. side of Market Street, 10 yards N.E. of Church Street. The upper storey projects in front and has original shaped brackets. Inside the building are original moulded ceiling-beams.

(25). *House*, N. of (24), was built late in the 16th century. The upper storey projects on the N.E. side and has a moulded bressumer carved with two leopards and a cartouche with the initials E.C. ; under one end is a carved bracket. The original doorway at the N.W. end has a four-centred head carved with the date 1588 flanked by two griffons ; the door-post is carved with the figure of a man in Elizabethan costume. In the S.E. wall of the building is a similar doorway with a pelican and a figure of a woman holding a mirror and a shield charged with a *fesse nebuly* ; below the figure are the letters OENS.

(26). *House*, two tenements, 10 yards N.E. of (23), was built probably late in the 16th century and has an original moulded ceiling-beam. N.E. of the house is a short piece of rubble walling possibly of 15th-century date.

(27). *House*, on S.E. side of Austin's Lane, 35 yards N.E. of (19), was built probably in the 16th century. The upper storey projects in front on curved brackets.

(28). *House* and shop, 30 yards N.E. of (27), has a projecting upper storey in front.

(29). *Duke of Norfolk Inn*, N.E. of (28), was built early in the 16th century but has a modern block on the N.E. side. The upper storey of the original block projects on the N.W. and N.E. sides. Inside the building is an original moulded ceiling-beam and an original window of three pointed lights and now blocked. Two rooms on the first floor are lined with 17th-century panelling. The cellar has in the E. wall a stone recess with a flat ogee head. There are two original fireplaces in the house, both with oak lintels.
Condition—Bad.

(30). *House*, standing back from King's Quay Street, 115 yards S.S.E. of (29).

(31). *Globe Inn*, 70 yards N.W. of (29). The upper storey projects on the N.E. and S.E. sides. Inside the building one room has an original plaster ceiling enriched with roses, foliage and fleurs-de-lis and divided into panels by moulded trabeations.

(32). *House*, 30 yards S.W. of (31), was built late in the 16th century. The upper storey projects on the S.W. side. The lower part of the N.E. wall is of stone rubble and may be mediaeval.
Condition—Bad.

———

Henny, see Great Henny and Little Henny.

———

44. HEYBRIDGE. (B.e.)

(O.S. 6 in. (a)liv. N.W. (b)liv. N.E.)

Heybridge is a parish and village on the N. side of the Blackwater, opposite Maldon. The church is interesting.

Ecclesiastical :—

a(1). Parish Church of St. Andrew stands in the village. The walls are of flint-rubble, boulder-clay and pudding-stone with dressings of lime-stone and clunch ; the roofs are tiled. The *Chancel* and *Nave* were built early in the 12th century and later in the same century the *West Tower* was added. In the 15th century the chancel was lengthened towards the E. and a clearstorey to the nave was begun but probably never completed. At some uncertain date the upper part of the tower was destroyed. The South Porch is modern.
The church is an interesting example of 12th-century work.

HEYBRIDGE *The* PARISH CHURCH *of* S.^T ANDREW.

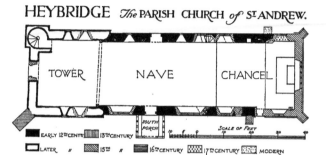

EARLY 12THCENT^Y 13THCENTURY LATER „ 15TH „ 16THCENTURY 17THCENTURY MODERN

SCALE OF FEET

Architectural Description—The *Chancel* (29 ft. by 24 ft. average) is structurally undivided from the nave. The 15th-century E. window is much restored and of five cinquefoiled lights with vertical tracery in a two-centred head. In the N. wall is a 15th-century window of two cinquefoiled lights in a square head with a moulded label ; there was a second similar window at the E. end of the wall now blocked by a monument but visible externally ; above the still existing window is the round external head of a 12th-century window with plastered splays and rear-arch. In the S. wall are two 15th-century windows similar to that in the N. wall but much restored ; above the western window is the head of a 12th-century window similar to that in the N. wall but only visible internally ; between the windows is a doorway with modern jambs and a 15th-century two-centred arch ; the thicker wall W. of this doorway indicates the junction of the 12th and 15th-century work ; between the doorway and the western window is an early 12th-century doorway, now blocked and with plain jambs, round arch and hollow-chamfered imposts, cut back on the face.

The *Nave* (42 ft. by 23 ft.) has in the N. wall three windows, the easternmost is of two plain pointed lights under a three-centred head and is probably 16th or 17th-century work partly restored; it is set in a recess containing the rood-loft staircase; the two western windows are of early 12th-century date and each of one round-headed light ; the western is much restored externally ; between these windows is the N. doorway of the same date and with plain jambs and round arch enclosing a diapered tympanum with a segmental arch springing from roll-moulded imposts. The S. wall has two 15th-century windows each of three cinque-foiled lights with tracery in a square head almost completely restored externally except for the label and defaced stops of the western window ; above the eastern window is an early 12th-century window, now blocked but visible externally ;

between the windows is the 12th-century S. doorway (Plate, p. 132) similar to the N. doorway but of two plain orders with grooved and hollow-chamfered imposts and partly restored jambs. The N. and S. walls have each the splayed lower parts of four clearstorey windows now cut off by the roof timbers.

The *West Tower* (22 ft. by 24 ft.) is of one stage (Plate, p. 131) and part of a second and rises little above the roof of the nave. The N.W. stair-turret is gabled and the tower has a pyramidal roof. At the S.W. angle is a heavy 16th-century buttress of brick. There is no tower-arch. In the N. wall are two windows, the eastern a 13th-century lancet and the western set at a higher level and a single 12th century light of two plain orders with a round head. In the S. wall are two windows similar to those in the N. wall. In the W. wall is a late 14th or early 15th-century doorway, with double cham-fered jambs and two-centred arch ; it is set in the blocking of a larger 12th-century doorway with a moulded semi-circular arch and a defaced label ; above the doorway is a 12th-century window similar but larger than those in the side walls ; the projection enclosing the turret staircase has a roll-moulded internal angle. The remaining part of the second stage has in the N., S. and W. walls remains of the jambs of a series of panels now flush with the rest of the wall.

The *Roof* of the chancel has three trusses, the eastern is a late 15th-century hammer-beam truss and the two western are of late 14th or early 15th-century date and of king-post type with rebated king-posts and four-way struts. The late 15th-century roof of the nave is of four bays with four king-post trusses and one truss with queen-posts ; the curved braces of the tie-beams have spandrels carved with foliage and shields bearing the initials S.T. and G. with various merchants' marks and the Bourchier knot. The modern roof of the S. porch incorporates a 15th-century moulded tie-beam.

Fittings—*Bells :* two ; 1st by John Danyell, inscribed " Vox Augustini Sonet in Aure Dei," 15th-century ; 2nd by John Darbie, 1684, now broken up. *Brasses :* In chancel—(1) of John Whitacres, 1627, with figure in civilian dress and inscription ; (2) to Elizabeth (Wiseman), wife of John Freshwater, 1681, inscription with shield of arms. *Coffin-lid :* Set in blocking of S. doorway to chancel—with calvary and ornamental stem, 13th-century. *Door* (Plate, p. 132): In S. doorway, of battens with ornamental iron hinges and straps with foliated ends, 12th-century, pierced scutcheon-plate, probably 13th-century. *Font :* In tower—part of font with square scalloped base, 12th-century, recut octagonal top, later. *Glass :* In chancel—in N.W. window, figure of female saint, 13th-century (Plate, p. 192) ; quarries with flower ornament and top of canopy, 14th-century. *Locker :* In chancel—in N. wall, plain square recess with wood lintel, date uncertain. *Monument* and *Floor-slabs.* Monument : In chancel —on N. wall, of Thomas Freshwater, 1638, and Sara, his third wife, 1634, marble wall-monument with kneeling figures of man and wife in double-arched recess flanked by Corinthian columns supporting an entablature, achievement and two shields of arms. *Floor-slabs :* In chancel—(1) Thomas Freshwater, 1690, with shield of arms ; (2) to Elizabeth (Freshwater), wife of William Aylett, 1690, with defaced shield of arms ; (3) to John Freshwater, 1686, with achievement of arms. *Panelling :* In tower—incorporated in seating, with carved frieze, 17th-century. *Piscinae :* In chancel—rough recess with projecting sill and round, ribbed drain, date uncertain. In nave— in E. splay of S.E. window, with pointed head and multifoiled drain, date uncertain. *Plate :* includes cup probably of 1705 and small paten of 1617. *Table :* In chancel—small with turned legs, 17th-century. *Miscellanea :* In nave—built into W. splay of rood-loft staircase, part of Purbeck marble *bowl* of font with shallow round-headed panels ; fragment with saltire ornament and other fragments of worked stone, 12th-century.
Condition—Fairly good.

Secular :—

ᵃ(2). HOMESTEAD MOAT, at Moat Cottage, 250 yards E. of the church.

MONUMENTS (3–6).

The following monuments, unless otherwise described, are of the 17th century and of two storeys, timber-framed and plastered or weatherboarded ; the roofs are tiled. Some of the buildings have exposed ceiling-beams and original chimneystacks.
Condition—Good, or fairly good.

ᵃ(3). *Heybridge Hall*, 650 yards S.E. of the church, is of L-shaped plan with the wings extending towards the N. and E. and some modern additions. Inside the building is an original dog-legged staircase, with turned balusters and heavy moulded handrail. One room has original panelling and on the first floor is a panelled door with a double shell-ornament at the top. A doorway on the same floor has a four-centred arch in a square head and appears to be of the 15th century and reused.

ᵃ(4). *Cottage*, 50 yards N.W. of (3), was built in the 15th century and has a cross-wing at the N. end. The upper storey projects at the E. end of the cross-wing. Inside the building the roof of the cross-wing has a king-post truss.

ᵃ(5). *Jacob's Farm*, house, ¼ m. N.E. of (4), was built in the 15th century with a central hall and cross-wings at the E. and W. ends. The W. wing is now included under the main roof and the projecting upper storey of the E. wing has been underbuilt. Inside the building the former hall has been divided into two storeys, but retains its original king-post truss ; the king-post has a moulded and embattled capital. The original king-post truss of the E. wing also remains. There are two original windows with diamond-shaped mullions and now blocked.

ᵃ(6). *Middle Farm*, house, 400 yards S.E. of (5), has a cross-wing at the E. end.

Unclassified :—

ᵇ(7). MOUND, 1 m. E.S.E. of the church and on the E. side of Basin Road, is large and flat-topped. Condition—Fairly good.

HOLLAND, see GREAT HOLLAND and LITTLE HOLLAND.

HORKESLEY, see GREAT HORKESLEY and LITTLE HORKESLEY.

45. INWORTH. (B.d.)

(O.S. 6 in. ⁽ᵃ⁾xxxv. N.E. ⁽ᵇ⁾xxxv. S.E. ⁽ᶜ⁾xlv. N.E.)

Inworth is a parish 3½ m. S.S.E. of Great Coggeshall. The church is the principal monument.

Ecclesiastical :—

ᵇ(1). PARISH CHURCH OF ALL SAINTS (?) stands in the middle of the parish. The walls are of coursed flint-rubble mixed with pudding-stone, freestone and Roman brick ; the dressings are of limestone and brick and the roofs are tiled. The *Chancel* and *Nave* were built about the middle of the 11th century. Probably in the 14th century the chancel was lengthened by a few feet.

INWORTH *The* PARISH CHURCH *of* ALL SAINTS.(7)

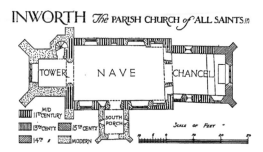

A south porch was built *c.* 1500. The church was restored in the 19th century when the *West Tower* and the *South Porch* were rebuilt.

The church is of great interest from its pre-Conquest date, and among the fittings the carved bench and remains of paintings are noteworthy.

Architectural Description—The *Chancel* (19½ ft. by 15 ft.) has a modern E. window. The side walls have each a straight joint about 6 ft. from the E. end, with pudding-stone quoins, showing the original termination of the 11th-century chancel. In the N. wall (Plate, p. 140) is an 11th-century window of one round-headed light with double splays; the external head is of pudding-stone with a course of Roman bricks at the springing level on the W. side. In the S. wall are three windows, the easternmost and westernmost are probably of the 14th century, much restored, and are each of two cinquefoiled lights with tracery in a two-centred head; the middle window (Plate, p. 142) is a single 11th-century light uniform with that in the N. wall, but with bricks at the springing level on both sides; below it is a modern doorway. The chancel-arch is probably of the 11th century but is entirely covered with plaster; it is semi-circular and of two square orders on the W. side; flanking the chancel arch are two squints, that on the N. with a two-centred head, probably of the 13th century, and that on the S. modern.

The *Nave* (33 ft. by 19¾ ft.) has in the E. wall two recesses with pointed heads enclosing the squints; the S. recess is modern. At the E. end of each side wall is a similar recess with a two-centred head, probably of the 13th century. In the N. wall are two windows, the eastern of late 15th-century date and of two cinquefoiled lights in a square head with a moulded label; the western window is apparently entirely modern. In the S. wall are two windows, the eastern of *c.* 1500 is of brick and of three plain lights in a four-centred head with a moulded label; the western window is modern; between the windows is the S. doorway of *c.* 1500 with double chamfered

jambs and segmental-pointed arch of brick; W. of the doorway are the splays and round head of a blocked window, possibly of the 11th or 12th century.

The *Roof* of the nave is of the 15th century and has moulded wall-plates, three cambered tie-beams and king-posts with moulded capitals and bases. The S. porch has moulded wall-plates of *c.* 1500.

Fittings—*Door:* In S. doorway—with hollow-chamfered frame and fillets and trellis framing at the back, probably *c.* 1500. *Glass:* In chancel—in middle S. window, fragments of foliage, figures, etc., 14th and 15th-century. *Niches:* In chancel—in N. wall, double, with trefoiled heads of brick, *c.* 1500, use uncertain; in E. splay of S.E. window, with trefoiled head; W. of S. door-way, with trefoiled head of brick, both *c.* 1500. *Paintings:* In nave—on E. wall, N. of chancel-arch, masoned diaper in red and traces of orna-mental border to arch, probably 12th-century; S. of arch, two tiers of figure subjects, top tier with much defaced figures, lower tier with (*a*) bishop standing beside a tower and three other figures, and (*b*) a boat with striped sail and a man standing beside it, late 13th-century. *Paving:* In chancel—slip-tiles with foliated ornament, etc., 13th and 14th-century. *Piscinae:* In chancel—with two-centred head and round drain, probably 15th-century. In nave—in recess in N. wall, with round head, all plastered; in recess in S. wall, similar but with pointed head, both with round drains, dates uncertain. *Plate:* includes cup and cover-paten of 1571, with incised ornament on cup. *Screen:* Under chancel-arch—of three bays with wide doorway having cinquefoiled and sub-cusped head with traceried spandrels; side bays with tre-foiled and traceried heads, modern beam with reset cresting; close lower panels, late 15th-century. *Seating:* In nave—bench (Plate, p. 181) with richly carved and traceried back with foliated spandrels, panels separated by foliated bands, *c.* 1500.

Condition—Good, much restored.

Secular :—

MONUMENTS (2–11).

The following monuments, unless otherwise described, are of the 17th century and of two storeys, timber-framed and plastered or weather-boarded ; the roofs are tiled or thatched. Many of the buildings have original chimney-stacks and exposed ceiling-beams.

Condition—Good or fairly good, unless noted.

b(2). *House,* 130 yards N.N.E. of the church, was built *c.* 1600, with a cross-wing at the N. end. The upper storey projects at the E. end of the cross-wing.

b(3). *Cottage,* 140 yards N.N.E. of (2). ·

a(4). *Bridge House,* nearly 1¼ m. N.W. of the church, was built probably in the 16th century. Inside the building is an original moulded ceiling-beam. The late 17th-century staircase has twisted balusters and square newels with turned pendants. There are also some 17th-century panelled doors.

b(5). *Theobald's Farm,* house, about ½ m. S. of the church, was built *c.* 1600.

b(6). *Cottage,* two tenements, 1 m. S.S.W. of (5).

c(7). *Cottage,* on N. side of road, 270 yards S.S.E. of (6).

c(8). *House,* two tenements, 1,000 yards E. of (7), was built early in the 16th century, with cross-wings at the E. and W. ends. Inside the building is an original window with bar mullions, now blocked. There is also part of the arched head of an original doorway.

Condition—Bad.

c(9). *Ship Inn,* 120 yards E. of (8), has been fronted with modern brick.

b(10). *House,* two tenements, ¼ m. N.E. of (9), was built early in the 16th century. The 17th-century chimney-stack has three square shafts with a common capping. Inside the building is an original moulded ceiling-beam. The late 17th-century staircase has turned balusters and a close string. There is also a door of moulded battens, of the same date.

b(11). *Cottage,* ¼ m. E. of (10), was built early in the 18th century and has walls of red brick.

---

46. KELVEDON. (B.d.)

(O.S. 6 in. *(a)*xxxv. N.W. *(b)*xxxv. N.E. *(c)*xxxv. S.W. *(d)*xxxv. S.E.)

Kelvedon is a parish and small town 3½ m. N.E. of Witham. The church is the principal monument, and there are many mediaeval houses in the parish.

Roman :—

(1). Vague statements have been made respecting : (*a*) The remains of Roman villa beneath the soil in some meadowland at Felix Hall (*Essex Arch. Soc. Trans.,* O.S., I (1858), 198), which lies about 1 m. N.W. of Kelvedon, and N. of the London and Colchester road ; (*b*) burial urns, with coins, bronze fibula, etc., found about 1855 or 1860 on Dorward's Hall estate, 1½ m. S.W. of Kelvedon, and S. of the road (*Proc. Soc. Ant.* (2), V, 30.) ; (*c*) Roman potsherds found close to the River Blackwater in a meadow opposite Little Barrows ; and many skeletons found immediately above in digging for gravel.

The 6-in. Ordnance Map (xxxv. S.W.) marks " Roman Urns," etc., found 1847 and 1850, on the N. side of the main road near Hole Farm and Crabb's Farm, perhaps the same as (*b*) ; also " Roman and Danish Coins and Roman Urns found 1873 " in the second field S.E. of the Vicarage.

Nothing can be made of these indefinite references. Perhaps allusion is made to the Villa at Rivenhall 1¼ m. S.W. of Felix Hall, and the burials may be connected with that building. (See *Sectional Preface,* p. xxvii.)

Ecclesiastical :—

c(2). PARISH CHURCH OF ST. MARY (Plate, p. 141), stands at the S.W. end of the village. The walls are of flint-rubble with limestone dressings ; the roofs are covered with tiles and lead. The *Nave* was built probably early in the 12th century, and of this the N.W. angle remains. About 1230 the *North Aisle* and arcade were built followed by the *South Aisle* and arcade *c.* 1250. About 1360 the *Chancel* was enlarged and rebuilt and the *West Tower* added or rebuilt. In the 15th century the clear-storey was added and the top stage of the tower built. Early in the 16th century the *North Chapel* and *Vestry* were added. The church was restored in the 19th century when the *South Porch* was largely rebuilt and the *South Chapel* added.

The 13th-century detail of the nave arcades is interesting.

Architectural Description—The *Chancel* (28 ft. by 20 ft.) has a modern E. window. In the N. wall is a 14th-century window, now opening into the vestry, of one cinquefoiled light with a moulded label ; further W. is a doorway inserted early in the 16th century and made up of the jambs and head of a 14th-century window formerly of two cinquefoiled lights in a two-centred head ; W. of the doorway is an early 16th-century plastered brick archway with a moulded and four-centred arch, moulded E. respond and splayed W. respond both with moulded capitals and bases ; at the W. end of the wall is a narrow recess with a four-centred head, possibly a doorway to the former

INWORTH : PARISH CHURCH.

Chancel from North-East, showing 11th-century Window and Quoins.

COPFORD : PARISH CHURCH OF ST. MICHAEL AND ALL ANGELS.

Apse and North Wall ; c. 1100.

KELVEDON : PARISH CHURCH OF ST. MARY.
Interior, showing Nave Arcades ; 13th-century.

KELVEDON. *The* PARISH CHURCH *of* S.^T MARY *the* VIRGIN.

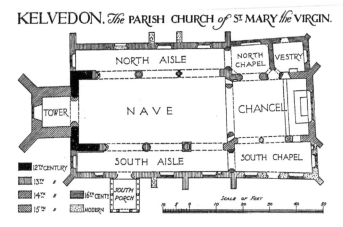

rood-loft staircase. In the S. wall is a modern arch and an arcade of two bays. The two-centred chancel-arch is of *c.* 1360 and of two moulded orders ; the responds have semi-octagonal attached shafts, with moulded capitals and bases, partly restored ; on each side of the chancel-arch is a 15th-century squint with a chamfered, four-centred head ; that on the S. has been much restored.

The *North Vestry* (11¼ ft. by 10½ ft.) has a reused 15th-century E. window of two cinque-foiled lights under a square head with a moulded label, partly restored. The N. wall is of 16th-century brickwork and has a modern doorway. In the S.W. angle is a 16th-century doorway of brick with a four-centred head, which opens into a triangular lobby with a second and similar doorway into the N. chapel.

The *North Chapel* (15 ft. by 9¾ ft.) has a N. wall of 16th-century brickwork with a stepped gable. In the N. wall is a brick window of four four-centred lights, with intersecting tracery in a four-centred head with a moulded label ; in the gable are two round-headed openings, now blocked. The 16th-century W. archway is of plastered brick and has a moulded and four-centred arch and moulded responds with moulded capitals and bases.

The *South Chapel* is modern but has reset in the E. wall a 15th-century window-head of two cinquefoiled lights ; reset in the S. wall are two windows, the eastern is of *c.* 1360 and of two trefoiled ogee lights with tracery in a two-centred head with a moulded label ; the western window is of the 15th-century and of two cinque-foiled lights with tracery in a two-centred head with a moulded label ; the doorway is perhaps

of the 14th century but is covered with cement. In the W. wall is a modern arch.

The *Nave* (55½ ft. by 23½ ft.) has in the E. wall N. of the chancel-arch a 15th-century doorway at the level of the rood-loft with a four-centred head. The N. arcade is of *c.* 1230 and of three bays with two-centred arches of two moulded orders and a chamfered label on the S. side ; the E. respond has a moulded corbel partly restored and carved with ' stiff-leaf ' foliage ; the first column is moulded and has four attached shafts with moulded and foliated capitals (Plate, p. 213), badly broken, and moulded bases ; the second column is cylindrical with a moulded and foliated capital and moulded base ; the W. respond has one attached shaft and two angle rolls ; the rolls have carved ' water-leaf ' capitals but that of the shaft is modern. Further W. are marks of a blocked opening, possibly a 12th-century window. The S. arcade is of *c.* 1250 and of three bays, with arches similar to those of the N. arcade ; above the first column and not *in situ* is a carved 15th-century shield (Plate, p. 213) of England quartering France (modern) with a label and surmounted by a crown ; the columns are cylindrical with moulded capitals and chamfered bases ; the second column is of later date ; the W. respond has three attached shafts with modern capitals and bases ; the E. respond is of the 14th-century with a semi-octagonal attached shaft and moulded capital and base. The 15th-century clearstorey has on each side four windows, each of two cinquefoiled lights under a square head and almost entirely restored. The N.W. angle of the nave externally has quoins of Roman brick.

The *North Aisle* (7½ ft. wide) has in the N. wall two 15th-century windows, the eastern of two cinquefoiled lights under a square head with a moulded label; the western window is of two cinquefoiled lights with tracery in a two-centred head with a moulded label; further W. is the 15th-century N. doorway, now blocked, with moulded jambs, two-centred arch and label. In the W. wall is a window similar to the eastern window in the N. wall.

The *South Aisle* (7½ ft. wide) has in the S. wall three windows and a doorway, all modern except the westernmost window, which is of late 14th-century date, recut and reset, and of two cinque-foiled ogee lights with tracery in a square head. In the W. wall is a modern window.

The *West Tower* (10⅔ ft. by 10 ft.) is of three stages with an embattled parapet having carved grotesques at the angles of the string-course and a small spire. The details of the two lower stages are of the 14th century and those of the bell-chamber of the 15th century. The two-centred tower-arch is of two moulded orders; the responds are of two chamfered orders with moulded capitals and bases; above the arch is a plain two-centred opening, now blocked. The W. window has been completely restored except the jambs, splays and rear-arch. The second stage has in the N., S. and W. walls a single light window with a trefoiled ogee head, all much restored. The bell-chamber has in each wall a window of two cinquefoiled lights in a square head, almost completely restored.

The *Roof* of the chancel is probably of the 14th century and is of trussed-rafter type with moulded wall-plates. The 15th-century roof of the nave is of four bays with modern tie-beams and moulded braces with traceried spandrels; the principals have a carved boss at the apex of each pair and the intermediate principals spring from carved half-figures holding shields, crowns, pipes and books. The flat pent roofs of the aisles have some 15th-century moulded timbers but most of the beams are plain.

Fittings—Bells: six; 3rd by Henry Pleasant, 1705; 5th by Miles Graye, 1615; 6th by Miles Graie, 1608. *Chest:* In S. aisle—made up of early 17th-century work. *Door:* In doorway to vestry —of studded battens, 16th-century, later frame planted on. *Glass:* In N. aisle—in second window in N. wall, fragments including sun and stars, leopards' heads and leaf-ornament, 15th-century. *Indent:* In churchyard—S. of S. chapel, of small figure and inscription - plate. *Monuments* and *Floor-slabs.* Monuments: In S. chapel—on S. wall, (1) to Thomas Crane, 1654, black and white marble oval tablet with cornice and skull at top. In S. aisle—on S. wall: (2) to Thomas Abdy, 1684, carved white marble tablet with pediment and cartouche of arms; (3) to Sir Anthony Abdy, Bart., 1704, white marble wall-monument with

carved frieze and shield of arms; (4) to Sir Thomas Abdy, Bart., 1685, Mary (Corselis), his wife, 1645, Abigail, his daughter, wife of Sir Marke Guyon, 1679, and William, son of Sir Thomas, 1682, white marble wall-monument with carved curtain flanked by Ionic pilasters, broken pediment, achievement, three cartouches and a shield of arms. In churchyard—E. of chancel, (5) to Abraham Clerke, 1700, slab with shield of arms. Floor-slabs: In N. aisle—at W. end, (1) to Anna, daughter of Sir Thomas Abdy, 1682, with shield of arms; (2) to William Abdy, 1682, with shield of arms. *Niche:* In N. chapel—in N.E. angle, with four-centred head, moulded cornice and shelf with cusped support, early 16th-century, now hidden by organ. *Panelling:* In N. vestry—various, including panels carved with a figure subject, Ahasuerus and Esther or Solomon and the Queen of Sheba, birds, foliage, etc., three linen-fold panels, etc., 16th and 17th-century. In S. aisle—incorporated in cupboard, four linen-fold panels, 16th-century. *Piscinae:* In S. chapel—reset, with moulded jambs and cinquefoiled ogee head, quatrefoiled drain, 14th-century. In S. aisle—in S. wall, with chamfered jambs and trefoiled ogee head, quatre-foiled drain, 14th-century. *Plate:* In N. aisle—cup of 1562 and cover-paten of about the same date. *Poor-box:* In S. aisle—incorporating two narrow strapwork panels, 17th-century and part of two carved flowers, early 16th-century. *Royal Arms:* In W. tower—on S. wall, on canvas, arms of Queen Anne, 1709. *Table:* In N. aisle—with turned legs and two drawers, late 17th-century.

The *Churchyard* has on the E. side a 16th-century brick wall with a moulded plinth on both sides.

Condition—Good, except N. aisle, which is much decayed.

Secular :—

a(3). HOMESTEAD MOAT at Woodhouse Farm, 2½ m. N.W. of the church.

a(4). PORTER'S FARM, house and moat, 1½ m. W.N.W. of the church. The *House* is of two storeys with attics, timber-framed and plastered; the roofs are tiled. It was built late in the 16th century. Inside the building are exposed ceiling-beams.

The *Moat* is incomplete.

Condition—Of house, good.

MONUMENTS (4–60).

The following monuments, unless otherwise described, are of the 17th century and of two storeys, timber-framed and plastered or weather-boarded; the roofs are tiled or thatched. Many of the buildings have exposed ceiling-beams, wide fireplaces and original chimney-stacks.

Condition—Good or fairly good, unless noted.

ias
45,
on,
92,
aim
nt,
of
to
ms.
na,
ith
ith
E.
ice
hli-
ng:
ved
her
rds,
6th
in
ry.
ded
lled
vith
tre-
cup
ate.
row
two
ms:
s of
with

6th-
both

uch

arm,

½ m.
two
red;
16th
iling-

rwise
two
ather-
Many
unde

d.

INWORTH.
Window, S. Wall of Chancel; mid 11th-century.

COLCHESTER, HOLY TRINITY.
West Doorway; pre-Conquest.

MIDDLETON.
South Doorway; 12th-century.

LITTLE TEY.
South Doorway; 12th century.

TOLLESBURY.
South Doorway; late 11th-century.

GREAT TEY.
South Doorway of Chancel; early
14th-century.

GREAT OAKLEY.
North Doorway of Chancel; c. 1500.

FINGRINGHOE.
ArchWay to South Porch; late 15th or early
16th-century.

CHURCH WINDOWS.

LITTLE OAKLEY.
East Window ; mid 14th-century.

GREAT BROMLEY.
Clearstorey Windows ; *c.* 1500.

STISTED.
N. Windows of Chancel ; 14th-century.

FEERING.
Window in North Aisle ;
14th-century.

LITTLE OAKLEY.
West Doorway and Window;
late 15th-century

LITTLE BENTLEY.
N. Wall of N. Aisle. Windows ; 15th and 16th-century.

Church Street, N.E. side :—

ᶜ(5). *Lawn Cottage*, house, and barn, 150 yards
E.S.E. of the church. The *House* has been much
altered and added to in the 18th and 19th centuries.
Inside the building is some late 17th-century
bolection-moulded panelling and a staircase of the
same date, with turned and twisted balusters,
square newels and close string. There is one early
17th-century panelled door.

The *Barn*, E. of the house, is small and incorporates part of a 16th-century building.

Condition—Of house, good ; of barn, poor.

ᶜ(6). *Block of Seven Tenements* (Plate, p. 123),
110 yards E.S.E. of (5), are probably of different
dates and not later than the 17th century. A projecting wing at the back of the S.E. end is probably
of the 15th century and has exposed timber-
framing. In front at the same end the upper storey
projects on curved brackets and is gabled.

ᶜ(9). *Range of Buildings*, house and two shops,
on the W. side of the cross-roads, 50 yards S.E. of
(6), has been much altered and partly refaced with
modern brick.

ᶜ(8). *Almshouses*, forming five tenements, 30
yards S.W. of (6).

Condition—Poor.

ᶜ(9). *House*, now two tenements, opposite (8),
is of two storeys with attics, and has been partly
refaced with modern brick.

Maldon Road, S.E. side :—

ᶜ(10). *Schoolmaster's House*, 60 yards S.E. of (8),
has been much altered. The upper storey projects
on the N.E. front but has been partly underbuilt.

ᶜ(11). *School*, S. of (10), is of one storey. The
walls are of brick in English bond. There are
modern additions at each end. In the old N.W.
wall is an original window, now blocked and of
three lights. In the original block is an early
18th-century fireplace with a moulded marble
architrave.

ᶜ(12). *Gray's Cottage*, 60 yards S.E. of (11), has
been almost entirely rebuilt, but incorporates
remains of a 17th-century cottage.

ᶜ(13). *House*, on N.E. side of cross-roads and
50 yards N.W. of (9), is of two storeys with attics.
It was built late in the 16th century but was
much altered and rebuilt late in the 18th century.
Inside the building are some original moulded
beams and four cambered tie-beams.

ᶜ(14). *Angel Hotel*, N.W. of (13), was built
early in the 16th century but has been much
altered in the 18th and 19th centuries. The upper
storey projects on part of the S.W. front. Inside
the building are some original and later moulded

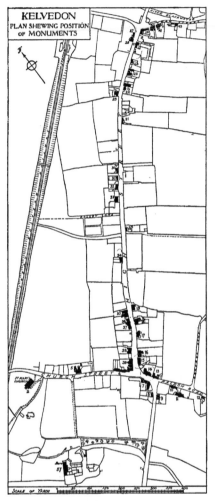

beams and at the N.W. end is an original king-
post roof-truss. There are also some remains of
early 17th-century panelling.

High Street, E. side (Plate, p. 122) :—

ᶜ(15). *White Hart Inn*, and house, 30 yards N.
of (14). The house has an original central chimney-
stack with five octagonal shafts.

*(16). *House*, three tenements, N.N.E. of (15), has cross-wings at the N. and S. ends. The upper storey projects on the whole of the W. front. In an outhouse at the back of the house is some original panelling.

*(17). *House*, 50 yards N.N.E. of (16), was built probably early in the 18th century.

*(18). *House*, two tenements, 30 yards N.N.E. of (17), has cross-wings at the N. and S. ends. The upper storey projected at the W. ends of the cross-wings, but in the S. wing it has been under-built.

*(19). *House*, three tenements, 30 yards N.N.E. of (18), is of two storeys with attics, and was built early in the 18th century.

*(20). *Cottage*, two tenements, 230 yards N.N.E. of (19).

*(21). *The Cedars*, house, 320 yards N.N.E. of (20), has been entirely refronted. The N. chimney-stack has an original moulded capping and a modern shaft.

*(22). *House*, now two tenements, 100 yards N.E. of (21), was built in the 15th century with a central hall and cross-wings at the N.E. and S.W. ends. The N.E. wing was extended at the back early in the 16th century. Inside the building the original hall has no ancient features but in the S.W. wall is an original doorway with an ogee head. The N.E. wing has original moulded ceiling-beams and joists, and in the N.E. wall is an embattled wall-plate and a fireplace with moulded jambs and depressed arch. The upper storey has an original cambered tie-beam with one curved brace. The S.W. wing has also original tie-beams.

*(23). *House* (Plate, p. xxxi), now five tenements, 30 yards N.E. of (22), was built probably in the first half of the 15th century with a central hall and cross-wings at the N.E. and S.W. ends. The N.E. wing was extended at the back in the 16th century and there is a 16th or 17th-century addition at the S.W. end. The upper storey projects at the front end of the N.E. wing and on the S.W. side of the extension of the same wing. Inside the building the ground floor of both wings has original main beams with curved braces ; the upper storey has original cambered tie-beams with curved braces. In the S.W. wall of the former hall is an original doorway with an ogee head. In the extension of the N.E. wing is the two-centred head of a doorway above the modern opening.

*(24). *House* and shop, 20 yards N.E. of (23), was built c. 1700 and has walls partly of brick. Inside the building one room has an original plaster ceiling with a large oval panel with a foliated wreath round it and spandrels enriched with flowers and shells. In the garden is a fire-back with the date and initials 1700 G.K. and a figure subject of the Return of the Spies from Canaan.

(25). *Star and Fleece Inn*, 30 yards N.E. of (24), has been much altered. The upper storey projects at the W. end of the N. front. Inside the building is a cupboard with an original panelled door.

*(26). *House*, with shop and tenement, at corner of Swan Street and 30 yards N.E. of (25), was built in the 15th century with a central hall and cross-wings at the E. and W. ends. In the 17th century the long extension fronting on Swan Street was added. The central chimney-stack has grouped diagonal shafts of the 17th century. Inside the building the original hall has hollow-chamfered wall-plates and posts. The cross-wings have remains of the original roof construction and the W. or solar wing has original moulded ceiling-beams.

N.W. side :—

*(27). *Britannia Inn* and shops, 30 yards W. of (26), had a projecting upper storey on the S.E. front, which has now been underbuilt.

*(28). *House*, now three tenements, S.W. of (27), has a cross-wing at the S.W. end. The upper storey projects at the front end of the cross-wing. Inside the building is an original door of moulded and nail-studded battens. The S.W. wing has a tie-beam with curved braces.

*(29). *House*, now three tenements, 160 yards S.W. of (28), was built probably in the 16th century, but has been extensively altered.

*(30). *House*, now three tenements, 230 yards S.W. of (29), is of two storeys with attics and was built possibly in the 15th century but much altered and rebuilt in the 17th century. The eaves have a cornice of plaster. Inside the building the 17th-century staircase has flat-shaped balusters.

*(31). *House*, 15 yards S.W. of (30), is of two storeys with attics. It has an early 18th-century addition of brick at the back.

*(32). *House* and shop, 15 yards S.W. of (31), has been much altered.

*(33). *Ormonde House*, 20 yards S.W. of (32), is of two storeys with attics. The walls are of brick. It was built early in the 17th century and late in the same century wings were added at the back. In the 18th century the front and side walls were faced with brick. The original chimney-stack has four octagonal shafts on a rectangular base with a moulded capping.

*(34). *Victoria Inn*, 180 yards S.W. of (33), was much altered and rebuilt in the 18th century.

*(35). *House*, 160 yards S.W. of (34), was almost entirely rebuilt in the 18th century, but contains some early 17th-century panelling not *in situ*.

*(36). *Range of Four Tenements*, 20 yards S.W. of (35), has an original chimney-stack, cross-shaped on plan.

^e(37). *House*, three tenements, S.W. of (36), has a projecting upper storey in front with a moulded fascia and two sunk panels inscribed 1685 $\begin{smallmatrix} F. \\ M. \ M. \end{smallmatrix}$

^e(38). *House*, three tenements, 60 yards S.W. of (37).

^e(39). *Range of Four Tenements*, at the corner of Church Street and 20 yards S.W. of (38), was built in the first half of the 16th century and has three wings projecting at the back. The front has been faced with modern brick, but the upper storey originally projected on this side. The upper storey projects on one side of two of the back wings and some original timber-framing is exposed. Inside the building the main block has original moulded ceiling-beams and there are three original doorways with four-centred heads.

SWAN STREET, S. side :—

^b(40). *House* and outbuilding, 10 yards E. of (26), is of two storeys with attics. The upper storey formerly projected in front, but has been underbuilt and the front faced with brick. The original central chimney-stack has three octagonal shafts. At the back is an original window of three lights with moulded jambs and mullions, now blocked. Inside the building are three original doors with moulded muntins and nail-studded.

^b(41). *House*, now four tenements, E. of (40), was built in the 15th century with a central hall and cross-wings at the E. and W. ends. The W. wing was extended at the back in the 17th century and the hall divided into two storeys. The front of the hall has been refaced with brick ; at the end of the W. wing is a bay-window with a moulded sill supported on early 17th-century shaped brackets. At the W. end is an early 17th-century chimney-stack with a moulded capping and two octagonal shafts. In the extension is a blocked window with a moulded mullion. Inside the building the hall has an original moulded wall-plate. The W. or solar wing has similar wall-plates and a ceiling-beam with curved braces. The other wing has remains of the original roof construction. In the extension is some early 17th-century panelling.

^b(42). *Cottage*, two tenements, 40 yards S.E. of (41).

^b(43). *House*, S.E. of (42), is of three storeys and has been much altered. Inside the building is a late 17th-century staircase, with turned balusters, close strings and square newels with turned pendants.

---

^a(44). *Mill Farm*, house, ¾ m. N.N.E. of the church, is of two storeys with attics.

^a(45) *Monk's Farm*, house, about 1 m. N.N.W. of the church, is of two storeys with attics.

(6405)

^a(46). *Cottage*, two tenements, 50 yards N. of (45).

^a(47). *Cottage*, three tenements, 50 yards N.E. of (45).

^a(48). *Park Farm*, house, 700 yards N.W. of the church, is of two storeys with attics and was built probably about the middle of the 16th century. The 17th-century central chimney-stack has diagonal pilaster strips. Inside the building is an original moulded ceiling-beam.

^a(49). *Cotcroft*, cottage, now four tenements, 350 yards S.W. of (48), has an added gable in the roof.

^a(50). *Leapingwells*, house and barn, nearly 1 m. W.N.W. of the church. The *House* is of two storeys with attics and was built probably late in the 16th century with 17th-century and modern additions on the S. side. Inside the building are two original windows, now blocked, one of six lights with diamond-shaped bar-mullions and one of two lights with a moulded frame and mullion. The *Barn*, W. of the house, is of five bays with a porch.

^a(51). *Allshot's Farm*, house, about 2 m. N.W. of the church.

^a(52). *Marylands*, house, now two tenements, nearly 1¼ m. W.N.W. of the church, was built in the 16th century with a cross-wing at the S. end. The upper storey projects on the W. front. On the S. end is an original chimney-stack with a crow-stepped offset. Inside the building is some early 17th-century panelling.

^a(53). *Cottage*, 200 yards S.S.E. of (52). Condition—Bad.

^e(54). *Clark's Farm*, house, nearly ¾ m. W.S.W. of the church, is of two storeys with attics. It has an 18th-century wing on the N. side.

^e(55). *Crabb's Farm*, house and barn, ¼ m. S.E. of (54). The *House* was built c. 1500 with a central hall and a kitchen wing on the W. There is a 17th-century extension on the W. and an early 18th-century wing on the N. side. Inside the building the former hall has an original roof with a king-post truss.

The *Barn* adjoins the house on the E. and may include the former solar wing. It is of four and a half bays with an original roof of king-post type.

^e(56). *Hole Farm*, house, 1 m. S.W. of the church, was built late in the 15th or early in the 16th century but a portion at the W. end has been destroyed. The roof has a central purlin and curved struts springing from the partitions.

^e(57). *Church Hall*, cottage and barn, 300 yards S. of the church. The *Cottage* was built in the 15th century and has exposed timber-framing and brick nogging to the lower storey.

The *Barn*, N.W. of the house, is of the 15th or 16th century with aisles.

*(58). *Bridgefoot Farm*, house, about 750 yards S.E. of the church, is of two storeys with attics. It was built *c.* 1500 or earlier but was much altered *c.* 1600 when the hall was raised. Late in the 17th century an addition was made at the S.W. end and the house was altered and added to in the 18th and 19th centuries. Inside the building the former central hall has an original screen at the N.E. end with plain chamfered posts, sill and rail. The roof of the hall incorporates some of the old timbers. The roof of the kitchen wing is original and has a king-post truss and central purlin. There is some early 17th-century panelling.

*(59). *Highfields*, house, 1 m. S.E. of the church, has been much altered and enlarged. Inside the building is some early 17th-century panelling.

*(60). *Ewell Hall*, house and barn, nearly ¾ m. E.S.E. of the church. The *House* is of two storeys with attics and was built early in the 17th century but was largely rebuilt *c.* 1700 with walls of brick. Inside the building is a staircase of *c.* 1700 with square newels, close string and turned balusters. There are also some panelling, doors, and a fireplace of the same date.

The *Barn*, N.W. of the house, is of eight bays with two porches.

---

47. KIRBY-LE-SOKEN. (F.c.)

(O.S. 6 in. xxxix. N.W.)

Kirby-le-Soken is a parish and small village 5 m. N. of Clacton.

Ecclesiastical :—

(1). PARISH CHURCH OF ST. MICHAEL stands in the village. The walls are of septaria and flint-rubble with limestone dressings. The roofs are tiled and lead-covered. The *Chancel* and *North Aisle* are probably of the 14th century ; there was also a S. chapel at this period. The *West Tower* was added in the 15th century. The church was restored in the 19th century when the *Nave* was rebuilt, the chancel refaced and the *South Chapel* and *Aisle* built.

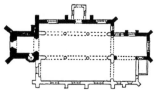

Architectural Description—The *Chancel* (24½ ft. by 14½ ft.) has a modern E. window. In the N. wall are two windows all modern except the splays and rear-arches ; below them is a 14th-

century doorway with a two-centred head and a moulded label ; it is now blocked. In the S. wall is a modern window and further W. a 14th-century segmental-pointed arch of one chamfered order opening into the S. chapel.

The *North Aisle* (6 ft. wide) has a much restored 14th-century E. window of two trefoiled light with a quatrefoil in a two-centred head with a moulded label. In the N. wall are two windows all modern except the 14th or 15th-century splays and rear-arches ; between them is the 15th-century N. doorway with moulded and shafted jambs and two-centred arch with a moulded label and head-stops.

The *West Tower* (13 ft. by 12 ft.) is of the 15th century and of three stages with a moulded and quatrefoiled plinth and an embattled parapet of chequer-work. The two-centred tower-arch is of two orders, the outer moulded and continuous and the inner chamfered ; the responds have semi-octagonal attached shafts with moulded capitals and bases. The much restored W. window is of three cinquefoiled lights with tracery in a two-centred head with a moulded label and head-stops ; the W. doorway has moulded and shafted jambs, moulded two-centred arch and label with head-stops. The second stage has in the S. and W. walls a cinquefoiled light. The bell-chamber has in each wall a window of two cinquefoiled ogee lights with an embattled transom and tracery in a two-centred head with a moulded label and head-stops.

Fittings—*Bells* : five ; 3rd by Miles Graye, 1641. *Chest* : In S. chapel—with iron bands and hasp, lid in two portions, 17th-century. *Door* : In doorway to turret of tower, modern and with strap-hinges, 15th-century. *Niche* : On external wall of N. aisle—with moulded jambs and two-centred head, 15th-century. *Piscina* : In chancel —double with pointed heads, round drains, 14th-century.

Condition—Good, much rebuilt.

Secular —

(2). INN, 150 yards N. of the church, is of two storeys with attics ; the walls are timber-framed and faced with modern brick ; the roofs are tiled. It was built probably late in the 16th century with a cross-wing at the W. end, but has been much altered. Inside the building are original exposed ceiling-beams and joists.

Condition—Good, much altered.

(3). COTTAGE, 150 yards W. of (2), is of two storeys, timber-framed and weather-boarded ; the roofs are tiled. It was built probably in the 16th century and has a cross-wing at the W. end. Inside the building are exposed ceiling-beams and joists and an original doorway with a three-centred head.

Condition—Fairly good.

(4). SADLER'S FARM, house, at Kirby Cross, ¾ m. S.S.W. of the church, is of two storeys, timber-framed and plastered ; the roofs are tiled. It was built late in the 17th century and has an original chimney-stack with a raised panel on the S. side.

Condition—Good.

(5). COTTAGE, on N. side of road, nearly ½ m. W.N.W. of (4), is of one storey with attics ; the roofs are thatched. It was built in the 17th century and has an original chimney-stack of two grouped diagonal shafts.

Condition—Good, much altered.

Unclassified :—

(6). RED HILLS, S. of Skipper's Island, about 1 m. N.N.W. of the church.

---

48. LAMARSH. (B.b.)

(O.S. 6 in. xii. S.E.)

Lamarsh is a small parish on the Suffolk border, 6 m. N.E. of Halstead.

Ecclesiastical :—

(1). PARISH CHURCH OF THE HOLY INNOCENTS (Plate, p. xxviii) stands in the middle of the parish. The walls are of flint-rubble rendered in cement and with dressings of clunch ; the roofs are tiled. The West Tower is of early 12th-century date and the Nave may be of the same period but of this there is no actual evidence. The Chancel was entirely or partly rebuilt probably early in the 14th century. Early in the 16th century the South Porch was added. Part of the tower fell in the 17th or 18th century and was restored in timber and brick. The church was restored in the 19th century when the tower-arch was rebuilt, the North Vestry added, and the E. wall rebuilt 3 ft. further E.

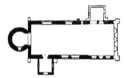

Architectural Description—The Chancel (18½ ft. by 22 ft.) has in the E. wall three lancet windows almost entirely modern. In the N. wall is a modern doorway and organ recess. In the S. wall are two windows ; the eastern is of the 14th century, of two pointed lights with a spandrel in a two-centred head, partly restored ; the western window has a lower sill and is of two

lights with a modern head ; between the windows is a 14th-century doorway with chamfered jambs and two-centred head, partly restored. There is no chancel-arch but a thickening of both walls indicates its original position.

The Nave (50 ft. by 21 ft.) has in the N. wall two windows, both modern except for the 14th-century rear-arches and splays ; at the E. end of the wall are the early 16th-century lower and upper doorways of the rood-loft staircase, both with chamfered jambs and four-centred heads of brick ; both are blocked and the upper one is partly covered by the modern roof. In the S. wall are two windows, the eastern is of late 15th-century date and of three cinquefoiled lights in a four-centred head, with moulded label and head-stops ; the early 14th-century western window is of two trefoiled ogee lights with flowing tracery in a two-centred head with a moulded label ; further W. is the early 16th-century S. doorway with moulded jambs and four-centred arch of brick.

The West Tower (10¾ ft. diameter) is circular and of three stages, undivided externally ; it is of early 12th-century date. Part of the wall has fallen out on the N.W. side and has been replaced by timber, plaster and brick ; the spire is modern. The tower-arch is modern. In the S. face is a lancet window of c. 1200. Higher up are two round-headed loops, one in the second stage and one in the bell-chamber.

The South Porch is of early 16th-century date and of red brick. The outer archway has double-chamfered jambs and four-centred head with a moulded label ; above is a window of one four-centred light and now blocked. In each side wall is a window of two four-centred lights in a depressed head.

The Roof of the porch is of early 16th-century date and has moulded ceiling-beams and joists, framed round an opening to the attic ; the barge-boards are moulded.

Fittings—Bell : one, by Henry Pleasant. 1695. Door : In S. doorway—of feathered battens with strap-hinges, early 16th-century. Monument : In chancel—on N. wall, to Thomas Stephen, 1654, marble tablet with side pilasters, broken pediment and achievement of arms. Niche : In nave—on jamb of N.E. window, with two-centred head, 14th-century. Painting : In nave—on N. and S. walls, traces of black-letter inscription and ornamental border, 16th-century. Plate : includes cup and cover-paten of 1691. Recesses : In S. porch—in S. angles, two with pointed heads, early 16th-century. Screen : Between chancel and nave—of ten bays with doorway of two bays, with moulded and buttressed posts, crocketed and traceried heads to upper panels, two to each bay, 15th-century, rails and lower panels modern, buttresses and cresting restored.

Condition—Fairly good.

Secular :—

(2). LAMARSH HALL, and moat, 100 yards N. of the church. The *House* is of two storeys, timber-framed and plastered ; the roofs are tiled. It was built in the 16th century and has an original central chimney-stack with grouped diagonal shafts ; a second stack has a stepped base. Inside the building are exposed ceiling-beams.

The *Moat* surrounds the house.

Condition—Of house, good.

MONUMENTS (3–12).

The following monuments, unless otherwise described, are of the 17th century, and of two storeys, timber-framed and plastered ; the roofs are tiled or thatched. Many of the buildings have original chimney-stacks and exposed ceiling-beams.

Condition—Good or fairly good, unless noted.

(3). *Daw's Hall,* 750 yards N.N.W. of the church, was built in the 16th century but has large modern additions. Fixed above a doorway at the N. end is a boss carved with a crowned female head and foliage of late 14th-century date. Inside the building a fireplace has an original moulded oak lintel.

(4). *Cottage,* three tenements, and barn, 400 yards N.N.W. of (3).

(5). *Valley Farm,* house, ¾ m. N.W. of the church, is of two storeys with attics and was built probably in the 16th century. The central chimney-stack has four grouped diagonal shafts. The modern porch incorporates some original moulded posts.

(6). *Brookhouse,* house, ¼ m. S. of the church, was built probably in the 16th century. Inside the building are original moulded ceiling-beams.

(7). *Cottage,* 40 yards W. of (6).

(8). *Street Farm,* house, 150 yards W. of (7), was built in the second half of the 16th century. The central chimney-stack has diagonal pilasters.

(9). *Newman's Farm,* house, 250 yards W.S.W. of (8), has a later addition at the W. end. In an outhouse are many reused timbers, including some moulded 16th-century joists.

(10). *Hall's Cottages,* 100 yards S. of (7), were built probably in the 16th century. The N. chimney-stack has two diagonal shafts and at the base of it is a doorway with a four-centred head. The main block has a coved and moulded cornice. Inside the building is an original moulded beam.

(11). *Chestnut Lodge,* about ½ m. S.S.E. of the church.

(12). *Hewitts,* cottage, nearly ¾ m. S.S.E. of the church.

49. LANGENHOE. (D.d.)

(O.S. 6 in. xxxvii. S.W.)

Langenhoe is a parish on the N. side of the Pyefleet Channel and 5 m. S.S.E. of Colchester.

Ecclesiastical :—

(1). PARISH CHURCH OF ST. ANDREW stands at the S.W. corner of the parish. The old church was destroyed by an earthquake in 1884. The modern church on the site was built largely of old material and incorporates the following old features : In the S. wall of the chancel is a 15th-century window of two cinquefoiled lights in a square head with a moulded label. In the N. wall of the nave are two 15th-century windows, one of three cinque-foiled lights with vertical tracery in a two-centred head ; the other is similar to that in the chancel. In the S. wall of the nave is a 15th-century doorway with moulded jambs and two-centred arch. The W. tower incorporates a two-centred tower-arch of two chamfered orders and a doorway, with a two-centred head, to the turret staircase ; these, with the W. doorway, which has moulded jambs, two-centred arch and label with one head-stop, are all of the 15th-century ; the windows incorporate many old stones.

Fittings—*Chair :* with carved and inlaid back, curved arms and turned legs, early 17th-century. *Chest :* In vestry—hutch type with panelled lid and enriched panels in front with arabesque ornament, 17th-century. *Doors :* In S. doorway, of battens with moulded fillets and frame, 15th-century. In doorway of turret staircase, of battens with strap-hinges, drop handle and plate, 15th-century. *Font :* octagonal bowl, each side with a quatrefoiled panel, enclosing a flower, octagonal stem with sunk panels having cinquefoiled heads, moulded base, 15th-century.

Condition—Rebuilt.

Unclassified :—

(2). MOUNDS, two on S. side of Gréton Creek and about 2 m. E. of the church.

(3). RED HILLS, a number from Peet Tie Hall eastwards, along the old high-water mark.

---

50. LANGHAM. (D.b.)

(O.S. 6 in. [a]xix. N.W. [b]xix. S.W.)

Langham is a parish and small village 6 m. N.N.E. of Colchester. The church and Valley House are the principal monuments.

Ecclesiastical :—

[a](1). PARISH CHURCH OF ST. MARY (Plate, p. 148) stands on the N. side of the parish. The walls are mostly of pebble-rubble with much iron pudding-stone in the extension of the chancel.

LANGHAM : PARISH CHURCH OF ST. MARY.

Interior, showing Chancel Arch, South Arcade, etc. ; 14th-century.

the

at
vas
em rial:
es :
ury
ead
ave
pe red
cel.
vay
The
rch
h a
ese,
nbs,
lop,
cor-

ick,
ary.
lid
que
vay,
5th-
tens
5th-
with
onal
ads,

and

Hall

; m.
alley

late,
The
iron
ncel.

LAWFORD : PARISH CHURCH OF ST. MARY ; 14th-century.

From the South-East.

LANGHAM. *The* PARISH CHURCH *of* ST MARY.

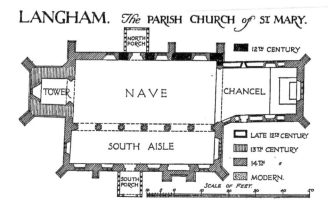

The dressings are of limestone and oolite. The roofs are tiled. Part of the N. wall of the *Nave* and the W. part of the *Chancel* are probably of the 12th century. The lower part of the *West Tower* is perhaps of the 13th century. Early in the 14th century the whole church was remodelled, the chancel extended towards the E., the chancel-arch rebuilt and subsequently widened, the S. wall being splayed to meet it, the *South Aisle* and arcade rebuilt, and the W. tower remodelled and heightened. The top stage of the tower appears to be a different ' build ' and may be rather later in date. The church was restored in the 19th century, when the *North* and *South Porches* were added.

The church contains some fairly good 14th-century detail.

Architectural Description—The *Chancel* (27½ ft. by 16¾ ft.) has a 14th-century E. window of three cinquefoiled lights with intersecting tracery in a two-centred head with a moulded label and head-stops. In the N. wall are two windows, the first is of early 14th-century date, much restored, and of two trefoiled ogee lights with tracery in a two-centred head with a modern label ; the western is a small single-pointed light probably of 12th-century origin but entirely restored. In the S. wall are two windows ; the eastern is uniform with the corresponding window in the N. wall ; the western (in the splayed wall) is similar to the eastern but with a moulded rear-arch and internal label with head-stops, one with a hood and one crowned ; there is also a moulded external label. Between them is a 14th-century doorway with double-chamfered jambs and moulded two-centred arch and label with grotesque beast-stops. The early 14th-century chancel-arch is two-centred and of two moulded orders, the outer continuous

and the inner resting on semi-octagonal shafts with moulded capitals and restored bases and a restored moulded band-course and a moulded label ; the capitals have a band of diapered flowers.

The *Nave* (52 ft. by 22¾ ft.) has Roman brick quoins at the N.E. angle, probably part of the 12th-century building. In the N. wall are three windows ; the easternmost is of early 14th-century date and of two plain pointed lights with a spandrel in a two-centred head and with moulded jambs, rear-arch and· label with head and beast-stops. The second window is similar in detail and tracery to the S.E. window of the chancel, but is of two cinquefoiled lights, partly restored. The western window is uniform with the second ; between them is the 14th-century N. doorway, with restored jambs and double-chamfered two-centred arch with a moulded label.

The *S. Arcade* is of the 14th century and of six bays with two-centred arches of two chamfered orders ; the octagonal columns and semi-octagonal responds have moulded capitals and bases ; the bays are small and the arches partly restored.

The *South Aisle* (11¾ ft. wide) has in the E. wall a 14th-century window of five trefoiled ogee lights and tracery in a square head, with moulded jambs and mullions. In the S. wall are four windows, the easternmost is early 14th-century date and of two trefoiled lights with a quatrefoil in a two-centred head with moulded jambs and label with head-stops ; the second is similar to the N.E. window in the nave but with a moulded label and head-stops ; the third and fourth windows are of early 14th-century date and similar to the chancel windows ; between the second and third windows is the 14th-century S. doorway, with modern jambs and moulded ·two-centred arch with a moulded label and head-stops. In the W. wall is a 14th-century window of two cinquefoiled lights with a quatrefoil in a segmental-pointed head with a moulded label, one head and one dragon stop.

The *West Tower* (9½ ft. square) is possibly of the 13th century, with an added 14th-century bell-chamber. It is of four stages with a late 16th or early 17th-century brick parapet with crude crocketed pinnacles at the angles. The two-centred 14th-century tower-arch is of two chamfered orders, the outer continuous and the inner resting on semi-octagonal shafts with moulded capitals and bases. The W. window is of one trefoiled ogee light with tracery in a two-centred head with a moulded label and head-stops. The second stage has in the W. wall a window of one trefoiled ogee light with tracery in a two-centred head with a moulded label, one beast-head and one human head-stop. The third stage has in each wall a window of one trefoiled light with a moulded label. The bell-chamber has in each wall a similar but smaller window.

The *Roof* of the nave is of the 14th century and of trussed-rafter type, with moulded wall-plates. The weathering of an earlier and higher roof remains on the E. face of the tower.

Fittings—*Bells :* six ; 4th by Miles Graye, 1618. *Chests :* In S. aisle—heavy dug-out with small compartment in middle and money slot, lock gone, 12th or 13th-century. In nave—framed, with panelled lid, date uncertain. *Coffin-lids :* In churchyard—W. of tower, (1) part of tapering slab, with hollow-chamfered edge and base of cross, 13th-century ; (2) with traces of cross ; (3) plain slab. *Monuments* and *Floor-slabs.* Monuments : In S. aisle—in S. wall, (1) tomb-recess with moulded jambs and segmental-pointed head with moulded label, recess set in an external projection, early 14th-century. In churchyard—S.W. of tower, (2) to Joseph Downes, 1714, and Debora, his wife, 1726, head-stone. Floor-slabs : In chancel—against N. wall, (1) to Jacob Nurth, 1714 ; against S. wall, (2) to Sir Arqlus Umfrevile, 1696, with two shields of arms. *Piscinae :* In chancel—with hollow-chamfered jambs and two-centred head, quatrefoiled drain, 14th-century. In S. aisle—in S. wall, with recut jambs and head, septfoiled drain, 14th-century. *Seating :* In chancel—reused in stalls, moulded rails and shaped bench-ends (Plate, p. 181), with popey-heads, two ends carved with crowns and rampant leopards and with angels holding scrolls on the popey-heads, early 16th-century.

Condition—Good.

Secular :—

ᵃ(2). PANELLING, etc., at Langham Hall, 250 yards W. of the church. A number of rooms in the modern house are lined with 16th and 17th-century panelling. There are also two fireplaces

of *c.* 1600 and an early 16th-century beam carved with running foliage. All these are said to have been brought from neighbouring houses.

ᵃ(3). VALLEY HOUSE, (Plates, pp. 101, 176) nearly 1 m. W.N.W. of the church, is of two storeys with attics ; the roofs are tiled. It was built probably early in the 16th century and is rectangular with a large early 17th-century stair-case-wing projecting towards the N.

The staircase is a fine example of the period.

On the S. front is an early 17th-century porch (Plate, p. 101), much restored, but with an original carved lintel over the outer archway and four large carved brackets with voluted ornament ; the inner doorway has an original moulded frame with carved stops. The brick staircase wing has early 17th-century windows with square heads and moulded labels and there are three chimney-stacks of the same date, each with three octagonal shafts with moulded caps and bases. Inside the building the entrance hall has original carved wall-plates and the western room has moulded ceiling-beams. There are several doorways with three-centred heads and a fireplace with chamfered jambs and four-centred head. There is also an original door of nail-studded battens. The early 17th-century staircase (Plates, pp. 7, 101) has a square well, symmetrically turned balusters and moulded hand-rails and strings ; the newels are richly carved and are surmounted by moulded and carved vases, the lowest one ending in a terminal figure.

Condition—Good.

MONUMENTS (4–18).

The following monuments, unless otherwise described, are of the 17th century and of two storeys, timber-framed and plastered ; the roofs are tiled. or thatched. Several of the buildings have original chimney-stacks and exposed ceiling-beams.

Condition—Good or fairly good, unless noted.

ᵃ(4). *Church Farm*, house, N. of the church, has a cross-wing at the E. end. The upper storey projects at the S. end of the cross-wing. The porch on the S. side is of two storeys and has an original bressumer carved with leaf ornament.

ᵃ(5). *Broomhouse* (Plate, p. xxxi), 1,100 yards N.N.W. of the church, was built probably early in the 16th century, with cross-wings on the E. and W. The upper storey projects at the S. end of the E. cross-wing.

ᵃ(6). *House*, now two tenements, about ½ m. S.W. of the church, was built probably in the 16th century with cross-wings on the E. and W. The upper storey projects at the S. end of the E. cross-wing and the timber-framing is exposed at each end of the house.

LAWFORD : PARISH CHURCH OF ST. MARY ; 14th-century.
Sedilia, etc., South Side of Chancel.

LAWFORD : PARISH CHURCH OF ST. MARY ; 14th-century.
North Wall of Chancel.

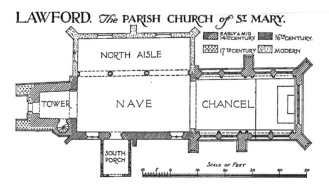

LAWFORD. *The* PARISH CHURCH *of* S.^T MARY.

NORTH AISLE

TOWER   NAVE   CHANCEL

SOUTH PORCH

EARLY & MID 14.TH CENTURY.   16.TH CENTURY.
17.TH CENTURY   MODERN

SCALE OF FEET

a(7). *Glebe Farm*, house, ½ m. S.S.W. of the church, was built probably in the 16th century with a cross-wing at the S. end. The upper storey projects at the E. end of the cross-wing.

a(8). *Priory Farm*, house, ¼ m. S.S.W. of (7), has a cross-wing at the W. end.

a(9). *Cottage*, 120 yards S.W. of (8), was built in the 16th century with a cross-wing at the W. end. The upper storey projects at the S. end of the cross-wing. Inside the building the roof has cambered tie-beams with curved braces.
Condition—Ruinous.

b(10). *Langford Hall*, about ¼ m. S. of (9), was built probably in the 16th century. The upper storey projects on the S. and W. sides and has a moulded diagonal angle-bracket.

a(11). *Hill Farm*, house, about 1¼ m. S.W. of the church, is of L-shaped plan with the wings extending towards the E. and S. The original chimney-stack has two octagonal shafts. Inside the building is some original panelling and a fire-place with a richly carved overmantel with two arcaded panels and flanking pilasters. There are three old panelled doors.

a(12). *Wybourne*, house, 600 yards S.E. of (11), was built early in the 16th century and is of L-shaped plan with the wings extending towards the E. and S. The upper storey formerly projected at the E. end. Inside the building are some shaped wall-posts and an original cambered tie-beam.

b(13). *House*, now two tenements, 350 yards S. of (12).

b(14). *House*, now two tenements, W. of (13).

b(15). *House*, now two tenements, at Langham Moor and 750 yards S.W. of (14).

b(16). *Chaplin's Farm*, house, 90 yards N.W. of (15), has a S. wing of 16th-century date. The main block is of the 17th century.

b(17). *Woodhouse Farm*, house, 170 yards S.S.W. of (16).

b(18). *Langham Lodge Farm*, house, nearly 1 m. S. of (17). The upper storey projects on one side.

---

51. LAWFORD.   (E.b.)

(O.S. 6 in. xix. S.E.)

Lawford is a parish on the S. bank of the Stour and 7 m. N.E. of Colchester. The church and Lawford Hall are the principal monuments.

Ecclesiastical :—

(1). PARISH CHURCH OF ST. MARY (Plate, p. 149) stands near the N. end of the parish. The walls are of flint and stone-rubble, septaria and brick ; the dressings are of limestone ; the roofs are covered with tiles and slates. The *Nave* was built at the beginning of the 14th century and about the middle of the same century the *Chancel* was rebuilt and the *South Porch* added. The *West Tower* is perhaps of the same period, but was extensively altered and the tower-arch rebuilt early in the 16th century ; it was again repaired late in the 17th century. The *North Aisle* was added in 1826 and the church has since been restored and the chancel-arch rebuilt.

The chancel is a remarkably rich example of 14th-century work and the woodwork of the S. porch is also noteworthy.

Architectural Description—The *Chancel* (36½ ft. by 20 ft.) is of mid 14th-century date. It has a moulded plinth and the walls below the window sills are faced with brick and flint chequer-work. The S.E. and S.W. buttresses were each enriched with two niches with trefoiled ogee and crocketed heads and side shafts with pinnacles ; the upper niche in the S.W. buttress has lost its head. The

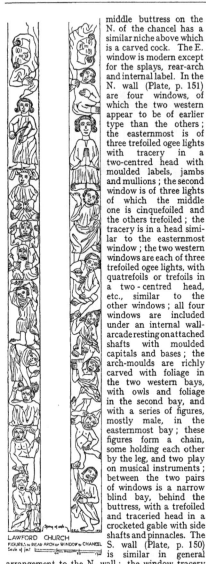

LAWFORD CHURCH
FIGURES IN REAR ARCH OF WINDOW IN CHANCEL
Scale of feet

middle buttress on the N. of the chancel has a similar niche above which is a carved cock. The E. window is modern except for the splays, rear-arch and internal label. In the N. wall (Plate, p. 151) are four windows, of which the two western appear to be of earlier type than the others; the easternmost is of three trefoiled ogee lights with tracery in a two-centred head with moulded labels, jambs and mullions; the second window is of three lights of which the middle one is cinquefoiled and the others trefoiled; the tracery is in a head similar to the easternmost window; the two western windows are each of three trefoiled ogee lights, with quatrefoils or trefoils in a two-centred head, etc., similar to the other windows; all four windows are included under an internal wall-arcade resting on attached shafts with moulded capitals and bases; the arch-moulds are richly carved with foliage in the two western bays, with owls and foliage in the second bay, and with a series of figures, mostly male, in the easternmost bay; these figures form a chain, some holding each other by the leg, and two play on musical instruments; between the two pairs of windows is a narrow blind bay, behind the buttress, with a trefoiled and traceried head in a crocketed gable with side shafts and pinnacles. The S. wall (Plate, p. 150) is similar in general arrangement to the N. wall; the window tracery varying in each case; each window is of three trefoiled lights, except the westernmost, which is of three cinquefoiled lights; the wall arcade has arch-moulds carved in foliage, fruit, birds and squirrels; below the second window is a door-way with moulded jambs and two-centred arch carved with diaper ornament and a moulded label carved with running foliage; the rear-arch is in range with the sedilia (see Fittings). The chancel-arch is modern.

The *Nave* (41½ ft. by 20½ ft.) has a modern N. arcade. In the S. wall are two windows both of early 14th-century date with an 18th-century wooden frame and mullion in a two-centred head with a moulded label; between them is the late 14th-century S. doorway with moulded jambs, two-centred arch and label with defaced head-stops

The *West Tower* (11 ft. by 9 ft.) is of three stages and is much repaired, if not largely rebuilt, with 17th-century brick. The early 16th-century brick tower-arch is two-centred and of two chamfered orders, the outer continuous and the inner resting on attached shafts with moulded capitals and modern corbels. The W. window and doorway are modern. On the outer face of the N. wall are remains of a window design, in pudding-stone with flint-inlay. The second stage has in the E. wall an opening into the roof; in the N. wall is a broken quatrefoiled window of early 16th-century date and of brick. The bell-chamber has in each wall a late 17th-century brick window of two square-headed lights.

The *South Porch* is of mid 14th-century date and of timber-framing on dwarf rubble walls. The outer archway is modern but flanking it are a pair of lights with cinquefoiled ogee heads and traceried spandrels. The side walls are partly plastered externally and each consist of three bays, each bay containing three cinquefoiled lights (Plate, p. 133) with more or less elaborate tracery above them; the N.E. bay has lost its lights and tracery and the middle bay on both sides its mullions.

The *Roof* of the S. porch is of the 14th century and is flat and divided into twelve square bays by moulded ribs with round bosses at the intersections, all defaced except two which have a face and a rosette respectively.

Fittings— *Bells:* three; 1st by Miles Graye, 1667; 3rd by John Thornton, 1714. *Communion Table:* In N. aisle—with turned legs, fluted top rail and carved brackets, early 17th-century. *Cupboard:* In tower—in N. wall of second stage, rectangular with slots for shelves, 17th-century. *Door:* In turret staircase to tower, of one piece with strap-hinges, early 16th-century. *Glass:* In chancel—in N.E. window, fragments of tabernacle work, etc.; in tracery of second N. window, trefoil with geometrical roundel, vine leaves and border, *in situ;* in third window, fragments only; in N.W. window, in tracery a considerable amount of oak leaf and acorn designs with borders, *in situ,* in heads of lights fragments of tabernacle work;

in S.E. window and third S. window, fragments of foliage ; in S.W. window, oak leaf and acorn design, with fragment of tabernacle work, sun, rosettes, etc. ; all 14th-century. *Monuments* and *Floor-slabs.* Monuments : In chancel—on N. wall, (1) of Edward Waldegrave, 1584, and Johan (Ackworth), his wife, alabaster and marble wall-monument, with kneeling figures of man in armour and wife, in arched recesses, divided and flanked by Corinthian columns supporting an entablature, cresting and three shields of arms. In churchyard —S. of chancel, (2) to John Edes, 16(5)8, slab on modern base. Floor-slabs : In chancel—(1) to Sarah (Bingham), wife of Edward Waldegrave, 1634 ; (2) to Thomas Harris, 1699, rector of the parish, with achievement of arms ; (3) to Edward Waldegrave, 1621. *Niches :* In chancel—flanking E. window, two, modern, but incorporating moulded jambs and bases, 14th-century. On S.W. buttress of nave—with cinquefoiled head, 15th-century. See also Architectural Description *under* Chancel. *Piscina* and *Sedilia :* In chancel—in one range, with rear-arch of doorway, piscina and three bays of sedilia divided by square piers with diapered faces and attached shafts with moulded and foliated capitals and moulded bases, cinquefoiled ogee heads with moulded and crocketed labels and finials carved on front of horizontal moulded string-course ; piers or buttresses between bays, carried up as pinnacles also crocketed and finialed, moulded ogee rear-arch of doorway similarly treated ; the spandrels are carved with vine and oak leaves and have a series of figures in high relief playing musical instruments, one in each spandrel ; the spandrels of the doorway have each a large crowned head and a number of much mutilated smaller figures ; the string-course is carved with grotesque beasts and heads, round drain to piscina, all mid 14th-century. *Plate :* includes cup and cover-paten of 1663 and a paten of 1695 given in 1696. *Stoup :* In S. porch—with moulded jambs and cinquefoiled head, broken bowl, late 14th-century. *Sundial :* On middle S. buttress of nave, scratched dial.

Condition—Good, except tower.

Secular :—

(2). LAWFORD HALL, 300 yards N.N.W. of the church, is of two storeys, partly timber-framed and plastered and partly of brick ; the roofs are tiled. It was built *c.* 1580 on an H-shaped plan, with the cross-wings at the E. and W. ends. The S. front was entirely refaced about the middle of the 18th century. The upper storey projects at the N. ends of the cross-wings with original moulded bressumers; the projection of the E. wing has moulded brackets. In the N. part of both wings are some original windows with moulded oak mullions ; that at the end of the W. wing is of five transomed lights, and, reused as a sill, is an original moulded bressumer

carved with griffons, etc., and two shields with the initials A. and C.B. Two of the chimney-stacks are original and have octagonal shafts, more or less rebuilt and moulded bases ; at the back of the main block is a stack with 17th-century grouped hexagonal shafts.

Inside the building is some 17th-century panelling and an original doorway with a moulded frame. Reset in two windows on the N. of the main block is a collection of stained glass roundels and shields, including (*a*) royal arms within a crowned wreath, and crowned initials E.R., 16th-century ; (*b*) two quartered coats of Bowyer, one dated 1596, and Bowyer impaling Brabant, dated 1599 ; (*c*) quartered coats of Fifield, one dated 1599 ; (*d*) quartered coat of Bulstrode, late 16th-century ; (*e*) figure of a coped bishop with inscription Scs Rycarde, probably St. Richard of Chichester, late 15th-century ; (*f*) 16th-century roundels of foreign glass, including a shield dated 1547 ; armorial device of the Imperial City of Fribourg with other towns ; angel with a shield dated 1541 ; group of women playing instruments ; St. John ; and St. Quirinus (Plate, p. 192).

Condition—Good, much altered.

(3). DALE HALL, nearly ½ m. E. of the church, is of two storeys ; the walls are of brick and plastered timber-framing ; the roofs are tiled. It was built late in the 17th century, with cross-wings at the E. and W. ends. The S. front is of brick, with a band between the storeys. Inside the building are original ceiling-beams and some exposed timber-framing.

Condition—Good.

MONUMENTS (4–9).

The following monuments, unless otherwise described, are of the 17th century and of two storeys, timber-framed and plastered ; the roofs are tiled or thatched. Some of the buildings have original chimney-stacks and exposed ceiling-beams.

Condition—Good or fairly good.

(4). *Cottage,* at S.W. corner of churchyard, has been mostly refaced with brick.

(5). *Cottage,* now two tenements, on S. side of Mill Hill, 1,100 yards W. of the church.

(6). *House,* now three tenements, on S. side of road in W. outskirts of Manningtree and about 1 m. E.N.E. of the church, was built probably in the 15th century with the cross-wings at the N. and S. ends. Inside the building are original cambered tie-beams with curved braces.

(7). *House,* now four tenements, on W. side of road, 30 yards S. of (6), was built probably in the 16th century and has an early 17th-century extension on the N.

(8). *House,* now three tenements, 30 yards E. of (6), was built probably early in the 16th century.

There is a 17th-century extension at the E. end. The upper storey formerly projected on the N. front, but has been underbuilt. Inside the building is an original doorway with a four-centred head. The middle room has original moulded joists and ceiling-beams and the roof has a king-post truss.

(9). *House*, now five tenements, 40 yards E. of (8), was built in the 16th century. There are late 17th-century additions on the E. and S. The timber-framing is exposed on the W. side.

52. LAYER BRETON. (C. d.)

(O.S. 6 in. xxxvi. S.W.)

Layer Breton is a small parish 5½ m. S.W. of Colchester.

Ecclesiastical :—

(1). PARISH CHURCH OF ST. MARY has recently been pulled down, but the traces of foundations indicate a building about 46 ft. by 25 ft. Lying on the site are various worked and moulded stones of the 15th century, including the greater part of one window of two cinquefoiled lights in a square head with a moulded label.

Secular :—

HOMESTEAD MOATS.

(2). At Stamp's Farm, 1 m. N.N.W. of the site of the church.

(3). At Whitehouse Grove, 100 yards E.N.E. of the site of the church.

(4). COTTAGE, 130 yards S.S.E. of (2), is of two storeys, timber-framed and weather-boarded ; the roofs are tiled. It was built in the 16th century and the upper storey projects on the N.E. side. Inside the building are exposed ceiling-beams. Condition—Good.

(5). ST. CATHERINE'S COLLEGE FARM, house, about ¼ m. S. of (2), is of two storeys, timber-framed, partly plastered and partly weather-boarded ; the roofs are tiled. It was built late in the 16th or early in the 17th century. The upper storey projects at the E and W. ends. Condition—Good.

53. LAYER DE LA HAYE. (C.d.)

(O.S. 6 in. xxxvi. N.E.)

Layer de la Haye is a parish and small village 4 m. S.W. of Colchester. The church is interesting.

Ecclesiastical :—

(1). PARISH CHURCH (dedication unknown)stands near the middle of the parish. The walls are of mixed rubble and septaria, with dressings of lime-stone ; the roofs are tiled. The S.E. angle of the nave is of the 12th century and the *Chancel* from its

form and the absence of buttresses is probably also of early date, but all definite evidence is concealed by cement. The *Nave* was rebuilt *c*. 1350 and the *West Tower* and *North Porch* added about the middle of the same century. The chancel-arch was built in the 15th century. The church was restored in the 19th century, when the *South Aisle* was added and the N. wall of the nave refaced or rebuilt.

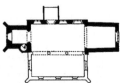

Architectural Description—The *Chancel* (21 ft. by 15½ ft.) has an E. window, all modern except the two-centred rear-arch. In the S. wall are two blocked windows, but in both cases the head has been destroyed and they are of uncertain date. The 15th-century chancel-arch is two-centred and of two hollow-chamfered orders, the outer continuous and the inner carried down as a plain chamfer on to the hollow-chamfered base.

The *Nave* (39½ ft. by 21 ft.) has S.E. quoins of Roman brick. In the N. wall are three windows ; the easternmost is modern and the two western are of the 14th century, partly restored, and each of two trefoiled ogee lights with a quatrefoil in a two-centred head with a moulded label ; between these two windows is the modern N. doorway. The S. arcade is modern.

The *West Tower* (11¼ ft. by 10 ft.) is of *c*. 1350 and of three stages with an embattled parapet. The two-centred tower-arch is of two continuous chamfered orders, hollow in the arch and plain in the responds, with hollow-chamfered bases. In the S. wall is a doorway to the stair-turret, with chamfered jambs and two-centred arch ; a blocked doorway of similar form and at a higher level indicates the former existence of a gallery. The W. window is of two cinquefoiled lights with a quatrefoil in a two-centred head with a moulded label. The second stage has in both the N. and W. walls a window of one trefoiled light in a square head with a moulded label. The bell-chamber has in each wall a similar window, but of two lights.

The *North Porch* is timber-framed, the outer archway being formed with a cambered tie-beam and two curved braces ; the gable has mid 14th-century trefoiled and sub-cusped barge-boards, the top main cusp being of ogee form.

The *Roof* of the nave is of trussed-rafter type and probably of the 14th century. The roof of the N. porch has moulded wall-plates and chamfered tie-beams of the 14th century.

LAYER MARNEY : THE PARISH CHURCH AND THE HALL FROM THE SOUTH.

Painting on North Wall of Nave ; early 16th-century.

West Tower and South Porch ; early 16th-century.

LAYER MARNEY : PARISH CHURCH OF ST. MARY.

Fittings—*Bells :* five ; 1st by Miles Graye, 1673 ; 2nd by Johanna Sturdy, inscribed "In Multis Annis Resonet Campana Johannis I.S.," mid 15th-century ; 3rd by Miles Graye, 1622. Bell-frame, probably 15th-century. *Monument :* In chancel—against N. wall, altar-tomb of Purbeck marble with moulded edge and plinth, defaced panelling in front, recessed canopy with coved and quatrefoiled vault, flanked by attached shafts and surmounted by a frieze with a band of quatrefoils and carved cresting, early 16th-century. *Piscina :* In chancel—with hollow-chamfered jambs and tre-foiled head, round drain, 15th-century. *Plate :* includes a late 16th-century cup with a band of incised ornament and a stem probably of later date ; the late 16th-century cover-paten has the sacred monogram.

Condition—Fairly good, but some ivy on tower.

Secular :—

(2). HOMESTEAD MOAT, at Rye Farm, ½ m. E.N.E. of the church.

(3). BLIND KNIGHTS, house, about ¾ m. E. of the church, is of two storeys, timber-framed and plastered ; the roofs are tiled. It was built possibly in the 15th or early in the 16th century, with a cross-wing at the W. end and later additions beyond it. The upper storey projects on the N. side of the original building and some of the timber-framing is exposed.

Condition—Fairly good.

(4). GREAT HOUSE FARM, house, about ¾ m. N.E. of the church, is of two storeys, timber-framed and faced with modern brick ; the roofs are tiled. It was built in the 15th century, with a central hall and cross-wings at the E. and W. ends. Inside the building are some exposed ceiling-beams and the W. wing has an original roof with a king-post truss.

Condition—Good.

(5). COTTAGE, on S. side of road, 1,200 yards N. of the church. It is of two storeys, timber-framed and plastered ; the roofs are thatched. It was built early in the 17th century and has exposed timber-framing inside the building.

Condition—Good.

(6). COTTAGE, two tenements, ½ m. N.E. of (5), is of two storeys, timber-framed and plastered ; the roofs are tiled. It was built early in the 16th century, with a cross-wing at the W. end. Inside the building the timber-framing and ceiling-beams are exposed.

Condition—Poor.

———

54. LAYER MARNEY. (C.d.)

(O.S. 6 in. [a]xxv. S.E. [b]xxxvi. S.W.)

Layer Marney is a parish 6½ m. S.W. of Colchester. The church and Layer Marney Towers (Plate, p. 154) are both important monuments.

Ecclesiastical :—

[b](1). PARISH CHURCH OF ST. MARY (Plate, p. 156) stands about the middle of the parish. The walls are of plastered brick, with dressings of limestone and brick ; the roofs are tiled. The whole building consisting of *Chancel* with *South Porch, Nave* with *South Porch, West Tower, North Chapel* and *North Aisle* with *Priest's Lodging*, was built during the first quarter of the 16th century ; the chapel and aisle being added probably *c.* 1525.

The church is a good example of Tudor brick-work and among the fittings the monuments, especially those of the early Renaissance, and the paintings are noteworthy.

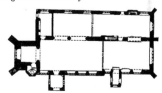

Architectural Description—The walls have embattled parapets and moulded plinths ; the details where unrestored are all of early 16th-century date.

The *Chancel* (35½ ft. by 21ft.) has a partly restored E. window of stone and of five trefoiled ogee and transomed lights with vertical tracery in a four-centred head with a moulded label and shield stops ; the jambs are moulded ; the base of the window has a stepped filling for a former reredos ; below the internal sill is a moulded and embattled string-course, returned a short distance along the side walls ; the E. gable has a crow-stepped parapet. In the N. wall is a plastered segmental arch containing monument (5) ; further W. is a doorway with chamfered jambs and four-centred head ; W. of the doorway is a window of one trefoiled light lighting the rood-loft staircase. In the S. wall are three windows ; the two eastern are partly restored and each of three cinquefoiled and transomed lights in a four-centred head with a moulded label ; the rear-arch is of three chamfered orders ; the westernmost window is much restored and is of two cinquefoiled lights in a square head with a moulded label ; E. of it is an opening to the S. porch, now used as an organ chamber.

The *North Chapel* (44¼ ft. by 16½ ft.) has an E. window similar to the S.E. windows in the chancel, but with a plain rear-arch. In the N. wall are two windows, the eastern is probably of the 18th century with some reused 16th-century work ; the western window is of brick and of three four-centred and transomed lights in a four-centred head with a moulded label ; the head and mullions have been rebuilt ; W. of the eastern window is an external projection with a crow-stepped head and enclosing a recess, said to be a fireplace, but now plastered over ; further W. is a doorway with moulded jambs, four-centred arch and label. In the S. wall, W. of the doorway is a second doorway to the rood-loft staircase, with rebated jambs and four-centred head ; the staircase is set in a projection with a stepped head.

The *Nave* (46¼ ft. by 22½ ft.) has a N. arcade of two bays with four-centred arches of three moulded orders and moulded labels on both sides and a shield stop on the S. side above the column ; the column is an irregular octagon on plan, with moulded capital and base and fluted faces to the shaft ; the responds have attached half columns ; E. of the arcade is the upper doorway to the rood-loft staircase, with a four-centred head ; W. of the arcade is a doorway to the priest's lodging with chamfered jambs and four-centred head. In the S. wall are four windows each of three four-centred and transomed lights in a four-centred head with moulded jambs, mullions and label ; between the two western windows is the S. door way with moulded jambs, four-centred arch and label ; the jambs have a moulded plinth.

The *North Aisle* (16¼ ft. wide) has in the N. wall two windows uniform with the N.W. window in the N. chapel, but not rebuilt.

The *Priest's Chamber* at the W. end of the N. aisle has in the N. wall a window uniform with those in the N. aisle. In the W. wall is a restored doorway with a four-centred head and moulded label ; further S. is a fireplace, now blocked, and a recess set in a projection with a stepped external head, terminating in an octagonal chimney-shaft with moulded capping and base.

The *West Tower* (11¼ ft. square) is of three stages (Plate, p. 155) and of unplastered red brick, with black brick diapering with an embattled parapet having pierced water-chutes. The plastered tower-arch is four-centred and of three orders, two chamfered and one moulded, with a moulded label ; the semi-octagonal responds have moulded capitals and bases. The partly restored W. window is of brick and of three transomed and four-centred lights with intersecting tracery in a four-centred head with moulded jambs and label. The second stage has in the N. wall a window of one four-centred light with a moulded label ; at the N.E. angle is a splayed projection or corbelling enclosing a gangway to the roof of the N. aisle. In the W. wall is a partly restored brick window of two four-centred lights in a four-centred head with a moulded label. The bell-chamber has in each

wall a window similar to that just described but with a transom.

The *South Porch* of the *Chancel* (Plate, p. xxix) is now used as an organ chamber and has E. and W. archways, the western now blocked ; each archway has moulded jambs, four-centred arch and label, and is set in a slight projection with a moulded and crow-stepped capping. In the S. wall is a window of two four-centred lights in a four-centred head and with moulded jambs and label.

The *South Porch* of the *Nave* has a moulded and four-centred outer archway of brick, with double-chamfered responds having moulded capitals and bases ; above the archway is a projecting niche with a four-centred head and a coved soffit. The side walls have each a window of three transomed and four-centred lights with moulded jambs and label.

The *Roof* of the chancel is of four bays with moulded principals and moulded and braced collars ; the middle principal has short hammer-beams. The flat roof of the N. chapel has moulded wall-plates and main timbers dividing it into square panels. The roof of the nave is similar to that of the chancel, but there are no hammer-beams.

Fittings—*Altar :* see Monument (6). *Bells :* three ; 1st uninscribed, but probably late 14th or early 15th-century ; 3rd by John Thornton, 1711. Bell-frame, probably 16th-century. *Brasses :* see Monument (3). *Chair* (Plate, p. 157): In chancel—with turned front legs, carved and panelled back and shaped arms and cresting, mid 17th-century. *Chest :* In N. aisle—large iron-bound, with two locks, 14th or 15th-century. *Communion Table :* With turned legs, mid 17th-century, top modern. *Doors :* In S. doorway—of overlapping nail-studded battens, with strap-hinges and grip-latch, early 16th-century. In door-way to priest's chamber—similar, but without latch, early 16th-century. *Glass* (Plate, p. 192) : In N. chapel—in E. window, four shields of arms, (*a*) with the garter and Marney—*gules a leopard rampant argent,* quartering Sergeaux and Venables ; (*b*) the quartered coat of Marney impaling Arundel —*sable six swallows argent,* quartering Chideock and Carminow, with supporters and wreath ; (*c*) similar to (*b*), but without supporters and with a garter surrounding it ; (*d*) a mutilated shield of Radcliffe—*argent a bend engrailed sable,* quartering two destroyed coats, and *barry gules and argent,* and encircled by the garter ; also several quarries with a wing, the Marney badge, all early 16th-century ; hanging loose, small panel of foreign glass with figure of St. Peter, 16th-century. *Monuments :* In chancel—on N. wall, (1) to John and William Bridge, 1674, white marble tablet with cornice and corbelled base ; (2) to Nicholas Corsellis, 1674, marble wall-monument with Ionic side columns, cornice, pedestal and achievement of arms ; against S. wall, (3) to

LAYER MARNEY: PARISH CHURCH OF ST. MARY; early 16th-century.
Interior, showing original Roofs, Wall Painting, etc., and Screen; 15th-century.

LAYER MARNEY : PARISH CHURCH OF ST. MARY.
Monument to Henry, Lord Marney, K.G., 1523.

Robert Cammocke, 1585, and Elizabeth (Badby) and Mary (Everton), his wives, also to Thomas, his son, and Ursula (Wyrley), and the daughter of Robert, Lord Riche, his wives, altar-tomb with plain slab and flat classic canopy on two Doric columns, at back inscription and three shields of arms on brass plates. In N. chapel—in middle, (4) probably of Sir William Marney, c. 1360, alabaster tomb (Plate, p. 158) with moulded top and plinth, sides and ends with elaborate cusped panelling in squares each with a blank shield; effigy (Plate, p. 159) in armour with bascinet, camail, jupon with the arms of Marney, hip-belt and remains of sword and dagger, head of helm with crest of a hat between two wings, and feet on lion, front band of bascinet inscribed " Ihs nazarenus " ; round tomb, six oak posts spirally reeded (except one), and with moulded capitals and bases and supporting seated leopards holding shields, one with the arms of Marney and the rest with the Marney badge, early 16th-century. Under arch between chapel and chancel, (5) of Henry, Lord Marney, K.G., 1523, Lord Privy Seal, etc., altar-tomb (Plates, pp 157, 158), effigy and canopy of terra-cotta and touch, altar-tomb of terra-cotta with four square panels on each side enriched with egg and tongue and acanthus ornament and divided by enriched Renaissance shafts supporting the slab, each panel with a gartered shield of the arms of Marney impaling Venables ; below each panel on the S. side a deeply cut quatrefoil in a square panel ; slab of touch with moulded edge and on it recumbent effigy (Plate, p. 159), of touch of man in armour of the period with bare head, long mantle, tabard of the arms of Marney quartering Sergeaux and Venables, garter on left leg and feet on lion ; flat-topped canopy of terra-cotta flanked by outer shafts terminating in Composite capitals and surmounted by vases and inner shafts with enriched baluster ornament and Composite capitals supporting an enriched entablature carried across the width of the monument, the end walls of which are carved and divided into two panels by another shaft uniform with the inner shafts just described ; from the entablature springs the canopy proper, divided into four bays by pilasters terminating in Composite pendants and forming part of a continuous main entablature with rich Italian decoration ; above are two segmental pediments enclosing a shield and surmounted by richly carved and foliated cresting ; the soffit of the canopy has moulded trabeations and richly carved panels. In middle of W. part of chapel, (6) of John, 2nd Lord Marney, 1525, altar-tomb and altar of terra-cotta with slabs and effigy of touch ; altar-tomb with square panels at sides and end with pilasters and enrichments similar to panels on monument (5) and each enclosing a shield of Marney impaling Venables and surrounded

by a wreath ; slab of touch with moulded edge and effigy of the same material and almost a replica of that on monument (4) but without the garter ; altar across W. end of tomb with pilasters, panels, shields, etc., all similar to those on altar-tomb and with a modern slab of touch. Painting : In nave —on N. wall, rectangular panel with large figure of St. Christopher (Plate, p. 155) bearing the Christ and holding a ragged staff in his right hand ; he is dressed in hose, tunic and cloak ; background of river and rocks with small figure of fisherman ; traces of foliage in the top W. corner, early 16th-century. Piscinae : In chancel—with moulded jambs and four-centred arch in a square head, square drain, early 16th-century. In N. chapel— in wall, with chamfered jambs and four-centred head, oak shelf, early 16th-century. Pulpit : semi-octagonal and made up of early 16th and 17th - century woodwork, including linen - fold panels, upper and middle moulded rails with running foliage ornament and upper rail with the Marney badge, carved 17th-century bookboard ; sounding-board with panelled soffit, jewel ornament dentilled cornice, acorn pendants, mid 17th - century. Screens : Between chancel and nave (Plate, p. 156)—with central doorway and six bays on each side, moulded posts and mullions, doorway with four - centred head and traceried spandrels, side bays each with trefoiled and sub-cusped head and tracery, close lower panels 15th-century, partly restored, cornice modern. Between chapel and aisle—of twelve bays two forming the doorway and all with moulded posts and rail, plain lights with an iron stancheon, close lower panels with linen-fold ornament, moulded head-beam with diaper ornament, early 16th-century. Seating : In nave—some pews incorporate early 16th-century linen-fold panelling, early 17th-century panelling and 16th-century moulded rails. Stoup : In S. porch—recess with four-centred head, early 16th-century, basin destroyed. Miscellanea : In N. chapel and aisle— various worked stones, including 12th-century cheveron and billet ornament and fragments of 16th-century terra-cotta.

Condition—Fairly good, but unsatisfactory foundations tend to render the structure insecure.

Secular :—

b(2). LAYER MARNEY TOWERS or HALL (Plates, Frontispiece and p. 160), N.E. of the church, is generally of two storeys with a gatehouse of three storeys. The walls are of brick, with terra-cotta dressings to the gatehouse ; the roofs are tiled. The house was begun early in the 16th century by Henry, 1st Lord Marney, but at the time of his death in 1523, and that of his son in 1524, the building was probably incomplete, and it has never since been finished. It has been restored in the

20th century, when the gap between the gatehouse and the E. wing was filled in. A short N. wing is also modern and the barn has been rebuilt.

The gatehouse is a valuable example of early Renaissance ornament and the roof of the long gallery is interesting.

The house appears to have been designed on the courtyard plan with an irregular outer court on the S. side. Of this the S. range of the main courtyard and the three sides of the outer court remain standing.

Elevations—The S. Elevation of the main block consists of the great gatehouse with a short wing on the W. and a long wing on the E. The gatehouse is of three storeys and is flanked by semi-octagonal towers, each of eight stages; the walls have diapering in black bricks and stand on a moulded plinth. The outer archway has moulded jambs and four-centred arch with traces of a square label; between the two lower storeys is a band of cusped panelling continued round the turrets and much broken away; the two upper storeys have each a large window of five transomed and trefoiled lights of terra-cotta with a moulded label; the mullions and transoms are enriched with moulded Italian ornament and the mullions have Corinthian capitals; the trefoiled heads are formed of Renaissance scroll work with winged *putti* in the spandrels; the parapet has a series of segmental pediments with radiating panels and moulded and shaped terminals. The side turrets have angle-pilasters and are divided into four main storeys by bands of cusped panelling, and each face of the eight stages has a window with a four-centred head; windows in alternate stages have moulded labels; the turrets are finished with a trefoiled corbel-table with a cresting similar to that of the main building but retaining a pair of conventional dolphins to each pediment; the cresting of the E. turret is much damaged. The terminals have each a true lover's knot and the initials M Ɔ. Flanking the outer sides of these turrets are two subsidiary turrets, each seven stages high, but otherwise similar to the main turrets and with windows only in the S. face of the W. turret and two faces of the E. turret. The return walls of the gatehouse have trefoiled corbel-tables and some original windows above the adjoining roofs. The W. wing has in the ground storey three windows and a doorway covered with modern cement. The upper storey has four transomed windows, two of four and two of two lights; they are similar in character to the main windows of the gatehouse, but have no *putti* in the spandrels. In the middle dividing these windows are two small lights with four-centred heads. The E. wing has a modern building adjoining the gatehouse. The remainder of the wing has a moulded band between the storeys. The westernmost bay of the old work is gabled and has a moulded plinth; the lower

storey has a window of three four-centred lights with a square moulded label continued as a string-course; the upper window is set in a projection with a corbelled and moulded head; the window is of three four-centred lights in a four-centred head with a moulded label, voluted stops and spandrels ornamented with shields bearing the initial H. and a device of doubtful meaning. The rest of the wing has in the upper storey several original two-light windows and an original doorway with a four-centred head and a moulded label; the projecting chimney-stack has tabled offsets and the moulded base of an original shaft.

The N. Elevation of the main block. The gatehouse has moulded string-courses between storeys, an embattled parapet and square turrets at the angles with trefoiled corbel-tables and traces of former cresting. The inner archway of the gatehouse is set in a projection with a square moulded head and has moulded jambs and a four-centred arch. The two main windows above it are similar to those in the S. face of the gatehouse. The turrets have each seven two-light windows in the return walls. The gatehouse has six chimney-shafts (Plate, p. 176) all with moulded bases and above these four have been rebuilt, but the other two have spiral flutings and moulded caps with spurs. The W. wing (Plate, p. 176), has trefoiled corbelling between the storeys; the three lower windows are each of two four-centred lights in a four-centred head with a moulded label; they are covered largely with cement; further E. is a doorway with moulded jambs and a four-centred arch with a square moulded label. The three upper windows are each of three lights and are similar to the corresponding windows on the S. side of this wing. The end of this range is covered by the modern wing. The E. wing beyond the modern block has several original windows and doorways of stone in the lower storey and four original windows of brick in the upper storey; these are each of two four-centred lights with a square moulded label; one is now blocked. A short distance from the E. end is a stepped gable wall with a chimney-stack at the apex resting on trefoiled corbelling and having the bases of two shafts.

The W. End of the main block has a crow-stepped gable with a moulded coping and some original windows of brick with four-centred lights and two with moulded labels; the top window has a projecting brick sill. This wing has the bases of two original chimney-stacks.

The Outer Court is bounded on the N. by the E. wing described above, on the E. by a large modern barn incorporating much old timbering and on the S. by the 'Gallery' range. This building is of brick and of two storeys with diapering in black bricks. The N. side has a number of original doorways of stone with four-centred heads; in the upper storey are nine original windows with

LAYER MARNEY : PARISH CHURCH OF ST. MARY.

North Chapel, showing Monuments to Sir William Marney, c. 1360, and Lord Marney, K.G., 1523.

Effigy of Sir William Marney ; *c.* 1360.

Effigy of Henry, Lord Marney, K.G., 1523.

LAYER MARNEY: PARISH CHURCH OF ST. MARY.

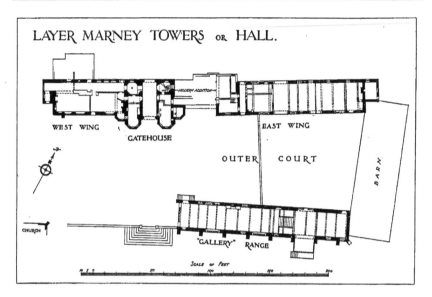

moulded labels. The S. side is divided into eight bays by buttresses of three stages. There are remains of several original windows. The E. end has an original doorway with a four-centred head and now blocked. The W. end has a crow-stepped gable. At the S.W. angle are traces of the moulded jamb of a former window showing that the range extended further W.

Interior—The main block contains many original doorways with moulded or chamfered jambs and four-centred arches. The eastern room in the W. wing has a fireplace made up of original moulded oak jambs and four-centred head; the mantel-shelf incorporates a 17th-century carved cornice. The western room has a 17th-century marble fireplace of foreign work, with terminal pilasters, consoles, carved frieze and shelf. In the passage N. of this room is a fireplace (Plate, p. xxxiii) with an overmantel incorporating early 17th-century woodwork including two terminal figures, carved frieze, consoles, etc. All the above rooms have panelling partly of the 16th century and partly modern. A room in the modern wing has a reset original fireplace (Plate, p. xxxiii) of terra-cotta; it has enriched Corinthian pilasters, acanthus consoles and an enriched entablature. On the first floor the room adjoining the S.W. turret of the gatehouse has an original fireplace with moulded jambs and four-centred arch in a square head; the spandrels are carved with

shields and vine ornament. Two rooms in the W. wing have stone fireplaces of similar character, but different detail to that just described. These rooms also retain original plaster ceilings with moulded ribs, in one room forming a geometrical pattern and in the other a similar design of inter-secting lines. The W. wing has the main timbers of the roof exposed. The E. wing has at the E. end on the ground floor a large fireplace with a four-centred arch surmounted by a moulded horizontal set-back; adjoining it on the S. is a large recess now communicating with the fireplace by a modern arch. The first floor is divided into two main rooms, each with an original roof of five and four bays respectively; the trusses have arched principals and above the collar-beams are scissor-shaped braces; the purlins have wind-braces of ogee form. The gallery range has an original open roof (Plate, p. 161) of similar character to that just described. In the N. wall of the main room is a modern fireplace with an overmantel made up of mid or late 17th-century material and divided into five bays with a carved and arched panel in the middle and diminishing pilasters enriched with jewel ornament.

Condition—Good.

[b](3). DUKE'S FARM, house and moat, about ½ m. N.N.E. of the church. The *House* is of two storeys with attics; the walls are of brick and the roofs are tiled. The W. cross-wing was built in the

second half of the 16th century but the main block was rebuilt in the 17th century. There are modern additions on the N. side. The original wing has a moulded string-course and a splayed plinth. The two windows at the S. end are each of five transomed lights with moulded jambs and mullions of brick. The return walls have similar windows but of a single light each. The entrance has a 17th-century nail-studded door with moulded ribs. Inside the building is a considerable quantity of early 17th-century panelling and some original moulded beams. On the first floor one room has an original fireplace with a moulded and four-centred head. In the S. window is some late 16th-century glass with a Tudor rose and the initials E.R. On this floor are some 17th-century doors with cock's head hinges.

The *Moat* is fragmentary.

Condition—Of house, good.

b(4). WICK FARM, house, 280 yards E. of the church, is of two storeys, timber-framed and plastered; the roofs are tiled. It was built in the 16th century and has an addition of *c.* 1700 at the N. end. One chimney-stack is original and has diagonal pilaster strips and a square base with a moulded capping.

Condition—Of E. part, bad.

b(5). PARKGATE FARM, house, now two tenements, about ½ m. W. of the church, is of two storeys, timber-framed and plastered; the roofs are tiled. It was built in the 15th century and has a cross-wing at the E. end. The upper storey projects at the N. end of the cross-wing, on curved brackets. Inside the building the cross-wing has an open timbered ceiling.

Condition—Bad.

b(6). COTTAGE, about ¾ m. N.W. of the church, is of two storeys, timber-framed and plastered; the roofs are thatched. It was built late in the 17th century; inside the building the ceiling-beams are exposed.

Condition—Bad.

b(7). THORRINGTON'S FARM, house, about 270 yards N.E. of (6), is of two storeys, timber-framed and plastered; the roofs are tiled. It was built in the 16th century, but has large 18th-century and modern additions. Inside the building are exposed ceiling-beams and joists and moulded wall-posts.

Condition—Poor.

Unclassified :—

a(8). DYKE, about 1 m. W. of the church, extends for about 470 yards from E. to W. and consists of a ditch about 9 ft. deep and 35 ft. wide with a slight bank on each side.

Condition—Fairly good.

55. LITTLE BENTLEY. (E.c.)

(O.S. 6 in. xxix. S.W.)

Little Bentley is a parish 8 m. E. of Colchester. The church is the principal monument.

Ecclesiastical :—

(1). PARISH CHURCH OF ST. MARY stands towards the S.E. corner of the parish. The walls are of mixed rubble with some Roman and some 16th-century bricks, the dressings are of limestone and brick. The roofs are covered with tiles, slates and lead. The *Nave* and *Chancel* are of 12th-century date. In the 13th century the chancel was rebuilt and the *North Chapel* and a N. aisle added. Late in the 14th century the *North Aisle* was rebuilt. About the middle of the 15th century the *West Tower* was built. About 1520 a pre-existing priest's house adjoining the N. aisle was removed and the aisle wall heightened. The church has been restored in the 18th century and in modern times.

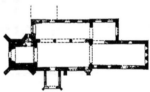

Architectural Description—The *Chancel* (38½ ft. by 15½ ft.) has in the E. wall three mid 13th-century lancet-windows with shafted splays and moulded rear-arches; the middle window has also a moulded internal label with mask-stops. In the N. wall is a 13th-century lancet window; further W. is a 13th-century two-centred archway of one chamfered order with chamfered imposts; cut through the E. respond is a squint with a roughly rounded head; about 6 ft. W. of the window are the Roman brick quoins of the 12th-century chancel. In the S. wall are three windows, the easternmost is of early 15th-century date, partly restored, and has two cinque-foiled lights with tracery in a two-centred head with a moulded label; the splays are probably of the 13th century; the second window is similar to that in the N. wall; the westernmost window is set low in the wall and is of early 16th-century date; it is of one light with a modern head; between the two eastern windows is the modern doorway. The early 16th-century chancel-arch is two-centred and of two chamfered orders; the responds are semi-octagonal with moulded capitals and bases, mostly cut away; the upper part of the wall is of early 16th-century date and has a crow-stepped gable.

The *North Chapel* (17 ft. by 13 ft.) has a late 15th-century E. window of three cinquefoiled lights with vertical tracery in a four-centred head with

LAYER MARNEY : LAYER MARNEY HALL.
Gatehouse from the North-East ; early 16th-century.

LAYER MARNEY: LAYER MARNEY HALL.
Interior of Long Gallery ; early 16th-century.

a moulded label. In the N. wall are two early 15th-century windows, partly restored, and each of two cinquefoiled lights in a two-centred head with moulded labels. In the W. wall is a late 15th-century archway, two-centred, and of two chamfered orders, the inner resting on moulded corbels carved with leopards' faces.

The *Bayning Vault*, below the N. chapel, is of brick and was built *c.* 1647 ; it has a semi-circular barrel-vault.

The *Nave* (38¼ ft. by 17½ ft.) has an N. arcade of early 13th-century date, and of three bays with two-centred arches of one chamfered order, circular columns with moulded capitals, circular to square on plan, and moulded bases with square plinths ; the responds are semi-octagonal and have similar capitals and bases. In the S. wall at the E. end is the rood-loft staircase of *c.* 1520 ; the lower doorway has rebated jambs and a three-centred head ; the upper doorway is blocked with 17th-century brick ; further W. is an early 16th-century window, partly restored, and of three transomed and four-centred lights in a four-centred head with moulded jambs and label ; all of brick ; the S. doorway is of the same date, but of stone ; it has moulded jambs and four-centred head. The S. wall has brick buttresses and parapet.

The *North Aisle* (39¾ ft. by 11¾ ft.) has in the N. wall three windows ; the two eastern are similar to the S.E. window in the chancel ; the westernmost window is of *c.* 1520 and of brick ; it is of two four-centred lights in a four-centred head with a moulded label ; further W. is a doorway of brick of the same date and now blocked ; it has double-chamfered jambs and a four-centred arch with a moulded label ; the N. wall (Plate, p. 143) has a moulded plinth with trefoil-headed panels, except in the W. bay, where the wall was made good *c.* 1520 in brick after the removal of the pre-existing priest's house. In the W. wall is a window similar to the two eastern in the N. wall.

The *West Tower* (13 ft. by 11¾ ft.) is of three stages (Plate, p. 221) with an embattled parapet and carved gargoyles. The 15th-century tower-arch is two-centred and of one chamfered order on the E. face. The W. window is modern, except for the moulded label, splays and rear-arch ; below it is the mid 15th-century W. doorway, with moulded jambs, two-centred arch in a square head with a moulded label and head-stops ; the spandrels are carved with foliage and shields. The existence of a former ringing gallery is indicated by a blocked opening in the N. wall. The second stage has in the E. wall a brick doorway opening into the roof and above it is a blocked window. The N., S. and W. walls have each a mid 15th-century brick window of one pointed light. The bell-chamber has in each wall a mid 15th-century window, each of two cinquefoiled lights in a two-centred head with moulded jambs and labels.

The *South Porch* is of *c.* 1520 and of brick, with an embattled parapet. The outer archway has moulded jambs, four-centred arch and label. The side walls have each a window, now blocked, of three pointed lights in a square head with a moulded label ; the mullions of the E. window have been removed.

The *Roof* (Plate, p. xxxvi) of the nave is of early 16th-century date and of six bays with hammer-beam trusses with moulded main timbers ; the wall-plates are embattled and the hammer-beams are carved with angels holding shields, all much defaced ; below the hammer-beams are curved braces with foliated spandrels and wall-posts resting on carved figures holding shields. The early 16th-century pent roof of the N. aisle is of five bays with moulded main timbers.

Fittings—Bells : five ; 2nd, 3rd and 4th by Robert Mott, 1599 ; 5th by Miles Graye, 1625. *Brass :* In N. chapel—of [Sir William Pyrton, 1490], figure of man in armour, lower part lost, with SS. collar and portcullis clasp, [wife, Katherine, 1501] in widow's veil, three sons and five daughters, and shield of arms, *ermine a cheveron engrailed with three leopards' heads thereon*, indents of three more shields and inscription-plate. *Chest* (Plate, p. xxxii) : In N. chapel—large, with cambered lid, iron-bound and nail-studded, three locks and two bolts, ring handle at each end, 14th or 15th-century. *Coffin-lid :* In N. chapel—coped slab with moulded edge and carved with cross in low relief, 13th-century, lower part missing. *Communion Table :* In chancel—with moulded and turned legs, moulded and carved top-rail with consoles at the angles, mid 17th-century. *Door :* In turret staircase to tower—of two battens with sexfoiled scutcheon-plate, early 16th-century. *Font :* octagonal, one face of bowl with octofoiled panel enclosing a shield of the arms of Pyrton, moulded under-edge, carved with plain shields and rosettes alternately, plain stem and moulded base, *c.* 1500. *Funeral-helm :* In chancel—on N. wall, with comb and visor, late 16th-century. *Glass :* In N. chapel—in N. windows, fragments of canopy work, borders and black-letter inscription, 15th and 17th-century. *Hour-glass Stand :* On pulpit—of wrought iron, probably 17th-century. *Monuments :* In Bayning vault—in W. wall, to Penelope, widow of Paul, Viscount Bayning, 1647, arched recess with inscription on brass shield. *Niche :* In N. chapel—in N.E. angle, with hollow-chamfered jambs and trefoiled ogee head, crocketed and finialed, moulded shelf at bottom, 15th-century. *Painting :* In N. aisle—on N. wall, part of black-letter inscription, 15th-century, now covered. *Piscina :* In chancel —with hollow-chamfered jambs and trefoiled head, one round and one octofoiled drain, 14th-century. *Plate* (Plate, p. xxxv) : includes cup of 1623, with an achievement of the Bayning arms, flagon of 1623, both with original wooden cases covered with stamped leather. *Scratchings :* In tower—on N. jamb of W. window, indecipherable graffiti, and initials and date I.S. 1608. *Seating :* In nave—four benches with moulded and embattled rails with bench-ends with carved popey heads, eight other bench-ends and eight popey heads, 15th-century. *Sedilia :* In chancel—recess with double two-centred head springing from moulded corbel in middle, probably 14th-century. *Stoup :* In S. porch—recess with broken bowl, date uncertain. *Miscellanea :* In blocked entrance to ringing gallery, reused worked stones. In external quoins, reused trefoiled panels.

Condition—Good.

Secular :—

(2). OUTBUILDING, called the "Castle," in the grounds of the hall, 500 yards S. of the church, is a small square building of brick, probably a garden pavilion. It was built about the middle of the 16th century and has a thatched roof. In the E. wall is an original doorway with moulded jambs ; the head has been destroyed. In the N. wall is a round-headed doorway and in the W. wall is a similar doorway, now blocked, with remains of a square external label. In the S. wall is an original window, with moulded jambs and now blocked.

Condition—Ruinous.

(3). WARREN'S FARM, house, nearly 1 m. S.S.W. of the church, is of two storeys, timber-framed and plastered ; the roofs are tiled. It was built in the 16th century and has a projecting upper storey with curved brackets on the E. side. Inside the building are exposed ceiling-beams and joists.

Condition—Good.

(4). COTTAGE, on N. side of road, nearly ¾ m. N.W. of the church, was built late in the 17th century. It is of two storeys, timber-framed and plastered ; the roofs are tiled. Inside the building the ceiling-beams and timber-framing are exposed.

Condition—Good.

(5). FISH STEWS, S.W. of the hall.

---

56. LITTLE BRAXTED. (B.d.)

(O.S. 6 in. xlv. N.W.)

Little Braxted is a small parish adjoining Witham on the E. The church is interesting.

Ecclesiastical :—

(1). PARISH CHURCH OF ST. NICHOLAS stands at the N. end of the parish. The walls are of flint-rubble with pudding-stone ; the dressings are of limestone and the roofs are tiled. The apsidal *Chancel* and the *Nave* were built in the 12th century. The church was restored in the 19th century, when the *North Aisle, Vestry* and *South Porch* were added and the bell-turret rebuilt.

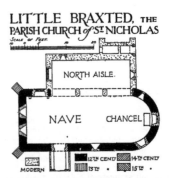

LITTLE BRAXTED, THE PARISH CHURCH of ST NICHOLAS

NORTH AISLE.

NAVE   CHANCEL

MODERN   12TH CENT   14TH CENT   13TH   15TH

Architectural Description—The *Chancel* and *Nave* (45½ ft. by 16½ ft.) are structurally undivided. The apse has three windows, the eastern is apparently modern ; the N. window is a single 12th-century light with a round head, but that on the S. is of the 14th century, much restored, and of one trefoiled light. In the N. wall is a modern arcade and window. In the S. wall is a single-light window, completely restored externally, but with splays and rear-arch, perhaps of the 12th century ; further W. is the much restored 14th-century S. doorway of one chamfered and one rounded order, with a two-centred arch and a moulded label with head-stops. In the W. wall are two 13th-century lancet windows and a modern round arch.

The *North Aisle* is modern, but reset in the E. wall is a much restored 13th-century round-headed window and parts of a 14th-century doorway with a moulded label and defaced head-stops. Reset in the N. wall is a 14th-century window with a cinque-foiled head and in the W. wall a 15th-century window of two cinquefoiled lights in a square head with a moulded label.

The *Roof* of the chancel is modern, but incorporates a few old timbers. The 15th-century roof of the nave has collar-beams, purlins and wind-braces.

Fittings — *Brass :* In chancel — of William Roberts, 1508, and Joyce and Margaret, his wives, figures of man in armour and two women in pedimental head-dresses, four groups of children and four shields of arms (*a*) and (*b*), *three pheons, a chief with a running and collared greyhound therein* for Roberts ; (*c*) Roberts impaling *three crescents* for Peryent ; (*d*) Roberts impaling *a cheveron with three leopards' heads thereon* for Pyrton. *Chests :* In nave—plain, with scutcheon-plate, 17th-century, lid modern. In N. aisle—panelled, with moulded muntins and lid, 17th-century. *Floor-slab :* In nave—to Thomas Roberts, 1680, with shield of arms. *Glass :* In N. aisle—in N.W. window, maple leaf quarries, 14th-century. *Piscina :* In chancel — with trefoiled head, probably 14th-century, drain modern. *Plate:* includes cup (with added base) and cover-paten of 1567 and an alms-dish of 1683.

Condition—Good, much restored.

Secular :—

(2). LITTLE BRAXTED HALL, house, summer-house, barn and moat, W. and N. of the church. The *House* is of two storeys, partly of brick and partly of plastered timber-framing ; the roofs are tiled. It was built in the 16th century and has modern additions on the N. and W. The S. chimney-stack has two original octagonal shafts with moulded bases and partly rebuilt. Inside the building is some early 17th-century panelling and some exposed timber-framing.

The *Garden Wall* is of 16th-century brickwork with a projecting coping on brick corbels. At the S.W. angle is a square summer-house of two storeys and of brick and timber-framing, it is buttressed on the N. and S. sides.

The *Barn*, N. of the house, is timber-framed and square on plan. It was formerly of two storeys, and was built in the 15th century, but the floor has been removed. The roof is supported by an arched truss in the middle. The barn may possibly have been the hall of the former house.

The *Moat* surrounds the barn.

Condition—-Of house, etc., good.

----

57. LITTLE BROMLEY. (E.c.)

(O.S. 6 in. (a)xix. S.E. (b)xxviii. N.E.)

Little Bromley is a parish 6 m. E.N.E. of Colchester.

Ecclesiastical :—

(b)(1). PARISH CHURCH OF ST. MARY stands on the S.W. of the parish. The walls are of pudding-stone rubble ; part of the tower is of brick ; the dressings are of limestone and the roofs are tiled. The *Nave* was built probably early in the 12th century. In the 14th century the *Chancel* was re-built. The *West Tower* was added in the first half of the 15th century but the top stage was rebuilt in the 16th century when the *South Porch* was added. The church has been restored in the 19th century.

Architectural Description—The *Chancel* (26½ ft. by 18½ ft.) is of early 14th-century date and has an E. window of three pointed lights with inter-secting tracery in a two-centred head. In the

N. wall is a window of one trefoiled light. In the S. wall are two windows, the eastern of one cinque-foiled light and the western trefoiled and set low in the wall ; between them is a doorway with moulded jambs and two-centred head. There is no chancel-arch.

The *Nave* (35 ft. by 17 ft.) has in the N. wall two windows ; the eastern is modern and the western is a single round-headed light of early 12th-century date and covered with cement ; further W. is the N. doorway with chamfered jambs and two-centred arch ; it is probably of the 14th century and is now blocked. In the S. wall are two windows, the eastern is of late 15th-century date, partly restored and of three cinquefoiled lights in a four-centred head with a moulded label and head-stops ; the western window is similar to the corresponding window in the N. wall ; further W. is the early 14th-century S. doorway with moulded jambs, and two-centred arch with a moulded label and head-stops.

The *West Tower* (10¾ ft. square) is of three stages ; the third stage and the embattled parapet are of brick. The two-centred tower-arch is covered with cement and of uncertain date. The 15th-century W. window is of three cinquefoiled lights with vertical tracery in a two-centred head with a moulded label and head-stops ; below it is the W. doorway of the same date ; it has moulded jambs and two-centred arch in a square head with a moulded label and defaced head-stops. The ground-stage had a gallery at half its height. The second stage has in the N. wall a round-headed loop of brick. The bell-chamber has in each wall an early 16th-century window of two cinquefoiled lights with vertical tracery in a two-centred head with a moulded label.

The *Roof* of the nave is modern but has 14th-century moulded wall-plates partly restored. The early 16th-century roof of the S. porch has two tie-beams with curved braces, wind-braces and chamfered posts.

Fittings—*Bells :* four ; 3rd and 4th by Robert Burford, early 15th-century and inscribed " Sancta Katerina Ora Pro Nobis " and ". Sit Nomen Domini Benedictum." *Communion Rails :* with turned balusters and moulded rails, c. 1700. *Doors :* In nave—in S. doorway, with moulded fillets, strap-hinges, studded with nails, 16th-century. In tower—in doorway to turret, of nail-studded battens, 16th-century. *Font* (Plate, p. xxxiv): octagonal bowl with panelled sides carved alternately with roses and the symbols of the evangelists, under-edge with four half-angels holding hearts or shields, buttressed stem, early 16th-century. *Glass :* In W. window—coloured fragments. *Piscina :* In chancel—with moulded jambs and two-centred head, quatrefoiled drain, 14th-century. *Plate :* includes cover-paten, possi-bly Elizabethan, but without mark. *Miscellanea :*

Preserved at Rectory, round silver brooch with black-letter inscription " Ihs est amor cordis mei," 15th-century, found in churchyard.

Condition—Good, much restored.

Secular :—

^b(2). BRAHAM HALL, ¾ m. E.N.E. of the church, is of two storeys, timber-framed and plastered ; the roofs are tiled. It was built probably in the 17th century but has been almost completely altered.

Condition—Good.

^a(3). COTTAGE, on E. side of road, nearly ¾ m. N. of the church, is of two storeys, timber-framed and weather-boarded ; the roofs are thatched. It was built late in the 17th century and has exposed ceiling-beams.

Condition—Poor.

---

58. LITTLE CLACTON. (F.d.)

(O.S. 6 in. xxxviii. S.E.)

Little Clacton is a parish and small village 2½ m. N. of Clacton. The church is interesting.

Ecclesiastical :—

(1). PARISH CHURCH OF ST. JAMES stands in the village. The walls are of rubble, entirely covered with plaster ; the dressings are of limestone ; the roofs are covered with tiles and slates. The *Chancel* was built probably in the 12th century. The *Nave* was much lengthened and perhaps rebuilt early in the 14th century. The timber *South Porch* is probably of the 14th century and the bell-turret of the 15th century. The church was restored in the 19th century.

Architectural Description—The *Chancel* (28½ ft. by 17½ ft.) has an early 14th-century E. window of three pointed lights with pierced spandrels in a two-centred head with a moulded label. In the N. wall is a 12th-century window of one small round-headed light, plastered. In the S. wall are two windows, the eastern of early 14th-century date and of two pointed lights with a plain spandrel in a two-centred head ; the western window is of the 15th century and of two cinquefoiled lights in a square head with a moulded label ; between the windows is a doorway with plain jambs and rough two-centred head. There is no chancel-arch.

The *Nave* (61½ ft. by 19½ ft.) has in the N. wall two windows ; the eastern is of the 16th century and of three round-headed uncusped lights in a four-centred head ; the western window is of early 14th-century date and similar to that in the S. wall of the chancel, but with a moulded label ; between the windows is the 14th-century N. doorway, with chamfered jambs and two-centred arch. In the S. wall are three windows, all originally of early 14th-century date ; the two eastern are uniform with the western window in the N. wall, but almost entirely modern ; the westernmost window is a single pointed light ; E. of it is the 14th-century S. doorway with chamfered jambs and two-centred arch. In the W. wall is a modern window set in a blocked doorway ; above it is the W. window similar in date and detail to the eastern windows in the S. wall but not restored. The bell-turret at the W. end of the nave stands on four chamfered posts with heavy tie-beams and curved braces ; it is now partitioned off to form a vestry and stair to the modern gallery.

The *South Porch* is timber-framed and of the 14th-century, much restored. The two-centred archway is flanked by two trefoiled lights. The sides have each six open lights. The gable has foiled barge-boards.

Fittings—*Bells :* three ; said to be, 1st by Miles Graye, 1652 ; 2nd by Robert Crowch, early 15th-century and inscribed " Sancta Margareta Ora Pro Nobis." *Brasses* and *Indents*. Brasses : In chancel—on N. wall, (1) to Giles Bageholt alias Badger, 1581 ; (2) to Thomas Bageholt, 1568, brother of above, inscriptions only. Indents : In nave—(1) of inscription-plate ; (2) of two figures. *Chairs :* In chancel—two, incorporating 17th-century carving. *Font :* square bowl of Purbeck marble with shallow round-headed arcades on sides ; under each arch on N. side, a raised cross, late 12th-century. *Lockers :* In chancel—in N. wall, three, one round-headed and two square, two rebated for doors and one chamfered, date uncertain. *Piscina :* In chancel—with two moulded two-centred heads, two drains and in middle remains of shaft and moulded base, 13th-century. *Sedile :* In chancel—sill of S.E. window carried down to form seat. *Table :* In nave—with turned legs and carved top-rail, 17th-century.

Condition—Fairly good.

Secular :—

(2). BOVILL'S HALL, house and moat, nearly ¾ m. S.W. of the church. The *House* is of two storeys, timber-framed and plastered ; the roofs are tiled. It was built probably in the 17th century and has an 18th-century wing on the E.

The *Moat* surrounds the house.

Condition—Of house, good.

(3). CLAPGATE FARM, house, ¼ m. N.W. of the
church, is of two storeys, timber-framed and
plastered; the roofs are tiled. It was built
probably in the 16th century, with cross-wings at
the N. and S. ends. The upper storey projects at
both ends of the N. cross-wing. Inside the building
are some exposed ceiling-beams and joists.

Condition—Good (since burnt down).

59. LITTLE COGGESHALL. (B.d.)

(O.S. 6 in. (a)xxvi. S.W. (b)xxxv. N.W.)

Little Coggeshall is a small parish adjoining
Great Coggeshall on the S. St. Nicholas' Chapel
and Abbey are the principal monuments.

Roman :—

b(1A). A very curious find, probably a burial,
made apparently early in the 16th century, seems
worthy of record and possibly indicates occupation somewhere in the western end of the parish.
"In a place called Westfield, ¾ m. distant from
Cogeshall and belonging to the Abbay there, was
found by touching of a plough a great brasen
potte . . . . the mouth of the potte was closed
with a white substance like past or claie, as hard
as burned bricke, when that by force was
remooued, there was found within it another
potte, but that was of earth; that beeing opened
there was found in it a lesser potte of earth of the
quantitie of a gallon covered with a matter like
veluet, and fastned at the mouth with a silke-lace.
In it they found some whole bones and many
peeces of small bones wrapped up in fine silke
of fresh colour" (Philemon Holland's ed. of
Camden's Britannia, 1610, p. 449). Westfield has
been located to the N. of Cuthedge Lane, and
somewhere between it and Curd Hall, and not
near Highfields in Great Coggeshall parish as
marked on the Ordnance map (Beaumont, Hist.
of Coggeshall (1890), pp. 7, 85). A denarius of
M. Antonius and a 'third brass' of Hadrian
have been found at Curd Hall and Scripps Farm
respectively (Ibid.).

Ecclesiastical :—

b(1). ST. NICHOLAS' CHAPEL (Plate, p. 127),
formerly the "capella extra portas" of the
Cistercian Abbey, stands in the N.E. corner of
the parish. The walls are of flint-rubble mixed
with brick and tiles and with quoins and dressings of
13th-century bricks; the roof is tiled. The Chapel
was built c. 1220 and remains without structural
alteration.

It is of exceptional interest, both from its original
purpose and from the extensive use of 13th-century
bricks.

Architectural Description—The Chapel (43½ ft.
by 20 ft.) is a plain rectangular building with brick
quoins. In the E. wall is a brick window of three
lancet lights enclosed in a two-centred outer order
and with roll-moulded splays and two-centred rear-
arch. In the N. wall are four lancet-windows of
brick and of similar detail to the E. window; all
are slightly restored. In the S. wall are four
windows similar to those in the N. wall, but the
third window is much restored or perhaps rebuilt;
W. of it is a modern S. doorway. In the W. wall
is a window similar to the E. window, but badly
weathered externally.

The Roof has been entirely reconstructed, but
is of the trussed-rafter type and incorporates some
old timbers.

Fittings—Chair: with curved arms, panelled
back and sides, 17th-century. Chest: with
carved, panelled and inlaid front, one lock, early
17th-century. Locker: In N. wall—rectangular
recess with oak sill and lintel, date uncertain.
Painting: On sedilia, on soffit of E. bay, remains
of red masonry lines; at back of middle bay
remains of cruciform nimbus or consecration cross,
13th-century. Paving: In threshold of S. doorway,
of cut and shaped bricks forming pattern, 13th-
century. Piscinae: In S. wall—at E. end, with
chamfered jambs and trefoiled head, 13th-century,
probably not in situ; in range with sedilia, of
brick with hollow-chamfered E. jamb and rough
two-centred head, remains of sill, 13th-century.
Sedilia: In range with piscina, of three bays
with defaced two-centred arches, hollow-chamfered
W. jamb and modern piers between the bays,
13th-century. Table: small, with turned legs,
17th-century.

Condition—Good.

Secular :—

a(2). COGGESHALL ABBEY (Plates, pp. 166, 167),
house, foundations, outbuildings and fish-ponds, 150
yards E.S.E. of the chapel. The abbey was founded
for monks of the order of Savigny by King Stephen
and Queen Maud, probably in 1140. It became
Cistercian in 1147. The foundations of the Nave
arcades appear to be of mid 12th-century date and
the existing pier and respond of the supposed
Farmery Hall are of about the same date. The
rest of the church, as represented by marks in the
turf, appears to indicate a 13th or 14th-century
extension of the eastern arm and the addition of
a large chapel N. of the nave. The Dorter Range
appears to have been extended to the S. c. 1220,
and this extension is the only part now surviving;
very shortly after the two-storeyed corridor E. of
the extension and the cross-wing at its S. end were
built. The detached building S.E. of the dorter
range was built c. 1200. The abbey was dissolved
in 1539, and c. 1581 the existing dwelling-house
was built or rebuilt, to the E. of the dorter range.

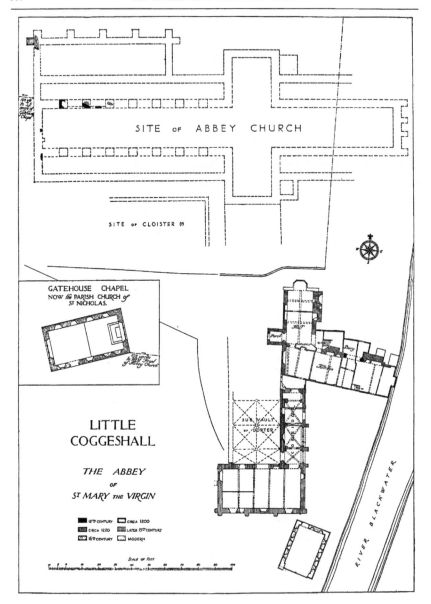

SITE of ABBEY CHURCH

SITE of CLOISTER (?)

GATEHOUSE CHAPEL
NOW the PARISH CHURCH of
St NICHOLAS.

LITTLE
COGGESHALL

THE ABBEY
of
St MARY the VIRGIN

SCALE of FEET

Vaulting, Southernmost Bay of Corridor;
13th-century.

Blocked Doorway in East Wall of Dorter
Subvault; 13th-century.

Doorway in North Wall of Corridor;
13th-century.

Column in East Wing of House, from
North; 12th-century.

Roof of Upper Storey of Corridor; 16th-century.

Vaulting Shaft, East Wall of Dorter
Subvault; 13th-century.

Chimney-stack, East Side of House;
mid 16th-century.

East side of Corridor, next Subvault of Dorter; 13th and 16th-century.

Archway, South End of West Vault of Corridor;
13th-century.

East wall of Subvault of Dorter; 13th-century and later.

Cross-wing, 13th-century; and detached Building, c. 1200, at South End of Dorter Range.

The remains are of great interest as those of a Cistercian Abbey of unusual plan. The early use of brick both here and in the gatehouse chapel (1) is noteworthy.

The *Abbey Church* is represented only by marks in the turf after a long drought. It appears to have had a total internal length of about 210 ft. by 80 ft. across the transepts. Excavations undertaken in 1914 revealed the brick bases of the western piers of the nave, together with fragments of the screen-walls between them. Portions of the N. and W. walls of a large chapel N. of the nave were also uncovered. It is probable that the E. arm of the church was extended at some period subsequent to the 12th century.

There are no traces of the buildings immediately adjoining the church on the S., but the S. end of the *Dorter Range* still exists about 153 ft. S. of the transept of the church. From the slightly divergent alignments of this building and the 16th-century house it appears probable that this part is an extension of the earlier dorter range, the line of which is probably represented by the house. The existing remains are of *c.* 1220 and consist of the S. and part of the E. walls. It was covered by a stone vault with a row of columns down the centre and quadripartite bays. The keying of the vault remains on the two walls, together with parts of the vaulting shafts on the E. side ; these are semi-circular on plan with moulded capitals ; in the S.E. angle is a moulded corbel. In the E. wall the S. bay is occupied by a brick doorway of *c.* 1220 with jambs and two-centred arch of two moulded orders ; in the next bay is a blocked doorway of the same date with external stone jambs of two shafted orders and richly moulded head, partly destroyed ; the unusually lofty rear-arch is also moulded ; the third bay has a small opening with a four-centred head.

Adjoining the dorter range on the E. is a two-storeyed *corridor*, evidently built to provide direct communication between the Farmery Hall and the cross-wing at the end of the dorter. It is of slightly later date than the dorter extension and is of three bays with a narrow half-bay at the N. end ; each of the full bays is covered by a quadripartite vault with ribs of brick : the E. wall is divided into bays by brick buttresses and has arches either two-centred or semi-circular, formerly open but now partly closed in ; the arches have a chamfered inner order stopping at imposts below which the order is continued as two roll-mouldings ; the northernmost of these arches was partly destroyed probably in the 16th century and replaced by a pointed brick arch enclosing a doorway with a four-centred head and a window of three four-centred lights. The N. half-bay of the corridor is covered by a barrel-vault and between it and the N. bay is a detached shaft with a moulded capital, from which springs the cross-arch of the

vault. In the N. wall of the corridor is a doorway generally similar to that in the E. wall of the dorter extension but now plastered and painted.

The *Cross-wing* at the S. end of the dorter range is of the same date as the corridor. It may possibly have served as the Misericorde on the ground floor and as the Farmery Chapel on the first floor. The building has original buttresses of brick and several doorways and windows inserted late in the 16th century and subsequently altered. The ground floor has an opening in the N. wall, from the corridor ; on the W. side of it is the original buttress of the dorter range. In the S. wall at the E. end is an opening with an original rear-arch. The first floor has in the N. wall the remains of the three buttresses at the end of the dorter range. The doorway from the corridor at this level is similar in date and detail to that at the N. end of the lower corridor. In the E. wall are two original lancet-windows and between them is a recess with a two-centred head. In the S. wall near the E. end is a recess with a two-centred head, possibly for a piscina. In the building are various scratchings of mediaeval and later date.

The detached *building* to the S.E. is of very unusual type and doubtful purpose. It is of *c.* 1200 and built of flint-rubble, with a large admixture of brick ; all the dressings are of brick. The S. wall has been destroyed but otherwise the building is intact. The E. and W. walls have each four lancet-windows with recessed jambs of two orders ; below the windows is a series of plain recesses with pointed heads, four in the E. and five in the W. wall. The N. wall has a blocked doorway with a round rear-arch and further E. is a wide recess with a modern pier in the middle. The roof has a large tie-beam and curved wind-braces of the 16th or 17th century.

The *House* is of two storeys, partly of brick and partly of plastered timber-framing. It was built about the middle of the 16th century. The W. front has a two-storeyed porch wing with a projecting gable on curved brackets. The outer doorway has a flat four-centred head and is set in a projection with a moulded entablature ; above it is a shield with the initials R. A. and a device, and below it the date 1[5]81. On each side of the porch is a 16th-century window, now blocked. N. of the porch is a window of the same date and of five lights with brick mullions and transom. On the E. side of the house is a large chimney-stack with an embattled offset and four octagonal shafts with moulded bases ; at the base of the stack is a fireplace with a four-centred head, showing that the building formerly extended further in this direction. Other stacks are partly of 16th-century date. At the E. end of the timber-framed back wing is a 16th-century bay-window of five lights, with moulded frame and mullions ;

flanking this window are two small windows each of two lights and now blocked. Inside the building the main N. room has 16th-century moulded ceiling-beams and joists and the walls have early 17th-century panelling to half their height. At the S. end is part of an early 17th-century screen, consisting of three arcaded bays with foliated spandrels and divided by fluted Doric pilasters supporting an entablature with a fluted frieze ; the middle bay appears to have been a doorway and the spandrels have the initials R.B. Other rooms on the ground floor have 16th-century ceiling-beams and doors. In the kitchen is some late 16th or early 17th-century panelling. On the first floor the room over the hall (now divided up) has panelled walls divided into bays by pilasters ; the fireplace in the E. wall is flanked by fluted pilasters standing on tall pedestals ; the overmantel has three arcaded panels with foliated spandrels and divided by pilasters, all of early 17th-century date. The upper part of the staircase has early 18th-century turned balusters.

Incorporated in the E. wing of the house is a W. respond and a cylindrical pier of mid to late 12th-century date and probably forming part of the former Farmery Hall. They are built of brick and the pier has a scalloped stone capital, much damaged. The upper part of the pointed arch resting upon them is visible in a room on the first floor.

Condition—Of house, good ; of ruins, fairly well preserved.

Monuments (3–7).

The following monuments, unless otherwise described, are of the 17th century and of two storeys, timber-framed and plastered or weather-boarded ; the roofs are tiled. Many of the buildings have original chimney-stacks and exposed ceiling-beams.

Condition—Good, or fairly good.

b(3). *Coggeshall Hall* (Plate, p. 177), house and barn, about 1 m. S.S.E. of St. Nicholas' Chapel and partly in Kelvedon parish. The *House* was built late in the 16th century and extended to the N. early in the following century ; there is a modern wing at the S. end. The upper storey projects on most of the W. front and has an original bressumer carved with grotesque monsters. The central chimney-stack has grouped diagonal shafts.

The *Barn*, N.W. of the house, is probably of the same date and is of six bays.

b(4). *Curd Hall* (Plate, p. 177), about 1¼ m. W.S.W. of St. Nicholas' Chapel, has a modern addition on the S.W. The original chimney-stack has diagonal pilaster strips. There are two projecting gables on the N. front with original moulded bressumers and barge-boards. Inside the building the original staircase has flat wavy balusters and moulded handrail.

a(5). *Grange Farm*, house and barn, 500 yards W. of St. Nicholas' Chapel. The *House* was built *c.* 1600 and is of three storeys with 18th-century and modern additions on the S.W. Inside the building a room on the first floor is lined with original panelling having an enriched frieze and dentilled cornice ; the overmantel has two arcaded panels flanked by grotesque terminal figures. In the S. wall is a window of six transomed lights with moulded frames and mullions. The upper part of the staircase is original and has symmetrically turned balusters and octagonal newels with acorn-shaped tops. In the attic is an original fireplace with chamfered jambs and three-centred arch of brick.

The *Barn*, N. of the house, is probably of late 15th or early 16th-century date and is of six bays with aisles and two porches. It is about 130 ft. by 45 ft., and has a roof of king-post type.

a(6). *House*, now tenements, on E. side of road, N. of Long Bridge, has an original chimney-stack with five octagonal shafts.

a(7). *House*, now tenements, on W. side of road, 70 yards N. of (6).

---

a(8). *Long Bridge*, about ¼ m. W. of the chapel, is of three spans and of red brick. It was built probably in the 13th century, as the brickwork is similar to that employed at the Abbey, and has been widened on the E. side in modern times. The arches are slightly pointed and the 'cut-waters' are additions of doubtful date.

Condition—Good, much restored.

a(9). *Stone*, set in wall of modern house, on E. side of the road, ¼ m. W. of the chapel, is carved with a shield of arms and an inscription to Edward Larke and Ann, his wife, 1699.

---

60. LITTLE HENNY. (B.a.)

(O.S. 6 in. xii. N.E.)

Little Henny is a very small parish 5 m. N.N.E. of Halstead.

Ecclesiastical :—

(1). Foundations of the former parish church, 70 yards E.S.E. of the Ryes, are much overgrown, but appear to indicate a small rectangular building. In it is a semi-octagonal bowl, probably of a stoup.

Condition—Overgrown.

Secular :—

(2). Cottage, about 300 yards W. of (1), is of two storeys, timber-framed and plastered ; the roofs are thatched. It was built probably in the 17th century and has exposed ceiling-beams.

Condition—Bad.

61. LITTLE HOLLAND. (F.d.)

(O.S. 6 in. xxxix. S.W.)

Little Holland is a small parish on the sea, 2 m. N.E. of Clacton.

Ecclesiastical :—

(1). PARISH CHURCH (dedication unknown) stood about 200 yards from the cliff. All that remains is a fragment of brick and rubble walling representing the E. wall, with diagonal buttresses at the angles.

Unclassified :—

(2). MILL PONDS, at Little Holland Hall, N. of the site of the church. Two ponds and a large basin, embanked at the N. end, remain.

Condition—Fairly good.

---

62. LITTLE HORKESLEY. (C.b.)

(O.S. 6 in. (a)xviii. N.E. (b)xviii. S.E.)

Little Horkesley is a parish on the right bank of the Stour, 5 m. N.N.W. of Colchester. The principal monuments are the church, Josselyns and Lower Dairy Farm.

Ecclesiastical :—

a(1). PARISH CHURCH OF SS. PETER AND PAUL stands on the E. side of the parish. The walls are probably of rubble, but are covered externally with Roman cement ; the rubble of the tower is much mixed with brick ; the dressings are of limestone and the roofs are lead-covered. The Priory of Little Horkesley was founded *temp.* Henry I by Robert, son of Godebold, and Beatrice, his wife, for Cluniac monks and as a cell to the priory of Thetford. There is no remaining work of this period, except perhaps the N. wall of the *Nave*, which is 3 ft. thick. About 1340 the *West Tower* was built and a South Aisle added ; the W. wall of the existing aisle is of this date (see Scratchings). About the middle of the 15th century the S. arcade was built or rebuilt and the *South Chapel* and *Aisle* rebuilt. Early in the 16th century a N. chapel was added and the *South Porch* built. The priory was suppressed in 1525. It appears probable that the priory chapel extended E. from the existing chancel and that the cloister lay to the N. of it with the domestic buildings on the site of the existing house (2). There is no evidence of cloister or adjoining buildings on the N. side of the existing nave. If the priory chapel extended E. then the E. wall of the existing parish *Chancel* must be of post-suppression date. The S. porch was largely rebuilt probably in the 18th century. The church was extensively restored in the 19th century when the *North Chapel* was rebuilt.

The church though much restored is interesting as the parochial portion of a small monastic church. Among the fittings is a fine series of Brasses and Monuments.

Architectural Description—The *Chancel* (24½ ft. by 19 ft.) has an E. window, all modern except the splays and hollow-chamfered segmental-pointed rear-arch, possibly of early 16th-century date. In the N. wall is an early 16th-century arch, four-centred and of three orders, the two outer continuous and the inner resting on attached shafts with moulded capitals and bases, all much scraped : the E. capital is modern ; further W. is a doorway with wave-moulded jambs and four-centred arch entirely recut ; further W. is a modern arch. In the S. wall is a low four-centred arch of the 15th century, over a tomb, with stop hollow-chamfered jambs and arch. Further W. is the first bay of the arcade (see Nave). The clearstorey has on the N. side two windows, each of two trefoiled lights in a four-centred head and both much restored.

The *Nave* (31¼ ft. by 21 ft.) has in the N. wall two windows, the eastern is modern except for the E. splay and two-centred, hollow-chamfered rear-arch which are probably 14th-century ; the western is modern except for the splays and hollow-chamfered, segmental-pointed rear-arch which are probably of the 16th century ; E. of the windows are the upper and lower doorways and the rood-loft staircase in the thickness of the wall ; the lower doorway has a square and the upper a rounded head, and the stairs are of brick, all of early 16th-century date. The S. arcade (overlapping the chancel by one bay) is of four bays and of mid 15th-century date ; the two-centred arches are of two moulded orders and the piers have each four attached shafts with moulded capital and bases ; the moulded responds have each one attached shaft.

The *North Chapel* is modern, but reset in the N. wall is a 15th-century window of two cinquefoiled lights in a square head ; the mullion and middle part are modern.

The *South Chapel* and *Aisle* (12¼ ft. wide) are without structural division. In the E. wall is a window, modern except the splays and hollow-chamfered segmental-pointed rear-arch. In the S. wall are four windows, all modern except the splays and segmental-pointed rear-arches and parts of the moulded labels of the two western, which are of the 15th century ; further W. is the 15th-century S. doorway with moulded jambs, two-centred arch in a square head with a moulded label with angel stops and spandrels carved with foliage and a rose. In the W. wall is a window, all modern except the splays, which have (on N. splay) the same mason's mark as the tower, and are therefore of the 14th century.

The *West Tower* (11 ft. by 12 ft.) is of three stages with a modern embattled parapet and is of

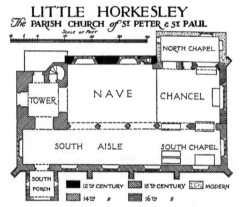

LITTLE HORKESLEY
The PARISH CHURCH of St PETER & St PAUL

SCALE OF FEET

NORTH CHAPEL

TOWER N A V E CHANCEL

SOUTH AISLE SOUTH CHAPEL

SOUTH PORCH

■ 12 TH CENTURY ▨ 15 TH CENTURY ▨ MODERN
▨ 14 TH ″ ■ 16 TH ″

c. 1340. The tower-arch is two-centred and of one continuous hollow-chamfered order. In the N. wall is a doorway to the stair-turret, with chamfered jambs and two-centred arch ; further W. is another similar but larger doorway with the rebate on the outside. In the S. wall is an arch similar but lower than the tower-arch. The W. window is modern except the splays ; the W. doorway has double hollow-chamfered jambs and restored two-centred arch with a moulded label and head-stops. The second stage has in the S. and W. walls a window of one plain pointed light. The bell-chamber has in each wall a window of two cinque-foiled ogee lights with flowing tracery in a two-centred head with a moulded label ; the S. and W. windows have been restored externally.

The *South Porch* has a modern outer archway and openings in the side walls ; the early 16th-century roof has moulded and embattled wall-plates and cambered tie-beam at the S. end, also moulded and embattled.

Fittings— *Altar :* In chancel—under communion table, slab, broken in three pieces, and formerly used as threshold, three incised consecration-crosses, back part cut away. *Bells :* five ; 2nd by Miles Graye, 1686 ; 3rd by Miles Graye, 1615 ; 5th by John Bird, 15th-century and inscribed "Eternis Annis Resonet Campana Johannis." *Bracket :* In chancel—on E. respond of N. arch, early 16th-century, scraped. *Brasses and Indent.* Brasses : In S. chapel—(1) of [Katherine ? Leventhorp, 1502], figure in shroud with shield of arms— quarterly 1 and 4 *a bend gobony between two cotises,* 2 and 3 *a fesse engrailed between three bulls' heads cut off at the neck,* indent of inscription-plate ; (2) shield of arms, *fretty on a chief three roundels,* indents of figure of woman and inscription-plate ; (3) of John, 1430, and Andrew Swynborne, 1418,

mutilated marginal inscription and indents of two figures in armour, four shields and evangelistic symbols. Indents : In S. chapel—(1) of shield and inscription-plate ; (2) of shield. See also Monuments (1), (2), (3). *Chest :* In vestry—of oak, bound with iron and 6½ ft. long, two round lock plates and money-slot, 16th-century, lid partly repaired. *Coffin-lids :* In S. chapel—(1) part of slab with raised cross and 'omega' ornament, 13th-century, also detached portion with similar ornament. In S. porch (2) and (3), plain tapering slabs, one much broken. *Coffin-stool :* In S. chapel—with carved rail and brackets and turned legs, 17th - century. *Font :* plain octagonal bowl, stem and base on one step ; remains of red colour ; hard limestone, 15th-century. *Font-cover :* of oak (covered with modern paint) in three stages ; octagonal base with cresting, lowest stage with traceried projections ; middle stage with canopied niches divided by buttresses and having pinnacles and crocketed finials ; top stage with range of crocketed gables and above them a central crocketed spire ; early 16th-century, partly restored. *Glass :* In S. chapel—in E. window, tracery lights, fragments and roundels with blue and green borders and large initials M, S, M, W, also two suns in splendour, 15th-century. In S. aisle—in S.E. window, in tracery, oak foliage in white and yellow, fragments and four roundels as above, with initials M, I, B, S. In heads of lights, three scrolls with remains of black-letter inscriptions, 15th-century. *Lectern :* made up of 15th-century tracery probably from a screen. *Monuments and Floor-slabs.* Monuments : In chancel— on N. side, (1) of Brygete, wife successively of Thomas Fyndorne, and John, Lord Marney, 1549, low altar-tomb with moulded slab inlaid with brass figure of woman in pedimental head-dress

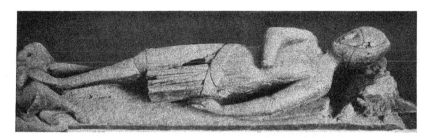

Oak Effigy of Knight in South Chapel ; *c.* 1310.
ELMSTEAD : PARISH CHURCH OF ST. LAURENCE.

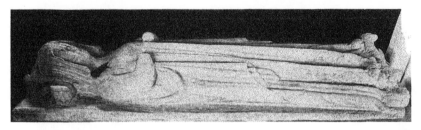

Oak Effigy of Woman ; late 13th-century.

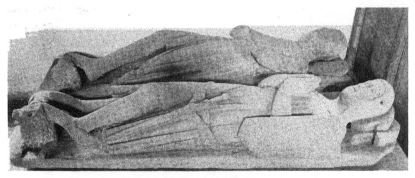

Oak Effigies of Knights ; *c.* 1250 and 1270.
LITTLE HORKESLEY : PARISH CHURCH OF SS. PETER AND PAUL.

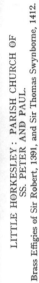

LITTLE HORKESLEY: PARISH CHURCH OF
SS. PETER AND PAUL.

Brass Effigies of Sir Robert, 1391, and Sir Thomas Swynborne, 1412.

PEBMARSH: PARISH CHURCH OF
ST. JOHN THE BAPTIST.

Brass Effigy of Sir William Fitzralph;
c. 1323.

and heraldic mantle with the arms of Waldegrave quartering Montchensy, and figures of two husbands in armour with tabards of arms : (a) Fyndorne, and (b) Marney quartering Sergeaux and Venables ; two shields of the arms (a) and (b) impaling Waldegrave quartered with Montchensy ; on S. side —(2) altar-tomb with moulded base and slab and indents of figures of man in armour and wife, double canopy, inscription-plate, six shields and several monograms, c. 1425. In S. chapel—(3) of Sir Robert Swynborne, 1391, and his son, Sir Thomas Swynborne, 1412, lord of Hammes, mayor of Bordeaux and captain of Fronsac, low altar-tomb with moulded slab inlaid with large brass figures (Plate, p. 171) of two men in armour, one in camail, jupon and hip-belt, the other in complete plate with SS. collar, palettes, taces, diagonal sword-belt, etc., elaborate triple-arched canopies with middle and side standards, the latter with five attached shields of arms—(a) *crusily three boars' heads ; (b) paly wavy ; (c) as (a) ; (d) a scutcheon in an orle of owls ; (e) a fesse between two cheverons,* indents of ten shields on sides of tombs ; (4) oak effigy (Plate, p. 170) of man in mail armour with legs crossed, long surcoat, knee-cops, feet on lion, and the whole on a moulded oak slab, c. 1250, much broken ; (5) similar figure of man (Plate, p. 170), with remains of shield on left arm, and hands of figures formerly supporting head, crossed legs, feet on lion, c. 1270 ; (6) oak effigy (Plate, p. 170) of woman, with head on two cushions supported by angels, feet against two dogs, long gown, wimple and veil, chamfered oak board, late 13th-century, much decayed ; (7) loose in S. chapel, part of side of altar-tomb of Purbeck marble, with cusped panelling enclosing shields with rivets of former brasses, late 15th-century. Floor-slabs : In chancel—(1) to Elizabeth, wife of Edward Husbands, 1687, and to Elizabeth, their daughter, 1707 ; (2) to Azariah Husbands, 1666 ; (3) to Elizabeth, wife of Richard Knight and widow of Azariah Husbands, 1684, also to Azariah Husbands, —76 ; (4) to Susanna, daughter of Thomas Lock, 1649 ; (5) to Anne Gardiner, 1706 ; (6) to Audery (Wates), wife of William Lynne, 1625, John Lynne, 1680, and Jacob Lynne, 1708. In nave—(7) to Margaret, wife of Thomas Smith, 1641. *Niches :* In nave—in E. jamb of N.E. window, shallow, with 14th-century trefoiled head not fitting the recess, recess plastered with remains of red colour, 15th-century. In S. aisle—in E. splay of middle window, plain plastered niche as in nave, but with restored pointed head, 15th-century. *Paintings :* In S. aisle—on E. splay of N.W. window, remains of conventional ornament, uncertain date. *Piscina :* In S. chapel—in S. wall, plain plastered niche with two-centred head, date uncertain. *Plate :* includes cup and cover-paten and flagon of 1705, paten of 1684 and dated 1685, all pieces have original cases with stamped leather

lining. *Scratchings :* On tower arches and on N. splay of W. window of aisle, several mason's marks, all the same, 14th-century. *Screen :* Between S. chapel and aisle—of five bays, one forming doorway, with moulded rail, buttressed posts and moulded head with carved flowers and cresting, side bays with double cinquefoiled and traceried heads, trefoiled and sub-cusped head to doorway with remains of pendant in middle, close lower panels with two groups of six round holes for peep-holes, 15th-century, partly repaired. Between the chancel and N. chapel, grille of wrought iron forming a screen, standards with fleur-de-lis heads and attached to each other by curved ornamental ironwork, late 17th-century. *Table :* In vestry—with fluted top-rail, shaped brackets and turned legs, c. 1660. *Miscellanea :* In porch—nine carved heads from label-stops, etc., 14th and 15th-century. Condition—Good, much restored.

Secular :—

MONUMENTS (2–7).

The following monuments, unless otherwise described, are of two storeys, timber-framed and plastered ; the roofs are tiled. Some of the buildings have original chimney-stacks and exposed ceiling-beams.
Condition—Good, or fairly good.

ᵃ(2). *Priory Farm*, house, N.E. of the church, was built probably late in the 16th century but may occupy the site of the priory buildings. In an addition on the N. side is a reset original window of five lights with moulded mullions.

ᵃ(3). *Josselyns* (Plate, p. xxx), house, nearly ½ m. N.N.E. of the church, was built probably late in the 15th or early in the 16th century, with a central hall and cross-wings at the N.E. and S.W. ends. In the 16th or 17th century the S.W. cross-wing was included in the main block and large additions made on the N.E. and S.E. The timber-framing is exposed throughout the house. The upper storey projects on the N.W. front of the original house, on curved brackets ; the doorway has original moulded jambs and a door with moulded fillets, planted on. Inside the building is some 17th-century panelling and a mutilated overmantel with two arched panels and inlaid ornament. On the first floor one room has the walls largely covered with stencilled decoration of c. 1600 in red, blue and brown ; above the fireplace in another room are remains of painted decoration. The roof of the main block has remains of the original construction and the N.E. cross-wing has a king-post roof-truss.

ᵃ(4). *Cottage*, 110 yards N.E. of (3), on opposite side of road, was built early in the 17th century and has exposed timber-framing.

a(5). *Lower Dairy Farm* (Plate, p. xxx), house,
¼ m. N.E. of (4), was built *c.* 1601, with a cross-wing at the S. end. The timber-framing is exposed
and the cross-wing has original bressumers to the
first floor and to the projecting gable, carved with
foliage, conventional monsters and the date and
initials 1601, I. H. K. ; each floor has a pair of
original windows of three and four lights, now
blocked ; the gable has an original barge-board
carved with running foliage. Inside the building
is an original moulded ceiling-beam.

b(6). *Cottage* (Plate, p. 188), 250 yards S.S.E.
of the church, was built *c.* 1600. The upper storey
projects on the S. front on curved brackets. The
original central chimney-stack has six dwarf
octagonal shafts with moulded bases.

b(7). *Hammond's Farm*, house, 1¼ m. S. of the
church, was built probably in the 17th century.
The upper storey projects in front.

---

63. LITTLE OAKLEY. (F.c.)

(O.S. 6 in. xxx. N.W.)

Little Oakley is a small parish 3¼ m. S.W. of
Harwich.

Ecclesiastical :—

(1). PARISH CHURCH OF ST. MARY stands on the
W. side of the parish. The walls are of septaria
and flint-rubble, with dressings of limestone ; the
roofs are tiled. The *Nave* was built early in the
12th century. About the middle of the 14th
century the *Chancel* was rebuilt and a N. vestry
added but subsequently destroyed. The *West
Tower* was added *c.* 1490–1500. The church has
been restored in modern times, when the tower
was partly rebuilt and the *South Porch* added.

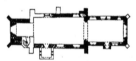

Architectural Description—The *Chancel* (26½ ft.
by 15¾ ft.) has a mid 14th-century E. window
(Plate, p. 143) of three trefoiled ogee lights with
net tracery in a two-centred head with moulded
labels ; the external work is much restored ; above
this window is a small square-headed opening,
now blocked. On the apex of the gable is an
enriched 14th-century cross, partly broken. In the
N. wall are three windows ; the easternmost is of
the 14th century and of one cinquefoiled light ;
the middle window, now blocked, is of doubtful
date and of two square-headed lights with the
splays outwards ; it communicated with the former
vestry ; the westernmost window is of mid 14th-

century date and of two cinquefoiled ogee lights
with flowing tracery in a two-centred head with a
moulded label ; E. of the blocked window is a
blocked doorway, probably of the 14th century,
with a segmental-pointed head. In the S. wall are
two mid 14th-century windows, partly restored
and each of two cinquefoiled lights with tracery in
a two-centred head with a moulded label ; between
them is a doorway, all modern except the 14th-century splays and rear-arch ; covering this door
and under a buttress is a small porch (Plate, p. xxix)
having an outer archway of the 14th century with
moulded jambs and two-centred head. The mid
14th-century chancel-arch is two-centred and of
two chamfered orders ; the responds have each
an attached octagonal shaft with moulded capital
and base.

The *Nave* (37½ ft. by 19½ ft.) has in the N. wall
a mid 14th-century window of two cinquefoiled
lights in a two-centred head with a moulded label ;
further E. is the 15th-century rood-loft staircase ;
the lower doorway has hollow-chamfered jambs
and two-centred heads ; the upper doorway, in the
E. wall, has a roughly rounded head ; near the
W. end of the N. wall is the 14th-century N. doorway with double hollow-chamfered jambs, two-centred arch and label ; it is now blocked. In the
S. wall are two windows ; the eastern is of the
14th century and of two trefoiled ogee lights with
tracery in a two-centred head with a moulded
label ; the western window is modern, between
them is an early 12th-century window of one
round-headed light, now blocked ; W. of the
windows is the mid 14th-century S. doorway, with
moulded jambs, two-centred arch and label with
defaced head-stops.

The *West Tower* (9¾ ft. square) is of one stage,
partly of late 15th-century date and partly modern ;
it has a moulded plinth with cusped panels formerly
of flint-inlay work, but now filled with cement.
The tower-arch has been rebuilt, but incorporates
material of *c.* 1500. The W. window is of three
cinquefoiled lights with vertical tracery in a
segmental-pointed head with a moulded label ;
below it is a doorway (Plate, p. 143) with moulded
jambs and two-centred arch in a square head with
a moulded label and stops carved with crowned
lions ; the jambs and arch-mould are carved with
square flowers and the spandrels have shields of
the arms of Vere and Howard ; above the label is
a range of trefoiled panels with blank shields in
alternate panels.

The *South Porch* is modern but reset in the
E. and W. walls are 14th-century cinquefoiled
window-heads.

The *Roof* of the chancel is of the 14th century
and of trussed-rafter type with moulded wall-plates. The roof of the nave is of similar form
but the wall-plates are partly and the tie-beams
entirely modern.

Fittings—*Bells :* four, all by Miles Graye and dated respectively 1612, 1615, 1633 and 1652. *Doors :* In nave—in S. doorway, battened with strap-hinges, late 15th-century, restored. In tower —in doorway to staircase, of ridged panels with moulded fillets and frame, late 15th-century ; in W. doorway, of two folds with moulded battens, late 15th-century. *Floor-slabs :* In chancel—(1) to ...., 1699 ; (2) to John ...., late 17th-century ; (3) to Robert Blacksell, 1680 ; (4) to Robert Blacksell, 1674, and Rachel, wife of John Scarpe, 1693 ; (5) to ...., 1672. *Glass :* In chancel—in N.E. and two S. windows, fragments of borders, tabernacle work, etc., 14th-century. *Indents :* In chancel—two, of inscription-plates. *Niches :* In chancel—flanking E. window, two with shafted and buttressed jambs, canopy with ribbed soffit, cinquefoiled, gabled and crocketed heads and crocketed and finialed spire, 14th-century, partly restored. *Painting :* remains of blue and gold, now restored, on vaults of niches and of red colour on backs of niches. *Piscina :* In chancel—with shafted and buttressed jambs, cinquefoiled head, with tall crocketed gabled enclosing blind tracery, flanking pinnacles, sexfoiled drain, 14th-century. *Scratching :* In chancel— on E. jamb of S. doorway, circular design. *Sedile :* Sill of S.E. window of chancel, carried down to form seat. *Tiles :* In nave—incised tiles with geometrical or rose designs, late 13th-century. *Miscellanea :* Built into S.E. buttress of tower, six trefoiled heads of panels, from plinth.
Condition—Fairly good.

Secular :—

(2). WHITEHOUSE FARM, house, 750 yards N. of the church, is of two storeys with attics, timber-framed and plastered ; the roofs are tiled. It was built probably in the 16th century and has a later addition at the back. The upper storey projects at the W. end of the N. front. Inside the building are exposed ceiling-beams.

(3). COTTAGE, three tenements, 500 yards E. of (2), is of two storeys, timber-framed and weather-boarded ; the roofs are tiled. It was built late in the 17th century.
Condition—Good.

(4). COTTAGE, 100 yards S.E. of (3), is of two storeys, timber-framed and weather-boarded ; the roofs are thatched. Inside the building are exposed ceiling-beams.
Condition—Good.

---

64. LITTLE TEY. (B.c.)

(O.S. 6 in. xxvi. S.E.)

Little Tey is a very small parish about 3 m. E.N.E. of Great Coggeshall. The church is interesting.

Ecclesiastical :—

(1). PARISH CHURCH OF ST. JAMES (Plate, p.xxviii) stands about the middle of the parish. The walls are of coursed flint-rubble with some pudding-stone the dressings are of limestone and the roofs are tiled. The *Chancel* and *Nave* were built *c.* 1130. Probably early in the 16th century the bell-turret was built. The church was restored in the 19th century when the *North Vestry* and *South Porch* were added.
The church is interesting as having an apsidal E. end.

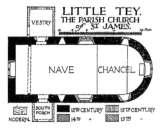

Architectural Description — The *Chancel* and *Nave* (47½ ft. by 18 ft.) are structurally undivided. The plain semi-circular apse has at the E. end a window of two pointed lights in an elliptical head ; it is perhaps of the 14th century, subsequently altered. At the spring of the apse on each side is a 12th-century window, that on the N. modern externally but old internally and that on the S. enlarged and with an inserted lancet-window. The N. wall has two windows, the eastern of the 14th century, partly restored, and of two pointed lights in a two-centred head ; the western window is a single round-headed light of the 12th century ; further N. is the N. doorway, modern externally but with 12th-century splays and round rear-arch. In the S. wall are two windows uniform with those in the N. wall except that the spandrel of the eastern window is quatrefoiled ; further W. is the 12th-century S. doorway (Plate, p. 142) with jambs of two plain orders, grooved and chamfered imposts and a moulded, semi-circular arch enclosing a diapered tympanum ; the door-head has been subsequently raised and an oak lintel inserted in the tympanum. In the W. wall is an early 15th-century window of two cinquefoiled lights with vertical tracery in a two-centred head with a moulded label ; above it is a single 12th-century light with a round head and altered internally.
The *Roof* of the apse is gabled and has a large projecting gusset-piece on each side under the eaves. The roof of the nave is of trussed-rafter type and ceiled.

Fittings—Bell : one, by Henry Pleasant, 1701. *Chair :* In chancel—with cane back, carved front legs and rail, turned back legs, early 18th-century. *Chest :* In vestry—of hutch-shape with one lock, three locks missing, probably 16th-century. *Font :* In garden of rectory, lower part of octagonal bowl with moulded under-edge, 15th-century. *Glass :* In E. window, fragments with small flower-ornament, 15th-century. *Plate :* includes late 16th-century cup and cover-paten, the cup with bands of incised ornament.
Condition—Good.

Secular :—

(2). HOMESTEAD MOAT, at Little Tey House, ½ m. N. of the church.

(3). GODBOLT'S FARM, house, 600 yards S.E. of the church, is of two storeys, timber-framed and plastered ; the roofs are tiled. It was built probably in the 15th-century, with a central hall and cross-wings at the E. and W. ends. The hall has been divided into two storeys. Inside the building the W. wing has an original cambered tie-beam and flat joists.
Condition—Good.

_____

65. LITTLE TOTHAM. (B.e.)

(O.S. 6 in. xlv. S.E.)

Little Totham is a small parish 4 m. N.E. of Maldon. The Church is interesting.

Ecclesiastical :—

(1). PARISH CHURCH OF ALL SAINTS stands about the middle of the parish. The walls are probably of flint-rubble but except for the tower they are plastered ; the dressings are of limestone and brick and the roofs are tiled. The *Nave* was built in the 12th century. In the 13th century the *Chancel* was rebuilt and perhaps enlarged. Probably in the 15th century the N. wall of the nave was rebuilt except for the lowest 3 ft. Early in the 16th century the *West Tower* was added but the upper part of it was rebuilt in the 17th or 18th century. The church was restored in the 19th century when the *South Porch* was added.
The S. doorway is an interesting example of 12th-century work.

Architectural Description—The *Chancel* (24½ ft. by 17 ft.) has in the E. wall three early 13th-century graduated lancet-windows ; they are partly restored and have a moulded internal string-course below the sills. In the N. wall is a 13th-century lancet-window, partly recut ; further W. is a blocked window, probably also of the 13th century. In the S. wall are two windows ; the eastern is a 13th-century lancet, subsequently widened and much restored ; the 16th-century western window is of terra-cotta and of two cinquefoiled lights in a square head. There is no chancel-arch.

The *Nave* (38 ft. by 18½ ft.) has in the N. wall two 18th-century or modern windows ; between them is the early 12th-century N. doorway (Plate, p. 132) with plain jambs, round arch and chamfered imposts, now blocked. The N. wall has an internal ledge of diminishing width and about 3 ft. above the floor, which indicates the line of the 12th-century window. In the S. wall are two windows, the eastern is of late 15th-century date, partly restored, and of two cinquefoiled lights in a square head with a moulded label ; the western window is a 13th-century lancet with restored jambs ; further W. is the S. doorway (Plate, p. 115) of *c.* 1160 with a round arch of three orders, the inner square and diapered and the two outer moulded, with embattled and billet ornament respectively ; the moulded label has billet-ornament ; the jambs have each a square inner order and two detached shafts with simply foliated capitals, moulded bases, and banding bosses, each with a disc on the face, enriched with diapering.

The *West Tower* (9¼ ft. square) is of two stages, the lower of 16th-century brick faced with knapped flint-work, and the upper timber-framed and weather-boarded and now divided into three storeys. The tower-arch which was probably never completed has semi-octagonal responds with moulded bases. The W. doorway has moulded jambs and four-centred arch in a square head with traceried spandrels and a moulded label ; above it is a shield bearing the date 1527. The upper stage incorporates 16th-century timbers but was probably rebuilt in the 17th or 18th century.

The *Roof* of the chancel has a plain tie-beam and moulded wall-plates of the 15th century. The 15th-century roof of the nave is of four bays with moulded and embattled wall-plates and moulded or chamfered tie-beams ; the moulded tie-beams have curved braces, and there are two carved grotesque corbels of wood. Incorporated in the modern porch is a reused beam with the mortices for diamond mullions.

Fittings—Bells : three ; 1st inscribed " Sancte Petre Ora Pro Nobis, A," 15th-century ; 2nd (Plate, p. 133) by John Sturdy and inscribed " Sancta Maria Ora Pro Nobis, I.S.," 15th-century ; 3rd by Miles Graye, 1663 ; bell-frame old. *Chair :* In chancel—with turned legs and rails, upholstered back with turned posts, probably late 17th-century. *Doors :* In N. doorway (Plate, p. 132)—of plain battens with ornamental iron hinges and strap with foliations, late 12th or early 13th-century. In S. doorway—of feathered battens with strap-hinges, 15th-century, elaborately foliated scutcheon-plate, late 13th-century. In W. doorway—of battens with strap-hinges, 16th-century. *Font* (Plate, p. xxxiv) : octagonal, each face of bowl with different form of window tracery, moulded top-edge, 15th-century, stem and base modern. *Monuments* and *Floor-slab*. Monuments : In chancel—against S. wall, of Sir John Samms (buried at Isendike) and Isabell (Garrard), his wife, mid 17th-century, marble monument (Plate, p. 97) with large kneeling figure of man in armour and wife with a recess in the middle ; at back of figures two arched recesses, flanked by panelled pilasters ; loose in lower recess, kneeling figure of man in armour, probably Sir Garrard Samms, son of the above ; monument reset. Floor-slab : In chancel—to John Sames, 1606, with achievement of arms and bevelled edge to slab. *Piscina :* In chancel—with defaced moulded and trefoiled head, shafted jambs with moulded capitals and bases, chamfered shelf and round drain, 13th-century. *Pulpit :* modern incorporating early 17th-century panelling and frieze with carved foliage. *Scratchings :* On tower-arch—various masons' marks and 17th and 18th-century names and dates.

Condition—Good.

Secular :—

(2). MOOR'S FARM, house and moat, ½ m. N. of the church. The *House* is of two storeys, timber-framed and plastered ; the roofs are tiled. It was built early in the 17th century, and has an original chimney-stack with two diagonal shafts.

The *Moat* surrounds the house.

Condition—Of house, good.

(3). LITTLE TOTHAM HALL, N.W. of the church, is of two storeys, timber-framed and plastered ; the roofs are tiled. The middle part of the house is of the 15th century, and appears to have been the original great hall, the cross-wings of which have been destroyed. On the N.E. is an irregular addition, partly in brick and of the 16th century ; it formed part of a much larger building, extending towards the N.E. There are various modern additions. In the S. wall of the original block is a blocked window of three lights with original moulded mullions. The E. end of the 16th-century addition has clasping pilasters at the angles and a blocked doorway with a four-centred head. Inside the building is an original window-head with the mortices for diamond-shaped mullions ; it now forms a ceiling-beam. There is also some exposed timber-framing, and on the first floor a braced tie-beam.

Condition—Good.

66. LITTLE WIGBOROUGH. (D.d.)
(O.S. 6 in. xlvi. N.E.)

Little Wigborough is a small parish 7 m. S. of Colchester.

Ecclesiastical :—

(1). PARISH CHURCH OF ST. NICHOLAS stands on the W. side of the parish. The walls are of stone-rubble roughly coursed and with dressings of limestone ; the roofs are tiled. The whole building consisting of *Chancel*, *Nave*, and *West Tower* was built or rebuilt late in the 15th century. The church was restored in the 19th century when the walls of the nave were heightened and the upper part of the tower rebuilt.

Architectural Description—The *Chancel* (16¾ ft. by 17½ ft.) is of late 15th-century date and has an E. window partly restored, of three cinquefoiled lights with vertical tracery in a two-centred head with a moulded label and defaced angel-stops. In the N. wall is a much restored window of two cinquefoiled lights in a square head. In the S. wall is a window uniform with that in the N. wall ; further E. is a doorway with double hollow-chamfered jambs and four-centred arch with a modern square head and label. There is no chancel-arch.

The *Nave* (28¼ ft. by 17½ ft.) is of late 15th-century date and has in the N. wall a window similar to that in the chancel but almost entirely modern externally ; further W. is the partly restored N. doorway with moulded jambs, two-centred arch, and label with stops carved with angels. In the S. wall is a window similar to that in the N. wall ; further W. is the S. doorway with moulded jambs, two-centred arch and label, all much restored. Flanking the doorway are the broken ends of the side walls of a former S. porch, now destroyed.

The *West Tower* (7½ ft. by 6 ft.) is of three stages, the lowest of late 15th-century date and the two upper rebuilt in the 19th century. The tower-arch is two-centred and of two hollow-chamfered orders, the outer continuous and the inner dying on to the side walls. The W. window is modern except the splays and rear-arch.

The *Roof* of the nave is of the 15th century and of three bays with moulded tie-beams and curved and moulded braces.

Fittings—*Floor-slab :* In nave—to Isaac Mazengarb, 1698, and Mary, his wife, 1714. *Painting :* In nave—on splay of N. window, traces of red colour.

Condition—Fairly good, but some cracks in walls.

Secular :—

(2). GROVE FARM, house about ⅓ m. N. of the church, is of two storeys, timber-framed and plastered ; the roofs are tiled. It was built early in the 17th century with cross-wings at the N. and S. ends. Inside the building some original ceiling-beams and joists are exposed.
Condition—Good.

Unclassified :—

(3). RED HILLS, several along the line of the old high-water mark W. of Sampson's Creek and about ½ m. S.E. of the church.

----

67. MANNINGTREE. (E.b.)

(O.S. 6 in. xx. S.W.)

Manningtree is a parish and small town on the S. side of the Stour and 8½ m. N.E. of Colchester. The principal monuments are those numbered (2), (4), and (13).

Ecclesiastical :—

(1). PARISH CHURCH OF ST. MICHAEL stands on the S. of the main street. The N. wall is of brick with some septaria and flint ; the rest of the building is either of timber or is modern ; the roofs are tiled. The church was built *c.* 1616 when it consisted of *Nave* and *North* and S. *Aisles*. The church has been much altered in modern times, most of the columns replaced, the *Chancel* added, and the *South Aisle* rebuilt and galleries inserted. The early 17th-century hammer-beam roof is interesting.

Architectural Description—The *Nave* (50 ft. by 15½ ft.) is of four bays with timber arcades (Plate, p. xxxvi) formed of curved braces, springing from columns, which are now all of iron except the westernmost on the N. and the W. respond post, these being early 17th-century octagonal or semi-octagonal posts of oak.
The *North Aisle* (15½ ft. wide) is mainly of early 17th-century brick with some rubble. The windows and doorway are modern.
The *Roofs* of the nave and N. aisle are of early 17th-century date and of simple hammer-beam type with curved braces to the hammer-beams and collars ; the shields at the end of the hammer-

beams are modern except those in the N. aisle which are variously designed. The roofs are boarded below the rafters.
Fittings—*Chair :* In chancel—with turned legs, twisted rails, carved frame and uprights, late 17th-century. *Font :* In churchyard—octagonal bowl with quatrefoiled panels enclosing shields, also plain octagonal stem, 15th-century. *Gallery :* In nave—at W. end, incorporates 16th-century moulded beams ; the staircases incorporate symmetrically turned balusters of *c.* 1600. *Floor-slab :* In nave—to John Scarpe, jun., 1706 ; Hannah Scarpe, 1706 ; Elizabeth (Scarpe), wife of Robert Godfrey, 1712, and her infant daughter Elizabeth. *Glass :* In chancel—in E. window, three panels in enamel of SS. Paul, Jerome, and John, 17th-century, foreign. *Plate :* includes cup, given by William Laud, Bishop of London in 1633 and with his arms and two stand-patens with the same arms. *Miscellanea :* In wall of N. aisle—flanking N. doorway, externally, two stone panels, one carved with a Tudor rose and one with defaced figure, possibly St. Michael, 15th-century.
Condition—Good.

Secular :—

MONUMENTS (2–15).

The following monuments, unless otherwise described, are of the 17th century and of two storeys, timber-framed and plastered or weather-boarded ; the roofs are tiled. Many of the buildings have original chimney-stacks and exposed ceiling-beams.
Condition—Good, or fairly good.

(2). *House*, with shop and outbuilding, W. of the church. The *House* (Plate, p. 177) was built probably late in the 16th century and the remaining wing is of brick ; the front block has been entirely rebuilt ; there are 17th-century additions on the S. and E. The original wing has two windows of two and three lights respectively, with moulded mullions, square heads and labels, all of brick ; the original chimney-stack has six octagonal shafts with elaborately moulded bases.
The *Outbuilding*, S. of the house, was built in the 15th century. The upper storey projects at the S. end on curved brackets. Inside the building are remains of the original roof-construction.

(3). *House* and shop, 90 yards W. of (2), was built early in the 16th century and has an 18th-century addition at the back. There is one 17th-century window at the back, of three transomed lights. Inside the building is an original ceiling-beam, elaborately moulded. In the attic are two 17th-century battened doors.

(4). *White Hart Inn*, 20 yards N.W. of (3), was built early in the 16th century. There is a long

SECULAR BRICK-WORK.

LAYER MARNEY HALL.
Chimneys and North Turret of Gatehouse ;
early 16th-century.

LANGHAM.
(3) Valley House ; early 17th-century.
From the West.

RAMSEY.
(2) Roydon Hall; mid 16th-century.
West End of Main Block.

BRIGHTLINGSEA.
(4) Jacobes Hall.
Turret ; early
16th-century.

LAYER MARNEY HALL.
North Elevation of West Wing ; early 16th-century.

COLCHESTER.
(160) Winnock's Almshouses.
Main Doorways ; dated 1678.

BRICK CHIMNEY-STACKS.

MARKSHALL.
(4) Cradle House; late 16th-century.

GREAT TEY.
(30) Cottage; late 16th-century.

GREAT COGGESHALL.
(94) Stock Street Farm;
late 16th-century.

EARLS COLNE.
(16) Cottage, Back Lane; 17th-century.

TWINSTEAD.
(4) Smith's Farm; 17th-century.

FEERING.
(4) Feeringbury; early 17th-century.

MANNINGTREE.
(2) House W. of Church; late 16th-centu

(4) Curd Hall; 17th-century.

LITTLE COGGESHALL.

(3) Coggeshall Hall; late 16th-century.

17th-century addition on the N. and an 18th-century addition on the E. The upper storey formerly projected on the S. front, but has been underbuilt and the whole refaced with brick. The upper storey projects on the W. side of part of the 17th-century addition. Inside the building the former central hall has been divided up and part now forms a cartway ; the hall has original moulded ceiling-beams and joists and two moulded wall-posts carved at the top with the heads of a man and a woman. A room further E. has also original moulded ceiling-joists.

(5). *House* and shop, on E. side of road, 60 yards E.N.E. of (4), was built probably early in the 15th century, but all except the E. part was rebuilt in the 16th century. The upper storey projects at the W. end on curved brackets springing from buttressed shafts ; below the capitals runs a band of carved conventional foliage. Inside the building is some early 17th-century panelling and doors. The cellar has a series of brick niches with four-centred heads. There are remains of the original roof-construction in the E. part of the house.

(6). *House*, two tenements, 40 yards E. of (5), was built probably in the 15th century on an L-shaped plan with the wings extending towards the E. and N. A wing was added on the N. of the E. wing in the 17th century. The upper storey projects on the E. side of the N. wing ; it formerly projected also in the S. front but has been under-built. Inside the building are some 16th-century moulded ceiling-beams. The roof of the N. wing has an original king-post truss.

(7). *House*, opposite the church, contains some original panelling.

(8). *House* and shop, 30 yards E. of (7), has an 18th-century block on the street front.

(9). *House*, 30 yards E. of (8).

(10). *House*, on the quay, 30 yards N. of (9).

(11). *House*, 100 yards W. of (10), was built probably in the 16th century.

(12). *House* and offices, on W. side of South Street, 50 yards S. of High Street.

(13). *House*, E. of (12), on opposite side of road, was built late in the 15th century with a cross-wing at the W. end. The hall was subsequently divided into two storeys. Inside the building the hall has an original middle roof-truss with a cambered tie-beam and octagonal king-post with moulded capital and base. The ground floor has an early 17th-century moulded bracket. The circular newel-staircase is probably of the 16th century and has four 17th-century turned balusters at the top. A room on the first floor has a 17th-century plaster ceiling enriched with a central rosette and fleurs-de-lis.

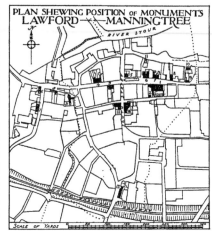

PLAN SHEWING POSITION of MONUMENTS
LAWFORD—*—MANNINGTREE
RIVER STOUR
SCALE OF YARDS

(14). *House* and shop, S. of (13), was built probably late in the 16th century and has a 17th or 18th-century addition at the back incorporating original moulded and chamfered beams. In the cellar is an original fireplace with a four-centred head of brick.

(15). *House*, four tenements, 200 yards S. of (14), was built probably in the 16th century.

---

68. MARKSHALL. (B.c.)

(O.S. 6 in. (a)xxvi. N.W. (b)xxvi. S.W.)

Markshall is a small parish 2 m. N. of Great Coggeshall. The Hall is an important monument.

Ecclesiastical :—

a(1). PARISH CHURCH OF ST. MARGARET was entirely rebuilt in 1875 but retains from the old church the following :—

Fittings—*Bell :* one, by Richard Bowler, 1595. *Monument :* In nave—on N.E. wall, of Mary (Waters), wife of Robert Honywood, 1620, marble wall-monument with kneeling figure of a lady flanked by Ionic columns supporting a pediment, lozenge and two shields of arms. *Plate :* includes cup and cover-paten of 1628.
Condition—Good, rebuilt.

Secular :—

a(2). MARKS HALL, house, and dovecote, N. of the church. The *House* is mainly of three storeys ; the walls are of brick and the roofs are covered with tiles, slates and lead. It was almost entirely rebuilt *c.* 1609 except for a small portion on the N. side which is of *c.* 1566 and is of different

M

alignment to the rest of the building. The servants' wing, between this fragment and the main block, is of early 18th-century date. The house was much altered and added to late in the 18th century and was generally restored in the 19th century.

The house is important as a 17th-century building of some size and contains some good contemporary woodwork.

Elevations—The *S. Front* is symmetrical and has two projecting bays and an embattled parapet, all of late 18th-century date ; the windows are of the same period. The projecting porch in the middle of the front is of *c.* 1609, and of three storeys, divided by plaster cornices with coupled pilasters at the sides, of the Doric, Ionic and Corinthian orders superimposed ; the frieze of the Doric order has rosettes and ox-skulls between the triplighs ; above its cornice is a shield of the quartered coat of Honywood impaling Browne. The round-headed outer archway has moulded imposts, fluted key-block and sunk spandrels with a band of arabesque ornament above them. The inner doorway has moulded jambs and four-centred arch in a square head with sunk spandrels all in plaster ; the panelled door has radiating flutings in the head.

The *E. Side* has a top storey largely reconstructed late in the 18th century. The windows of the two lower floors are mainly of early 17th-century date ; they are of three transomed lights, except the semi-octagonal bay window of two storeys at the N. end, which has four lights in front and one at each side ; on the ground floor these lights have two transoms. All the windows are of plastered brick. The early 18th-century wing has some original sash windows, with plain sunk panels above them.

The *N. Elevation* includes the remains of the mid 16th-century house but the walls of this part are plastered. The *W. Elevation* has no ancient features of interest. Some of the chimney-stacks are of early 17th-century date with octagonal shafts and moulded bases, but all are much restored.

Interior—The *Great Hall* has at the W. end an early 17th-century oak screen (Plate, p. 180) of five bays of which the middle one forms a doorway with a four-centred head ; the side bays are close-panelled and the other two bays are open and fitted with a rail and flat, shaped and pierced balusters below it ; the posts are moulded and the four side bays have a fluted frieze ; the cornice is surmounted by two pediments, each with turned terminals at the base and apex. The walls of the room have late 16th-century panelling with a later fluted frieze. The fireplace is plastered and has a four-centred head with the spandrels carved with two shields of arms and on the stops of the jambs are the initials and date R.H. 1609, for Robert Honywood ; the fireplace is flanked by pilasters supporting an arcaded overmantel divided into two main bays and flanked by diminishing pilasters. the 'screens' have a pavement of white stone

but the rest of the room is paved with black and white squares set diagonally. A doorway has early 17th-century stop-moulded jambs and square head. The *Library*, W. of the Hall, has early 17th-century panelling and an altered fireplace flanked by fluted Ionic pilasters and having an overmantel of two stages, each of three bays with arcaded panels and Ionic pilasters. The "*Prayer Room*" (Plate, p. 180), N. of the Hall, has early 17th-century panelled walls with a frieze enriched with triplighs and arabesques. The fireplace has a flat lintel with a shield in the middle and is flanked by terminal pilasters supporting an entablature with arabesque ornament ; the overmantel is of three bays, divided and flanked by carved Corinthian columns ; the middle bay is panelled and the side bays have each an enriched arch with a female figure—Justice and Charity—standing on a bracket. The back stairs are of late 17th-century date with turned newels and balusters and moulded rails. The *Servants' Hall* has a moulded ceiling-beam with a shield inscribed 1566 I.C. (for John Cole). On the first floor the room over the "Prayer Room" has early 17th-century panelling and a fireplace with moulded jambs and square head and flanked by Ionic pilasters ; the overmantel is divided into three bays by terminal pilasters ; the bays have arched panels, the middle one with a shell head and the side bays with the sun and moon. The room over part of the Hall has similar panelling and fireplace flanked by coupled pilasters supporting a panelled overmantel of two bays with coupled pilasters at the sides and a single pilaster in the middle. Another room has a similar fireplace flanked by Ionic pilasters supporting an overmantel of two bays with double-arched panels and Ionic pilasters. *Glass :* In S.E. window of Hall a quartered coat of Wentworth impaling *gules three scutcheons argent* set in a green chaplet, 16th-century ; also fragments of figures, a saint's head and borders, 15th and 16th-century. In S.W. window a coat of Waldegrave impaling Wentworth and quarterings ; the royal arms (Tudor) crowned ; and a crowned fleur-de-lis with initials E.R., 16th-century. In the Library in S.E. window, a quartered coat of Browne of Bechworth impaling Guilford and quarterings within a coloured chaplet ; and, at sides of shield, crests of these families, 16th-century, set in fragments of 15th and 16th-century glass. In S.W. window, a quartered coat of Poynings impaling Browne and quarterings, 16th-century ; also 15th and 16th-century fragments. In bedroom on first floor, small enamel-painted panel of a man on horseback inscribed ' equestris principis vel Baronis Germani ' (black-letter), 16th-century, and heraldic fragments 17th-century.

The *Dovecote*, N.E. of the house, is octagonal and of red brick ; it is probably of mid 16th-century date. E. of the servants' wing is a *Cottage* partly of brick and partly of plastered timber-framing. It is probably of the 16th century but has been much altered.

Condition—Of house, etc., good.

a(3). BRICKHOUSE FARM, house, about 1,150 yards N. of the church, is of two storeys, timber-framed and plastered; the roofs are tiled. It was built probably early in the 17th century and has exposed ceiling-beams and joists.

Condition—Good, much altered.

b(4). CRADLE HOUSE (Plate, p. 177), 1 m. S. of the church, is of two storeys, timber-framed and plastered; the roofs are tiled. It was built late in the 16th century and has a S. wall of brick with a projecting chimney-stack having numerous tabled offsets and some black diapering; the two shafts are set diagonally.

Condition—Good.

---

69. MARKS TEY. (C.c.)

(O.S. 6 in. *(a)*xxvi. S.E. *(b)*xxvii. S.W.)

Marks Tey is a parish and small village 5½ m. W.S.W. of Colchester. The church is interesting.

Ecclesiastical :—

(1). PARISH CHURCH OF ST. ANDREW stands at the N. end of the parish. The walls are of mixed rubble, coursed and including septaria and iron pudding-stone in the nave, and random in the chancel and tower. The upper part of the tower and the S. porch are of timber and the roofs are tiled. The *Nave* was built *c.* 1100. The *Chancel* was rebuilt *c.* 1330 and there was possibly a late 14th-century *West Tower*, which was rebuilt early in the 16th century; the *South Porch* was added in the 16th century. The church was restored in the 19th century.

Architectural Description—The *Chancel* (30 ft. by 16½ ft.) has a modern E. window. In the N. wall are two uniform windows, the western is set lower in the wall; each is of two trefoiled lights with tracery in a two-centred head with a moulded label, all of *c.* 1330; the mullions have been restored. In the S. wall are two windows uniform with those on the N. but partly restored externally; between the windows is a 14th-century doorway with wave-moulded jambs and two-centred arch. The chancel-arch is of mid to late 14th-century date and is two-centred and of two hollow-chamfered orders dying into plain chamfered orders in the responds.

(6405)

The *Nave* (38 ft. by 19 ft.) has quoins of Roman brick and pudding-stone. In the N. wall are two windows; the eastern is all modern except the W. splay and the segmental-pointed rear-arch, which is probably of the 14th century; the western is entirely modern; between the windows is the N. doorway of *c.* 1100 with Roman-brick jambs and round arch with an oak lintel at the springing level, supporting a rubble tympanum; E. of the eastern window is the lower doorway to the rood-loft staircase with a two-centred head of late 14th or early 15th-century date; In the S. wall are three windows, the easternmost is all modern except the splays which are probably of the 15th century; the second window is of *c.* 1100 and of one round-headed light in Roman brick; the westernmost window is of mid 14th-century date, partly restored and of two cinquefoiled lights with a quatrefoil in a two-centred head with a moulded label and angel-head stops; between the two western windows is the S. doorway uniform with the N. doorway.

The *West Tower* (10 ft. square) is of three stages, the lowest of rubble below and brick above, the two upper of timber with a small spire. The tower-arch is two-centred and modern but the chamfered responds are possibly of late 14th-century date. The W. window is of early 15th-century date, probably reset, and is of two cinquefoiled lights with vertical tracery in a two-centred head with a moulded label and head-stops; it is partly restored externally; the W. doorway is of late 14th or early 15th-century date reset and has hollow-chamfered jambs and two-centred arch with a moulded label and head-stops; S. of the doorway externally is a cross of bricks on a calvary of two steps, let into the wall. The second stage has cross-braces to the timber-framing and the bell-chamber has in each wall a 16th-century window of oak and two four-centred lights in a square head. The spirelet has a square-framed base resting on two tie-beams with curved braces running E. and W., and the spire itself has a central post with struts, all of the 16th century.

The *South Porch* is timber-framed and of 16th-century date, and stands on dwarf brick walls, partly old. It has chamfered main posts and modern intermediate ones.

The *Roofs* of the chancel and nave are of the trussed-rafter type, of uncertain date. The porch has two king-post trusses, one at each end and with struts to a central purlin, all of the 16th century.

Fittings — *Chair:* In chancel - - modern incorporating two panels carved with lozenge and other ornament, early 17th-century. *Chest:* In chancel—of hutch type with carved lid and front, early 17th-century. *Font* (Plate, p. xxxiv) : of oak, octagonal bowl, panelled sides divided by buttresses, each panel formerly enclosing a carved figure—probably a seated figure—on a throne and an evangelistic

M 2

symbol alternately, but now mostly cut away, modern traceried heads to panels ; moulded underside of bowl carved with roses, panelled and traceried stem with carved roses and moulded base, 15th-century. Cover of octagonal pyramid form with moulded fillets, early 17th-century. *Niche :* In chancel—N. of E. window, recess with plastered back, moulded jambs removed to stoup in S. porch and replaced by modern work, possibly 15th-century. *Piscina :* In chancel—with moulded jambs and trefoiled head, cinquefoiled drain, 14th-century. *Plate :* includes Elizabethan cup and cover-paten, 1567· *Sedile :* In chancel—sill of S.E. window carried down to form seat. *Stoup :* In S. porch—recess with damaged head, date uncertain.

Condition—Good.

Secular :—

(2). MARKS TEY HALL, house and moat, ½ m. S.E. of the church. The *House* is of two storeys with attics ; the walls are timber-framed and plastered, and the roofs are tiled. It was built probably in the 17th century with projecting cross-wings at the E. and W. ends. On the N. front the main block has a gabled and two-storeyed porch and a projecting staircase wing.

The *Moat* is fragmentary.

MERSEA, see EAST MERSEA and WEST MERSEA.

---

70. MESSING. (B.d.)

(O.S. 6 in. (a)xxxv. N.E. (b)xxxv. S.E.)

Messing is a parish and small village 4¼ m. S.E. of Great Coggeshall. The church is the principal monument.

Ecclesiastical :—

a(1). PARISH CHURCH OF ALL SAINTS stands in the village. The walls are of stone rubble with conglomerate and Roman bricks ; the dressings are of limestone and the roofs are tiled. The earliest detail in the church is a 13th-century window in the *Chancel* but the character of the masonry of the chancel seems to indicate an earlier date. The chancel-arch was rebuilt probably early in the 17th century. The church was restored in the 19th century, when the E. wall was apparently rebuilt, the *Nave* lengthened and practically rebuilt, and the *West Tower, South Chapel* and *South Porch* added. There is said to have been a modern N. transept, now destroyed.

Among the fittings the 17th-century panelling and royal arms are noteworthy.

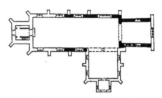

Architectural Description—The *Chancel* (21½ ft. by 15¼ ft.) has an E. window, perhaps of the 17th century, and of three lights with net tracery in a two-centred head. In the N. wall is a mid 14th-century window of two ogee lights, with tracery in a two-centred head with a moulded label. In the S. wall is a window uniform with that in the N. wall, but not *in situ ;* further W. is a 13th-century lancet-window, now blocked ; between the windows and partly destroyed by the eastern is an early 16th-century doorway of brick, with chamfered jambs and four-centred arch in a square head ; it is now blocked. The two-centred chancel-arch is probably of early 17th-century date and of plastered brick ; it is of two chamfered orders, the outer continuous and the inner resting on crudely moulded corbels.

The *Nave* (63½ ft. by 21½ ft.) has no ancient features except the remains of a late 14th-century doorway under the second window in the N. wall ; it has moulded jambs and defaced head-stops to the former label.

The *Roof* of the nave is of the 15th century and of six bays, of which the two western are mostly modern ; the others have moulded wall-plates, curved principals and trussed-rafters ; at the feet of the principals are small carved angels, two holding shields, charged with *three cheverons ermine* and *a label of five points* for Baynard ; at the apex of each truss is a flowered boss ; against the E. wall is a hammer-beam truss with carved angels at the ends of the hammer-beams.

Fittings — *Brasses* and *Indent.* Brasses : In chancel—(1) of woman in pedimental head-dress, *c.* 1540. In nave—(2) to John Porter, 1600, inscription only. Indent : In nave—of inscription-plate. *Chairs :* In chancel—two with elaborately carved and pierced backs, turned legs, late 17th-century. *Chests :* In S. chapel—(1) (Plate, p. xxxii) iron-bound, with three locks, lid in two sections, 13th or 14th-century ; (2) with feet and panelled sides and lid, top-rail in front, fluted, 17th-century. *Communion Table :* with two pairs of turned legs with round arches, shaped lower rail, upper rail ornamented with turned drops, 17th-century. *Glass :* In chancel—in E. window, and including the six of the seven works of mercy with titles, figures of Faith, Hope and Charity, and cherub-heads and stars, early 17th-century. *Monument :* In nave—fragments, with two quatrefoiled panels

MARKS HALL.
Screen and Panelling in Hall; late 16th and early 17th-century.

MARKS HALL.
Panelling and Fireplace in 'Prayer Room'; early 17th-century.

ST. OSYTH'S PRIORY OR ABBEY.
Panelling in 'Bishop's Lodging'; *c.* 1527.

TOLLESHUNT D'ARCY HALL.
Panelling in middle room; early 16th-century.

MESSING CHURCH.
Carved Royal Arms; 1634.

WHITE COLNE CHURCH.
Pulpit; early 17th-century.

EAST MERSEA CHURCH.
Pulpit and Sounding board
early 17th-century.

LANGHAM CHURCH.
Bench-end; early
16th-century.

INWORTH CHURCH.
Back of Bench in Nave; c. 1500.

ARDLEIGH CHURCH.
Chancel Screen; late 15th-century.

FINGRINGHOE CHURCH.
Font-cover; 15th-century.

MESSING CHURCH.
Chancel Stalls; c. 1640.

enclosing shields, probably part of monument, 15th-century. *Panelling :* In chancel—on E., N. and S. walls, elaborate oak panelling divided into bays by enriched Corinthian pilasters and having an entablature with dentilled cornice and enriched frieze with cherub-heads, each bay normally with two panels, each with an enriched and masoned arch in perspective, panelling raised in middle of E. wall to form reredos and entablature interrupted and stopped at the windows by pierced and carved scrolls ; stalls (Plate, p. 181) included in same design, with panelled fronts and ends, each panel containing a masoned oval and carved spandrels, dentilled book-board, *c.* 1640 ; around responds of chancel-arch, modern panelling incorporating linen-fold panels, early 16th-century. *Pavement :* In chancel—of black and white marble, part set diagonally and some inscribed with text, late 17th-century. *Piscina :* In chancel—plain round drain, probably 13th-century, recess modern. *Plate :* includes two cups with cover-patens, two flagons and a standing-dish, all of 1634 and each with a shield of arms and inscription. *Reredos :* see Panelling. *Royal Arms* (Plate, p. 181) : In S. chapel—gabled panel with pierced, supporting scrolls and the Stuart arms and date 1634 on the N. face and on 'the S. face the Prince of Wales' feathers, crown, initials C.R., and the same date, below main panel, rectangular panel with dentilled entablature, texts on one side and an impaled achievement of arms of Hananeel Chibborne and his wife. *Stalls :* see Panelling.

Condition—Good, but some cracks in walls of nave.

Secular :—

MONUMENTS (2–22).

The following monuments, unless otherwise described, are of the 17th century and of two storeys, timber-framed or weather-boarded ; the roofs are tiled or thatched. Some of the buildings have original chimney-stacks and exposed ceiling-beams.

Condition—Good, or fairly good.

*(2). *Bourchier's Hall,* 180 yards S. of the church, was built in the 15th century with a cross-wing at the E. end. The hall block was subsequently divided into two storeys and probably now includes a former cross-wing at the W. end. Inside the building are remains of the original roof construction. There are some 17th-century battened doors and a staircase of the same period, with turned balusters, close strings and square newels with turned heads and pendants.

*(3). *House,* two tenements, 100 yards N.N.E. of (2), has a lower storey of brick.

*(4). *Old Crown Inn,* 100 yards N. of (3), has a modern front.

*(5). *House,* two tenements, on E. side of church-yard, has a modern front.

*(6). *House,* two tenements, 30 yards W. of (4), has a W. cross-wing of the 15th century, with remains of original king-post roof-trusses ; the rest of the house is modern.

*(7). *Queen's Head Inn,* W. of (6).

*(8). *House,* 10 yards W. of (7), has an E. cross-wing and part of the main block of a 15th-century building, but the rest of the house has been rebuilt. The upper storey projects on the S. end of the cross-wing and in the same wing is an original king-post roof-truss.

*(9). *Cottage,* two tenements, 36 yards W. of (8).

*(10). *Cottage,* two tenements, W. of (9).

*(11). *Messing Lodge,* house, ½ m. N.E. of the church, has been very much altered.

*(12). *Yewtree Farm,* house, 1,100 yards W. of the church, was built in the 16th century. The upper storey projects on the S. front on curved brackets. The short back wing has an original king-post roof-truss.

ᵇ(13). *Stubbers,* house, now two tenements, about ¼ m. S.W. of (12), was built probably late in the 15th or early in the 16th century, but has been extensively altered and added to.

ᵇ(14). *Parsonage Farm,* house, 500 yards E. of (13), has a large modern block, added in front. Inside the building are some original doors of moulded battens.

ᵇ(15). *Hill Farm,* house, 1¼ m. S.W. of the church, has a late 17th-century addition on the N.E. The front has been refaced with modern brick.

ᵇ(16). *Cottage,* 800 yards E.S.E. of (15).

ᵇ(17). *Cottage,* on N. side of Tiptree Heath and ¼ m. S.S.E. of (16).

ᵇ(18). *Cottage,* at cross-roads, ¼ m. E. of (16).

ᵇ(19). *Cottage,* 260 yards N.E. of (18), has an original chimney-stack, cross-shaped on plan.

ᵇ(20). *The Elms,* house, 180 yards N. of (18), has been considerably altered. The upper storey projects on the W. front on original shaped brackets.

ᵇ(21). *Cottage,* 300 yards S.E. of the church, was built probably early in the 18th century.

ᵇ(22). *Harborough Hall,* house and outbuilding, 500 yards S.E. of the church. The *House* has been almost completely altered, but in the N. wall is a blocked window with an original moulded mullion. The *Outbuilding* adjoins the house on the S. and is of L-shaped plan.

Unclassified :—

ᵇ(23). MOUND, probably tumulus, in Coneyfield Wood, about ½ m. S. of the church, is about 6 ft. high and 75 ft. in diameter at the base.

Condition—Fairly good.

71. MIDDLETON.   (B.a.)

(O.S. 6 in. xii. N.E.)

Middleton is a small parish on the Suffolk border, 7 m. N.E. of Halstead. The church is interesting.

Ecclesiastical :—

(1). PARISH CHURCH OF ALL SAINTS (?) stands about the middle of the parish. The walls are of flint-rubble covered with cement and with dressings of Barnack stone and clunch ; the roofs are tiled. The *Chancel* and *Nave* were built about the middle of the 12th century, but the chancel was extended perhaps in the 13th century. The *South Porch* was added probably early in the 16th century. The church was restored in the 19th century, when the *North Vestry* and *Organ Chamber* were added and the bell-turret rebuilt and the S. porch partly rebuilt.

The mid 12th-century chancel-arch and S. doorway and the incised floor-slab (see Fig., p. 183) are noteworthy.

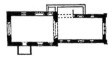

Architectural Description—The *Chancel* (34 ft. by 16 ft.) has a 14th-century E. window, partly restored, and of three pointed lights with intersecting tracery in a two-centred head. In the N. wall are two windows, the eastern of late 13th or early 14th-century date and of a single trefoiled light ; the western window is modern ; further W. is a modern opening. In the S. wall are four windows ; the easternmost is of the 14th century and of a single cinquefoiled light in a two-centred head with a moulded label ; the second window is modern ; the third window is a mid 13th-century lancet ; the westernmost window is similar to the easternmost, but all modern externally. The mid 12th-century chancel-arch is semi-circular and of two orders enriched with cheveron-ornament ; the responds are of three orders and have each two shafts, the inner octagonal and enriched and with a foliated capital and the outer round and with a scalloped capital ; the bases are moulded ; the chamfered impost has carved lozenge-ornament ; the respond on the S. side is modern and the other partly restored.

The *Nave* (32 ft. by 19 ft.) has in the N. wall two modern windows ; further W. is the N. doorway, now blocked, with a segmental arch. In the S. wall at the E. end is an early 13th-century recess probably to provide more room for a nave altar ;

the chamfered two-centred arch has dog-tooth ornament and springs from a plain respond on the E. and a reused shaft on the W., octagonal and with diapered faces and scalloped capital of the 12th century ; in this recess is a 13th-century lancet window ; further W. is a coupled lancet-window of the 13th century, much restored ; W. of this window is the mid 12th-century S. doorway (Plate, p. 142), partly restored and with a round arch of two orders with cheveron-ornament and a billety label ; the jambs have each two shafts with scalloped capitals, grooved and chamfered abaci and moulded bases. In the W. wall is a modern window.

The *Roof* of the nave is of the 15th century and of four bays, with moulded and embattled wall-plates and with tie-beams with traceried spandrels and curved braces springing from moulded corbels. The roof of the S. porch incorporates some old timbers and at the sides are diamond-shaped mullions, mostly of the 16th century.

Fittings—*Chest :* In nave—plain iron-bound, with drop-handles and two locks, 16th-century. *Door :* In S. doorway, of battens, panelled with moulded fillets worked from the solid, cusped head and embattled transom, lower panels cusped and with carved spandrels, late 15th-century. *Monuments* and *Floor-slab.* Monuments : In nave—in N. and S. walls (1 and 2), tomb-recess with moulded segmental-pointed arch and label ; triple-shafted jambs with moulded capitals and bases, early 14th-century. Floor-slab : In chancel—of James Samson (Fig., p. 183), rector of the church, 134(9 ?), Purbeck marble slab with incised figure in mass-vestments, diapered apparel to alb and swastika ornament to maniple, holding chalice, elaborately cusped and crocketed canopy with side-pinnacles and marginal inscription, head, hands and chalice formerly inlaid but now missing except face, which is in white marble, probably modern, marginal inscription with symbols of the evangelists, probably Flemish work. *Painting :* In nave—above chancel-arch, painting on canvas probably of the Annunciation, Italian, said to be by Schiavone, 16th-century. *Piscina :* In chancel—with moulded two-centred head and sexfoiled drain and oak shelf, 14th-century.

Condition—Good.

Secular :—

(2). HOMESTEAD MOAT, at Middleton Hall, ¼ m. N. of the church.

(3). COTTAGE, 300 yards S.W. of the church, is of two storeys, timber-framed and plastered ; the roofs are thatched. It was built in the 17th century and has exposed ceiling-beams.

Condition—Good.

Incised Floor-slab of James Samson, mid 14th-century. (1/11th full size.)

72. MISTLEY. (E.b.)   .
(O.S. 6 in. xx. S.W.)

Mistley is a parish and village on the S. side of the Stour estuary, adjoining Manningtree on the E.

Ecclesiastical :—

(1). CHURCH OF ST. MARY, now in ruins, stands about 1 m. S.E. of the modern church. The walls are of flint and septaria-rubble, with dressings of limestone. There is little evidence of the date of the main building, but the *South Porch* was built *c.* 1500. The church became ruinous in the 17th or early in the 18th century, and now consists only of the lower parts of the former E. wall, most of the S. wall, the S. porch and a fragment further W., which may be the W. end of the N. wall or part of a former W. tower.

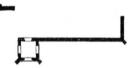

Architectural Description—The *Chancel* and *Nave* (85 ft., including fragment, by 19 ft.) have no remaining details.

The *South Porch*, built *c.* 1500, has a moulded plinth with flint-inlay panels having capital letters (Plate, p. 133) RA, DAE, D, DMD, RA. The S. front with the buttresses has traceried panels inlaid with knapped flint. The buttresses have sunk panels with cusped and crocketed heads. The outer archway is two-centred and of three moulded orders, the inner and the label resting on attached shafts with moulded capitals and bases; the moulded label is double, the outer one enclosing a square head with carved foliage and two shields, each with a merchant's mark. The side walls have each a blocked window with a four-centred head. In the N. wall, the former S. doorway of the nave has a segmental head and is now blocked.

Fitting—*Plate :* At new church—17th-century cup.

Condition—Ruined.

Secular :—

(2). HOUSE, two tenements, 600 yards W.N.W. of the modern church, is of two storeys with attics, timber-framed and plastered ; the roofs are tiled. It was built early in the 16th century and has a 17th-century addition at the back. Inside the building is an original moulded ceiling-beam.

Condition—Good.

73. MOUNT BURES. (C.b.)
(O.S. 6 in. [a]xvii. N.E. [b] xviii. N.W. [c]xvii. S.E. [d] xviii. S.W.)

Mount Bures is a parish on the Suffolk border, 6 m. E. of Halstead. The church and mount are monuments of interest.

Ecclesiastical :—

[a](1). PARISH CHURCH OF ST. JOHN stands at the N. end of the parish. The walls are of coursed flint-rubble with Roman brick quoins ; the dressings are of limestone and clunch ; the roofs are tiled. The *Chancel* and *Nave*, with a Central Tower, were built early in the 12th century. Late in the 15th century the *South Porch* was added. The church was restored in the 19th century when the *Central Tower* was rebuilt and *North* and *South Transepts* and the *North Vestry* added.

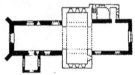

Architectural Description—The *Chancel* (26 ft. by 19½ ft.) has E. quoins of Roman brick and a 14th-century E. window of three cinquefoiled lights with modern tracery in a triangular head. In the N. wall is a modern doorway with a two-centred head. In the S. wall are two windows, the eastern is modern, except for the splays and rear-arch, which are of the 14th century ; the 14th-century western window is partly restored and of three trefoiled ogee lights in a square head.

The *Central Tower* (15 ft. by 15¾ ft.), *North Transept* and *South Transept* have no ancient features except the reused Roman brick quoins of the S. transept.

The *Nave* (34½ ft. by 17½ ft.) has in the N. wall two windows, the eastern is modern but the western is a single, early 12th-century, round-headed light ; further W. is the early 12th-century N. doorway, now blocked, and with plain jambs of Roman brick and a round head. In the S. wall is a 15th-century window, much restored, of two cinquefoiled lights with vertical tracery in a two-centred head with a moulded label and jambs ; further W. is a blocked round-headed window of the 12th century, only visible internally ; further W. is the late 14th-century S. doorway with moulded jambs, two-centred arch and a moulded label with head-stops. In the W. wall is a late 14th-century window of three trefoiled lights with net tracery in a two-centred head, but almost entirely restored externally ; above it is a 12th-century window with a round head of Roman brick.

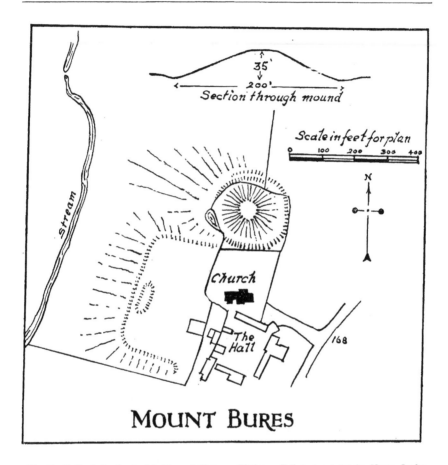

MOUNT BURES

The *South Porch* is of mixed brick and flint-rubble and has a late 15th-century outer archway with moulded and shafted jambs and two-centred arch in a square head with a moulded label, head-stops and spandrels carved with vine foliage and shields, one with IHC and one *quarterly over all a bend vair*, for Sackville ; above it is a small pointed light. The side walls have each a partly restored late 15th-century window of three cinquefoiled lights in a square head.

The *Roof* of the S. porch is of the 15th-century and has moulded wall-plates and tie-beams with king-posts.

Fittings—*Bells :* two ; 1st by Henry Jordan, inscribed " Sancte Necolae Ora Pro Nobis," mid 15th-century ; 2nd by Robert Burford, inscribed " Sit Nomen Domini Benedictum," early 15th-century. *Chest :* In S. transept—plain, with three locks, probably 17th-century. *Communion Table :* In vestry—with turned legs and carved top rail, early 17th-century. *Door :* In N. doorway—of feathered and nail-studded oak battens, 15th-century. In S. doorway—of nail-studded battens, with strap-hinges and pierced scutcheon-plate, 15th-century. *Font :* plain octagonal bowl, with moulded under-edge and plain stem, probably

15th-century. *Monument:* In churchyard—N. side, to Prudence Turner, 1662, headstone. *Niche :* In N. splay of E. window, with ribbed vault and cinquefoiled and crocketed head, 15th-century. *Piscina :* In chancel—two octofoiled drains, one with spiral flutings, 13th or 14th-century, recess modern. *Plate :* includes a cup and cover-paten of 1641. *Sedile :* In chancel—sill of S.E. window carried down low to form seat. *Stoup :* In S. porch —E. of doorway, with cinquefoiled head, no bowl, 15th-century.

Condition—Good, much restored.

Secular :—

ᵃ(2). FORTIFIED MOUNT, N. of the church, is about 35 ft. high and 200 ft. in diameter at the base. Round the mount is a ditch, now nearly dry. There are no definite traces of outer works, but the Norman church stands immediately S. of the mount and perhaps originally stood within the Bailey.

The work is situated on high ground, which drops sharply towards a stream to the W. ; on the slope is a nearly rectangular area scarped on three sides, with an oblong depression near the W. side. This is probably the site of a terraced garden belonging to the Hall. (Plan, p. 185.)

Condition—Fairly good. The summit of the mount is uneven and appears to have been opened by digging.

MONUMENTS (3–10).

The following monuments, unless otherwise described, are of the 17th century and of two storeys, timber-framed and plastered or weather-boarded ; the roofs are tiled or thatched. Some of the buildings have original chimney-stacks and exposed ceiling-beams.

Condition—Good, or fairly good.

ᵃ(3). *Cottage* (Plate, p. 188), 300 yards N. of the church, was built probably in the 16th century. The upper storey projects on the S. side. Inside the building is a large cambered tie-beam with curved braces.

ᵇ(4). *House,* 650 yards E. of the church, was built probably late in the 15th century. The upper storey projects at the N. end of the cross-wing at the E. end of the house. Inside the building is a doorway with a three-centred head ; the main block has an original king-post with rebated angles and four-way struts.

ᵇ(5). *Cottage,* 700 yards E. of (4), has ornamental plaster-work in front, with roses, fruit, and birds, all much defaced.

ᵇ(6). *Elm's Farm,* house, and barn, nearly ¾ m. E.S.E. of the church.

ᵇ(7). *Wither's Farm,* house, 100 yards S. of (6).

ᵇ(8). *Josselyns,* house, ¼ m. S.W. of (7). The upper storey projects at the W. end of the S. side.

ᵈ(9). *Norton's Farm,* house (Plate, p. 189), now two tenements, about ¾ m. S.S.E. of the church, has an original chimney-stack with two attached hexagonal shafts.

ᵉ(10). *Cottage,* at Jinke's Green, about 1½ m. S. of the church, has an original chimney-stack with grouped diagonal shafts.

OAKLEY, see GREAT OAKLEY and LITTLE OAKLEY.

74. PATTISWICK. (A.c.)

(O.S. 6 in. ⁽ᵃ⁾xxvi. N.W. ⁽ᵇ⁾xxv. S.E. ⁽ᶜ⁾xxvi. S.W.)

Pattiswick is a small parish 2½ m. W.N.W. of Great Coggeshall.

Ecclesiastical :—

ᶜ(1). PARISH CHURCH OF ST. MARY THE VIRGIN (formerly St. Mary Magdalene) stands in the middle of the parish. The walls are of plastered flint-rubble, with dressings of limestone and clunch ; the roofs are tiled. The *Nave* was built about the middle of the 13th century. Early in the 14th century the *Chancel* was rebuilt. The bell-turret was added probably early in the 15th century. The church was restored in the 19th century, when the *North Vestry* was rebuilt and the *South Porch* added.

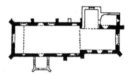

Architectural Description—The *Chancel* (26¼ ft. by 15¾ ft.) has an E. window entirely modern except for the 14th-century splays. In the N. wall is a 14th-century doorway, with moulded jambs and two-centred arch ; further W. is a modern arch. In the S. wall are two 14th-century windows, each of two pointed lights in a two-centred head ; the eastern window has been completely restored externally ; between the windows is a much restored 14th-century doorway, with chamfered jambs and two-centred arch. There is no chancel-arch.

The *North Vestry* has in the E. wall a reset 13th-century lancet window, with chamfered and rebated jambs and head. Reset in the N. wall of the modern *Organ Chamber* is a 14th-century window uniform with those in the S. wall of the chancel and partly restored.

The *Nave* (48 ft. by 20¼ ft.) has in the N. wall three windows, the easternmost is uniform with that in the organ chamber, but partly restored ; the two western windows are modern and between them is the 13th-century N. doorway, with a two-centred arch and a double-chamfered label. In the S. wall are three windows, the easternmost is modern except for the 14th-century splays and chamfered rear-arch ; the second is of the 14th century and of two trefoiled lights with a plain spandrel in a two-centred head ; the westernmost window is a mid 13th-century lancet with chamfered and rebated jambs and head ; between the two western windows is the 14th-century S. doorway, with jambs and two-centred arch of two chamfered orders, partly restored. In the W. wall is a 15th-century window of three cinquefoiled lights in a square head, all modern externally.

The *Roof* of the chancel is probably of the 14th century and of the trussed-rafter type, with moulded and embattled wall-plates. The 14th or early 15th-century roof (Plate, p. xxxvi) of the nave is of trussed-rafter type with two tie-beams ; the western tie-beam has an octagonal king-post with moulded capital and base ; the wall-plates are moulded. The bell-turret at the W. end of the nave rests on a heavy 15th-century tie-beam with a plain king-post.

Fittings—Bells : three, said to be, 1st by Miles Graye, 1668 ; 2nd by Miles Graye, 1632. *Communion Table :* with turned legs and shaped brackets to top rail, early 17th-century. *Glass :* In chancel—in spandrels of windows in S. wall, jumbled fragments ; in nave—in N.E. window and in two eastern S. windows, similar fragments, 15th to 17th-century. *Piscinae :* In chancel—in E. wall, with moulded jambs, two-centred head and octofoiled drain, 14th-century. In nave—in S. wall, with chamfered jambs, two-centred head and sexfoiled drain, 14th-century. *Seating :* In nave—at W. end, four pews with moulded top rails and panelled bench-ends, early 16th-century, made up with modern work. *Miscellanea :* In vestry—broken half of stone mortar, date uncertain.

Condition—Good.

Secular :—

ᶜ(2). CHURCH FARM, house and moat, 500 yards E.N.E. of the church. The *House* is of two storeys, timber-framed and plastered ; the roofs are tiled. It was built late in the 17th century, and has exposed ceiling-beams.

The *Moat* surrounds the house.

Condition—Of house, good.

MONUMENTS (3–14).

The following monuments, unless otherwise described, are of the 17th century and of two storeys, timber-framed and plastered ; the roofs

are tiled. Many of the buildings have original chimney-stacks and exposed ceiling-beams.

Condition—Good, or fairly good, unless noted.

ᶜ(3). *Pattiswick Hall*, house and barn, 250 yards W. of the church. The *House* was built late in the 16th century and has a late 17th-century wing on the N.E. side. There are modern additions at the S.E. end and in the angle between the wings. The upper storey projects on the whole of the S.W. front. Inside the building are some original moulded ceiling-beams and some 17th-century wall-posts, with moulded heads. The roof of the original block has moulded and wind-braced purlins and shaped collars. The garden has a late 16th-century boundary wall.

The *Barn* stands N. of the house.

ᶜ(4). The *Rectory*, 480 yards N.E. of the church, was originally of T-shaped plan, with the cross-wing at the W. end. There are various modern additions.

ᵃ(5). *Woodhouse Farm*, house, 1,100 yards N.N.E. of the church.

ᵃ(6). *Hawkes Cottages*, three tenements, 600 yards N.W. of (5). The house is of L-shaped plan with the wings extending towards the N. and E. The upper storey projects on the N. side of the E. wing. The original central chimney-stack has grouped diagonal shafts.

ᵃ(7). *Warley Farm*, house, 650 yards N.E. of (6). Condition—Poor.

ᵃ(8). *Nunty's Farm*, house, about ½ m. N.E. of (7), is of T-shaped plan with the cross-wing at the E. end. The original chimney-stack has three detached octagonal shafts.

ᵇ(9). *House*, now two tenements, 500 yards N.W. of the church, has an original central chimney-stack with detached octagonal shafts on a square base with a moulded capping.

ᵇ(10). *Cottage*, three tenements, on the N. side of the road at Blackwater Bridge.

ᵇ(11). *House* (Plate, p. 188), S.W. of (10), was built late in the 16th century on an L-shaped plan with the wings extending towards the W. and S. The upper storey projects on the N. front and at the W. end and has a curved diagonal bracket at the angle. On the S. side of the W. wing is an original chimney-stack with two crow-stepped offsets and three octagonal shafts with moulded bases. Inside the building are two original moulded wall-plates and some old battened doors.

ᵇ(12). *Cottage*, E. of (11). The upper storey projects on the N. front and under it is an original bay window with moulded angle-posts and mullions.

ᶜ(13). *Whiteshill Farm*, house, about ¾ m. E.S.E. of (12), has an original chimney-stack with six octagonal shafts on a rectangular base with a moulded capping.

ᵉ(14). *Cottage*, two tenements, at Stock Street, nearly ½ m. E. of (13), was built probably late in the 16th century. The chimney-stack at the E. end has tabled offsets and the stack at the back has a shaft, cross-shaped on plan.

75. PEBMARSH. (B.b.)

(O.S. 6 in. ⁽ᵃ⁾xvii. N.W. ⁽ᵇ⁾xvii. N.E.)

Pebmarsh is a parish and small village 3 m. N.E. of Halstead. The church and Stanley Hall are the principal monuments.

Ecclesiastical :—

ᵃ(1). PARISH CHURCH OF ST. JOHN THE BAPTIST (Plate, p. xxviii) stands near the middle of the parish. The walls are of flint-rubble with dressings of lime-stone ; the porch and parapets are of red brick. The roofs are covered with tiles and lead. The *West Tower* is the earliest part of the building and was added early in the 14th century to a pre-existing nave lower and narrower than the present one ; shortly afterwards the *Chancel* and *Nave* were rebuilt and the *North* and *South Aisles* added or rebuilt. Early in the 16th century the chancel was shortened, the *South Porch* added and most of the parapets rebuilt. The church was restored in the 19th century, when the *Organ Chamber* was added.

The porch is a good example of early 16th-century brickwork and among the fittings the early 14th-century brass is particularly noteworthy.

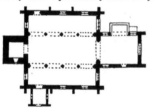

Architectural Description—The *Chancel* (28 ft. by 20 ft.) has an early 16th-century E. wall and a modern E. window. The N. and S. walls have moulded internal and external string-courses of the 14th century. In the N. wall are two 14th-century windows, partly restored and each of two cinque-foiled lights in a two-centred head with moulded label and head-stops ; between the windows is a modern opening to the organ chamber. In the S. wall are three windows, the two eastern, set high in the wall, are of the 14th century and of two trefoiled ogee lights with tracery in segmental-pointed heads with moulded labels and head-stops ; the western window is similar to those in the N. wall, but much restored ; below the second window

is a 14th-century doorway, with moulded jambs and two-centred arch with a moulded label and head-stops. The 14th-century chancel-arch is two-centred and of two chamfered orders, the outer continuous and the inner resting on semi-octagonal shafts with moulded capitals.

The *Nave* (50½ ft. by 20 ft.) has in the E. wall above the chancel-arch a small opening with a two-centred head and now blocked. The N. and S. arcades are of mid 14th-century date and are each of four bays with two-centred arches of two chamfered orders ; the columns consist of four attached shafts, two semi-octagonal and two semi-circular, with moulded capitals and bases ; the responds have semi-circular shafts, with moulded capitals and bases. The 14th-century clearstorey has on both sides three windows each of two trefoiled ogee lights with a quatrefoil in a two-centred head.

The *North Aisle* (12 ft. wide) is of the 14th century and has an E. window of three cinquefoiled lights with tracery in a two-centred head. In the N. wall are two windows, each of two cinquefoiled lights with tracery in a two-centred head ; further W. is the N. doorway, with moulded jambs, two-centred arch and label. In the W. wall is a 14th-century window of two cinquefoiled lights in a two-centred head with a moulded label and head-stops.

The *South Aisle* (12 ft. wide) has windows in the E., S. and W. walls uniform with the corre-sponding windows in the N. aisle. W. of the windows in the S. wall is the 14th-century S. door-way with moulded jambs, two-centred arch and crocketed and finialed label springing from flanking buttresses with crocketed pinnacles. The em-battled brick parapet is of the 16th century.

The *West Tower* (11¼ ft. square) is of early 14th-century date and of three stages with an embattled parapet and angle pinnacles of early 16th-century brick. The tower-arch is modern. In the S. wall is a window of one cinquefoiled light. The second stage has in the N., S. and W. walls a window of one pointed light with a moulded label ; the S. window is trefoiled. In the E. wall is a pointed opening and the weathering of the earlier and lower roof of the nave. The bell-chamber has a pointed window in each wall.

The *South Porch* (Plate, p. xxix) is of brick and of early 16th-century date with a crow-stepped gable. The outer archway has moulded jambs, two-centred arch and label and is set in a pro-jection with a crow-stepped head. In the head of the main gable is a niche flanked by two square cusped panels and surmounted by a rectangular panel enclosing a rose. The side walls have each a window of two four-centred lights with a pierced spandrel.

The *Roof* of the nave is of five bays and has 16th-century tie-beams and modern queen-posts.

SMALL TIMBER-FRAMED AND PLASTERED HOUSES.

FEERING.
(2) Houchin's Farm ; c. 1600.

EARLS COLNE.
(13) House South side of High Street ; c. 1500.

BRADWELL-JUXTA-COGGESHALL.
(6) Cottage ; early 16th-century.

GREAT COGGESHALL.
(19) House, Church Street ;
16th-century.

EASTHORPE.
(5) House opposite Church ; late 15th century.

MOUNT BURES.
(3) Cottage North of Church ; 16th-century.

LITTLE HORKESLEY.
(6) Cottage. S.S.E. of Church : c. 1600.

PATTISWICK.
(11) House at Blackwater Bridge ; late 16th-century.

PEBMARSH.
(9) Oak Farm ; early 17th-century.

DEDHAM.
(26) House, Lamb Corner ; 16th-century.

EARLS COLNE.
(25) Cottage, near Colneford Bridge ; dated 1640.

GREAT HENNY.
(4) Cottage, Henny Street ; 17th-century.

PEBMARSH.
(8) Cottage, South-West of Church ; 17th-century.

MOUNT BURES.
(9) Norton's Farm ; early 17th-century.

BRADFIELD.
(4) Cottage ; early 17th-century.

GREAT HORKESLEY.
(4) Barrack Yard ; 15th-century.

The aisle roofs have old rafters. The roof of the porch has early 16th-century moulded and embattled plates carved with running foliage.

Fittings—*Bells:* five; 5th by John Bird and inscribed " Sum Rosa Pulsata Mundi Maria Vocata" early 15th-century. *Brasses:* In chancel—(1) of [Sir William Fitzralph, *c.* 1323], large cross-legged figure (Plate p. 171) of knight in mixed mail and plate, feet on dog, prick spurs, greaves, knee-cops and arm-pieces with elbow and shoulder roundels, mutilated shield of arms of Fitzralph on left arm, indent of gabled canopy and marginal inscription of which two fragments are kept in vestry; on S. wall—(2) to Joseph Birch, M.A., 1674, rector of the parish, inscription in wooden frame. *Chairs:* In chancel—two, with carved backs, turned rails and shaped front legs, late 17th-century. *Chest:* In tower—plain, with moulded edge to lid, 17th or 18th-century. *Coffin-lid:* In S. aisle—tapering slab with foliated cross,14th-century. *Door:* In S. doorway—on modern door, domed scutcheon-plate with drop-handle, mediaeval. *Floor-slabs:* In chancel—on S. wall—(1) to Thomas Crosse, 1634, pastor of the parish; (2) to Elizabeth, widow of Steven Crosse, 1667. *Glass:* In chancel—in N.E. window, in spandrel, foliage *in situ,* 14th-century; in N.W. window, three shields of arms, two set in bordered quatrefoils, (*a*) *quarterly argent and gules on a bend sable five rings or,* for Bourguylon; (*b*) *or three cheverons gules each charged with three fleurs-de-lis argent,* for Fitzralph; (*c*) as (*b*) but restored; 14th-century. In N. aisle—in E. window, remains of tabernacle work, etc.; in N.W. window, in tracery, flowers, foliage and leopards' faces; in W. window, in spandrel, foliage, all 14th-century, mostly *in situ.* In S. aisle—in S.W.window, headless figure with staff, fragmentary; in W. window, foliage, 14th-century. *Niche:* On S. porch—above archway, of brick with three-centred head, early 16th-century. *Panelling:* Incorporated in pulpit, four traceried heads of panels, 15th-century. *Piscina:* In S. aisle—in S. wall, with shafted jambs and cinquefoiled and sub-cusped head, sexfoiled drain, 14th-century. *Plate:* includes cup of 1567 and stand-paten of 1696–7 with shield of arms. *Sedilia:* In chancel—now of two bays, but formerly extending further E. and cut off by later E. wall, moulded two-centred arches with ogee crocketed and finialed labels with head-stops, middle shaft of Purbeck marble, jamb-shaft and shafts at back of recess of clunch, all with moulded capitals and bases, 14th-century, partly restored. Condition—Good.

Secular :—

ª(2). HOMESTEAD MOAT, at the Rectory, 400 yards E. of the church.

ª(3). STANLEY HALL, house and moat, 1¼ m. W.S.W. of the church. The House is of two storeys with attics; the walls are timber-framed and plastered and the roofs are tiled. It was built late in the 16th century on an L-shaped plan with the wings extending towards the S. and E. The upper storey projects and is gabled at the S. end of the W. front; there are two other gables on this side, both projecting, with original bressumers enriched with billet ornament. At the back of the E. wing is an original bay-window supported on shaped brackets, of six lights with moulded mullions, now blocked. Inside the building the ceiling-beams and joists are exposed in many of the rooms and there are a number of blocked windows with moulded mullions.

The *Moat* surrounds the house and outbuildings. Condition—Of house, fairly good.

ª(4). WORLDSEND, house and moat, ½ m. S.E. of (3). The *House* is of two storeys, timber-framed and plastered; the roofs are tiled. It was built in the 16th century and has a gabled staircase-wing on the N.E. side. The upper storey projects on the whole of the S.W. front. The original front door is of nail-studded battens, with strap-hinges, and there is a similar door at the back. Some of the windows have original diamond-shaped mullions. Inside the building there are some original moulded ceiling-beams and panelled doors.

The *Moat* is fragmentary.

MONUMENTS (5–20).

The following monuments, unless otherwise described, are of the 17th century and of two storeys, timber-framed and plastered or weather-boarded; the roofs are tiled or thatched. Many of the buildings have original chimney-stacks and exposed ceiling-beams.

Condition—Good, or fairly good, unless noted.

ª(5). *Post Office,* house, 40 yards W. of the church, was built probably in the 16th century with cross-wings at the E. and W. ends. The roof has been rebuilt.

ª(6). *King's Head Inn,* 120 yards W. of (5), with modern additions.

ª(7). *Street Farm Cottages,* house, 100 yards N.W. of (6).

ª(8). *Cottage* (Plate, p. 189), two tenements, 50 yards S.E. of (6).

ª(9). *Oak Farm,* house (Plate, p. 189), nearly ½ m. N.W. of the church, has been partly refaced with modern brick. The original chimney-stack has grouped diagonal shafts.

ª(10). *Dagworth Farm,* house, 750 yards N. of (9), was built probably in the 16th century with a cross-wing at the N. end. The upper storey projects at the E. end of the cross-wing. Inside the building the cross-wing has an original queen-post truss.

^a(11). *Byndes Cottages*, ¾ m. W. of the church. The original chimney-stack has grouped diagonal shafts.

^a(12). *Spoons Hall*, house and barn, ¼ m. E.S.E. of (11). The *House* was built in the 16th century on an L-shaped plan with the wings extending towards the S. and W. In the 17th century a block was added at the N. end and an addition made between the wings. The upper storey of the original building projects on the E., S. and W. sides, the last part being also gabled. The three 17th-century chimney-stacks have grouped diagonal shafts. Inside the building is an original doorway with a four-centred head and a window with a three-centred head, both now blocked. In the 17th-century block is a door of moulded battens. The roof of the main block has original queen-post trusses.

The *Barn*, E. of the house, is probably of early 16th-century date and has a roof of king-post type.

^a(13). *Hunt's Hall*, nearly ½ m. S.S.W. of (12), was built probably early in the 16th century, with cross-wings at the N. and S. ends. The N. cross-wing has an extension on the N. side. The upper storey projects at the E. ends of the cross-wings. Inside the building is some late 16th-century panelling. The late 17th-century staircase has turned balusters, square newels and close strings. The N. wing has an original cambered tie-beam and the extension has a king-post truss.

^a(14). *Abbot's Farm*, house, 550 yards S. of (13), was built late in the 16th century on an L-shaped plan with the wings extending towards the S. and W. The original chimney-stack has three octagonal shafts. Inside the building are original cambered tie-beams, morticed for the former queen-posts.

^a(15). *Marvel's Garden*, house, about ½ m. S.S.W. of the church, was built in the 16th century on an L-shaped plan with the wings extending towards the N.E. and N.W. Inside the building one room has original moulded ceiling-beams. Condition—Poor.

^a(16). *Greathouse Farm*, house and barns, about ¼ m. E.N.E. of the church. The *House* is modern, but beneath it are cellars of 16th-century brick and a nail-studded door of the same date.

The *Barns*, N.E. of the house, are of five and seven bays and of the 16th and 17th century respectively. A granary of two storeys and of brick was built probably late in the 16th century.

^b(17). *Cottage*, ½ m. S.E. of the church.

^b(18). *Valiant's Farm*, house, 300 yards S.E. of (17), was built probably early in the 16th century and has a cross-wing at the N. end. The upper storey projects at the W. end of the cross-wing.

^b(19). *Garland's Farm*, house and outbuilding, 600 yards E. of (18), was built early in the 16th century on an L-shaped plan with the wings extending towards the W. and N. and with a staircase-wing in the angle between them. Inside the building two rooms have original moulded ceiling-beams and joists.

^b(20). *Bluepale Farm*, house, ½ m. N.E. of the church, has been refronted with modern brick.

---

76. PELDON. (D.d.)

(O.S. 6 in. ^(a)xxxvi. S.E. ^(b)xlvi. N.E.)

Peldon is a parish and scattered village 5 m. S. of Colchester. The church is the only monument of importance, though the secular monuments are all of the 15th century.

Ecclesiastical :—

^a(1). PARISH CHURCH OF ST. MARY stands in the middle of the parish. The walls are of mixed rubble except the clearstorey and part of the porch which are of brick ; the dressings are of limestone and the roofs are tiled. The *Nave* was built probably in the 12th century. The *West Tower* was added c. 1400, and the *South Porch* rebuilt during the 15th century. Early in the 16th century the clearstorey was added and the walls below strengthened with buttresses. The church was restored in the 19th century, when the *Chancel* was rebuilt, the *North Vestry* added and the S. porch rebuilt.

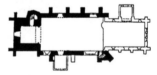

Architectural Description—The *Nave* (47¼ ft. by 24¼ ft.) has early 16th-century buttresses of brick. In the N. wall is a 14th-century window, partly restored, and of two trefoiled ogee lights with tracery in a two-centred head with a moulded label ; further W. is the N. doorway of c. 1400, with richly moulded and shafted jambs, moulded two-centred arch and label with defaced angel-stops ; the splays are shafted and the rear-arch is moulded. The clearstorey is of early 16th-century brick and has on this side three windows, each of two four-centred lights with a pierced spandrel in a four-centred head. In the S. wall are two windows, all modern except for some reused stones in the western window ; at the E. end of the wall are the upper and lower doorways of the rood-loft staircase, both with segmental heads and of early 16th-century date ; between the two windows is the mid 14th-century S. doorway, with moulded jambs, two-centred head and label with a defaced head-stop. The clearstorey on this side has four windows uniform with those on the N. side.

The *West Tower* (12½ ft. by 13¼ ft.) is of *c.* 1400 and of four stages with a moulded plinth and embattled parapet with grotesques at the angles. The two-centred tower-arch is of two hollow-chamfered orders ; the responds have each two attached shafts with moulded capitals and bases. In the N. wall is the doorway to the stair-turret, with moulded jambs and two-centred arch. The partly restored window is of three cinquefoiled lights with tracery in a two-centred head ; the W. doorway has moulded jambs and two-centred arch in a square head with traceried spandrels and a restored label with defaced head-stops ; N. of it is a small cross of flint and there are four similar crosses in the S. wall of the third stage. The second stage has in the S. and W. walls a window of one cinquefoiled light, that in the W. wall having been rebuilt. The third stage has in the W. wall a restored window of one trefoiled light. The bell-chamber has in each wall a partly restored window of two cinquefoiled lights in a square head with a moulded label.

The *South Porch* incorporates in the W. wall an early 16th-century brick buttress ; in its E. face is a recess with a four-centred head and above it'part of a trefoiled corbel-table of brick, partly restored.

The *Roof* of the nave is of early 16th-century date, partly restored, and of six bays with hammer-beam trusses resting on wall-posts forming shafts with moulded capitals and bases and restored except in the easternmost truss ; all the main timbers are moulded and the curved braces to the collars form four-centred arches. The 15th-century roof of the S. porch has a central king-post truss and a moulded tie-beam at the base of the S. gable.

Fittings—*Bells :* two ; 1st by Miles Graye, 1613. *Doors :* In tower—in two doorways to turret, with chamfered fillets and nail-studded battens, *c.* 1400. *Font :* octagonal bowl of Purbeck marble, with central pier and eight small shafts, double chamfered base, late 12th-century, much restored or recut. *Indents :* In tower—(1) of priest, with inscription-plate. (2) much defaced. *Stoup :* In S. porch—E. of S. doorway, with moulded jambs, four-centred head and foliated spandrels, 15th-century. *Miscellanea :* Loose in stoup, capital with conventional foliage, 12th-century. On quoins of N.E. angle of nave incised geometrical pattern. Condition—Fairly good.

Secular :—

ª(2). HOUSE, 50 yards S. of the church, is of two storeys with attics. The walls are timber-framed

and the roofs are tiled. It appears to be the remaining wing of a 15th-century house, but has been refaced at the W. end with modern brick. The upper storey originally projected at the E. end but has been underbuilt. Inside the building are some 17th-century battened doors ; the roof has an original king-post truss.

Condition—Good.

ª(3). HARVEY'S FARM, house, 700 yards S.W. of the church, is of two storeys, partly timber-framed and partly of brick ; the roofs are tiled. It was built in the 15th century, probably with a central hall and cross-wings at the N. and S. ends. The S. wing was rebuilt in the 17th century and the main block in the 18th century. The upper storey formerly projected at both ends of the N. wing and at the W. end of the S. wing, but on the W. side these projections have been underbuilt. Inside the building is some exposed timber-framing and an original cambered tie-beam.

Condition—Good.

ª(4). KEMP'S FARM, house, 1,450 yards S.E. of the church, is of two storeys, timber-framed and plastered ; the roofs are tiled. It was built in the 15th century, with a central hall and cross-wings at the E. and W. ends. Inside the building are some original moulded ceiling-beam with curved braces and some of the timber-framing is exposed. The roof has original cambered tie-beams.

Condition—Poor.

ª(5). ROSE INN, 1¼ m. S.E. of the church, is of two storeys, timber-framed and plastered ; the roofs are tiled. It was built in the 15th century, with a cross-wing at the N. end and possibly one at the S. end, now roofed with the main block. Inside the building the N. room has an original moulded beam and chamfered joists with foliated stops. Other rooms have exposed ceiling-beams and there are several 17th-century panelled doors.

Condition—Fairly good.

Unclassified :—

ᵇ(6). RED HILLS, a number, starting from the head of the "Ray," about 1 m. S.E. of the church and extending southwards along the old high-water mark.

---

77. RAMSEY. (F.b.)

(O.S. 6 in. ⁽ᵃ⁾xx. S.E. ⁽ᵇ⁾xxi. S.W.)

Ramsey is a parish and village on the S. of the Stour estuary, 3½ m. W.S.W. of Harwich. The church is the principal monument.

Ecclesiastical :—

ᵇ(1). PARISH CHURCH OF ST. MICHAEL stands E. of the village. The walls are probably of septaria and flint-rubble but except those of the tower they are covered with plaster ; the dressings are of limestone, and the roofs are tiled. The *Nave* is of early

12th-century date. The *Chancel* was rebuilt in the 13th or 14th century. Early in the 15th century the *West Tower* was added and late in the same century the upper walls of the chancel were built. The tower was restored in the 17th century and the upper part rebuilt in the 18th century. The *South Porch* was rebuilt in 1816 and the church has since been restored.

Architectural Description—The *Chancel* (27½ ft. by 18¼ ft.) has a late 16th-century E. window of three square-headed and double-transomed lights with 13th-century splays. In the N. wall is a similar window, but of two transomed lights; further E. is the E. part of a 13th-century window with a two-centred head; at the W. end of the wall is a blocked square-headed window. In the S. wall is a window similar to that in the N. wall; further W. is an early 16th-century doorway, partly restored, with moulded jambs and five-centred arch; immediately W. of it is part of the rear-arch of a blocked doorway, probably of the 13th century; at the W. end of the wall is a blocked window similar to the corresponding window in the N. wall. The late 14th-century chancel-arch is partly restored; it is two-centred and of two moulded orders, the outer continuous and the inner resting on attached shafts with moulded capitals carved with half-angels and moulded bases; below the base on the N. side is a plinth.

The *Nave* (56½ ft. by 20½ ft.) has in the N. wall four windows; the easternmost is of early 14th-century date and of two pointed lights in a two-centred head; the second window is a single, 12th-century, round-headed light; the third window is of late 14th-century date and of two trefoiled lights with tracery in a square head with a moulded label; the westernmost window is a 13th-century lancet; between the second and third windows is the early 12th-century N. doorway, partly restored; the round arch is of one plain order and the imposts have diaper ornament and a chamfered under-edge carved with zigzags; at the E. end of the wall is the late 15th or early 16th-century rood-loft staircase, set in a brick projection; the lower doorway has double-chamfered jambs, partly restored, and four-centred arch; the upper doorway has a square head. In the S. wall are four windows; the easternmost is of the 16th or 17th century, partly restored, of two square-headed lights; the second is of mid 14th-century date, partly restored, and of two pointed lights with uncusped tracery in a square

head with a moulded label and grotesque head-stops; the third window is of early 14th-century date, partly restored, and of two pointed lights in a two-centred head with a moulded label; the westernmost window is similar to the third window in the N. wall; E. of it is the early 15th-century S. doorway, with jambs and two-centred arch of two moulded orders with a moulded label and head-stops; the inner order is carved with moons, stars, crowned initials I.M., heads, and leopards' heads; the outer order is carved with a Coronation of the Virgin, crowns and hanging shields; the label is carved with shields, winged hearts and leaves.

The *West Tower* is of three stages with a modern parapet. The early 16th-century tower-arch is two-centred and of two orders, the outer moulded and continuous, and the inner chamfered and resting on attached shafts with moulded capitals and bases. The W. window, of the same date but much restored, is of three ogee lights with plain vertical tracery in a four-centred head with moulded label; the early 16th-century W. doorway with moulded jambs, two-centred arch in a square head with traceried spandrels and a moulded label. The second stage has in the N. and W. walls an early 16th-century window of one trefoiled light in a square head with a moulded label; the window in the S. wall was similar, but has now a 17th-century head to the light. The bell-chamber has 15th-century E., N. and W. windows, each of two cinquefoiled lights with vertical tracery in a four-centred head with a moulded label; the window in the S. wall is of 18th-century or modern date.

The *Roof* of the chancel is dated 1597 on the middle collar-beam; it is of four bays and of collar-beam type, at the junctions of principals and collars are carved double consoles with enriched spandrels; the collars and wall-plates are moulded and carved with running ornament. The roof of the nave is mostly modern, but incorporates some old material, including three tie-beams probably of the 17th century.

Fittings—*Bells*: five; 3rd by Miles Graye, 1638; 4th by John Darbie, 1676. *Chest*: In tower—plain, possibly 17th-century. *Door*: In S. doorway—with moulded frame and vertical fillets, shafts with moulded bases and capitals, cut from the solid, to support former figures, 15th-century, partly restored. *Font*: octagonal bowl, mostly recut, octagonal stem and moulded base, 15th-century. *Floor-slabs*: In chancel—(1) to William Whitmore, 1678, with shield of arms; (2) to Penelope, his wife. *Indent*: In chancel—of inscription-plate. *Niches*: In nave—in E. wall, N. of chancel-arch, two, narrow with triangular heads, date uncertain. *Paintings*: In nave—on second and westernmost windows on N. side, remains of decorative designs, probably

GLASS.
(Approximately one-eighth full size, from drawings.)

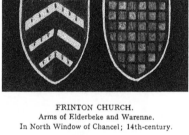

WORMINGFORD CHURCH.
Shields of Arms in South-West Window of Chancel, made up of
14th-century material.

HEYBRIDGE CHURCH.
Figure in North Window of
Chancel ; 14th-century.

FRINTON CHURCH.
Arms of Elderbeke and Warenne.
In North Window of Chancel; 14th-century.

LAWFORD HALL.
Figure of St. Quirinus ;
16th-century.

Arms of Marney quartered, impaling Arundel
quartered with Chideock and Carminow.

Arms of Marney quartering Sergeaux and
Venables surrounded by the Garter.

LAYER MARNEY CHURCH.
Glass in East Window of North Chapel ; early 16th-century.

'Robert Lemaire'; 13th-century.

The Virgin and Child; late 12th-century.

RIVENHALL: PARISH CHURCH OF ST. MARY AND ALL SAINTS.

Glass in East Window of Chancel.

(Approximately one-sixth full size—from drawings.)

15th-century. In nave—on S. wall, head of large figure with nimbus and remains of decorative band above; on W. jamb of second window, similar ornament, probably 15th-century. On soffit of middle tie-beam in nave, running stencilled ornament, 16th or 17th-century. *Piscinae :* In chancel—with triangular head and round drain, date uncertain. In nave—in S. wall, with chamfered jambs and cinquefoiled head, 14th-century. *Plate :* includes cup of 1576, with modern base; Elizabethan cup and secular dish of 1707. *Pulpit :* octagonal, with modern stem and base, tub divided into three ranges with bolection-moulded panelling, enriched arcading and carved conventional foliage, respectively, early 17th-century. *Recess :* In chancel—in N. wall, with moulded cinquefoiled head and shafted jambs with moulded capitals and bases, 14th-century, possibly Easter sepulchre. *Sedile :* In chancel—sill of S.E. window, carried down to form seat. *Stoup :* In S. porch—with chamfered jambs and two-centred head. *Miscellanea :* In nave—in N. wall, sawn-off end of moulded *rood-beam.* In rood-loft staircase, architectural fragments of *stonework ;* trefoiled head of window used as step in second stage of tower. In bell-chamber—carved on head of N. window, small mitre ; on key-stone of W. window, I. H. S. monogram.

Condition—Generally good, but, of tower, bad.

Secular :—

ᵃ(2). ROYDON HALL (Plate, p. 176), 1¾ m. W. of the church, is of two storeys ; the walls are of brick and plastered timber-framing ; the roofs are tiled. It was built about the middle of the 16th century and has a 17th-century wing projecting S. from the E. end. The upper storey projects on the S. front and on the W. side of the S. wing. The W. end is of brick with octagonal turrets at the angles carried up as pinnacles with panelled sides ; the gable has a moulded coping and a similar pinnacle at the apex ; there are two blocked windows, each with a pediment and in the gable is a round opening. The chimney-stack on the N. side has two original octagonal shafts with panelled ornament and moulded capitals and bases. The E. end of the house is also of brick and retains the lower part of octagonal turrets similar to those at the W. end. The N.E. chimney-stack is original, with modern shafts. Inside the building are some original moulded ceiling-beams.

Condition—Good.

MONUMENTS (3–6).

The following monuments, unless otherwise described, are of two storeys, timber-framed and plastered ; the roofs are tiled. Some of the buildings have exposed ceiling-beams and original chimney-stacks.

Condition—Good.

ᵃ(3). *Stourwood Farm,* house, ½ m. N.N.E. of (2), was built in the 17th century.

ᵇ(4). *Bridgefoot Farm,* house, about 600 yards W. of the church, was built early in the 16th century and has been refaced with modern brick. The doorway has moulded jambs and head carved with spiral leaf pattern. Inside the building the N.E. room has an original moulded and carved ceiling-beam and moulded joists ; another room at the back also has moulded beams and joists.

ᵇ(5). *Whitehouse Farm,* house, 350 yards S.W. of (4), was built early in the 16th century, with a cross-wing at the S.W. end. Inside the building is an original moulded ceiling-beam and at the back is an original window of four lights, now blocked.

ᵇ(6). *Mill Farm,* house (Plate, p. 234), ¼ m. S.E. of (5), was built late in the 16th century. The walls are of original brick, except on the S.E. side, which is modern. On the N.W. front are two gables with moulded corbelling to the base of the parapets and octagonal pinnacles at the apex. The porch on this side has an original embattled parapet and a doorway with chamfered jambs, two-centred arch and moulded label. Two windows in the gables have original moulded labels.

78. RIVENHALL. (B.d.)

(O.S. 6 in. ⁽ᵃ⁾xxxiv. N.E. ⁽ᵇ⁾xxxv. N.W. ⁽ᶜ⁾xxxv. S.W.)

Rivenhall is a parish 2 m. N. of Witham. The church and Rivenhall Place are the principal monuments.

Roman :—

ᶜ(1). A large house existed near a stream at the lower end of the field E. of the church. It was opened during draining works in 1846 and again in 1894, but unfortunately has never been properly excavated. A red tessellated pavement 400 ft. long and 4½ ft. wide, presumably belonging to a corridor, with concrete foundation 18 in. thick, was found with other foundations, marble tesserae, hypocaust tiles, bits of coloured wall stucco, pottery and coins of Hadrian and Probus. Pieces of tile and pottery have been found in the churchyard and school garden adjoining.

The Roman brick at Faulkbourne and in the walls of Witham church, and the burials noted at Kelvedon may be connected with this building. (*Brit. Arch. Assoc. Jour.,* 1846, II, 281, 339 ; *Gent's. Mag.,* 1847, I, 185 ; *Essex Rev.,* 1894, III, 145, quoting *Chelmsford Chron.,* 15th May, 1846.) (See also *Sectional Preface,* p. xxvii.)

Ecclesiastical :—

*(2). PARISH CHURCH OF ST. MARY AND ALL
SAINTS stands about 1 m. N.W. of the village.
The walls are probably of flint-rubble but are
thickly covered with plaster ; the roofs are covered
with slates. The church was almost entirely re-
built in 1838–9, but the walls of the *Chancel* and
Nave and *West Tower* may be partly old ; the
South Porch is modern.

Architectural Description—The *Chancel* (39 ft.
by 20 ft.) has a plastered E. window of three
uncusped lights with intersecting tracery in a
two-centred head, all of doubtful date. In the
N. wall are three windows, of which the two
eastern are dummy or blocked windows ; they are
all of similar character to the E. window, but of
two lights each. In the S. wall are three windows
uniform with those in the N. wall ; between the
two western is a doorway of doubtful date with
moulded jambs and two-centred arch, all covered
with plaster. The chancel-arch is mostly modern.

The *Nave* (47 ft. by 24 ft.) has, in the N. wall,
three windows ; the easternmost is of the 16th
century and of one square-headed light set low in
the wall ; the second and westernmost windows
are uniform with the E. window ; between the
two western windows is the 15th-century N. doorway, now blocked ; it has jambs and two-centred
arch of two chamfered orders ; the internal splays
and rear-arch are moulded. In the S. wall are
four windows ; the easternmost is uniform with
that opposite in the N. wall, and the others are
uniform with the E. window ; between the two
western windows is the 15th-century S. doorway
with moulded jambs and two-centred arch ; the
middle member of each jamb has a moulded
capital and base ; the segmental rear-arch is also
moulded.

Fittings—*Chair :* In chancel—modern, incorporating one 17th-century carved panel. *Chest :*
At rectory—iron-bound, 17th-century. *Coffin-lids :*
(1) On floor of chancel, coped coffin-slab with raised
stem and trefoiled head and foot, late 13th-century ;
(2) coped coffin-slab, ridged, with traces of cross,
probably 13th-century. *Communion Rails :* moulded,
with twisted balusters, *c.* 1700. *Glass :* In chancel
—in E. window, four large roundels with borders,
etc., and representing a Majesty, entombment
of the (?) Virgin, the Virgin and Child (Plate,
p. 193), and the Annunciation, late 12th-century ;
two large figures of bishops or abbots, 12th-century ;
a figure on horseback in banded mail with background, possibly heraldic, and inscription " Robert
Lemaire " (Plate, p. 193), 13th-century ; the
Adoration of the Magi, fragmentary, late 15th or
early 16th-century, a bishop and various panels
with figure subjects, fragments, etc., various dates ;
in S.W. window—three roundels including one of
God the Father, late 15th and 16th-century. In

nave—in middle N. window, shields of arms,
various fragments and two roundels one with a
skull and one with the handkerchief of St. Veronica,
16th and 17th-century ; in tracery, 14th-century
ornament ; in middle S. window, in tracery, 14th
and 15th-century fragments. Nearly all this glass,
with some other pieces at the Rectory, was brought
here in 1840 from France by the then rector ; the
12th-century panels are said to have come from
the church of St. Martin at Chenu in Sarthe.
Monuments and *Floor-slabs.* Monuments : In
chancel—on S. side, (1) of Raphe Wyseman [1608],
and Elizabeth (Barley), his wife, 1594, alabaster
and black-marble altar-tomb (Plate, p. 197) with
effigies of man in plate armour with ruff and feet
on sea-horse, of lady in farthingale and rich head-
dress ; on front of tomb, kneeling figures of three
sons and three daughters, against wall at back
pilasters, cornice and cresting with three shields
of arms ; hanging above, a funeral helmet (Plate
p. 133) with sea-horse crest ; on N. wall, (2) to
Samuel, son of Thomas Western,1699,veined marble
tablet with cherub-head, drapery and shield of
arms. Floor-slabs : In chancel—under organ, name
covered, 1706, of cast-iron, with achievement of
arms. In tower—(2) to Jeremy Aylett, 1657, of
Doreward Hall, with impaled shield of arms.
Royal Arms : Above tower-arch—of James II,
painted.

Condition—Good, much restored or rebuilt.

Secular :—

*(3). BOWSER'S HALL, house and moat, about
1¼ m. N.W. of the church. The *House* is of two
storeys, timber-framed and plastered ; the roofs
are tiled. It was built early in the 17th century
on an L-shaped plan with the wings extending
towards the W. and N. ; there are modern additions
on the S. and E. The original central chimney-
stack has diagonal pilaster strips. Inside the
building the ceiling-beams and some joists are
exposed and there is an iron fire-back with the
royal Stuart arms.

The *Moat*, N.E. of the house, is rectangular.

Condition—Of house, good.

*(4). RIVENHALL PLACE, 1 m. N.N.W. of the
church, is of two storeys with attics ; the walls
are of brick ; the roofs are tiled. The E. part of
the house was built in the second half of the 16th
century with a cross-wing at the N. end. The
main staircase was added *c.* 1700, and in the
18th century the E. front was refaced and three
ranges added on the W. side making the plan
quadrangular. The elevations have no ancient
features except the N. end and W. side of the
original block. At the N. end is an original
chimney-stack with three octagonal shafts having
modern tops. The W. side of the original block
has at the N. end a gable with a brick coping and

at the apex the base of a pinnacle, set diagonally ; in the gable is an original window of three lights ; further S. is a chimney-stack with the bases of three octagonal shafts. Inside the building the original staircase has a central newel-post. The staircase of c. 1700 has turned and twisted balusters and a moulded rail ramped over square newels ; the walls have a bolection-moulded and panelled dado. The house contains a considerable quantity of reset 16th and 17th-century panelling and two fire-backs dated 1651 and 1652 respectively.

Condition—Good, much altered.

MONUMENTS (5–20).

The following monuments, unless otherwise described, are of the 17th century and of two storeys, timber-framed and plastered ; the roofs are tiled or thatched. Several of the buildings have original chimney-stacks and exposed ceiling-beams.

Condition—Good, or fairly good, unless noted.

ᵃ(5). *Groom's Farm*, house, three tenements, about 1¼ m. N.W. of the church, has a cross-wing at the S. end.

ᵃ(6). *Boarstye Farm*, house and barn, ¼ m. N.N.W. of (5). The *House* is of L-shaped plan with the wings extending towards the S. and W.

The *Barn*, S.E. of the house, is of five bays.

ᵃ(7). *Rolphe's Farm*, house, 600 yards N.N.W. of (6), has a cross-wing at the N.W. end. The original central chimney-stack has three diagonal shafts. Inside the building is a door made up of linen-fold panelling and an original window with diamond-shaped mullions and now blocked.

ᵃ(8). *Wright's Farm*, house, 550 yards N.W. of (7).

ᵃ(9). *Egypt Farm*, house, 260 yards W.S.W. of (8), was built about the end of the 15th century with cross-wings at the N. and S. ends. The N. cross-wing has an 18th-century addition at the E. end and the upper storey projects at the E. end of the S. cross-wing. Inside the building the two cross-wings have original roofs of king-post type with central purlins ; in the main roof only a cambered tie-beam is visible. In the S. wing are two original windows with diamond-shaped mullions, and now blocked.

ᵃ(10). *Sheepcote Farm*, house and barn, nearly 2 m. N.N.W. of the church. The *House* was built late in the 16th or early in the 17th century, on an L-shaped plan with the wings extending towards the S. and E.

The *Barn*, S.W. of the house, is of five bays and of early 16th-century date with a roof of king-post type.

ᵇ(11). *Parkgate Farm*, house, two tenements, ¼ m. E.N.E. of (4), has been largely rebuilt in the 18th century.

ᵇ(12). *Ford Farm*, house and barn, ½ m. N. of the church. The *House* was built in the 15th

century with cross-wings at the N.W. and S.E. ends. There is a 17th-century addition on the N.W. side and modern additions at the N.E. and S.W. ends. Inside the building the main block has an original collar-beam roof-truss with curved braces ; the cross-wings probably both have original roofs with king-post trusses, but one is now ceiled. There is one 17th-century door of moulded battens.

The *Barn*, E. of the house, is of five bays and of 17th-century date.

ᵇ(13). *Rivenhall Hall* (Plate, p. xxxi), 300 yards N. of the church, was built early in the 16th century with cross-wings at the E. and W. ends. There is a large 17th-century addition on the N. side. The upper storey projects at the S. end of both cross-wings. The 17th-century chimney-stack at the W. end has the base of attached diagonal shafts. Inside the building one room has late 16th-century panelling and there are remains of the original roof construction.

ᶜ(14). *Hoo Hall*, ½ m. E.S.E. of the church, was largely rebuilt in brick late in the 18th century.

ᶜ(15). *Cottage*, two tenements, 600 yards W.S.W. of (14), has two gabled dormers on the E. front.

ᶜ(16). *Cottage*, two tenements, 600 yards S. of the church.

ᶜ(17). *Stovern's Hall*, two tenements, 300 yards W.S.W. of (16), has a modern addition of red brick. One original chimney-stack has a shaft of cross-shaped plan.

Condition—Poor.

ᶜ(18). *Rickstones*, house, ¼ m. S.W. of (17), has been much altered within recent years.

ᵃ(19). *Pond Farm*, house, nearly 1 m. S.E. of the church, was built about the middle of the 16th century with cross-wings at the N. and S. ends. The S. cross-wing has been destroyed. The upper storey projects at the E. end of the N. cross-wing on curved brackets. The chimney-stack on the W. side has three 17th-century shafts, set diagonally.

ᶜ(20). *Fox Inn*, 250 yards S.E. of (19), was built c. 1700 and has 18th-century additions.

---

79. ST. OSYTH. (E.d.)

(O.S. 6 in. ⁽ᵃ⁾xxxviii. S.W. ⁽ᵇ⁾xlviii. N.W.)

St. Osyth is a parish and village 3½ m. E. of Clacton-on-Sea. The church, abbey and St. Clairs Hall are the principal monuments.

Roman :—

ᵃ(1). In 1906 a pavement of red and buff tile tesserae was found about 50 ft. above sea-level in Priory Park, near an old gravel-pit, about ¾ m. N.W. of the Priory and 100 yards N.W. of the pond in Nun's Wood. Nothing else was found,

S⸍ OSYTH.   THE PARISH CHURCH _of_ S.S. PETER & PAUL.

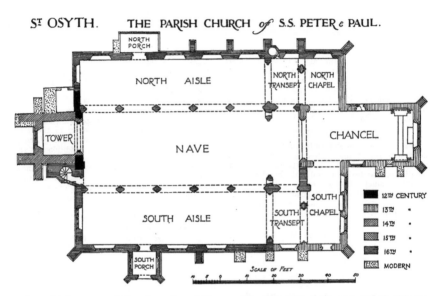

and no details are recorded.   A portion of the same pavement was again uncovered in 1921. (*Essex Arch. Soc. Trans.* (N.S.), X, 88.) (See also *Sectional Preface*, p. xxvii.)

Ecclesiastical :—

_b_(2). PARISH CHURCH OF SS. PETER AND PAUL (Plate, p. 196) stands in the village.   The walls are generally of septaria and flint-rubble, with limestone dressings ; the nave, S. aisle and S. porch are of red brick ; the roofs are tiled.   The W. wall of the *Nave*, and perhaps part of the W. wall of the N. aisle, are of early 12th-century date, when the nave was aisled.   The E. arcades of the *North* and *South Transepts* are of *c.* 1250-70, the N. transept being probably the earlier.   The date of the *Chancel* is uncertain, but it is perhaps late 13th-century work.   The *West Tower* was added *c.* 1340.   In the 15th century the chancel-arch was rebuilt.   Earlier in the 16th century a general reconstruction was begun, the nave was rebuilt and widened towards the S., the *North* and *South Aisles* rebuilt, and the *South Porch* added ; the N. transept was shortened at the same time.   The tower was much repaired in the 18th century and the whole church was restored in the 19th century.

The church is of considerable architectural interest, the brick arcades of the nave being a remarkable feature ; among the fittings the 16th-century monuments of the Darcy family are note-worthy.   The roofs of the nave and N. aisle are also noteworthy.

Architectural Description—The *Chancel* (39½ ft. by 17¾ ft.) has a late 14th-century E. window, partly restored, and of three cinquefoiled ogee lights with tracery in a two-centred head with a moulded label.   In the N. wall is a late 13th-century two-centred arch of one chamfered order ; further E. is a 14th-century window, much altered, with a two-centred head and a moulded label ; below it is a doorway with a two-centred head, probably of the 14th century but much altered and restored ; it probably opened into a former vestry.   In the S. wall is an arch similar to that in the N. wall ; further E. is a window similar to that in the N. wall ; and beyond it is a blocked window with a shouldered head, probably of the ·13th century.   The chancel-arch is two-centred and of three chamfered orders ; it is probably of the 13th century, but has 15th-century splayed responds, each with three moulded and attached capitals at the top.

The *North Transept* (14½ ft. by 10 ft.) was reduced to the width of an aisle and also shortened in the early 16th-century alterations.   The mid 13th-century E. arcade is now of one and a quarter bays with two-centred arches of three chamfered orders ; the round pier has four attached shafts with continuously moulded capitals and bases ; the S. arch springs from a moulded corbel, the

ST. OSYTH : PARISH CHURCH OF SS. PETER AND PAUL.

Interior, showing Nave Arcades, early 16th-century, and Transept Arcades, 13th-century.

ST. OSYTH : PARISH OF SS. PETER AND PAUL.
Monument to John, 2nd Lord Darcy, 1580-81, and Frances, his wife.

RIVENHALL : PARISH CHURCH OF ST. MARY AND ALL SAINTS.
Monument to Raphe Wyseman, 1608, and Elizabeth, his wife, 1594.

stem of which is carved with stiff flowers ; below it is a round shaft, apparently of earlier work, as it is not central with the arch above ; between the arches on the E. face is a moulded corbel. In the N. wall is an early 16th-century window of three trefoiled lights in a four-centred head with a moulded label and partly restored ; further W. are three early 16th-century doorways to the rood-loft staircase, at different levels but all with four-centred heads and now blocked ; the two upper are of brick. In the N. wall is a brick four-centred arch of three moulded orders ; the responds are also of three orders and have moulded bases and continuous moulded capitals.

The *North Chapel* (12 ft. by 14¾ ft.) has a blank E. wall, probably owing to the former existence of a vestry E. of it. In the N. wall is a window uniform with that in the N. transept.

The *South Transept* (19 ft. by 10 ft.) has been reduced in depth like the N. transept, but retains its original S. wall. In the E. wall is an arcade of *c.* 1270 and of two bays of which the northern is partly blocked by an early 16th-century brick pier ; the two-centred arches are of three chamfered orders and the pier has eight attached shafts with moulded capitals and bases ; the S. respond has three similar attached shafts. In the S. wall is a window all modern except the splays, jambs, two-centred arch and label, which are probably of late 14th-century date. In the W. wall is an arch uniform with the corresponding arch in the N. transept.

The *South Chapel* (12 ft. by 27¾ ft.) has in the E. wall two windows, the northern is all modern except the 14th-century splays and rear-arch ; the southern is of early 14th-century date, much restored externally, and of two cinquefoiled lights with tracery in a two-centred head. In the S. wall is an early 16th-century window, partly restored and of three cinquefoiled lights with vertical tracery in a four-centred head ; below it is a modern doorway.

The *Nave* (80 ft. by 26½ ft.) is entirely of early 16th-century date and of brick except the W. wall. The E. bay is separated from the rest by the responds of a chancel-arch which was never completed ; they are each of three orders and behind each is a squint with a four-centred head. The E. bay has on the N. and S. an arch opening into the transepts ; they are similar but lower and narrower than the arches in the W. walls of the transepts. The nave proper has N. and S. arcades of five bays with arches, etc., all similar to those in the W. walls of the transepts. On the W. wall, S. of the tower-arch, is an early 12th-century respond to the former S. arcade ; it is plain with a chamfered impost.

The *North Aisle* (16 ft. wide) is of septaria and flint-rubble, with a moulded plinth and is entirely of early 16th-century date, except part of the

W. wall. In the N. wall are four windows each of four trefoiled four-centred lights with vertical tracery in a four-centred head with a moulded label and partly restored ; between the two western windows is the N. doorway with moulded and shafted jambs and two-centred arch in a square head with a moulded label and spandrels carved with the crowned monogram of the Virgin and the arm of an angel with a sword breaking the wheel of St. Katherine. In the W. wall is a window of three cinquefoiled lights in a segmental-pointed head ; further S. is a small circular window, now blocked, and of 12th or 13th century date.

The *South Aisle* (19 ft. wide) is of red brick with black brick diapering and stone dressings and a moulded plinth ; it is entirely of early 16th-century date. In the S. wall are three windows uniform with those in the N. aisle ; between the two western is the S. doorway with moulded and shafted jambs, four-centred arch and label. In the W. wall is a window uniform with those in the S. wall.

The *West Tower* (12 ft. square) is of *c.* 1340, much altered and repaired in the 18th century. It is of three stages with an 18th-century parapet and an early 16th-century stair-turret. The 14th-century tower-arch is two-centred and of two wave-moulded orders ; the chamfered responds have each an attached semi-octagonal shaft with moulded capital and base of unusually wide projection. The mid 14th-century W. window is of two pointed lights in a two-centred head. The second stage has a window in the W. wall, completely altered in the 18th century. The bell-chamber has a similar window in each wall.

The *South Porch* is of early 16th-century date and of red brick and stone. The outer archway has splayed brick and stone jambs and a four-centred arch of three chamfered orders with a moulded label, all of brick. The side walls have each a stone window of two four-centred lights in a square head with a moulded label.

The *Roof* of the chancel is of four bays with curved principals or braces springing from moulded brackets above the plates ; the spandrels are carved with a cinquefoil, for Darcy, in each ; the roof is perhaps of *c.* 1560, with modern gilding, etc. The early 16th-century flat roof of the N. transept has moulded main timbers and joists. The S. transept has a similar roof. The S. chapel has one early 16th-century tie-beam with twisted foliage ornament. The early 16th-century roof of the nave is of nine bays with hammer-beam trusses and moulded plates, principals, purlins, collars, hammer-beams and wall-posts ; there are curved braces to the collars and hammer-beams. The early 16th-century flat roof of the N. aisle is of five bays with moulded and elaborately carved tie-beams, intermediates, purlins and wall-plates ; each beam has a different type of running foliage and under the centres of the main tie-beams are richly carved pendants ; the main ties have also curved braces one of which (between the first and second bays) springs from a shaped wall-post or large bracket, carved on the E. face with vine ornament and on the W. face with conventional foliage ; the intermediate in the first bay is a 17th-century insertion with a series of cinquefoils and the initials S.L. ; the intermediate in the fifth bay is similar, but without initials, and other timbers were renewed at the same time. The early 16th-century flat roof of the S. aisle is of five bays with moulded main timbers, except two tie-beams, curved braces under the tie-beams, some of which were renewed in the 18th century, hollow-chamfered joists and moulded brackets under the wall-posts.

Fittings—*Altar :* In chancel—part of slab with chamfered under-edge and two consecration-crosses. *Bells :* six ; 3rd, 4th and 6th by Miles Graye, 1663. *Brackets :* In S. chapel—at N. end of E. wall, a corbel capital, 14th-century, and at S. end a plain corbel, date uncertain. *Brass :* see Monument (3). *Door :* In S. doorway—of nail-studded oak battens with strap-hinge, early 16th-century. *Font :* octagonal bowl with cusped panels enclosing two shields with crossed keys and sword and three crowns ; head of the Baptist ; half-angel with shield ; knot and heart ; on under-edge carved flowers, knot and shield with plain cross ; panelled and traceried stem and moulded base ; late 15th-century. *Monuments* and *Floor-slabs.* Monuments : In chancel—against N. wall (1) of John, 2nd Lord Darcy, 1580–1, and Frances (Rich), his wife, altar-tomb and monument (Plate, p. 197) of alabaster and marble with recumbent effigies of man in plate armour, ruff and long mantle (effigy broken below knees), and wife with ruff, fur-lined cloak, etc. ; canopy resting on carved and panelled pilasters supporting a cornice, which carries two cartouches with shields and in the middle an achievement of arms ; against S. wall (2) of Thomas, 1st Lord Darcy, K.G. [15—] and Elizabeth (Vere), his wife ; alabaster and marble monument (erected *c.* 1580), similar in general design to (1), but with panelled centre-piece above the cornice ; effigies similar to those in monument (1) but the knight wears the garter (his left leg broken below the knee) ; two cartouches with shields, and an achievement of arms. In S. chapel —against E. wall (3) of John Darcy, 1638, sergeant-at-law, altar-tomb and recess with alabaster effigy in robes with cloak and cap ; on wall at back, brass inscription-plate with name of artist, Fr. Grigs, 1640 ; on S. wall (4) to Briant Darcie, 1587, Bridget (Corbet), his wife, and a number of their children and grandchildren, marble tablet with Corinthian side-columns and achievement of arms. Floor-slabs : In nave—(1) to Marget, wife of James Kenarley, 1690, and Isaac, their son, 1705. In S. aisle—(2) to Richard Tnbman, 1620, cook to

Thomas, Lord Darcy, a prayer for his soul, and a small incised stepped cross have been partly obliterated. *Piscina :* In chancel—in E. wall, with moulded jambs and three-centred head, round drain, 13th-century, possibly reset. *Plate :* includes a large cup of 1574, and cover-paten of same date, inscribed ANNO DŌM 1575 ; inside of bowl gilded. *Miscellanea :* On S. bracket in S. chapel, a man's head label-stop, 14th-century. In churchyard—many worked stones, shafting, window-tracery, etc., 12th-century and later, probably partly from abbey.

Condition—Good.

Secular :—

ᵃ(3). HOMESTEAD MOAT, in Nun's Wood, 1,100 yards N.N.W. of (4).

ᵇ(4). ST. OSYTH'S PRIORY, or Abbey, house (Plate, p. 198), outbuildings, gatehouse, precinct wall, etc., 200 yards N.W. of the church. The walls are of flint and septaria-rubble or of red brick with limestone dressings ; the roofs are covered with tiles and lead. The Priory (later Abbey) was founded before 1127, for Austin Canons, by Richard de Belmeis, Bishop of London. The earliest remaining work is the sub-vault of the *Dorter* range which is of the period of the foundation ; the still existing portions of the walls bounding the *Cloister* on the N. and W. are possibly also of this date. The remains of what was probably the *Kitchen* are of early 13th-century date ; to the same period belong the remains of the early gate-house ; *c.* 1230–40 the *Frater* was rebuilt with the vaulted *Passage* to the E. of it ; about the end of the 13th century the vaults in the *W. Range* were built. Late in the 15th century the *Great Gatehouse* was built and the ranges flanking it and projecting S. from it are of about the same date ; the eastern of these ranges incorporates an earlier gatehouse. About 1527 extensive additions were made by Abbot Vintoner who built the range running N. from the W. range and the *Bishop's Lodging,* a wing projecting towards the W. The Abbey was suppressed in 1539 and in 1553 came into the possession of Lord Darcy who transformed the buildings into a house, destroying some parts and making additions in others. At this time the conventual church, which flanked the cloister on the S., was destroyed together with the major portion of the E. and W. ranges of the cloister quadrangle ; the ends of the remaining portions of these ranges were faced with chequer-work, the *Abbot's* and *Clock Towers* built and the upper part of the dorter range rebuilt. The added buildings must have been extensive, but the precise form of the house as reconstructed, is uncertain ; remains of these additions are standing, N. of the Dorter range, N. of the modern house, and a patch of tile-paving has recently been uncovered about 100 ft.

Abbey Buildings from the South-West ; 16th-century.

Gatehouse and adjacent Buildings from the South-East ; late 15th-century.

ST. OSYTH'S PRIORY OR ABBEY.

ST. OSYTH'S PRIORY OR ABBEY.

Bishop's Lodging, and West Range ; North Half, early 16th-century, South Half, mid 16th-century.

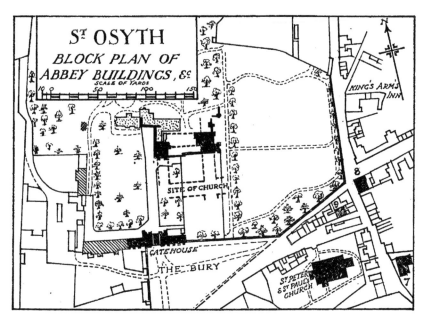

W. of the modern house. The monastic Frater appears to have done duty as the Great Hall. To this period must also be assigned the great barn, the outbuilding on the W. of the gardens, and many of the boundary-walls of the stable-yards and gardens. The Frater as a Hall seems to have been abandoned and a large red-brick building was erected, c. 1600, on the area of the N. part of the cloister. In the 17th or 18th century the whole of the eastern part of the house fell into ruin and about the middle of the 18th century the wing extending W. from the Bishop's Lodging was built. In 1866 almost the whole of the Bishop's Lodging except the S. wall was rebuilt and about the same time the modern wing was built, extending E. from it and covering part of the site of the monastic kitchen.

The house is of great interest both for the remains of monastic work and for the work of Lord Darcy. The gatehouse is amongst the finest examples of this class of structure in the country.

The *Cloister* (106 ft. E. to W.) lay on the N. side of the conventual church and was mostly destroyed by Lord Darcy. Portions of the outer walls remain on the E., N. and W., and there are indications of the former level of the pent roof preserved in

offsets on the S. side of the Clock tower and on the E. face of the S.E. buttress of the W. range. There are no remains of the conventual church, but the foundations of the nave were encountered in making the sunk lawn S. of the house.

The *Dorter Range* (Plate, p. 202), now mostly ruined, is substantially of early 12th-century work with a mid 16th-century upper storey. The S. end is faced with the chequer-work (ashlar and septaria) of Lord Darcy. In this wall are several mid 16th-century windows with four-centred lights and square heads with moulded labels, all now blocked; opening into a modern shed on the ground floor is a much damaged doorway of the same date, with remains of a four-centred arch. The sub-vault generally has early 12th-century piers of Roman brick with moulded stone imposts and rough rubble vaults groined in the two southern bays where they remain intact and of barrel form in the fifth bay where the springing only remains and probably groined in the third and fourth bays; the southern-most bay has a 16th-century doorway in the W. wall, modern externally, and in the E. wall a semi-circular 14th-century arch and a 16th-century filling with moulded jambs and segmental-pointed head. The wall between this bay and the next is

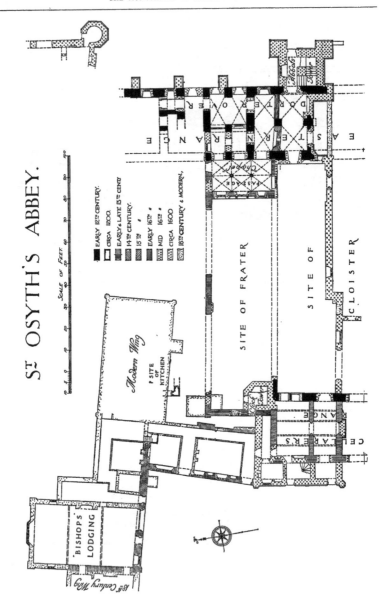

an insertion and in the western part has an early 16th-century brick recess with moulded jambs and a four-centred arch. The N. wall of the second bay is an original cross-wall and in the E. wall are the splays of an old doorway with a mid 16th-century filling and window in it. In the N. wall is a mid 16th-century doorway with a four-centred head of brick and W. of it is part of a round 12th-century arch, possibly of a former recess. The third and fourth bays had in the E. wall two open 12th-century arches of Roman brick ; both are now blocked and fitted with mid 16th-century windows. The western parts of these two bays form annexes of the building now used as a chapel and have with the second bay 16th-century arches pierced in the W. wall. The fourth bay has a paving of mediaeval tiles, some with patterns. The N. wall of the fourth bay was an original cross-wall and the fifth bay formed a passage open at the E. end but now filled in and fitted with a mid 16th-century window. The sixth bay is very narrow and has the appearance of being the channel for a drain ; it has an original round arch in the W. wall resting on the W. on a square 12th-century pier ; E. of this is the moulded head of a blocked 14th-century doorway, now much buried. Of the seventh bay only the E. wall remains with traces of a wide archway, blocked and fitted with a mid 16th-century three-light window ; this bay has traces of the former vault. The rest of the range has been destroyed and there is no evidence of its original length. The upper storey is entirely of mid 16th-century date and has been destroyed except for the E. wall which has the whole of one chequer-work gable and part of another ; the windows are all of the same type with four-centred lights and square heads with moulded labels ; they are all more or less damaged. This wall has a series of mid 16th-century buttresses and a chimney stack with an embattled offset and two diapered brick shafts with concave octagonal caps and moulded stone bases. Below this stack, inside the building, are three mid 16th-century fireplaces, two with moulded jambs, all with depressed heads.

The "Abbot's Tower" (Plate, p. 202) is entirely of mid 16th-century date and adjoins the Dorter range on the S.E. It is of three stages with turrets at three angles, square at the base and octagonal above and carried up above the parapet ; the parapets have a low gable on each face of the tower. The walls are of ashlar and septaria chequer-work and have a moulded plinth. The windows are all of the same type as those in the Dorter range and the doorway in the E. wall has a segmental-pointed arch and a square-moulded label. The great staircase in the tower has a solid pier in the middle and rises only to the first floor ; from this point a circular staircase in the S.W. turret gives access to the second floor and roof.

At the N.W. angle are two stone chimney-shafts, with moulded caps and bases and diapered shafts.

The Frater Range flanked the cloister on the N. and overlapped the W. range. The Frater itself (97½ ft. by 28½ ft.) has been destroyed except for the E. and W. ends and a fragment of the N. wall. The E. end has a wall-arcade (Plate, p. 202) of which the three middle bays remain ; they are of c. 1230-40 and have moulded two-centred arches with a moulded trefoiled inner order ; the points of the trefoil of the middle bay have defaced carving ; the arches rest on restored free shafts with old Purbeck marble capitals and bases. The W. end of the Frater is partly occupied by the Clock tower ; in the W. wall is a blocked mid 16th-century doorway with a four-centred head. In the adjoining fragment of the N. wall are remains of two doorways formerly opening into the kitchen-wing ; one of these has been partly destroyed by an inserted mid 16th-century doorway, now itself ruined.

The Passage (26½ ft. by 14½ ft.), now a chapel (Plate, p. 203), at the E. end of the Frater is roofed in six bays with a ribbed quadripartite vault of c. 1230-40 ; the web is of chalk, but the moulded ribs are of Reigate stone springing from round Purbeck marble columns with moulded capitals and bases ; the corbels against the W. wall have Purbeck marble abaci and carved crowned heads but those in the angles and on the E. wall are simply moulded ; the corbels on the E. wall appear to be of 14th-century date. The passage is lit by modern windows, that on the S. being inserted in the blocking of a former doorway ; the northern window on the W. is set in a mid 16th-century doorway with a four-centred head and now blocked. In the N. wall is a doorway of c. 1500 with moulded jambs and four-centred arch ; further W. is the E. jamb of another opening, now blocked ; in the blocking is a mid 16th-century window and below it a reset square drain in a recess with a four-centred head.

The Clock Tower is entirely of mid 16th-century date, except the lower part of the S. wall ; it is faced with chequer-work and is square below and octagonal above ; the windows are of two four-centred lights in square heads.

N. of the Frater is a double respond of early 13th-century date, with half-round attached piers with moulded capitals and bases and the springers of arches N. and E. There is little doubt that this formed part of the Kitchen-wing but its precise significance is uncertain.

The Western Range has a mid 16th-century chequer-work gable to the S. wall with the stumps of the two side walls transformed into buttresses ; in the middle is a projection with an embattled top and above and to the W. of it is a chimney-stack with two restored shafts with reeded ornament. The E. wall has been much patched and altered ; it has a mid 16th-century doorway with double hollow-chamfered jambs and a four-centred arch with a square head and a label. The range has a narrow mid 16th-century addition on the W. side (Plate, p. 199), of red brick, with octagonal projections at the angles ; it is of two storeys with two gables to the attics on the W. side and has windows of the usual form and a doorway with moulded jambs and rounded head with a moulded cornice ; the spandrels have a cinquefoil (for Darcy) and a molet (for Vere) with inlaid work of composition. The western range contains two late 13th-century cellars on the ground floor, roofed with barrel-vaults divided into five bays by chamfered ribs ; the wall between the cellars has an archway with jambs and segmental-pointed head of two chamfered orders. A similar archway in the S. wall has been blocked on the outside. At the N. end of the range is a narrow added bay probably of mid 16th-century date and with door-ways of that period. The upper floor of the range has a mid 16th-century doorway with moulded jambs and four-centred arch of oak.

Between the E. and W. ranges and cutting across the site of the cloister is a lofty red brick wall of c. 1600 ; it formed the S. wall of a range of buildings of two storeys. Between the storeys is a moulded brick cornice and above it is a moulded parapet-string. The wall contains a modern archway and nine windows of c. 1600 all of brick with square heads and moulded labels ; they are now blocked.

N. of the W. range is a red brick *Wing* (Plate, p. 199) of c. 1527. The W. wall is original and has a moulded stone parapet-coping and two low gables; the original window openings have four-centred heads on the ground floor and square heads on the upper floor ; all these windows have been partly blocked and fitted with smaller square-headed stone windows of mid 16th-century date with moulded labels. The southern doorway is of c. 1527 and has a four-centred head. The wall has black brick diapering. The E. side and the interior has been almost entirely altered.

The *"Bishop's Lodging"* (Plate, p. 199) extends W. at right angles to the range last described. It was almost entirely rebuilt in 1866 except the S. front. This front is of c. 1527 and of red brick with black brick diapering ; the dressings are partly of stone and partly of brick. The moulded parapet has a band of cusped brick panelling below it. In the middle of the ground floor is a wide stone archway with stop-moulded jambs and four-centred arch in a square head with moulded labels ; the traceried spandrels have each a shield with defaced carving, that on the W. apparently a beast with a scroll. The main archway is flanked by doorways, that on the W. modern but that on the E. generally similar to the large arch and with a tun and crown carved in the spandrels. Above the main archway

is a large oriel window, modern externally, except for the moulded and carved head and the panelled and carved base and corbelling. The head has a band of early Renaissance ornament with foliage and small nude figures. The base has two bands of panelling the upper consisting of cusped squares enclosing shields and trefoil-headed panels with Tudor roses ; the shields have (a) crossed keys and sword of SS. Peter and Paul, with a papal tiara in chief ; (b) three crowns and a sword palewise, for St. Osyth ; (c) a crowned heart pierced by three swords and encircled by a crown of thorns ; (d) crowned monogram of the Virgin ; (e) dimidiated rose and pomegranate, crowned ; (f) a stag supporting a scutcheon charged with three crowns ; (g) rebus of Abbot John Vintoner ; (h) Bouchier. Below this the lower band has lozengy, cusped panelling with a carved flower in the middle of each main panel. The moulded corbelling has two bands of carved foliage each with shields ; the upper band contains six shields all defaced except a crowned M and a dolphin with a mitre in chief. The lower band has running vine ornament with remains of lettering intertwined, apparently the name Johannes Vintoner, but much broken, and five shields—(a) SS. Peter and Paul ; (b) three crowns ; (c) chalice and host ; (d) vine and tun, for Vintoner ; (e) three combs, for Tunstall, bishop of London. The reveals and rear-arch of the oriel window have rich cusped panelling in stone with 88 small shields. These shields bear the various devices of Abbot Vintoner, St. Osyth, Tunstall bishop of London, Henry VIII, the later arms of the Abbey—*parted cheveronwise, in chief a ring between a mitre and a crozier* and the arms of Bourchier, Tunstall, Henry VIII, France, etc. There are also monograms of the Virgin, Vintoner, the five wounds and two small standing figures, probably of canons. A series of four shields on each side give the date 1527, one in Roman and one in Arabic numerals. Flanking the oriel window on each side are windows with four-centred heads and moulded labels of red brick ; they are partly blocked and fitted with modern windows. Inside the building are many carved oak panels (Plate, p. 180) of c. 1527 all reset ; some have vine ornament and double ogee enrichment and a large number have shields with the initials N, I, H, V, O, A, S and T, Bourchier knot, water-bouget, dolphin, stag, mitre, molets, three curry-combs, crossed swords and keys, mitre, tun, crown, portcullis, etc.

N. of the Dorter range is an isolated ruin of part of the mid 16th-century house ; it has an octagonal turret of chequer-work at the S.E. angle with two-light square-headed windows. The main wall running N. is faced with brick and has two square-headed windows on the first floor. A window on the ground floor has been turned into an archway ; further N. is a stone doorway with a four-centred head.

Remains of Frater Range, 13th-century and later ; Dorter Range, Subvault 12th-century,
Upper Part 16th-century.   From the North-West.

Remains of Frater Range, 13th-century and later, and 'Abbot's Tower,' 16th-century.   From the West.

ST. OSYTH'S PRIORY OR ABBEY.

ST. OSYTH'S PRIORY OR ABBEY.

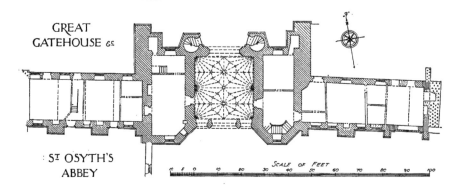

GREAT
GATEHOUSE &c

Sᵗ OSYTH'S
ABBEY

SCALE OF FEET

N. of the modern house is an isolated buttress or gate-pier of mid 16th-century date.

In the garden N.E. of the house is part of a 13th-century coffin-lid.

The *Gatehouse* (Plate, p. 198) S. of the house is of late 15th-century date and of two storeys with a double moulded plinth and an embattled parapet of chequer-work, mostly set diagonally. The S. front (Plate, p. 204) has elaborate knapped flint-inlay in cusped and crocketed panels ; between the storeys is a moulded string-course and the entrances are flanked by two semi-octagonal projections ; the windows are all of two cinquefoiled lights in a square head with a moulded label, except a small single light spy-window in the plinth of the porters' room. The main outer archway has stop-moulded jambs and four-centred arch in a square head with a double label and carved stops ; the spandrels have figures carved in high relief of St. Michael and the dragon. The two small footway arches are of similar character to the main arch with head-stops to the labels and carved foliage and a rose in the spandrels. Flanking the main arch are a pair of niches with ogee cusped and crocketed canopies with flint-inlay and ribbed vaults ; the moulded brackets have angels holding scrolls ; above the arch is a similar but taller niche, with traceried instead of inlaid panels and an angel on the bracket holding a shield. The N. front has a parapet and windows similar to those on the S. front ; the two semi-octagonal stair-turrets have external doorways with four-centred heads, quatrefoiled lights, and rise above the parapet. The great inner archway (Plate, p. 205) has stop-moulded jambs and two-centred arch in a square head with moulded labels and traceried spandrels, enclosing blank shields ; above the head is a band of flint chequer-work. The Gate-hall has

a ribbed lierne vault (Plate, p. 205) of two bays springing from grouped triple shafts with moulded capitals and bases ; the intersections of the ribs have richly carved bosses the three central ones being (*a*) the Annunciation ; (*b*) crowned and veiled head of St. Osyth ; and (*c*) a couched hart in a park paling and with a napkin round its neck, powdered with crowns ; the smaller bosses include foliage, flowers, various grotesque heads and faces, lions' faces, bishop's head, kings' heads, a double face, pelican, half-angel with scroll, shields with the later arms of the Abbey and three crowns and a head of St. John on a charger. The Porter's room on the W. of the Gate-hall has a doorway with moulded jambs and two-centred arch ; in the E. wall is a recess with a large square basin and drain and a niche for a lantern at the back ; in the W. wall is a fireplace with moulded jambs and four-centred arch ; above it is a triangular-headed niche ; further S. is a blocked doorway. In the room over it is a similar fireplace in the E. wall. In the main N.W. buttress of the gatehouse is a garderobe or cupboard. The rooms E. of the Gate-hall have no features of interest, but there is a garderobe or cupboard in the main N.E. buttress.

The *Range* E. of the gatehouse is possibly of rather earlier date ; it is of three bays with an embattled parapet and windows similar to those of the gatehouse. The easternmost bay is an early 13th-century gatehouse, refronted in the 15th century to match the rest of the range. Incorporated in the S. wall and only visible internally is a wide early 13th-century archway, two-centred and of two moulded orders ; in the N. wall is a wide blocked archway with a segmental-pointed head ; the difference in walling between this and the other bays of the range is visible on the N. face. Between the two pairs of windows on the S. face are rectangular cusped panels enclosing shields with (*a*) the later arms of the Abbey, and (*b*) *three birds* (? popinjays or pheasants). At the E. end of the range is a heavy brick chimney-stack of the 17th century with grouped diagonal shafts.

The *Range* W. of the gatehouse is of late 15th-century date and of two storeys with an embattled parapet of knapped flint on the S. side; the windows on this side have been much altered. The projecting stone chimney-stack has two mid 16th-century brick octagonal shafts with spurred caps and moulded bases. The N. side has one original and one mid 16th-century doorway both with four-centred heads. The windows on this side are mostly original but some of them blocked.

The *Barn* adjoins the range last described on the W. ; it is of mid 16th-century date and timber-framed, except for the N. wall, which is of rubble with three doorways, each with a four-centred head and a square-moulded label. There are three porches on the S. side. The roof has plain tie-beams with curved braces and plain collar-beams. The W. wall is of rubble.

Extending S. from the W. side of the gatehouse is a wall with an embattled parapet, which once formed the E. side of a building and is mainly of late 15th-century date. It has four windows, in pairs, similar to those in the gatehouse ; between them is a doorway with moulded jambs and two-centred arch ; it is now blocked. Further S. is a large archway (Plate, p. 205) of mid 14th-century work reset ; it is semi-circular and of three moulded orders with a moulded label and head-stops ; the jambs have each three attached shafts with moulded capitals.

The *Outbuilding* S.W. of the house is of two storeys with rubble walls and a brick coping and pinnacle to the S, gable. It is probably of mid 16th-century date, but has been much patched and altered.

The *Precinct Wall* is of various dates ; the part at the S.E. angle is perhaps of late 14th-century date and has a moulded string-course and an embattled parapet with the crenels subsequently filled in and finished with a continuous stone coping. The wall between this and the gatehouse wing is of mid 16th-century date with small buttresses and a large round-headed archway with a square-moulded label, now blocked ; further E. is a smaller doorway with a three-centred head and a square label. The cross-walls of the garden are of the same date and have similar doorways. The walls of the kitchen garden and yards are partly of brick and probably all of mid 16th-century date.

Condition—Good, ruins well preserved.

Secular :—

a(5). NUN'S HALL, ruin in Nun's Wood 100 yards N.W. of (3), is of flint and septaria rubble with dressings of limestone. The remaining fragment is the S. gabled end of a building probably of the 14th century. There are remains of an internal moulded string-course. The ruin has been much patched and has an inserted doorway and above it are various reset details including a 14th-century niche with cusped and sub-cusped head.

Condition—Poor.

b(6). FRAGMENT of WALLING on S. side of stream, ¼ m. S.E. of the church. The fragment is of rubble and about 10 ft. in length and may have formed part of the revetment of a former dam.

Condition—Poor.

b(7). ST. CLAIR'S HALL, house (Plate, p. xxxi) and moat, ¼ m. S.S.E. of the church. The *House* is of two storeys, timber-framed and plastered ; the roofs are tiled. It was built in the 14th century with an aisled central hall and cross-wings at the E. and W. ends. Early in the 16th century the cross-wings were largely altered or rebuilt and later in the same century the E. cross-wing was extended towards the S.

The house is an important example of an aisled Hall retaining its aisles.

The upper storey of both cross-wings projected on the N. front, but that of the W. wing has been underbuilt ; the gable of this wing also projects and all have early 16th-century moulded bressumers. The 16th-century extension of the E. wing is mainly built of red brick and has a projecting chimney-stack on the E. side incorporating a garderobe pit. There is a small added bay of early 16th-century date on the S. side of the Hall, in which is a window of four lights with moulded mullions.

Interior—The *Hall* is now divided up by an inserted chimney-stack, but retains its two octagonal oak columns with moulded capitals dividing it into two bays ; the main roof-truss has been removed but the original moulded and curved braces remain. The roof is continued down over the aisles without interruption. In the W. wall are remains of an early 16th-century screen with moulded posts and on the E. wall is a moulded and embattled plate. A door is made up of early 16th-century linen-fold panels. The upper floor of the E. wing has an arched plaster ceiling divided up into square panels by moulded ribs ; there are two early 16th-century windows with moulded mullions and now blocked. The main staircase appears to have been much altered but probably incorporates 17th-century material.

The *Moat* surrounds the house and was formerly divided by a cross-arm.

Condition—Of house, good except W. wing.

MONUMENTS (8–16).

The following monuments, unless otherwise described, are of two storeys, timber-framed and

ST. OSYTH'S PRIORY OR ABBEY.
South Entrance to Gatehouse ; late 15th-century.

Gatehouse: Details of Vaulting; late 15th-century.

Gatehouse: North Archway; late 15th-century.

Archway in Wall S.W. of Gatehouse; mid 14th-century.

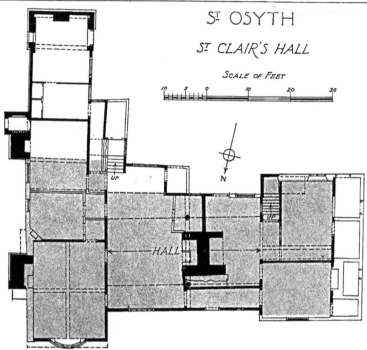

ST OSYTH

ST CLAIR'S HALL

SCALE OF FEET

plastered or weather-boarded; the roofs are tiled. Many of the buildings have original chimney-stacks and exposed ceiling-beams.

Condition—Good, or fairly good, unless noted.

[b](8). *Priory Cottage* (Plate, p. xxxi), house, 50 yards E. of the church, was built probably late in the 15th century with a central Hall and cross-wings at the N. and S. ends; the Hall was subsequently divided into two storeys and there are 17th-century and modern additions at the back. The upper storey projects at the W. end of both cross-wings on curved brackets; the brackets of the N. wing spring from shafts with moulded capitals. The main block has a projecting and gabled bay and below it is the moulded head of an original window now destroyed. Inside the building one room has original moulded ceiling-joists. The Hall has an original moulded tie-beam with curved braces and the N. wing has an original king-post roof-truss.

[b](9). *House*, at cross-roads, 70 yards N. by W. of (8), was built probably late in the 16th century and has a modern addition on the E.

[b](10). *House*, 30 yards S.W. of (9), has been pulled down except for the lower part of the S. wall which is *c.* 1500 and has two doorways with four-centred heads and a window with a trefoiled head.

Condition—Bad.

[b](11). *House*, two tenements, on N. side of Mill Street, 500 yards W. of the church, was built probably in the first half of the 16th century and has a cross-wing at the E. end. The upper storey projects at the S. end of the cross-wing on curved brackets.

[b](12). *House*, on E. side of Colchester road, 350 yards N. of the church, was built probably late in the 15th century with a cross-wing at the N. end and a back wing. The upper storey projected on the whole of the W. side but has been underbuilt; it still projects on the N. side of the back wing. Inside the building an original cambered tie-beam is exposed.

[a](13). *The Hill*, cottage, 600 yards S.E. of the church, was built late in the 16th century and has several original windows with moulded frames and mullions.

Condition—Poor.

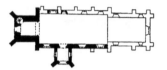

ᵃ(14). *Park Farm*, house, 1 m. N.E. of the church, was built probably in the 15th century but has been much altered. Inside the building, on the first floor is a framed partition with two doorways and a blank space dividing them ; above the N. doorway (Plate, p. 101) is a painted black-letter inscription " Hic deum adora . . ." and on the upright is an inscribed scroll, forming part of a painted panel removed from here and now in the Colchester Museum. The work can hardly be *in situ* and may possibly, from the position of the two doorways, have formed the rood-screen in the Abbey church. The roof of the house has remains of the original construction.

ᵃ(15). *Frowick Hall*, house, nearly 1¾ m. N. of the church, was built probably late in the 16th century on an L-shaped plan with the wings extending towards the N. and E. There is an added 17th-century wing on the S.W., with a chimney-stack on the N. side having grouped diagonal shafts.

ᵃ(16). *Highbirds*, house, 1½ m. N.E. of (15), was built probably in the 16th century and has a 17th-century addition on the N.E. The upper storey projects at the W. end of the S. front.

Unclassified :—

ᵇ(17). MOUND, in grounds of St. Osyth's Priory, N.E. of the house. The mound is circular and is surrounded by a shallow ditch.

ᵇ(18). MOUND, about 250 yards N.W. of (17).

---

80. SALCOTT.   (C.e.)
(O.S. 6 in. xlvi. N.W.)

Salcott is a small parish and village on the S. side of Salcott Creek and 7½ m. N.E. of Maldon.

Roman :—

(1). Mr. Wire's Diary (Colchester Museum), under 21st May, 1845, has the hearsay record of the discovery of some foundations of Roman character at " Sorker," near Virley.

Ecclesiastical :—

(2). PARISH CHURCH OF ST. MARY stands at the E. end of the village. The walls, where ancient, are of flint-rubble and septaria with dressings of limestone ; the roofs are tiled. The *Nave* was built probably early in the 14th century. Late in the 15th century the *West Tower* was added and early in the 16th century the *South Porch* was built. The church suffered severely in the earthquake of 1884 and was drastically restored in 1893 when the *Chancel* and most of the N. and S. walls of the nave were rebuilt.

Architectural Description—The *Nave* (50 ft. by 21½ ft.) has in the N. wall, which has been largely rebuilt, three modern windows and a blocked N. doorway with a two-centred head and incorporating some 14th-century stones. In the S. wall are three windows ; the easternmost is modern ; the middle window is of mid 14th-century date partly restored and of two pointed lights with a plain spandrel in a two-centred head with a moulded label ; the rear-arch and splays are moulded ; the westernmost window is modern except for the late 15th-century rear-arch and splays ; between the two western windows is the early 16th-century S. doorway with moulded jambs and four-centred arch in a square head ; the spandrels are carved with blank shields and foliage ; above the doorway externally is a roughly pointed relieving-arch of brick.

The *West Tower* (10 ft. square) is of three stages, of which the two lower with the moulded plinth are of late 15th-century date ; the top stage has been largely rebuilt but incorporates old material ; it has an embattled parapet. The tower-arch is two-centred and of two orders, the outer moulded and continuous and the inner hollow-chamfered and springing from attached shafts with moulded capitals. The W. window is modern except for the rear-arch ; below the window is the W. doorway with moulded jambs, two-centred arch and label. The second stage has in the N. wall a single light window all modern except the rear-arch and splays. The bell-chamber has in each wall a modern window.

The *South Porch* is of early 16th-century date, partly restored and has a four-centred outer archway of two moulded orders, the outer continuous and the inner resting on attached shafts with moulded capitals and bases ; the moulded label has square voluted stops. The side walls have each a much restored window of two cinquefoiled lights in a square head ; the jambs and head are moulded.

Fittings — *Chair :* In chancel — high panelled back with guilloche ornament, shaped arms and turned front legs, early 17th-century. *Coffin-lids :* In churchyard—W. of tower, (1) coped slab with double hollow-chamfered edge, cross with foliated ends on stepped calvary, 13th-century ; (2) broken slab with hollow-chamfered edge, probably 13th-century. *Door :* In S. doorway—of two folds each with two panels filled with ridged battens cut ogee-shaped at the top, early 16th-century.

Indents : In churchyard—W. of tower, (1) of half-figure of civilian and inscription-plate ; (2) of man and wife with inscription-plate ; both 15th-century. *Niche :* In S. porch—over S. doorway, with moulded jambs and cinquefoiled head, early 16th-century. *Painting :* In nave—on splays and rear-arch of S. doorway, remains of black paint and pattern of red foliage, date uncertain. *Plate :* includes cup and cover-paten of 1574, the cup with a band of engraved ornament. *Pulpit :* hexagonal with moulded styles and rails, raised panels, with inlay, ogee-shaped stem with moulded base, early 18th-century. *Sloup :* In nave—E. of S. doorway, with chamfered jambs and trefoiled head, 14th or 15th-century. *Miscellanea :* In nave—on E. splay of middle S. window, two round cut panels in stonework, one enclosing quatrefoil and one a sexfoiled design, probably late 14th-century.

Condition—Good, but much ivy on tower.

Secular —:

(3). COTTAGE, two tenements, on S. side of road, 230 yards W. of the church, is of two storeys, timber-framed and weather-boarded. The middle part is one wing of a 15th or early 16th-century house, with a modern building on each side of it. The upper storey projects in front. Inside the building is a 17th-century door and an original tie-beam with curved braces.

Condition—Good, much altered.

(4). HOUSE, 180 yards W. of (2), is of two storeys, timber-framed and plastered ; the roofs are tiled. The W. cross-wing was built probably in the 15th century but the rest of the house is modern. The upper storey projects at the N. end of the cross-wing. In the W. wall are two original windows with diamond-shaped mullions. Inside the building are some exposed ceiling-beams and framing. The roof has braced tie-beams and a king-post.

Condition—Good.

(5). COTTAGE and post office, on N. side of road, 300 yards W. of the church, is of two storeys, timber-framed and plastered ; the roofs are tiled. It was built early in the 17th century.

Condition—Good.

---

81. STANWAY. (C.c.)

(O.S. 6 in. [a]xxvii. N.W. [b]xxvii. S.W. [c]xxvii. S.E. [d]xxxvi. N.W. [e]xxxvi. N.E.)

Stanway is a parish adjoining that of Colchester on the W. The two churches are the principal monuments.

Roman :—

[d](1). A house was excavated in 1842 in a field called Cheshunt, on Gosback Farm, a quarter of a mile S. of All Saints' Church, Bottle End. The

remains were only about six inches below the sur-face, and were in very fragmentary state, and nothing now survives except bits of tile, tesserae, &c., scattered over the field. A corridor, 14 ft. wide, ran round a square, each side of which was about 288 ft. in length. The walls were 3 ft. thick. There were traces of rooms on the E. and W. In the centre of the quadrangle were foundations 4 ft. thick, strongly built of septaria and Kentish rag, connected with which had been rooms of which only vestiges remained. The earth excavated to the depth of 10 ft. was entirely composed of debris— tiles, coloured stucco and tesserae.

On the W. side, for 60 ft. parallel to the S. wall, at a distance of 12 ft., was the foundation of a wall 2 ft. wide, ' composed of the chippings of Kentish rag laid in alternate layers with concrete.'

In the same field, almost parallel to the E. wall, at a distance of 170 ft., the foundations of a wall, with a return wall at the N. end, were traced for about 450 ft. The wall was from 2 to 3 ft. thick, and at two spots along it, and in two other parts of the field, large quantities of oyster shells, boars' tusks and broken pottery were found in deep pits. The stones were mostly removed soon after the excavations.

This must once have been a large house, and, to judge from the thirty coins found there, which range from Vespasian to the Constantine family, it was occupied from the second century to the end of the fourth.

(C. R. Smith, *Collectanea Antiqua*, 1852, II, 41 ; Jenkins, in *B. A. A. J.*, 1846, II, 45 ; *Gent.'s Mag.*, 1842, II, 526.) (See also *Sectional Preface*, p. xxvii.)

Ecclesiastical :—

[b](2). PARISH CHURCH OF ST. ALBRIGHT (= St. Ethelbert) stands on the S. side of Stane Street. The walls are of flint and ragstone rubble, with dressings of limestone and Roman brick. The *Nave* was built early in the 12th century. In the 15th century the E. part of the present nave, then forming the chancel, was rebuilt and the *North Porch* added. The church was restored in the 19th century when the existing *Chancel, South Chapel* and *South Aisle* were added. The S. arcade of the chancel is of late 15th or early 16th-century date and was brought here from the destroyed church of St. Runwald, Colchester.

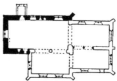

Architectural Description — The *Chancel* is modern but reset in the S. wall is a late 15th or early 16th-century arcade of two bays with four-centred arches of two moulded orders, the outer continuous and the inner resting on attached shafts with moulded capitals and bases.

The *South Chapel* is modern but reset in the E. wall is a partly restored 15th-century window of three cinquefoiled lights with vertical tracery in a two-centred head.

The *Nave* (45 ft. by 20½ ft.) has in the N. wall a slight difference in the masonry and a rough raking plinth showing the junction of the 12th and 15th-century work. In this wall are four windows, the easternmost is of the 15th century and of two cinquefoiled lights with vertical tracery in a two-centred head; the second and western-most windows are each a single 12th-century light with Roman brick jambs and a round head of stone; the third window is of mid 14th-century date and of two cinquefoiled lights with a quatre-foil in a two-centred head with a moulded label and head-stops; between the two eastern windows is the late 15th or early 16th-century upper door-way to the rood-loft staircase, with a rounded head; the lower doorway is said to exist but is not now visible; below the westernmost window is the 15th-century N. doorway with moulded jambs, two-centred arch and label. In the S. wall is a modern arcade of two bays; further W. is a 12th-century window similar to those in the N. wall and just E. of it is the 12th-century S. door-way with plain jambs and round arch of Roman bricks. The W. wall has quoins of Roman brick and in it is a much restored 14th-century window similar to that in the N. wall but with head-stops to the label; below the window are rough joints possibly indicating the jambs of three openings or recesses and now filled in flush with the rest of the wall; they possibly represent a 12th-century W. doorway flanked by two recesses. In the gable is a 12th-century window similar to the others but restored.

The *South Aisle* is modern but reset in the W. wall is a much restored 15th-century window similar to that in the N. wall of the nave.

The *Roof* of the nave has old trussed-rafters and collar-beams. The bell-turret rests on a 15th-century tie-beam at the W. end of the nave, with modern braces springing from carved grotesque corbels, one mostly cut away. The 15th-century roof of the N. porch has a cambered tie-beam with curved braces, king-post with four-way struts and central purlin.

Fittings—*Bell :* one, said to be by Miles Graye, 1610. *Coffin-lid :* In S. chapel—coped slab with large formy cross (two arms only remain), incised ornament at base, early 13th-century. *Door :* In N. doorway—modern but with strap-hinges of the 15th century. *Floor-slab :* In nave—to William Eldred, 1701, and Joannah (Goodwin), his wife, 1696. *Font :* octagonal bowl with panelled sides,

panels with blank shields and irradiated chalice and host alternately, moulded lower edge and base, 15th-century. *Painting :* In chancel—on piers of S. arcade, traces of red colour. *Piscina :* In chancel—with cinquefoiled head and rectangular drain, 15th-century, reset. *Plate :* includes two pewter plates, probably early 18th-century.

Condition—Good.

[d](3). CHURCH OF ALL SAINTS (Plate, p. 6), formerly the parish church, stands about 1½ m. S.S.E. of St. Albright's church. The walls are of pebble and ragstone rubble, with a large admixture of tiles and brick; the tower is of alternate courses of brick and flint; the N. porch is of brick; the dressings are of limestone. The *Nave* and *West Tower* with a chancel and N. aisle were built probably late in the 14th century. The bell-chamber is perhaps of slightly later date. Probably after the Reformation the church fell into disrepair and was restored by Sir John Swinerton early in the 17th century, when the chancel-arch and N. arcade were built up and the *North Porch* added on part of the site of the N. aisle. The church again fell into disuse probably later in the same century and is now roofless and ruinous.

The vault of the tower is of unusual form.

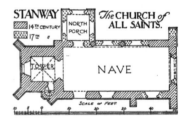

Architectural Description—The *Chancel* has entirely disappeared except for the late 14th-century two-centred chancel-arch now blocked with brick and with an early 17th-century window of brick in the blocking; the window was formerly of three lights in a four-centred head, but the mullions have been destroyed.

The *Nave* (39 ft. by 15¾ ft.) has a late 14th-century N. arcade of three bays with two-centred arches of two chamfered orders; the columns have each four attached shafts with moulded capitals and defaced bases; the responds are chamfered; the arcade has an early 17th-century blocking of brick with two square-headed windows and a doorway with a three-centred head and a moulded label; the head of one window has gone. In the S. wall are two windows, the eastern of early 17th-century date and of brick with a three-centred head; the western window is of the 14th century, with a two-centred head restored with

17th-century brick ; both windows have lost their mullions ; further W. is the S. doorway, with a segmental-pointed relieving arch of brick, much damaged and altered.

The *West Tower* (9 ft. square) is of late 14th-century date and of three stages with an embattled parapet and a moulded plinth. The ground stage has a domed vault of concentric rings of brickwork with chamfered stone ribs on the soffit springing from head corbels some with crowns. The two-centred tower-arch is of two chamfered orders ; the responds have each a semi-circular attached shaft with moulded capital and defaced base. In the S. wall is the doorway to the turret staircase, with moulded jambs and two-centred arch. The W. window has a two-centred head and a moulded label, but the mullion and tracery have been destroyed. The second stage has on the N., S. and W. sides a small square-headed loop ; in the E. wall is a brick opening with a three-centred head and now blocked. The bell-chamber has in each wall a window formerly of two transomed and cinquefoiled lights with a quatrefoil in a two-centred head with a moulded label ; all these windows are much weathered and partly destroyed.

The *North Porch* is of early 17th-century date and of brick with a crow-stepped gable ; the four-centred outer archway is plastered and of two chamfered orders ; it has a moulded label and shafted jambs with moulded capitals and bases ; the relieving - arch has counterfeit masonry in plaster ; above it is a sunk panel with a quartered shield of the Swinerton arms. The side walls have each a window without mullions, tracery or head.

Condition—Ruinous.

Secular :—

a(4). STANWAY HALL, 100 yards W. of (3), was built probably about the middle of the 16th century but has been almost entirely rebuilt in modern times. Inside the building one room is lined with early 17th-century panelling and contains an original stone fireplace (Plate, p. xxxiii) flanked by diminishing fluted pilasters with Ionic capitals supporting a frieze carved with scrolled foliage, small figures and a cartouche.

Condition—Good, much altered.

MONUMENTS (5–18).

The following monuments, unless otherwise described, are of the 17th century and of two storeys, timber-framed and plastered or weatherboarded ; the roofs are tiled. Many of the buildings have original chimney-stacks and exposed ceilingbeams.

Condition—Good, or fairly good, unless noted.

b(5). *Oldhouse Farm*, house, 700 yards S.E. of the parish church, has been refronted with brick.

STANE STREET, N. side :—

b(6). *House*, two tenements, 620 yards W. of the parish church, was built in the 16th century or earlier and has a cross-wing at the W. end.

b(7). *House*, 20 yards E. of (6), was built probably in the 15th century with cross-wings at the N. and S. ends. The late 16th-century central chimney-stack has four octagonal shafts on a square base. Inside the building two original doorways in the N. wing, probably in the former ' screens,' have four-centred heads ; the roof of the S. wing has an original king-post truss.

Condition—Poor.

b(8). *White Hart Farm*, house, formerly an Inn, 300 yards W. of the parish church, was built probably in the 16th century with cross-wings at the E. and W. ends.

b(9). *The Cedars*, house, 100 yards N.E. of the parish church, was built probably in the 16th century but has been extensively altered and refaced with brick ; there are cross-wings at the E. and W. ends.

b(10). *Wiseman's*, house, 300 yards E. of (9), has been refaced with brick.

b(11). *Cottage*, about ½ m. E.N.E. of (10).

b(12). *Beaconend Farm*, house, 110 yards E. of (11), was built probably in the 15th century with cross-wings at the E. and W. ends. It has been refronted with brick. Inside the building the roof has an original roof-truss with octagonal king-post having a simple capital.

S. side :—

b(13). *Judd's Farm*, house, opposite (11).

b(14). *Abbot's Farm*, house (Plate, p. xxxi), about ¾ m. N.N.E. of the parish church, was built probably in the 15th or early in the 16th century with cross-wings at the N. and S. ends. The upper storey projects at the E. ends of both cross-wings. Inside the building the main block and both wings have original king-post roof-trusses.

b(15). *House*, 50 yards N. of (14), has been refaced with modern brick.

a(16). *"Brick Stables,"* house, ¾ m. N.E. of the parish church, has an 18th-century block added in front.

c(17). *Olivers*, house, about 2½ m. S.E. of the parish church, has a back wing with a king-post roof-truss of the 15th century. The rest of the house was added or rebuilt in the 18th century. There is a large fish-pond N.E. of the house.

c(18). *House*, N. of (17), has large 18th-century additions.

STISTED. *The* PARISH CHURCH *of* ALL SAINTS.

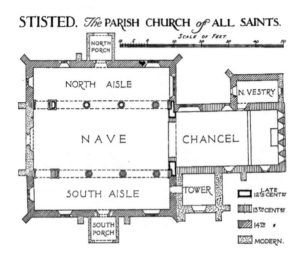

82. STISTED. (A.c.)

(O.S. 6 in. (ª)xxv. N.E. (ᵇ)xxv. S.E.)

Stisted is a parish and small village 3 m. E.N.E. of Braintree. The church is a monument of importance.

Ecclesiastical :—

ᵇ(1). PARISH CHURCH OF ALL SAINTS (Plate, p. xxviii) stands at the S. end of the village. The walls are of flint and pebble-rubble with some boulder-clay ; the dressings are of limestone and clunch and the roofs are covered with tiles and lead. The N. arcade of the *Nave* is of late 12th-century date. Early in the 13th century the S. arcade and aisle were built, the arches of the N. arcade rebuilt, and a narrow arch inserted instead of the former E. respond ; at the same time or shortly after the nave was lengthened by a narrow bay at the W. end and the *Chancel* was rebuilt. In the first half of the 14th century the *South Aisle* was rebuilt and shortly after the *North Aisle* and *North Vestry* were rebuilt. The church was restored in the 19th century, when the *South Tower* and the W. wall of the nave were rebuilt. the *North* and *South Porches* built and the clear-storey refaced.

The late 12th-century columns in the nave are noteworthy.

Architectural Description—The *Chancel* (37½ ft. by 19¾ ft.) has in the E. wall five graduated 13th-century lancets with chamfered and rebated jambs and heads, all partly restored ; above them is a round window apparently entirely modern. In the N. wall are two windows, the eastern is a 13th-century lancet with chamfered jambs and head ; the western window (Plate, p. 143) is of the 14th century and of three trefoiled ogee lights with tracery in a segmental-pointed head with a moulded label and grotesque stops ; further E. is a 14th-century doorway with chamfered jambs and two-centred head. In the S. wall are two 13th-century lancet-windows with chamfered jambs and heads, both much restored. The 13th-century chancel-arch is two-centred and of one moulded order ; the square responds have moulded imposts.

The *North Vestry* (15¼ ft. by 18¼ ft.) has a modern E. wall and window and a modern doorway in the W. wall.

The *Nave* (50½ ft. by 22 ft.) has a N. arcade (Plate, p. 212) of five bays, with early 13th-century, two-centred arches of one chamfered order ; the easternmost arch was probably inserted in the deep 12th-century respond and the E. respond has a late 12th-century chamfered impost reset ; the column in place of the former respond is circular and has a moulded capital carved with three grotesque heads and a rose with a dragon and a bird feeding off it ; the base is modern ; the second and third columns are circular and of late 12th-century date and have square moulded abaci and moulded capitals elaborately carved with conventional foliage (Plate, p. 213) ; the bases are modern except for one stone ; the fourth pier is square and has a late 12th-century respond on the E. face, with a chamfered impost foliated at the angles ; the westernmost arch springs from a lower level and has 13th-century moulded imposts. The S. arcade is of five bays, the E. and W. bays corresponding in width and character to those of the N. arcade ; the whole arcade is of the 13th century and has arches uniform with those on the N. ; the easternmost column is similar to the corresponding one on the N. side, but has the capital carved with one grotesque and one foliage boss, the others being left uncarved ; the second and third columns are circular and have moulded square capitals. The clearstorey has on each side three quatrefoiled windows probably of the 14th century, but entirely modern externally. In the W. wall are five modern windows ; the W. doorway is also modern but incorporates many 13th or 14th-century stones.

The *North Aisle* (12 ft. wide) has in the E. wall a window all modern except for part of the splays and the segmental rear-arch, which are of the 14th century. In the N. wall are two windows and the N. doorway all modern except for the splays and rear-arches which are probably of the 14th century. In the W. wall is a window all modern except the 14th-century splays and rear-arch.

The *South Aisle* (11½ ft. wide) has in the E. wall a modern doorway. In the S. wall are two windows all modern except the 14th-century splays and rear-arches ; between them is the reset 13th-century S. doorway with jambs and two-centred arch of two chamfered orders, with a moulded label, mostly modern. In the W. wall is a window modern except for the 14th-century moulded splays and rear-arch.

The *Roof* of the nave is of three bays and has four trusses having tie-beams and octagonal king-posts with moulded capitals and bases and four-way struts, trussed rafters, and central purlin ; the tie-beams and wall-plates are modern, the rest is of the 15th century. The roof of the N. aisle has late 15th or 16th-century chamfered tie-beams with curved braces, moulded purlins and flat rafters; the roof of the S. aisle is similar. The roof of the modern N. porch has old lead with a stamped inscription with the churchwardens' names, etc., the date 1677 and a shield of the arms of Turner of Suffolk.

Fittings—*Brass* and *Indent*. Brass : In chancel —on N. wall, of Elizabeth (Glascock), wife of John Wyseman, 1584, with figures of woman and daughter kneeling at prayer-desk and shield of arms. Indent : In S. porch—part of Purbeck marble slab, with inscription in Lombardic letters, early 14th-century. *Chairs :* In chancel—(1) with panelled and arcaded back, curved arms and turned legs, early 17th-century ; (2) with carved and panelled back, formerly inlaid, shaped arms and turned legs, early 17th-century. *Chest :* In S. aisle—dug-out chest, with iron-bound lid and iron

rings, date and initials 1676 T.B., I. F. on lid, iron straps with foliations at ends, probably mediaeval. *Floor-slabs :* In chancel—(1) to William Lynwood, 1699–1700, and Elizabeth, his wife, 1719 ; (2) to Mary, wife successively to Sir Thomas Wyseman, Sir Henry Appleton, Bart., and Thomas Turnor, 1685. *Glass :* In chancel—in E. lancets, Flemish glass arranged in panels and borders of various fragments, panels include numerous figure subjects, figures and parts of figures among them, St. John the Evangelist ; Adam and Eve ; the Last Judgment ; the Conversation on the Road to Emmaus ; St. John the Baptist ; the Betrayal ; a High Priest ; the Assumption of Elijah, etc., early and late 16th-century. In round window in E. gable, the Ascension, probably 17th-century. In N.E. window, similar glass including the date 1554, the Virgin supported by two women, man's head and fragments. In S.E. window, panels of the Return of the Prodigal and the head of a crowned female saint and fragments; in head late 14th or early 15th-century tabernacle work. In S.W. window, two panels with figures and fragments, 16th-century. *Panelling :* In vestry— dado of late 16th-century panelling. *Piscinae :* In chancel—in E. wall, with moulded segmental head, moulded and shafted jambs with capitals and bases, shelf and octofoiled drain, 13th-century. In S. aisle—in S. wall, with moulded jambs and cinquefoiled ogee head, sexfoiled drain, early 14th-century. *Pulpit :* semi-octagonal, with panelled and bolection-moulded sides and inlaid centres, one panel with shield of arms, early 18th-century, base modern. *Seating :* In nave—incorporated in pew-front, four linen-fold panels with traceried heads, early 16th-century. *Sedile :* In S. aisle— sill of S.E. window carried down to form seat, splays stopped with cinquefoiled ogee heads, one restored, 14th-century. *Miscellanea :* In S. aisle —fixed to E. wall, tile with boundary inscription, 17th-century.

Condition—Good, much restored.

Secular :—

^a(2). MOAT FARM, house and moat, 1¾ m. N.N.E. of the church. The *House* is of two storeys, timber-framed and plastered ; the roofs are tiled or thatched. It was built in the 17th century but has been largely rebuilt in the 19th century.

The *Moat* surrounds the house.

Condition—Of house, good.

MONUMENTS (3–20).

The following monuments, unless otherwise described, are of the 17th century and of two storeys, timber-framed and plastered or weather-boarded ; the roofs are tiled. Many of the buildings have original chimney-stacks and exposed ceiling-beams.

Condition—Good, or fairly good, unless noted.

ᵃ(3). *Brook's Farm*, house and barn, 1¼ m. N.E. of the church. The *House* was built probably in the 16th century on a half H-shaped plan with the wings extending towards the N. There are later extensions to both wings.

The *Barn*, W. of the house, is of four bays, with aisles and a porch.

ᵃ(4). *Cottage*, now three tenements, S. of Lambert's Farm and 500 yards S.W. of (3).

Condition—Poor.

ᵃ(5). *Baines Farm*, house, now three tenements, 500 yards W. of (4), is of L-shaped plan with the wings extending towards the S. and W.

ᵃ(6). *Tan Office Cottages*, three tenements, 570 yards S. of (5). The house was built late in the 16th century on a half H-shaped plan with the wings extending towards the N.W. The upper storey projects on the S.E. front. The original central chimney-stack has modern octagonal shafts with old moulded bases ; the other chimney-stack has original octagonal shafts. Inside the building are two original fireplaces of brick with chamfered cambs and four-centred heads.

ᵃ(7). *Cottage*, 60 yards S.W. of (6), has an original square chimney-stack with a moulded capping and a modern shaft.

ᵇ(8). *Cottage*, on the E. side of road, 280 yards N.E. of the church. The upper storey projects on the W. front.

ᵇ(9). *Cottage*, 50 yards S. of (8), is modern but incorporates two early 16th-century moulded bressumers carved with running foliage. Inside the building are some moulded ceiling-beams and joists of the same date.

ᵇ(10). *Red Lion Inn*, S. of (9), has inside the building a reused doorway with a four-centred head.

ᵇ(11). *Cottage*, in Stisted Hall Park and 200 yards W.N.W. of the church, is modern but contains a large quantity of early 16th-century panelling said to have come from the original Stisted Hall, now destroyed.

STANE STREET, N. side :—

ᵇ(12). *Cottage*, two tenements, W. of Blackwater Bridge.

ᵇ(13). *Cottage*, four tenements, 550 yards W. of (12), may be of the 16th century or earlier and has gabled cross-wings at the N. and S. ends.

ᵃ(14). *Dolphin Inn*, and tenements, 650 yards W. of (13), has modern extensions at both ends.

S. side :—

ᵃ(15). *Cottage*, two tenements, 400 yards E. of (14), has an original central chimney-stack with a cross-shaped shaft set diagonally.

ᵃ(16). *Baytree Farm*, house, 750 yards W. of (15), was built early in the 16th century but the W. part of the house is an early 17th-century addition. The upper storey projects on the N. front and there are two projecting gables to the 17th-century addition. The 17th-century central chimney-stack has grouped diagonal shafts. Inside the building the original block has king-post roof-trusses.

ᵇ(17). *Jenkin's Farm*, house, nearly 1 m. W.S.W. of the church, was built probably early in the 16th century with cross-wings at the N. and S. ends. The porch on the W. front has been rebuilt but incorporates the 16th-century symmetrically turned balusters at the sides and other old material. Inside the building was a considerable quantity of late 16th-century panelling, lately removed to Stisted Hall. The roof of the N. wing has original king-post roof-trusses.

ᵃ(18). *Kentish Farm*, house, about 1 m. N.N.W. of the church, was built on an L-shaped plan with the wings extending towards the S. and W. The original entrance door is of moulded and nail-studded battens with strap-hinges. The original chimney-stack at the S. end has three detached octagonal shafts. The stack at the N. end has original tabled offsets. Inside the building are some original moulded ceiling-beams, a door similar to the entrance door and a panelled dado. The staircase is original and has heavy turned newels and turned balusters ; the staircase to the cellar has a balustrade with original flat-shaped balusters and newel.

ᵃ(19). *Rayne Hatch Farm*, house, 1,100 yards N. of (18), is possibly of the 16th century but has been much altered.

ᵃ(20). *Covenbrook Hall*, ¾ m. W. by N. of the church, was largely rebuilt in the 18th century. Inside the building are two 17th-century doors.

83. TENDRING. (F.c.)

(O.S. 6 in. xxix. S.W.)

Tendring is a parish about 9 m. S.W. of Harwich. The church is the principal monument.

Ecclesiastical :—

(1). PARISH CHURCH OF ST. EDMUND stands about the middle of the parish. The walls are of stone and flint-rubble, largely covered with plaster ; the dressings are of limestone and the roofs are tiled. The *Chancel* was built about the middle of the 13th century. The *Nave* was rebuilt probably c. 1300 and the *North Porch* and a bell-turret added about the middle of the 14th century. The church has been drastically restored in modern times when the *South Chapel* and *Aisle* and the *West Tower* were added and the E. wall rebuilt.

STISTED : PARISH CHURCH OF ALL SAINTS ; late 12th-century and later.
Interior, looking East.

DETAILS OF CARVED STONEWORK.

KELVEDON CHURCH.
Carved Shield, South Arcade ; 15th-century.

DEDHAM CHURCH.
Soffit of Ground Stage of Tower ; c. 1519.

STISTED CHURCH.
Capital, North Arcade ; late 12th-century.

GREAT BROMLEY CHURCH.
Capital, South Arcade ; early 14th-century.

STISTED CHURCH.
Capital, North Arcade ; late 12th-century.

KELVEDON CHURCH.
Capital, North Arcade ; c. 1230.

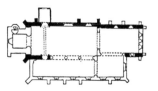

Architectural Description—The *Chancel* (28½ ft. by 17½ ft.) has three modern windows in the E. wall. In the N. wall are two mid to late 13th-century lancet-windows, the western being partly restored. In the S. wall is a modern window and an archway, also modern. The chancel-arch is modern.

The *Nave* (48¾ ft. by 21¼ ft.) has in the N. wall two windows ; the eastern is of *c.* 1300, partly restored and of two trefoiled lights with a trefoil in a two-centred head ; the western window is modern except for some stones in the splays and rear-arch ; further W. is the N. doorway, all modern except the 14th-century splays. In the S. wall is a modern arcade and further W. is the 14th-century S. doorway with recut chamfered jambs and two-centred arch.

The *North Porch* (Plate, p. xxxvi) is timber-framed and of mid 14th-century date. The outer archway has a moulded two-centred head and is flanked by two open lights with trefoiled ogee heads and tracery (one restored). The side walls have each six open lights with cinquefoiled ogee heads, cusped spandrels and modern mullions.

The *Roof* of the nave has, above the two door-ways, a 14th-century hammer-beam truss with curved braces under the hammer-beams springing from framed timber arches (Plate, p. xxxvi), enclosing the doorways ; the framing is moulded and the spandrels have traceried panelling ; the truss supported a former bell-turret. The 14th-century roof of the N. porch has foiled barge-boards, a cambered tie-beam and moulded wall-plates.

Fittings—Font : octagonal bowl with panelled sides carved with foliage or pomegranates and four with blank shields, moulded lower edge with scroll ornament, stem with cinquefoil-headed panels, moulded base, early 16th-century. *Glass :* In nave—in N.E. window, a rose and fleurs-de-lis, 14th-century. *Monument :* In chancel—on S. wall, of Edmund Saunder, 1615, alabaster wall-monument with kneeling figure of man in civil dress, at prayer-desk, all within a round-headed recess with flanking pilasters, cornice and defaced shield of arms. *Piscina :* In chancel—with chamfered jambs, 13th-century, head modern. *Plate :* includes cup of 1567. *Miscellanea :* In rectory garden—remains of window jambs and mullions, etc.

Condition—Good, much altered.

Secular :—

(2). TENDRING HALL, 200 yards N.W. of the church, is of two storeys with attics, timber-framed and plastered ; the roofs are tiled. It was built probably late in the 17th century on an H-shaped plan with the cross-wings at the N. and S. ends. Inside the building are some exposed ceiling-beams and an original door.

Condition—Good, much altered.

(3). CHURCH FARM, house, about 1,000 yards N.N.E. of the church, is of two storeys, timber-framed and plastered ; the roofs are tiled. It was built early in the 16th century, but only the W. cross-wing of the original building remains. The upper storey projects on the W. and N. sides with projecting joists and a moulded plate beneath them ; the angle-post forms a pilaster with a moulded and enriched capping and a curved diagonal bracket. In the N. wall is a bay-window of *c.* 1600, of five lights with moulded mullions. Inside the building are original ceiling-beams, one moulded, and a cambered tie-beam with braces.

Condition—Good.

(4). FISHER'S FARM, house, nearly 1½ m. S.W. of the church, is of two storeys, timber-framed and plastered ; the roofs are tiled. It was built probably in the 16th century and has a projecting upper storey on the S. side. The W. chimney-stack has two attached shafts.

Condition—Good.

TEY, see GREAT TEY and LITTLE TEY.

84. THORPE-LE-SOKEN. (F.c.)

(O.S. 6 in. [a]xxix. S.E. [b]xxxviii. N.E.)

Thorpe-le-Soken is a parish and village 4½ m. N. of Clacton-on-Sea.

Ecclesiastical :—

(1). PARISH CHURCH OF ST. MICHAEL stands in the village. The *West Tower* is of red brick with some limestone dressings. It was built early in the 16th century ; the rest of the church was rebuilt in 1876.

Architectural Description — The *West Tower* (13 ft. by 11 ft.) is of three stages with a moulded plinth, modern parapet and a stair-turret at the S.E. angle ; the walls have diapering in black brick. The two-centred tower-arch is of five chamfered orders with plain cemented responds. The much restored W. window is of four cinque-foiled lights with vertical tracery in a two-centred head with a moulded label ; the W. doorway has splayed brick jambs and a two-centred arch of three moulded orders with a moulded label. The second stage has in the N. and W. walls a window of one four-centred light with a moulded label. The bell-chamber has in each wall a partly restored window of two rounded lights with a quatrefoil in a four-centred head with a moulded label.

The *North Porch* is modern but incorporates a 16th-century moulded beam and chamfered joists in the roof.

Fittings—Bells : five ; 4th by Charles Newman, 1688. *Doors :* In doorway to stair to room over porch—nail-studded battens, foiled scutcheon-plate. In doorway of tower stair-turret—of nail-studded battens with hollow-chamfered fillets, 16th-century, partly restored. *Font :* octagonal bowl, faces with plain shields in star-shaped panels, panelled and cusped stem, 15th-century, moulded base, with spur ornaments, 12th-century. *Monuments :* In chancel—in arch in S. wall, (1) freestone effigy in mail with surcoat, remains of shield and sword, legs missing, feet on lion, mid 13th-century, arch with high cinquefoiled and sub-cusped ogee head, spandrels carved with foliage moulded label with very naturalistic crockets, on each side diapered buttresses carried up with crocketed finials, early 14th-century; upper part of arch with crockets restored. In tower—in S. wall, (2) to Thomas Wharton, 1669, inscribed slab with alabaster achievement of arms. *Plate :* includes stand-paten of 1695. *Screen :* In S. chapel—of three bays and double entrance bay, one bay destroyed ; each bay with trefoiled ogee heads, moulded mullions and head-beam and carved cresting ; below cresting, carved angels holding shields, chalice and host, crossed keys and swords, scroll with inscription in black letter " This cost (? loft) is the bachelers made by Alles . . . . Jhesu be the(r ?) med," early 16th-century.

Condition—Of tower, good.

Secular :—

b(2). BELL INN, N. of the church, is of two storeys, timber-framed and plastered ; the roofs are tiled. It was built early in the 16th century and has a projecting upper storey and gable on the N. front ; the bressumers are carved with running foliage. There is a later wing on the W. Inside the building are exposed ceiling-beams.

Condition—Good.

b(3). THE " ABBEY," house, 150 yards E. of the church, is of two storeys with attics ; the walls are of brick ; the roofs are tiled. It was built in the 16th century but has been much altered and the walls are covered with cement. The main block has crow-stepped gables and the two-storeyed porch has an embattled parapet ; the entrance arch is four-centred and the jambs are shafted ; above it is an original window with a four-centred head and a moulded label. There is one original chimney-stack with two octagonal shafts and a 17th-century stack with two shafts set diagonally.

Inside the building is one original moulded ceiling-beam, carved with running foliage.

Condition—Fairly good.

a(4). HOUSE, now tenements, on W. side of Thorpe Green, and ¾ m. N.W. of the church, is of two storeys, timber-framed and weather-boarded ; the roofs are tiled. It was built in the 17th century and has a cross-wing with a projecting upper storey at the S. end. Inside the building are exposed ceiling-beams.

Condition—Good.

---

85. THORRINGTON. (E.d.)

(O.S. 6 in. *(a)*xxxvii. N.E. *(b)*xxxvii. S.E.)

Thorrington is a small parish 2 m. N. of Bright-lingsea. The church is interesting.

Ecclesiastical :—

a(1). PARISH CHURCH OF ST. MARY MAGDALENE stands on the E. side of the parish. The nave, N. aisle and S. porch are of rubble composed of septaria pebbles and flint pebbles, but the S. wall is largely of flint pebbles. The tower is faced with knapped flint with limestone dressings. The roofs are tiled. The *Chancel, Nave* and *North Aisle* appear to be of early 14th-century date but the aisle wall is much patched and the upper part possibly rebuilt. The S. wall is very neat and may have been refaced. The *South Porch* was added in the second half of the 14th century. In the 15th century the N. aisle was probably extended towards the W. ; the *West Tower* was added *c.* 1480 (see brass of J. Deth). The church was drastically restored in the 19th century when the N. arcade was rebuilt and the E. gable and tops of walls also rebuilt.

The W. tower is a good example of the period and is of interest as being approximately dated.

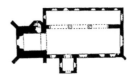

Architectural Description—The *Chancel* (21¼ ft. by 18 ft.) has an early 14th-century E. window of three uncusped lights in a two-centred head with a moulded label and partly restored. In the N. wall is the E. bay of the modern arcade. In the S. wall are two windows ; the eastern is of early 14th-century date and of two trefoiled lights in a two-centred head. The western is of the 14th century, partly restored, and of one obtusely pointed light ; below it in continuation is a doorway of the same date with a segmental head. There is no division between chancel and nave.

The *Nave* (31 ft. by 18 ft.) has a modern N. arcade. In the S. wall are two windows ; the eastern is of three cinquefoiled lights and all modern except parts of the jambs and splays which are of the 15th century ; the western window is modern ; between the windows is a modern doorway.

The *North Aisle* (10 ft. wide) has in the E. wall a modern window. In the N. wall are five windows ; the easternmost is of early 14th-century date, partly restored, and is of one trefoiled ogee light ; the second is similar ; the third is also of the 14th century, partly restored, and reset, it is of one obtusely pointed light ; the fourth and westernmost are of 15th-century date, partly restored, and each of two trefoiled lights in a square head. Between the two western windows is the 15th-century N. doorway, with chamfered jambs and moulded two-centred head with a moulded label and head-stops. In the W. wall is a 15th-century window of one trefoiled light.

The *West Tower* (12 ft. square) is of late 15th-century date and of three stages (Plate, p. 220), faced with knapped flint ; it has a moulded plinth and a damaged embattled parapet enriched with cusped and crocketed panels of flint-inlay. The tower-arch is two-centred and of two moulded orders on the E. side, the outer continuous and the inner resting on semi-octagonal shafts with moulded capitals and bases. In the N. wall is a doorway with chamfered jambs and four-centred head. The W. window is of three cinquefoiled lights with vertical tracery in a four-centred head ; below it is the W. doorway with moulded jambs, two-centred arch and a moulded label with head-stops. The second stage has in the S. and W. walls a window of one pointed light with an inner order of brick. The bell-chamber has in each wall a window of two trefoiled ogee lights, with flowered points and vertical tracery in a two-centred head with a moulded label.

The *South Porch* is of the 14th century and has quoins and the jambs of the outer archway built of tiles. The archway has jambs of tiles and two-centred arch of brick of two chamfered orders. The side walls have each a window of two trefoiled lights in a square head and much restored.

The *Roof* of the ground stage of the tower has four curved braces meeting in the middle with a round carved boss with a quatrefoil enclosing a rose.

Fittings—*Altar :* In chancel—formerly in tower, slab of Bethersden marble 5 ft. by 2 ft. 3 in., with chamfered under-edge. Plain cross at each corner and large cross of unusual form in the centre, mediaeval. *Bells :* six ; 5th by Henry Jordan, 15th-century, and inscribed " Sit Nomen Domini Benedictum."

Brasses and *Indent.* Brasses : In N. aisle—(1) to John Clare, 1564, and his two wives, Joan and Katherine (Pirton), figure of woman, two sons and three daughters, scroll, mutilated inscription and two shields of arms. In tower—(2) to John Deth, 1477, and Margery, his wife, 1483, " specialis benefactor isti' ecclīe et campanil' ejusdm," inscription only. Indent : In nave—of two figures, inscription-plate and groups of children. *Chest :* In vestry—plain oak, with strap-hinges, 17th-century. *Coffin-lid :* In vestry—tapering slab, partly hidden in wall. *Font :* octagonal bowl with panelled sides, three with instruments of the passion, others with pomegranate and flower, buttressed stem with trefoil-headed panels, moulded base, early 16th-century. *Hour-glass Stand :* In vestry—of wrought iron, late 17th-century. *Lockers :* In tower—in turret staircase, two plain recesses, late 15th-century ; in side walls, two plain recesses, same date. *Monument :* In churchyard—S. of tower, to John Wilkins, 1700, head-stone. *Niche :* In porch—with pointed head, 14th-century. *Piscina :* In chancel—with trefoiled head and moulded label with head-stops, octofoiled drain, 14th-century. *Scratchings :* On tower-arch—various masons' marks. On jamb of west doorway—a rough five-pointed molet, the date 1659 and other marks. On buttress of tower, three molets. *Sedile :* In chancel—sill of S.E. window cut down to form seat. *Sundials :* On buttress of tower, two scratched. *Table :* In vestry—with heavy turned legs and carved upper rail, c. 1600.

Condition—Good, much restored.

Secular :—

b(2). GATEWAY, at Gatehouse Farm, 1 m. W.S.W. of the church, is of early 16th-century date and of brick with stone jambs, and four-centred arch of two chamfered orders. It is finished with a moulded and crow-stepped coping of brick and forms part of the garden wall of the house.

Condition—Wall, out of perpendicular.

MONUMENTS (3–9).

The following monuments, unless otherwise described, are of two storeys, timber-framed and plastered or weather-boarded ; the roofs are tiled or thatched. Many of the buildings have original chimney-stacks and exposed ceiling-beams.

Condition—Good or fairly good.

b(3). *Thorrington Hall*, 30 yards N. of the church, was built in the 16th century with cross-wings at the N. and S. ends. The S. wing was extended in the 17th century and there is a modern extension to the N. wing. The E. front has been faced with modern brickwork.

ᵃ(4). *Glebe Farm*, house, about ¼ m. W.N.W. of the church, was built probably in the 16th century and has a 17th-century addition on the E. side. The doorway on the W. side has 17th-century shaped brackets to the hood.

ᵃ(5). *Red Lion Inn*, ¼ m. N.N.W. of the church, was built in the 17th century.

ᵃ(6). *House*, 360 yards W.N.W. of (5), was built probably in the 16th century on an L-shaped plan, with the wings extending towards the N.E. and S.E.

ᵃ(7). *House*, three tenements, at Thorrington Cross, ¾ m. N.W. of the church, was built probably early in the 16th century, with a central hall and cross-wings at the N. and S. ends. The W. side of the main block has been refaced with modern brick.

ᵃ(8). *Goldacre Farm*, house, 700 yards N.N.E. of (7), was built probably early in the 16th century. The 17th-century central chimney-stack has three diagonal shafts. Inside the building some timber-framing is exposed.

ᵃ(9). *White House Farm*, house, 1,200 yards N.N.W. of the church, was built in the 16th century on an L-shaped plan, with the wings extending towards the N. and E. The upper storey projects at the N. end and on the S. side; at the N. end it has an original moulded bressumer. The central chimney-stack has five attached diagonal shafts. Inside the building the roof has an original cambered tie-beam and curved braces.

---

86. TOLLESBURY. (C.e.)

(O.S. 6 in. ⁽ᵃ⁾xlvi. N.W. ⁽ᵇ⁾xlvi. S.W. ⁽ᶜ⁾xlvi. S.E. ⁽ᵈ⁾lv. N.W.)

Tollesbury is a parish and village on the N. side of the estuary of the Blackwater and 7½ m. E.N.E. of Maldon. The church, Bourchier's Hall and Black Cottages are the principal monuments.

Roman :—

(1). At the restoration of the church about 1875 many Roman tiles, including flue-tiles, were found in the nave, tower and S. doorway. If these were not brought 3 miles from Tolleshunt Knights, or from West Mersea, they presumably indicate the site of a Roman building. (*Brit. Arch. Assoc. Jour.*, XXXII, 418.) (See also *Sectional Preface*, p. xxvii.)

Ecclesiastical :—

ᵇ(2). PARISH CHURCH OF ST. MARY stands S.E. of the village green. The walls are of boulder-clay and the upper part of the tower of red brick; the dressings are of clunch and Roman brick and the roofs are tiled. The *Nave* and the ground stage of the *West Tower* were built probably late

in the 11th century. Probably in the 14th century the tower-arch was rebuilt. In the 16th or early in the 17th century the two upper stages of the tower were rebuilt. The church was restored in 1872 when the *Chancel* was lengthened and rebuilt and the *South Porch* added.

The nave is an interesting example of early work.

Architectural Description—The *Nave* (41¾ ft. by 21½ ft.) has in the N. wall two windows, the eastern modern and the western of mid 15th-century date and of three cinquefoiled lights with vertical and transomed tracery in a two-centred head; the jambs and label are moulded and the mullions are modern; further W. is the N. doorway, all modern except a few stones in the jambs and rear-arch; in this wall are three original windows, now blocked and all to the W. of the modern window; they are only visible externally and are set regularly spaced and high in the wall; the jambs and rough semi-circular heads are of boulder-clay; one of these windows has recently been opened out. In the S. wall are four windows, the easternmost and westernmost are modern; the second is uniform with the 15th-century window in the N. wall but the transom is embattled; the third window is of late 11th-century date and similar to the blocked windows in the N. wall, but more carefully built and perhaps lengthened and widened; W. of and below this window is the S. doorway (Plate, p. 142) with 15th-century double chamfered jambs and two-centred arch with a moulded label; the splays round rear-arch and tympanum are of late 11th-century date and of Roman brick; between the two eastern windows is a 15th-century doorway with a two-centred head and now blocked; it formerly opened into the rood-loft staircase.

The *West Tower* is of three stages, the lowest of late 11th-century date and the two upper of brick and of the 16th or early 17th century. The embattled parapet was probably repaired in the 18th century. The tower-arch is probably of late 14th-century date, much scraped, and is of four chamfered orders, the inner order two-centred and dying on to the chamfered responds and the other orders segmental-pointed; above the arch is a rough relieving-arch partly of Roman brick and perhaps built of the materials of the 11th-century tower-arch. The W. doorway and window are modern. The second stage has in the N., S. and W. walls a 16th or 17th-century window, each of one light; the S. window has a reused trefoiled head of stone; the W. window has a rounded head of brick; both have square labels of brick; the N. window is covered by a clock. The bell-chamber has in each wall a brick window of two lights in a square head with a moulded label; the E. window has lights with rounded heads but the others have cinquefoiled stone heads reused.

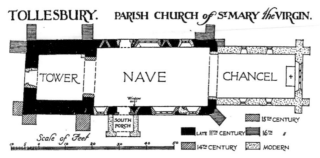

TOLLESBURY. PARISH CHURCH of S.T. MARY the VIRGIN.

The *Roof* of the tower is probably of early 17th-century date and is pyramidal with diagonal ties and an upright post in the middle.

Fittings—Bells : six; 3rd by Miles Graie, 1604 ; 5th by Miles Graye, 1661, bell-frame probably early 17th-century. *Book :* some pages of a Great Bible of 1540. *Brass* and *Indent. Brass :* In nave—on S. wall, of [Thomas Freshwater, 1517, and Margaret, his wife], with figures of man in fur-lined gown and woman with pedimental head-dress, group of nine daughters, indents for inscription-plate and two sons. Indent : In nave—in S. wall externally, fragment of Purbeck marble slab with a few letters of a Lombardic inscription, early 14th-century. *Chest :* In tower —plain with iron straps at angles, possibly 17th-century. *Monument :* In chancel—on N. wall, to Jane (Kempe), wife of Thomas Gardiner, 1654, richly carved, veined marble tablet with pediment and four shields of arms. *Plate :* includes cup of 1562 with three bands of incised ornament and a plated pewter flagon, late 17th-century. *Stoup :* In S. porch—with rounded head, 16th-century, bowl broken.

Condition—Good.

Secular :—

b(3). BOURCHIER'S HALL, nearly 1¼ m. N.W. of the church, is of two storeys, timber-framed and plastered ; the roofs are tiled. It was built in the 14th century and originally consisted of a great Hall with aisles probably on both sides and cross-wings at the N. and S. ends. In the 16th century the staircase wing was added on part of the site of the former E. aisle, the S. cross-wing destroyed and the Hall divided into two storeys. There are 17th-century additions on the E. side and a modern addition at the N.W. angle.

The house has interesting timber construction of the 14th century.

The W. front has the main roof carried down low over the former W. aisle and in it have been inserted two gabled dormers. Inside the building the former great hall has been cut up into rooms and the oak columns which must have supported the middle roof-truss have apparently been removed. The main roof of this building remains and the original roof-truss has a cambered and moulded tie-beam, with curved and moulded braces forming a two-centred arch ; the octagonal king-post has a moulded capital and base and four-way struts ; the common rafters are continued down over the former aisle on the W. side and there are definite indications that they continued over a corresponding aisle on the E. side which has been destroyed. All the original timbers are much blackened with smoke. The S. bay of the main roof has two intermediate collar-beams supporting upright posts. In the E. wall of the staircase wing is a 16th-century window of three lights with moulded mullions and now blocked. The 17th-century addition has exposed ceiling-beams.

At Guisnes Court, 150 yards W. of Bourchier's Hall, is a considerable quantity of early 16th-century linen-fold panelling said to have been removed from Bourchier's Hall ; there is also an early 17th-century overmantel (Plate, p. xxxiii) probably of the same provenance and with fluted Ionic pilasters flanking the fireplace, a fluted frieze with carved lions' heads and an overmantel of three bays divided by coupled Ionic columns on pedestals ; the panels have arched heads and enclose an achievement and two cartouches with painted arms of the Gardner family.

Condition—Good.

b(4). THE CAGE, at the N.W. corner of the churchyard, is a square building, timber-framed and weather-boarded ; the pyramidal roof is also boarded. It was built probably early in the 18th century but many of the timbers have been renewed. At the apex of the roof is an acorn-shaped finial.

Condition—Fairly good.

MONUMENTS (5–28).

The following monuments, unless otherwise described, are of the 17th century and of two storeys, timber-framed and plastered or weather-boarded ; the roofs are tiled. Many of the buildings have original chimney-stacks and exposed ceiling-beams.

Condition—Good, or fairly good, unless noted.

ᵇ(5). *Tollesbury Hall*, now three tenements, S. of the churchyard, was built probably in the 15th century with a central Hall and cross-wings at the E. and W. ends. The W. cross-wing has since been altered and the main roof extended over it. The central chimney-stack has the lower parts of three 16th-century octagonal shafts, now covered with cement. Inside the building the roof of the E. wing has an original king-post truss.

ᵇ(6). *Cottage*, two tenements, 50 yards S.W. of (5).

ᵇ(7). *House*, two tenements, on W. side of the Green, 70 yards N. of (6), was built probably in the 16th century with cross-wings at the N. and S. ends. It has been refronted with modern brick.

ᵇ(8). *House*, three tenements, on E. side of the Green, 60 yards N. of the church, was built late in the 16th or early in the 17th century. The ground storey in front has been refaced with modern brick and there is a cross-wing at each end.

EAST STREET :—

ᵇ(9). *Cottage*, two tenements, on S. side of street, 100 yards E. of (8).

ᵇ(10). *Range of four tenements*, E. of (9).

ᵇ(11). *Cottage*, three tenements, on N. side of street, 70 yards N.N.W. of (9).

Condition—Poor.

MAIN STREET, N. side :—

ᵇ(12). *House*, two tenements, at N. end of the Green, 100 yards N.N.W. of the church, has been refronted with modern brick.

ᵇ(13). *House*, two tenements, 100 yards W. of (12), has been refronted with modern brick.

ᵇ(14). *House* and three shops, 70 yards W. of (13), has been in part refronted with modern brick.

ᵇ(15). *House*, two tenements, W. of (14).

ᵇ(16). *Cottage*, three tenements, 360 yards W. of (15), has an original central chimney-stack with a moulded capping and plain pilasters to the shafts.

S. side :—

ᵇ(17). *House*, two tenements, 200 yards E. of (16).

ᵇ(18). *Black Cottages*, house, E. of (17), was built *c.* 1520 with a cross-wing at the E. end. A W. cross-wing has probably been destroyed. Inside the building the two W. tenements formed the *Hall* and the ground floor has moulded ceiling-beams and plates, elaborately carved with twisted

leaf ornament (Plate, p. xxxvii) ; the joists are also moulded. The upper storey formerly projected in front. The E. wing has an original cambered tie-beam with curved braces.

ᵇ(19). *House*, three tenements, 110 yards E. of (18), was built probably *c.* 1666, which date with the initials R.B.C. appears in a sunk panel in the central chimney-stack ; the shafts have diagonal pilaster-strips.

ᵇ(20). *House* (Plate, p. xxxi), three tenements, 60 yards E. of (19), was built late in the 15th or early in the 16th century, with a central Hall and cross-wings at the E. and W. ends. The Hall was subsequently divided into two storeys. The upper storey projects at the front ends of the cross-wings. Inside the building the former hall has a passage representing the 'screens' at the E. end and in the E. wall is an original doorway with chamfered jambs and ogee head, now blocked ; a second doorway, said to be similar, is now papered over. In the N. wall of the W. wing is an original window with a rounded head and one diamond-shaped mullion still *in situ*. Both cross-wings have remains of the original roof-trusses.

ᵇ(21). *House*, three tenements, 120 yards E. of (20), was built probably early in the 16th century and formerly had cross-wings at the E. and W. ends, both now covered by the main roof. The upper storey projects at the front end of the former E. wing.

ᵇ(22). *Prentice Hall Farm*, house, 1,000 yards W.S.W. of the church, has a later wing on the W. side. The original central chimney-stack has plain pilasters at the angles and oversailing courses at the top.

ᵇ(23). *Bohun's Hall*, house and barn, ¼ m. S. of the church. The *House* has a wing at the N. end of 16th or early 17th-century date, but the rest of the house was rebuilt probably late in the 18th century. The old wing has original moulded barge-boards.

The *Barn*, W. of the house, is of six bays with two porches ; the roof has queen-post trusses.

ᵈ(24). *Roll's Farm*, house, nearly 1½ m. S.W. of the church, was built probably early in the 16th century and has a cross-wing at the E. end. At the W. end is a modern addition perhaps on the site of a former W. wing. The upper storey projects at the N. end of the cross-wing. Inside the building the ground floor of the E. wing has original moulded ceiling-beams and joists and in the W. wall is a doorway with a four-centred head. In the main block is a chamfered ceiling-beam supported by a moulded bracket.

ᵇ(25). *Bourchier's Lodge*, house, 20 yards S. of (3), has modern additions on the E. side.

ᵇ(26). *Cottage*, 300 yards N. of (3).

b(27). *Old Hall Cottage*, ½ m. E. of (26), has been rebuilt except the central chimney-stack which has attached diagonal pilasters.

a(28). *Salcottstone Farm*, house, 1¾ m. N.N.W. of the church, was built in the 15th or early in the 16th century, with a central Hall and cross-wings at the E. and W. ends. The E. wing has been destroyed and the W. wing is now included under the main roof. The 17th-century chimney-stack has two diagonal and one square shaft. Inside the building the former Hall, now divided into two storeys, has an original king-post truss in the roof.

Unclassified :—

c(29). RED HILL, N. of Woodrolfe Farm, and about ¾ m. E. of the church. There are others on Wick Marshes.

———

87. TOLLESHUNT D'ARCY. (C.e.)

(O.S. 6 in. xlvi. S.W.)

Tolleshunt D'Arcy is a parish and village 6 m. N.E. of Maldon. The church and Hall are the principal monuments.

Ecclesiastical :—

(1). PARISH CHURCH OF ST. NICHOLAS stands in the village. The walls are of rubble with dressings of limestone or clunch ; the roofs are covered with tiles and slates. The lower part of the *West Tower* has an early 14th-century window and may be of this date but it with the nave was remodelled or rebuilt late in the 14th century. Early in the 15th century the *Chancel* was rebuilt and later in the same century the *North Chapel* and *South Porch* were added. Early in the 16th century the *North Vestry* was added. The church was restored in the 19th century when the vestry was reduced in size by rebuilding the E. wall further W.

Architectural Description—The *Chancel* (20½ ft. by 16½ ft.) has a modern E. window. In the N. wall is an early 15th-century window of two cinquefoiled lights with vertical tracery in a two-centred head with a moulded label ; it was formerly covered by the vestry ; further W. is a modern archway. In the S. wall are two windows, the eastern similar to that in the N. wall and the western of a single cinquefoiled light in a square

head and set lower in the wall. The early 15th-century chancel-arch is two-centred and of two chamfered orders ; the responds have each a semi-octagonal attached shaft with moulded capital and base. N. of the arch is a rectangular squint.

The *North Vestry* has a modern E. wall in which is a reset 15th-century window of two cinquefoiled lights under a square head with a moulded label. In the N. wall is a 15th-century window of one cinquefoiled light in a square head ; further W. is a modern doorway incorporating old material. In the W. wall is a 16th-century doorway with a wooden frame and two-centred head with sunk spandrels.

The *Nave* (38½ ft. by 26½ ft.) has a moulded plinth and an embattled parapet. In the N. wall is a 15th-century archway four-centred and of two hollow-chamfered orders, dying on to the hollow-chamfered responds ; further W. is a late 14th-century window of three trefoiled lights with tracery in a segmental head with a moulded label ; further W. is a late 14th-century doorway with moulded jambs and two-centred arch ; it may incorporate reused material of the 13th century and has been converted into a window. In the S. wall are two windows uniform with that in the N. wall, but the head of the western window is modern and above it is the mark of the 18th-century head ; further W. is the late 14th-century S. doorway, with moulded jambs and two-centred arch ; the splays have sockets for a draw-bar.

The *North Chapel* (16½ ft. by 11 ft.) has in the E. wall, above the doorway already described, a blocked window with a segmental rear-arch. In the N. wall is an early 16th-century window of brick with a later mullion ; the window is of two lights in a four-centred head with a moulded label. In the W. wall is a 15th-century window of two lights similar to that in the N. wall of the chancel ; it has been partly repaired in brick.

The *West Tower* (9¼ ft. square) is of three stages with a moulded plinth and embattled parapet. The late 14th-century tower-arch is two-centred and of two hollow-chamfered orders, dying into the side walls. The early 14th-century W. window is of two trefoiled ogee lights with a quatrefoil in a two-centred head with a moulded label and head-stops. The second stage has a rectangular opening in the S. and W. walls. The bell-chamber has in each wall a late 14th-century window of two cinquefoiled lights under a square head with a moulded label, partly restored.

The *South Porch* is of late 14th-century date and has carved figures at the angles of the parapet. The outer archway has moulded jambs and two-centred arch with a moulded label and much defaced stops carved with half-angels holding shields. The side walls have each a window of two trefoiled lights under a square head with a moulded label ; they are now blocked.

The *Roof* of the chancel is of the 15th century and of two bays with a central truss having moulded tie-beam, king-post, struts and wall-plates, which are also embattled and returned along the E. wall. The late 15th or early 16th-century roof of the N. chapel is flat with moulded principal and purlin; the principal has curved braces springing from carved head-corbels of a man and woman.

Fittings — *Brasses* and *Indents*. Brasses: In N. chapel—on E. wall, (1) of man in plate-armour, sword mutilated, and wife (figure on N. wall) in veil head-dress and with dog at feet, *c.* 1420; (2) of Anthony Darcy, J.P., 1540, curious figure of man in plate-armour, copy of a much earlier figure, and now fixed on N. wall, palimpsest on back of inscription-plate, inscription to Robert le Wale and Maud, his wife, both died 1362; (3) of Philippe (Bedyngfeld), wife of Thomas Darcye, 1559, figure of woman in French hood, etc.; on N. wall, (4) of woman in pedimental head-dress, *c.* 1540; palimpsest on reverse, part of figure of an abbot or bishop in mass vestments with staff, *c.* 1400; (5) to Thomas Darce, 1624, inscription only; (6) two shields of arms of Darcy and Darcy impaling *a fesse between three oak-leaves* for FitzLangley (?), 16th-century; palimpsest on reverse, parts of figures of priests, 15th-century; on S. wall, (7) rectangular plate of Flemish design, engraved on both sides with figures of apostles, etc., a ribbon with portions of the Creed and vine decoration; the figures are St. Bartholomew, the Virgin and Child, St. Philip and the symbols of St. Mark and St. Luke on the one side and St. James the Less with the symbol of St. Mark on the other side, late 14th-century. Indents: In S. porch—of cross. See also Monuments. *Doors:* In S. doorway—of two folds with moulded ribs, trellis framing at back, early 15th-century, partly restored. *Font:* octagonal, with panelled bowl, panels filled with roses and shields one with a plain cross, moulded upper and lower edge, buttressed stem and hollow-chamfered base, late 15th or early 16th-century. *Glass:* In chancel—in N. window, plain foliage and a cinque-foil, 14th-century; in S.W. window, fragments, including tabernacle work, part of inscription, borders, etc., 14th to 16th-century. In N. vestry—in E. window, head of tabernacle work, 15th-century. In N. chapel—in N. window, quatrefoiled panel enclosing blank shield, late 14th-century, and other fragments. In nave—in tracery of N. window, small fragments, 13th and 15th century. In W. tower—in W. window, various fragments of uncertain date. *Monuments:* In chancel—in S. wall, (1) recessed and canopied tomb of Sussex marble, tomb cut down to form seat, canopy with shafted and panelled jambs, flat arch with traceried spandrels, quatrefoiled frieze with embattled cresting, soffit and reveals of recess panelled and at back indents of a cross, inscription-plate and

four shields; reset in N. wall of chancel, front of this tomb, with three diamond-shaped panels enclosing the indents of as many shields; in S. porch, slab of this tomb, now broken, early 16th-century. In N. chapel—on N. wall, (2) of Thomas D'Arcy, 1593, and Camylla (Guycciardyne), his wife, marble wall-monument (Plate, p. 97) with moulded and enriched base having thereon kneeling figures of man in armour and wife at prayer-desk, and set in a recess flanked by square pilasters and surmounted by obelisks and an achievement of arms, in front of base, figures of three sons and six daughters. *Piscina:* In N. chapel—in S. wall, with moulded jambs and cinquefoiled arch in a square head with traceried spandrels, 15th-century, drain destroyed. *Plate:* includes cup and cover-paten of *c.* 1570, with bands of engraved ornament, and stand-paten of 1699. *Stoup:* In S. porch—remains of hollow recess for stoup. *Table:* In chancel—made up of 16th and 17th-century wood-work, including linen-fold panelling and fluted rails.

Condition—Fairly good, but some stonework much decayed.

Secular :—

(2). TOLLESHUNT D'ARCY HALL, house, dove-cote, outbuilding, bridge and moat, S. of the church. The *House* is of two storeys, timber-framed and plastered; the roofs are tiled. The main block of the house was built *c.* 1500 and at that time probably included a cross-wing at the E. end and a wing projecting southwards from the W. end. The E. wing has been destroyed and the S. wing was rebuilt late in the 17th century. There is a modern addition at the N.E. angle. On the S. side of the main block is the original entrance (Plate, p. 100) with moulded jambs and lintel carved with a band of conventional ornament, above it are three plain panels divided by studding; the door is of moulded and overlapping battens and is nail-studded. Further E. is an original doorway and window with moulded jambs and now blocked. In the N. wall is an original window, at the back of the staircase, of six transomed lights with moulded frame and mullions; most of the lights are now blocked.

Interior—The main block consists of five bays of building of which the second and third from the E. formed the Great Hall with the 'screens' at the E. end. The wall at the back of the 'screens' has two original doorways with stop-moulded jambs and four-centred heads with spandrels carved with pomegranate and leaf ornament; the post between the doorways is carved with twisted leaf ornament and above the door-heads is a moulded, carved and embattled cornice; the southern doorway has a door of linen fold panelling. At the N. end of the 'screens' and

THORRINGTON : PARISH CHURCH OF ST. MARY MAGDALENE.
West Tower ; c. 1480.

TOLLESHUNT MAJOR : PARISH CHURCH OF ST. NICHOLAS.
West Tower ; early 16th-century.

LITTLE BENTLEY: mid 15th-century.

EARLS COLNE: about 1460, partly rebuilt 1539.

ARDLEIGH: late 15th-century.

WEELEY: early 16th-century.

behind the staircase is part of the four-centred head of an original external doorway. Another doorway has a door of linen-fold panelling and there is some early 17th-century panelling on the staircase and in the hall itself. The great fireplace has a chamfered oak lintel and niches in the side walls. The middle room of the late 17th-century wing is lined with reused early 16th-century panelling (Plate, p. 180), mostly linen-fold but with a range of carved panels at the top and near the middle of the walls ; the upper carved panels have conventional foliage and various heads and figures, including a mermaid, eagle and child, grotesques, etc., also the initials A.D. for Anthony Darcy ; the lower carved panels have conventional foliage and cartouches with the Darcy arms differenced by a crescent, the initials A.D., etc. ; the panelling is finished with an embattled cornice. The ceiling of this room has reused moulded and traceried ceiling-beams with moulded ribs forming geometrical designs. There are two wall-posts in the form of Ionic pilasters and having carved foliage ; another wall-post with cusped panelling has been reused as a ceiling-beam. On the first floor the roof of the main block has original king-post trusses with hollow-chamfered tie-beams, four-way struts and central purlin. In the E. wall and at the E. end of the S. wall are blocked doorways, indicating the position of the destroyed E. wing.

The *Dove-cote* (Plate, p. 231) at the N.E. corner of the site is of brick with a tiled roof. It was built probably late in the 16th-century, and the interior is fitted with nests on each wall. In the W. wall is an original window of two four-centred lights. The doorway has an oak frame and a four-centred rear-arch.

The *Outbuilding* at the S.E. corner of the site is of brick and timber-framing and of eight bays. It was built probably late in the 16th-century.

The *Bridge* (Plate, p. 231) over the S. arm of the moat is of brick and stone and was built *c*. 1585. It has four semi-circular arches and the wall above is of alternate bands of brick and stone. At the S. end are two square piers of brick with moulded cappings ; each has a carved achievement of the arms of Darcy impaling Sulyard (?) and inscriptions " Ao. Dni. 1585 " and " Ao Regny Regina Elyzabeth 27." The island has a brick revetment wall, buttressed at intervals.

The *Moat* surrounds the house.

MONUMENTS (3–10).

The following monuments, unless otherwise described, are of the 17th century and of two storeys, timber-framed and plastered or weather-boarded ; the roofs are tiled. Some of the buildings have original chimney-stacks and exposed ceiling-beams.

Condition—Good, or fairly good.

(3). *Red Lion Inn*, 200 yards N.E. of the church, is partly built of brick.

(4). *Spring Farm*, house and cottage, 300 yards E. of (3).

(5). *House* and shop, on E. side of road, 200 yards N. of (3), has been rebuilt except the middle portion.

(6). *Rolfe's Farm*, house, on N. side of road, 100 yards N.W. of (5), was of L-shaped plan with the wings extending towards the W. and N. There is an 18th-century addition making the plan T-shaped.

(7). *Cottage*, two tenements, 40 yards W. of (6).

(8). *Cottage*, 40 yards W. of (7), was built *c*. 1700.

(9). *Limesbrook Farm*, house, ½ m. W.N.W. of (8), was built late in the 15th century and of this building the E. cross-wing remains. The main block was rebuilt late in the 16th century and there are modern additions on the N. side. The upper storey projects on the S. side, the overhang being carried across the earlier E. wing in the 16th century. The W. chimney-stack has five octagonal shafts on a rectangular base of late 16th-century date. Inside the building is some early 17th-century panelling and a ceiling-beam with billet ornament. The roof of the E. wing has an original king-post truss.

(10). *Freme Farm*, house, 600 yards S.S.W. of (9).

Unclassified :—

(11). MOUNDS, on E. side of stream, 1½ m. S.S.W. of the church, are probably the remains of a dam.
Condition—Fairly good.

(12). RED HILLS, about ½ m. S.E. of (11).
Condition—Poor.

88. TOLLESHUNT KNIGHTS. (C.e.)

(O.S. 6 in. xlvi. N.W.)

Tolleshunt Knights is a parish with a small village at Tiptree, 6 m. N.E. of Maldon.

Roman :—

(1). Possibly a Roman house stood near Barne Walden, now called Barn Hall, N.E. of the church, where Morant records that " Roman pavements were dug up near it some years ago several feet under ground." Nothing more is known of this find. (Morant, *Essex*, 1768, I, 393 ; hence Gough's *Camden's Britannia*, 1789, II, 53 ; *Essex Arch. Soc. Trans.*, O.S., I, 199.) (See also Tollesbury (1) and *Sectional Preface*, p. xxvii.)

Ecclesiastical :—

(2). PARISH CHURCH OF ALL SAINTS stands near the middle of the parish. The walls are plastered except in one place where pudding-stone is visible ; the dressings are of limestone and the roofs are tiled. The proportions of the *Nave* and the thickness of the walls indicate a 12th-century building but none of the details are earlier than the 15th century. The *Chancel* was rebuilt in the 13th or 14th century. The *South Porch* was added late in the 16th or early in the 17th century. The church was extensively restored in the 19th century.

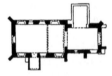

Architectural Description—The *Chancel* (23 ft. by 16 ft.) has no ancient features, in the E. or N. walls. In the S. wall is a lancet-window completely restored and E. of it is part of a square-headed window with a 14th-century moulded label and defaced stop, now blocked. The chancel-arch is probably of the 15th century and is two-centred and of two hollow-chamfered orders dying on to the hollow-chamfered responds.

The *Nave* (37 ft. by 20 ft.) has in the N. wall three windows ; the easternmost and westernmost are modern ; the middle window is of the 15th century and of two cinquefoiled lights in a square head with a moulded label ; W. of it is the 15th-century N. doorway, now blocked and with moulded jambs, two-centred arch and label ; the shafted splays have moulded capitals. In the S. wall are three windows similar in date and details to the corresponding windows in the N. wall ; between the two western is the 15th-century S. doorway partly restored and with moulded jambs, two-centred arch and moulded label with head-stops of two bishops. In the W. wall is a modern single-light window with splays and two-centred rear-arch possibly of the 13th century.

The *South Porch* is of modern timber-framing set on dwarf brick walls of late 16th or early 17th-century date.

The *Roof* of the chancel incorporates some 15th or 16th-century timbers. The roof of the nave has two late 15th-century moulded tie-beams with curved braces and straining-beams. The roof of the S. porch incorporates some old timbers.

Fittings—*Bells :* two ; said to be 1st by Miles Graye, 1664 ; 2nd by Richard Bowler, 1595. *Door :* In N. doorway—of overlapping battens and strap-hinges, probably 15th-century. *Font :* In chancel—square tapering bowl, of Barnack

stone, sides each with two square traceried panels ; late 14th-century panelling probably cut on earlier bowl. *Monument :* In chancel—in N.E. angle, mutilated stone effigy of man in armour with bascinet, camail with a series of lappets each with a crescent on it, surcoat and sword-belt, head on helm, hands holding heart, *c.* 1380, legs and arms broken off and figure much scratched and defaced. *Piscina :* In chancel—with chamfered and rebated jambs and two-centred head, 13th-century. *Miscellanea :* In nave—set in wall over haunch of chancel-arch, carved head on a moulded bracket, probably 15th-century.

Condition—Good, much restored.

---

89. TOLLESHUNT MAJOR. (C.e.)

(O.S. 6 in. xlv. S.E.)

Tolleshunt Major is a parish and scattered village 4 m. N.E. of Maldon. The principal monuments are the church and Beckingham Hall.

Ecclesiastical :—

(1). PARISH CHURCH OF ST. NICHOLAS stands S.E. of the village. The walls are of boulder clay, flint and pudding-stone rubble with dressings of limestone ; the tower is of red brick ; the roofs are tiled. The material used seems to indicate the existence of a 12th-century *Chancel* and *Nave* but there is no detail of this period remaining and the side walls appear to have been subsequently lowered. Probably in the 15th century the chancel was extended about 8 ft. to the E. Early in the 16th century the *West Tower* was added ; later in the same century a N. chapel with a vestry W. of it was built, but the vestry was subsequently destroyed. The church was restored in the 19th century when the N. chapel was rebuilt as a *North Vestry* and the *South Porch* added.

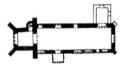

Architectural Description—The *Chancel* (21 ft. by 16 ft.) has a much restored 15th-century E. window of three cinquefoiled lights with vertical tracery in a four-centred head. In the N. wall is a 16th-century archway of plastered brick with a four-centred arch of two chamfered orders and semi-octagonal responds with moulded capitals and bases. In the S. wall are two windows, the eastern is of the 15th century, partly restored and is of two cinquefoiled lights in a square head ; the western window is modern ; between them is a 15th-century doorway with moulded jambs and two-centred arch in a square head with traceried spandrels and square foliated bosses ; E. of the western window is a plastered groove, part of the W. splay and part of the arch of a window perhaps of the 12th century. There is no chancel-arch.

The *Nave* (34 ft. by 16 ft.) has in the N. wall a 15th-century window of two cinquefoiled lights in a square head with a moulded label ; E. of the window is a 16th-century doorway of plastered brick, with double-chamfered jambs and four-centred arch ; it is now blocked ; at the W. end of the wall is an early 16th-century doorway with moulded jambs, two-centred arch and label ; it is now partly blocked and fitted with a wooden window. In the S. wall are two modern windows ; between them is the late 14th or early 15th-century S. doorway with a two-centred arch of two moulded orders and jambs of two hollow-chamfered orders.

The *West Tower* (11 ft. by 10½ ft.) is of early 16th-century date and of red brick with blue brick diapering. It is of three stages (Plate, p. 220) and has an embattled parapet with the merlons cut down. The tower-arch is plastered and has semi-octagonal responds with moulded capitals and bases and a four-centred arch of two chamfered orders. The stair-turret has doorways with four-centred heads and the brick stairs are supported by a four-centred arch at every quarter turn. The W. window is of three four-centred and transomed lights with tracery in a four-centred head with a moulded label. The second stage has in the S. wall a loop and in the W. wall a window of two four-centred lights in a four-centred head with a moulded label. The bell-chamber has in each wall a window similar to the W. window but without a transom. The angles of this stage have counterfeit masonry quoins of plaster.

The *Roof* of the chancel is of late 15th-century date and of braced collar-beam type with a moulded wall-plate and tie-beam ; the plain W. tie-beam has a king-post. The 15th-century roof of the nave is of three bays of which the western is of later date than the others ; of the two main tie-beams, the eastern has a king-post with moulded capital and base ; the western tie-beam supports a timber-framing probably for a former bell-turret which rested further W. on an intermediate collar-beam with similar framing.

Fittings—*Bells :* three ; 1st, uninscribed but probably pre-Reformation ; 2nd inscribed " Vox Edwardi sonet in Aure Dei," late 14th-century. *Coffin-lid :* In chancel—with raised cross and omega ornament, 13th-century, formerly used as a window head. In porch—tapering slab of Purbeck marble. *Font :* built against S. wall, semi-octagonal, Purbeck marble bowl, two faces with trefoiled-headed panels, one face with a shield and two faces with rosettes, moulded under-side, early 14th-century. *Glass :* In E. window—in

tracery, fragments with rosettes, 16th-century. *Niches :* In nave—in N. wall, shallow, with remains of double vaulted canopy in brick ; in S. wall, similar niche, much defaced, both early 16th-century. *Paintings :* In nave—on N. wall, L-shaped panel with traces of colour, date uncertain ; on S. wall, remains of head and hand of figure ; on W. wall, remains of strap-work frames and black-letter inscription, 16th-century. *Piscina :* In chancel, rough segmental-headed recess, with oak shelf and quatrefoiled drain. *Plate :* includes 17th-century cup. *Sedile :* In chancel—sill of S.E. window carried down to form seat. *Stoup :* In nave—in N.W. angle, with four-centred head and plastered bowl, early 16th-century.

Condition—Good.

Secular :—

(2). HOMESTEAD MOAT, at Wicks Manor Farm, nearly 1 m. N.W. of the church.

(3). BECKINGHAM HALL, house, gatehouse, walls and moat, 200 yards N.E. of the church. The *House* is of two storeys, partly of brick and partly of plastered timber-framing ; the roofs are tiled. It was built *c.* 1546, the date on a panel (now at the Victoria and Albert Museum, South Kensington). Early in the 17th-century a wing was added on the W. side and there are modern additions on the S. and N. The fact that the house is unimportant in comparison to the gatehouse and walls implies either the former existence of a much larger building or at any rate the intention to erect such a building. The E. side of the house has an original moulded string-course and a blocked window. Inside the building is some early 17th-century panelling and some exposed timber-framing.

The *Gatehouse* (Plate, p. 230) W. of the house is of *c.* 1546 and forms the central feature of the boundary wall of a large courtyard, 130 ft. by 120 ft., with the house adjoining the S.E. angle. The gatehouse is of two storeys and of red brick with remains of plaster having painted decoration in black and white, the ground white in the one part and black in the other, the pattern remaining the same ; at each angle is a circular turret, the inner pair partly solid and the outer hollow and entered by external doorways with four-centred heads ; these turrets are lit by cruciform loops and have internal doorways opening into the room above the gatehouse. Above the S.W. turret is a circular chimney-shaft with a moulded necking on which stands an ornamental cap with four attached shafts. The outer archway has moulded jambs and four-centred arch in a square head with a double label ; the spandrels have remains of painted tracery on plaster. The upper floor has a window of two four-centred lights in a square head with remains of a moulded label. The responds of the inner archway have each an attached semi-circular shaft with a moulded capital; only the springers of the original moulded arch remain, the rest being replaced with modern brickwork. The inner turrets have embattled parapets. The building has no floor or roof but in the thickness of the S. wall are straight staircases entered by doorways with four-centred heads. The upper floor had in the N. wall a fireplace with a four-centred head now partly destroyed; there are remains also of a barrel-vaulted roof.

The boundary wall of the great courtyard is of red brick with black brick diapering and a broad coping set on oversailing courses. At the N.W. angle is a circular hollow turret, with a top of pepper-box form and finished with a truncated cone. At the S.W. angle is a plain circular turret forming with a similar turret further S. a pair flanking an outer gateway; these turrets have embattled parapets, but the gateway arch has been removed. Near the middle of the N. and S. sides of the main courtyard are the bases of two more turrets, corbelled out below the coping of the walls.

The *Moat* probably surrounded the house but only the E. arm remains.

Condition—Of house, good; of gatehouse and walls, poor.

MONUMENTS (4–7).

The following monuments are of two storeys, timber-framed and plastered or weather-boarded; the roofs are tiled. All have exposed ceiling-beams.

Condition—Good, or fairly good.

(4). *Manor Farm*, house, ½ m. S.S.E. of the church, was built in the 16th century with a cross-wing at the S. end. Inside the building the roof of the main block has a queen-post truss.

(5). *Cottage*, on N. side of road, 1,100 yards W. of the church, was built early in the 16th century with a cross-wing at the E. and W. ends.

(6). *Cottage*, 100 yards S.W. of (5), was built probably in the 15th century with a cross-wing at the E. end. A former W. cross-wing has been destroyed. The upper storey projects at both ends of the cross-wing. Inside the building is an early 17th-century panelled door and the roof of the E. wing has original cambered tie-beams.

(7). *Long's Farm*, house, 220 yards S.W. of (6), was built early in the 17th century on an L-shaped plan with the wings extending towards the S. and E. Inside the building are some original battened doors.

Unclassified :—

(8). MOUND, 220 yards S.W. of the church. A circular mound about 8 ft. high and 50 ft.

in diameter with slight traces of a ditch at the base.

Condition—Fairly good.

TOTHAM, see GREAT TOTHAM and LITTLE TOTHAM.

---

90. TWINSTEAD. (B.b.)

(O.S. 6 in. [a]xii. S.W. [b]xii. S.E.)

Twinstead is a small parish 5 m. N.E. of Halstead.

Ecclesiastical :—

[b](1). PARISH CHURCH OF ST. JOHN THE EVANGELIST was entirely rebuilt in 1860 but retains from the old church the following :—

Fittings—*Bell :* one, probably by John Bird, early 16th-century. *Brasses :* In organ-chamber —(1) to Mary, wife of Thomas Wyncoll, 1658, inscription and shield of arms. In nave—on N. wall, (2) of Marie (Gaudy), wife of Isake Wyncoll, 1610, with figures of man, wife and five daughters, figure of son missing. *Chair :* In chancel—with carved top-rail and turned and twisted posts, *c.* 1700. *Chest :* In vestry—hutch-type with panelled front and ends, early 18th-century. *Floor-slabs :* Outside porch—(1) to Hannah, daughter of Isaac Wyncoll, 1680, with lozenge of arms ; (2) to Isaac Wyncoll, 1681 ; (3) to Thomas Wyncoll, 1675. *Weather-vane :* Loose in churchyard—copper cock, early 18th-century.

Condition—Rebuilt.

Secular :—

MONUMENTS (2–5).

The following monuments are of the 17th century and of two storeys, timber-framed and plastered ; the roofs are tiled. They have exposed ceiling-beams.

[b](2). *The Rectory*, W. of the church, is modern except for the S.W. wing.

Condition—Good, much altered.

[a](3). *Lodge Farm*, house, ¾ m. W. of the church, is of L-shaped plan with the wings extending towards the S. and W.

Condition—Fairly good.

[a](4). *Smith's Farm*, house (Plate, p. 177), ¼ m. S.S.E. of (3), has an original chimney-stack with four stunted octagonal shafts. Inside the building is a moulded ceiling-beam and a window of three lights with moulded mullions.

Condition—Poor.

[b](5). *Sparrow's Farm*, house, 1,200 yards E. of the church, is of L-shaped plan with the wings extending towards the N. and E.

Condition—Poor.

91. VIRLEY. (C.e.)

(O.S. 6 in. xlvi. N.W.)

Virley is a very small parish 8 ,m. S.W. of Colchester. The church is of interest.

Ecclesiastical :—

(1). PARISH CHURCH OF ST. MARY THE VIRGIN stands on the S. side of the parish. The walls are of mixed rubble with some Roman bricks. The *Chancel* and *Nave* were built probably early in the 13th century but the later windows may indicate partial rebuilding of both parts. The church fell into disuse in the second half of the 19th century and is now roofless and ruinous.

Architectural Description—The *Chancel* (20½ ft. by 14½ ft.) has the E. and S. walls ruined to the floor level. In the N. wall are two 15th-century windows, both formerly of two lights with tracery in a four-centred head ; the mullions and tracery have been destroyed and both windows have been repaired with 17th-century brick. The early 13th-century chancel-arch has semi-octagonal responds with moulded capitals and a round arch of two chamfered orders.

The *Nave* (19 ft. wide) has in the N. wall a window probably of the 14th century and of two pointed lights in a two-centred head ; the mullions and sub-heads are modern ; further W. is the E. jamb of the former doorway with a blocking of 17th-century bricks ; the rest of the N. wall has been completely destroyed. In the S. wall is a window similar to that in the N. wall but without mullion or sub-heads ; further W. is the E. jamb of the 14th-century S. doorway, of two moulded orders ; the rest of the S. wall with the whole of the W. wall has been destroyed.

Condition—Ruinous and overgrown with ivy.

Unclassified :—

(2). MOUND, about ⅛ m. N. of the church, is circular and partly surrounded by a dry ditch. It was possibly a mill-mound.

Condition—Fairly good.

---

92. WAKES COLNE. (B.c.)

(O.S. 6 in. xvii. S.E.)

Wakes Colne is a parish and small village 5 m. E. of Halstead. The church is the principal monument.

Ecclesiastical —

(I). PARISH CHURCH OF ALL SAINTS stands at the S. end of the parish. The walls are of flint-

rubble coursed in the earlier work and with lime-stone dressings ; the roofs are tiled. The *Nave* and a central tower were built about the middle of the 12th century. In the 14th century the *Chancel* was rebuilt probably of greater length than the existing building. Probably in the 14th century the central tower with its E. arch was removed. Early in the 15th century the W. bell-turret was erected and the *North Porch* added. The church was restored in the 19th century when the E. wall was rebuilt and the *South Vestry* and organ-chamber added.

Architectural Description—The *Chancel* (34½ ft. by 17½ ft.) has a modern E. wall and window. The side walls have each a set-back showing the eastern extent of the former central tower. In the N. wall is a 14th-century window, very much restored and of two cinquefoiled lights with a quatrefoil in a two-centred head ; further W. is an early 16th-century doorway with a three-centred head, opening into a staircase in the thickness of the wall ; the top of the staircase is at a suitable level for a rood-loft but its easterly position is more appropriate to a lenten-veil screen. In the S. wall is a window uniform with N. window and further W. is a modern arch and doorway to the organ-chamber and vestry. The two-centred chancel-arch, formerly the W. arch of the tower, is of 14th-century date and of three chamfered orders ; the plain responds are thicker at the base and have on the W. face the angle roll of the outer order of the 12th-century responds.

The *Nave* (49½ ft. by 22 ft.) has in the N. wall four windows ; the easternmost is of early 14th-century date and of two trefoiled ogee lights with a quatrefoil in a two-centred head with a moulded label ; the other three windows are of the 12th century and each of a single round-headed light set high in the wall ; the 12th-century N. doorway is round-headed and of two orders, one plain and continuous the other moulded and springing from a shaft with cushion capital and defaced moulded base. In the S. wall are four windows ; the easternmost is similar to the easternmost in the N. wall ; further W. were three 12th-century windows similar to those in the N. wall, but of these the middle one is now blocked and the western has been widened and a modern two-light window inserted in the opening ; below the blocked window is a late 16th-century window of brick, of three transomed lights in a square head ; the 12th-century S. doorway has plain jambs and round arch. In the W. wall is a modern window. The bell-turret at the W. end of the nave stands on tie-beams, the eastern resting on wall-posts with curved braces and moulded corbels and the western with four posts carried down to the floor and all of early 15th-century date ; the two middle posts are octagonal with moulded stops.

The *North Porch* is of timber standing on modern brick walls. The framework is partly of the 15th century together with the cusped and sub-cusped barge-boards.

Fittings—*Bells :* three; said to be, 1st by Henry Pleasant, 1707.; 2nd by Henry Jordan, inscribed " Wox Augustine Sonet in Aure Dei," late 15th-century ; 3rd by Miles Graye, 1662. *Brasses :* In chancel—on S. wall, (1) to William Tyffin, 1617, and Mary (Jenour), his wife, 1616, also John Tyffin, 1616, and Mary, his wife, 1620, inscription only. In nave—(2) to Edmund Sandford, 1611, with three shields of arms. *Coffin-lid :* In nave—on sill of W. window, tapering slab with double hollow-chamfered edge and remains of cross, 13th-century. *Door :* In N. doorway—of oak battens, with strap-hinges and domed handle-plate, 16th-century. *Font :* hexagonal bowl, each face with three round-headed panels, late 12th-century, base modern. *Glass :* In nave—in tracery of N.E. window, white and yellow foliage, 15th-century. *Monument :* In chancel—on S. wall, to William Tyffin, 1617, and Mary (Jenour), his wife, 1616, alabaster tablet with Jacobean frame, cresting and shield of arms. *Painting :* In nave—on E. wall, diaper of black roses on white ground, 16th-century. *Plate :* includes a cup of 1702. *Stoup:* In N. porch —with moulded jambs and cinquefoiled head, 15th-century, basin removed.

Condition—Good.

Secular :—

(2). HOMESTEAD MOAT, at Alcock's Green, about 1 m. N.N.E. of the church.

(3). FISHER'S FARM, house and moat, 300 yards S.W. of (2). The *House* is of two storeys, timber-framed and plastered ; the roofs are tiled. It was built probably late in the 16th century and has a later E. wing. The original chimney-stack has six octagonal shafts.

The *Moat,* W. of the house, is fragmentary.

Condition—Of house, good, much altered.

(4). LITTLE LOVENEY HALL, house and moat, 1¾ m. N. of the church. The *House* is of two storeys, timber-framed and plastered ; the roofs are tiled. It was built probably late in the 16th century. The central chimney-stack has three diagonal shafts. Inside the building are exposed ceiling and tie-beams.

The *Moat* surrounds the house.

Condition—Of house, good.

(5). CREPPING HALL, house and moat, 1¼ m. E. of the church. The *House* is of two storeys, timber-framed and plastered ; the roofs are tiled. It was built probably in the 15th century but has been almost entirely altered. Inside the building is an original doorway with chamfered jambs and two-centred head and remains of an original king-post roof with smoke-blackened timbers.

The *Moat* is fragmentary.

Condition—Of house, good, much altered.

MONUMENTS (6–16).

The following monuments, unless otherwise described, are of the 17th century and of two storeys, timber-framed and plastered or weather-boarded ; the roofs are tiled or thatched. Many of the buildings have original chimney-stacks and exposed ceiling-beams.

Condition—Good or fairly good, unless noted.

(6). *Oldhouse Farm,* house, ½ m. N.E. of the church, was built in the 16th century, with cross-wings at the N. and S. ends.

(7). *The Watch House,* 750 yards E. of the church, was built in the 16th century, with a cross-wing at the E. and W. ends. Inside the building the main block has original moulded ceiling-beams and joists.

(8). *House,* now three tenements, 80 yards E. of the church, was built in the 16th century and has inside the building an original doorway with a four-centred head.

(9). *House* and Post Office, S.E. of the church, has an original chimney-stack with four octagonal shafts.

WAKES COLNE GREEN :—

(10). *Cottage,* two tenements, 350 yards W.N.W. of (3).

(11). *Jordan's Farm,* house, 170 yards S.W. of (10), has an original chimney-stack with one hexagonal shaft.

(12). *Cottage,* 200 yards W. of (11).

(13). *Sturgeon's Farm,* house, 130 yards N.W. of (12), has in front the date 1715, probably that of the plastering only.

(14). *Cottage,* 170 yards N. of (13).

Condition—Bad.

(15). *Norman's Farm,* house, ¼ m. W. of (14), was built in the 16th century with a cross-wing at the E. end. The upper storey projects at the N. end of the cross-wing.

Condition—Poor.

(16). *Cottage,* ½ m. S.E. of (4).

93. WALTON-LE-SOKEN. (G.c.)

(O.S. 6 in. xxxix. N.W. and N.E.)

No monuments known.

94. WEELEY. (F.d.)

(O.S. 6 in. [a]xxxviii. N.W. [b]xxxviii. N.E.)

Weeley is a small parish and village 4½ m. N. of Clacton.

Ecclesiastical :—

[b](1). PARISH CHURCH OF ST. ANDREW stands near the middle of the parish. The church was entirely rebuilt in 1880 with the exception of the early 16th-century tower, which is of red brick the lowest 10 ft. being built of large bricks (11¼ in. by 5¼ in.) and the upper parts of brick of normal size.

Architectural Description — The *West Tower* (11 ft. square) is of three stages (Plate, p. 221) with diagonal western buttresses and a turret at the S.E. angle having two loops each fitted with a 17th-century turned baluster of oak. There is a little diapering in black brick and the embattled parapet has modern tops to the merlons. The two-centred tower-arch is of three chamfered orders dying on to plain responds. The W. window is of three cinquefoiled lights with vertical tracery in a four-centred head with a moulded label and head-stops. The W. doorway has splayed jambs and two-centred arch of two moulded orders. The bell-chamber has in each wall a window of two four-centred lights in a square head with a moulded label.

Fittings—*Bells :* two ; 1st by Robert Burford, *c.* 1400, and inscribed " Sce. Michael " and " Sancta Katerina Ora Pro Nobis " ; 2nd by Thomas Bullisdon, *c.* 1500, and inscribed " Sancte Edwarde Ora Pro Nobis " and " Pray for Vyllam Brooke and Agnes his Wyff." *Font :* octagonal bowl with quatrefoiled sides enclosing blank shields and foliage, much recut, moulded underside with square flowers, stem with traceried panels, 15th-century. *Plate :* includes small cup and cover-paten, cup with band of incised ornament, late 16th-century. *Miscellanea :* In chancel—shaft with scalloped capital, Barnack stone, recut, 12th-century, now used for credence table.

Condition—Good.

Secular :—

[a](2). HOMESTEAD MOAT, at Willow Lodge, about 1,000 yards S.S.W. of the church.

[a](3). BARN and moat, at Guttridge Hall, 1 m. W.S.W. of the church. The *Barn* is timber-framed and probably of the 15th century. It is of five bays with aisles and king-post roof-trusses.

The *Moat* is fragmentary.

Condition—Of barn, fairly good.

[b](4). FOUNDATIONS, at Weeley Hall, N. of the church, are of red brick and probably of the 16th

century. Some arches of the former cellars remain and adjoining them are brick garden walls, probably of the 17th century.

Condition—Bad.

MONUMENTS (5–8).

The following monuments, unless otherwise described, are of the 17th century and of two storeys, timber-framed and plastered or weather-boarded ; the roofs are tiled. Some of the buildings have exposed ceiling-beams.

Condition—Good, or fairly good.

[a](5). *Black Boy Inn,* ¾ m. N.W. of the church, has been practically rebuilt but incorporates some old timber-framing.

[a](6). *Ash Farm,* house, 100 yards E. of (5), was built early in the 16th century with cross-wings at the E. and W. ends. The E. cross-wing has been destroyed and there is a 17th-century wing added on the N. of the main block. The upper storey projects on the N. side of the main block and at the N. end of the original cross-wing where it has curved brackets and an original moulded capital under one of them. The gable of the wing has original barge-boards with much weathered carved foliage. Inside the building the main block has an original cambered tie-beam with curved braces.

[a](7). *Cottage,* on W. side of road, 300 yards S. of (5), was built probably early in the 16th century with a cross-wing at the N. end. The upper storey projects at both ends of the cross-wing.

[a](8). *Pond Farm,* 700 yards S.W. of the church, has an 18th-century addition on the N.E.

---

95. WEST BERGHOLT. (C.c.)

(O.S. 6 in. [a] xxvii. N.W. [b] xxvii. N.E.)

West Bergholt is a parish 3 m. N.W. of Colchester. The church is the principal monument.

Ecclesiastical :—

[b](1). PARISH CHURCH OF ST. MARY stands to the W. of the modern village. The walls are of rubble covered with rough-cast ; the dressings are of limestone and the roofs are tiled ; the bell-turret is boarded. The thickness of some of the walls and the irregularity of the plan seem to indicate a fairly early date for parts of the *Chancel* and *Nave* but the earliest detail is of early 14th-century date when the whole church was remodelled and the *South Aisle* added. The *South Porch* may also be of the 14th century and the bell-turret is perhaps of the 15th. The church was restored in the 18th century when the W. gallery was built.

Among the fittings the 17th-century lectern is interesting.

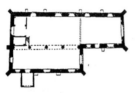

Architectural Description—The *Chancel* (28½ ft. by 18½ ft.) is structurally undivided from the nave. The E. window is of the 18th century or modern, set in the blocking of a 14th-century opening with a two-centred head. In the N. wall are two windows ; the eastern is of the 14th century with a modern mullion and tracing and is of two segmental-pointed lights under a segmental-pointed head and rear-arch ; the western is also of the 14th century and of two pointed lights in a two-centred head, with a modern mullion. In the S. wall are two windows ; the eastern is uniform with the eastern window in the N. wall but is all modern except the rear-arch ; the western is modern except the 14th-century splays and two-centred, moulded rear-arch ; between the windows is a 14th-century doorway with moulded jambs and two-centred arch. The two western windows have low internal sills and the lower halves of the lights are now filled in, showing that they were probably used as ' lowsides.'

The *Nave* (47½ ft. by 20 ft.) has in the N. wall three windows all of the 18th century but the middle retains parts of the 14th-century jambs and sill and the westernmost is set in the 14th-century N. doorway which has chamfered jambs and two-centred arch. The S. arcade is of four bays with two-centred early 14th-century arches of two chamfered orders ; the octagonal columns and semi-octagonal responds have moulded capitals and bases. In the roof are two 18th-century dormer windows. In the W. wall is a 14th-century window of two trefoiled lights in a square head.

The *South Aisle* (13½ ft. wide) is of early 14th-century date and gabled at each end ; on the gables are mutilated stone gable-crosses. In the E. wall is an 18th-century or modern wood window set in a 14th-century opening with a two-centred head and a moulded label. In the S. wall are three windows ; the two eastern are each of two trefoiled ogee lights with tracery in a two-centred head and a moulded label ; the westernmost is similar but of one trefoiled light ; between the two western windows is the S. doorway with jambs and two-centred arch of two wave-moulded orders with a moulded label. In the W. wall is a window uniform with the eastern windows in the S. wall.

The *South Porch* is probably of the 14th century ; it is timber-framed with modern dwarf walls and

front. The sides are each of six lights with diamond-shaped mullions.

The *Roof* of the chancel is ceiled but has 14th-century moulded plates ; the roof of the nave is similar but has one heavy grooved and stop-chamfered tie-beam. At the W. end of the nave is the timber bell-turret probably of the 15th century and standing on eight posts with curved braces but much covered by modern partitions. The roof of the S. aisle is similar to that of the nave and has two tie-beams. The S. porch has old rafters and collar-beams.

Fittings—*Chest :* In S. aisle—large iron-bound, with six hinges to lid, which is half the width of the top and in two lengths, 16th-century. *Coffin-lid :* In S. aisle—tapering stone slab. *Door :* In S. doorway—of battens with strap-hinges and old key-plate, date uncertain. *Floor-slabs :* In chancel—(1) to wife of— Parker (?), 1700 ; (2) to Mary Poilard, widow of Francis Poilard, 1676 ; (3) to Rebecka, wife of Peter Sadler, 1676 ; (4) to Peter Sadler, 1670 ; (5) to Thomas Scarlet, 1705. *Font :* cylindrical bowl, probably 13th-century, square stem with chamfered angles and repaired with brick. *Glass :* In S. aisle—in tracery of S.E. window, green glass with one foliated roundel 14th-century ; in W. window, two similar roundels. *Lectern :* square base with elaborate ornament of conventional foliage, turned baluster-stem, early 17th-century, book-rest modern. *Niches :* In chancel—flanking E. window, plain pointed and plastered recesses, possibly 15th-century. *Panelling :* In chancel on E. wall and on W. wall of nave, panelling with fluted frieze, 17th-century. *Piscinae :* In chancel—with moulded jambs and two-centred head, sexfoiled drain, 14th-century. In S. aisle—in S. wall, with moulded and chamfered jambs and trefoiled head, octofoiled drain, 14th-century. *Sedile :* In S. aisle—sill of S.E. window carried down to form seat, 14th-century.

Condition—Poor, very damp.

Secular :—

[a](2). COOK'S HALL, ½ m. S.S.W. of the church, is of two storeys, timber-framed and plastered ; the roofs are tiled. The back wing was built late in the 16th or early in the 17th century. The main block was built in the 18th century. On the W. side of the wing is the sill with two window-brackets of a former oriel window. Inside the building the ceiling-beams are exposed.

Condition—Good.

[a](3). HORSEPIT'S FARM, house, about ¼ m. S.E. of (2), is of two storeys, timber-framed and plastered ; the roofs are tiled. It was built probably early in the 16th century with cross-wings at the N. and S. ends. The upper storey projects on the whole of the W. side. Inside the building one room

has original moulded ceiling-beams and joists. In the roof is an original king-post truss.

Condition—Fairly good.

b(4). HIGHTREES FARM, house, 650 yards E. of the church, is of two storeys, timber-framed and plastered; the roofs are tiled. It was built probably late in the 15th century with cross-wings at the N. and S. ends. The upper storey projects at the E. ends of the cross-wings. Inside the building are two original doorways with four-centred heads and the ceiling-beams are exposed. The N. wing has an original king-post roof-truss.

Condition—Good.

96. WEST MERSEA. (D.e.)

(O.S. 6 in. (*a*)xlvi. N.E. (*b*)xlvi. S.E. (*c*)xlvii. N.W.)

West Mersea is a village and parish including the W. half of Mersea Island. The Romano-British barrow and the Roman circular building are both important monuments, and the church has features of interest.

Roman :—

c(1). MERSEA MOUNT.—This barrow stands ½ m. S.E. of the Strood crossing, and about the same distance due S. of an old ford, and adjoining the highway to E. Mersea, about 1¼ m. N.E. of W. Mersea church. It stands at an elevation of 60 ft. above sea-level, and, though now much worn, is about 110 ft. in diameter and 22½ ft. high, and the top is flat over a space of 16 ft. Excavations carried out by the Morant Club in 1912 showed that in the centre a chamber 18 in. square by 21½ in. in height was sunk so that the floor was 15 in. below the original surface. The floor consisted of two roof tiles, laid on two courses of septaria; the walls were made of seven courses, of flanged roof-tiles and the roof was composed of a single bonding tile, 21½ in. square. Over the chamber was a dome of seven courses of tile set in mortar. On the original surface soil beneath the barrow was a thin red stratum, 2 in. or less in thickness, made of crushed tile and yellow ochre. Above this for 12 ft. was a core of grey earthy

quartz sand, very compact, with repetitions of the red stratum for the first 18 in., and the rest of the barrow consisted of looser sand and gravel. Mixed with these were a few fragments of Samian, Belgic and Upchurch pottery, a few flints, and a little briquetage.

In the chamber was a leaden casket, 12½ in. square and 13 in. deep, covered with two pieces of board and containing a glass bowl, 11½ in. high, and nearly 13 in. in diameter, with a small mouth and a broad, flat rim. The glass was pale green and transparent. The vessel contained the cremated remains of an adult. It would seem to date from the latter half of the first century, and to have belonged to a Romano-Briton of good position. (*Essex Arch. Soc. Trans.* (N.S.), XIII, 116. F. Haverfield, *Roman Britain in 1913* (Brit. Acad. Suppl. Papers, II, p. 42. See also *Sectional Preface*, p. xxvii.)

b(2). ROUND BUILDING.—About 200 yards E. of W. Mersea church, and 150 yards E. of the Hall Farm, foundations were met with in December, 1896, in the course of digging a saw-pit. They were about 9 in. below the surface in undisturbed soil, and were those of a circular building, with walls 3 ft. in thickness, and having twelve buttresses or bases for columns, projecting 4 ft. beyond the main wall. Alternate buttresses were continued on the inner side to the angles of a central hexagon. The hexagon was about 5 ft. across, and the entire building was 65 ft. in diameter. The walls were composed of brick and mortar laid in concrete, with an offset 6 in. wide of a course or two of tiles and rubble foundations; the bricks measured on an average 17 in. by 11 in. by 1½ in. No indications of doors or floors were observed. The debris included many roof-tiles with red mortar. There were three pieces of stone, each a yard long and 7 in. in width, flat on one edge, convex at the other, and not moulded. There were signs of fire, but no coins or pottery were noted which could give a date to the edifice. (*Proc. Soc. Ant.*, XVI, 425, with plan. *Essex Arch. Soc. Trans.* (N.S.), VI, 173, 284.) The foundations were still exposed in 1922.

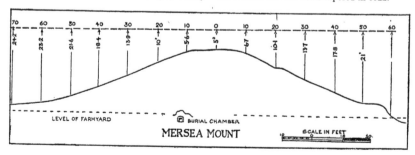

MERSEA MOUNT

LEVEL OF FARMYARD   BURIAL CHAMBER

SCALE IN FEET

WEST MERSEA   ROMAN FOUNDATIONS

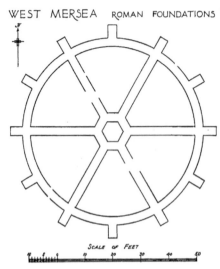

SCALE OF FEET

It is well known that the Romans employed towers as lighthouses, block-houses, watch-towers, and for purposes of harbour defence, but this building does not conform to any common type, and the foundation cannot have supported a very lofty structure, unless it were of wood. A pair of somewhat similar buildings exhibiting the same plan exist at old Cairo ("Babylon of Egypt"), but as these appear to have guarded the entrance to the Red Sea Canal, which, according to Ptolemy, IV, 5, 24, flowed through "Babylon," they can afford but a superficial analogy to the Mersea structure. (A. J. Butler, *Ancient Coptic Churches of Egypt*, 1884, Chap. IV. A. J. Butler, *Arab Conquest of Egypt*, 238, 249. Strabo., XVI, 21. See also *Sectional Preface*, p. xxvii.) Perhaps a better suggestion is that the buttress-like projections are really platforms to carry columns, the whole thus forming a circular peristyle monument of well-known classical type. (See L. Canina, *Via Appia*, for examples.)

b(3). DWELLING HOUSE.—The church and churchyard at West Mersea cover the site of one or more houses of Roman date. The remains are not completely recorded and from the nature of the site it is impossible to reconstruct any ground-plan. The principal finds have been :—

(*a*) About 1730, pavements were discovered over an area of 100 ft. by 50 ft. in the churchyard just N.E. of the church, 10 ft. from the stile and also in the hall-yard, W. of the gravel path from the village. In the churchyard it lay 4 ft. below the surface; outside, 1 ft. only. The chief pavement, 21 ft. by 18½ ft., was of geometrical pattern with ivy-leaves and roses, with guilloche ornament on the outside and a white border. White, black, blue, red and yellow colours were employed. (Salmon, *Hist. of Essex* ·(1743), pp. 434–5, and Lysons quoting Mortimer in *Arch.*, XVI, 149; also plan in Gough's copy of Salmon in the Bodleian, and a drawing of the pavement in a red portfolio at the Society of Antiquaries.)

(*b*) In 1740 a red tessellated floor was found under the chancel and to the S.E. of the church red tiles 14 in. square. (Salmon.)

(*c*) Gough saw remains of floors W. of the church in 1764, and within recent years the footway of the road by the churchyard wall had red tessellation actually exposed. (Gough's *Tours* in Bodl. Library, MS. Top. Gen., e. 18, fol. 215.)

(*d*) Further W. in 1920 a similar pavement was met with in fixing a telegraph-pole 40 ft. S. of Yewtree House, in the corner of the garden at the angle of the road about 180 ft. S.W. of (3). (Information from the occupier of Yewtree House.)

The small finds included coins of which the dates are not given, and also (from the orchard of the Hall) bronze buckles, styles, etc. The fabric of the church and tower is largely composed of rubble, thought to have come from Roman buildings.

Ecclesiastical :—

b(4). PARISH CHURCH OF SS. PETER AND PAUL stands in the village. The walls are of ragstone, septaria, Roman bricks and later bricks. The dressings are of limestone, brick and Roman bricks. The roofs are tiled. The *West Tower* was built late in the 11th century. Probably in the 14th century the *Chancel* and *Nave* were rebuilt and the *South Aisle* added. The *North Porch* was added in the 15th century. Early in the 16th century the upper part of the chancel was rebuilt and the roof added. Late in the 18th century the walls of the Nave were heightened, the existing ceilings inserted and the *South Vestry* added.

The W. tower is a good example of early masonry.

Architectural Description—The *Chancel* (25½ ft. by 21¾ ft.) has 14th-century walls of coursed and

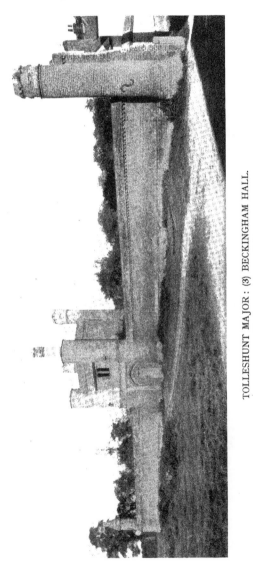

TOLLESHUNT MAJOR : (3) BECKINGHAM HALL.

Gatehouse, etc. ; c. 1546.

WIX.
(2) Wix Abbey, late 16th-century; West Front.

GREAT COGGESHALL.
(80) House, East Street; *c.* 1700.

TOLLESHUNT D'ARCY HALL.
Bridge over Moat; *c.* 1585.

TOLLESHUNT D'ARCY HALL   Dovecote; late 16th-century.

squared ragstone to a height of about 9 ft.; above, the walling is of later rebuilt ragstone and bricks. The E. window is modern. In the N. wall are two early 16th-century windows of three lights with four-centred main heads and labels of brick and modern mullions; the jambs and heads of lights are of stone. Between the windows is a doorway with an early 16th-century head of brick and earlier jambs of stone. There is no structural division between the chancel and nave.

The *Nave* (42¼ ft. by 21½ ft.) has in the N. wall two windows both with modern frames, but set in partly blocked larger openings; the eastern has a four-centred moulded label with one head-stop of late 14th-century date, and is partly destroyed by the N. porch; the western, also partly hidden by the porch, has a badly decayed moulded label; between the windows is the late 14th-century N. doorway with moulded and shafted jambs, two-centred arch and label with defaced stops and triangular rear-arch; E. of the eastern window is a recess with a segmental head, possibly in connection with a former nave altar. The S. arcade is of four bays, partly overlapping the chancel, with two-centred arches of three chamfered orders; they are possibly of the 14th century but the piers, responds and arches are covered with 18th-century plaster.

The *South Aisle* (12 ft. wide) has in the E. wall an early 16th-century window of three four-centred lights under a square-head in a four-centred outer order with a moulded label. In the S. wall are two windows of the 17th or 18th century with reused material probably in earlier openings; the western has a reused 14th-century mullion; each is of three lights; further W. is an 18th-century doorway. In the W. wall, which is built chiefly of reused septaria and Roman bricks, is a mid 14th-century window of two plain pointed lights in a two-centred head with a moulded label.

The *West Tower* (14¼ ft. by 13½ ft.) is of late 11th-century date and of three stages, with an embattled parapet; the quoins are of Roman bricks and the rubble is of coursed ragstone and septaria mostly set herring-bone-wise. The plain semi-circular tower-arch has plain jambs and imposts formed of three oversailing courses. In both the N. and S. walls are late 11th-century windows with round heads and narrow splays. In the W. wall is a 15th-century window of two lights (formerly cinquefoiled), with reset vertical tracery in a four-centred head with a moulded label. The second stage has a small circular opening in the W. wall. The bell-chamber has in each wall a late 14th-century window of two cinquefoiled and transomed lights and a quatrefoiled head with a moulded label.

The *North Porch* has a 15th-century outer archway with a moulded two-centred arch and moulded label with head-stops, the moulded

and shafted responds have moulded capitals and bases. The E. and W. walls have each a two-light window with original jambs and modern heads and mullions.

The *Roof* of the chancel is of two bays with early 16th-century arched and moulded trusses, wall-plates and plain trussed rafters and collar-beams. The N. Porch has two stone corbels, for the former roof-truss, with carved half-figures of angels, one holding a book, the other a heart.

Fittings—*Chests*: In tower—(1) iron-bound with large lock-plates and two staples, probably 16th-century; (2) covered with leather, three locks with pierced ornamental hasp-plates, drop-handles, probably 17th-century. *Coffin-lid*: In chancel—tapering slab with hollow-chamfered edge and raised foliated cross, 13th-century; lower part of slab gone. *Consecration crosses*: On E. wall of chancel, two, circular, painted red, 14th-century or earlier. *Font*: octagonal bowl of Purbeck marble, each face with two shallow panels with pointed heads; also Purbeck marble base, early 13th-century. *Niche*: On N. porch over outer archway with moulded jambs and cinquefoiled head, 14th-century, probably reset. *Painting*: On E. wall of chancel, lower part, remains of geometrical and foliage pattern in red, probably 14th-century. In nave, on W. wall, pattern with repeats of sacred monogram in black and rosettes in red, probably 15th-century. *Miscellanea*—In S. aisle—on S. wall, lunette in glazed Della Robbia ware of the dead Christ with angels, Italian, possibly early 16th-century. In S. aisle loose on E. window ledge, several square tiles with remains of glazing, mediaeval.

Condition—Poor.

Secular :—

ᶜ(5). GARDEN FARM, house ½ m. N.E. of the church, is of two storeys, timber-framed and plastered; the roofs are tiled. It was built probably early in the 16th century, with cross-wings at the E. and W. ends. The upper storey projects at the N. end of the E. wing. Inside the building some of the ceiling-beams are exposed and the W. wing has original cambered tie-beams.

Condition—Good.

ᵃ(6). HOUSE at Mersea Lane, 1,100 yards N.W. of the church, is of two storeys, timber-framed and weather-boarded; the roofs are tiled. It was built probably in the 17th century.

Condition—Fairly good.

Unclassified :—

ᶜ(7). RED HILL, on line of sea-wall behind Strood House. There are several others in the parish.

---

97. WHITE COLNE. (B.c.)

(O.S. 6 in. xvii. S.E.)

White Colne is a parish 4 m. E. of Halstead.

Ecclesiastical :—

(1). PARISH CHURCH OF ST. ANDREW (early dedication unknown) stands near the middle of the parish. The walls are of roughly coursed flint-rubble with some brick and tiles ; the dressings are of limestone except the quoins of the nave which are of Roman brick ; the roofs are tiled. The *Chancel* and *Nave* were built probably in the 12th century and early in the 14th century a W. tower was added ; in modern times the whole church has been drastically restored, the *West Tower* wholly or partly rebuilt, and the *South Vestry* and *South Porch* added. The 17th-century pulpit is noteworthy.

Architectural Description—The *Chancel* (20¼ ft. by 14½ ft.) has in the E. wall a window entirely modern except for the 14th-century splays. In the N. wall is a window modern except for the splays and moulded two-centred rear-arch which are of the 14th century ; the sill is carried down to form a seat ; further W. are traces of a former doorway. In the S. wall is a window similar to that in the N. wall, but with a normal sill ; further W. is a modern arch. The 14th-century chancel-arch is moulded and two-centred ; the plain responds are now largely plastered.

In the *Nave* (32½ ft. by 18½ ft.) in the E. wall N. of the chancel-arch traces are said to have been found of the former rood-loft staircase. In the N. wall are two windows entirely modern except for the splays and moulded two-centred rear-arches which are of the 14th century. In the S. wall is a window all modern except for the splays which are possibly of the 14th century ; further W. is the S. doorway, all modern except the splays.

The *West Tower* (10 ft. by 9 ft.) has a modern W. window. The chamfered, two-centred tower-arch has plain cemented responds ; above it is a small square-headed opening, now blocked. The upper stage is entirely modern.

Fittings—Chair : In chancel—with richly carved back, semi-gothic tracery and shield of arms, square legs with sunk panels, late 16th-century, probably foreign. *Font :* In churchyard—plain octagonal bowl, mediaeval. *Niches :* In nave—N. of chancel-arch, three, one pointed and two round-headed, one with plain pedestal, all cemented

over but probably reredos to former nave altar, date uncertain. *Painting :* In nave—on E. wall, traces of stars, fleur-de-lis, etc., probably 15th-century. *Piscina :* In chancel—with trefoiled ogee head, 14th-century, scraped. *Plate :* includes small cup of 1563 with band of engraved leaf-ornament ; cover-paten, probably of same date. *Pulpit* (Plate, p. 181) : hexagonal, sides with bolection-moulded panels flanked by pilasters enriched with jewel-ornament ; three panels carved with figures in relief of St. James the Great, St. Augustine of Hippo, and Charity ; cornice enriched with masks and conventional foliage, early 17th-century. *Recesses :* In chancel—in N. wall, (1) with hollow-chamfered jambs and trefoiled head, 14th-century. In nave—in E. wall S. of chancel arch, (2) with cinquefoiled two-centred head and hollow-chamfered jambs, 14th-century.

Condition—Good.

Secular :—

(2). FOX AND PHEASANT FARM, house, 1,100 yards S. of the church, is of two storeys ; the walls are of plastered timber-framing ; the roofs are tiled. It was built probably early in the 17th century, but has a late 17th-century addition at the E. end and a modern wing at the back. On the S. front the upper storey of the original block projects. Inside the building are exposed ceiling-beams, and in a room at the W. end is a plastered fireplace with figures of a fox and a pheasant.

Condition—Good.

(3). COTTAGE, ½ m. W. of (2), is of similar construction. It was built probably early in the 17th century on an L-shaped plan with the wings projecting towards the E. and S. ; on the E., W. and S. are modern additions. In the gable at the E. end are remains of rough pargeting. The original central chimney-stack has four octagonal shafts. Inside the building are chamfered ceiling-beams.

Condition—Good.

WIGBOROUGH, see GREAT WIGBOROUGH and LITTLE WIGBOROUGH.

98. WIVENHOE. (D.d.)

(O.S. 6 in. xxxvii. N.W.)

Wivenhoe is a parish and small town on the left bank of the Colne, 3½ m. S.E. of Colchester. The church, Wivenhoe Hall and the house (6) are the principal monuments.

Ecclesiastical :—

(1). PARISH CHURCH OF ST. MARY stands in the town. The walls are of mixed rubble, with some Roman brick in the aisle walls and in the ground stage of the tower. The dressings are of Reigate and hard limestone. The roofs are covered with slates. The chancel-arch and the arches of the N. arcade incorporate 13th-century worked voussoirs but there is no work *in situ* of this date. The North Arcade and *Aisle* of the *Nave* were built *c.* 1340 and the South Arcade and *Aisle* *c.* 1350. The *West Tower* was added *c.* 1500. The church was extensively restored and the E. parts enlarged in 1859 and another restoration took place after the earthquake of 1884, so that the *Chancel* and *North* and *South Chapels* are modern. The *North* and *South Porches* are modern. There was a N. but no S. chapel before the restoration.

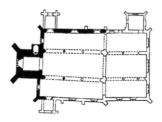

Architectural Description—The *Chancel* (29½ ft. by 16½ ft.) is modern but the chancel-arch incorporates some 14th-century stones and the outer order on the E. is largely of 13th-century voussoirs, reworked in the 14th century.

The *North* and *South Chapels* are modern but incorporated in the W. arch of the S. chapel are a few old stones. There are also old stones in the rear-arch of the N.W. window of the N. chapel.

The *Nave* (44½ ft. by 17¾ ft.) has a N. arcade of *c.* 1340, of three bays with two-centred arches of two wave-moulded orders and octagonal columns with moulded capitals and bases and responds with attached half-columns ; the E. respond, first arch, part of the second arch and the first column are modern ; the arches incorporate reworked 13th-century voussoirs. The S. arcade is generally similar to the N. arcade but rather later ; the E. respond, first arch, first column and the lowest stone of the second arch are modern ; the base of the W. respond is restored.

The *North Aisle* (12¼ ft. wide) has in the N. wall two windows the eastern modern except the 14th-century splays and moulded two-centred rear-arch ; further W. is the N. doorway modern except for the 14th-century splays and hollow-chamfered, two-centred rear-arch. The eastern part of this wall appears to have been refaced. In the W. wall is a window modern except for the 14th-century splays and segmental-pointed rear-arch.

The *South Aisle* (13 ft. wide) has in the S. wall two modern windows incorporating a few old stones

internally. Further W. is the S. doorway modern except for the 14th-century splays and the segmental-pointed rear-arch, partly restored. In the W. wall is a window all modern except for the 14th-century splays and moulded two-centred rear-arch.

The *West Tower* (12 ft. by 10 ft.) is of *c.* 1500 and of three stages with a modern embattled parapet and a moulded plinth with flint chequerwork. The tower-arch is two-centred and of two hollow-chamfered orders ; the semi-octagonal responds have moulded capitals and bases. The W. window is modern except the splays and two-centred hollow-chamfered rear-arch. The second stage has in the N., S. and W. walls a plain rectangular light. The bell-chamber has a modern two-light window in each face. The N.E. stair-turret is modern.

Fittings—*Brasses* and *Indents*. Brasses : In chancel—(1) of William, Viscount Beaumont and Lord Bardolfe [1507], large figure in Tudor armour, head on helm with lion crest, feet on elephant, with castle, standing on a broom-pod ; elaborate triple-arched canopy with crocketed gables and pinnacles, horizontal super-canopy, shafts gone, mutilated marginal inscription with elephant and castle-stops ; (2) of [Elizabeth, widow of above and wife of John, Earl of Oxford, 1537], large figure of woman in heraldic cloak with the arms of Scrope quartering Tiptoft, pedimental head-dress with coronet, triple canopy with crocketed gables and pinnacles, side buttresses, embattled super-canopy with cresting, four shields of arms— (a) and (b) Scrope quartering Tiptoft ; (c) Vere quartering Howard impaling (a) ; (d) a quartered shield of Beaumont impaling (a) ; side-shafts and part of canopy missing, remains of marginal inscription ; (3) of Thomas Westeley, chaplain to the Countess of Oxford, 1535, figure of priest in mass vestments with chalice and host. Indents : In chancel—(1) and (2) of marginal inscription with roundels and shield ; (3) of man in armour and wife, groups of children, four shields and inscription-plate, late 15th-century. In N. aisle—(4) of figure, 15th-century ; (5) of civilian and two shields in panels, 15th-century ; (6) defaced ; (7) of canopy, four shields and marginal inscription, 15th-century, much worn ; (8) of marginal inscription in Lombardic capitals to Margerie de Sutt(on)e, early 14th-century ; (9) of civilian, scroll, shield, inscription-plate and two other plates, 15th-century ; (10) of man in armour, marginal inscription and four shields, *c.* 1500. *Chest :* In vestry —with elaborate arabesque ornament in iron, two monograms on lid surmounted by coronets, ornamental handles and key-plate, 16th-century, foreign. *Font :* In N. aisle—octagonal bowl, traceried panels to sides with alternate shields and foliage, 15th-century, stem and base modern.

Monuments : In churchyard—S. side (1) to . . . ,
1686, head-stone ; W. side (2) to Joseph Townson,
1690, head-stone. *Plate :* includes cup of 1562,
17th-century cover-paten and flagon of 1709 given
in 1729.
Condition—Fairly good.

Secular :—

(2). WIVENHOE HALL (Plate, p. 234), nearly ¼ m.
N. of the church, is of two storeys. The walls are
of brick and plastered timber-framing ; the roofs
are tiled. It was built *c.* 1530 but only the N.
wing remains ; the rest of the building includes
some original work but was very much altered
and rebuilt in 1844. The N. wing has, at the
E. and W. ends, original crow-stepped gables with
pinnacles set diagonally ; there is a second smaller
but similar gable at the W. end ; the stepped
parapets are partly supported by trefoiled corbelling
and each gable has a shallow niche with a double-
trefoiled head ; flanking the niches of the main
gables are small round-headed windows set in
square sinkings. In the E. wall is a wide wall-arch
with moulded jambs and four-centred head with
a moulded label. There are also other original
windows with square heads and moulded labels,
but fitted with modern frames. Inside the building
the N. wing has original moulded ceiling-beams
and joists. The rest of the building retains a
moulded ceiling-beam, part of an original doorway
and a staircase incorporating some 16th-century
material. Under the S. wing is an original cellar
with a barrel-vaulted roof of brick.
Condition—Good, much altered.

MONUMENTS (3–8).

The following monuments, unless otherwise
described, are of the 17th century and of two
storeys, timber-framed and plastered or weather-
boarded ; the roofs are tiled. Many of the buildings
have original chimney-stacks and exposed ceiling-
beams.
Condition—Good, or fairly good, unless noted.

(3). *House* and shop, on W. side of High Street,
30 yards W.N.W. of the church, has in front an
original coved eaves-cornice of plaster, enriched
with running foliage. The upper storey formerly
projected at the W. end but has been underbuilt.

(4). *House,* on N. side of street, 20 yards W.
of (3).

(5). *House* and shop, W. of (4). The upper
storey projects at the end of the back wing. The
front has been refaced with 18th-century brick.
Condition—Bad.

(6). *House* (Plate, p. 235), on S. side of street,
30 yards S.S.W. of the church, was built about the
middle of the 17th century.
The pargeting is noteworthy.

The upper storey projects on the S. side on three
moulded and shaped brackets ; the projecting
eaves have a moulded cornice, and there is an
original doorway with a moulded frame and a
modern window with an original moulded sill.
The N. front has the upper storey completely
covered with elaborate pargeting with a running
band of foliage at the base and large panels of
foliage and strap-work above. In the roof is a
dormer with an original moulded frame and a
pargeted gable. Inside the building one room on
the first floor has monochrome decoration of
swags and scrolls over the fireplace and traces of
painted pilasters under the beams and in the
angles of the room.
Condition—Bad.

(7). *House,* three tenements, on W. side of road,
60 yards E. of the church. The upper storey
projected on the E. front but has been underbuilt ; the two projecting gables on the same side
have original shaped and moulded brackets.

(8). *House,* on W. side of road, near the Quay,
and 60 yards S.S.E. of the church. The E. gable
has original dentilled barge-boards, carved with
arabesque ornament.

---

99. WIX. (F.c.)

(O.S. 6 in. [a]xxix. N.W. [b]xxix. N.E.)

Wix is a parish 6½ m. W.S.W. of Harwich.
Wix Abbey is the principal monument.

Ecclesiastical :—

[b](1). PARISH CHURCH OF ST. MICHAEL stands
near the middle of the parish. The ancient portions
are of rubble with dressings of limestone ; the
roofs are covered with slates. The church was
attached to a priory of Benedictine nuns founded
temp. Henry I and dissolved in 1525. Parts of
the W. wall may be of the 12th century ; the
N. arcade of the *Nave* is of mid 13th-century date.
The whole of the rest of the church appears to have
been rebuilt about the middle of the 18th century.
The foundations of the N. aisle are reported to
have been uncovered in recent years.

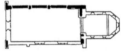

Architectural Description—The *Nave* (48 ft.
by 18 ft.) has in the E. wall, S. of the chancel-
arch a blocked 14th-century doorway with moulded
jambs and two-centred arch. The mid 13th-
century N. arcade is of three bays with two-centred
arches of two chamfered orders ; the octagonal
columns have moulded capitals and chamfered

BRICK HOUSES.

RAMSEY.
(6) Mill Farm ; late 16th-century.

WIVENHOE.
Wivenhoe Hall. North Block,
West End ; c. 1530.

WIVENHOE.
Wivenhoe Hall. North Block,
East End ; c. 1530.

GREAT BRAXTED.
(2) Tiptree Priory ; c. 1570.

BEAUMONT-CUM-MOZE.
(3) Beaumont Hall, late 17th-century ; from the West.

BEAUMONT-CUM-MOZE.
(3) Beaumont Hall, late 17th-century ; South-East Side.

DEDHAM.
(22) Boxhouse Farm. Ceiling; late 17th-century.

HARWICH. (3) The Three Cups Hotel.
Ceiling; late 16th-century.

WIVENHOE. (6) House S.S.W. of Church. Pargeting; mid 17th-century.

EARLS COLNE. (23) Colneford House. Pargeting on North-West Front; 1685.

bases and the responds have attached half-columns : the arcade is now blocked with brickwork. The W. wall is modern except perhaps for the core of the buttresses, which may be of the 12th century and are partly faced with reused 12th and 13th-century ashlar.

Fittings—*Bells :* one, by John Danyell, mid 15th-century, and inscribed "Sit nomen Domini Benedictum," cracked ; bell-frame, partly old. *Coffin :* In nave—of stone with shaped head, probably 13th-century.

Condition—Good, mostly rebuilt.

Secular :—

b(2). WIX ABBEY, house (Plate, p. 231), 60 yards S. of the church, is of two storeys with attics. The walls are of brick with some stone dressings ; the roofs are tiled. The foundations of the destroyed S. wing are of stone and may be of mediaeval date but the house was built in the second half of the 16th century and was of half H-shaped plan with the wings extending towards the W. The porch, between the wings, was added shortly after. The S. wing was destroyed at some uncertain date and the house has been much altered. The W. front has a projecting porch of three storeys with a crow-stepped gable. The outer archway has a rounded head and moulded imposts ; above it is a moulded entablature and a steep pediment flanked by small pedestals. The upper storeys have each a window with a moulded pediment above it ; the lower window has a modern frame, but the upper one is of three transomed lights and is now blocked. The inner doorway of the porch has stop-moulded jambs and a square head. The nail-studded door has moulded fillets, planted on. The rest of the house has been entirely altered.

Condition—Fairly good.

MONUMENTS (3–7).

The following monuments, unless otherwise described, are of the 17th century and of two storeys, timber-framed and plastered or weather-boarded ; the roofs are tiled or thatched. Some of the buildings have original chimney-stacks and exposed ceiling-beams.

Condition—Good, or fairly good, unless noted.

b(3). *Carbonalls*, house, 300 yards N.N.E. of the church, was rebuilt in the 18th century except the back wing which is of the 15th century and has in the N. and S. walls an original doorway with a four-centred head and now blocked. In the E. wall is an original window, with mortices for former bar-mullions. Inside the building is an original tie-beam with a curved brace.

b(4). *Park Hall*, two tenements, about ½ m. S.W. of the church, has cross-wings at the N. and S. ends.

a(5). *Cottage*, in Honeypot Lane, nearly 1 m. S.S.W. of (4).

Condition—Poor.

b(6). *Bardox Farm*, house, ¼ m. E.S.E. of (4).

b(7). *White Hart Inn*, ½ m. S.E. of the church, is of L-shaped plan, with the wings extending towards the E. and S. Inside the building one room has some original panelling with some carved panels above the fireplace.

---

100. WORMINGFORD. (C.b.)

(O.S. 6 in. *(a)*xviii. N.W. *(b)*xviii. S.W.)

Wormingford is a parish on the right bank of the Stour, 6½ m. N.W. of Colchester. The church, Church House and Jenkin's Farm are the principal monuments.

Ecclesiastical :—

a(1). PARISH CHURCH OF ST. ANDREW stands near the N. end of the parish. The walls are of flint-rubble with some admixture of brick ; the dressings are of limestone and Roman brick. and the roofs are tiled. The *Nave* and the *West Tower* were built early in the 12th century. At the beginning of the 14th century the *North Aisle* was added and about the middle of the same century the *Chancel* was rebuilt. A South Porch was added in the 15th century. The church was generally restored in 1870 when the *North Vestry* and *Organ Chamber* were added and the *South Porch* rebuilt.

The W. tower and the N. arcade are interesting examples of their respective periods.

Architectural Description—The *Chancel* (31½ ft. by 19 ft.) has a modern E. window. In the N. wall are two mid 14th-century windows, much restored and each of two trefoiled lights with tracery in a two-centred head with a moulded label ; between them is a modern opening. In the S. wall are two windows similar to those in the N. wall. The mid 14th-century chancel-arch is two-centred and of two orders, the outer moulded and the inner sunk-chamfered ; the chamfered responds have each a semi-octagonal shaft with a moulded capital and base.

The *Nave* (41 ft. by 23½ ft.) has an early 14th-century N. arcade of four bays with two-centred arches of two moulded orders ; the octagonal columns have moulded capitals and bases ; the responds have attached semi-octagonal shafts with moulded capitals and bases. In the S. wall are three windows, the easternmost is of early 14th-century date, much restored and of two trefoiled ogee lights with a quatrefoil in a two-centred head ; the second window is also of two trefoiled ogee lights with tracery in a segmental-pointed head of mid 14th-century date ; the westernmost window is modern, but incorporates some old stones ; further W. is a blocked 12th-century window with a round internal head and Roman brick jambs ; further E. some Roman bricks may indicate the position of a second 12th-century window ; W. of the modern window is a mid or late 14th-century doorway with jambs and two-centred arch of two moulded orders ; above the E. haunch of the arch, externally, is the line of the round head of the 12th-century doorway.

The *North Aisle* (8 ft. wide) is of mid 14th-century date and has in the E. wall a window of two trefoiled lights in a two-centred head almost entirely modern. In the N. wall are three windows similar to that in the E. wall and much restored ; further W. is the N. doorway with chamfered jambs and restored two-centred arch. In the W. wall is a window of a single trefoiled light.

The *West Tower* (13½ ft. square) is of three stages with Roman brick quoins and an early 17th-century embattled parapet of brick, with crocketed pinnacles at the angles. The tower-arch is modern. The N., S. and W. walls have each a narrow early 12th-century window of brick with a round head. The second stage has a similar window in the S. and W. walls, but of 15th or 16th-century brick externally. The bell-chamber has in each wall a larger 12th-century window of brick and with a round head ; that in the E. wall is partly covered by the nave roof and is now blocked.

The *South Porch* is modern, but has a reset outer archway of early 15th-century date, with moulded jambs and two-centred arch in a square head with a moulded label ; the spandrels and label-stops are carved with the symbols of the evangelists each holding a shield with the arms—(*a*) a defaced coat impaling *a lion rampant* (?) ; (*b*) *three cheverons* for Clare ; (*c*) *a fesse indented between three martlets* for Rokell ; and (*d*) *a lion rampant*. The *Roof* of the N. aisle is of early 16th-century date with moulded wall-plates and tie-beams with curved braces.

Fittings—*Bells :* four, said to be, 1st and 2nd by Richard Bowler, 1591 ; 3rd by Joanna Sturdy, 15th-century and inscribed " Sit Nomen Domini Benedictum I.S." *Brasses and Indents.* Brasses : In tower—(1) of civilian and two wives in large hats, indents of inscription-plate and groups of children, early 17th-century ; (2) of civilian in long gown and pointed shoes, collar inlaid with lead, indents of inscription-plate and two shields,

c. 1450. Indents : In tower—of woman, inscription-plate and four shields, 15th-century ; (2) of inscription-plate. *Font :* In churchyard—octagonal bowl, 14th or 15th - century, much weathered. *Floor-slab :* In tower — to John Potter, 1710, with achievement of arms. *Glass :* In chancel—in N.W. window, borders, grisaille, tops of tabernacle work and a foliated roundel, 14th-century ; in S.W. window, two shields of arms, probably for Hoskyns (Plate, p. 192), not in their original state but of 14th-century material ; in tracery foliated roundel and grisaille, 14th-century, and a 16th-century shield of arms. *Piscina :* In chancel—with trefoiled ogee head and septfoiled drain, 14th-century, sill partly restored. *Plate :* includes Elizabethan cup with band of incised ornament. *Screen :* modern, but incorporating parts of moulded and buttressed posts, moulded rail, four trefoiled and sub-cusped heads with elaborate tracery, and sub-cusped ogee head with tracery, to doorway, 15th-century. *Sedilia :* In chancel—sill of S.E. window carried down to form seats, 14th-century. *Stoup :* In S. porch—with moulded jambs and four-centred head, 15th-century, bowl destroyed. Condition—Good, much restored.

Secular :—

a(2). HOMESTEAD MOAT, at Bowdens, nearly 1 m. N.E. of the church.

a(3). GARNONS, house and moat, 1¼ m. E.N.E. of the church. The *House* is of two storeys, timber-framed and plastered ; the roofs are tiled. It was built in the 17th century and has two gabled cross-wings at the W. end and a long outbuilding to the S.W.

The *Moat* partly surrounds the house and there are traces of an outer enclosure.

Condition—Of house, good.

b(4). WOOD HALL, house and moat, ½ m. S. of the church. The *House* is of two storeys, timber-framed and plastered ; the roofs are tiled. It was built probably late in the 16th century with a cross-wing at the E. end. There are modern additions on the E. and W. The upper storey projects at the N. end of the cross-wing and has a bressumer carved with a form of guilloche ornament.

The *Moat* surrounds the house.

Condition—Of house, good, much altered.

b(5). ROTCHFORDS, house and moat, nearly ¾ m. S. of (4). The *House* is of two storeys, timber-framed and plastered ; the roofs are tiled. It was built probably in the 15th century and has a 16th-century staircase-wing on the E. side. The house was much altered and refronted in the 18th century. The early 17th-century central and N. chimney-stacks have grouped diagonal shafts.

Inside the building the middle room has a 16th-century moulded ceiling-beam and the N. room is lined with panelling of the same date. In the wall between the main block and the staircase are remains of an original window, with mortices for diamond-shaped mullions. On the first floor one room has early 17th-century panelling with a fluted frieze. The E. wing has an original king-post roof-truss.

The *Moat* partly surrounds the house.

Condition—Of house, good, much altered.

a(6). CHURCH HALL, N. of the church, is of two storeys, timber-framed and plastered; the roofs are tiled. It was built probably early in the 16th century with cross-wings at the N. and S. ends. Adjoining the N. wing is a small staircase-wing of red brick. The early 17th-century chimney-stack to the N. wing has grouped diagonal shafts. Inside the building the front room of the N. wing has an original moulded ceiling-beam and some late 16th-century panelling with fluted pilasters. The S. wing has remains of the original projecting upper storey, now underbuilt. A window in the main block has a roundel of 16th-century glass with a crowned double rose and the initials E.R. On the first floor is an original doorway with a three-centred head. The main block has an original king-post roof-truss and the N. wing has a cambered tie-beam.

Condition—Good.

a(7). CHURCH HOUSE, E. of church, is of two storeys, timber-framed and plastered except the S. wing which is of red brick; the roofs are tiled. It was built in the 16th century and has cross-wings at the N. and S. ends. The S. wing has a shaped Dutch gable at the W. end and two five-light transomed windows with square heads. In the S. wall of the same wing is a similar three-light window and in the E. wall are two more windows of similar character. The central chimney-stack has grouped diagonal shafts. Inside the building are some exposed ceiling-beams and an early 18th-century dog-gate to the staircase.

Condition—Good.

MONUMENTS (8–13).

The following monuments, unless otherwise described, are of the 17th century and of two storeys, timber-framed and plastered; the roofs are tiled or thatched. Some of the buildings have original chimney-stacks and exposed ceiling-beams. Condition—Good, or fairly good.

a(8). *Cottage*, 30 yards S. of (7).

a(9). *Cottage*, 60 yards S. of (8), has exposed timber-framing externally.

a(10). *The Grange*, house, about ¼ m. E. of the church, has been much altered and enlarged. Inside the building is some panelling of *c.* 1600, brought from elsewhere.

b(11). *Crown Inn*, ½ m. S.S.W. of the church, has exposed timber-framing on the S. front.

b(12). *Jenkin's Farm*, house, ½ m. S. of (11), was built *c.* 1583. Probably early in the 17th century the N. wall and the N. part of the W. front were refaced with brick. In the middle of the W. front is a porch with a projecting upper storey and a projecting gable both with carved bressumers; the angle posts of the ground floor have moulded capitals and curved brackets carved with the initials and date W.L. A.D. 1583. In the brick wall of the N. part of the front is a square-headed window of three lights, with a moulded label; a second window is now all modern except the label. On the first floor is a third window of two lights and now blocked. There are similar windows in the N. wall. At the back is an original window, now blocked, and with moulded mullions. On the first floor are two original projecting windows with moulded sills and mullions. The S. chimney-stack has the bases of two octagonal shafts. Inside the building are three original doorways with three-centred heads and one old panelled door.

b(13). *The Grove*, house, about 1¼ m. S.E. of the church, is largely modern, but incorporates a rectangular block, probably of the 16th century.

---

101. WRABNESS. (F.b.)

(O.S. 6 in. xx. S.E.)

Wrabness is a small parish on the S. side of the Stour estuary and 5½ m. W. of Harwich.

Ecclesiastical :—

(1). PARISH CHURCH OF ALL SAINTS stands near the middle of the parish. The walls are of septaria-rubble and brick with dressings of limestone; the roofs are tiled. The *Nave* was built early in the 12th century. Early in the 14th century the *Chancel* was rebuilt. In the 15th century the upper part of the nave was rebuilt and in 1697 the E. wall was rebuilt. The church has been restored in modern times, the nave lengthened towards the W., and the *North Vestry* and *South Porch* added.

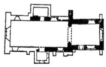

Architectural Description—The *Chancel* (20¾ ft. by 15½ ft.) has a modern E. window. In the N. wall is a window all modern except the 14th-century rear-arch. In the S. wall is a window similar to that in the N. wall and further W. is a modern doorway. The early 14th-century chancel-arch is two-centred and of two chamfered orders, the outer continuous and the inner resting on attached shafts with moulded capitals.

The *Nave* (42½ ft. by 18¾ ft.) has in the N. wall two windows ; the eastern is modern except the 15th-century moulded label with head-stops and perhaps the plastered rear-arch ; the western is entirely modern ; between them is the early 12th-century N. doorway with a round arch of two plain orders enclosing a rubble tympanum supported by a segmental arch ; the jambs have each a free shaft with cushion capital and a chamfered abacus continued round the inner order ; at the E. end of the wall is the late 15th-century lower doorway of the former rood-loft staircase ; it has hollow-chamfered jambs and four-centred arch and is now blocked. In the S. wall are two windows all modern except the 15th-century moulded label of the eastern ; between them is the early 15th-century S. doorway partly restored and with moulded jambs, two-centred arch and label ; the moulding is enriched with carved flowers and two shields ; above the doorway is part of the head of the early 12th-century doorway with a billety label.

The *Roof* of the E. part of the nave is of late 15th-century date and of simple hammer-beam type with moulded main timbers ; the spandrels of the braces below the hammer-beams are carved with foliage.

In the churchyard is a square timber-framed structure, to hold the bells, probably of the 17th century.

Fittings —- *Coffin-lid :* In porch — of Purbeck marble, with foliated cross on stepped calvary, 13th-century. *Font :* octagonal bowl with panelled sides, each carved with an evangelistic symbol or a seated saint, all defaced ; underside of bowl with half-angels at the angles and rosettes between them, buttressed stem with defaced figures under canopies, 15th-century. *Miscellanea :* In church-yard and rectory garden, fragments of window jambs, etc.

Condition—Good, much altered.

Secular :—

(2). WRABNESS HALL, 120 yards E. of the church, is of two storeys, timber-framed and plastered ; the roofs are covered with slate. The E. wing of the house was built in the 15th century and the W. wing was added or rebuilt in the 16th century. Inside the building the W. wing has original moulded ceiling-beams and there are exposed ceiling-beams in the E. wing.

Condition—Good.

(3). COTTAGE, two tenements, on S. side of road, about ¾ m. S. of the church, is of two storeys, timber-framed and plastered ; the roofs are thatched. It was built early in the 17th century and has some exposed ceiling-beams.

Condition—Good.

Colchester, Holy Trinity Church. Label-stop, 14th-century.

OF THE MEANING ATTACHED TO THE TECHNICAL TERMS USED IN THE INVENTORY.

Abacus.—The uppermost member of a capital.

Alb.—Long linen robe, with close sleeves ; worn by clerks of all grades.

Alettes *or* **Allettes.**—In armour, plates usually rectangular, of metal or leather covered with cloth or other light material, fastened by a lace to the back or sides of the shoulders ; they commonly display armorial bearings ; worn *c.* 1275 to *c.* 1325.

Altar-tomb.—A modern term for a tomb of stone or marble resembling, but not used as, an altar.

Amess.—Fur cape with hood, and long tails in front ; worn by clerks of the higher grades.

Amice.—A linen strip with embroidered apparel, placed upon the head coifwise by a clerk before vesting himself in an alb, after which it is pushed back, and the apparel then appears like a collar.

Ankar-hold.—The dwelling house of an ankorite or recluse.

Apparels.—Rectangular pieces of embroidery on alb, amice, etc.

Apse.—The semi-circular or polygonal end of a chancel or other part of a church.

Arabesque.—A peculiar kind of strap-ornament in low relief, common in Moorish architecture, and found in 16th and 17th-century work in England.

Arcade.—A range of arches carried on piers or columns.

Arch.—The following are some of the most usual forms :—
Segmental :—A single arc struck from a centre below the springing line.
Pointed or two-centred :—Two arcs struck from centres on the springing line, and meeting at the apex with a point.
Segmental-pointed :—A pointed arch, struck from two centres below the springing line.
Equilateral :—A pointed arch struck with radii equal to the span.
Lancet :—A pointed arch struck with radii greater than the span.
Three-centred, elliptical :—Formed with three arcs, the middle or uppermost struck from a centre below the springing line.
Four-centred, depressed, Tudor :—A pointed arch of four arcs, the two outer and lower arcs struck from centres on the springing line and the two inner and upper arcs from centres below the springing line. Sometimes the two upper arcs are replaced by straight lines.
Ogee :—A pointed arch of four or more arcs, the two uppermost or middle arcs being reversed, *i.e.*, convex instead of concave to the base line.
Relieving :—An arch generally of rough construction, placed in the wall above the true arch or head of an opening, to relieve it of some of the superincumbent weight.
Stilted :—An arch with its springing line raised above the level of the imposts.
Skew :—An arch not at right angles laterally with its jambs.

Archbishops' Vestments.—Buskins, sandals, amice, alb, girdle, stole, fanon, tunic, dalmatic, chasuble, pall ; gloves, ring, mitre ; an archbishop carries a crosier but, in later times, holds a cross-staff for distinction.

Architrave.—A moulded enrichment to the jambs and head of a doorway or window opening ; the lowest member of an entablature (*q.v.*).

Argent.—In heraldry, white or silver, the latter being the word used in mediaeval English blazonry.

Armet.—*See* " Helmet."

Arming Doublet.—Sleeved coat worn under armour ; 15th and 16th-centuries.

Arming Points.—Laces for attaching parts of armour together.

Arris.—An edge or angle.

Articulation.—The joining of several plates of armour to form a flexible defence.

Ashlar.—Masonry wrought to an even face and square edges.

Aumbry.—*See* " Locker."

Azure.—In heraldry, blue.

Baberies.—The " childlike conceits " and other carvings on the underside of misericords.

Badge of Ulster.—A silver scocheon charged with a red hand upraised, borne in the arms of baronets of England, Ireland, and the United Kingdom.

Bailey.—A court attached to a mount or other fortified enclosure.

Ball-flower.—In architecture, a decoration peculiar to the first quarter of the 14th century, consisting of a globular flower of three petals enclosing a small ball.

Banded Mail.—Mail shown with narrow bands, between rows of rings ; construction uncertain.

Bar.—*See* " Fesse."

Barbe.—Pleated linen covering for chin and throat, worn by widows and women under vows.

Barbican.—An advanced protective work before the gate of a town or castle, or at the head of a bridge.

Barbican Mount.—A mound advanced from the main defences to protect an entrance.

Barge-board. — A board, often carved, fixed to the edge of a gabled roof, a short distance from the face of the wall.

Barnack stone.—A shelly oolitic limestone ; from Barnack, Northamptonshire.

Barrel-vaulting.—*See* " Vaulting."

Barrow.—A burial mound.

Barry.—In heraldry, an even number of horizontal divisions in a shield, normally six, but sometimes four or eight. When a greater and indefinite number of divisions appear the word **Burely** is used.

Bascinet.—Steel head-piece worn with camail, sometimes fitted with vizor.

Baston.—*See* " Bend."

Battled.—In heraldry, the edge of a chief, bend, bar, or the like drawn in the fashion of the battlements of a wall.

Bead.—A small round moulding.

Bell-capital.—A form of capital of which the chief characteristic is a reversed bell between the neck moulding and upper moulding ; the bell is often enriched with carving.

Bend.—In heraldry, a band aslant and across the shield, commonly from the dexter chief. A narrow bend over other charges is called a **Baston.** The baston with the ends cut off, drawn in the other direction across the shield is a mark of bastardy in post-mediaeval heraldry. A field or charge divided bend-wise into an equal number of parts, normally six, is said to be **bendy.**

Bendwise.—In the direction of a bend.

Bendy.—In heraldry, divided bendwise into an equal number of divisions, normally six.

Berm.—A platform on the slope of a rampart.

Besagues.—Small plates worn in front of the arm-pits.

Bevor.—Plate defence for chin and throat.

Bezant.—In heraldry, a gold roundel or disc.

Billet.—In heraldry, a small oblong figure; also an architectural ornament chiefly used in the 11th and 12th centuries.

Billety.—In heraldry, a field or charge powdered with billets.

Bishops' Vestments.—Same as an archbishop's, but without pall, and a bishop carries a crosier, and not a cross.

Bolection-moulding.—A moulding raised above the general plane of the framework of the door or panelling in which it is set.

Border.—In heraldry, an edging round a coat of arms, whether simple or quartered.

Boss.—A projecting square or round ornament, covering the intersections of the ribs in a vault, panelled ceiling or roof, etc.

Bouget *or* **Water-bouget.**—A pair of leather bottles, borne as a heraldic charge.

Bowtell.—A continuous convex moulding; another term for roll-moulding.

Brace.—In roof construction, a subsidiary timber inserted to strengthen the framing of a truss. *Wind-brace,* a subsidiary timber inserted between the purlins and principals of a roof to resist the pressure of the wind.

Brassart.—Plate armour defence for the arm.

Bressumer.—A beam forming the direct support of an upper wall or timber-framing.

Brick-nogging.—The brick-work filling the spaces between the uprights of a timber-framed building.

Brick-work.—*Header :*—A brick laid so that the end only appears on the face of the wall.
Stretcher :—A brick laid so that one side only appears on the face of the wall.
English Bond :—A method of laying bricks so that alternate courses on the face of the wall are composed of headers or stretchers only.
Flemish Bond :—A method of laying bricks so that alternate headers and stretchers appear in each course on the face of a wall.

Brigandine.—Coat of padded cloth and very small plates (of metal).

Broach-spire.—*See* " Spire."

Broach-stop.—A half-pyramidal stop against a chamfer to bring out the edge of a stone or beam to a right angle.

Buff Coat.—Coat of heavy leather.

Burgonet.—*See* " Helmet."

Buskins.—Stockings reaching to the knee; worn by archbishops, bishops, and mitred abbots.

Butterfly Head-dress.—Large, of lawn and gauze on wire, late 15th-century.

Buttress.—A mass of masonry or brick-work projecting from or built against a wall to give additional strength.
Angle-buttresses :—Two meeting, or nearly meeting, at an angle of 90° at the corner of a building.
Diagonal-buttress :—One placed against the right angle formed by two walls, and more or less equi-angular with both.
Flying-buttress :—A butting arch transmitting thrust from a wall to an outer buttress.

Cable-moulding.—A moulding carved in the form of a cable.

Camail.—Hood of mail; first worn attached to hauberk, then separate from it with tippet of mail over shoulders, and, in the 14th century, attached to bascinet.

Cambered (applied to a beam).—Curved so that the middle is higher than the ends.

Canonical Quire Habit.—Surplice, amess, cope.

Canopy.—A projection or hood over a door, window, etc., and the covering above a tomb or niche; also the representation of the same on a brass.

Cantilever.—A beam supported at a point short of one end, which end carries a load, the other end being fixed.

Canton.—A word applied in modern heraldry to the Quarter which is commonly given less space than in the older examples.

Caryatid.—Pillar carved as a woman.

Casement.—1. A wide hollow moulding in window jambs, etc.
2. The hinged part of a window.
3. The sinking for a brass in a slab.

Cassock.—Long, close-sleeved gown; worn by all clerks.

Cellarer's Building *or* **Cellar.**—In monastic planning that part of the Convent under the control of the cellarer containing store-rooms, wine-vaults, etc. In Cistercian monasteries it also included the Frater and Dorter of the Lay brethren (conversi). Its ordinary position in all orders was on the W. side of the cloister.

Central-chimney Type of House.—*See* " Houses."

Chamfer.—The small plane formed when the sharp edge or arris of stone or wood is cut away, usually at an angle of 45°; when the plane is concave it is termed a *hollow chamfer,* and when the plane is sunk below its arrises, or edges, a *sunk chamfer.*

Chantry-chapel.—A small chapel usually occupying part of a large building, specially attached to a chantry.

Chasuble.—A nearly circular cape with central hole for head, worn by priests and bishops at mass. It is put on over all the other vestments.

Chausses.—Leg defences of mail.

Checky.—In heraldry, a field or charge divided into squares or checkers.

Cheveron.—In heraldry, a charge resembling a pair of rafters of a roof; sometimes used decoratively.

Chief.—In heraldry, the upper part of the shield. Cut off from the rest of the field by a horizontal line and having its own tincture, it becomes one of the charges of the shield, covering a space which occupies from a third to a half, or even more of it.

Chrismatory.—A box containing the holy oils for anointing.

Chrisom-child.—Child swaddled in a chrisom-cloth.

Cinquefoil.—1. *See* " Foil."
2. An heraldic flower of five petals.

Clearstorey.—An upper storey, pierced by windows, in the main walls of a church. The same term is applicable in the case of a domestic building.

Close-helmet.—*See* " Helmet."

Clunch.—A local name for the lower chalk limestone, composed of chalk and clay.

Cockatrice.—A monster with the head and legs of a cock and the tail of a wyver.

Coif.—Small close hood, covering head only.

Collar-beam.—A horizontal beam framed to and serving to tie a pair of rafters together some distance above the wall-plate level.

Combed Work.—The decoration of plaster surfaces by " combing " it into various patterns.

Console.—A bracket with a compound curved outline.

Cope.—A processional and quire vestment shaped like a cloak, and fastened across the chest by a band or brooch ; worn by clerks of most grades.

Coped-slab.—A slab of which the upper face is ridged down the middle, sometimes hipped at each end.

Cops, Knee and Elbow.—Knee and elbow defences of leather or plate.

Corbel.—A projecting stone or piece of timber for the support of a superincumbent weight.

Cotises.—In heraldry, pairs of narrow bands, in the form of bends, pales, fesses, or cheverons, and borne accompanying one of those charges on each side of it.

Counter-coloured.—In heraldry, term applied in cases where the field and charges exchange tinctures on either side of a dividing line.

Counter-scarp.—The reverse slope of a ditch facing towards the place defended.

Courtyard Type of House.—*See* " Houses."

Cove.—A concave under-surface.

Cover-paten.—A cover to a communion cup, sometimes used as a paten.

Credence.—A shelf, niche, or table on which the vessels, etc., for mass are placed.

Crest, cresting.—1. A device worn upon the helm. 2. An ornamental finish along the top of a screen, etc.

Crockets.—Carvings projecting at regular intervals from the vertical or sloping sides of parts of a building, such as spires, canopies, hood-moulds, etc.

Crosier, or Pastoral Staff.—A tall staff ending in an ornamental crook carried as a mark of authority by archbishops, bishops, and heads of monastic houses, including abbesses and prioresses.

Cross.—In its simplest form in heraldry, a pale combined with a fesse, as the St. George's Cross ; there are many other varieties, of which the following are the most common :—*Crosslet*,—with a smaller arm crossing each main arm ; *Crosslet fitchy*,—having the lowest arm spiked or pointed ; Crosslet *flowered* or *flory*,— having the arms headed with *fleurs-de-lis* ; *Crosslet formy*,—arms widening from the centre, and square at the ends. The old forms of the crosslet have, as a rule, the arms ending as in trefoils with rounded petals ; *Plain crosses*,—with four equal arms not extending to the edges of the shield ; *Moline* (or *mill-rind*), —with the arms split or forked at the ends ; *Paty*,—as a cross *formy*, but with the arms notched in two places at the ends, giving them a form which may approach that of a blunt head of a fleur-de-lis ; *Potent* (or *Jerusalem*),—having a small transverse arm at the extreme end of each main arm ; *Tau* (or *Anthony*),— in the form of a T.

Cross-loop.—Narrow slits or openings in a wall, in the form of a cross, generally with circular enlargements at the ends.

Cross-staff.—Staff terminating in a cross ; carried before archbishops, who are usually shown holding it on effigies, brasses, etc.

Cross-vaulting.—*See* " Vaulting."

Crow-stepped.—A term applied to gables, the coping of which rises in a series of steps.

Crusily.—In heraldry, covered or powdered with crosslets.

Cuirass.—Breast and back plates of metal or leather.

Cushion-capital.—A cubic capital with its lower angles rounded off to a circular shaft.

Cusps (*cusping, cusped heads, sub-cusps*).—The projecting points forming the foils in Gothic windows, arches, panels, etc. ; they were frequently ornamented at the ends, or *cusp-points*, with leaves, flowers, berries, etc.

Dagging.—Cutting of edges of garments into slits and foliations.

Dalmatic.—The special vestment at mass of a deacon ; a loose tunic of moderate length, slit up sides, with wide sleeves and fringed edges.

Dance.—In heraldry, a fesse or bar drawn zigzagwise, or *dancetty*.

Deacons' Vestments (Mass).—Amice, alb, stole (worn over left shoulder), dalmatic, and fanon.

Demi-brassart.—Plate defence for outside of arm.

Dexter.—In heraldry, the right-hand side of a shield as held.

Diaper.—Decoration of surfaces with squares, diamonds, and other patterns.

Dimidiated.—In heraldry, applied to the halving of two shields and joining a half of each to make a new shield.

Dog-legged Staircase.—Two flights of stairs in opposite directions.

Dog-tooth Ornament.—A typical 13th-century carved ornament consisting of a series of pyramidal flowers of four petals ; used to cover hollow mouldings.

Dormer-window.—A vertical window on the slope of a roof, and having a roof of its own.

Dorter.—In monastic buildings, the common sleeping apartments or dormitory.

Double-ogee.—*See* " Ogee."

Dovetail.—A carpenter's joint for two boards, one with a series of projecting pieces resembling doves' tails fitting into the other with similar hollows ; in heraldry, an edge formed like a dovetail joint.

Drawbar.—A wood bolt inside a doorway, sliding when out of use into a long channel in the thickness of the wall.

Dressings.—The stones used about an angle, window, or other feature when worked to a finished face, whether smooth, tooled in various ways, moulded, or sculptured.

Drip-stone.—*See* " Hood-mould."

Easter Sepulchre.—A locker in the north wall of a chancel wherein the Host was placed from Good Friday to Easter Day, to typify Christ's burial after His crucifixion. A temporary wooden structure in imitation of a Sepulchre with lights, etc., was often placed before it, but in some parts of the country this was a more permanent and ornate structure of stone.

Eaves.—The under part of a sloping roof overhanging a wall.

Embrasures.—The openings, indents, or sinkings in an embattled parapet.

Enceinte.—The main outline of a fort.

Engaged Shafts.—Shafts cut out of the solid or connected with the jamb, pier, respond, or other part against which they stand.

Engrailed.—In heraldry, edged with a series of concave curves.

Entablature.—In Classic or Renaissance architecture, the horizontal superstructure above the columns or jambs of an opening, consisting of an *architrave*, *frieze*, and *cornice*.

Ermine or Ermines.—The fur most frequently used in heraldry; white powdered with black tails. Other varieties are sometimes found, as sable ermined with silver, and in more modern heraldry, gold ermined with sable, and sable ermined with gold.

E Type of House.—*See* " Houses."

Fanon.—A strip of embroidery probably at one time a handkerchief, held in the left hand, or worn hanging from the left wrists by bishops, priests and deacons. It is often called a maniple.

Fan-vaulting.—*See* " Vaulting."

Fascia.—A plain or moulded board covering the plate of a projecting upper storey of timber, and masking the ends of the cantilever joists which support it.

Feretory.—A place or chamber for a shrine.

Fesse.—In heraldry, a horizontal band athwart the shield. When more than one fesse is borne they are known as **Bars.**

Finial.—A formal bunch of foliage or similar ornament at the top of a pinnacle, gable, canopy, etc.

Fitchy.—*See* " Cross."

Flanches.—In heraldry, the side portions of a shield, bounded by convex lines issuing from the chief.

Foil (*trefoil, quatrefoil, cinquefoil, multifoil*, etc.).—A leaf-shaped curve formed by the cusping or feathering in an opening or panel.

Foliated (of a capital, corbel, etc.).—Carved with leaf ornament.

Fosse.—A ditch.

Four-centred Arch.—*See* " Arch."

Frater.—The refectory or dining-hall of a monastery.

Fret or Fretty.—In heraldry, a charge formed of a number of bastons drawn from each side of the shield, and interlaced like lattice-work. In modern heraldry, the charge of a fret takes the form of a narrow saltire interlacing a voided lozenge, while the word *Fretty* is kept for the older form.

Frieze.—The middle division in an *entablature*, between the architrave and the *cornice ;* generally any band of ornament or colour immediately below a cornice.

Funeral helm.—A trophy, in the form of a crested head-piece, carried at the funerals and placed over the tombs of important personages.

Fusil.—In heraldry, a word applied to the pieces into which a fesse is divided by engrailing or indenting.

Fylfot.—A peculiar cruciform figure, each arm of which is bent to form a right angle.

Gable.—The wall at the end of a ridged roof, generally triangular, sometimes semi-circular, and often with an outline of various curves, then called *curvilinear.*

Gadlings.—Spikes or knobs on plate gauntlets.

Galleted or garretted Joints.—Wide joints in rubble or masonry into which thin pieces of flint or stone have been inserted.

Gambeson.—Garment of padded cloth worn under hauberk or as sole defence.

Gardant.—In heraldry, an epithet of a beast whose full face is seen.

Gargoyle.—A carved projecting figure pierced to carry off the rain-water from the roof of a building.

Gimel-bar or Gemel-bar.—In heraldry, a pair of narrow bars lying close to one another.

Gipon.—Close-fitting vest of cloth, worn over armour *c.* 1350 to *c.* 1410.

Gobony.—In heraldry, checkers or panes of a metal alternating with a colour, or either with a fur.

Gorget.—Plate defence for neck and throat.

Greek Cross.—A plain cross with four equal arms.

Griffon or Griffin.—A winged monster with the fore parts of an eagle, and the hinder parts of a lion.

Groining, Groined Vault.—*See* " Vaulting."

Guige.—Strap from which shield was suspended.

Guilloche-pattern.—An ornament consisting of two or more intertwining wavy bands.

Gules.—In heraldry, red.

Gussets.—Pieces of flexible armour placed in gaps of plate defences.

Gyronny or Gironny.—In heraldry, the field of a shield divided into six, eight or more gussets meeting at a point in the middle.

Haketon.—Studded, stiffened or quilted body defence, of cloth, leather and metal, with moderately long skirts.

Half-H type of House.—*See* " Houses."

Hall and cellar type of House.—*See* " Houses."

Hammer-beams.—Horizontal brackets of a roof projecting at the wall-plate level, and resembling the two ends of a tie-beam with its middle part cut away ; they are supported by braces (or struts), and help to diminish lateral pressure by reducing the span. Sometimes there is a second and even a third upper series of these brackets.

Hatchment.—A heraldic display in a rectangular frame, commonly set lozenge-wise.

Hauberk.—Shirt of chain or other mail.

Helm.—Complete barrel or dome-shaped head defence of plate.

Helmet.—A light headpiece ; various forms are : Armet, Burgonet, close Helmet, all similar in principle.

Hipped roof.—A roof with sloped instead of vertical ends. *Half-hipped,* a roof whose ends are partly vertical and partly sloped.

Hood-mould (*label, drip-stone*).—A projecting moulding on the face of a wall above an arch, doorway, or window ; in some cases it follows the form of the arch, and in others is square in outline.

Houses.—These are classified as far as possible under the following definitions :—

1. *Hall and cellar type :*—Hall on first floor ; rooms beneath generally vaulted ; examples as early as the 12th century.

2. *H type :*—Hall between projecting wings, one containing living rooms, the other the offices. The usual form of a mediaeval house, employed, with variations, down to the 17th century.

3. *L type :*—Hall and one wing, generally for small houses.

4. *E type :*—Hall with two wings and a middle porch ; generally of the 16th and 17th centuries.

5. *Half-H type :*—A variation of the E type without the middle porch.

6. *Courtyard type :*—House built round a court ; sometimes only three ranges of buildings with or without an enclosing wall and gateway on the fourth side.

7. *Central-chimney type :*—(Rectangular plan), small houses only.

Impaled.—*See* " Parted."

Indent.—The sinking or casement in a slab for a monumental brass.

Indented.—In heraldry, notched like the teeth of a saw.

Infirmary.—In monastic planning, a distinct block of buildings, generally including a hall, misericord, kitchen and chapel, and devoted to the use of the infirm or aged.

Invected.—In modern heraldry, edged with a series of convex curves.

Jambs.—1. The sides of an archway, doorway, window, or other opening.
2. In heraldry, legs of lions, etc.
3. In armour, plate defences for lower leg.

Jazerine.—Armour of small plates on leather or cloth.

Keep.—The great tower or stronghold in a castle; of greater height and strength than the other buildings.

Keystone.—The middle stone in an arch.

King-post.—The middle vertical post in a roof truss.

Kneeler.—Stone at the foot of a gable.

Label.—*See* "Hood-mould." In heraldry, a narrow horizontal band (lying across the chief of a shield), from which small strips, generally three or five, called *pieces*, depend at right angles.

Lancet.—A long narrow window with a pointed head, typical of the 13th century.

Latin Cross.—A plain cross with the bottom arm longer than the other three.

Latten.—A term applied to the alloy of copper, zinc, &c., used in the manufacture of memorial brasses, &c.

Lenten Veil.—A cloth or veil hung across the chancel or presbytery between the stalls and the altar, during Lent.

Leopard.—In heraldry, a lion showing its full face; always passant (unless otherwise emblazoned), as in the three leopards of England.

Lierne-vault.—*See* "Vaulting."

Linces, linchets or lynchets.—Terraces on a hill-side formed by the gradual banking of ploughed earth between the main furrows.

Linen-fold panelling.—Panelling ornamented with a conventional representation of folded linen.

Lintel.—The horizontal beam or stone bridging an opening.

Lion.—In heraldry, face in profile and (unless otherwise emblazoned) always rampant.

Liripipe.—Long tail of cloth attached to hooded tippet of the 14th century; the whole finally developed into a form of turban called *Liripipe head-dress.*

Locker (*Aumbry*).—A small cupboard formed in a wall.

Loop.—A small narrow light in a turret, etc.; often unglazed.

Louvre *or* **luffer.**—A lantern-like structure surmounting the roof of a hall or other building, with openings for ventilation or the escape of smoke, usually crossed by slanting boards to exclude rain.

Low-side window.—A grated, unglazed, and shuttered window with a low sill, *i.e.*, within a few feet of the floor, in the N. or S. wall of the chancel near its W. end, probably the window at which the sacring bell was rung.

Lozenge.—In heraldry, a charge like the diamond in a pack of cards.

L type of house.—*See* "Houses."

Luce.—In heraldry, a fish (pike).

Lychgate.—A covered gateway at the entrance of a churchyard, beneath which the bier is rested at a funeral.

Mail Skirt.—Skirt of chain mail worn under taces and tuiles.

Mail Standard.—Collar of chain mail.

Manche, Maunche.—A lady's sleeve with a long pendent lappet; a heraldic charge.

Maniple.—*See* "Fanon."

Mantle or Mantling.—In heraldry, a cloth hung over the hinder part of a helm; the edges were fantastically dagged and slit.

Martlet.—A martin, shown sometimes in heraldry without feet.

Mask-stop.—A stop at the end of a hood-mould, bearing a distant resemblance to a human face; generally of the 12th and 13th centuries.

Mass Vestments.—These included the amice, alb, and girdle (which were worn by all clerks) to which a sub-deacon added the tunicle, fanon and stole (over one shoulder only) and the priest the fanon, stole (over both shoulders) and chasuble. Bishops and certain privileged abbots wore the tunicle and dalmatic under the chasuble, with the mitre, gloves, and ring, and buskins and sandals. Archbishops used the pall in addition to all the foregoing. Bishops, abbots, and archbishops alike carried crosiers, and in the same way, but an archbishop had likewise a cross carried before him for dignity, and he is generally represented holding one for distinction. The mass vestments were sometimes worn over the quire habit, and the hood of the grey amess can often be seen on effigies hanging beyond the amice apparel at the back of the neck.

Merlon.—The solid part of an embattled parapet between the embrasures.

Mezzanine.—A subordinate storey between two main floors of a building.

Mill-rind (*Fer-de-moline*).—The iron affixed to the centre of a millstone; a common heraldic charge. In early heraldry the name given to the mill-rind cross, or cross moline.

Misericord.—1. An indulgence in the form of a folding seat of a quire-stall, having a broad edge or bracket on the underside, which can be used as a seat by the occupant when standing during a long office.
2. In monastic planning, a small hall, generally attached to the Infirmary, in which better food than the ordinary was supplied for special reasons.

Mitred Abbots' Vestments.—Same as a bishop's.

Modillions.—Brackets under the cornice in Classic architecture.

Molet.—In heraldry, a star of five or six points, drawn with straight lines. When the lines are wavy it is called a *Star.* A molet with a round hole in the middle is called a *Rowel.*

Morse.—Large clasp or brooch fastening cope across the breast.

Mullion.—A vertical post, standard, or upright dividing an opening into lights.

Muntin.—The intermediate uprights in the framing of a door, screen, or panel, butting into or stopped by the rails.

Mutules.—In Classic and Renaissance architecture, small flat brackets under the cornice of the Doric order.

Nasal.—Plate of a headpiece to protect nose.

Nebuly.—Heraldic term for a line or edge, following the fashion of the mediaeval artists' conventional cloud.

Neck-moulding.—The narrow moulding round the bottom of a capital.

Newel.—The central post in a circular or winding staircase; also the principal posts at the angles of a dog-legged or well-staircase.

Nogging.—The filling, generally of brick, between the posts, etc. of a timber-framed house.

Ogee.—A compound curve of two parts, one convex, the other concave; a *double-ogee* moulding is formed by two ogees meeting at their convex ends.

Or.—In heraldry, gold ; a word which, like *argent*, was established in English blazon in the second half of the 16th century.

Orders of Arches.—Receding or concentric rings of voussoirs.

Oriel Window.—A projecting bay-window carried upon corbels or brackets.

Orle.—In heraldry, a term used to describe a voided scocheon, or a number of small charges, as martlets or the like.

Orphreys.—Strips of embroidery on vestments.

" Out of the Solid."—Mouldings worked on the styles, rails, etc., of framing, instead of being fixed on to them.

Oversailing Courses.—A number of brick or stone courses, each course projecting beyond the one below it.

Ovolo moulding.—A Classic moulding forming a quarter round in section.

Pale.—In heraldry, a vertical band down the middle of a shield.

Palimpsest.—1. Of a brass : reused by engraving the back of an older engraved plate.
2. Of a wall-painting : superimposed on an earlier painting.

Pall.—1. In ecclesiastical vestments, a narrow strip of lambswool, having an open loop in the middle, and weighted ends ; it is ornamented with a number of crosses and forms the distinctive mark of an archbishop ; it is worn round the neck, above the other vestments.
2. A cloth covering a hearse.

Paly.—In heraldry, a shield divided by lines palewise, normally into six divisions, unless otherwise emblazoned.

Panache.—A plume or bush of feathers worn on the helm.

Pargeting.—Ornamental plaster work on the surface of a wall.

Parted or Party.—In heraldry, a term used when a shield is divided down the middle. When two coats of arms are marshalled, each in one of these divisions, the one is said to be party or parted with the other, or, in the words of the later heraldry, to be impaling it. The word *party* or *parted* is also used for other specified divisions, as *party bendwise*.

Parvise.—Now generally used to denote a chamber above a porch.

Passant (of beasts, etc.).—In heraldry, walking and looking forward—head in profile.

Pastoral Staff.—*See* " Crosier."

Paten.—A plate for holding the Bread at the celebration of the Holy Communion.

Paty (*cross*).—*See* " Cross."

Pauldron.—Plate defence for the shoulders.

Pediment.—A low-pitched gable used in Classical and Renaissance architecture above a portico, at the end of a building, and above doors, windows, niches, etc. ; sometimes the middle part is omitted, forming a " *broken* " *pediment*.

Perk.—A perch on which to hang vestments.

Pheon.—In heraldry, a broad arrow head.

Pilaster.—A shallow pier attached to a wall.

Pile.—In heraldry, a triangular or wedge-shaped charge, issuing from the chief of the shield unless otherwise blazoned.

Piscina.—A basin with a drain, set in or against the wall to the S of an altar.

Plinth.—The projecting base of a wall or column, generally chamfered or moulded at the top.

Popey.—The ornament at the heads of bench-standards or desks in churches ; generally carved with foliage and flowers, somewhat resembling a *fleur-de-lis*.

Portcullis.—The running gate, rising and falling in vertical grooves in the jambs of a doorway.

Pourpoint.—A body defence of cloth or of leather, padded or quilted.

Powdered.—A shield or charge with small charges scattered indiscriminately thereon is said to be powdered with them.

Presbytery.—The part of a church in which is placed the high altar, E. of the quire.

Priests' Vestments (*Mass*).—Amice, alb, girdle, stole crossed in front, fanon, chasuble.

Principals.—The chief trusses of a roof, or the main rafters, posts, or braces, in the wooden framework of a building.

Processional Vestments.—Same as canonical.

Pulvinated Frieze.—In Classical and Renaissance architecture, a frieze having a convex or bulging section.

Purlin.—A horizontal timber resting on the principal rafters of a roof-truss, and forming an intermediate support for the common rafters.

Purple or Purpure.—One of the colours in heraldry.

Pyx.—Any small box, but usually a vessel to contain the reserved Sacrament.

Quarry.—In glazing, small panes of glass, generally diamond-shaped or square, set diagonally.

Quarter.—In heraldry, the dexter corner of the shield ; a charge made by enclosing that corner with a right-angled line taking in a quarter or somewhat less of the shield and giving it a tincture of its own.

Quartered or Quarterly.—A term which, in its original sense, belongs to a shield or charge divided crosswise into four quarters. After the practice of marshalling several coats in the quarters of a shield had been established, the quarters themselves might be quartered for the admission of more coats, or the four original divisions increased to six or more, each being still termed a quarter.

Quatrefoil.—In heraldry, a four-petalled flower. *See* also " Foil."

Queen-posts.—A pair of vertical posts in a roof-truss equi-distant from the middle line.

Quillon.—Bars forming cross-guard of sword.

Quilted Defence.—Armour made of padded cloth, leather, etc.

Quire-habit.—In secular churches : for boys, a surplice only over the cassock ; for clerks or vicars, the surplice and a black cope-like mantle, partly closed in front and put over the head, which was exchanged for a silk cope on festivals ; canons put on over the surplice a grey amess. In monastic churches, all classes, whether canons regular, monks, friars, nuns, or novices, wore the ordinary habit with a cope on festivals.

Quoin.—The dressed stones at the angle of a building.

Ragged, Raguly.—In heraldry, applied to a charge whose edges are ragged like a tree trunk with the limbs lopped away.

Rampant (of beasts, etc.).—In heraldry, standing erect on one foot, as if attacking or defending.

Rampart.—A mound or bank surrounding a fortified place.

Rapier.—Cut and thrust sword.

Razed.—Of a head, etc. in heraldry, having a ragged edge as though torn off.

Rear-arch.—The arch on the inside of a wall spanning a doorway or window opening.

Rear-vault.—The space between a rear-arch and the outer stonework of a window.

Rebate (*rabbet, rabbit*).—A continuous rectangular notch cut on an edge.

Reliquary.—A small box or other receptacle for relics.

Rerebrace.—Plate or leather defence for upper arm.

Rere-dorter.—The common latrine of a monastic house.

Reredos.—A hanging, wall, or screen of stone or wood at the back of an altar or daïs.

Respond.—The half-pillar or pier at the end of an arcade or abutting a single arch.

Revetment.—A retaining wall of masonry against a bank of earth.

Roll-moulding *or* **Bowtell.**—A continuous convex moulding cut upon the edges of stone and woodwork, etc.

Rood (*Rood-beam, Rood-screen, Rood-loft*).—A cross or crucifix. The *Great Rood* was set up at the E. end of the nave with accompanying figures of St. Mary and St. John ; it was generally carved in wood, and fixed on the loft or head of the rood-screen, or in a special beam (the *Rood-beam*), reaching from wall to wall. Sometimes the rood was merely painted on the wall above the chancel-arch or on a closed wood partition or tympanum in the upper half of the arch. The *Rood-screen* is the open screen spanning the E. end of the nave, shutting off the chancel ; in the 15th century a narrow gallery was often constructed above the cornice to carry the rood and other images and candles, and it was also used as a music gallery. The loft was approached by a staircase (and occasionally by more than one), either of wood or in a turret built in the wall wherever most convenient, and, when the loft was carried right across the building, the intervening walls of the nave were often pierced with narrow archways. Many of the roods were destroyed at the Reformation, and their final removal, with the loft, was ordered in 1561.

Roundel.—In heraldry, a round plate or disc of any tincture other than gold.

Rubble.—Walling of rough unsquared stones or flints.

Rustic work, rusticated joints.—Masonry in which only the margins of the stones are worked.

Sabatons or Sollerets.—Articulated plate defences for the feet.

Sable.—In heraldry, black.

Salade or Sallet.—Light steel headpiece, frequently with vizor.

Saltire.—In heraldry, an X-shaped cross ; also called St. Andrew's cross.

Sanctus-Bell.—A small bell, usually hung in a bell-cot over the E. gable of the nave, or in the steeple, and rung at the Elevation of the Host during mass. The name is also applied to small bells of post-Reformation date.

Scallop.—A shellfish, a common charge in heraldry.

Scalloped capital.—A development of the cushion capital in which the single cushion is elaborated into a series of truncated cones.

Scapple, to.—To dress roughly, of masonry or timber.

Scarp.—A vertical or sloping face of earth in a ditch or moat, or cut in the slope of a hill, facing away from the place which it helps to defend.

Scribe.—A term applied to timber cut or fitted to an irregular surface or moulding.

Scroll-moulding.—A rounded moulding of two parts, the upper projecting beyond the lower, thus resembling a scroll of parchment.

Scutcheon or Scocheon.—1. A shield, a charge in heraldry, *Voided Scutcheon*, a scutcheon whose border alone is seen ; termed in modern heraldry an *Orle*.
2. A metal plate pierced for the spindle of a handle or for a keyhole.

Sedilia (sing. *sedile*, a seat), sometimes called presbyteries.—The seats on the S. side of the chancel, quire, or chapel near the altar, used by the ministers during the Mass.

Sexpartite vault.—*See* " Vaulting."

Shaft.—A small column.

Shafted jambs.—A jamb containing one or more shafts either engaged or detached.

Shell-keep.—A ring wall cresting a castle mount and sometimes enclosing buildings.

Shingles.—Tiles of cleft timber, used for covering spires, etc.

Sinister.—In heraldry, the left hand side of a shield as held.

Slip-tiles.—Tiles moulded with a design in intaglio which was then filled in, before burning, with a clay of a different colour.

Slype.—A mediaeval term for a narrow passage between two buildings ; generally used for that from the cloister to the cemetery of a monastic establishment.

Soffit.—The under side of a staircase, lintel, cornice, arch, canopy, etc.

Soffit-cusps.—Cusps springing from the flat soffit of an arched head, and not from its chamfered sides or edges.

Solar.—An upper chamber in a mediaeval house adjoining the daïs end of the Hall, and reserved for the private use of the family.

Sollerets.—*See* " Sabatons."

Spandrel.—The triangular-shaped space above the haunch of an arch ; the two outer edges generally form a rectangle, as in an arched and square-headed doorway ; the name is also applied to a space within a curved brace below a tie-beam, etc., and to any similar spaces.

Spire, Broach-spire, Needle-spire.—The tall pointed termination covered with lead or shingles, the roof of a tower or turret. A *Broach-spire* rises from the sides of the tower without a parapet, the angles of a square tower being surmounted, in this case, by half-pyramids against the alternate faces of the spire, when octagonal. A *Needle-spire* is small and narrow, and rises from the middle of the tower-roof well within the parapet.

Splay.—A sloping face making an angle more than a right-angle with the main surface, as in window jambs, etc.

Springing-line.—The level at which an arch springs from its supports.

Sprocket-pieces.—Short lengths of timber covering the ends of roof-rafters to flatten the angle of pitch of the roof at the eaves.

Spurs.—*Prick* : in form of plain goad ; early form.
Rowel : with spiked wheel ; later form.

Squinch.—An arch thrown across the angle between two walls to support a superstructure, such as the base of a stone spire.

Squint.—A piercing through a wall to allow a view of an altar from places whence it could otherwise not be seen.

Stages of Tower.—The divisions marked by horizontal string-courses externally.

Stanchion, stancheon.—The upright iron bars in a screen, window, etc.

Stole.—A long narrow strip of embroidery with fringed ends worn above the alb by a deacon over the left shoulder, and by priests and bishops over both shoulders.

Stops.—Projecting stones at the ends of labels, string-courses, etc. against which the mouldings finish; they are often carved in various forms, such as shields, bunches of foliage, human or grotesque heads, etc.; a finish at the end of any moulding or chamfer bringing the corner out to a square edge, or sometimes, in the case of a moulding, to a chamfered edge. A splayed stop has a plain sloping face, but in many other cases the face is moulded.

Stoup.—A vessel, placed near an entrance doorway, to contain holy water; those remaining are usually in the form of a deeply-dished stone set in a niche, or on a pillar. Also called *Holy-water Stones*, or *Holy-water Stocks*.

String-course.—A projecting horizontal band in a wall; usually moulded.

Strut.—A timber forming a sloping support to a beam, etc.

Style.—The vertical members of a frame into which are tenoned the ends of the rails or horizontal pieces.

Sub-deacons' Vestments (*Mass*).—Amice, alb, tunicle, fanon.

Surcoat.—Coat, usually sleeveless, worn over armour.

Tabard.—Short loose surcoat, open at sides, with short tab-like sleeves, sometimes worn with armour, and emblazoned with arms; distinctive garment of heralds.

Taces or tonlets.—Articulated defence for hips and lower part of body.

Terminal figure.—The upper part of a carved human figure growing out of a column, post, or pilaster, diminishing to the base.

Tie-beam.—The horizontal transverse beam in a roof, tying together the feet of the rafters to counteract the thrust.

Timber-framed building.—A building of which the walls are built of open timbers and covered with plaster or boarding, or with interstices filled in with brickwork.

Totternhoe stone.—Clunch from Totternhoe, Bedfordshire.

Touch.—A soft black marble quarried near Tournai and commonly used in monumental art.

Tracery.—The ornamental work in the head of a window, screen, panel, etc., formed by the curving and interlacing of bars of stone or wood, and grouped together, generally over two or more lights or bays.

Transom.—A horizontal bar of stone or wood across the upper half of a window opening, doorway, or panel.

Trefoil.—In heraldry, a three-lobed leaf with a pendent stalk.

Tressure.—In heraldry, a narrow flowered or counter-flowered orle, often voided or doubled, as in the arms of the King of Scots.

Trimmer.—A timber, framing an opening in a floor or roof.

Tripping.—Applied, in heraldry, to stags, etc., walking or passant.

Truss.—A number of timbers framed together to bridge a space or form a bracket, to be self-supporting, and to carry other timbers. The *trusses* of a roof are generally named after a peculiar feature in their construction, such as *King-post, Queen-post, Hammer-beam*, etc. (*q.v.*).

Tuiles.—In armour, plates attached to and hanging from the edge of taces, or tonlets.

Tunicle.—Similar to dalmatic.

Tympanum.—An enclosed space within an arch, doorway, etc., or in the triangle of a pediment.

Types of Houses.—*See* "Houses."

Vair.—In heraldry, a fur imitating grey squirrels' skins, usually shown as an alternating series, often in rows, of blue and white bell-shaped patches. If of other tinctures it is called *vairy*.

Vallum.—A rampart.

Vambrace.—Plate defence for lower arm.

Vamplate.—Funnel-shaped hand-guard of lance.

Vaulting.—An arched ceiling or roof of stone or brick, sometimes imitated in wood. *Barrel-vaulting* (sometimes called *waggon-head-vaulting*) is a continuous vault unbroken in its length by cross-vaults. A *groined vault* (or cross-vaulting) results from the intersection of simple vaulting surfaces. A *ribbed vault* is a framework of arched ribs carrying the cells which cover in the spaces between them. One bay of vaulting, divided into four quarters or compartments, is termed *quadripartite;* but often the bay is divided longitudinally into two subsidiary bays, each equalling a bay of the wall supports; the vaulting bay is thus divided into six compartments, and is termed *sexpartite.* A more complicated form is *lierne-vaulting;* this contains secondary ribs, which do not spring from the wall-supports, but cross from main rib to main rib. In *fan-vaulting* numerous ribs rise from the springing in equal curves, diverging equally in all directions, giving fan-like effects when seen from below.

Veil.—A sweat-cloth attached to the head of the crosier. (*See also* "Lenten Veil.")

Vernicle.—A representation of the face of Christ printed on St. Veronica's handkerchief.

Vert.—In heraldry, green.

Vestments (ecclesiastical).—*See* alb, amess, amice, apparels, archbishops' vestments bishops' vestments, buskins, canonical quire habit, cassock, chasuble, cope, crosier, cross staff, dalmatic, deacons' vestments, fanon, mitred abbots' vestments, morse, orphreys, priests' vestments, processional vestments, quire habit, sub-deacons' vestments, stole, tunicle.

Vizor.—Hinged face-guard of bascinet, salade, close helmet, etc.

Voided.—In heraldry, with the middle part cut away, leaving a margin.

Volute.—A spiral form of ornament.

Voussoirs.—The stones forming an arch.

Vowess.—A woman, generally a widow, who had taken a vow of chastity, but was not attached to any religious order.

Waggon-head-vault.—*See* " Vaulting."

Wall-plate.—A timber laid lengthwise on the wall to receive the ends of the rafters and other joists.

Warming-house.—In monastic planning, an apartment in which a fire was kept burning for warmth.

Water-bouget.—*See* " Bouget."

Wattle and daub.—An old form of filling in timber-framed buildings.

Wave-mould.—A compound mould formed by a convex curve between two concave curves.

Weather-boarding.—Horizontal boards nailed to the uprights of timber-framed buildings and made to overlap ; the boards are wedge-shaped in section, the upper edge being the thinner.

Weathering (to sills, tops of buttresses, etc.).—A sloping surface for casting off water, etc.

Well-staircase.—A staircase of several flights and generally square, surrounding a space or " Well."

Wimple.—Scarf covering chin and throat.

Wyver or Wyvern.—A dragon-like monster with a beaked head, two legs with claws, and tail sometimes coiled in a knot. The earlier examples show wings.

ROYAL COMMISSION ON HISTORICAL MONUMENTS (ENGLAND).

THIRD

REPORT OF THE INDEX COMMITTEE.

To the Chairman, the Earl of Plymouth.

MY LORD,

We desire to make the following additional recommendations with regard to the method of indexing the Inventories of the Commission :—

(1) Following the precedent set in Volume II, where only certain monuments are so indexed, the references to *all* monuments in Volumes III and IV to be confined to the *Parish*, and to the *number of the monument* within the parish, and in the combined Index in the final Volume to the *number of the Volume* as well. All page references outside those that are necessary for the proper indexing of the Sectional Preface to be excluded.

Thus :—iii Colchester (8) will denote that the monument in question is to be found in Volume III under monument (8) of the Parish of Colchester.

(2) A note to be included at the beginning of the Index explaining the manner in which the Index has been compiled.

(3) The special advantages accruing from the method of indexing suggested above are that :—

(*a*) It will give a closer reference in all cases where the accounts of more than one monument are printed on the same page.

(*b*) It will save time by enabling the Index to be compiled as the accounts of monument are put into typescript without waiting for the arrival of a printed and paged proof.

(*c*) It will save labour in checking page references.

We have the honour, My Lord, to remain,

Your obedient, humble servants,

(*Signed*) W. PAGE,

C. R. PEERS,

GEORGE H. DUCKWORTH.

25th February, 1922.

INDEX.

How to use the Index :—The Parishes are printed alphabetically in the Inventory which, so far as the Parishes are concerned, is in itself an index. The number or numbers in brackets after the name of the Parish refer to the number of the Monument within the Parish. Thus, Masons' Marks : Dedham (1), means that an instance of Masons' Marks will be found under Monument (1) in the Parish of Dedham. Look for Dedham in its alphabetical sequence in the volume and then to the *monument numbered* (1) and the reference will be found. Page references in Roman figures are to the Sectional Preface only.

· *For the general headings and the method used in compiling this Index readers are referred to the three Reports of the Index Committee printed in this and previous volumes on Essex. The recommendations of this Committee were considered and adopted by the Commission.*

(8405)

R 2

Tiles, with designs : *cont'd.*
14TH OR 15TH-CENTURY : Bradwell (1)
17TH-CENTURY :
Colchester (11) ; Messing (1)
UNDATED : Colchester (16)
Tiptoft, arms : Wivenhoe (1)
Tiptree, see Great Braxted
Tiptree Heath, see Messing
Tiptree Priory, Great Braxted (2)
Tnbman (*sic*), Richard, cook to Thomas, Lord Darcy, floor-slab to, 1620 : St. Osyth (2)
Toller, George and Elizabeth, initials probably for : Earls Colne (23)
Tollesbury
Tollesbury Hall, Tollesbury (5)
Tolleshunt D'Arcy
Tolleshunt D'Arcy Hall, Tolleshunt D'Arcy (2)
Tolleshunt Knights
Tolleshunt Major
Tombs, see under **Monuments, Funeral**
Totham, see **Great Totham** *and* **Little Totham**
Towers, see also Sectional Preface, p. xxx
CENTRAL :
Great Tey (1) ; Mount Bures (1) (rebuilt)
ROUND : Lamarsh (1)
Town Hall, Colchester (19)
Townsend, Hannah, floor-slab to, 1691 : Great Coggeshall (2)

Umfreville, arms : Langham (1)
Umfrevile, Sir Arqlus, floor-slab to, 1696 : Langham (1)
Upper Goulds Farm, Alphamstone (5)

Valiant's Farm, Pebmarsh (18)
Valley Farm, Lamarsh (5)
Valley House, Langham (3)
Vaults :
BRICK :
13th-century : Little Coggeshall (2)
14th-century : Stanway (3)
16th-century :
Colchester (8) ; Feering (1) ; Wivenhoe (2)
17th-century : Little Bentley (1)
STONE :
11th-century : Colchester (18)
c. 1100 : Copford (1)
12th-century :
Colchester (16) ; Great Clacton (1) (remains of)
13th-century :
Little Coggeshall (2) (remains of) ; St. Osyth (4)
14th-century : Fingringhoe (1)
15th-century :
Colchester (15) ; Great Coggeshall (1) (mostly modern) ; St. Osyth (4)
16th-century :
Colchester (128) ; Dedham (1) ; Tolleshunt D'Arcy (3)
RUBBLE :
11th-century : Colchester (18)
12th-century : St. Osyth (4)
Venables, arms : Layer Marney (1) ; Little Horkesley (1)
Vere :
Arms : Earls Colne (1), (2), (9), (13) ; Feering (1) ; Little Oakley (1) ; Wivenhoe (1)
Badge : Colne Engaine (1) ; Earls Colne (1), (2), (9), (13) ; St. Osyth (4)
Vere, de :
Elizabeth, see **Darcy**
Elizabeth, widow of William, Viscount Beaumont and Lord Bardolfe, and wife of John, Earl of Oxford, brass of, 1537 : Wivenhoe (1)
(6405)

Townson, Joseph, headstone to, 1690 : Wivenhoe (1)
Tread-wheel :
c. 1700 : Harwich (2) (of oak)
Trinity, The :
Arms : Brightlingsea (3) ; Copford (1) ; Dedham (1) ; Great Clacton (1) (on font) ; Great Horkesley (1)
Painting : Bradwell (1)
Trumpington's, Great Tey (5)
Trussell, arms : Earls Colne (1)
Tunstall, arms and badge : St. Osyth (4)
Turnor of Suffolk, arms : Stisted (1)
Turnor, *or* **Turner :**
Mary, wife successively to Sir Thomas Wyseman, Sir Henry Appleton, Bart., and Thomas Turnor, 1685 : floor-slab to, Stisted (1)
Prudence, headstone to, 1662 : Mount Bures (1)
Turpin, Susanna, wife of Ralph, headstone to, 1706 : East Donyland (1)
Twinstead
Tye Homestead, Great Bentley (10)
Tyffin, arms : Wakes Colne (1)
Tyffin :
William, 1617, and Mary (Jenour), his wife, 1616 ; John, 1616, and Mary his wife, 1620, brass to : Wakes Colne (1)
William, 1617, and Mary (Jenour), his wife, 1616, tablet to : Wakes Colne (1)
Tymperleys, Colchester (141)

Upper Hill Farm, Birch (8)
Upper Jennys, Bures (9)

Vere, de : *cont'd.*
John, 15th Earl of Oxford, Tower of St. Andrew Church, Earls Colne (1), restored and partly rebuilt by, 1534
Richard, K.G., 11th Earl of Oxford, 1417, and Alice (Sergeaux) his wife, altar-tomb of : Earls Colne Priory, Earls Colne (2)
Robert, 5th Earl of Oxford, 1296, altar-tomb of, *c.* 1340 ; effigy, *c.* 1296 : Earls Colne Priory, Earls Colne (2)
Robert, 9th Earl of Oxford and Duke of Ireland, 1392, part of monument of : Earls Colne Priory, Earls Colne (2)
Thomas, 8th Earl of Oxford, altar-tomb of, 1371 : Earls Colne Priory, Earls Colne (2)
Veronica, St., Handkerchief of, glass : Rivenhall (2)
Vespasian, coins of : Stanway (1)
Vicarage, St. Peter's, Colchester (75)
Vicarage, The, Feering (18)
" " Great Tey (2)
Vineyard Cottages, Copford (2)
Vintner, arms and badge : St. Osyth (4)
Vintoner, Abbot, additions made by, *c.* 1527, to St. Osyth's Priory, St. Osyth (4) ; rebus of, and probably name (Johannes Vintoner), "Bishop's Lodging," St. Osyth's Priory, St. Osyth (4)
Virgin, The :
Coronation of, carving, on doorway, Ramsey (1)
Entombment of ?, glass, Rivenhall (2)
Figure of, Great Coggeshall (2)
Glass : Stisted (1)
Virgin and Child :
Brass : Great Coggeshall (2) (indent) ; Tolleshunt D'Arcy (1)
Glass : Rivenhall (2)
Painting : Fingringhoe (1)
Virley